SPATIALLY INTEGRATED SOCIAL SCIENCE

SPATIAL INFORMATION SYSTEMS

General Editors

M. F. Goodchild
P. A. Burrough
R. A. McDonnell
P. Switzer

SPATIALLY INTEGRATED SOCIAL SCIENCE

Edited by

Michael F. Goodchild

Donald G. Janelle

OXFORD
UNIVERSITY PRESS

2004

OXFORD

UNIVERSITY PRESS

Oxford   New York
Auckland   Bangkok   Buenos Aires   Cape Town   Chennai
Dar es Salaam   Delhi   Hong Kong   Istanbul   Karachi   Kolkata
Kuala Lumpur   Madrid   Melbourne   Mexico City   Mumbai   Nairobi
São Paulo   Shanghai   Taipei   Tokyo   Toronto

Publised by Oxford University Press, Inc.
198 Madison Avenue, New York, New York, 10016

www.oup.com

Oxford is a registered trademark of Oxford University Press

Library of Congress Cataloging-in-Publication Data
Spatially integrated social science / edited by Michael F. Goodchild
and Donald G. Janelle.
p.   cm. — (Spatial information systems)
Includes bibliographical references and index.
ISBN 978-0-19-515270-8
1. Spatial analysis (Statistics). 2. Population geography—Statistical
methods. I. Goodchild, Michael F.   II. Janelle, Donald G., 1940–
III. Series.
HA30.6 .S665 2003
300'.1'5195—dc21   2002156669

Printed in the United States of America
on acid-free paper

Foreword

Space is one of the fundamental categories within which we experience the world. Behavior takes place in space, and the geographical context of the behavior is important in shaping that behavior. While space by itself explains very little, the spatial patterning of behavior has long been viewed as a key to understanding and explaining much of human behavior. Yet, until recently, there has been surprisingly little work in the social sciences, except in the field of geography, based on analysis of spatial data.

The advent of geographic information systems (GIS) has enabled an explosion of interest in and ability to study the spatial patterns of behavior. GIS not only makes it possible to store in digital form vast amounts of spatial data, it makes possible statistical analysis, modeling, and visual display of geographical data. It provides a powerful new tool that has stimulated new and exciting social science research using geographical concepts and data. At last, long-held but unverified hypotheses about the importance of locational and spatial variables can be tested. We are at the dawn of a revolution in a spatially oriented social science.

In 1998, the National Science Foundation undertook a program designed to develop the infrastructure for social science research. In the first round of competition, one of the outstanding proposals was for a Center for Spatially Integrated Social Science (CSISS), submitted by the University of California, Santa Barbara, with Professor Michael Goodchild as the Principal Investigator. CSISS was to develop new computational and analytic tools for spatial data, facilitate the development of social science data archives based on geographical data, train scientists in the use of the most advanced tools, and foster the development of the emerging community of social scientists who integrate spatial data into their research.

CSISS began operation in the fall of 1999. This book is one of the fruits of its work. We hope that it will not only exemplify the breadth and depth of social science research that integrates spatial analyses but also stimulate others to continue and expand the type of work displayed here.

Norman M. Bradburn
Assistant Director for the Social, Behavioral and Economic Sciences
National Science Foundation
September 2002

Preface

The editors' objective for this book is to make available outstanding examples of the uses of spatial thinking in the social sciences. Chapters were selected to illustrate how spatial analysis fosters theoretical understanding and empirical testing. Each chapter exemplifies the founding principle for the Center for Spatially Integrated Social Science (CSISS)—that the analysis of social phenomena in space and time enhances our understanding of social processes. It is our hope that this book will help cultivate an integrated approach to social science research that recognizes the importance of location, space, spatiality, and place.

The chapters that follow offer substantive empirical content for illustrating the interpretation of specific spatial analytic approaches suited to an advanced transdisciplinary audience. In identifying contributors, we looked for authors of articles with relevant content who were widely cited, supported from major peer-reviewed funding programs, and noted for use of spatial approaches within their disciplines. Though the authors represent several disciplines, they have one major attribute in common—the application of spatial thinking in their research designs and execution. We are indebted to the authors for rising to the challenge of communicating their research in ways that cross the usual disciplinary divides.

The domain of the social sciences spans hundreds of thousands of scholars. Though capable of adding substantive analytical power and theoretical insight to most areas of social science research, the notion of "spatial social science" is in its formative stages. It is drawing momentum from rapidly expanding applications of new geographic information technologies, improved software, and newly available geographically referenced data of relevance to social science issues. We anticipate that spatial thinking and analysis will expand greatly over the next few years, and we hope that this book will assist this important transition.

Aside from demonstrating applications of spatial analysis in research, it is anticipated that this book will also be suited for teaching. To this end, the editors have established an associated Web page that includes material to supplement selected chapters.
At http://www.csiss.org/best-practices/siss/ readers have access to additional data associated with analyses, presentations that document further the research arguments of
authors, color representations of graphics, and software that can be downloaded for
experimentation.

Readers are encouraged to explore the Web site of the Center for Spatially Integrated Social Science for further background on spatial analysis in the social sciences
(http://www.csiss.org). It features smart search engines designed to retrieve materials
on spatial analysis from the World Wide Web. A collection of course syllabi, arranged
by discipline, illustrate actual examples of how spatial approaches are currently used in
university courses at undergraduate and graduate levels. In addition, the *GIS Cookbook*
and *CSISS Classics* are resources designed for social scientists—researchers, teachers,
and students.

The *GIS Cookbook* is a collection of simple descriptions and illustrations of geographic information systems (GIS) methods written with minimal jargon. It provides
introductory "recipes" for those who are new to GIS and who seek guidance about
fundamental GIS concepts for spatial analysis and mapping—geocoding, buffers, projections, datums, density estimation, and (especially for social scientists) uses of census
data at the tract level.

CSISS Classics recognize that the foundations of spatial analysis span many disciplines over many generations of researchers and practitioners. *CSISS Classics* provide illustrations that attempt to capture and acknowledge the repository of spatial
thinking in the social sciences for the last few centuries. Summaries of innovations,
along with key references, are intended as guides for those interested in exploring the
intellectual inheritance from previous generations. Thus, nineteenth-century mapping
projects by sociologists document poverty in London (Charles Booth) and Chicago
(Florence Kelley). The work of planner Constantinos Doxiadis illustrates the importance of geographic scale in settlement systems design. Geographer Vernor C. Finch
pioneered multi-variable mapping techniques for land use classifications in the 1930s.
Economic historian Robert W. Fogel applies distance buffers in an historical analysis
of transportation development in the United States. And political scientist Valdimer Or-
lando Key mapped and interpreted voting patterns in the American South in the 1940s,
adding insight to regional political thinking. These are a few of the many examples of
innovative uses of spatial thinking that predate the development of GIS in the 1980s.
CSISS Classics highlight several dozen examples of such important early contributions
to spatial reasoning in the social sciences—precursors to some of the research issues
and methods featured in this book.

Many people have contributed to the development of this volume. In the early phases,
we benefited enormously from suggestions and critiques by the multi-disciplinary scientific advisory board of CSISS, chaired by geographer Brian J. L. Berry. This body
has included anthropologist Emilio Moran; criminologist Nancy LaVigne; demogra-
pher Peter Morrison; geographers Amy Glasmeier and Billy-Lee Turner II; GIS innovator and entrepreneur Jack Dangermond; economists Kerry Smith, Karen Polen-
ski, and Susan Wachter; historian Myron Gutmann; political scientists Carol Kohfeld

and Michael Ward; psychologist Bennett Bertenthal; sociologists John R. Logan and Robert Sampson; and statistician Dick Berk. We also benefited from members of the CSISS executive committee: anthropologist Barbara Herr-Harthorn, economist Peter Kuhn, sociologist Richard Appelbaum, and fellow geographers Luc Anselin, Helen Couclelis, and Stuart Sweeney. We owe a special thanks to Norman Bradburn, author of this book's Foreword, and to Brian Berry for his epilogue on spatial analysis in retrospect and prospect.

In addition to CSISS advisors and chapter authors, we thank Ben Sprague, who undertook much of the final assembly of material for the book; Jorge Sifuentes, who conducted citation research for helping us to locate authors; Gamaiel Zavala, who assisted with graphics and with the design of the Web page that supplements the book; and the staff of CSISS, including Christian Brown, LaNell Lucius, and Ann Ricchiazzi. Finally, we owe special thanks to the National Science Foundation, without whose funding under NSF BCS 99788058 this project would not have been possible. They have all contributed in important ways to this outcome. We as editors are, of course, solely responsible for any errors.

Michael F. Goodchild and Donald G. Janelle
Center for Spatially Integrated Social Science
University of California, Santa Barbara
November 2002

Contents

Part IV. Multi-Scale Spatial Perspectives

Contributors

Luc Anselin is Professor of Agricultural and Consumer Economics at the University of Illinois, Urbana-Champaign, holds appointments in the Department of Economics and the Department of Geography, and is Senior Research Professor at the Regional Economics Applications Laboratory (REAL). He is a member of the National Consortium on Violence Research, is on the faculty of the Summer Program in Quantitative Methods of the Interuniversity Consortium on Political and Social Research (ICPSR), and serves on the Executive Committee of the Center for Spatially Integrated Social Science (CSISS). His research deals with the development, software implementation, and application of spatial analytical methods to social science research questions, with a focus on exploratory spatial data analysis and spatial econometrics. Dr. Anselin is also the developer of the SpaceStat™ software packages for spatial data analysis. He is an editor of the *International Regional Science Review* and serves on six other journal editorial boards in regional science and analytical geography.

Paul Bélanger is a geography graduate of the University of Victoria, British Columbia, and the University of Kentucky (M.A.). He received his Ph.D. in geography from the University at Buffalo—The State University of New York, in 2002. His research interests are in political geography, the electoral geography of Canada, and the application of spatial and GIS-based analysis to the study of political behavior. He has written on electoral districting, the geography of campaign tours, voter turnout, and party financing.

Itzhak Benenson is a Senior Lecturer at the Department of Geography and Human Environment, Tel Aviv University. His scientific interests include theoretical and applied urban, social, and ecological modeling and simulation, GIS and its applications in archaeology, social science, demography, urban studies and management, software for agent-based simulation, spatial analysis, and data mining. He is a Deputy Head of the Environmental Simulation Laboratory of the Porter School of Environmental Studies University Tel Aviv and is Head of the GIS Special Interest Group of the Israeli Geographic Society.

Brian J. L. Berry is Lloyd Viel Berkner Regental Professor and Professor of Political Economy at the University of Texas at Dallas. He received his B.Sc. (Economics) degree at University College, London in 1955, the M.A. in geography from the University of Washington in 1956 and the Ph.D. in 1958. He was a faculty member at the University of Chicago (1958–1976), where he chaired the geography department and directed the Center for Urban Studies; at Harvard (1976–1981), where he chaired the doctoral program in urban planning and directed the Laboratory for Computer Graphics and Spatial Analysis; and at Carnegie-Mellon (1981–1986), where he was dean of the Heinz School of Public Policy and Management. He joined UTD in 1986, and was the founding director of the Bruton Center for Development Studies. The author of more than 500 books and articles, he was the most-cited geographer for more than 25 years from the early 1960s. In his work he has attempted to bridge theory and practice via involvement in development activities in both advanced and developing countries. When elected to the National Academy of Sciences in 1975, he was the youngest social scientist so honored. Among others, he also is a fellow of the British Academy and of the American Academy of Arts and Sciences and received the Victoria Medal from the Royal Geographical Society in 1988. In 1999 he was elected a member of the Council of the National Academy of Sciences, the first geographer to be so honored.

Bruce W. Boucek received both B.A. and M.A. degrees in geography from Temple University in Philadelphia. He is currently a graduate research assistant at the Anthropological Center for Training and Research on Global Environmental Change (ACT) and a Ph.D. student in the Department of Geography at Indiana University. His recent work includes prediction of deforestation at the farm property level for ACT's study region in the Amazon. His primary research interest is in the link between land use and land cover change and urbanization in the developing world. In the past, he has also worked as a graduate research assistant for the Center for the Study of Institutions, Population, and Environmental Change (CIPEC) at Indiana University.

Norman M. Bradburn is Assistant Director for the Social, Behavioral, and Economic Sciences Directorate (SBE) of the National Science Foundation. He is on leave from the University of Chicago, where he is the Tiffany and Margaret Blake Distinguished Service Professor Emeritus and Vice President and Director of Research at the National Opinion Research Center. He served three terms as Director of the center, from 1967 to 1992, and was Provost of the University of Chicago from 1984 to 1989. Dr. Bradburn pioneered applications of cognitive psychology to questionnaire design and methodological problems in survey research. He is a member and former chair of the Committee on National Statistics, National Research Council/National Academy of Sciences; and a member of the Panel to Review the Statistical Procedures for the Decennial Census. He also is a member of the American Academy of Arts and Sciences and the International Statistical Institute, and a fellow of the American Statistical Association and the American Association for the Advancement of Science.

Ted Bradshaw received his Ph.D. in Sociology from the University of California, Berkeley, and currently he is an Associate Professor in the Human and Community Development Department at the University of California, Davis. He teaches community development and economic development, and has recently published *Planning Local Economic Development* (Third Edition, with Edward Blakely) and journal articles on small business loan guarantees, land use and farmland conversion in the California central valley, complex community development organizations, and the environmental technology industry. He is currently working on a book on the California energy crisis. Prior to joining the faculty at the UC Davis in 1995, Bradshaw was a Research Sociologist at the Institute of Urban and Regional Development at UC Berkeley, where he headed a series of studies on California's economic development. He is the editor of the *Journal of the Community Development Society*.

Hugh Calkins is Research Professor of Geography at the University at Buffalo—The State University of New York, and a Research Scientist with the National Center for Geographic Information and Analysis (NCGIA). He received his Ph.D. in Urban Planning from the University of Washington in 1972 and recently completed a term as Chair of the Geography Department at UB. His primary research involves the use and value of geographic information in decision-making, and the use of GIS in understanding the human and social capital stock of communities.

Gilberto Câmara is Director for Earth Observation at INPE. He is an electronics engineer (ITA, 1979) with a Ph.D. in Computer Science (INPE, 1995). His research interests are geographical information science, spatial databases, spatial analysis, and remote sensing image processing. He has published more than 80 full papers in refereed journals and scientific conferences in Brazil and abroad. He has also been the leader in the development of GIS and image processing technology in Brazil, including the SPRING software, freely available on the Internet.

Jacqueline Cohen is Principal Research Scientist in the H. John Heinz III School of Public Policy and Management at Carnegie Mellon University. Her research, which spans 30 years, analyzes many aspects of crime and criminal justice policy, including demographic trends in crime and prison populations, criminal careers, and incapacitative effects of incarceration. Her work also examines various aspects of illegal drug use and its relationship to violent offending and investigates the effectiveness of policing strategies. Her most recent work pursues issues relating to firearm involvement among youthful offenders, including exploration of its links to youthful violence and the potential effectiveness of various law enforcement strategies pursued by local police. Dr. Cohen also has contributed to the work of several panels convened by the National Research Council to examine research on deterrence and incapacitation, sentencing policy, patterns of offending during criminal careers, and the understanding and control of violent behavior.

Patrick Daly is conducting research at the Institute of Archaeology, University of Oxford, focusing upon the development of cultural landscapes from the Late Bronze Age through the Iron Age in South Central England. As part of this research, GIS has been used extensively to explore the movement and deposition of material culture across the landscape. His academic interests lie in landscape archaeology, long-term regional development, material culture and social theory, and the practical and theoretical application of GIS in anthropology and archaeology. He has conducted fieldwork and led teams in northern Scandinavia, Karalia, the United Kingdom, Jordan, Syria, Peru, and Borneo. He has published a number of papers on the use of GIS in archaeology and eth-noarchaeology and is currently editing a volume, *Digital Archaeology,* for Routledge Press.

Munroe Eagles is an Associate Professor of Political Science and Associate Dean for Graduate Studies in the College of Arts and Sciences, University at Buffalo—The State University of New York. He is also a Research Scientist with the National Center for Geographic Information and Analysis (NCGIA). He received his Ph.D. in Political Science from the University of California, Irvine, in 1988. His main research interests are in the political and electoral geography of advanced industrial societies.

Guy Engelen is Director of the Research Institute for Knowledge Systems in Maastricht, The Netherlands. Following graduate work in geography at the (Flemish) Free University of Brussels in Belgium, he worked on spatial modeling with the interdisciplinary group headed by Nobel laureate I. Prigogine in Brussels. Since coming to Maastricht, he has built the Institute into a leading research and consultancy group in geographical systems. Two of his current areas of interest are the extension of geoinformatics to encompass the effects of dynamic processes and the development of effective spatial decision support systems.

Edward J. Feser is an Assistant Professor in the Department of City and Regional Planning at the University of North Carolina at Chapel Hill, where he teaches courses in urban and regional economics and local development policy. His research focuses on industry cluster analysis and policy, regional influences on process technology adoption in manufacturing, external economies and industrial productivity, regional distress and economic adjustment, and the development of improved data and spatial-analytical techniques for local development practice. The National Science Foundation, the U.S. Economic Development Administration, the Appalachian Regional Commission, the German Marshall Fund of the United States, and state and local development agencies in eight states have funded his research. He is co-author of *Understanding Local Economic Development*, published by Rutgers' CUPR Press in 1999.

Tony Gatrell is Professor of the Geography of Health at Lancaster University and also Director of the Institute for Health Research, which was created in 1996. He has a First Class Honours degree from Bristol University and a Ph.D. from Pennsylvania State University, where the influence of Peter Gould was considerable. He began his career at Salford University, before subsequently moving to Lancaster. His research interests lie primarily in geographical epidemiology, spatial analysis, and the geography of health care provision, but with an underlying interest in health inequalities. He has recently written *Geographies of Health: An Introduction*, published by Blackwell in 2002, and is the author or editor of three other books and numerous research papers. Currently, he is involved in several projects, including "Cultivating health," a project that is assessing the mental health and well-being benefits of gardening among older people in deprived areas. Other recent and ongoing projects include care preferences for people with cancer and local geographies of health inequality. He hopes that a spatial imagination informs all this work.

Michael F. Goodchild is Professor of Geography at the University of California, Santa Barbara, Chair of the Executive Committee of the National Center for Geographic Information and Analysis (NCGIA), and Director of the Center for Spatially Integrated Social Science. He was elected member of the National Academy of Sciences and Foreign Fellow of the Royal Society of Canada in 2002, and holds honorary doctorates from Laval University and Keele University. He is a past editor of *Geographical Analysis* and the current editor of the Methods, Models, and Geographic Information Sciences section of the *Annals of the Association of American Geographers.* Dr. Goodchild is a member of editorial boards for ten other journals and book series and is the author of some 300 scientific papers and several books. He was Chair of the National Research Council's Mapping Science Committee and is currently a member of NRC's Committee on Geography. His research interests center on geographic information science, spatial analysis, the future of the library, and uncertainty in geographic data.

Jean-Michel Guldmann is Professor of City and Regional Planning at the Ohio State University (OSU). He holds a master's degree in Industrial and Systems Engineering from Ecole des Mines, Nancy, France, and a Ph.D. in Urban and Regional Planning from the Technion—Israel Institute of Technology, Haifa, Israel. He is also a Faculty Associate at Argonne National Laboratory. At OSU, he teaches courses in energy planning and policy, and in quantitative methods. His research interests center on environmental, energy, and telecommunication issues, including: (1) the development of optimization models for air-quality management and pollution sources location, and of statistical models explaining pollution concentrations in urban areas; (2) the development of management, planning, and pricing models for natural gas utilities, and of econometric models of the cost structure of local gas and electricity distribution networks; and (3) the analysis of economies of scale and density of local telephone systems, and the estimation of point-to-point spatial interaction models of telephone traffic at the regional and international scales. The National Science Foundation and the Ameritech Foundation have supported his telecommunications research.

Donald G. Janelle is a Research Professor and Program Director for the Center for Spatially Integrated Social Science at the University of California, Santa Barbara. His Ph.D. in geography is from Michigan State University. He is former Chair of the Geography Department at the University of Western Ontario. Research interests include urban-regional spatial-systems development and time-space convergence, information technologies and the transformation of social space, transportation geography, and the time geography of cities and human activity patterns. A recently co-edited book *Information, Place, and Cyberspace: Issues in Accessibility* (Springer-Verlag, 2000) captures the interrelationship among his research interests. He is the North American co-leader of the STELLA Transatlantic Thematic Network's focus group on ICT, Innovation and the Transport System, and he is a recipient of the Association of American Geographers' Ullman Award for career research contributions to transportation geography.

John Kantner is an Assistant Professor in the Department of Anthropology and Geography at Georgia State University in Atlanta. He received his doctoral degree from the University of California, Santa Barbara in 1999, where he studied archaeology, geography, and GIS. His research focuses on how evolutionary theory and human behavioral ecology can help us understand the emergence of sociopolitical differentiation and complexity. These issues are investigated in the prehistoric Southwest, in particular reference to the evolution of the Chaco Anasazi tradition. Dr. Kantner employs a variety of methodological approaches in his research, including geochemical techniques, GIS and geographical analyses, and ceramic stylistic approaches. Publications have appeared in *Historical Archaeology, Journal of Anthropological Archaeology, Human Nature,* and in numerous edited volumes. He recently co-edited *Great House Communities Across the Chacoan Landscape,* published by University of Arizona Press, and he is editor of the Society for American Archaeology's trade magazine, *The SAA Archaeological Record.*

Mei-Po Kwan is Associate Professor of Geography at Ohio State University and holds a Ph.D. in Geography from the University of California, Santa Barbara. She is currently an associated faculty of the Center for Urban and Regional Analysis and the John Glenn Institute for Public Service and Public Policy at OSU. Dr. Kwan is associate editor of *Geographical Analysis* and serves on the International Editorial Advisory Board of *The Canadian Geographer.* She has also served as the guest editor of special issues for *Gender, Place and Culture, Journal of Geographical Systems*, and *Cartographica.* Her research interests include GIS-based geocomputation and 3D geovisualization, qualitative GIS, gender/ethnic issues in transportation and urban geography, new information technologies, feminist methodologies, cybergeography, and cyberspatial cognition. Her recent project explores the impact of Internet use on women's activity patterns in space-time and the gender division of household labor.

Jiyeong Lee holds a Ph.D. in Geography from the Ohio State University, and is Assistant Professor of Geography at Minnesota State University. He received first prizes in the Association of American Geographers GIS Specialty Group Student Paper Competition and the Integraph Student Award from the University Consortium for Geographic Information Science (UCGIS). His research and teaching interests focus on feature-based 3D GIS data models, land information systems in urban and regional planning, internal spatial structure of urban forms, pedestrian accessibility in 3D urban space, and 3D urban virtual reality systems. His current project develops a Community Geospatial Data Hub, accessed through the Internet.

Gary Lock is a University Lecturer in Archaeology at the University of Oxford, based in both the Institute of Archaeology and the Department for Continuing Education. He has a long-standing interest in the use of computers in archaeology, especially the application of GIS to landscape studies based on his fieldwork projects in England, Spain, and Italy. He is an editor of the *Archaeological Computing Newsletter*, has published many papers, has written *Virtual Pasts: Using Computers in Archaeology* (Routledge, due 2003) and *Digging Numbers: Elementary Statistics for Archaeologists* (with Mike Fletcher, Oxford University and Oxbow Books, 1991), and has edited *Archaeology and Geographic Information Systems: A European Perspective* (with Zoran Stančič,

Taylor and Francis, 1995), *Beyond the Map: Archaeology and Spatial Technologies* (IOS Press, 2000), and *On the Theory and Practice of Archaeological Computing* (with Kayt Brown, Oxford University and Oxbow Books, 2000).

John R. Logan is Distinguished Professor of Sociology at the University at Albany, SUNY, and Director of the Lewis Mumford Center for Comparative Urban and Regional Research. His books include *Urban Fortunes: The Political Economy of Place* (California, 1987), *Beyond the City Limits: Urban Policy and Economic Restructuring in Comparative Perspective* (Temple, 1990), and *The New Chinese City: Globalization and Market Reform* (Blackwell, 2002). He is a member of the editorial boards of *Urban Affairs Review, Sociological Forum, Journal of Urban Affairs,* and *City and Community*. He also founded and directs the Urban China Research Network, supported by the Andrew W. Mellon Foundation.

Steven F. Messner is Professor of Sociology and Chair at the University at Albany, SUNY, and a member of the National Consortium on Violence Research (NCOVR). His research has focused primarily on the relationship between social organization and crime, with a particular emphasis on criminal homicide. Recently, he has been studying the spatial distribution of violent crime, social capital and homicide rates, crime and delinquency in China, and the situational dynamics of violence. In addition to his publications in professional journals, he is co-author of *Crime and the American Dream* (Wadsworth), *Perspectives on Crime and Deviance* (Prentice Hall), *Criminology: An Introduction Using ExplorIt* (MicroCase), and co-editor of *Theoretical Integration in the Study of Deviance and Crime* (SUNY Press) and *Crime and Social Control in a Changing China* (Greenwood Press).

Emilio F. Moran is the James H. Rudy Professor of Anthropology at Indiana University, Professor of Environmental Sciences, Adjunct Professor of Geography, Director of the Anthropological Center for Training and Research on Global Environmental Change (ACT), and co-Director of the Center for the Study of Institutions, Population and Environmental Change (CIPEC). He is also Lead Scientist of the Land Use Cover Change (LUCC) Focus 1-Land Use Dynamics Office. Dr. Moran is the author of six books, nine edited volumes, and more than 100 journal articles and book chapters. He is trained in anthropology, tropical ecology, tropical soil science, and remote sensing. His research has focused on the Amazon for the past 30 years.

Jeffrey Morenoff is an Assistant Professor of Sociology and a Faculty Associate at both the Population Studies Center and the Survey Research Center of the University of Michigan. His major interests include crime, health, urban neighborhoods, and the analysis of spatial data. He is currently conducting research on the neighborhood context and spatial dynamics of infant health, differences across generations of Mexican immigrants and racial/ethnic groups in adolescent crime and problem behavior, and the systematic social observation of urban neighborhoods.

Brian Muller is an assistant professor at the University of Colorado at Denver. Brian received his B.A. from Yale University and his Ph.D. in urban and regional planning from the University of California, Berkeley. He teaches in the areas of environmental planning, planning methods, and spatial analysis, and his research interests include urban and regional growth dynamics, application of decision support systems, and environmental assessment methods.

David O'Sullivan is an Assistant Professor of Geography at the Pennsylvania State University. Research interests include modeling socio-spatial phenomena, particularly urban growth and social change at the micro-scale of parcels, blocks, and neighborhoods. He is also interested in developing methods for the detailed representation of spatial configuration in contemporary "complex" modeling techniques such as cellular automata and multi-agent simulations, while at the same time exploring the rich possibilities of these approaches for the representation of individuals and societies in geographical information science and systems.

Sergio J. Rey earned his Ph.D. in Geography from the University of California, Santa Barbara. He is an Associate Professor of Geography at the San Diego State University and an Adjunct Associate Research Professor at the Regional Economics Applications Laboratory (REAL) at the University of Illinois, Urbana-Champaign. Rey's research interests include regional economic growth and income inequality, spatial econometrics, open source geocomputation, integrated multiregional socioeconomic modeling, and regional industry cluster analysis. He has published widely on these areas in such journals as *Geographical Analysis, Regional Studies, Growth and Change, Environment and Planning A, The International Regional Science Review*, and *Economic Systems Research*, as well as in several edited volumes. His research has been funded from such public agencies as the U.S. Environmental Protection Agency, the California Employment Development Department, and the Southwest Center for Environmental Policy and Research. In 1998 he received the Geoffrey J.D. Hewings Distinguished Young Scholars Award from the North American Regional Science Council. Rey is an editor of the *International Regional Science Review*, and he serves on the editorial boards of *Geographical Analysis* and *Papers in Regional Science*.

Jan Rigby's career as a geographer began in 1990 with the M.Sc. course in GIS at Edinburgh University. After a few years of lecturing in GIS within a business school environment, she moved to Lancaster University to study for a Ph.D. in breast cancer epidemiology, which was completed in 1999. Tony Gatrell, from whom she is still learning, supervised the work. Following lectureships in geography departments at Bristol and Lancaster universities, she moved to New Zealand to develop the GIS courses at Victoria University of Wellington. She is currently working to establish a joint health geoinformatics facility with the Ministry of Health, aimed at public health applications of GIS. Her main research interests are spatial epidemiology, poverty, and the health of underserved populations.

Robert J. Sampson is the Henry Ford II Professor of Social Sciences in the Department of Sociology at Harvard University. He is also a Senior Research Fellow at the American Bar Foundation and Scientific Director of the Project on Human Development in Chicago Neighborhoods. His book with John Laub, *Crime in the Making: Pathways and Turning Points Through Life* (Harvard, 1993), received the outstanding scholarship award from the American Society of Criminology, the Academy of Criminal Justice Sciences, and the Crime, Law, and Deviance Section of the American Sociological Association. For 2002–2003, Sampson was a Fellow at the Center for

Advanced Study in the Behavioral Sciences, Stanford, California. He was formerly the Fairfax M. Cone Distinguished Service Professor in the Department of Sociology at the University of Chicago.

Qing Shen is Associate Professor of Urban Studies and Planning at the University of Maryland, College Park. He holds a Ph.D. degree in City and Regional Planning from the University of California, Berkeley. His areas of research and teaching are urban modeling, analytical methods, and metropolitan planning, with a special interest in the effects of transportation, telecommunication, and information technologies on the spatial structure of cities and regions. Funding for his research has come from various foundations and government agencies, including the Lincoln Institute of Land Policy, the National Science Foundation, and the U.S. Department of Transportation. He is the author of many scholarly publications, which include "A Spatial Analysis of Job Openings and Access in a U.S. Metropolitan Area," in *Journal of the American Planning Association*; "New Telecommunications and Residential Location Flexibility," in *Environment and Planning A*; "An Approach to Representing the Spatial Structure of the Information Society," in *Urban Geography*; and "Spatial and Social Dimensions of Commuting" in *Journal of the American Planning Association*. He was formerly Associate Professor in the Department of Urban Studies and Planning at MIT.

Aldaíza Sposati is Secretary for Social Services for the City of São Paulo and Full Professor in the Social Services Graduate School at the Catholic University of São Paulo (PUC/SP). She holds a Ph.D. in Social Services (PUC/SP, 1987) and a post-doctorate at the University of Coimbra, Portugal. Her research deals with public policies for social security, with an emphasis on the use of census data and maps for exploring social inequalities. She has published ten books, and advised six Ph.D. and 28 M.Sc. students at PUC/SP.

Bas Straatman took a master's degree in mathematics at the University of Utrecht, The Netherlands, and has since worked with the Maastricht Technological Research Institute for Knowledge and Systems, primarily in the area of applications of cellular automata to spatial decision support systems. He is currently working toward a Ph.D. in geography at Memorial University of Newfoundland.

Stuart H. Sweeney is an Assistant Professor of Geography at the University of California, Santa Barbara. He is an executive committee member of the Center for Spatially Integrated Social Science and a faculty affiliate/advisor for the Quantitative Methods for Social Sciences graduate emphasis at UC Santa Barbara. His research is broadly focused on modeling local labor market dynamics in an interregional setting. Specific research themes related to local labor markets include modeling occupational migration and mobility processes, studying the economic effects of depopulation, and modeling agglomeration as a spatial point process. He is currently engaged in research projects funded by the U.S. Department of Labor and the National Science Foundation.

George E. Tita is an Assistant Professor in the Department of Criminology, Law, and Society at the University of California, Irvine. He received his Ph.D. (1999) from the Heinz School of Public Policy and Management at Carnegie Mellon University. His research interests include the study of inter-personal violence, urban street gangs, the intersection of social network and spatial analysis, and the community context of crime. Dr. Tita has employed GIS and spatial analysis in his publications focusing on the territories of urban youth gangs, the spatial diffusion of homicide, and the design and implementation of a gun-violence reduction strategy within several neighborhoods of Los Angeles. He (along with Jacqueline Cohen) has served as a guest editor for a special edition of the *Journal of Quantitative Criminology* dedicated to research examining the diffusion of violence. Dr. Tita is also a member of the National Consortium on Violence Research (NCOVR), a research and training center funded by the National Science Foundation, specializing in violence research.

John R. Weeks is Professor of Geography and Director of the International Population Center at San Diego State University. He received his A.B. in Sociology from the University of California, Berkeley, in 1966, his M.A. in Demography from the University of California, Berkeley, in 1969, and his Ph.D. in Demography from the University of California, Berkeley, in 1972. He taught at Michigan State University for 3 years prior to accepting an appointment at San Diego State University in 1974. He is the author of the best-selling text in demography, *Population: Introduction to Concepts and Issues*, which is now in its eighth edition, and he is currently the principal investigator on a National Science Foundation funded project that aims to integrate remotely sensed imagery, GIS, and spatial statistical analysis into the study of the Arab fertility transition in Egypt and Jordan.

Roger White is University Research Professor at Memorial University of Newfoundland, Canada, and since 1990 has also been associated with the Research Institute for Knowledge Systems in Maastricht, the Netherlands, as Senior Scientist. A geographer, he works primarily in the area of urban and regional modeling, and is particularly interested in developing new approaches to understanding the dynamics and evolution of geographical systems.

Wenquan Zhang is a doctoral candidate in the Department of Sociology, University at Albany, SUNY. He is co-author of several articles on ethnic residential patterns. His dissertation focuses on secondary migration of Asian and Hispanic immigrants, analyzing population flows to areas outside the traditional points of entry in the United States.

Introduction

1

Thinking Spatially in the Social Sciences

Michael F. Goodchild
Donald G. Janelle

The table of numbers or statistics is such a common way to organize information that we scarcely if ever think about its significance. Tables are used to organize information about states from the decennial census, to report the comparative performance of national economies, to summarize the performance of individual schools in a state, and for a host of other purposes. In most cases a simple convention will have been followed in preparing the table (Nicol and Pexman 1999). The rows of the table will represent the instances, objects, or cases whose attributes are being reported, and all such objects will be drawn from a homogeneous class, such as counties, states, or nations. Each column of the table represents one of the attributes, allowing the reader to make comparisons by running the eye up or down a column or by computing statistics such as column means. In all of the instances just listed the objects happen to be geographic, in the sense that they occupy distinct locations on the earth's surface; in the case of the census these objects might range from regions to states, counties, municipalities, census tracts, or block groups.

Tables succeed in organizing information for easy comparison and for analysis in spreadsheets or statistical packages, but they do so by largely ignoring one particular property of each object: its geographic location. A table of U.S. states ordered alphabetically, for example, places Alabama at the top and Wyoming at the bottom, and in only two instances (Florida and Georgia, Illinois and Indiana) do states that are adjacent geographically appear in adjacent rows in the table. In effect, the table discards any importance that one might attach to geographic location: do states that are near each other geographically tend to share common properties, and do such tendencies contribute greater insight into the processes at work on the landscape; or are there instances of states whose attributes are out of line with those of neighboring states? The Census Bureau often addresses this issue by ordering tables by region, so that

3

all states in New England occur together in the table, for example, with each region's states ordered alphabetically within region. But, while this allows for easy comparison within regions and serves to link the contents of the table to whatever else the reader happens to know about New England, it still allows neighboring states to appear far apart in the table, if they happen to lie in different regions; and it can place states that are in the same region next to each other, although they are far apart in space. Clearly it is impossible to order states such that proximity in the table fully captures relative geographic proximity, or a state's geographic context (Abel and Mark 1990).

At another level, one might ask whether states are actually the appropriate units for reporting statistics. Of course, one can use larger units that are aggregations of states, such as regions or nations, or smaller units that themselves aggregate to states, such as counties, but the larger question is whether any of the standard reporting units are optimal—whether some quite different way of dividing the United States might lead to greater insight. For example, metropolitan regions frequently cross the state boundaries that were drawn somewhat arbitrarily many years ago, and yet are much less than the aggregations of their respective states (e.g., the New York or Kansas City metropolitan regions). States also vary vastly in area, from the more than 1.5 million sq km of Alaska to the 3,144 sq km of Rhode Island, confusing any effort to link state-level analysis with processes operating on the landscape over particular ranges of distances. Perhaps the geographic world is better seen as continuous, with reporting zone boundaries somewhat arbitrarily imposed on it.

But does this matter, or are geographic location and context irrelevant? Clearly geographic location is important for many purposes, such as wayfinding, but is it important for the purposes of social science, which is the focus of this book? Social science addresses a multitude of domains, using a wide range of methods, but in essence its purposes boil down to three:

- Understanding and explanation of human behavior, and processes involving humans and their actions;
- Prediction of such behaviors and processes, for purposes of planning or commerce;
- Solution of problems that face society, and can be alleviated through knowledge of human behavior.

This book is about the role of space, geographic location, and related concepts in such tasks. It rests on two related assertions, which will be addressed in detail in subsequent sections of this introduction and exemplified in the studies that are described by the book's contributors. First, location (and more generally space) is important and can contribute substantially to all three of the objectives identified above. Second, location and space provide a powerful mechanism for integrating the efforts of the various social sciences. Multidisciplinary efforts are increasingly important in pursuing the objectives of social science and in understanding the coupling of social and physical processes on the landscape. We argue in the third section of this introduction that space provides one of the few, and perhaps the only basis for such integration.

These are the arguments that we made in our successful proposal to the National Science Foundation that led to the establishment in 1999 of the Center for Spatially Integrated Social Science (CSISS) within the National Center for Geographic Information and Analysis at the University of California, Santa Barbara (see http://CSISS.org).

In the fourth section of this introduction, we briefly review CSISS and expand on our purposes in putting together this book.

Although the focus of this book is on the role of space, many of the points made here can equally well be made about time, or the combination of space and time (Peuquet 2002). For many purposes, *spatial* should be read as shorthand for *spatiotemporal*, especially for dynamic phenomena.

The Importance of Space

In this section, we present three arguments for the importance of space as a source of insight and understanding and as a basis for prediction and the solution of problems. We do not suggest that the set of three is exhaustive—rather, it seems likely that other arguments can also be made. The discussion expands on the arguments presented by Goodchild et al. (2000). It is followed by a short introduction to geographic information systems (GIS), and their impacts on the social sciences.

Spatial Analysis

The terms *spatial analysis* or *spatial data analysis* suggest an emphasis on location in the conduct of analysis or, more formally, suggest that results of analysis using any of the techniques falling into this category are dependent in some way on the locations of the objects being analyzed—if the locations change, the results change. Spatial analysis examines data in *cross-section*, as opposed to *longitudinal* analysis, or the analysis of temporal series. The decennial snapshots provided by the census are a prominent example of cross-sectional data, because each snapshot provides a picture of the nation's population at one specific date. Successive snapshots can, in principle, be assembled to provide longitudinal series, but the long time intervals between census years and the tendency for the definitions of variables and reporting zones to change makes this a challenging task. Nevertheless, the National Historic GIS project at the University of Minnesota is attempting to build a Web-based resource that will make this possible for the entire period since the first U.S. census (see http://www.nhgis.org).

Despite such efforts, however, social scientists must face the fact that cross-sectional data of relevance to social science are much easier to acquire than longitudinal data. Yet the processes that social scientists study occur in time and reveal their effects in changes on the landscape. How can the study or analysis of data in cross section lead to insights into behavioral processes—or more broadly, how can spatial analysis lead to scientific understanding in social science? This theme is explored in detail in many chapters of this book; in Chapter 12, for example, Sweeney and Feser discuss our ability to understand business processes from cross-sectional data.

The techniques of spatial analysis address the issue that opened this chapter: the loss of spatial context when cross-sectional information is displayed in the form of tables. Suppose, for example, that the same information on comparative performance of national economies, or percentage of home ownership by state, were displayed in the form of a map rather than as a table. In this form it is easy to compare each state's level of home ownership to those of its neighbors, to identify anomalies in the form of states whose levels are out of line with those of their neighbors, and to compare the patterns seen in the map with prior knowledge of each state's characteristics and those of its neighbors. In essence, the creation of a map is a very simple and intuitive form of spatial analysis or, perhaps more correctly, a way of empowering the human eye and brain to perform intuitive spatial analysis. Just as with any form of information presentation, it is subject to manipulation by the map designer, through the inappropriate choice of colors and class intervals (see, e.g., Monmonier 1991); and by insisting on planimetric accuracy, maps tend to overemphasize large states and may make small states almost impossible to see (though *cartograms* provide an interesting way of adjusting visual emphasis (Dorling 1995).

A multitude of more elaborate forms of spatial analysis have been described in the past few decades, and several excellent texts provide surveys. Bailey and Gatrell (1995) organize their review by data type, providing surveys of techniques suited for the analysis of data based on (1) point observations, such as records of crime locations; (2) aggregations by reporting zones, such as the summary data produced by the census; and (3) interactions between reporting zones, such as data on migrations, trade flows, or commuting patterns. The survey by Fotheringham et al. (2000) is one of the most recent, and includes many techniques developed in the past decade for place-based analysis (see the next section). Mitchell (1999) provides an intuitive survey that is most helpful as a key to understanding the role of GIS in spatial analysis.

Spatial analysis can play important roles in both inductive and deductive approaches to science. In an inductive context, the display of data in spatial context may reveal patterns and anomalies and suggest processes that might account for them. The story of John Snow's use of a map to reinforce the notion that drinking water from a pump in London might have been the cause of an outbreak of cholera in 1854 remains one of the most compelling instances of inference from data viewed in cross section (Gilbert 1958; Goodchild 1992; Tufte 1983). The map clearly shows a clustering of cholera cases around the pump, reflecting the tendency for people to draw water from the nearest available source (Figure 1.1). Since then, many other potential causes of disease have been investigated as a result of similar observations of anomalous clustering in cross-sectional data, suggesting causal mechanisms associated with residential or workplace locations that are in turn reflected in georeferenced mortality or morbidity records. Clustering is also the focus of Chapter 6, in which Logan and Zhang examine the varying character of ethnic neighborhoods in contemporary Los Angeles, and of Chapter 19, where Weeks describes the role of clustering in understanding demographic processes. In Chapter 18, Gatrell and Rigby review the role of spatial perspectives in many areas of public health, from epidemiology to health care service delivery.

Cross-sectional data can also be used to test existing theories and principles, in an approach that is more deductive than inductive. But here one must confront an important principle: that the same spatial pattern can be produced by a range of different processes—in other words, that there is no 1:1 correspondence between process through time and pattern in space. For example, even Snow's simple symmetrical clustering of cholera cases around the Broad Street pump could have been caused by contagion, the popular hypothesis for cholera transmission at the time, if the original carrier had also been located in Broad Street, given the tendency for social networks to cluster in space. The principle of Occam's razor might be invoked to justify adopting

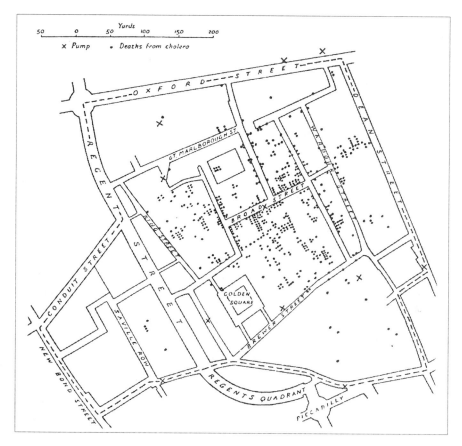

Figure 1.1. The map made by Dr. John Snow of the incidence of cholera during an outbreak in the Soho district of London in 1854. The contaminated water pump is to the right of the D in Broad Street. Snow's map first appeared in his *On the Mode of Communication of Cholera,* 2nd Edition, much Enlarged (London: John Churchill, 1855); it is included in *Snow on Cholera, being a reprint of two papers by John Snow, M.D.* (New York: The Commonwealth Fund: Oxford University Press, 1936) and is reproduced here from Gilbert (1958, 174).

the simpler drinking water hypothesis, but although this is amply justified by scientific practice, it seems a weak argument in the circumstances. Snow himself was able to have the pump handle removed and to observe the consequent effect on the outbreak, but today few social scientists can enjoy the luxury of such a controlled experiment on a human population. Thus, spatial pattern and spatial analysis can rarely if ever be used to confirm theories, though they can certainly be used to deny false ones and to justify controlled experiments or longitudinal analysis where these are possible.

In summary, spatial analysis is perhaps best seen as an exploratory technique, more suitable for the generation of hypotheses and insights than to strict confirmation of theory (a process ably illustrated by Kantner in Chapter 16 in his efforts to reconstruct past behavior from the evidence of prehistoric roadways). As such, however, its presentation of data in visual form, its use of spatial context, and the power of the eye and brain to detect patterns and anomalies and to recall other information about places from memory form a potent environment for scientific understanding, as the authors demonstrate in several of the chapters of this book.

Recently, much technical progress has been made in taking advantage of the capabilities of modern computing environments to go well beyond what has traditionally been possible with data displayed in the form of maps, and the application of routine and somewhat mechanical methods of spatial analysis. In Chapter 3, Kwan and Lee use GIS-based tools to visualize individual behavior in space and time, using the capabilities of software to generate dynamic, three-dimensional displays of vast amounts of data. Such methods can reveal patterns and anomalies in behavior that might never be evident in more conventional two-dimensional mapping. *Exploratory spatial data analysis* (ESDA) builds on the broad success of exploratory data analysis (EDA), a trend toward a more interactive and visual approach to statistical analysis initiated by Tukey and others in statistics in the 1970s (Tukey 1977). ESDA research has explored several distinct avenues that are variously unique to spatial data. Anselin (1999) emphasizes the importance of *spatial autocorrelation*, or the tendency for observations that are near each other in space to have similar values—for "locational similarity matched by value similarity." In Chapter 7, Messner and Anselin demonstrate the use of the concept in understanding patterns of homicide. Others have pursued the idea of *linked windows*. In this approach, several distinct views of a data set are presented to the observer simultaneously in a series of windows, with dynamic linkages between them. For example, a data set might be displayed as a map, a table, a histogram of one variable, and a scatterplot of two variables. Pointing to an observation or group of observations in one window automatically causes the corresponding observations to be highlighted in other windows. Thus, one can highlight the outliers from the main trend in a scatterplot and observe their locations on a map.

Place-Based Analysis

Generalization is a cornerstone of the scientific method, and there is much greater interest in discovering things that are generally true than things that are true only at certain times or in certain places. This *nomothetic* approach to science has obvious value in such disciplines as physics and chemistry, where scientific truths, such as chemical reactions and the laws of motion, have an absolute validity. But in the social sciences there is no realistic prospect of discovering such absolute truths about human behavior; as the nuclear physicist Sir Ernest Rutherford is reputed[1] to have said or written, "The only possible conclusion the social sciences can draw is: some do, some don't." One might dream of a model of human behavior that accounts for all variance ($R^2 = 1$), but in reality, rejection of the null hypothesis that the model accounts for *no* variance is more often the basis for claims of progress.

If a model fits imperfectly, then it is reasonable to expect that its residuals will show geographic patterns, and perhaps that the model will fit better (residual variation will be smaller) in some areas than others—in other words, it will exhibit spatial *nonstationarity*. If so, then the results obtained from an analysis over any limited study area will depend explicitly on the bounds of the study area, and will be different if the study area is changed. It is common, when analyzing cross-sectional data, to make maps of residuals, hoping that spatial context will suggest factors that might explain the residual variation and improve the model's fit. One might observe, for example, that residuals were uncommonly high in certain parts of a city or in certain states, and prior knowledge of those areas, or maps of other factors, might suggest modifications to the model. But these arguments lie firmly within the nomothetic tradition: the purpose of analysis is to discover universal truths.

By contrast, the *idiographic* approach seeks to identify and record the unique properties of places. The effort may still be scientific, in the sense that results are reproducible and described in terms whose meanings are widely understood, but generalization is much less important as a motivation. A follower of the idiographic approach might become an expert in some particular area of the earth's surface, and his or her students might become experts in parts of that area, in a potentially infinite regress. The debate between nomothetic and idiographic approaches to the discipline of geography peaked in the 1950s (Johnston 1991), and remains an important dimension of the discipline's methodological tensions.

Recently, however, a middle position has emerged that adds a new stimulus to the debate. *Place-based* or *local* analysis (Fotheringham and Brunsdon 1999) attempts to identify the properties that distinguish places, within the context provided by a general framework. Consider, for example, the technique of *geographically weighted regression* (GWR) developed by Fotheringham and his group at the University of Newcastle (Brunsdon et al. 1999; Fotheringham et al. 1998, 2000). Suppose a simple linear model is to be fitted to data from geographically dispersed observations. Normally, one would use ordinary least squares, maximum likelihood, or some other suitable criterion to obtain a single set of estimates of the universal parameters of the model. Suppose, instead, that observations are weighted, using weights that are inversely related to distance from some chosen location. The fitted parameters of the model will now be dependent on the location chosen and will vary as the regression is recentered on different locations. By recentering the regression many times, one can build up a complete map of the spatial variation of the parameter estimates, which can now be interpreted based on spatial context and known characteristics of the study area.

Many other methods of local analysis have been developed in the past few years. Anselin's Local Indicators of Spatial Association (LISA; Anselin 1995) decompose universal measures of pattern into local measures, allowing much more detailed and insightful interpretation (Cohen and Tita apply these methods in Chapter 9). For example, measures of spatial autocorrelation such as Moran's I can be decomposed into local Moran scatterplots, a useful means of detecting local anomalies (in Chapter 11, Câmara et al. apply these techniques to analyze social exclusion in São Paulo). Getis and Ord (1992) describe locally centered measures of clustering in point patterns. In Chapter 12 Sweeny and Feser provide a thorough evaluation of measures for assessing the clustering and dispersal of manufacturing firms in Los Angeles and Atlanta.

In essence, place-based analysis relies on a simple expectation: that any model or theory in the social sciences will fail to account perfectly for the phenomena that it describes, and that in such circumstances phenomena will almost certainly exhibit nonstationarity. If this is the case, then more will be learned by exploring patterns of nonstationarity than by averaging them within a universal model or analytic technique. As in the previous section, space provides the necessary link to other potentially interesting factors and to the context of observations.

Spatially Explicit Models and Theory

A model is said to be spatially explicit when it differentiates behaviors and predictions according to spatial location. Consider a model that attempts to predict the behavior of the U.S. economy. If the model lumps all aspects of the economy together without respect to location, assuming in effect that there is perfect communication between all regions of the United States, then its predictions similarly apply uniformly to the entire country. But the model would acquire some degree of spatial explicitness if it regarded the economy as a system of regional economies, with processes coupling the different regional parts together, and if it predicted distinct outcomes in each region. Regions could be broken down into constituent states; states might be broken down into counties; and the number of spatial components of the economy might be progressively increased to a very large number. In the limit, the economy might be modeled as a collection of actors moving across continuous space, rather than confined to lumped geographic areas.

This same continuum from one, to a few lumps, to a continuum underlies the models that are increasingly used to predict the behavior of large systems, in disciplines ranging from economics to communications, hydrology, ecology, and even physics. The field of *geocomputation* (Atkinson and Martin 2000; Longley et al. 1998; Openshaw and Abrahart 2000) specializes in spatially explicit models that make use of high-speed computation to simulate future outcomes on the earth's surface. Such models have been developed for the behavior of individuals in crowds (Haklay et al. 2001); for the impacts of human decisions on land use (White et al. in Chapter 21; Clarke et al. 1997; http://www.cipec.org/research/biocomplexity/); and for many other spatially distributed social phenomena. In Chapter 4, Benenson shows how a spatially explicit model of agent behavior can be used to gain insights into processes of residential segregation. In Chapter 5, O'Sullivan examines broader issues of agent-based modeling, including data requirements and model validation.

A spatially explicit theory might be defined as a theory whose outcomes depend on the locations of the objects that are the focus of the theory. It follows that one or more spatial concepts, such as distance, location, connectivity, adjacency, or direction, must appear in the theory. A good example is the spatial interaction model, a basis for predicting migration, communication, or travel between places over space (Fotheringham and O'Kelly 1989; Haynes and Fotheringham 1984) that has several theoretical roots. The quantity of interaction is modeled as the product of an origin factor or tendency to generate interaction, such as population; a destination factor or tendency to attract interaction, such as the number of job opportunities; and a factor that is a decreasing function of the spatial separation between origin and destination.

One of the significant attractions of space as a basis for modeling stems from the means used to assess a model's success. Consider, for example, the use of a spatially explicit model to predict the evolution of land use in an area, as a result of urban growth. The model will make use of spatially explicit starting conditions, such as the existing state of urbanization at the beginning of the modeled period, the availability of developable land, and proximity to existing transportation infrastructure. Included in the model's algorithm are random components, designed to produce a range of outcomes in the form of future patterns of development. None of these outcomes can be reasonably expected to match the actual future pattern of land use, raising the question of how the model can be validated. Typically, success is measured by the degree to which the gross spatial characteristics of the outcome match actual patterns—in terms of the degree of fragmentation of urban land use or the degree of dispersion around urban centers and infrastructure.

In summary, space is important in modeling and theory because it accounts for the effects of separation and imperfect communication between parts of a social system; because it allows the modeler to include the impact of heterogeneous spaces on model outcomes; and because the spatial properties of predictions are an important basis for assessment of model success. But although space is important, it is not at all clear that space can actually *explain*, or whether the spatial concepts that appear in a spatially explicit theory are not merely surrogates for something else (Harvey 1969; Sack 1972). For example, the distance term that appears in the spatial interaction model can be interpreted as measuring the costs of transportation that ultimately account for decreasing interaction with distance, or as reflecting the correlation that exists between distance and human communication (this issue of the relationship between social interaction and space is the focus of Chapter 10, where Eagles et al. examine the spatial structure of political networks, and of Chapter 20, where Guldmann describes models of international telecommunication flows). The information-theoretic basis for the spatial interaction model popularized by Wilson (1970) ascribes a rather different role to distance, arguing that the model represents merely the most likely allocation of trips, given knowledge of the average or total distance traveled, but again, this can hardly be interpreted as using distance to *explain* interaction.

Geographic Information Systems

At least some of the current interest in space in social science, and in other areas of science that deal with the earth's surface, has to do with the emergence over the past three decades of a class of software known as geographic information systems (GIS). Like many other classes of software, this one owes its success in part to the economies of scale that result from integrating computer functions that operate on a particular class of information, in this case geographic information. Similar scale-economies obtain for word-processing software (functions operating on digital text) or spreadsheets (functions operating on digital tables). Although geographic information seems particularly well defined, as information about phenomena on the earth's surface, the large number of ways of creating digital representations of such information has ensured that GIS is a particularly complex computer application. Nevertheless it has become popular, in areas ranging from resource management to marketing, and from academic research to the operations of utility companies. Longley et al. (2001) provide an introductory text, and Longley et al. (1999) a comprehensive review of the state of the GIS art. Social science applications are reviewed in many of the major texts, and particularly in the text by Martin (1996).

A modern GIS contains functions for the creation, acquisition, editing, and storage of geographic information; for query, analysis, and modeling; and for visual display, report generation, and other forms of output. It supports geographic features represented as points, lines, or areas, defining their locations with the use of coordinates in so-called *vector* representations, and also continuous geographic variation over regular grids known as *rasters*. It supports the easy integration of tabular data with representations of reporting zone boundaries and thus, the preparation of maps and other more sophisticated forms of data display, such as ESDA.

GIS is grounded in geographic space and treats the boundaries of reporting zones as features superimposed on the geographic continuum. Standard tools allow data from neighboring zones to be compared and aggregated, and *areal interpolation* tools allow statistics for one set of reporting zones to be estimated from known values for a second, incompatible set of reporting zones (Goodchild et al. 1993). Openshaw (1983) and others have explored the importance of reporting zone boundaries in conditioning what can be learned about social processes, a theme that is explored further by Sampson and Morenoff in Chapter 8 and by Rey in Chapter 14.

GIS has made tools for mapping and many of the methods of spatial analysis readily accessible to researchers. GIS courses and programs are now taught on almost all university campuses, in community colleges, and even in high schools, and courses and programs are readily available over the World Wide Web. In effect, a GIS is to spatial social science as a word processor is to writing, or a statistics package is to statistical analysis—an indispensable modern tool for working with a particular type of information. Some of the reasons for the popularity of GIS are explored in the next section, on the role of space in the integration of data, processes, and disciplines.

Space as a Basis for Integration

A neophyte's first view of GIS is often of some version of the *layer-cake* model, a representation of phenomena on the earth's surface as a series of layers, each layer representing a distinct variable or class of phenomena. The model graces the cover of several introductory GIS texts (e.g., Star and Estes 1990), and its roots extend back several centuries. McHarg (1969) was influential in promoting the model as a basis for landscape architecture and other design disciplines, arguing that one could represent the factors impacting a development, or impacted by it, as a series of transparent layers, with the strongest impact corresponding to the greatest opaqueness; by overlaying the layers, one could visualize the locations of least total impact.

McHarg's concept received a massive boost with the advent of GIS, since the tools to perform the necessary redrafting of maps onto transparencies, reclassification into measures of impact, registration of layers to a common base, and if necessary transformation to a common projection could all be handled easily by standard functions. The layer-cake thus became an important icon of the ability of GIS to integrate data on different topics from different sources, and to support the investigation of spatial correlations and spatial context. Users could easily compare one layer to another, combining information on environmental pollution with the ethnicity of neighborhoods, or rates of disease. Today, it is possible to use standard interfaces between GIS software and the Internet (e.g., the Geography Network, http://www.geographynetwork.com), along with the resources of massive public archives of geographic information (e.g., http://www.alexandria.ucsb.edu, http://www.fgdc.gov/clearinghouse/) to integrate, visualize, and analyze data about virtually any location on the planet, at spatial resolutions ranging down to 1 m.

The role of space as a mechanism of integration appears to be unique; although one might imagine integrating information based on time, it makes much more sense to integrate data about a historic period specifically for some geographic location, than for all locations. For example, there would be much more interest in all information about fifteenth-century Paris than about the fifteenth century anywhere; but someone researching contemporary Paris might well be interested in information about Paris in earlier periods. In essence, we argue that space trumps time alone as a basis for integration, but space and time trump space.

Recently, the idea of using space to integrate information has been extended beyond digital maps and images to any information that can be related to the earth's surface—in other words, information with a geographic *footprint*. The traditional library has relied on author, title, and subject as the keys to its catalog. Although one might imagine using geographic location as a key, the technical difficulties associated with doing so in a traditional library are profound. But they are comparatively trivial in a digital library, and several Web sites now support search of their information archives using geographic location as a primary key. One can, for example, search the site of the Environmental Protection Agency (http://www.epa.gov) for all information related to a particular area, such as a ZIP code. A *geolibrary* (NRC 1999) is defined as a digital library that is searchable by geographic location, returning maps, images, reports, photographs, and even pieces of music identified with a particular location.

But the integration argument can be extended further. The behavior of human societies is best understood in terms of distinct processes—economic, political, or social—that are studied somewhat in isolation by different disciplines (economics, political science, and sociology respectively). Although researchers pursue knowledge that is general, the implications of that knowledge are felt locally, in the particular circumstances of specific locations. In the development of local policy, the reductionist approach that allocates processes to different disciplines is counterproductive, since it encourages social policies that ignore economics, and economic policies that ignore politics. Just as space provides an integrating mechanism for data, then, we argue that space can provide an integrating mechanism for the social sciences and a mechanism for linking science to policy. In Chapter 2, Boucek and Moran show the importance of this principle in their studies of land cover changes in Brazil and Thailand, where a spatially explicit landscape proves to be the essential key to unraveling and understanding the complex interactions of social and physical processes. And in a very different context, Shen in Chapter 13 shows the value of space as an integrating mechanism for research on urban transportation and communication.

This concept is aptly captured in the design of GIS. Essentially, a GIS consists of two components: the database, representing the conditions on the earth's surface in the studied area; and the functions, algorithms, methods, models, and database design that are largely independent of location, in the sense that they could potentially be applied to data from anywhere. The database is thus idiographic and specific to the studied area, while the other components of the system are nomothetic, representing general procedures and scientific knowledge. Thus the GIS is a potential key to linking science to local policy—both a tool for scientific discovery and a means for delivering discovered scientific knowledge in local areas. Bradshaw and Muller use two examples in Chapter 15 to demonstrate this principle.

Toward Spatially Integrated Social Science

The previous two sections outlined the arguments for space as important in social science, and as a basis for integrating the work of social science disciplines and delivering that work in practical contexts. As we noted earlier, these are the arguments we used in founding the Center for Spatially Integrated Social Science (CSISS) at the University of California, Santa Barbara. This section outlines the work of the center, and its role in this book.

In the physical sciences, the concept of research infrastructure has a long and successful history. Systems like the Hubble Telescope are extremely expensive, and can only be justified if designed to serve the needs of many different scientific experiments, by many different research groups. Just as insurance companies spread risk over large groups of insured, so such infrastructure projects spread their costs over large research communities. But the concept of research infrastructure has never penetrated the social sciences to the same degree, except in the case of large surveys and large data archives, in part because infrastructure is too strongly associated with large items of equipment. But computational tools, research skills, and the publication system are also arguably research infrastructure, and the costs of the investments they represent are spread over large communities, even in the social sciences. We argued in the CSISS proposal that, because spatial methods are relevant to many social scientists, investments in learning about them, automating them in computational tools, and sharing success with them could legitimately be regarded as research infrastructure.

Funding for CSISS began in October 1999, with an initial five-year commitment by the National Science Foundation. The CSISS mission "recognizes the growing significance of space, spatiality, location, and place in social science research. It seeks to develop unrestricted access to tools and perspectives that will advance the spatial analytic capabilities of researchers throughout the social sciences." CSISS has since developed seven programs, all aimed at facilitating the use of spatial perspectives in the social sciences:

- A program of national workshops, offered each summer for one-week periods to young researchers in the social sciences, and focusing on GIS, mapping, spatial analysis, and related topics;
- Specialist meetings, which bring together senior researchers interested in major themes in the social sciences, such as spatial equity, to identify needed investments in infrastructure to support research in the theme;
- A virtual community of scholars interested in spatial perspectives, with Web resources that include search engines and bibliographies;
- A program to enhance the computational tools available for GIS and spatial analysis, being conducted at the University of Illinois at Urbana-Champaign under the directorship of Luc Anselin;

- Efforts to develop facilities for searching social science data archives based on geographic location;
- A collection of learning resources, and pointers from the CSISS Web site to other resources aimed at facilitating a spatial perspective;
- A program to encourage best practices in spatially integrated social science.

This book is the most important outcome of the last of these programs, and in the next section we describe our objectives and the process used to assemble the book.

Objectives of the Book

Our objective in assembling this book has been to illustrate the application of spatial perspectives across the breadth of the social sciences, without respect to discipline, and by doing so to encourage others to follow similar paths, to improve on them, and to apply them in new areas. The objective is thus fully consistent with our theme of spatially integrated social science. The term "best practices" is controversial and misleading, but it does convey the notion of leading by example and reflects our attempt to identify leaders in the application of spatial perspectives in different disciplines and subdisciplines.

We used a fairly complex process to assemble the book. We began by searching the social science literature and citation indices to find publications that used spatial perspectives and that were frequently cited—in other words, publications that were in some sense seminal or groundbreaking. From this analysis, we selected a tentative group of authors and commissioned them to write to the theme of the book, with an emphasis on the process of science, from problem formulation to generalizable conclusions. We deliberately allowed the subject matter to span the range from largely empirical studies, to surveys of studies, to more theoretical contributions, hoping thereby to represent the range of research styles in the social sciences. We also allowed the chapters to range from the very intuitive to the conceptually complex, again reflecting the range of practice. We reviewed and edited the drafts, striving for a consistent style and adherence to the objectives.

Such a diverse collection of material might be organized in any number of ways, each reflecting one dimension of the range of material. After much debate we decided to use a cross-cutting theme that speaks directly to the spatial focus and our desire to blur the boundaries of the disciplines: the spatial resolution of the project, from the local to the global. To study the individual from a spatial perspective one needs sufficient spatial resolution to identify the individual, which means on the order of 1 m; while to study the interactions between large aggregates, such as nations, a spatial resolution as coarse as 10 km might be adequate. Of course, few if any studies in the social sciences use such strictly uniform notions of spatial resolution, preferring to work with units such as counties, which may vary by as much as a factor of several hundred in linear dimension in the United States (between a Virginia city-county and San Bernardino County, for example), and in Chapter 17 Daly and Lock demonstrate the value of an explicitly multi-scale approach in spatial archaeology. Nevertheless, there are clear differences between studies of individuals, neighborhoods, cities, regions, and nations that are reflected in distinct methodologies and theoretical frameworks.

The book is structured as a series of sections, each containing chapters using a similar level of spatial resolution, and each beginning with an introduction that explains the relationship between the chapters and between the section and the rest of the book. The book is not intended to be read from cover to cover, though we would of course be very happy if some chose to do that. Rather, we hope the book will be mined for examples, parallels, analogies, and other aids to lateral thinking about research in the social sciences. As such, we hope we have contributed to the development of research infrastructure and to the growing importance of space in the social sciences.

Note

1. Although it is frequently cited, we have been unable to find a documented source of this comment.

References

Abel, D.J., and D.M. Mark. 1990. A comparative analysis of some 2-dimensional orderings. *International Journal of Geographical Information Systems* 4(1): 21–31.

Anselin, L. 1995. Local indicators of spatial association—LISA. *Geographical Analysis* 27: 93–115.

Anselin, L. 1999. Interactive techniques and exploratory spatial data analysis. In P.A. Longley, M.F. Goodchild, D.J. Maguire, and D.W. Rhind (eds.), *Geographical Information Systems: Principles, Techniques, Management and Applications*. New York: Wiley, 253–266.

Atkinson, P., and D. Martin (eds.). 2000. *GIS and Geocomputation*. London: Taylor and Francis.

Bailey, T.C., and A.C. Gatrell. 1995. *Interactive Spatial Data Analysis*. New York: Wiley.

Brunsdon, C., A.S. Fotheringham, and M. Charlton. 1999. Some notes on parametric significance tests for geographically weighted regression. *Journal of Regional Science* 39(3): 497–524.

Clarke, K.C., S. Hoppen, and L. Gaydos. 1997. A self-modifying cellular automaton model of historical urbanization in the San Francisco Bay area. *Environment and Planning B: Planning and Design* 24(2): 247–261.

Dorling, D. 1995. *A New Social Atlas of Britain*. Chichester, U.K.: Wiley.

Fotheringham, A.S., and C. Brunsdon. 1999. Local forms of spatial analysis. *Geographical Analysis* 31(4): 340–358.

Fotheringham, A.S., C. Brunsdon, and M. Charlton. 2000. *Quantitative Geography: Perspectives on Spatial Data Analysis*. London: Sage.

Fotheringham, A.S., M.E. Charlton, and C. Brunsdon. 1998. Geographically weighted regression: A natural evolution of the expansion method for spatial data analysis. *Environment and Planning A* 30(11): 1905–1927.

Fotheringham, A.S., and M.E. O'Kelly. 1989. *Spatial Interaction Models: Formulations and Applications*. Dordrecht: Kluwer.

Getis, A., and J.K. Ord. 1992. The analysis of spatial association by use of distance statistics. *Geographical Analysis* 24: 189–206.

Gilbert, E.W. 1958. Pioneer maps of health and disease in England. *Geographical Journal* 124: 172–183.

Goodchild, M.F. 1992. Analysis. In R.F. Abler, M.G. Marcus, and J.M. Olson (eds.), *Geography's Inner Worlds: Pervasive Themes in Contemporary American Geography*. New Bruswick, N.J.: Rutgers University Press, 138–162.

Goodchild, M.F., L. Anselin, and U. Deichmann. 1993. A framework for the areal interpolation of socioeconomic data. *Environment and Planning A* 25: 383–397.

Goodchild, M.F., L. Anselin, R.P. Appelbaum, and B.H. Harthorn. 2000. Toward spatially integrated social science. *International Regional Science Review* 23(2): 139–159.

Haklay, M., T. Schelhorn, D. O'Sullivan, and M. Thurstain-Goodwin 2001. 'So go down town': Simulating pedestrian movement in town centres. *Environment and Planning B: Planning and Design* 28(3): 343–59.

Harvey, D. 1969. *Explanation in Geography*. London: Edward Arnold.

Haynes, K.E., and A.S. Fotheringham. 1984. *Gravity and Spatial Interaction Models*. Beverly Hills, Calif.: Sage.

Johnston, R.J. 1991. *Geography and Geographers: Anglo-American Geography since 1945*. 4th edition. London: Edward Arnold.

Longley, P.A., S.M. Brooks, R. McDonnell, and W. Macmillan (eds.). 1998. *Geocomputation: A Primer*. New York: Wiley.

Longley, P.A., M.F. Goodchild, D.J. Maguire, and D.W. Rhind (eds.). 1999. *Geographical Information Systems: Principles, Techniques, Management and Applications*. New York: Wiley.

Longley, P.A., M.F. Goodchild, D.J. Maguire, and D.W. Rhind. 2001. *Geographic Information Systems and Science*. New York: Wiley.

Martin, D. 1996. *Geographic Information Systems: Socioeconomic Applications*. 2nd edition. London: Routledge.

McHarg, I.L. 1969. *Design with Nature*. Garden City, N.Y.: Natural History Press.

Mitchell, A. 1999. *The ESRI Guide to GIS Analysis*. Redlands, Calif.: ESRI Press.

Monmonier, M.S. 1991. *How to Lie with Maps*. Chicago: University of Chicago Press.

National Research Council. 1999. *Distributed Geolibraries: Spatial Information Resources*. Washington, D.C.: National Academy Press.

Nicol, A.A.M., and P.M. Pexman. 1999. *Presenting Your Findings: A Practical Guide for Creating Tables*. Washington, D.C.: American Psychological Association.

Openshaw, S. 1983. *The Modifiable Areal Unit Problem*. Concepts and Techniques in Modern Geography No. 38. Norwich, U.K.: GeoBooks.

Openshaw, S., and R.J. Abrahart (eds.). 2000. *Geocomputation*. New York: Taylor and Francis.

Peuquet, D.J. 2002. *Representations of Space and Time*. New York: Guilford.

Sack, R.D. 1972. Geography, geometry, and explanation. *Annals of the Association of American Geographers* 62: 61–78.

Star, J., and J.E. Estes. 1990. *Geographic Information Systems: An Introduction*. Englewood Cliffs, N.J.: Prentice Hall.

Tufte, E.R. 1983. *The Visual Display of Quantitative Information*. Cheshire, Conn.: Graphics Press.

Tukey, J.W. 1977. *Exploratory Data Analysis*. Reading, Mass.: Addison-Wesley.

Wilson, A.G. 1970. *Entropy in Urban and Regional Modelling*. London: Pion.

Part I

Spatial Analysis at Individual and Household Levels

The chapters in this section focus on two of the most fundamental units of human behavior—the individual and the household. Individual and household behaviors are important in their own right and are major areas of social science investigation. It is suggested that spatial contextual information adds significantly to the social meaning of data at these levels of analysis. For example, an individual's actions are conditioned, in part, by the locations and attributes of neighbors. In addition, behavior at the individual level is seen to influence patterns of occurrence and processes at more aggregate spatial levels, such as the neighborhood. While these chapters share scale of analysis in common, their analytic approaches differ in important ways. The chapters by Kwan and Lee and by Boucek and Moran treat observed phenomena and draw meaning from empirical analyses. In contrast, the chapters by Benenson and O'Sullivan, using Agent-Based Models (ABM), focus on the representation of behavior through artificial agents operative in environments that correspond spatially to real-world or representative situations.

Boucek and Moran use remotely sensed data from satellite imagery and large-scale aerial photography to document a time series of household-level land use changes in the Amazon region of Brazil. A spatially explicit research design links these inventories to the concept of an urban-rural transition, with separate but interrelated analyses for within-urban areas, for rural areas where households are located in villages, and for rural areas where household residences are dispersed on individual land holdings. The authors employ traditional social survey methods to establish ground truth for their observations on housing modifications, crop patterns, road extensions, and other changes in local phenomena. Successful inferring about household behavior from remotely sensed imagery would offer exceptional value for monitoring the environmental consequences of land cover changes in comparatively isolated regions of the world. While the authors

acknowledge difficulties in this task, the coupling of environmental and human processes is essential if society is to resolve issues of sustainable global change. Their work
has clear policy relevance for linking the impact of social processes to environmental
consequences.

Kwan and Lee make use of possibly the most explicit individual behavioral model of
how people engage in daily rounds of activities and travels—Torsten Hägerstrand's time-
geography model. They attempt to wed the model with the capabilities of GIS-based
three-dimensional visualization tools. They demonstrate the mapping of daily activity
paths for more than 4,400 individuals in the metropolitan region of Portland, Oregon.
This set of two-day, space-time diaries captured nearly 72,000 trips, disaggregated by
the authors to reveal different activity patterns based on gender and ethnicity. In addition, they illustrated space-time aggregations to map activity density surfaces (e.g.,
non-employment activities) at different times of the day. Although the activity resolution
is quite coarse for treating in-home episodes (only activities of at least 30 minutes in duration), it did capture all changes in location outside of the home. This research suggests
possibilities for treating even greater behavioral detail, especially with the integration
of modern wireless tracking systems linked for geo-referenced online computation.

Benenson develops an agent-based model (ABM) to simulate the decision choices
of households (agents) by establishing plausible behavioral rules for their selection of
houses and locations. The model is used as an exploratory forecasting tool for investigating housing choices, migration, and segregation processes in Yaffo, an area of Arab
and Jewish households within Tel Aviv, Israel. The environmental context for this simulated behavior is provided by a detailed GIS rendering of infrastructure, population
patterns, and housing characteristics for individual streets within the study area and by
demographic parameters determined from census data. These data are used to calibrate
the model and to validate its use for exploring individual choices made by household
agents about where to live. These decisions generate patterns of residential moves that,
in turn, influence future individual choices. This dynamic is seen as constituting an explicit space-time model. It is based on the distancing behavior and spatial interactions
of individual households in response to the behavior of others and to internal desires
for housing.

David O'Sullivan offers an interesting general argument for why it might be more
honest or useful to generate data from an artificial base of behavioral rules than to base
social science research on census or social surveys. This is especially the case for what
he describes as dynamic micro-scale modeling, for which he provides two examples: an
ABM approach to pedestrian movement in an urban setting, and a cellular automata
simulation of neighborhood gentrification. He alerts social scientists to some standard
criticisms of census-based research: arbitrary temporal discontinuities that pose problems for studying social processes and inappropriate levels of spatial aggregation that
camouflage the behavioral units. On the other hand, he also elaborates on issues regarding validation of simulation methods and representativeness of modeled agent
behavior.

While sharing commonality in scale of analysis, the chapters of Part I demonstrate
the value of different spatial methodologies. A primary advantage to assembling research data by individuals and households is the capability provided for aggregating
respondents to higher levels of generalization, in some cases to match with auxiliary

data sets organized at the levels of blocks, tracts, districts, or regions, and in other cases at the level of higher-ordered behavioral units, such as extended families, groups, communities, and neighborhoods. The availability of data at these scales is an issue of concern—high-resolution remote sensing data only indirectly capture human behavior and are subject to validation of inferred human actions and decisions. Space-time diary surveys are rare, expensive, and difficult to implement except for short durations. Tracking technologies may reduce this problem but pose ethical issues on the detail of surveillance that is acceptable, even for strictly scientific ends.

Possibly more than at any other scale of analysis, spatial social science at individual and household levels poses ethical issues for the researcher. The protection of individual privacy and the confidentiality of personal information may run counter to scientific interest. Locational information can be a powerful tool of science, yet its ability to provide identification may be seen as threatening and invasive, and politically sensitive. This is an issue that is even more telling in a world of wireless communication and locational technologies that people carry with them on a routine basis. Putting human choice behavior within a spatial or spatio-temporal context remains a challenge for social science research—the chapters in this section point to some of the issues and possible solutions.

2

Inferring the Behavior of Households from Remotely Sensed Changes in Land Cover

Current Methods and Future Directions

Bruce Boucek

Emilio F. Moran

F or the past 15 years, thanks in great part to the availability of 30-meter resolution Landsat Thematic Mapper (TM) digital data, a number of researchers have been able to carry out studies of land use and land cover change, focusing on issues such as landscape ecology, deforestation, and desertification and more recently, exploring the connection between climate change and health. Most of these analyses have focused on meso- and macro-scales with spatial resolution that is either global, national, or macro-regional (e.g., Amazon Basin, Southeast Asia). However, in the past 5 years a small community of scientists has begun to explore empirically the possibilities of more spatially detailed work that permits the examination of processes taking place at the household level. This chapter reviews these efforts, giving particular attention to the methods used: how they contribute to theory-building and methodological advances in a number of disciplines wherein the focus of research is on households, families, and other small social units.

Inferring the behavior of households from remotely sensed data is not commonplace—but it is now within reach. The spatial resolution of satellite data is improving, and so are the tools used to manipulate these data. These on-going improvements also benefit from the increased temporal frequency of data acquisition that improves the possibilities for the assemblage of finely grained spatial and temporal data. A number of important ethical challenges are presented by this opportunity: who should have access to these data, how should the behavior of individuals and households be protected, and what is appropriate and inappropriate use of these behavioral inferences? The scope of this chapter does not address these questions, but readers should take time to reflect on the ethical implications posed by this growing capacity to link spatial data to the behavior of households and communities. A number of expert meetings are planned for 2004 that will try to bring scholarly order and reflection to these issues. While it may be desirable to carry out research at the finest grained scale possible, given the explicitness of spatial information, research results may need to be aggregated to protect the confidentiality of the subjects.

This chapter reviews current approaches taken by a number of investigators examining urban areas, rural areas where people live in villages and commute to their landholdings, and rural areas where people reside on the land they use. Each of these contrasting settings presents distinct challenges to linking households to land cover change and for inferring the behavior of households using remotely sensed data within a geographic information system (GIS). A detailed discussion of concept, methodology, and empirical findings is based on approaches developed by our research group in the Brazilian Amazon. In this work we have linked demographic, social survey research to a time-series of Landsat TM, multispectral scanner (MSS), and aerial photography to construct a temporally and spatially fine-grained analysis of changes in land cover at both the landscape and individual property scales so as to achieve accurate inferences about the behavior of households. This accuracy is possible because we can check our inferences against the survey research data collected from households.

Methods for Studying Land Use in Urban Areas

Most researchers studying land use and land cover change have ignored the role of urban areas in driving land cover conversion and bringing about environmental change. The data from orbital satellites are well suited for providing information to analyze a number of important environmental changes. However, there is very little agreed upon with regard to the methods for systematically characterizing urban land cover and examining land use in an urban context. Part of the challenge is defining the difference between urban and rural so that change can be adequately assessed (e.g., the expansion of urban areas into peri-urban and rural landscapes over time accompanying population growth and development). Land cover is the most important source of anthropogenic change on the planet (Turner et al. 1994; Lambin et al. 1999). The conversion of forest and grasslands to agropastoral uses has received the most attention by scientists, because of its link to deforestation, biodiversity loss, and carbon emissions (Walker and Steffen 1997).

Much of the research conducted by the remote sensing community in the urban context has been concerned either with management and planning or with the general problem of urban expansion (Jensen 1983; Jensen et al. 1994). This focus on urban and suburban expansion (and sprawl in the North American context), though implicitly connected to larger concerns about the environment and the consumption and exploitation of material resources and energy, has not been explicitly linked to regional land use and land cover conversion processes occurring on the periphery of urban centers or their surrounding regions, particularly in the developing world. There are a few cases where urban expansion and influences upon the urban fringe have been analyzed. However, these analyses have focused on North American (Canadian), European, and Chinese locations (examples include, respectively, Treitz et al. 1992; Antrop 2000; Wu 1998) that have a long history of dense urbanization. These studies focus on the general measure of urban expansion, rather than on regional land use and conversion.

This is a serious oversight, albeit partly produced as a consequence of technological limitations. All around the globe, including areas like the Amazon region, a process of rapid urbanization is underway. Urban areas are the loci of human activities, and urban interests increasingly drive rural land cover change (Browder and Godfrey 1997). Urbanization concentrates populations, and this results in significant impacts on land, water, materials, and energy. Thus, to understand land cover change, one must study the process of urbanization itself.

Currently there is no standardized description of urban land cover, nor is there a generally accepted definition of a city (Davis 1969; Whyte 1985; Lambin et al. 1999; Foresman et al. 1997). In Peru, urban areas are defined as "populated centers with 100 or more dwellings," while in Japan, urban is defined as places having 50,000 or more inhabitants (UN 1994). There is a mismatch between administrative boundaries and actual built-up land, and the human population is therefore over- or under-represented depending on city boundaries (UN 1994). This problem is a result of administrative boundaries routinely lagging behind urban growth and areal expansion. Despite the lack of a globally recognized definition of a city, it is possible to determine urban characteristics of land cover and land use using remotely sensed imagery gathered from satellites and airplanes. Land cover classification approaches that rely on Landsat MSS and TM imagery (79-meter and 30-meter resolutions, respectively) often fail to capture urban land cover because the resolution is too coarse for capturing adequately the complexity of the urban landscape. This is also due in part to the use of image classification techniques that rely primarily on the spectral information in the image without adequately incorporating texture or spatial structure. The primary limitation in the developing world, however, is access to adequate financial resources and technology to acquire and make use of detailed remotely sensed imagery. High spatial-resolution imagery in the form of aerial photographs has been available for close to a century in some parts of the world but is costly to acquire and process. In the past forty years, with the advent of remotely sensed satellite imagery, it has become possible to classify and analyze much larger portions of the earth's surface. Concurrently, a greater range of classification and accuracy has become possible as a result of technological improvements that have increased the range of observations of physical properties of the objects/surfaces being imaged. These advantages result from the use of a wider range of the electromagnetic spectrum—beyond normal human vision—and the use of radar and laser systems (see, e.g., textbooks on remote sensing and image analysis by Jensen 1996 and 2000). At the same time that advancements have been made using a variety of methods to determine the physical properties of the earth's surface and the objects on it, there have also been improvements in the resolution or grain at which those properties can be observed. Cowen and Jensen (1998) suggest that in order to capture better than a USGS Level 1 urban classification[1] it is necessary to use imagery with a ground resolution of better than 20 meters and for many urban applications, better than half a meter. For information on appropriate spatial and temporal scales see Cohen and Jensen (1998, 167). They also state that remote sensing can only provide a suggestion of the details of human activity.

To capture the complexity of the urban landscape, it would be useful to create an urban-rural gradient or transect of the transitions from one condition to the other (including urban areas that may end up over time as abandoned and reclaimed for other uses). One can begin such an approach by defining the elements that characterize urbanization (McDonnell and Pickett 1990) and standardizing them across world regions (Whyte 1985). In doing this, there are considerable advantages to using remote sensing. However, the use of remote sensing in capturing urban elements is challenging, particularly in representing accurately the complex mosaic of human modifications and built structures (Zipperer et al. 2000). Urban areas vary in terms of density of dwellings, the three-dimensional structure of buildings, the types of construction materials used, and the amount and type of vegetation present, among other factors.

The first requirement of developing standardized methods is to represent the range of physical, biological, and socioeconomic variations present (Moran 1995). In urban areas this means coming up with a gradient of cities that combines population size, spatial settlement patterns, and differences in settlement history. Population size and differences in settlement history can be obtained largely from census and archival research and help in defining the number of urban area types that might be desirable to characterize. The spatial settlement pattern, particularly as it relates to the type and distribution of land covers, can probably best be done by combining Landsat TM with aerial videography. Aerial videography captured in digital image format can be made into a mosaic, visually analyzed, and then classified using automated methods to compare with TM imagery (Hess et al. 2002). This can be further improved with the use of either Quickbird or IKONOS imagery[2] (the former with 61 cm spatial resolution in panchromatic and 2.4 m in multispectral, and the latter with 1 m panchromatic and 4 m multispectral) should funds be available for this detailed imagery. The drawbacks of using aerial videography and the high spatial resolution IKONOS and Quickbird imagery are the cost, storage, and processing requirements.

Aerial videography can help to identify the components of urban land cover precisely. The better-than-one-meter resolution of aerial videography permits a refined observation of components of the landscape, such as types of roofs, number of trees in backyards, quality of roads, size of buildings, types of infrastructure, and water bodies. These observations can be used to build a library of reflectance spectra for urban materials. It is then possible to derive Vegetation-Impervious Surface-Soil (VIS) fractions (Ridd 1995) for each TM pixel using spectral mixture analysis, eventually resulting in the development of maps of land cover change based on the VIS components (Powell et al. 2001; Madhavan et al. 2001). This approach seeks to address the problem of spatial resolution associated with that Landsat TM. Its 30-m pixels capture multiple urban surface materials; hence each pixel is made up of heterogeneous urban structures that hide the distinct urban components (Roberts et al. 1998). Selecting endmembers for spectral mixture analysis is particularly problematic in urban areas because of the great variety of materials used in the construction of buildings, roads, and other urban surfaces. Simple spectral mixture analysis will not model successfully the components of the urban landscape. A variation of spectral mixture analysis that allows each pixel to be modeled as different end member combinations (known as multiple end-member spectral mixture analysis) seems to overcome this problem (Roberts et al. 1998). Urban materials can then be grouped minimally into three classes: vegetation, impervious surfaces, and soils. These quantities can be compared regardless of local environment or construction materials (Ridd 1995). This approach eventually permits the comparison of urban land cover change with the socio-economic structure of cities over time and space. If a sufficiently detailed time series is constructed (Powell et al. 2001), it is then possible to develop inferences about the behavior of households in and around their buildings and other structures of land cover. This approach is advantageous in that it provides a gradient of change that can be used to determine transition from urban to rural, although this is also dependent on the land cover of the surrounding region.

One approach to linking urban households to the satellite imagery at a cluster-of-households level is to infer the behavior of households by generating historical maps of change in the urban-rural gradient. This can provide valuable information about the transformations experienced by households in urban areas over time. For example, if one takes a small urban area in the Amazon frontier, one will see thatch roofs dominating cover of houses, with only a few tile roofs indicative of the elite families, from the period before growth and development that began in the 1970s across that region (Moran 1993; Wood and Perz 1996). After that, one sees replacement of many of the thatch roofs with corrugated fiberglass, and the thatch roofs moving to the outskirts in what may be called shantytowns. Over time, one will see these shanty towns improve in quality, and this can be measured by the shift in materials used in houses and roofs, by the paving of roads, by the dispersion of warehouses from the riverside towards the roadsides, and by the planting of trees on promenades and in large patios surrounding the houses of the elite. These too will be more numerous and move towards peri-urban areas and away from the river toward the road, to indicate the shift in economic infrastructure that marks the importance of road transportation and the decline of river transport. As the urban area grows and the number of warehouses increases, indicating the growth of commerce, one can see shifts in land cover in the rural areas. This may be measured by the shift from smaller to larger properties, and from subsistence cultivation plots to larger pasture-dominated ranches—a preferred form of land use by absentee owners living in the city. The measurement of these shifts is possible using the techniques mentioned above, and inferences about economic development, population change, and social stratification can be derived with reasonable accuracy.

Since videography is a costly and intensive effort, it may be possible and more appropriate in some cases to use coarser analytical methods, including remote sensing image analysis and GIS spatial analysis techniques, to identify and characterize larger peri-urban landscapes and to evaluate their internal dynamics, as well as their relationship to urban cores and to the extensive rural and possibly even wilderness/frontier landscapes that they provide linkages between. Below, we provide one example of a method that uses available classified Landsat TM imagery for determining a general transition or gradient in land use and land cover, in this case for the city of Altamira, in Pará State, Brazil (Figure 2.1). This method uses previously produced land use/land cover classifications (LULC) (Brondizio et al. 2002) that have been simplified to five classes and that use 1-kilometer buffers from a derived settlement/urban center to extract the percent of each class for each buffer zone. The classes were generated using data derived from a 1996 TM image with 30×30-meter pixels using a land use/land cover classification that was developed for the larger rural and forested region to the west of the city. Training samples were collected to inform the spectral classification of the Landsat TM image for 1996. The variety of classes was reduced to provide for a simplified analysis. The metrics for each of these zones are provided in Table 2.1, and Figure 2.2 provides a graph for easier visualization. This form of exploratory analysis

Table 2.1. Altamira: Percent land use/land cover for 8 1-kilometer buffer regions (1996).

km	Mature Forest	Secondary Succession	Bare Soil and Pasture	Water	Urban
1	12	14	1	1	72
2	14	21	11	9	45
3	23	20	12	20	26
4	29	22	21	15	12
5	42	23	24	14	0
6	42	24	19	15	0
7	42	26	19	14	0
8	34	33	20	13	0

is not complex, but it does clearly show a transition in land cover from majority urban near the urban center (as expected) to larger percent cover in mature forest and secondary succession forest further out from the urban center.

The two figures and the table do not show anything beyond what one would expect in a predominantly rural region where the city chosen for description is the dominant mercantile center. What the table and figures illustrate is that it is possible to quantify relationships between the different LULC classes. This method does not identify explicitly individual components in the heterogeneous landscape that most urban areas are, but it does provide a simple and effective method for determining general changes in land use and land cover as one moves from the center of an urban area or settlement to its periphery, or beyond. Simple descriptive measures of land use and land cover classes for each buffer can be used for comparative analysis between buffers, across time, and across sites. The urban core is within the first 1-kilometer buffer, and in this buffer the percentage of the landscape classified as urban is 72 percent. This figure quickly drops to 45 percent, 26 percent, and then 12 percent for each successive buffer of 1 kilometer out from the urban center. The complexity and interaction of land cover classes increases between 3 and 5 kilometers out from the center. In this region there is a complex mix of urban, forest, secondary succession, and pasture and bare soil. It is in the area of Altamira's urban fringe that one can pursue questions about spatially explicit patterns and processes. Multiple dates can provide a model of the trajectory of urbanization and landcover change over time and space that can be related to general events in the economy and in regional development.

There are problems associated with the arbitrary nature of buffers that are not linked to any specific phenomenon. The total area within each region created from the concentric circular buffers is not equal, nor is the perimeter. Therefore, even if percent measures are used, the regions may not be comparable. Despite such problems, this example provides a conceptualization of methods and ideas that can be used to develop gradients or transition measures on the impact of urbanization and its relationship to peri-urban and rural landscapes on land use and land cover change. This method provides general information about the landscape that may be useful in deriving parameters for more complex analyses. Using similar methods for other cities in the Amazon and around the world would provide for cross-comparison.

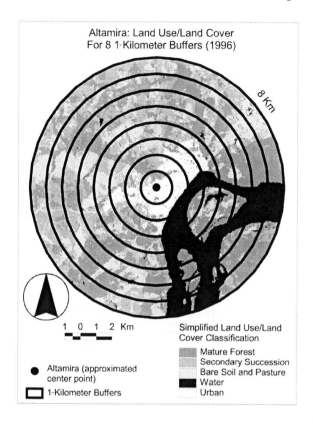

Figure 2.1. Map of Altamira: land use/land cover for eight 1-kilometer buffer regions for 1996.

It is clear that more complex but similar methods may be appropriate for characterizing, describing, and explaining the dynamics of land use and land cover change for urban-fringe and peri-urban regions. Though the method provided above is not complex, it does lay the groundwork for more complex analyses. Analysis of land use and land cover in urban areas, along the urban-fringe and urban periphery, and analyses that incorporate holistic objectives, seeking to characterize and model processes of urbanization in relation to the surrounding landscape, would include methods that incorporate a larger variety of LULC classes and buffering techniques that take into account the shape and the population density of urban centers. Frequently, in spatial analyses that use buffers, the buffers are arbitrary (as presented in the example above), or they are derived using linear distances from a given point, line, or polygon. Other buffer methods are possible, which use shapes that take into account human or biophysical processes, including ellipses that incorporate directional processes, and region boundaries that are produced using raster rule-based boundaries that incorporate topography (or a cost distance) and natural barriers (rivers, water bodies, cliffs, etc.) (for examples, see Evans 1998). Alternative methods for quantifying LULC for the regional landscape would also include alternative spatial sampling procedures, such as hexagonal, triangular, or rectangular (square) grids of predetermined size, providing a strategy that compares many like-size regions rather than the unequal areal extents

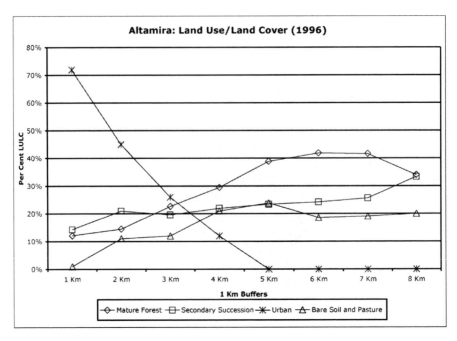

Figure 2.2. Graph of Altamira: land use/land cover for eight 1-kilometer buffer regions for 1996 as percent of cover class.

that are frequently produced by using uniform buffers. Alternatives also include the use of different classification techniques that produce change-based LULC classes, rather than hard single-time-period classes or classifications that are based on fuzzy or gradient classes (continuous rather than discrete). Methods should also be borrowed from landscape ecology that derive landscape fragmentation metrics for landscapes, individual classes, and patches. Methods for deriving landscape fragmentation metrics have found great utility in landscape ecology (Turner 1989; Baker and Cai 1992) and should also be considered for use in the analysis of urban-rural landscape processes. A final methodological component for the improvement of and incorporation into such analyses is the use of texture or spatial structure. Much LULC research uses remotely sensed imagery that is classified by methods that rely on spectral differences but that do not take into account very well the texture or overall spatial structure of the data. Two ways to address this are to (1) incorporate image (spatial) texture derived from neighborhood-based (kernel) calculations and (2) include geostatistical metrics derived from spatial variation in the data via the use of the semivariogram. Incorporation of texture is important in urban regions because of the spectral heterogeneity that is often encountered in such regions, but it has also recently found application in forest analyses. The semivariogram is used most frequently for modeling continuous (and often sparse) data; however, recent applications have used it for modeling differences between urban and non-urban regions from remotely sensed imagery (Brivio and Zilioli 2001). These methods, when incorporated with methods already developed that use image-derived data and spatial data, such as census tract or block group population and household structure (i.e., Cowen and Jensen 1998), provide many opportunities for improving the description and modeling of urban, urban-rural, and environmental change.

Methods for Studying Rural Areas Where People Live in Villages

One of the most common settings one finds in rural communities involves populations living in villages and commuting to nearby fields. Since their residential location does not have a one-to one relationship to the property (see Figure 2.3B), this presents particular problems to understanding how households use the land. A particularly well-studied site can serve to illustrate this type of situation and some of the methods that have been used to address this challenge. A team of sociologists, geographers, and demographers has been studying Nang Rong District in Thailand since 1992. The district, an area of 1,300 square kilometers, has an undulating landscape cultivated with paddy rice in the lower elevations and with manioc in the higher elevations to the east. The study began by linking GIS to survey data. It then acquired several Landsat images to evaluation of the land use and land cover changes in the region.

One important strength of this project in Thailand was the thorough development of spatially explicit social survey data. This approach is recommended for similar studies that link households to plots. These surveys followed up individuals, households, and villages using a community profile, a household survey, and migrant follow-ups. The village profiles provide information about cropping, use of fertilizer, water sources, and deforestation that serve to cross-check the satellite image analysis. It also provides a basis to decide when a village should be treated alone, and when it makes more sense to treat it as part of a cluster of villages due to exchanges and interconnections (Walsh et al. 1999; Entwistle et al. 1997). The household survey consisted of a complete household census in each of the 51 villages, which included: demographic information, visits and exchanges between households, migration patterns, plots of land owned and rented, use of agricultural equipment, crop mixes, planting and harvesting behavior, and debts. These data have a lot to offer when used in conjunction with remotely sensed data. Aggregated to the village level, the household data offer a contrasting perspective to the satellite image analysis and the community profile. The timing of planting and other activities further informs the interpretation of spectral data from Landsat images.

This kind of prospective research design allowed the investigators to link a 1984 survey to a 1994 survey by finding all households from the former in the latter. This allowed the 51 villages to be studied for population change in population composition (age, education, occupation, assets) over the 10-year period. Most importantly, it allowed the examination of population processes prospectively, i.e., examining the out-migration of young adults in relation to the availability of undeveloped land, the fragmentation of land use, and competition from other villages (Rindfuss et al. 1996). The final component of the study followed migrants from 22 of the 51 villages, chosen randomly.

The Nang Rong situation has the locations of household residences in villages and therefore does not provide any indication about the location of farms for households;

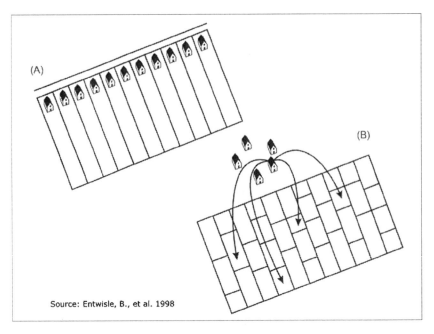

Source: Entwisle, B., et al. 1998

Figure 2.3. Nang Rong household and farm property relationship (adapted from Entwisle et al. 1998) is represented in (B).

further, single households often farm multiple plots that are scattered throughout the area. Trying to locate the coordinates of every single one of those multiple plots is prohibitive for investigators. This leads to the use of the village as the unit of observation. The population surveys at the household and village level are represented in the GIS as discrete point locations at the village centroid. Such a spatial representation is correct, given the nuclear nature of the settlement pattern. Integration of social and environmental data requires transformation whereby a polygon representation is used to denote the pattern and variability of landscape conditions associated with discrete village locations. This transformation requires defining village boundaries, a complicated issue where political boundaries change over time.

The investigators generated radial buffers around the nuclear village centroids at distances of 2 and 3 km. This is a simple solution that takes into account the fact that villagers rarely walk further than that to fields, allows for village overlapping boundaries, and represents well the village settlement concept. Figure 2.4 illustrates the 3-km buffers for the 51 villages overlaid on a 1993 TM image. The figure makes clear that villages may be competing with one another for land. Other approaches can also be used in setting village boundaries, such as Thiessen (Thiessen and Alter 1911) polygons, population-weighted Thiessen polygons, and Triangulated Irregular Networks (TINs) (Entwisle et al. 1998). Thiessen polygons are polygons that are derived from the spatial relationship between points distributed over a surface. They are derived by a mathematical operation that divides the space between points and connects the lines that result from this division. This results in an optimal division of a region based upon

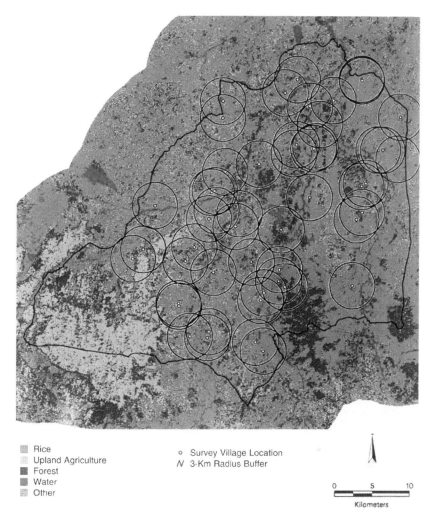

Rice
Upland Agriculture
Forest
Water
Other

○ Survey Village Location
N 3-Km Radius Buffer

0   5   10
Kilometers

Figure 2.4. Land use/land cover with survey villages and 3-km buffers, Nang Rong, Thailand, 1993.

the points distributed within it. Such approaches produce non-overlapping and irregular village boundaries. Figure 2.5 illustrates the use of a Thiessen polygon approach using the same 1993 TM image. This kind of analysis allows one to make reasonable inferences about the behavior of households. The overlapping boundaries of villages in Nang Rong suggest intermarriage between different villages, perhaps as a way of reducing competition over land, a pattern later confirmed by the survey data. Further, the competition for land, evident in the manioc area to the west, results in less forested land available, and indeed this absence in some villages is associated with higher rates of outmigration of young men, who see a limited future due to scarcity of forested land for future farms.

Village Location
Thiessen Polygon

0   5   10
Kilometers

Figure 2.5. Raw Landsat TM (4, 3, 2) and Thiessen polygons, Nang Rong, Thailand, 1993.

Methods for Studying Rural Areas Where People Live on the Property

In contrast to the Nang Rong setting where human communities have populations that commute out to their nearby farm fields (see Figure 2.3B), there are also places throughout the world where people live not in villages but on rural farm properties, engaging in extractive, agricultural, and pastoral practices for both subsistence and market production. In this case, a majority of farm property households live upon the land that they use (see Figure 2.3A). Frequently these farm property households have a nearly one-to-one relationship between the household and the farm property being used. An example of this type of situation would be our study area in Pará State, Brazil, to the immediate west of Altamira City and the Xingú River. This site has been studied from the early 1970s to the present (Moran 1975, 1976, 1981; Moran et al. 1994, 1996, 2000). Currently, there is a multi-disciplinary team of anthropologists, geographers, sociologists, and ecologists studying the relationship between farm property, household structure, health, and deforestation for a region of roughly 4,000 square kilometers. The area has a complex physiography ranging between 20 and 350 meters above sea level, with rolling hills in many areas and steep slopes in others. Farm property activities vary from cocoa and coffee production to manioc, and pasture used for cattle production.

This work linking remote sensing and GIS at the household-property level, with the use of sample surveys and a property boundary map/grid, draws heavily on previous work of our research group on secondary succession (Mausel et al. 1993; Moran et al. 1994, 1996; Brondizio et al. 1994, 1996; Tucker et al. 1998). This study was undertaken to more fully understand land use and land cover change through the acquisition of aerial photography, Landsat Multispectral Scanner, and Thematic Mapper satellite imagery. GIS methods were incorporated in an effort to link classified remote sensing imagery and farm property household surveys in a spatially explicit manner. Along with the desire to link household survey data and land use/land cover information derived from classified images, GIS could be used to model other physiographic, geophysical, and biophysical characteristics of the region, along with human impacts on the landscape from the creation, extension, and improvement of road networks, other infrastructure, settlements, and urban centers. In the context of the Altamira study region, the combination of social science survey data, ecological field studies, remote sensing imagery, and the use of a GIS to bring these disparate data types together allows for a complex analysis and understanding of a diversity of variables that affect and in turn are affected by farm property, family structure, development processes, and deforestation in the region.

The research design for this project does, however, have significant differences from the research design described previously for the Nang Rong region. The initial design for the Altamira study concentrated on farm property land use/land cover and household family structure. This, on the one hand, could be seen as a constraint on our ability to scale down to the individual or to scale up to a community, but on the other hand, it allows for a more in-depth look at householders' strategies and the local decisions that have repercussions for a fairly large forest frontier region in the Amazon. Our focus on the farm household, and by extension the farm property, also allows for a more finely grained spatial-explicitness than that of Nang Rong, where spatial analysis for the past decade was only possible by aggregating individuals and households to a community or village level. This constraint is now being addressed by detailed parcel land research. In the Altamira site the initial development plan was designed to accommodate one family on one 100-hectare property. For Altamira, because our study is at the property level, we did not encounter the problems associated with the delineation of village/community boundaries that were encountered in Nang Rong. Therefore, it is also an easier task to link field-gathered ecological and social data with our land use/land cover image classifications in a GIS, without having to make decisions about how to infer household impacts upon an aggregated landscape.

In reality, however, linking farm households and properties with survey data and land use/land cover change classifications in a spatially explicit manner is not as straightforward as it might seem from the above description. A number of different steps were required to derive the property grid that we are currently using for analysis. For spatially explicit analysis of farm property household structure and land use/land cover change, it is necessary to have information or data that can be used to define a given property, its location, and its spatial extent. In the case of Altamira, it was necessary to build or acquire a property parcel map (i.e., the property grid) that could be used in the production and selection of our survey sample and then be linked with the survey data. Creating such a property grid GIS layer with unique identifiers provides a powerful tool for data extraction from the classified satellite imagery that we have developed. Exploratory analysis of these data permitted the development of a stratified sampling frame for selecting properties and households based on (1) timing of settlement from the period of initial forest clearing and (2) extent of deforestation. Other sampling criteria could be used with these data, based on the questions of interest and concerns with patterns of land cover and land use, or for identifying farm properties associated, for example, with particular soil types or topographic positions.

For purposes of generating a stratified sampling frame congruent with our research questions focusing on episodes of deforestation, a property-level analysis seemed very useful. Explicit in our model is the need to disentangle *period effects* (e.g., credit policies for cattle and cocoa) from *cohort* (e.g., groups of immigrants) and *age effects* (e.g., length of time of a household on the farm) that may be related to farm development and stages of the domestic life cycle of households. Because in this region the majority of farm properties were settled between 1970 and 1978, we were particularly interested in over-sampling early and late colonist households for comparison and analysis. By stratifying our sampling frame, first by timing of initial clearing and subsequently by level of deforestation in 1991, we were able to obtain a sample to address our research questions. With this strategy, we were able to compare households at similar stages of farm development and stages of the household life cycle for different periods.

There are a number of different ways in which one can produce or acquire a property grid. Development of the property grid overlay proceeded by deriving perceived boundaries in individual satellite images and through their temporal comparison. Pre-fieldwork development of the property grid was carried out in three stages: (1) tablet digitizing of roads, (2) on-screen property definition and digitizing, and (3) property identifier assignment. The technique outlined here may not work in all regions. The Altamira colonization scheme divided land into roughly rectangular lots of similar spatial extent, distributed around a network composed of feeder or side roads evenly spaced along the highway (see Figure 2.6). The farm lots average 100 hectares in size (500 m by 2,000 m) and are, therefore, represented by approximately 1,100 pixels (per lot) in a TM image where pixels are generally 30 by 30 meters. These similarities make the definition of properties more apparent than in other areas, where it may not be possible to approximate the size and shape of properties ahead of time. However, where plat maps are available, the approach should be similar. Distinguishing property boundaries facing the road often required only a quick visual analysis. However, determining the interior or back border of properties in this grid scheme was not always so straightforward and required interpolation of a medium distance between the two properties

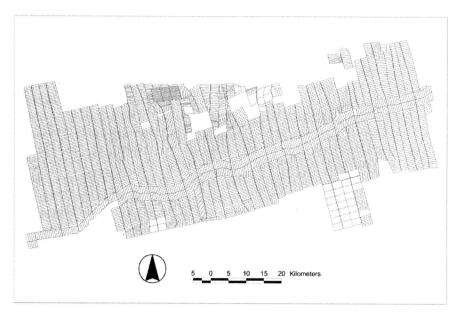

Figure 2.6. The Altamira property grid.

that shared back ends. This method proved useful and adequate for initial analyses but contained spatial error as a result of the uncertainty in the location and extent of the real property boundary, especially for the back end of the property parcels that are commonly covered in 100 percent forest canopy and thus cannot be discriminated by the TM sensor. This approach would also prove problematic as property settlement extended further into the forest frontier where properties were less developed and a majority of properties were still close to 100 percent forested. The other concern with continuing to use this technique is the large number of properties (over 4000) that were planned for this settlement project. This work also took advantage of data gathered in the field, where a number of teams were involved in data collection. One set of teams carried out extensive interviews with the male and female heads of households with two survey instruments, one on land use history and another on demographic characteristics of households. Another team focused on collecting differential GPS points along side roads and at property boundaries to test the accuracy and correct the property grid developed in advance of fieldwork, when appropriate. The field team used a Trimble Pathfinder system and also had a Magellan, ten-channel differentially capable, pair of units as a backup system. The GPS data were collected in a differential mode (with a base station in town and a mobile unit) to ensure accuracy. This often included looking at land titles with the respective farmers and permitted the redevelopment of a geo-corrected property grid based on differentially calculated GPS points.

The pre-field property grid, in addition to aiding in the development of a stratified sampling frame, helped the interview teams locate households and farms for interviews. In the field, laminated composites of bands 5–4–3 of the 1985, 1988, and 1991 TM images and aerial photographs from 1970 and 1978 were carried to discuss land use and land cover with farm families. GPS points were also collected at the houses interviewed and, during discussion with farmers, their properties were identified. This identification process assisted in the evaluation of the property boundary, as well as the investigation of the quality of our remotely sensed land-cover classification. In many cases it was possible to show farmers single-page printouts of the composite and classified land-cover class images for the above dates for their farm and adjoining properties. The data gathered in this way were particularly useful in verifying previous classification procedures and for refining this work after leaving the field. These printouts also aided in the land-use history interviews carried out with farmers, often improving recall of previous use of the land.

While in the field, more recent property maps were obtained from the colonization agency, or Instituto Nacional de Colonização e Reforma Agraria (INCRA). These maps were developed over different periods for different sections of the Transamazon highway feeder roads and were pieced together to cover the entire area covered by our study region. These maps were produced at a 1:50,000 scale, using the Universal Transverse Mercator coordinate system, and although pieced together, appeared to be much more accurate survey maps of the region. There are two different approaches, each containing multiple steps that can be taken to transform a paper map into a spatial data set. One way is to use a digitizing tablet or table. The other is to use a scanner. When using a digitizing tablet, the source map is converted directly into a vector data format. One positive aspect of using a digitizing table for conversion of a paper map into a GIS dataset is that it is possible to acquire digitizing tables that can fit even the largest map sheets. A few drawbacks of digitizing tables and tablets include the technical difficulties related to software driver support and communication between the digitizer and the GIS or CAD software being used and the possibility of moving the map on the digitizer between digitizing sessions. With big digitizing projects (which can take weeks or months to complete), changes in environmental conditions can stretch and shrink the paper map being digitized. Digitizers also have limited resolution; though with very good ones resolution should not be a substantial issue.

The other approach that can be used to transform a paper map into a spatial data set is to scan the map and digitize it on-screen (sometimes referred to as on-the-fly or heads-up digitizing), but there are a few disadvantages to this method. Large maps are often difficult to properly scan, even when one has access to a large-format drum scanner. The raster image files that are produced can be very large and require large amounts of storage space and a large amount of memory to process. The necessity for large amounts of digital storage, ranging from less than a gigabyte up to terabytes in size, and the requirement of large amounts of RAM (random access memory) to manipulate raster data have in the past posed difficulties, both from a financial perspective and in terms of raw processing time necessary to accomplish given tasks. However, computer equipment continues to improve in quality and raw power, and the scanning and manipulation of large images is becoming an increasingly efficient and cost-effective method for transforming older non-digital map libraries into digital data that can be stored in and manipulated by GISs. Besides the decreasing physical and financial constraints, the scanning of maps for use in creating spatial data sets does still entail other problems, though generally different than those difficulties associated with digitizers. Scanning a map in pieces can lead to difficulties in properly merging and aligning images, particularly edges. Scanners themselves can also distort the images produced from the scan if the scanner is not properly calibrated. Scanning also has advantageous qualities. When a map is scanned, it is converted from its paper form to a digital raster graphic or image file. This image file can then be manipulated in various ways to automate the extraction of the data contained in the map, and the transformation and projection of the image to its coordinate system can be applied to the raster data set before any vector attributes are extracted.

For production of the new property grid based on the newly obtained maps, the latter method was chosen. Sections of the 1:50,000 scale property grid sheets were scanned. These scans were saved as digital images that were then registered, transformed, and projected to the appropriate coordinate system using both GPS points collected in the field and 1:100,000 scale topographic sheets as a reference. These were merged together and used as a raster base in a GIS, where the properties were then hand digitized. Resampling and geo-referencing resulted in overall RMS errors on the order of 39 meters, suggesting a very good fit of these maps and the satellite images.

A comparison of the pre-field and "new" property grid indicated that the digitizing of property boundaries from satellite images worked relatively well, but that there were a few errors along some roads. We also had the additional problem of property islands being created by detours in the roads. In some instances, farmers left these pieces of land idle. Others allowed neighboring farmers to use them or property boundaries were re-negotiated. These changes were not surprising, given the gap between 1991 and 1998 fieldwork and the probability that farmers adjust roads to meet their transportation needs and in response to local soil, hydrological, and topographic patterns. However, with further analysis, errors of mis-registration were identified. These errors were perceived initially to be errors in the production of the property grid from its source. However, upon further exploration, we found that not to be the case, but rather that the scans for the mid-section were mis-registered north to south by one property. This mis-registration in the center of the property grid caused distortions in the whole property grid, requiring realignment of individual sections. Though we had found this one striking error in our initial production of the property grid, we did continue to have other problems that had two different sources. One of these problems was the initial property grid. The further the properties were from the Transamazon highway, the less reliable they appeared to be, and the layout of the roads that the properties were aligned along changed over time as the constraints imposed by nature altered the usable road network and property grid from the ideal evenly spaced grid that had been planned. The second problem was related to the scale of the original property grid and our desire to match properties with image classifications using 30-meter pixels. It was necessary to check the boundaries of the properties created with the property grid with our classified image data. In most cases the properties were within a pixel or two of where our visual inspections, combined with our intimate knowledge of the study area and the drawings and notes collected in the field for the properties that were surveyed, believed they should be. It was therefore necessary for us to move the boundaries of the properties one or two pixels in a given direction. It became obvious that engaging in such a process for all of the properties of the study area would be difficult and time-consuming (being based on intuitive and experiential shifts in the data, rather than on a quantitative or mathematical transformation), so the decision was made to concentrate on aligning the properties that we had surveyed as closely as we could.

Work on a new property grid, independent of the pre-fieldwork grid, has been completed for the area of colonization from 20 to 120 kilometers west of Altamira. Example subsets of the original property grid and the derived spatial data are provided (Figure 2.7), along with a map of the overall property grid overlaid onto a 1996 Landsat TM Image (Figure 2.8) of the total study region.

The example subsets illustrate clearly the differences between the original map product (once scanned) and the derived property grid. The property grid produced has already been used to extract farm property and household data for a number of research publications (Moran et al. in press; Brondizio et al. in press).

Additionally, we have also converted the data from the IBGE 1:100,000 scale topographical sheets into digital format. The spatial data derived from these maps includes topography, hydrography, and roads. The topographic (contours and spot elevations) and hydrographic data provide the necessary data for the creation of detailed digital terrain models (DTM). These models can either be vector based as in triangulated irregular networks (TINs) or raster based in the form of a digital elevation model (DEM). Both DTM types can be used to create additional secondary data sets, including slope, aspect, curvature, and others, for the landscape. In combination with the classified imagery, the farm property household data, and the ecological field training sample data gathered in the field, we have a complex combination of spatially and temporally explicit data for analysis.

Conclusions: What Have We Learned About Inferring Household Behavior in a Spatially Explicit Landscape?

In this chapter we began with a review of current approaches and issues for examining household behavior in a number of different spatially explicit landscapes including urban areas, rural areas where people live in villages and commute to their landholdings, and rural areas where people reside on the land they use. For each of these spatially explicit settings, we presented distinct challenges for the linking of households to land cover change, and for inferring the behavior of households, using remotely sensed data within a geographic information system (GIS). Each of these three area types has distinct challenges and problems associated with the analysis of household impact upon the landscape. In the urban setting, inferring the behavior of households on the landscape is currently a very difficult prospect, as a result of either the density of the population (and therefore housing) or a lack of data taken at a fine enough spatial resolution. This limitation is being overcome with the arrival of extremely fine-resolution satellites. This is less of a problem when an urban family owns a farm property. In this case it is possible to analyze the impact of that family upon the farm property with remote sensing and GIS data, but still difficult to do so for the urban property (unless the household is wealthy and the property in the city is a large estate). In the urban setting it is also difficult to adequately separate household impacts on the surrounding landscape, because households influence land that they do not own in aggregate with other house-

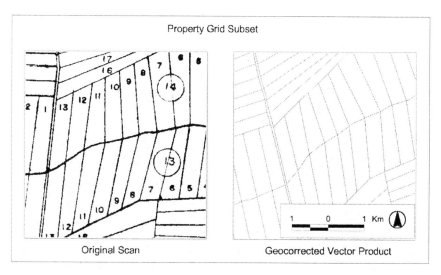

Figure 2.7. Example of property grid—original scan and derived product.

holds in the surrounding neighborhood and throughout the overall urban landscape. In the case of villages or settlements where households live and commute out to their farm properties, it is difficult to fully disentangle the household from the community properties, and it is difficult to fully disentangle the household from the community, but village-level inferences can be made about marriage patterns, land ownership, and likely migration patterns. This is why the Nang Rong study chose to aggregate households to the village level. For the Altamira site, where most of the households and farm properties are synonymous, the problem of disentangling the household from the community is less difficult, though as time passes this will become more difficult, as properties are consolidated, single households acquire multiple unattached properties, farm properties become subdivided, and households move to the city while continuing to manage their farm properties. For example, we can see, by the geometry of land clearing, where land consolidation is taking place, whether it is driven by pasture formation or intensive cropping, and infer the social dynamics of land cover change at the level of the individual property. In this work we have linked demographic, social survey research to finely detailed time-series of Landsat TM, MSS, and aerial photography to construct a temporally and spatially fine-grained analysis of changes in land cover at both the landscape and individual property, so as to achieve accurate inferences about the behavior of households. We have been able to infer that land consolidation is preferentially taking place close to town and on poorer soils—subsequently confirmed by survey data.

Integration of social and spatial data provides an effective mechanism to explore the inter-relationship between human behavior and landscape change. A number of spatial operations allow spatial and social data to be integrated. Collectively, these methods are referred to as data transformations. For example, population data collected at the community level (point data) can be interpolated to provide a continuous surface of

The Altamira Site, Brazil

Property grid of 3,800 parcels.
The average property parcel is 1 square kilometer.

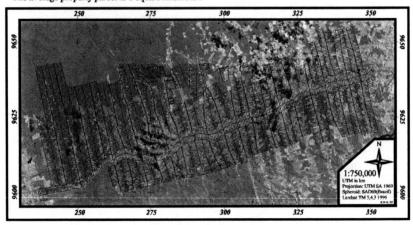

Figure 2.8. The Altamira study region with property grid overlay (TM bands 5-red, 4-green, 3-blue, converted to grayscale for publication). See color version at http://www.csiss.org/best-practices/siss/02

population density. Such a population density, or distribution, surface can be overlaid with a landcover change map to find a correlation between high population density and areas where deforestation is occurring. However, one must be careful, since interpolated surfaces do not always represent adequately the true distribution of phenomena, nor are some variables amenable to interpolation (e.g., nominal data such as ethnicity and occupation). A one-to-one-to-many linkage can also be made between social units of observation (e.g., households) and the landscape associated with that spatial unit. A one-to-one linkage associates the social unit to a single partition of the landscape, such as a household, which resides on a single land parcel (as in the case of Thailand discussed in this chapter). A one-to-many linkage associates the social unit of observation to multiple partitions of the landscape, as when a household is associated with multiple landholdings scattered across the landscape (as is often the case with minifundios or micro-parcels). Inferring the behavior of households from spatial data needs to take into account the varying definitions of communities. In the case of Nang Rong, Thailand, the administrative definition of a village differed from the spatial and the social definitions—and over time, the political definition administratively partitioned a social village into multiple political villages. This is not an unsolvable problem, but it does require adequate ground truthing of what constitutes the units of observation of socially and politically driven spatial divisions (Evans and Moran 2002).

The three examples provided in this chapter present distinct challenges to inferring the behavior of households from the use of spatial data, using remotely sensed information such as Landsat TM. Certainly, the ability to link a particular household to a particular landscape partition is a powerful tool for understanding human behavior over time and space. The pattern of land settlement plays a key determining role in the procedures likely to work in making such inferences. Private land parcels associated with distinct households provide the opportunity to create distinct partitions in the landscape and to link the behavior of households to landscape changes within that property space. When this one-to-one association is not present, spatial data transformations can be used to understand community-level behavior within a larger landscape unit, and even larger regional units.

The discussion that we have provided here has led to a number of conclusions about conducting research into the spatially explicit behavior of households using remotely sensed imagery, household surveys, and GIS techniques. It is clear that it is possible to link rural households in some contexts to spatially fine-grained LULC classifications, but that it is costly in that it requires many skilled, knowledgeable, and motivated research team members. Such research also requires extensive use of GPS equipment, GIS and remotely sensed image laboratory work, and extensive fieldwork, which all require time and adequate financial resources. In many situations, especially in the developing world and less developed frontier regions such as in the Amazon, property maps and property boundary data will be spatially imprecise. This will change over time, as more cities and roads develop in these regions, along with the infrastructure to maintain them. This is often accompanied by increased surveying and more accurate and up-to-date creation of spatial data. The increasing availability of fine-grained satellite imagery, such as IKONOS and Quickbird (previously mentioned), may accelerate this process but this will only be seen in time. The most important component to all of this is that, for spatial analysis, positional accuracy is of the utmost importance, along with methods that provide data that are finely grained enough for household-level analysis and for precise spatial modeling.

This type of study requires a multi-faceted team of researchers with a great diversity of skills. It is unlikely that one person would be expected to master all of the individual skills necessary to conduct this type of research. There needs to be a small core of researchers who can develop and refine the questions to be asked and the theories to be addressed. It is then necessary to have individuals who can work in the laboratory as well as in the field. In order to engage in spatially explicit analysis of households, it is necessary to have spatial data that clearly define the household unit (or possibly even the individual) in a meaningful and analytical manner. This means that to do such research it is necessary to have spatial data that represents explicitly the location and extent of household property holdings. These data also need to be available at a scale that is reasonable in relation to the average, minimum, and maximum sizes of the properties in question. This type of analysis is difficult when households own multiple dispersed properties of varying sizes. Another significant problem is that analyses of this type are often the result of interest in dynamics in frontiers or economically less developed regions. These regions frequently have poorly developed spatial data sets, and even if they have reasonable maps, those maps are not very likely to be available in a digital format. The best practice for engaging in spatially explicit analysis of household scale dynamics is for a very large team to first go to the location and hand survey the extent of all properties in the region of interest. However, this is unlikely to occur, as it would be prohibitively expensive and labor-intensive. Despite this expense, it may be productive for researchers engaged in similar projects to engage in partnerships and data sharing that encourage the exchange of higher quality spatial data and maintain ties with local planning agencies in order to achieve a high degree of contextual awareness.

Notes

1. The USGS/Anderson Classification system was designed to provide a systematic hierarchy of land cover and land use characteristics for use in the classification of satellite remote sensing imagery. The system has a number of different levels that are hierarchically organized and become increasingly complex. The first level in this system includes: urban or built-up land, agricultural land, rangeland, forest land, water, wetland, barren land, tundra, and perennial snow or ice (Anderson et al. 1976). Most remote sensing imagery acquired from satellites is suitable for Level 1 to Level 2 classification. Improvements in remote sensing technology are quickly improving the possibility for classification of the landscape to four hierarchical levels within this system of classification. It should be noted that this is only one classification system, and that its popularity is driven partially by its adoption by the USGS. Many other classification systems are possible, but they frequently have substantial similarity to this system.

2. Space Imaging Inc. IKONOS, launched in 1999, and Digital Globe's Quickbird, launched in 2001, provide commercial satellite imagery products available to the general public and the research community that is on par with or slightly coarser than aerial photography and that has much higher spatial resolution than previously available imagery, such as Landsat MSS (79 m), Landsat TM (30 m), Landsat Enhanced Thematic Mapper Plus (ETM+) (30 m multispectral, 15m panchromatic), or SPOT (20 m multispectral, 10 meter panchromatic) imagery. Both the IKONOS and Quickbird sensor provide panchromatic and multispectral image products. IKONOS panchromatic has an optimal spatial resolution of 1 meter, with a spectral range of 450 to 900 nm. IKONOS multispectral imagery has an optimal resolution of 4 meters in four bands: (1) blue, 450 to 520 nm; (2) green, 520 to 600 nm; (3) red, 630 to 690 nm; (4) near-infrared, 760 to 900 nm. Quickbird panchromatic has an optimal spatial resolution of 61 cm, with a spectral range of 450 to 900 nm. Quickbird multispectral imagery has an optimal resolution of 2.44 meters in four bands: (1) blue, 450 to 520 nm; (2) green, 520 to 600 nm; (3) red, 630 to 690 nm; (4) near-infrared, 760 to 900 nm. The spectral range is identical between these two image products and similar to TM and ETM+ satellite image sensors. For product and image sensor specifications see: (1) http://www.spaceimaging.com, and (2) http://www.digitalglobe.com.

References

Anderson, J.R., E. Hardy, J. Roach, and R. Witmer. 1976. *A Land Use and Land Cover Classification System for Use with Remote Sensing Data*. Washington, D.C.: U.S. Geological Survey Profession Paper 964, 28.

Antrop, M. 2000. Changing patterns in the urbanized countryside of Western Europe. *Landscape Ecology*. 15(3): 257–270.

Baker, W. L., and Y. Cai. 1992. The r.le programs for multiscale analysis of landscape structure using the GRASS geographical information system. *Landscape Ecology* 7(4): 291–302.

Brivio, P.A., and E. Zilioli. 2001. Urban Pattern characterization through geostatistical analysis of satellite images. In J.-P. Donnay, M.J. Barnsley, and P.A. Longley (eds.), *Remote Sensing and Urban Analysis*. London: Taylor & Francis, 43–59.

Brondizio, E., E.F. Moran, P. Mausel, and Y.Wu. 1994. Land use change in the Amazon Estuary. *Human Ecology* 22(3): 249–278.

Brondizio, E.S., E.F. Moran, P. Mausel, and Y. Wu. 1996. Land cover in the Amazon estuary: Linking of the thematic mapper with botanical and historical data. *Photogrammetric Engineering and Remote Sensing* 62(8): 921–929.

Brondizio, E.S., S.D. McCracken, E.F. Moran, A.D. Siqueira, D. Nelson, and C. Rodriguez-Pedraza. 2002. The colonist footprint: Towards a conceptual framework of deforestation trajectories among small farmers in Frontier Amazonia. In C. Wood, and R. Porro (eds.), *Deforestation and Land Use in the Amazon*. Gainesville: University of Florida Press, 133–161.

Browder, J.O., and B. Godfrey. 1997. *Rainforest Cities: Urbanization, Development, and Globalization of the Brazilian Amazon*. New York: Columbia University Press.

Cowen, D.J., and J.R. Jensen. 1998. Extraction and modeling of urban attributes using remote sensing technology. In D. Liverman, E. F. Moran, R. Rindfuss, and P. Stern (eds.), *People and Pixels: Linking Remote Sensing and Social Science*. Washington D.C.: National Academy Press, 164–188.

Davis, K. 1969. *World Urbanization 1950–1970*. Berkeley, Calif.: University of California Press.

Entwistle B., S. Walsh, and R. Rindfuss. 1997. *Population Growth and the Extensification of Agriculture in Nang Rong, Thailand*. Paper presented at the annual meeting of the Population Associaton of America, Washington D.C.

Entwistle, B., S. Walsh, R. Rindfuss, and A. Chamratrithirong. 1998. Land use/land cover and population dynamics , Nang Rong, Thailand. In D. Liverman, E. F. Moran, R. Rindfuss, and P. Stern (eds.), *People and Pixels: Linking Remote Sensing and Social Science*. Washington D.C.: National Academy Press, 121–144.

Evans, T.P. 1998. *Integration of Community Level Social and Environmental Data: Spatial Modeling of Community Boundaries in Northeast Thailand*. Ph.D. Dissertation. University of North Carolina: Chapel Hill.

Evans, T.P., and E.F. Moran. 2002. Spatial integration of social and biophysical factors related to landcover change. In W. Lutz, A. Prskawetz, and W.C. Sanderson (eds.), *Population and Environment: Methods of Analysis. Population and Development Review* Supplement to Vol. 28, 165–186.

Foresman, T. W., S. T. A. Pickett, and W.C. Zipperer. 1997. Methods for spatial and temporal land use and land cover assessment for urban ecosystems and application in the greater Baltimore-Chesapeake region. *Urban Ecosystems* 1(4): 201–216.

Hess, L.L., E.M.L.M. Novo, D.M. Slaymaker, J. Holt, C. Steffen, D.M. Valeriano, L.A.K. Mertes, T. Krug, J.M. Melack, M. Gastil, C. Holmes, and C. Hayward. 2002. Geocoded digital videography for validation of land-cover mapping in the Amazon Basin. *International Journal of Remote Sensing* 23(7): 1527–1555.

Jensen, J.R. 1983. Urban/suburban land use analysis. In R.N. Colwel (ed.), *Manual of Remote Sensing*. 2nd Ed. Falls Church, Va.: The American Society for Photogrammetry and Remote Sensing, 1571–1666.

Jensen, J.R., D.J. Cowen, J. Halls, S. Narumalani, N.J. Schmidt, B.A. Davis, and B. Burgess. 1994. Improved urban infrastructure mapping and forecasting for BellSouth using remote sensing and GIS technology. *Photogrammetric Engineering & Remote Sensing* 60(3): 339–346.

Jensen, J.R. 1996. *Introductory Digital Image Processing*. Upper Saddle River, N.J.: Prentice Hall.

Jensen, R.R. 2000. *Measurement, Comparison, and Use of Remotely Derived Leaf Area Index Predictors*. Ph.D. Thesis, Gainesville: University of Florida, 135.

Lambin, E.F., X. Baulies, N. Bockstael, G. Fischer, T. Krug, R. Leemans, E.F. Moran, R.R.

Rindfuss, Y. Sato, D. Skole, B.L. Turner II, and C. Vogel. 1999. Land Use and Land Cover Change (LUCC) Implementation Strategy. *IGBP Report* 48, *IHDP Report* 10.

Madhavan B.B., S. Kubo, N. Kurisaki, T.V.L.N. Sivakumar. 2001. Appraising the anatomy and spatial growth of the Bangkok metropolitan area using a vegetation-impervious-soil model through remote sensing. *International Journal of Remote Sensing* 22(5) March 20: 789–806.

Mausel, P., Y. Wu, Y. Li, E. Moran, and E. Brondizio. 1993. Spectral identification of successional stages following deforestation in the Amazon. *Geocarto International*. 8: 61–71.

McDonnell, M.J., and S.T.A. Pickett. 1990. Ecosystem structure and function along urban-rural gradients: An unexploited opportunity for ecology. *Ecology* 71(4): 1232–1237.

Moran, E.F. 1975. *Pioneer Farmers of the Transamazon Highway: Adaptation and Agricultural Production in the Lowland Tropics.* Ph.D. Dissertation: University of Florida, Department of Anthropology.

Moran, E.F. 1976. *Agricultural Development Along the Transamazon Highway.* Center for Latin American Studies Monograph Series. Bloomington: Indiana University Press.

Moran, E.F. 1981. *Developing the Amazon.* Bloomington: Indiana University Press.

Moran, E.F. 1993. *Through Amazonian Eyes: The Human Ecology of Amazonian Populations.* Iowa City: University of Iowa Press.

Moran, E.F. (ed.). 1995. *The Comparative Study of Human Societies*, Boulder: L. Reinner Publishers.

Moran, E.F., E.S. Brondizio, P. Mausel, and Y.Wu. 1994. Integrating Amazonian vegetation, land use, and satellite data. *BioScience* 44(5): 329–338.

Moran, E.F., A. Packer, E.S. Brondizio, and J. Tucker. 1996. Restoration of vegetation cover in the eastern Amazon. *Ecological Economics* 18: 41–54.

Moran, E.F., E.S. Brondizio, J.M. Tucker, M.C. Silva-Forsberg, S.D. McCracken, and I. Falesi. 2000. Effects of soil fertility and land-use on forest succession in Amazônia. *Forest Ecology and Management* 139: 93–108.

Moran, E.F., E.S. Brondizio, and S. McCracken. 2002. Trajectories of land use: Soils, succession, and crop choice. In C. Wood, and R. Porro (eds.). Deforestation and Land Use in the Amazon. Gainesville: University of Florida Press, 193–217.

Powell, R.L., D. Roberts, and L. Hess. 2001. *Long-Term Monitoring of Urbanization in the Brazilian Amazon using Optical Remote Sensing.* Poster presented at Human Dimensions of Global Change Conference, Rio de Janeiro, Brazil Oct. 6–8.

Ridd, M.K. 1995. Exploring a V-I-S (vegetation-impervious surface-soil) model for urban ecosystem analysis through remote sensing: Comparative anatomy for cities. *International Journal of Remote Sensing* 16(12): 2165–2185.

Rindfuss, R., S. Walsh, and B. Entwistle. 1996. *Land use, Competition and Migration.* Paper presented at the Annual Meeting of the Population Association of America, New Orleans, LA.

Roberts, D.A., M. Gardner, R. Church, S. Ustin, G. Scheer, and R.O. Green. 1998. Mapping chaparral in the Santa Monica Mountains using multiple endmember spectral mixture models. *Remote Sensing of Environment* 65(3): 267–279.

Thiessen, A.H., and J.C. Alter. 1911. Climatological data for July, 1911: District No. 10, Great Basin. *Monthly Weather Review* July: 1082–1089.

Treitz, P.M., P.J. Howarth, and P. Gong. 1992. Application of satellite and GIS technologies for Land-cover and land-use mapping at the rural-urban fringe—A case study. *Photogrammetric Engineering and Remote Sensing* 58(4): 4391—448.

Tucker J., E.S. Brondízio, and E.F. Moran. 1998. Rates of forest regrowth in Eastern Amazônia: A comparison of Altamira & Bragantina Regions, Pará State, Brazil. *Interciência* 23(2): 1–10.

Turner, B.L.II, W.B. Meyer, and D.L. Skole. 1994. Global land use / land cover change: Toward an integrated program of study. *Ambio* 23: 91–95.

Turner, M. 1989. Landscape ecology: The effect of pattern on process. *Annual Review of Ecological Systems* 20: 171–197.

United Nations. 1994. *Demographic Yearbook 1994—Special Topic: Population Census Statistics II*. Series: R No. 25. New York: United Nations Publications.

Walker, B., and W. Steffen. 1997. An overview of the implications of global change for natural and managed terrestrial ecosystems. *Conservation Ecology*. Special Focus on Global Change and Uncertainty. 1(2).

Walsh, S.J., T.P. Evans, W.F. Welsh, B. Entwisle, and R.R. Rindfuss. 1999. Scale-dependent relationships between population and environment in northeastern Thailand. *Photogrammetric Engineering and Remote Sensing* 65(1): 97–105.

Whyte, A. 1985. Ecological approaches to urban systems: Retrospect and prospect. *Nature and Resources*. 21(1): 13–20.

Wood, C.H., and S.G. Perz. 1996. Population and land-use changes in the Brazilian Amazon. In S. Ramphal, and S. W.Sinding (eds.), *Population Growth and Environmental Issues*. Westport, Conn.: Praeger.

Wu, F.1998. An empirical model of intrametropolitan land-use changes in a Chinese city. *Environment and Planning B: Planning and Design* 25(2): 245–263.

Zipperer, W.C., J. Wu, R.V. Pouyat, and S.T.A. Pickett. 2000. The Application of Ecological Principles to Urban And Urbanizing Landscapes. *Ecological Applications* 10(3): 685–688.

3

Geovisualization of Human Activity Patterns Using 3D GIS
A Time-Geographic Approach

Mei-Po Kwan

Jiyeong Lee

Human Activities in Space-Time

The study of human activities and movements in space and time has long been an important research area in social science. It covers a wide range of topics such as migration, residential mobility, shopping, travel, and commuting behavior. One of the earliest spatially integrated perspectives for the analysis of human activity patterns and movement in space-time is time-geography. Developed by a group of Swedish geographers associated with Torsten Hägerstrand (1970), the time geographic perspective has inspired generations of social scientists, especially geographers and transportation researchers, in the description and analysis of human activities in space-time. It conceives and represents an individual's activities and travel in a 24-hour day as a continuous temporal sequence in geographical space. The trajectory that traces this activity sequence is referred to as a space-time path, while the graphical representation of the three-dimensional space in which this path unfolds is referred to as the space-time aquarium. The number and location of everyday activities that can be performed by a person are limited by the amount of time available and the space-time constraints associated with various obligatory activities (e.g., work) and joint activities with others (Carlstein et al. 1978; Parkes and Thrift 1975; Thrift 1977).

Time-geography not only highlights the importance of space for understanding the geographies of everyday life, it also allows the researcher to examine the complex interaction between space and time and their joint effect on the structure of human activity patterns in particular localities (Cullen et al. 1972). This perspective has been particularly fruitful for understanding women's everyday lives, because it helps to identify the restrictive effect of space-time constraints on their activity choice, job location, travel, as well as occupational and employment status (Dyck 1990; England 1993; Friberg

1993; Hanson and Pratt 1995; Kwan 1999a,b, 2000a; Laws 1997; Palm 1981; Tivers 1985). Time geography has also been used as a framework for the study of migration and mobility behavior (Odland 1998), as well as the everyday life of children, dock-workers, and homeless people (Mårtensson 1977; Pred 1990; Rollinson 1998).

Despite the usefulness of time-geography in many areas of social science research, there are very few studies, except for some early attempts (e.g., Lenntorp 1976), that actually implemented its constructs as analytical methods. The limited development of time-geographic methods can be attributed to the lack of detailed individual-level data and analytical tools that can realistically represent the complexities of an urban environment (e.g., the transportation network and spatial distribution of urban opportunities). Another difficulty is that individual movement in space-time is a complex trajectory with many interacting dimensions. These include the location, timing, duration, sequencing, and type of activities and/or trips. This characteristic of activity patterns has made the simultaneous analysis of its many dimensions difficult (Burnett and Hanson 1982). However, with increasing availability of georeferenced individual-level data and improvement in the representational and geocomputational capabilities of geographical information systems (GIS), it is now more feasible than ever before to operationalize and implement time-geographic constructs. Further, the use of GIS also allows the incorporation of large amounts of geographic data that are essential for any meaningful analysis of human activity patterns. Because of these changes, time-geographic methods are undergoing a new phase of development as several recent studies indicate (Kwan 1998, 2000b; Miller 1999; Ohmori et al. 1999; Takeda 1998; Weber and Kwan 2002). Although the primary focus of these studies is on individual accessibility, there are many areas in social science research where time-geography can be fruitfully applied.

This chapter illustrates the value of time-geographic methods in the description and analysis of human activity patterns. It describes several GIS-based three-dimensional (3D) geovisualization methods that avoid the interpretative difficulties of conventional quantitative methods. These methods are used to study gender/ethnic differences in space-time activity patterns, using an activity diary data set collected in the Portland (Oregon) metropolitan area. The study shows that these geovisualization methods are effective in revealing the complex interaction between the spatial and temporal dimensions in structuring human behavior. They are also effective tools for exploratory spatial data analysis that can help the formulation of more realistic computational or behavioral models. Several significant substantive insights derived from using these methods will be discussed.

Scientific Visualization and Interactive 3D Geovisualization

Scientific visualization is the process of creating and viewing graphical images of data with the aim of increasing human understanding (Hearnshaw and Unwin 1994). It is based on the premise that humans are able to reason and learn more effectively in a visual setting than when using textual and numerical data (Tufte 1990; 1997). Visualization is particularly suitable for dealing with large and complex data sets, because conventional inferential statistics and pattern recognition algorithms may fail when a large number of attributes are involved (Gahegan 2000). In view of the large number of attributes that can be used to characterize human activity patterns, and given the capability of scientific visualization in handling a large number of attributes, visualization is a promising direction for exploring and analyzing large and complex data sets.

Geovisualization (visualization of geographic information), on the other hand, is the use of concrete visual representations and human visual abilities to make spatial contexts and problems visible (MacEachren et al. 1999). Through involving the geographical dimension in the visualization process, geovisualization greatly facilitates the identification and interpretation of spatial patterns and relationships in complex data in the geographical context of a particular study area. For the visualization of geographic data, conventional GIS has focused largely on the representation and analysis of geographic phenomena in two dimensions (2D). Although 3D visualization programs with advanced 3D modeling and rendering capabilities have been available for many years, they have been developed and applied largely in areas outside the GIS domain (Sheppard 1999). Only recently has GIS incorporated the ability to visualize geographic data in 3D (although specialized surface modeling programs have existed long before). This is so, not only in the digital representation of physical landscape and terrain of land surfaces, but also in the 3D representation of geographic objects using various data structures.

Despite the use of GIS-based 3D geovisualization in many areas of research in recent years, its application in the analysis of human activity patterns is rather limited to date. In many early studies, 2D maps and graphical methods were used to portray the patterns of human activity-travel behavior (e.g., Chapin 1974; Tivers 1985). Individual daily space-time paths were represented as lines connecting various destinations. Using 2D graphical methods, information about the timing, duration, and sequence of activities and trips was lost. Even long after the adoption of the theoretical constructs of the time-geographic perspective in the 1970s and 1980s, the 3D representation of space-time aquariums and space-time paths seldom went beyond the schematic representations used either to explain the logic of a particular behavioral model or to put forward a theoretical argument about human activity patterns. They were not intended to portray the real experience of individuals in relation to the concrete geographical context in any empirical sense.

There is, however, noticeable change in recent years. As more georeferenced activity-travel diary data become available, and as more GIS software incorporates 3D capabilities, it is apparent that GIS-based 3D geovisualization is a fruitful approach for examining human activity patterns in space-time. For instance, Forer (1998) and Huisman and Forer (1998) implemented space-time paths and prisms based on a 3D raster data structure for visualizing and computing space-time accessibility surfaces. Their methods are especially useful for aggregating individuals with similar socioeconomic characteristics and for identifying behavioral patterns. However, since the raster data structure is not suitable for representing the complex topology of a transportation network, the implementation of network-based computational algorithms is difficult when using their methods. On the other hand, Kwan (2000b, 2000c) implemented 3D visualization of space-time paths and aquariums using vector GIS methods and activity-travel diary data. These recent studies indicate that GIS-based geovisualization has considerable potential for advancing the research on human activity patterns. Further, implementing 3D visualization of human activity patterns can be an important first step in the development of GIS-based geocomputational procedures that are applicable in many areas of social science research. For example, Kwan (1998, 1999b), Miller (1999), Miller and Wu (2000) and Weber and Kwan (2002) developed different network-based algorithms for computing individual accessibility using vector GIS procedures.

There are several advantages in using GIS-based 3D geovisualization in the analysis of human activity patterns. First, since GIS has the capability to integrate a large amount of geographic data in various formats and from different sources into a comprehensive geographic database, it is able to generate far more complex and realistic representations of the urban environment than conventional methods. The concrete spatial context it provides can greatly facilitate exploratory spatial data analysis and the identification of spatial relations in the data. Results can also be exported easily to spatial analysis packages for performing formal spatial analysis (Anselin and Bao 1997). Second, 3D geovisualization provides a dynamic and interactive environment that is much more flexible than the conventional mode of data analysis in transportation research. The researcher can directly manipulate the attributes of a scene and its features, and change the views, alter parameters, query data, and see the results of any of these actions easily. Third, unlike quantitative methods that tend to reduce the dimensionality of data in the process of analysis, 3D geovisualization may retain the complexity of the original data to the extent that human visual processing is still capable of handling. Lastly, with many useful navigational capabilities such as fly-through, zooming, panning, and dynamic rotation, as well as the multimedia capabilities to generate map animation series such as 3D "walk-throughs" and "fly-bys", the researcher can create a "virtual world" that represents the urban environment with a very high level of realism (Batty et al. 1998).

Study Area and Data

Most examples described in this chapter are based upon an activity-travel diary data set collected in the Portland metropolitan region. This region consists of Multnomah, Washington, and Clackamas counties in Oregon and Clark County in Washington. These four counties had a population of 1.6 million in 1995, making up 93.15 percent of the population of the metropolitan region. Much of this area is included within the urban growth boundary of the Portland Metropolitan Service District (commonly known as Metro), which is the local metropolitan planning organization (MPO) for the Portland urban area. The urban growth boundary encompasses a total of 24 municipalities, of which the city of Portland is by far the largest city (with 498,747 people in 1995). A considerable portion of the study area's population resides within a large number of suburban municipalities, including Gresham, Beaverton, Hillsboro, Tigard, Lake Oswego, Milwaukie, and Tualatin. The study area includes geographic features that may have significant influence on human travel and mobility behavior. For instance, it is traversed by two major rivers, which are potentially important barriers to mobility. The Columbia River crosses from East to West along the north edge of the study area and the Willamette River bisects the study area as it flows from south to north and into the Columbia, northwest of the study area.

The activity data set was collected through a survey conducted in the Portland metropolitan region in 1994 and 1995. See Cambridge Systmatics, Inc. (1996) for details of the survey. The survey used a two-day activity diary to record all activities involving travel and all in-home activities with a duration of at least 30 minutes for all individuals in the sampled households. Of the 7,090 households recruited for the survey, 4,451 households with a total of 10,084 individuals returned completed and usable surveys. The data set logged a total of 129,188 activities and 71,808 trips. Besides the information commonly collected in a travel diary survey, this data set also provides the geocodes (geographical coordinates) of all activity locations, including the home and workplace of all individuals in the sample. This not only facilitates the incorporation of these data into a comprehensive geographic database of the study area but also allows analysis of the space-time behavior of the sampled individuals in fine spatial and temporal resolution.

In addition to the activity-travel diary data, geographic information about the Portland metropolitan region is also used in this study. Data for Oregon were obtained from Metro's Regional Land Information System (RLIS), while similar data for Clark County, Washington, were obtained from the local planning agency. The digital GIS database assembled from these two sources provides comprehensive data on many aspects of the urban environment and transportation system of the study area. These contextual data allow the activity-travel data to be related to the geographical environment of the region during visualization. A 3D representation of three geographical data layers used in the geovisualization sessions described in this chapter is shown in Figure 3.1. These layers are the residential parcels (top layer), commercial and individual parcels (bottom layer), and the transportation network. The next two sections describe several methods for the 3D geovisualization of human activity-travel patterns in space-time. These methods are implemented using ArcView 3D Analyst, where various segments of the original sample are used.

Geovisualization of Activity Density Patterns in Space-Time

The GIS-based 3D geovisualization methods discussed here are based upon the time-geographic perspective of Hägerstrand (1970) and his associates. In time-geographic conception, an individual's activities and trips in a day can be represented as a daily space-time path within a 'prism' defined by a set of constraints (Burns 1979; Hägerstrand 1970; Lenntorp 1976; Parkes and Thrift 1975). This time-geographic conception is valuable for understanding human activity patterns, because it integrates the temporal and spatial dimensions of human activity patterns into a single analytical framework. Although both time and space are significant factors structuring individual activity patterns, past approaches mainly focus on only one of these dimensions. Further, the significance of the interaction between the spatial and temporal dimensions in structuring individual daily space-time trajectories is often ignored. Yet, using the concepts and methods of time-geography that focus on the 3D structure of space-time

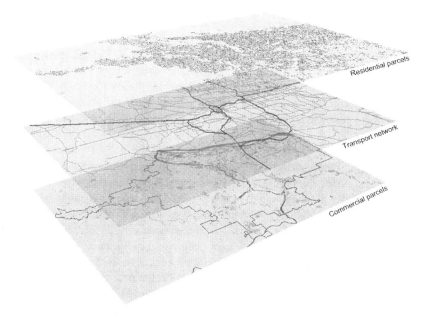

Figure 3.1. Three layers of geographical data used in the study.

patterns of activities, this kind of interaction can be examined, and many important behavioral characteristics of different population subgroups can be revealed.

This section focuses on interactive 3D geovisualizations of activity intensity in space-time. Geovisualizations of space-time paths will be discussed in the next section. Color versions of the figures are available on Web site http://geog-www.sbs.ohio-state.edu/faculty/mkwan/figures/best_links.htm. Since the dynamic process of knowledge discovery through interactive 3D geovisualizations cannot be illustrated using static screen captures, the figures in this chapter cannot convey the same amount and quality of information enabled by interactive 3D geovisualizations. The reader may find it difficult to follow the discussion simply by looking at these figures, because the text is based on observations enabled by the computer-aided interactive 3D visualization environment (which allows very complex manipulation of 3D objects or surfaces).

Simple Activity Patterns in Space-Time

A relatively simple method for visualizing human activity patterns in 3D is to use the two-dimensional (2D) activity-travel data provided in the original data set and to convert them to a format displayable in three dimensions. An important element in this conversion process is to identify the variable in the original data file that will be used as the Z value, which represents the value of a particular activity in the vertical dimension (besides the geographical coordinates X and Y). For a meaningful representation of activity patterns in space-time, the Z variable in this study represents the temporal dimension of activities and trips. In this particular example, activity start time is used as the Z variable in the conversion process. Using this Z value, each activity is first located in 3D space as a point entity, using its geographic location (X,Y) and activity start time (Z). To represent the duration of each activity, the activity points in 3D are extruded from their start times by a value equal to the duration of the activity. In 3D visualization, extruding a feature extends its geometric dimension and changes its form—for instance, from points into vertical lines, lines into vertical walls, and polygons into 3D blocks.

Figure 3.2 shows the result of this method for the 11,559 out-of-home, non-employment activities performed by the 3,147 European-American (white) men in the subsample. In the figure, the length of the vertical line that represents the temporal span of an activity indicates activity duration. Activity start time can be color-coded to represent the temporal distribution of activities during interactive visualization. A helpful background for relating the activity patterns to various locations in the study area is created by adding several layers of geographic information into the 3D scene. These layers include the boundary, freeways, and rivers of the Portland metropolitan region. For better visual anchoring and locational referencing during visualization, a 3D representation of downtown Portland, which appears as a partially transparent 3D pillar derived from extruding its 2D boundary along the Z dimension, is also added. For easier identification of the temporal span of these activities, two 3D grid lines representing noon and midnight are added in the 3D scene.

Interactive geovisualization of the activity patterns, shown in Figure 3.2, suggests that the highest concentrations of non-employment activities for the selected individuals are found largely in areas close to downtown Portland inside the "loop", east of downtown in the north, and south of Freeway 84. Important clusters of non-employment activities are also found in Beaverton in the west and Gresham in the east. Most of the non-employment activities are of very short duration (95.4 percent of them have durations under 5 minutes, and less than 1.6 percent have durations over 10 minutes). Further, non-employment activities were undertaken throughout the day with a rather even temporal distribution. This corroborates the findings of Kwan's (1999a) Columbus study not only that men's non-employment activities tend to be less temporally concentrated than women's, but also that there is a significant gender difference in activity patterns in space-time.

Activity Density Patterns in Geographic Space

Comparison of the patterns of different activities for the same population subgroup or the patterns of the same activity between different population subgroups using this simple representation, however, is difficult. As the number of activities involved will increase considerably when more population subgroups are included and the patterns may be difficult to compare visually, other methods that facilitate inter-group or inter-activity comparisons are needed. This subsection explores the use of 3D activity density surfaces for representing and comparing the density patterns of different activities in real geographic space. The same group of respondents discussed above is also used here. The purpose is first to represent the spatial intensity of the locations of workplace,

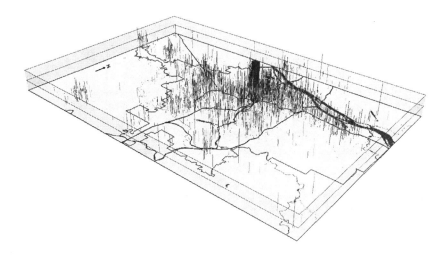

Figure 3.2. Simple activity patterns in space-time.

home, and non-employment activities of these individuals, and then to examine the spatial relationships between these density patterns.

To generate a density surface from a point distribution of n activity locations, a non-parametric density estimation method called kernel estimation is used (Gatrell 1994; Silverman 1986). Following Bailey and Gatrell's (1995) formulation, if $\Re$ represents the study area, x represents a general location in $\Re$ and $x_1, x_2 \ldots x_n$ are the locations of the n activities, then the intensity or density, $\lambda(x)$, at x is estimated by:

$$\lambda h(x) = \frac{1}{\delta_h(\mathbf{x})} \sum_{i=1}^{n} \frac{w_i}{h^2} k\left(\frac{(x - x_i)}{h}\right), \quad x \in \Re \tag{1}$$

where $k(.)$ is the kernel function, the parameter $h > 0$ is the bandwidth determining the amount of smoothing, w_i is a weighing factor, and $\delta_h(x)$ is an edge correction factor (Cressie 1993). In this study, the quartic kernel function

$$k(x) = \begin{cases} 3\pi^{-1}(1 - x^T x)^2 & \text{if } x^T x \leq 1 \\ 0 & \text{otherwise} \end{cases} \tag{2}$$

described in Silverman (1986) is used for generating space-time activity density surfaces. The method is implemented through covering the study area by a 1371×2105 grid structure (with 2.89 million cells) and using a bandwidth of 0.86. The density surfaces, originally created in the grid data structure, are then converted to 3D format and added into a 3D scene (Figure 3.3).

In Figure 3.3, the density surface of non-employment activities is displayed transparently on top of the density surface of home locations of the selected individuals. To help identify the location of density peaks and troughs, three geographic data layers, namely freeways, major arterials, and rivers, are draped over the density surface of home locations. The figure, oriented towards west, shows that the major peak of non-

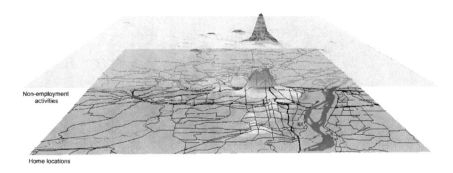

Figure 3.3. Activity density patterns in geographic space. The transparent surface for non-employment activities is above the surface of home locations.

employment activities is centered at downtown Portland within the "loop," and there are also considerable concentrations northeast of downtown and around Beaverton. The highest density of home locations for the selected individuals is found at two peaks in the northwest and east of downtown Portland.

Figure 3.4 provides a close-up view of the same 3D scene in which the transparent density surface of non-employment activities is not shown. Three distinctive peaks of home locations can be clearly seen in the figure. They are located at downtown Portland inside the "loop," in areas northwest and east of downtown. Other areas with high concentration of home locations are found in Beaverton and in the area north of Milwaukee. The major advantage of this visualization method is its capability for examining the spatial relationships between different surfaces in their concrete geographical context. To explore the temporal dimension and its interaction with the spatial dimension, another visualization method is needed.

Space-Time Activity Density Surfaces

For representing the intensity of activities in space-time, kernel estimation is used again to generate 'space-time activity density surfaces' (Gatrell 1994; Silverman 1986). In this implementation, a space-time region $\Re$ is established with a locational system similar to an x-y geographic coordinate system. The time-axis of this coordinate system covers a 24-hour day from 3 a.m., and the space-axis represents the distance of an activity from home. A fine grid structure of 1920×1920 space-time grids (with 3.69 million cells) is then created by dividing a day into 1920 0.75-minute time slices and distance from home into 1920 20.1-meter (66-foot) blocks. The quartic kernel function described above is also used here, with a bandwidth of 0.6. This method is used to generate three space-time activity density surfaces for individuals in the sample. One is for women employed full-time (Figure 3.5); the second one is for men employed full-time (figure not shown); and the third portrays the difference between these two density surfaces (Figure 3.6).

The density surface for full-time employed women (Figure 3.5) shows that there is a considerable amount of non-employment activities close to home (largely within

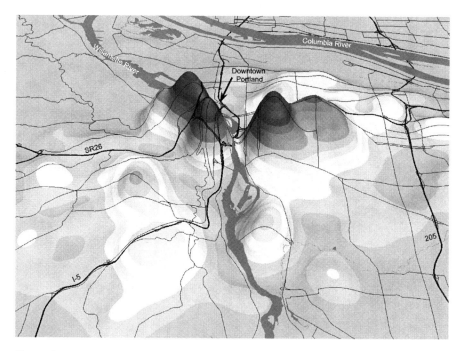

Figure 3.4. A close-up view of the density surface of home locations of the selected individuals.

8 km) around noon and 5:00 p.m. This suggests that most of the non-employment activities undertaken by these women are performed during lunch hours and shortly after work. There are two intensive peaks of non-employment activities. One is found at noon, about 6 km from home, and the other happens around 5 p.m., about 6 km from home. There is a considerable amount of non-employment activities within 8 km from home during the evening hours between 6 and 9 p.m. The density surface for full-time employed men (not shown) reveals a very similar space-time pattern when compared to that of the full-time employed women. The main difference is that the space-time density of non-employment activities for these full-time employed men is not as intensive as that of the full-time employed women.

Figure 3.6 shows the difference between these two density surfaces. It is obtained by using the map algebraic operator "minus" for the two surfaces, where the value in a cell in the output grid is obtained by deducting the value of the corresponding cell in the surface for men from the value of the corresponding cell in the surface for women. Peaks in this "difference surface" indicate areas where the intensity of women's non-employment activities is much higher than that of men, and vice versa. Since the two density surfaces are very similar, the resulting difference surface reveals only minor and random modulations. The greatest gender difference is found around 6:00 p.m. within 8 km of home.

There are two major advantages in using these 3D space-time activity density surfaces. First, they reveal the intensity of activities in space and time simultaneously, thus

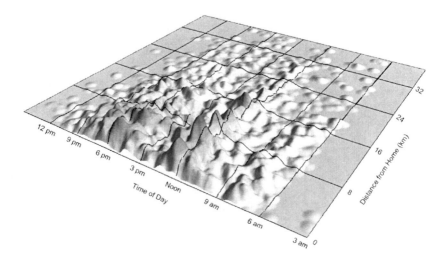

Figure 3.5. Space-time activity density of the non-employment activities of the full-time employed women in the sample.

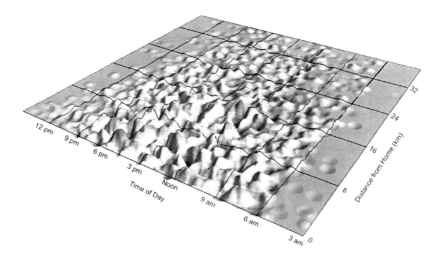

Figure 3.6. Gender difference in the space-time density of non-employment activities between the full-time employed women and men in the sample.

facilitating the analysis of their interaction. Second, the grid-based method is amenable to many map-algebraic operations that can be used to adjust the computed raw density for highlighting the distinctiveness in the activity patterns of a particular population subgroup. It also makes the derivation of a "difference surface" for two population subgroups relatively easy, thus facilitating the examination of inter-group differences. The next section explores the 3D geovisualization of space-time paths.

Geovisualization of Individual Space-Time Paths

The Space-Time Aquarium

The earliest 3D method for the visualization of individual space-time paths is the space-time aquarium conceived by Hägerstrand (1970). In a schematic representation of the aquarium, the vertical axis is the time of day, and the boundary of the horizontal plane represents the spatial scope of the study area. Individual space-time paths are portrayed as trajectories in this 3D aquarium. Although the schematic representation of the space-time aquarium was developed long ago, it has never been implemented using real activity-travel diary data. The main difficulties include the need to convert the activity data into "3Dable" formats that can be used by existing visualization software, and the lack of comprehensive geographic data for representing complex geographic objects of the urban environment. The recent incorporation of 3D capabilities into GIS packages and the availability of contextual geographic data of many metropolitan regions have ameliorated these two difficulties.

To implement 3D geovisualization of the space-time aquarium, four contextual geographic data layers are first converted from 2D map layers to 3D format and added to a 3D scene. These include the metropolitan boundary, freeways, major arterials, and rivers. For better close-up visualization and for improving the realism of the scene, outlines of commercial and industrial parcels in the study area are converted to 3D polygons and vertically extruded in the scene. Finally, the 3D space-time paths of the African and Asian Americans in the sample are generated and added to the 3D scene. These procedures created the scene shown in Figure 3.7.

The overall pattern of the space-time paths for these two groups shown in Figure 3.7 indicates heavy concentration of day-time activities in and around downtown Portland. Using the interactive visualization capabilities of the 3D GIS, it can be seen that many individuals of these two ethnic groups work in downtown Portland and undertake a considerable amount of their non-employment activities in areas within and east of the area. Space-time paths for individuals who undertook several non-employment activities in a sequence within a single day tend to be more fragmented than those who have long work hours during the day. Further, ethnic differences in the spatial distribution of workplace are observed using the interactive capabilities provided by the geovisualization environment. The space-time paths of Asian Americans are more spatially scattered throughout the area than those of the African Americans, whose work and non-employment activities are largely concentrated in the east side of the metropolitan region. This seems to suggest that racial segregation may involve dimensions other than residential segregation, since it may have a significant restrictive effect on the activity space of specific minority groups.

A close-up view from the west of the 3D scene is given in Figure 3.8, which shows some of the details of downtown Portland in areas within and around the "loop" and along the Willamette River. Portions of some space-time paths can also be seen. With the 3D parcels and other contextual layers in view, the figure gives the researcher a strong sense about the geographical context through a virtual reality-like view of the downtown area. This interactive virtual environment not only contextualizes the visualization in its actual geographical surroundings but also enables the analysis of local

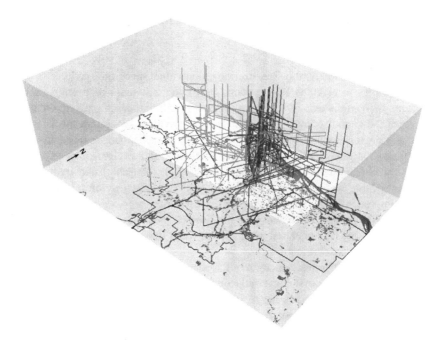

Figure 3.7. Space-time aquarium showing the space-time paths of African and Asian Americans in the sample.

variations at fine spatial scales. For instance, color codes can be used to represent different types of landuse or buildings, to provide the analyst a better sense of the urban environment and its context, which can then be used to compare the activities and paths of each individual in the sample. This approach will, therefore, have considerable potential for the analysis and understanding of individual activity patterns at fine spatial scales.

Space-Time Paths Based on GPS Data

Although the 3D space-time paths shown in Figures 3.7 and 3.8 are helpful for understanding the activity patterns of different population subgroups, these paths are not entirely realistic, since they only connect trip ends with straight lines and do not trace the travel routes of an individual. This limitation is due to the lack of route data in the Portland data set. When georeferenced activity-travel data collected by GPS are available and used in the geovisualization environment, the researcher can examine the detailed characteristics of an individual's travel pattern as actual travel routes. Figure 3.9 illustrate this possibility using the GPS data collected in the Lexington Area Travel Data Collection Test conducted in 1997 (Battelle 1997). The original data set contains information of 216 licensed drivers (100 male, 116 female) from 100 households with an average age of 42.5. In total, data of 2,758 GPS-recorded trips and 794,861 data

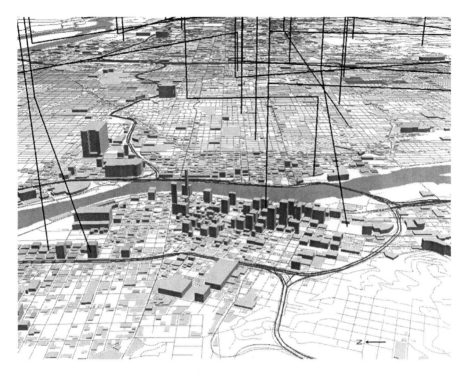

Figure 3.8. A close-up view of downtown Portland, Oregon.

points of latitude-longitude pairs and time were collected for a 6-day period for each survey participant.

To prepare for 3D geovisualization, three contextual geographic data layers of the Lexington metropolitan area are converted from 2D map layers to 3D format and added to a 3D scene. These include the boundary of the Lexington metropolitan region, highways, and major arterials. As an illustration, the 3D space-time paths of women without children under 16 years of age in the sample are generated and added to the 3D scene. These procedures created the scene shown in Figure 3.9. The overall pattern of the space-time paths for these women indicates that trips were undertaken using largely highways and major arterials. There is some regularity, as indicated by the daily repetition of trips in more or less the same time throughout the 6-day survey period. This suggests that distinctive activity-travel patterns can be revealed by 3D geovisualization.

Conclusions

The dynamic and interactive GIS-based 3D geovisualization methods discussed in this chapter are useful for the exploratory analysis of activity-travel patterns. They allow the researcher to interact and explore the 3D scene. The visual properties of objects can be altered to reflect their various attributes and the highly flexible viewing and navigational environment is also a great help to the researcher. As shown by the examples,

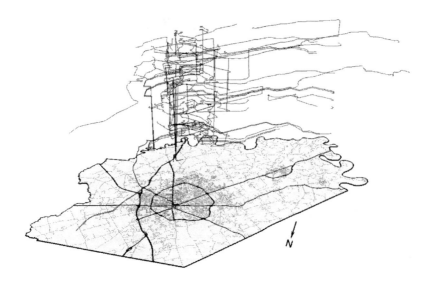

Figure 3.9. Space-time paths based on GPS data collected in Lexington, Kentucky.

these methods are capable of revealing many important characteristics of the space-time activity patterns of different population subgroups in relation to the concrete urban environment. They also facilitate the identification of complex spatial relations and the comparison of patterns generated by individuals of different gender/ethnic subgroups. As the rhythm of everyday life and life cycle events, such as migration, can be portrayed by these methods, they can be used to gain insight into the everyday life of a particular place and time (Hanson and Hanson 1993). As individual-level, geo-referenced data become increasingly available, the development and implementation of these kinds of 3D geovisualization methods is a promising direction for many areas of social science research.

There are, however, several difficulties in the development and use of these 3D methods. First, the researcher may encounter barriers to the effective visualization of large and complex activity-travel data sets. Four such potential barriers identified by Gahegan (1999) are: (1) rendering speed—the ability of the hardware to deliver satisfactory performance for the interactive display and manipulation of large data sets; (2) visual combination effects—problems associated with the limitation in human ability to identify patterns and relations when many layers or variables are simultaneously viewed; (3) large number of visual possibilities—the complexity associated with the vast range of possibilities that a visualization environment provides (i.e., the vast number of permutations and combinations of visual properties the researcher can assign to particular data attributes); and (4) the orientation of the user in a visualized scene or virtual world. Implementation of the interactive 3D methods in this study shows that a geovisualization environment that provides a geographical context for the researcher may alleviate the fourth problem. However, the other three barriers may still remain a significant challenge to researchers who want to use such methods. For instance, rendering the density surface in Figure 3.6, which involves a TIN (triangulated irregular network) of 494,076 triangles and 247,256 nodes, can be taxing on the hardware. Further, identifying patterns from the space-time paths covering 129,188 activities undertaken by the survey respondents may push our visual ability beyond its limit. It is therefore important for future research to examine how human cognitive barriers involved in the interpretation of complex 3D patterns may be overcome.

Second, there is the challenge of converting many types of data into "3Dable" formats for a particular geovisualization environment. Since every visualization software may have its unique data format requirements, and the activity and geographic data currently available are largely in 2D formats, the data preparation and conversion process can be time-consuming and costly. For example, considerable data preparation and pre-processing was required for converting the Portland activity-travel data for display as 3D space-time paths. Future research should investigate how the effort and time spent on data conversion could be reduced when data from various sources are used.

Third, the use of individual-level activity-travel data geocoded to street addresses, given their reasonable degree of positional accuracy, may lead to considerable risk of privacy violation. As Armstrong and Ruggles (1999) demonstrated, although "raw" maps composed of abstract map symbols do not directly disclose confidential information, a determined data spy can use GIS technology and other knowledge to "hack" the maps and make an estimate of the actual address (and hence, a good guess of the identity of an individual) associated with each point symbol. This practice, called "inverse address-matching," has the potential for serious confidentiality or privacy violation. As "map hackers" may be able to accurately recover a large proportion of original addresses from dot maps, any use of such kind of individual-level geocoded data should be conducted with great concern in protecting the privacy of survey respondents and maintaining the confidentiality of information. As apparent in the 3D geovisualization examples in this chapter (e.g., the details in Figure 3.8), releasing a 3D scene created from several accurate data layers in VRML (virtual reality markup language) format may lead to significant risk of privacy violation, because map hackers may be able to recover the identity of a particular survey respondent. This may further lead to the disclosure of other confidential information. As a result, researchers using 3D geovisualization methods should pay attention to this potential risk. Recent research on geographical masking as a method of privacy protection is particularly relevant and important in this context (Armstrong et al. 1998).

Acknowledgments   Support for this research by an NSF/ITR grant (BCS-0112488) and the College of Social and Behavioral Sciences of the Ohio State University to Mei-Po Kwan is gratefully acknowledged. In addition, Mei-Po Kwan thanks the Geography and Regional Science Program of the National Science Foundation for assistance.

References

Anselin, L., and S. Bao. 1997. Exploratory spatial data analysis linking SpaceStat and ArcView. In M. Fischer, and A. Getis (eds.), *Recent Developments in Spatial Analysis*. Berlin: Springer-Verlag, 35–59.

Armstrong, M.P., and A.J. Ruggles. 1999. *Map Hacking: On the Use of Inverse Address-Matching to Discover Individual Identities From Point-Mapped Information Sources*. Paper presented at the Geographic Information and Society Conference, University of Minnesota, 20–22 June.

Armstrong, M.P., G. Rushton, and D.L. Zimmerman. 1998. Geographically masking health data to preserve confidentiality. *Statistics in Medicine* 18(5): 497–525.

Bailey, T.C., and A.C. Gatrell. 1995. *Interactive Spatial Data Analysis*. New York: Longman.

Battelle. 1997. *Lexington Area Travel Data Collection Test: Final Report*. Columbus, Ohio: Battelle Memorial Institute.

Batty, M., M. Dodge, S. Doyle, and A. Smith. 1998. Modelling virtual environments. In P.A. Longley, S.M. Brooks, R. McDonnell, and B. MacMillan (eds.), *Geocomputation: A Primer*. New York: John Wiley and Sons, 139–161.

Burnett, P., and S. Hanson. 1982. The analysis of travel as an example of complex human behavior in spatially-constrained situations: Definition and measurement issues. *Transportation Research A* 16(2): 87–102.

Burns, L.D. 1979. *Transportation, Temporal, and Spatial Components of Accessibility*. Lexington, Mass.: Lexington Books.

Cambridge Systematics, Inc. 1996. *Data Collection in the Portland, Oregon Metropolitan Area*. Oakland, Calif. Cambridge Systematics, Inc.

Carlstein, T., D. Parkes, and N. Thrift. 1978. *Timing Space and Spacing Time II: Human Activity and Time Geography*. London: Arnold.

Chapin, F.S. Jr. 1974. *Human Activity Patterns in the City*. New York: John Wiley and Sons.

Cressie, N.A.C. 1993. *Statistics for Spatial Data*. New York: John Wiley and Sons.

Cullen, I., V. Godson, and S. Major. 1972. The structure of activity patterns. In A.G. Wilson (ed.), *Patterns and Processes in Urban and Regional Systems*. London: Pion, 281–296.

Dyck, I. 1990. Space, time, and renegotiating motherhood: An exploration of the domestic workplace. *Environment and Planning D* 8: 459–483.

England, K. 1993. Suburban pink collar ghettos: The spatial entrapment of women? *Annals of the Association of American Geographers* 83: 225–242.

Forer, P. 1998. Geometric approaches to the nexus of time, space, and microprocess: Implementing a practical model for mundane socio-spatial systems. In M.J. Egenhofer, and R.G. Golledge (eds.), *Spatial and Temporal Reasoning in Geographic Information Systems*. Oxford, England: Oxford University Press, 171–190.

Friberg, T. 1993. *Everyday Life: Women's Adaptive Strategies in Time And Space*. Translated by M. Gray. Lund, Sweden: Lund University Press.

Gahegan, M. 1999. Four barriers to the development of effective exploratory visualization tools for the geosciences. *International Journal of Geographic Information Science* 13(4): 289–309.

Gahegan, M. 2000. The case for inductive and visual techniques in the analysis of spatial data. *Journal of Geographical Systems* 2(1): 77–83.

Gatrell, A. 1994. Density estimation and the visualization of point patterns. In H.M. Hearnshaw, and D.J. Unwin (eds.), *Visualization in Geographical Information Systems*. New York: John Wiley and Sons, 65–75.

Hägerstrand, T. 1970. What about people in regional science? *Papers of Regional Science Association* 24: 7–21.

Hanson, S., and P. Hanson. 1993. The geography of everyday life. In T. Garling., and R.G. Golledge (eds.), *Behavior and Environment: Psychological and Geographical Approaches*. Amsterdam: North-Holland.

Hanson, S., and G. Pratt. 1995. *Gender, Work, and Space*. London: Routledge.

Hearnshaw, H.M., and D.Unwin (eds.). 1994. *Visualization in Geographical Information Systems*. Chichester, England: John Wiley and Sons.

Huisman, O.and P. Forer. 1998. *Towards a Geometric Framework for Modelling Space-Time*

Opportunities and Interaction Potential. Paper presented at the International Geographical Union, Commission on Modelling Geographical Systems Meeting, Lisbon, Portugal (IGU-CMGS), 28–29 August.

Kwan, M-P. 1998. Space-time and integral measures of individual accessibility: A comparative analysis using a point-based framework. *Geographical Analysis* 30(3): 191–216.

Kwan, M-P. 1999a. Gender, the home-work link, and space-time patterns of non-employment activities. *Economic Geography* 75(4): 370–394.

Kwan, M-P. 1999b. Gender and individual access to urban opportunities: A study using space-time measures. *The Professional Geographer* 51(2): 210–227.

Kwan, M-P. 2000a. Gender differences in space-time constraints. *Area* 32(2): 145–156.

Kwan, M-P. 2000b. Interactive geovisualization of activity-travel patterns using three-dimensional geographical information systems: A methodological exploration with a large data set. *Transportation Research C* 8: 185–203.

Kwan, M-P. 2000c. Human extensibility and individual hybrid-accessibility in space-time: A multi-scale representation using GIS. In D. Janelle, and D. Hodge (eds.), *Information, Place, and Cyberspace: Issues in Accessibility.* Berlin: Springer-Verlag, 241–256.

Laws, G. 1997. Women's life courses, spatial mobility, and state policies. In J.P. Jones III, H.J. Nast, and S.M. Roberts (eds.), *Thresholds in Feminist Geography: Difference, Methodology, Representation.* New York: Rowman and Littlefield, 47–64.

Lenntorp, B. 1976. *Paths in Time-Space Environments: A Time Geographic Study of Movement Possibilities of Individuals.* Gleerup: Lund.

MacEachren, A.M., M. Wachowicz, R. Edsall, and D. Haug. 1999. Constructing knowledge from multivariate spatiotemporal data: Integrating geographical visualization and knowledge discovery in database methods. *International Journal of Geographical Information Science* 13(4): 311–334.

Mårtensson, S. 1977. Childhood interaction and temporal organization. *Economic Geography* 53: 99–125.

Miller, H.J. 1999. Measuring space-time accessibility benefits within transportation networks: Basic theory and computational procedures. *Geographical Analysis* 31(2): 187–212.

Miller, H.J., and Y.H. Wu. 2000. GIS software for measuring space-time accessibility in transportation planning and analysis. *GeoInformatica* 4(2): 141–159.

Odland, J. 1998. Longitudinal analysis of migration and mobility spatial behavior in explicitly temporal contexts. In M. J. Egenhofer, and R. G. Golledge (eds.), *Spatial and Temporal Reasoning in Geographic Information Systems.* Oxford: University of Oxford Press, 238–260.

Ohmori, N., Y. Muromachi, N. Harata, and K. Ohta. 1999. A study on accessibility and going-out behavior of aged people considering daily activity pattern. *Journal of the Eastern Asia Society for Transportation Studies* 3: 139–153.

Palm, R. 1981. Women in nonmetropolitan areas: A time-budget survey. *Environment and Planning A* 13(3): 373–378.

Parkes, D.N., and N. Thrift. 1975. Timing space and spacing time. *Environment and Planning A* 7: 651–670.

Pred, A. 1990. *Lost Words and Lost Worlds: Modernity and the Language of Everyday Life in Late Nineteenth-Century Stockholm.* Cambridge: Cambridge University Press.

Rollinson, P. 1998. The everyday geography of the homeless in Kansas City. *Geografiska Annaler B* 80: 101–115.

Sheppard, S.R.J. 1999. Visualization software bring GIS applications to life. *GeoWorld* 12(3): 36–37.

Silverman, B.W. 1986. *Density Estimation for Statistics and Data Analysis.* London: Chapman and Hall.

Takeda, Y. 1998. Space-time prisms of nursery school users and location-allocation modeling. *Geographical Sciences* (*Chiri-kagaku*, in Japanese) 53: 206–216.

Thrift, N. 1977. *An Introduction to Time Geography*. Geo Abstracts, Norwich: University of East Anglia.

Tivers, J. 1985. *Women Attached: The Daily Lives of Women with Young Children*. London: Croom Helm.

Tufte, E.R. 1990. *Envisioning Information*. Cheshire, Connecticut: Graphics Press.

Tufte, E.R. 1997. *Visual Explanations: Images and Quantities, Evidence and Narrative*. Cheshire, Connecticut: Graphics Press.

Weber, J., and M.P. Kwan. 2002. Bringing time back in: A study on the influence of travel time variations and facility opening hours on individual accessibility. *The Professional Geographer* 54: 226–240.

4

Agent-Based Modeling
From Individual Residential Choice to Urban Residential Dynamics

Itzhak Benenson

H ouseholder residential choice and residential mobility are among the touchstones of theoretical and applied studies of urban systems. Sociology and human geography focus on these individual processes, which are inherently spatial and locally determined. Urban residential dynamics are an outcome of all the householders' simultaneous choices; hence, no programs, ranging from neighborhood rehabilitation to prevention of epidemics, can be planned without the ability to understand and foresee the global urban consequences of those individual decisions in the short and long term.

When confronting this challenge, conceptual as well as methodological issues have arisen that focus on the perspective we should adopt when analyzing residential choice, mobility, and their consequences. First, let us look at the problem in its simplest terms. When faced with the responsibility of changing residence, individuals are pitted against an often confusing if not threatening entity called the "city." A city's dwelling market is always in flux; transportation problems abound; the variety of social, economic, and cultural arrangements, neighborhoods, and so forth make finding a home a behaviorally complex endeavor. Based on their own partial and distorted image of the city (Golledge and Timmermans 1990), and driven by changing conditions and tastes, householders nevertheless do relocate. In the process, they determine the characteristics of the urban population, and the spatial patterns found in neighborhoods, boroughs, regions, and the entire city.

It is veritably impossible to anticipate the effects of the relationships derived from and in turn, inducing mobility among large numbers of residents—whether in individual neighborhoods or the city as a whole—without *dynamic models*: analytical, simulation, or mixed. During the last half-century, scholars' belief in modeling as the proper means to grasp the unexpected and sometimes counter-intuitive behavior of urban systems spread, together with the perception of the city as a complex, open system and with the notion of self-organization (Haken and Portugali 1995; Portugali 2000). Despite the general acceptance of this view, just how to develop a model of the urban residential dynamics resulting from householders' residential choices remained and still remains an open question. In this chapter, I will offer contemporary response to this question.

Approaches to Modeling Urban Residential Dynamics

There are two main approaches to modeling urban processes in general and residential dynamics in particular.

Regional Approach

The traditional regional approach, originating in economics, dates from the 1960s and 1970s (Anselin and Madden 1990; Bertuglia et al. 1994). This approach focuses on flows of assets, including jobs, information, and population between urban (usually municipal) regions; these make up the elementary units of the model. Averaging over regions depends on the scale of the regional partition; however, research of the "Modifiable Areal Unit Problem" has undeniably demonstrated that the conclusions reached on the basis of aggregate datasets can change significantly when the same data are considered at different scales (Openshaw 1983).

Regional models are also data-consuming. For a city divided into 20 to 30 regions, each described by ten state variables, the equations that describe flows between all possible pairs of regions have to account for astronomical numbers of parameters. To overcome this problem, regional modelers unify inter-regional flows in various ways (White and Engelen 2000); nonetheless, the dimension of parameter space required remains very high. I will consider regional models of residential dynamics in some detail below (Batty and Longley 1994; van Wissen and Rima 1988).

Averaging characteristics over units containing thousands of elementary independent decision-makers—householders—makes regional models insensitive to the behavior of particular individuals. Although such outcomes may be appropriate in the physical realm, researchers of social processes have always been aware of the conceptual inappropriateness of applying the regional approach to the behavior exhibited by the human constituents of the city, elements that exhibit "free will." This is not meant to be overly critical; rather, such limitations have driven researchers to search for another approach, one that takes the "human" nature of residential dynamics into account.

Agent-Based Approach

Formulated in early 1970s, the major alternative to the regional approach (Sakoda 1971; Schelling 1971, 1974) is seemingly simple. It requires that we populate computer memory with many explicitly located, distinct decision-makers, each of whom assesses the urban social and physical reality and makes residential decisions according to her own rules. Despite its inherent attractiveness for social research, this idea—agent-based (AB) modeling—remained somewhat buried in the methodological repertoire for years. Only in the last decade has it become a hotbed of social and urban modeling (Epstein and Axtell 1996; Gilbert and Conte 1995; Gilbert and Troitzsch 1999; Portugali 2000). The "agents" in a social AB model represent humans; they interact with other human agents as well as with the objects comprising the physical environment. Regarding residential dynamics, individual householder agents behave—choose and resettle in the new dwellings—and influence other agents accordingly. As a result, they affect urban infrastructure. From the perspective of an AB model, regional or global urban dynamics are the outcomes of agent behavior, yet influence individual agents' characteristics and behavior in turn. The emergence and persistence of ecological patchiness, traffic flows, and economic structures all are examples of processes for which AB models have recently been applied (Ligtenberg et al. 2001; Moss and Davidson 2000; Sichman et al. 1998). The general theory of AB systems (Ferber 1999) concentrates on agent behavior per se. The focus on *space* and *spatial interactions* clarifies our understanding of agent behavior; the resulting spatial models integrate various sources of information, allowing experts from various disciplines to coordinate their knowledge and propose social policy options.

The conceptual advantages of the AB approach extend beyond straightforward reflection of individual behavior. One can argue that quantitative and qualitative changes in urban systems can also be better understood within its framework, because they are dependent on actors who strongly and directly influence their immediate environment (Maes 1995; Portugali 2000). In contrast, aggregation by preset geographic partitions demands two-way "translation,"—of real-world events into parameters of interregional flows and of averaged regional dynamics into consequences at the individual level. The relationships between aggregate and individual characteristics always remain of uncertain validity, a problem known in geography as the "ecological fallacy" (Openshaw and Rao 1995; Wrigley et al. 1996).

The self-evident authenticity of the AB approach in the representation of social phenomena neither endows it with superiority over the regional approach nor automatically implies meaningful results, which are still scarce in coming. This chapter presents recent advances in AB modeling of residential choice and migration in addition to the effects of these processes on urban residential dynamics. As an introduction, I begin with a short description of current views on urban location processes and their experimental support. I then consider abstract AB models of residential behavior; these provide the foundations for understanding the system effects of feedback from neighborhood structure on individual residential behavior. Several examples of aggregate residential models are also presented. The last section presents real-world simulations of residential dynamics, including details of the AB simulation of the residential dynamics for an urban region having a population of 30,000.

How Residential Agents Make Choices—Ideas and Experiments

The agent-based model is, by definition, based on rules of agent (or individual) behavior. To make the model work, we must specify, at each moment in time and for each agent, what she "knows" about the city and how she reacts (if at all) to a perceived situation. The natural way to establish these rules for residential models is to mirror the behavior of the householders revealed in experiments on residential choice. These experiments are themselves rooted in theoretical perspectives on individual residential behavior that follow two main arguments.

Agents Optimize Their State

The view that reigned during the 1970s and 1980s assumed that residential choice belongs to the broader spectrum of individual economic behavior. *Homo economicus* (Sonis 1992) tends to optimize her state in various respects. Regarding residential choice, she maximizes the net sum of three components: benefits at the current location, costs of moving (or mobility), and benefits obtainable at the potential location; each can be calculated in different ways (Goodman 1981; DaVanzo 1981). A typical example is the trade-off between housing and commuting costs (Alonso 1964): the closer the residential location to work (i.e., the lower the commuting costs), the higher the probability that the agents will choose this location for residence.

Theoretically, the optimization hypothesis is consistent with the regional approach to modeling mainly because it adjusts residential distributions to the distribution of jobs, dwellings, commerce, and transport networks over regions (Alonso 1964; Mills and Hamilton 1989). However, it has failed to survive empirical tests. For instance, the trade-off between housing and commuting costs is either not true at all, or is so weak that it can be ascertained only after the effects of housing and neighborhood characteristics are eliminated (Herrin and Kern 1992; van Ommeren et al. 1996). Other analyses have demonstrated weak uni-directional dependence, with job location dependent on residence location (Deitz 1998) or vice-versa (Clark and Withers 1999).

The failure of the optimization hypothesis does not exclude economic factors from scholarly consideration; instead, it forces us to extend the framework to include other factors—social, cultural, and historical—as directly influencing residential choice.

The Stress-Resistance Approach

Even before firm empirical rejections of the optimization approach began to appear, social scientists felt profound discomfort with its view of residential behavior. This aversion was strongly supported by psychological research, where the *satisficing* hypothesis of human choice behavior, popular since the mid 1950s (Simon 1956, 1982; Gigerenzer and Goldstein 1996), was proposed as an alternative to optimization. The sociological models developed in the 1960s and established as theoretical mainstays in the 1970s liberated householders from the need to solve optimization problems. These models "allowed" householders to resettle to avoid unpleasant or negative conditions at their current locations and to search for better conditions at a new one. The new scenario thus maintained that an individual is influenced by local factors—state of the house, the ethnic and socio-economic structure of the neighborhood, distance to shops and transportation, among other things—but not by the average (or general) characteristics of the urban region in which her house is located.

To optimize a decision outcome, the householder should deal with all stages of residential choice simultaneously; if optimization is eliminated, we can break the process down into sequences of behavioral steps, each taking place in *time*. A typical choice process thus begins with assessment of one's residential situation, followed by the decision to attempt to leave; available alternatives are then investigated, their utility estimated and compared to that of the current location. All these result in the decision to resettle or to stay.

The *stress-resistance* approach (Wolpert 1965; Brown and Moore 1970; Speare 1974; Phipps and Carter 1984) formalized this view. In its standard application, householders take two basic steps: the first relates to the decision to leave the current location, the second to the decision to reside in the new location. At the first step, residents estimate the "stress" to move by comparing the current to the desired residential situation; if the stress is sufficiently high, they decide to move. At the second, those prepared to move estimate the "resistance" to moving by comparing available alternatives to their current location and then deciding either to relocate to one of the alternatives or to stay where they are. To avoid unnecessary associations with psychological stress, different authors have suggested the notions of dissatisfaction (Speare 1974), utility (Veldhuisen and Timmermans 1984), and *residential dissonance* (Portugali et al. 1994). I adopt the last in my description of the householder's situation.

The stress-resistance hypothesis had also compelled modelers to shift from the aggregate to the individual, that is, to the agent-based approach. Because householder stress, resistance, and choice-decisions are perceived as locally determined, images of the urban space must be sufficiently resolute to distinguish separate habitats. The ability to capture variation in householder and household characteristics likewise becomes crucial.

To verify the stress-resistance hypothesis, the economic and social "push" and "pull" factors (Sabagh et al. 1969; Ritchey 1976; Dorigo and Tobler 1983) that determine the householder's decision at each step of the choice process need to be identified. Speare proposed a natural classification of the factors that can determine the selection of a specific residence by a given householder (Speare 1974; Speare et al. 1975). His categories have been incorporated as a basis for experimental research and consistently used since their formulation.

Speare et al. (1975) assign decision factors to one of four categories: (1) individual, (2) household, (3) housing, and (4) neighborhood. This classification naturally fits the agent-based modeling scheme and can be extended if we wish to isolate factors related to higher levels of the urban hierarchy, such as time of trip to work, walking distance to the nearest commercial center, and so on.

Experimental Studies of Personal Residential Preferences

Two main approaches are used in experimental studies of residential choice. The *revealed preferences* approach uses real-world data on the outcomes of residential choice, while the *stated preferences* approach uses controlled experiments, where householders evaluate potential residences according to stated combinations of characteristics (Timmermans and Golledge 1990; van De Vyvere 1994). Revealed preferences tell us about real-world choices but can be biased by external constraints to making choices, such as lack of information about the dwelling. Alternatively, stated preferences reveal intentions; however, these may not necessarily be realized. Regarding model construc-

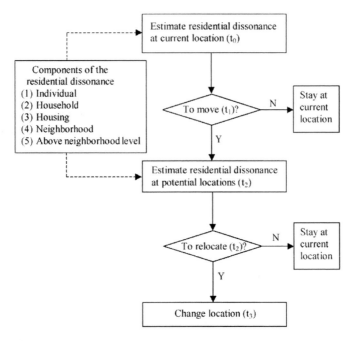

Figure 4.1. The stress-resistance hypothesis represented schematically; $t_0 < t_1 < t_2 < t_3$ denote consecutive moments of the *individual's time* sequence related to residential choice.

tion, the results obtained by the stated preferences approach help establish behavioral rules and their parameterization, while the revealed preferences approach helps verify the model.

Because the results of residential choice are qualitative in the main, the multinomial logit model is used as a basic tool for relating factors with choice outcomes; general statistical models are employed to account for factor hierarchies, latent variables, and so forth (Timmernams and van Noortwijk 1995). The research demonstrates that many factors, all belonging to the categories in Speare's taxonomy, are likely to significantly influence residential decisions (Phipps and Carter 1984; Deane 1990; van de Vyvere et al. 1998; van Ommeren et al. 1996; Fokkema and van Wissen 1997; Molin et al. 1999; Schellekens and Timmermans 1997; Tu and Goldfinch 1996):

- Householder: age, number of persons in a family, economic status/income, ethnicity;
- Household: size, number of rooms, floor, costs of maintenance, tenure;
- Housing: type of house, age of house;
- Neighborhood: housing structure, demographic structure, ethnic structure;
- Above-neighborhood level: distance to city center, frequency of public transport, travel time to work, travel time to school.

For different groups of householders, specific characteristics may be important, such as loneliness and need for home care among persons aged 55+ (Wiseman and Roseman

1979; Fokkema and Van Wissen 1997) or neighbors' ethnicity for minorities (Sermons 2000).

Among the factors investigated, characteristics of housing and of the social structure and housing options in the householder's vicinity are usually somewhat more important than factors such as location of the house relative to other infrastructure elements or distance to shopping or public transport (Louviere and Timmermans 1990). Nevertheless, no factor is, a priori, more salient than the others (Bolan 1997; van de Vyvere et al. 1998); pairwise correlations usually remain within an interval (-0.2 to 0.2), reaching ± 0.4 in some cases. Taken together, the investigated factors explain, according to R^2, about 20–30 percent of the variance in residential choice.

The low level of overall fitness exhibited in choice experiments has dimmed the optimism inspired by statistically significant relationships although they continue to be discussed intensively. It is difficult to believe that salient factors have been overlooked in so many experiments. Are weak correlations sufficient to explain the observed urban residential distributions? Can we agree that the essential components of a person's residential choice heuristics are irrational or that each type of stimulus induces a different type of response? Agent-based models can help to answer these questions by direct interpretation of qualitative assumptions and by experimentally discovered stated preferences of agents' behavioral rules.

From Modeling of Single Choice to Modeling of Residential Dynamics

Processes and factors beyond the standard framework of residential choice studies become important when we consider the population of householders and proceed to long-term modeling. Householders themselves change and make residential decisions again and again in evolving local and global circumstances. The stress-resistance approach ignores the recurrent character of residential behavior as well as the change in information available, initiated by changes in residential patterns, in- and out-migration, real estate markets, and other environmental conditions. The scheme displayed in Figure 4.1 is therefore incomplete in this respect and should be revised. Figure 4.2 demonstrates one way of doing so.

In this scheme, T represents time in an urban system; ΔT is a time interval between two consecutive observations of its state. In this paper, I do not discuss the meaning of "system state" and "system time" in relation to urban systems and base my arguments on an intuitive grasp of these notions (for an in-depth discussion see Nicolis and Prigogine 1977; Allen and Sanglier 1981; Haken and Portugali 1995). In what follows, it is convenient to consider ΔT to be in the order of several months and to assume that $\Delta T >> t_3 - t_0$; that is, an individual makes decisions at a pace faster than she observes the urban system.

Each component added to the residential dynamics scheme in Figure 4.2 could be elaborated into finer details. As our goal is to understand the long-term outcomes of residential choice rules, we can begin with the simplest demographic and infrastructure models or even set them as constant. Yet, from a systemic point of view, the outcome of a model can be complex because of limited capacity of an urban space. For example, the inherently competitive character of householder interactions entails *non-linear*

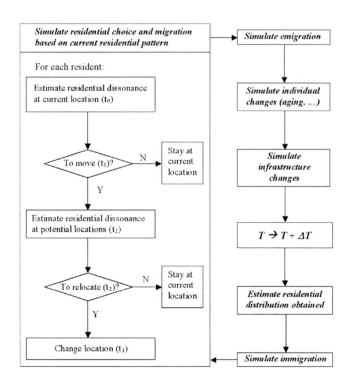

Figure 4.2. Agent-based description of urban residential dynamics based on stress-resistance hypothesis.

reactions of the system as a whole; one can easily imagine these effects when the numbers of householders looking for dwellings within an attractive area is beyond the area's capacity to respond. For open and non-linear systems, self-organizing effects are to be expected, such as "sudden" increases in dwelling prices, emergence of fashionable areas, and formation and dissolution of segregated residential patterns, all motivated by no clearly identifiable forces. Apparently, relatively simple urban systems exhibit this same kind of behavior (Benenson 1999; Portugali 2000).

Agent-based modeling offers several conceptual advantages over regional modeling when implementing the scheme shown in Figure 4.2. First, its convenience for representing rules of residential behavior naturally extends to the representation of individual changes as well as in- and out-migrations. Second, the urban physical environment consists of separate spatial (but immobile) objects, just as populations consist of agents. The most popular high-resolution tool for modeling infrastructure dynamics is the cellular automata, which can be easily combined with agent-based models of individual behavior (Portugali et al. 1997; Benenson 1999; Portugali 2000; Torrens 2000).

In what follows, I use the simplest possible description of demographic and infrastructure processes and concentrate on the outcomes of repeated acts of residential choice.

The Urban Consequences of Individual Residential Behavior

The factors in Speare's scheme are classified according to the level of urban hierarchy at which they operate. To analyze urban residential dynamics, it is important to distinguish between factors that influence residential choice but are not directly influenced by choice outcomes, and those that change together with the residential distribution. The characteristics of householders, houses, infrastructure, and in-migration do not directly follow changes in residential distributions and can be considered as *external* to residential distribution. Factors related to neighborhood structure act differently: a neighborhood's population directly reflects the residential behavior of the householders and should be considered as *internal* to residential distributions. Stated differently, a direct *feedback relationship* exists between neighborhood structure and urban residential distribution.

Examples of abstract models aimed at understanding the consequences of basic internal feedback relationships that entail the emergence and self-organization of urban segregation are presented first; models based on external factors are illustrated afterwards.

Agent-Based Modeling of Urban Segregation as Self-Organizing Phenomena

Residential distributions in cities populated by agents of two non-friendly types tend to display segregation. Two researchers, Thomas Schelling and James Sakoda independently published this basic result in the early 1970s (Schelling 1971, 1974; Sakoda 1971). They had no computers and played "urban games" on a chessboard, used to question the long-term consequences of individual tendencies to locate within friendly neighborhoods and to relocate when residential dissonance increases. Their models' assumptions and rules of agent behavior were intentionally primitive; namely, the chessboard was populated with constant numbers of agents of two types, say Black (B) and White (W), whose overall number was much below the number of cells. The cells themselves were set as designating location only. The residential behavior of the model agent was determined by the residential dissonance between the agent and her neighbors within the 3×3 square neighborhood around the agent's location. Schelling and Sakoda differed in the way they calculated local residential dissonance and formulated rules of agent reaction to dissonance. Sakoda (1971) defines the attitude—attraction (1), neutrality (0), or avoidance (-1)—of an agent to agents of her own and the other type; the agent reacts to the sum of attitudes to neighbors. Two versions of the model are considered: agents in both avoid representatives of the unfamiliar group; however, in the first they are attracted to the agents of their own type (Table 4.1a), while in the second they are neutral regarding these agents (Table 4.1b). Schelling's (1971) agents react to the fraction of familiar agents within the neighborhood, and also can be formulated in terms of attitude: agents are attracted by agents of their own type and neutral to agents of the other type (Table 4.1c).

In Schelling's (1971) experiments, agents located in cells where less than half of their neighbors are of their own type migrate to the closest free cell, where the fraction of agents of their own type is above 50 percent. Sakoda (1971) assumes that an agent

Table 4.1. Attitudes of agents to their neighbors.

a. Sakoda I			b. Sakoda II			c. Schelling		
	Neighbor type			Neighbor type			Neighbor type	
Agent type	B	W	Agent type	B	W	Agent type	B	W
B	1	−1	B	0	−1	B	1	0
W	−1	1	W	−1	0	W	0	1

tries to optimize her state and repeatedly estimates her potential dissonance at each empty cell within a 3 × 3 square neighborhood. If vacancies better than the current one are found, an agent migrates to the best of those options. Initially, agents are distributed randomly on the chessboard in each model; they make decisions in sequence, according to a preliminary order established in advance.

The main result of both papers is independent of the attitude scheme: B- and W-agents segregate after a number of migration loops, and the residential patterns obtained do not change qualitatively in subsequent time periods. Thus, both models show that socially determined local residential preferences do result in full segregation in the long run.

Schelling and Sakoda's basic result has been extended and generalized during the last decade, with computers replacing the chessboard. Hegselmann and Flache (1999) have applied the predecessors' choice rules on much larger grids. They reveal two additional effects after varying the number of urban agents and the agents' sensitivity threshold to their neighbors. First, they reveal qualitative differences in outcomes of the Sakoda I and Sakoda II models. In the case of mutual distrust (Sakoda I), agents of each type create many clusters (Figure 4.3a), while attitudes of avoidance only (Sakoda II) result in full separation of the two groups (Figure 4.3b); that is, uni-directional influences can induce sharper segregation than do bi-directional influences[1]. First, they demonstrate that the 50 percent threshold of familiar agents in the Schelling's model can be decreased: B- and W-agents segregate when an agent needs 30 percent or higher level of familiar neighbors, to initiate a search for housing.

Portugali et al. (1994) extended Schelling's and Sakoda's models to cover more "human" agent behavior and more realistic city dynamics. First, they introduce the simplest forms of in- and out-migration; in doing so, they partially implement the scheme shown in Figure 4.2 (infrastructure and agent properties remaining constant). Second, they eliminate the deterministic view of householder behavior and assume residential choice to be a stochastic process. Formally, they introduced the probability to leave (P) or to occupy (Q) a residence H as a function of the agent's local dissonance D(H) at H, that is $P = P(D(H))$ and $Q = Q(D(H))$. The rule for calculating residential dissonance D(H) in their model is complementary to Schelling's and Sakoda's; that is, D(H) depends on fractions of familiar and unfamiliar agents within a 5 × 5 square neighborhood. Regarding dependencies P(D) and Q(D) on D, they assume that the probability to leave a location P(D) increases and the probability to occupy a location Q(D) decreases monotonically with an increase in D.

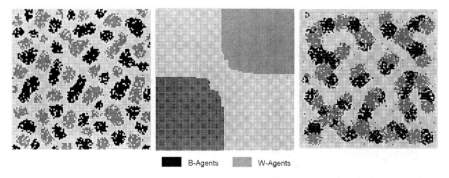

B-Agents   W-Agents

Figure 4.3. Typical stable spatial distribution of B and W agents in the Sakoda and Schelling models: left to right, (a) Sakoda I model; (b) Sakoda II model; and (c) Schelling model, 40 percent threshold.

To make their computer agents resemble humans more closely, Portugali et al. (1994) assume that the information on vacant residences available to an agent deciding to move is not limited to the agent's neighborhood. On the contrary, all residences in the city are potentially available to a migrating agent, and she can reside at any distance from her current location. At the same time, access to this information is limited to a finite number (usually ten) of vacancies that an agent can consider during a unit of system time ΔT. At the occupation stage of residential choice, the probability of occupying each new vacancy is set inversely proportional to the agent's dissonance at each vacancy. One more humanizing assumption is that agents of the same type behave differently: Some agents of both B- and W-types avoid the agents of the other type (Sakoda II scheme), while the rest are neutral towards those same strangers and are attracted by the agents of their own type (the Schelling scheme).

The above generalization of the model strengthens the basic result of Sakoda (1971): to cause and maintain stable residential segregation, uni-directional avoidance is sufficient. Segregation is maintained if a substantial portion of agents of both types are neutral regarding strangers; two-thirds of the agents, whose behavior is aimed at avoiding agents of the other type, are sufficient to obtain segregation between B- and W-agents (Figure 4.4a). The stochastic nature of the residential decision embodies a new, important feature of the segregated residential distribution modeled: At the boundaries between segregated groups, agents are always in flux (Figure 4.4b).

Portugali et al. (1994) conclude that boundary areas are especially important if the agents themselves (like the humans they represent) change: agents with new properties enter the unstable areas first. These agents can enter the city from the outside, but they can also be residents who have altered their residential behavior. To further investigate the latter possibility, Portugali and Benenson (1997), Portugali et al. (1997), and Benenson (1998) assume that agents can adapt their residential behavior to local and global urban environments. They consider the situation where the information on the local and global environment available to an agent is in conflict with the incentives available for agent adaptation. Specifically, they assume that the longer a scarcity of

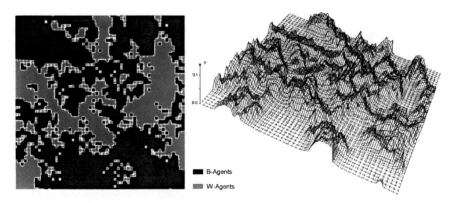

Figure 4.4. Typical stable spatial distribution of agents in the Portugali, Benenson, and Omer (1994) model: left to right, (a) distribution of agents, (b) probability that one agent can be substituted at the next iteration by an agent of the other type.

vacant habitats (i.e., migration options) forces an agent to remain within a neighborhood occupied by unfamiliar neighbors, the higher the probability that the agent will change her attitude toward these neighbors from avoidance to neutrality. In opposite, the higher the average level of segregation of individuals of the agent's type over the entire city space (not necessarily proximate to the agent's location), the higher the probability that the agent's avoidance of unfamiliar neighbors will persist.

Long-term residential dynamics in such a model evidently depend on the relative strength of the two opposing inclinations. If the tendency to adapt to local conditions is much stronger, then all agents become neutral to one another and the residential distribution of agents according to initial B- and W-types becomes random. If reaction to the global situation (of segregation) is stronger, initial behavior is preserved and complete segregation of B- and W-agents is obtained in the long run. The most interesting case occurs when both tendencies are strong: a sufficient number of agents become *neutral* towards members of the types initially present and then segregate and form a new group within the urban context (Portugali and Benenson 1995, 1997; Portugali et al. 1997). If agents' adaptation is regarded according to *several traits* simultaneously, then the groups of agents bearing new properties will *recurrently* emerge and vanish (Benenson 1998, 1999).

Abstract AB models elicit important qualitative conclusions regarding the internal factors motivating residential preferences and migration: first, permanent preferences to locate in friendly neighborhoods and/or avoid strangers are sufficient for urban residential patterns to (self-) organize; second, adaptation to the global state of the city entails emergence, persistence, and segregation of agents possessing novel properties. Before we proceed to the model that combines internal and external factors in a real-world situation, the relative influence of the latter on rules of agent behavior should be verified.

Agent-Based Modeling of Residential Reaction to the Physical Environment

To model the influence of the physical environment, data on the housing market should be incorporated into the model. Schellekens and Timmermans (1997) developed an agent-based simulation of residential choice aimed at comparing different rent subsidy policies. Model implementation differs for four different housing markets in Holland: four of the country's largest cities, other Dutch cities containing more than 100,000 residents, new towns, and other municipalities. Householders in the model are characterized by economic status, which does not change in time; residential decisions are based on household characteristics only, and markets are set as static. The model is limited to global external factors and ignores the spatial distributions of the habitats and the residents. For each market considered, it reveals likely and significant differences in the fraction of migrants and buyers, mean price of apartment, fraction of subsidized persons, amount of subsidy, and monthly rent in a subsidized versus a non-subsidized situation.

The agents in Schellekens and Timmermans (1997) model are purely mechanistic in their perception of the spatial situation as averaged over the entire city; their "human" characteristics are reflected by the rule according to which they select one specific habitat from the several options available. In the abstract models previously noted, choice is *parallel* and wholly rational—agents are cognizant of all the options before they decide which to select; the probability that a habitat will be chosen is set inversely proportional to dissonance between the agent and that habitat. Schellekens and Timmermans (1997), however, follow another—less rational and more human—*sequential* choice heuristic. The householders in their model examine available vacancies when they become available; if the first available vacancy is accepted, the choice procedure is cancelled; otherwise, the second vacancy is examined, and so forth. Sequential choice reflects the satisficing hypothesis of human choice behavior (Gigerenzer and Goldstein 1996) and as Benenson et al. (2002) demonstrate, essentially increases robustness of the system dynamics to changes in numerical values of the model parameters. It is applied in the real-world model of residential dynamics in Yaffo, below.

The rule of selection is unimportant for classical regional models, where the number of newcomers of different types into a region is determined by the capacity to develop dwelling infrastructure. If physical environment strongly governs the social structure, a regional model can provide good approximations and predictions of urban residential dynamics. This seems to be the case in the van Wissen and Rima (1988) model, which represents Amsterdam by means of 20 dwelling zones. In each zone, 11 dwelling types and 24 types of households of four different sizes are distinguished. The intensity of migration and the residential choice of each family are dependent upon the age of the head of household (according to five-year age categories) and on the number of family members (seven categories). Immigration, emigration, births, and deaths are included. The model's parameters were estimated on the database for 1971–1984. The resulting approximation of population and household dynamics was very good: for thirteen zones, the R^2 statistics of correspondence between actual data on population structure and model results are higher than 0.9; for the remaining zones, excluding one, they are not less than 0.5. Based on these correspondences, two scenarios of Amsterdam population and household dynamics for 1985–2000 are compared. The first reflects central government plans to build new dwellings in Amsterdam, while the second reflects local government measures to decrease construction quotas in the expanding suburbs, which diverge at the level of 10 percent or less during the period studied.

The van Wissen and Rima model (1988) still remains an outstanding example of exceptionally good approximation. The Batty and Longley model (1994) exhibits a common level of approximation for population dynamics in Greater London. In the model, the city is divided into 32 zones, each described by percentages of dwellings of four types. The probabilities of occupying dwellings of each type are considered as functions of the distance between the central business district (CBD) and the zone, and the mean age of the zone's dwellings. The overall percentage of the model's correct predictions, 0.432, is essentially lower than in the Amsterdam model. Spatially, prediction is much better for zones close to the CBD and for the outermost suburbs than for the intermediate zones.

To conduct a full study of the consequences of residential choice and migration for urban systems, we have to combine internal and external factors, which require high-resolution data on demography and infrastructure. The latter were unavailable until the 1990s; recent developments in GIS and census databases have corrected this situation. The remainder of the chapter is devoted, therefore, to a recently developed agent-based model of residential migration in the Yaffo area of Tel-Aviv, where I account for the influence of one internal and one external factor on residential choice. The detailed analysis of this model is presented in Benenson et al. (2002); here it is used to illustrate the implementation of the AB modeling approach in a real-world situation.

A Real-World Agent-Based Model of Residential Choice and Migration

The model presented here simulates the residential dynamics (1955–1995) of Yaffo, an area lying in the southern reaches of Tel-Aviv and populated by Arab and Jewish householders. The model scheme resembles that shown in Figure 4.2; for the present purposes, the model components that do not directly relate to residential choice and migration are severely simplified (see description below).

Why Yaffo?

The selection of Yaffo for construction of a real-world model of residential dynamics is not random. First, one can assume that ethnicity induces the residential behavior of Yaffo agents, and that the relationships between the agents, representing Arab and Jewish householders, are similar to the theoretical attraction-avoidance relations explored above. Second, quite a lot is known about Yaffo's infrastructure: during the Israeli Census of Population and Housing of 1995, high-resolution GIS coverage of streets and houses was constructed and released for all Israeli cities, including Tel-Aviv (ICBS 2000). Hence, individuals in the ICBS database are precisely geo-referenced: personal and family records of each person indicate the house where the person lives.

The individual census record contains age, education, origin, ethnicity, marital status, salaried income, and many other characteristics of the individual effective for 1995. The family record contains data on the house and the residence—the householder's estimate of the year the house was built, number of rooms in the apartment, home appliances, travel time to work, and so forth. The individual data are available for supervised study in the Israeli Central Bureau of Statistics (ICBS) offices; furthermore, the model is calibrated based on characteristics of Yaffo's residential distribution calculated from these data.

Yaffo's Infrastructure

Yaffo covers about 7km^2; its infrastructure was set in the early 1960s, when the majority of Yaffo's buildings were constructed. The GIS layers of houses and streets, constructed in 1995, are used as proxies for the entire 1955–1995 period; further proliferation of the infrastructure dynamics is avoided. Figure 4.5 presents the GIS view of Yaffo; houses are marked according to their architectural style, which enables use of this characteristic in the model. The architectural style of about 90 percent of Yaffo's buildings can be characterized as either "oriental" or "block," with the remaining 10 percent approaching one of these two styles; architectural style of a building (S) is defined as a continuous variable whose values range from 0 (oriental) to 1 (block). Only residential buildings are taken into account; the dwelling capacity of a building is estimated by the number of floors and the foundation area, assuming that an average apartment in Tel-Aviv covers 100m^2.

Yaffo's Demography

According to ICBS data, Yaffo's population in 1995 was about 40,000, composed of a Jewish majority (about 70 percent) and an Arab minority (the remaining 30 percent). After Israel's War of Independence (1948), only 3,000 of the original Arab inhabitants remained in Yaffo; almost all of whom were concentrated within the small neighborhood known as Adjami (Portugali 1991; Omer 1996). Beginning in 1948, the Arab population of Yaffo grew and spread throughout the area, whereas the Jewish majority declined by gradual out-migration. Precise percentages of the Arab population in Yaffo are available: 1961, 10 percent; 1974, 15 percent; 1985, 25 percent and 1995, 32 percent.

The fraction of ethnically mixed families in Yaffo is below 1 percent (ICBS 2000). The Arab population of Yaffo is divided into two major cultural groups—Muslims and Christians; the differences in their residential behavior are inconsequential for present purposes and are thus ignored.

Factors Determining Residential Choice in Yaffo

Direct data on the residential preferences of Yaffo inhabitants are not available. According to indirect evidence (Omer 1996; Omer and Benenson 2002), two factors, namely the Jewish/Arab ratio within the neighborhood and the architectural style of the buildings, can be considered as influencing the residential decisions made by Jewish and

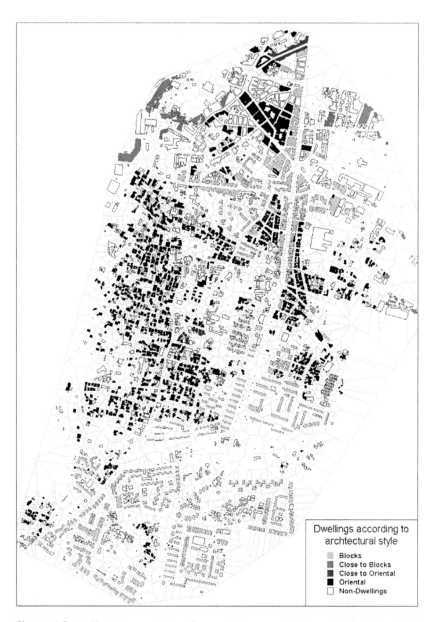

Dwellings according to archtectural style

- ▨ Blocks
- ▨ Close to Blocks
- ▨ Close to Oriental
- ■ Oriental
- □ Non-Dwellings

Figure 4.5. Yaffo at the resolution of separate houses and a Voronoi tessellation built on the base of house centroids. Levels of gray indicate architectural type. Reprinted from I. Benenson, I. Omer, and E. Hatna, 2002. Entity-based modeling of urban residential dynamics: The case of Yaffo, Tel Aviv. *Environment and Planning B: Planning and Design* 29: 491–512, with permission from Pion Ltd., London.

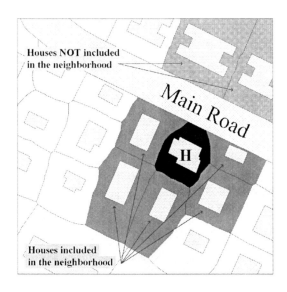

Figure 4.6. Definition of the neighborhood of the house H via Voronoi polygons.

Arab agents in Yaffo. The 1995 distributions of salaried income for Yaffo's Jews and Arabs are similar (Benenson et al. 2002); hence, the two factors of householder income and housing price are dispensed with here.

Neighborhoods

To determine the dissonance between an agent and her neighbors, "neighborhood" must be defined. The neighborhood for Yaffo's residential buildings is constructed according to a Voronoi tessellation[2] of the Yaffo area (Figure 4.5) on the basis of house centroids (Benenson et al. 2002; Halls et al. 2001); two buildings are considered as neighboring if their Voronoi polygons have a common boundary and they are on the same side of the main road (Figure 4.6).

Quantification of Residential Dissonance

Based on qualitative estimates of Omer (1996), six different levels of residential dissonance D are defined qualitatively for unmixed situations of the relationship between an agent and her local environment. These levels are then quantified as a stochastic variable; Table 4.2 presents average D_i, its standard deviation calculated as $STD_i = 0.05 \times \sqrt{(D_i \times (1 - D_i))}$, and 95 percent confidence intervals for each level i. Let us assume, for example, that the dissonance between an Arab agent located within purely Jewish neighborhood and her neighbors is "high". Her decision to leave will then be based on a dissonance value selected from the normal distribution with mean 0.8 and standard deviation 0.02.

Table 4.2. Residential dissonance estimates.

Dissonance Level	Zero	Very Low	Low	Intermediate	High	Very High
Average value	0.00	0.05	0.20	0.50	0.80	0.95
Standard deviation	0.000	0.011	0.020	0.025	0.020	0.011
95% confidence interval	(0.000, 0.000)	(0.029, 0.071)	(0.161, 0.239)	(0.451, 0.549)	(0.761, 0.839)	(0.929, 0.971)

Dissonance between an Agent and a Household and between an Agent and Her Neighbors

As shown in Table 4.3, for unmixed situations it is assumed that:

- Arab agents strongly avoid houses that are block and prefer houses of oriental architectural style; Jewish agents prefer the newly built block houses, although they accept oriental houses;
- Arab and Jewish agents strongly avoid homogeneous neighborhoods populated by agents of the other type; avoidance of Arab agents by Jewish is maximal.

Residential dissonance for mixed situations is linearly interpolated based on estimates set up for the unmixed ones. The dissonance $D_h(A_E, H_s)$ of an agent of identity A_E regarding dwelling in a house H of style S is calculated as

$$D_h(A_E, H_s) = D_h(A_E, H_0) \times (1 - S) + D_h(A_E, H_1) \times S \qquad (1)$$

where A_E is either A_J or A_R; H_0 stands for a house of oriental, and H_1 of block style.

For a mixed neighborhood $U(H)_r$ with fraction r of Arab agents (and $1 - r$ of Jewish agents), the dissonance regarding neighbors is calculated as:

$$D_p(A_E, U(H)_r) = D_p(A_E, U(H)_J) \times (1 - r) + D_p(A_E, U(H)_R) \times r \qquad (2)$$

where $U(H)_J$, $U(H)_R$ stand for homogeneous Jewish and Arab neighborhoods respectively.

The overall dissonance $D(A_E, H_s, U(H)_r)$ between an agent of identity A_E located in house H_s of style S within a neighborhood $U(H)_r$ having a fraction of Arab agents r is assumed to be high if it is high according to any one of its components:

$$D(A_E, H_s, U(H)_r) = 1-(1 - \alpha_h \times D_h(A_E, H_s))$$
$$\times (1 - \alpha_p \times D_p(A_E, U(H)_r)) \qquad (3)$$

where $\alpha_h, \alpha_p \in [0, 1]$ denote the influence of house style and ethnic factors.

Rules of Residential Choice and Migration

An agent's residential choice and decision to migrate do not depend on distance but on residential dissonance only. A three-step algorithm represents residential choice and migration of the Yaffo model agents.

Table 4.3. Initial estimate of the dissonance between an agent and a house (D_h) and between an agent and a homogeneous neighborhood (D_p). Values in italics stand for changes applied in "Arab Assimilation II" scenario.

	$D_h = D_h(A, H)$		$D_p = D_p(A, U(H))$	
	House's Architectural Style		Neighbors' Common Identity	
Agent's Identity	*Oriental (S = 0)*	*Block (S = 1)*	*Arab–U(H)$_R$*	*Jewish–U(H)$_J$*
Arab–A_R	Zero	High (*Low*)	Zero	High (*Low*)
Jewish–A_J	Intermediate	Zero	Very high	Zero

Step 1: Decide to migrate.   The probability P that an agent A will decide to move linearly depends on overall residential dissonance D at the agent's location:

$$P(D) = P_0 + (1 - P_0) \times D \qquad (4)$$

where $P_0 = 0.05$ is the probability of sporadic departure. If the decision is to move, A is marked as a potential migrant; otherwise, agent A remains at her current location (with probability $1 - P(D)$) and is ignored till the next step in time.

Step 2: Scan residence.   Each potential migrant A randomly selects ten houses H_v, $v = 1, \ldots, 10$, from the set of houses currently containing vacant residences. The probability $Q_v(D)$ (attractiveness) that agent A will decide to occupy vacancy v is calculated for each selected residence H_v as complementary to the probability to leave (4):

$$Q_v(D) = 1 - P_v(D) = (1 - P_0) \times (1 - D_v) \qquad (5)$$

where D_v is dissonance at potential location H_v.

Step 3: Occupy one of the scanned dwellings.   An agent A sorts information about all vacancies H_v according to their attractiveness $Q_v(D)$. After the sorted list of opportunities is constructed, A attempts to occupy the most attractive vacancy H_{best} with probability $Q_{\text{best}}(D)$; if A fails to occupy this vacancy, she turns to the second-best option, and so on.

Migration into and out of the City

Jewish or Arab potential migrants failing to resettle either leave the city with probability L_J (for Jewish agents) or L_R (for Arab agents) or remain at their current residence with probability $1 - L_J$ or $1 - L_R$. I assume that $L_J = 0.1$ per month and $L_R = 0.01$ per month, that is, L_R is ten times lower than L_J. The factor ten represents the ratio of areas available for resettlement of Jewish and Arab householders in Tel-Aviv, the latter having about ten times fewer options for resettlement than the former.

Based on partial data obtained by Omer (1996), the number of individuals who attempt to settle in Yaffo for the first time is set at 300 householders (natural increase and in-migration combined), with the ratio of Arabs to Jews equal to 1:2. The actual number of new householders remains below 150 per year in all model scenarios studied. Agents who failed to enter Yaffo do not repeat the attempt.

Initial Population Distribution

According to Omer's (1996) data for 1955, Yaffo's 3,000 Arab residents were located in Adjami neighborhood. In that year, full capacity of Adjami was three times higher, and Jewish householders populated the balance of the dwellings in Adjami as well as the remainder of Yaffo's territory (Figure 4.7).

Evaluation of the Model

The Yaffo model is calibrated by changing coefficients α_h, α_p in (3) and by varying the attitude of agents from each ethnic group toward houses of an unfamiliar type or an unfamiliar neighborhood; the initial values are shown in Table 4.3. The model results are then compared with the reality in Yaffo according to four characteristics:

1. The fraction of Arab population, present in 1961, 1974, 1985, and 1995.
2. The level of segregation of Arab and Jewish agents as estimated by means of Moran index I of spatial autocorrelation (Anselin 1995) at the resolution of buildings.
3. The non-correspondence of the population with the architectural style of the buildings.
4. The annual fraction of householders leaving a residence within Yaffo's boundaries.

The best correspondence is achieved with a scenario of low influence exerted by both factors explored ($\alpha_h = 0.05$ and $\alpha_p = 0.05$) and the tolerance of Arab agents adjusted two levels higher than initially suggested. In this "Arab Assimilation II" scenario, the dissonance between Arab agents and purely Jewish neighborhoods and "block" houses is set "Low" instead of "High", as marked by italics in Table 4.3. Table 4.4 and Figure 4.8 present the correspondence between real data and this scenario for 1995 and during the entire period of simulation. Confidence intervals of model characteristics are estimated based on 100 model runs under identical conditions.

The good correspondence between reality and the model in the case where Jews only experience dissonance within Arab neighborhoods coincides with the results of the theoretical models. Both in theoretical and the Yaffo models, if members of one group only either avoid strangers or prefer members of their own group as neighbors, then residential segregation occurs. The "common sense" view that two-sided competition is necessary for segregation to take place is shown to be irrelevant.

Spatial Determinism of Yaffo's Residential Dynamics

Table 4.4 and Figure 4.8 demonstrate global correspondence between the model and Yaffo reality. The agent-based approach makes it possible to investigate the finer properties of the residential distribution. The stochasticity of the model is extremely important in this analysis, as it represents the uncontrolled variation of the local factors to which the agents react. To test the "inevitability" of the residential distribution observed in Yaffo, maps representing the probability that the fraction of Arab or Jewish

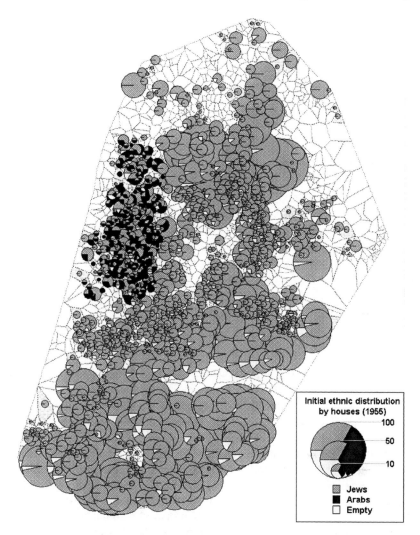

Figure 4.7. Initial (1955) distribution of Arab and Jewish agents in the Yaffo model. Reprinted from I. Benenson, I. Omer, and E. Hatna, 2002. Entity-based modeling of urban residential dynamics: The case of Yaffo, Tel Aviv. *Environment and Planning B: Planning and Design* 29: 491–512, with permission from Pion Ltd., London.

agents in a house is above a given threshold $F = 0.9$ are constructed based on 100 runs of "Arab Assimilation II" scenario (Figure 4.9).

These maps clearly indicate the areas where the variation in local processes has weakly influenced residential dynamics between 1955 and 1995; these areas contain about 80 percent of Yaffo's populated houses. The variation in the fraction of Arab agents in each house in the "Arab" part of Yaffo area is higher, both relatively and absolutely, than in the Jewish part. That is, the Arab area is more responsive to factors that the model does not account for. The ethnic structure within the houses over the re-

Table 4.4. Characteristics of Yaffo's population distribution in 1995 versus the most likely scenario of "Arab Assimilation II" in model year 40.

	Yaffo Data	Model Mean[†]	Model 95 Percent Confidence Interval[†]
Overall percentage of Arabs agents	32.2	34.8	(34.4, 35.2)
Moran index I of segregation for Arab agents	0.65	0.66	(0.63, 0.69)
Percentage of Arab agents in block houses	18.5	15.0	(12.8, 17.2)
Percentage of Jewish agents in oriental houses	28.1	8.0	(6.7, 9.3)
Annual percentage of migrants	3.5	3.7	(3.5, 3.9)

[†]Based on 100 runs

maining fifth of Yaffo's area is very sensitive to its agents' residential behavior; hence, it could be strongly influenced by other factors external to the model. The specific behavior of the human agents in these local areas—for instance, exaggerated reactions to the strangers and housing constructed for one specific population group—may have significantly influenced residential choice and resulted in Yaffo's unique residential distribution.

Discussion

Despite the limited number of implementations, I believe it appropriate to pose the basic question regarding the agent-based approach: Is it a step forward, one that provides social science with a truly adequate modeling tool, or is it merely a product of fashion? With respect to the modeling of residential behavior, I would argue that the former is true:

The concept of agent makes it possible for the model to directly reflect human behavior. AB models naturally reflect human capacities to perceive and react to information on different levels of the urban spatial hierarchy, to assess opportunities (vacant dwellings) before making a decision, to sort opportunities before exploring them on site, and so forth. All these cannot be directly projected onto the aggregate level; the concept of agent thus allows us to avoid problems related to the scale at which we observe social processes.

Agent-based models do not demand comprehensive knowledge of the phenomena studied. Changing the rules of residential behavior does not demand changing relationships between AB model components. This flexibility is a crucial asset for investigating different versions of the choice mechanism; we can begin with the simplest rules of agent behavior and increase their complexity while preserving the model's structure. For example, to study the economic aspects of residential choice in Yaffo, we can add prices to characterize dwellings, economic status to characterize agents, and revise the estimate of the residential dissonance to account for these characteristics; the other components of the rules of residential choice and migration will demand neither modification nor updating.

Formalization of behavioral rules reveals gaps in our knowledge of social processes. The ability to vary formal representation of agent behavior will reveal gaps in our

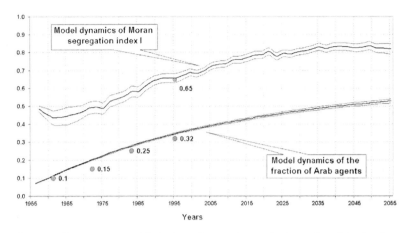

Figure 4.8. The "Arab Assimilation II" scenario: model dynamics of the fraction of Arab agents and of the Moran index *I* for the Arab population.

knowledge. As the residential models reveal, further research on choice heuristics—and not one more study of residential preferences—will make a more significant contribution to our understanding of urban residential dynamics.

Self-organizing consequences of human behavior can be investigated directly. Many urban phenomena are outcomes of local disturbances whose significance is recognized only long after the event. In the AB model framework, information regarding local changes in residential variables is made available to agents, and collective urban phenomena can be investigated directly through the study of the spatial outcomes of the model. The AB model's ability to reflect local indeterminacy opens the door to investigating urban self-organization and emergence at different spatial and temporal resolutions. Urban space itself integrates various sources of knowledge about social processes on the one hand and physical environment on the other. The maps of residential trends in Yaffo illustrate this point.

These conclusions are to be considered within the framework of rising standards of population census taking that make available the high-resolution geo-referenced urban data necessary for constructing agent-based models. The Israeli Census of Population and Housing of 1995 (ICBS 2000) demonstrates this trend. AB modeling makes possible *dynamic description* of the situations described by the census. It therefore enables explicit assessment of social and economic trends as well as the consequences of proposed planning decisions.

One final question should be asked: Does agent-based modeling invalidate the traditional regional paradigm? The response: Surely not! It remains an open question to what extent specific regional and AB models can be related *formally*, whether by disintegrating the parameters and interpreting the equations as if they were behavioral rules applicable to human agents and infrastructure objects, or visa versa, by integrating parameters and individual behavioral rules. It is clear, however, that the need to do so will eventually be salient, once we have formulated explicit ideas regarding the part played in urban dynamics by human factors—local interactions, short- or long-term

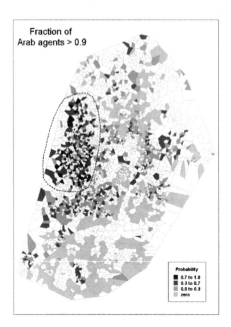
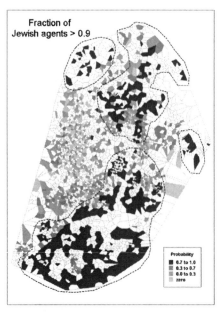

Figure 4.9. The "Arab Assimilation II" scenario: probability maps for $F = 0.9$. Contours mark areas where the sensitivity of the results to local effects is low. Left to right: (a) Probability that the fraction of Arab agents in a house is above 0.9. (b) Probability that the fraction of Jewish agents in a house is above 0.9.

expectations, processing of distant and incomplete information and of information pertaining to higher levels of the urban hierarchy, to name but a few. My prognosis is that in the future, students of urban dynamics will use agent-based and regional models *simultaneously* (see van Dyke et al. 1998 and Wilson 1998 as initial examples of this trend). The outcomes of the regional and AB models developed for the same situation should be compared; the differences will indicate when, where, and how human factors are important for the system.

Notes

1. The ideas captured by the Schelling and Sakoda models are very rich and can be implemented easily. When preparing Figure 4.3, a few experiments were sufficient to realize that the outcomes strongly depend on many factors ignored by the basic model—e.g., population density, behavior of an agent located within a fully occupied neighborhood, distance at which agents can relocate—all of which have to be investigated in depth.

2. An algorithm of Voronoi tessellation divides a plane into polygons, one for each building. A Voronoi polygon of a given building contains it and all points for which the building is the closest one (Halls et al. 2001). Voronoi tessellation is popular in geodesy and can be constructed by add-ins supplied with most desktop GIS. Usually, the algorithm's implementations account for constraints: open spaces can be excluded from Voronoi coverage; streets can be made boundaries of the Voronoi polygons, and so on.

Acknowledgments   The results presented in this chapter were obtained in part during the work performed in common with my colleagues, Prof. Juval Portugali, Dr. Itzhak Omer, and Mr. Erez Hatna; I am grateful for their assistance and fruitful comments. Thanks to Ms. Nina Reshef for valuable comments and language editing. Mr. Erez Hatna helped in preparing Figures 4.8 and 4.9. Development of the agent-based model of Yaffo residential dynamics was supported by a research grant provided by Israel's Ministry of Science.

References

Allen, P.M., and M. Sanglier. 1981. Urban evolution, self-organization and decision making. *Environment and Planning A* 13(1): 167–183.

Alonso, W. 1964. *Location and Land Use*. Cambridge: Harvard University Press.

Anselin, L. 1995. Local indicators of spatial association—LISA. *Geographical Analysis* 27(2): 93–115.

Anselin, L., and M. Madden (eds.). 1990. *New Directions in Regional Analysis. Integrated and Multi-Regional Approach*. London: Belhaven Press.

Batty, M., and P. Longley. 1994. *Fractal Cities*. London: AP.

Benenson, I. 1998. Multi-agent simulations of residential dynamics in the city. *Computers, Environment and Urban Systems* 22: 25–42

Benenson, I. 1999. Modeling population dynamics in the city: From a regional to a multi-agent approach. *Discrete Dynamics in Nature and Society* 3: 149–170.

Benenson, I., I. Omer, and E. Hatna. 2002. Entity-based modeling of urban residential dynamics—the case of Yaffo, Tel-Aviv. *Environment and Planning B* 29:491–512.

Bertuglia, C.S., S. Occelli, G.A. Rabino, and R. Tadei. 1994. An integrated urban model. In C.S. Bertuglia, G. Leonardi, S. Occelli, G.A. Rabino, R. Tadei, and A.G. Wilson (eds.), *Urban Systems: Contemporary Approach to Modeling*. London: Croom Helm, 178–191.

Bolan M. 1997. The mobility experience and neighborhood attachment. *Demography* 34(2): 225–237.

Brown L.A., and E.G. Moore. 1970. The intra-urban migration process: A perspective. *Geografiska Annaler* 52B: 1–13.

Clark, W.A.V., and S.D. Withers. 1999. Changing jobs and changing houses: Mobility outcomes of employment transitions. *Journal of Regional Science* 39(4): 653–673.

DaVanzo, J. 1981. Repeat migration, information cost, and location-specific capital. *Population and Environment* 4(1): 45–73.

Deane, G.D. 1990. Mobility and adjustments: Paths to the resolution of residential stress. *Demography* 27(1): 65–79.

Deitz, R. 1998. A joint model of residential and employment location in urban areas. *Journal of Urban Economics* 44(2): 197–215.

Dorigo, G., and W. Tobler. 1983. Push-pull migration laws. *Annals of the Association of American Geographers* 73(1): 1–17.

Epstein, J.M., and R. Axtell. 1996. *Growing Artificial Societies*. Washington, D.C.: Brookings Institution Press.

Ferber, J. 1999. *Multi-Agent Systems: An Introduction to Distributed Artificial Intelligence*. Harlow (U.K.): Addison-Wesley.

Fokkema, T., and L. van Wissen. 1997. Moving plans of the elderly: A test of the stress-threshold model. *Environment and Planning A* 29(2): 249–268.

Gigerenzer, G., and D.G. Goldstein. 1996. Reasoning the fast and frugal way: Models of bounded rationality. *Psychological Review* 103(4): 650–669.

Gilbert, G.N., and R. Conte. (eds.). 1995. *Artificial Societies: The Computer Simulation of Social Life*. London: UCL Press.

Gilbert, N.S., and K.G. Troitzsch. 1999. *Simulation for the Social Scientist*. Buckingham: Open University Press.

Golledge, R.G., and H. Timmermans. 1990. Applications of behavioral-research on spatial problems 1: Cognition. *Progress in Human Geography* 14(1): 57–99.

Goodman, J.L. 1981. Information, uncertainty, and the microeconomic model of migration decision making. In G.F. DeJong, and R.W. Gardner (eds.), *Migration Decision Making: Multidisciplinary Approaches to Microlevel Studies in Developed and Developing Countries*. New York: Pergamon Press, 13–58.

Haken, H., and J. Portugali. 1995. A synergetic approach to the self-organization of cities and settlements. *Environment and Planning B* 22(1): 35–46.

Halls, P.J., M. Bulling, P.C.L. White, L. Garland, and S. Harris. 2001. Dirichlet neighbors: Revisiting Dirichlet tessellation for neighborhood analysis. *Computers, Environment and Urban Systems* 25: 105–117.

Hegselmann, R., and A. Flache. 1999. Understanding complex social dynamics: A plea for cellular automata based modeling. *Journal of Artificial Societies and Social Simulation* 1(3): <http://www.soc.surrey.ac.uk/JASSS/1/3/1.html>.

Herrin, W.E., and C.R. Kern. 1992. Testing the standard urban model of residential choice-an implicit markets approach. *Journal of Urban Economics* 31(2): 145–163.

ICBS (Israeli Central Bureau of Statistics). 2000. Socio-economic characteristics of population and households in localities and statistical areas pub. No. 8 in the *1995 Census of Population and Housing series*. Jerusalem: State of Israel, Central Bureau of Statistics Publications.

Ligtenberg, A., A.K. Bregt, and R. van Lammeren. 2001. Multi-Actor-Based land use modeling: Spatial planning using agents. *Landscape and Urban Planning* 56: 21–33.

Louviere, J., and H. Timmermans. 1990. Hierarchical information integration applied to residential choice behavior. *Geographical Analysis* 22(2): 127–144.

Maes, P. 1995. Modeling adaptive autonomous agents. In Langton C.G. (ed.), *Artificial Life, An Overview*. Cambridge: MIT Press, 135–162.

Mills, E.S., and B.W. Hamilton. 1989. *Urban Economics 4th ed.*, Glenview, Ill.: Scott, Foresman.

Molin, E., H. Oppewal, and H. Timmermans. 1999. Group-based versus individual-based conjoint preference models of residential preferences: A comparative test. *Environment and Planning A* 31(11): 1935–1947.

Moss, S., and P. Davidson. (eds.) 2000. *Multi-Agent-Based Simulations*. Lecture Notes in Artificial Intelligence N1979. Berlin: Springer.

Nicolis, G., and I. Prigogine. 1977. *Self-Organization in Nonequilibrium Systems*. New York: Wiley.

Omer, I. 1996. *Ethnic Residential Segregation as a Structuration Process*. Unpublished Ph.D. Thesis, Tel-Aviv University, Tel-Aviv.

Omer, I., and I. Benenson. 2002. GIS as a tool for studying urban fine-scale segregation. *Geography Research Forum* 22: 41–60.

Openshaw, S. 1983. *The Modifiable Areal Unit Problem CATMOG 38*. Norwich: GeoBooks.

Openshaw, S., and L. Rao. 1995. Algorithms for re-engineering 1991 census geography, *Environment and Planning A* 27: 425–446.

Phipps, A.G., and J.E. Carter. 1984. An individual-level analysis of the stress-resistance model of household mobility. *Geographical Analysis* 16(1): 176–189.

Portugali, J. 1991. An Arab segregated neighborhood in Tel-Aviv: The case of Adjami. *Geography Research Forum* 11: 37–50.

Portugali, J. 2000. *Self-Organization and the City*. Berlin: Springer.

Portugali, J., and I. Benenson. 1995. Artificial planning experience by means of a heuristic sell-space model: Simulating international migration in the urban process. *Environment and Planning B* 27: 1647–1665.

Portugali, J., and I. Benenson. 1997. Human agents between local and global forces in a self-organizing city. In F. Schweitzer (ed.), *Self-Organization of Complex Structures: From Individual to Collective Dynamics*. London: Gordon and Breach, 537–546.

Portugali, J., I. Benenson, and I. Omer. 1994. Socio-spatial residential dynamics: Stability and instability within a self-organized city. *Geographical Analysis* 26(4): 321–340.

Portugali, J., I. Benenson, and I. Omer. 1997. Spatial cognitive dissonance and sociospatial emergence in a self-organizing city. *Environment and Planning B* 24: 263–285.

Ritchey, P.N. 1976. Explanations of migration. *Annual Review of Sociology* 2: 363–404.

Sabagh, G., M.D. van Arsdol Jr., and E.W. Butler. 1969. Some determinants of intrametropolitan residential mobility: Conceptual considerations. *Social Forces* 48(1): 88–98.

Sakoda, J.M. 1971. The checkerboard model of social interaction. *Journal of Mathematical Sociology* 1: 119–132.

Schellekens, M.P.G., and H.J.P. Timmermans. 1997. A conjoint-based simulation model of housing-market clearing processes: Theory and illustration. *Environment and Planning A* 29(10): 1831–1846.

Schelling, T. 1971. Dynamic models of segregation. *Journal of Mathematical Sociology* 1: 143–186.

Schelling, T. 1974. On the ecology of micro-motives. In R. Marris (ed.) *The Corporate Society*. London: Macmillan, 19–55.

Sermons, M.W. 2000. Influence of race on household residential utility. *Geographical Analysis* 32(3): 225–246.

Sichman, J.S., R. Conte, and G.N. Gilbert. 1998. *Multi-Agent Systems and Agent Based Simulations*. Lecture Notes in Artificial Intelligence N1524. Berlin: Springer.

Simon, H.A. 1982. *Models of Bounded Rationality*. Cambridge: MIT Press.

Simon, H.A. 1956. Rational choice and the structure of the environment. *Psychological Review* 63: 129–138.

Sonis, M. 1992. Innovation diffusion, Schumpeterian competition and dynamic choice: A new synthesis. *Journal of Scientific & Industrial Research* (51). New Dehli: J. Nerhu University.

Speare, A. 1974. Residential satisfaction as an intervening variable in residential mobility. *Demography*, 11: 173–188.

Speare, A., S. Goldstein, and W.H. Frey. 1975. *Residential Mobility, Migration and Metropolitan Change*. Cambridge: Bollinger.

Timmermans, H., and L. van Noortwijk. 1995. Context dependencies in housing choice behavior. *Environment and Planning A* 27(2): 181–192.

Timmermans, H., and R.G. Golledge. 1990. Applications of behavioral-research on spatial problems—2. Preference and choice. *Progress in Human Geography* 14(3): 311–354.

Torrens, P. M. 2000. How cellular models of urban systems work, CASA Working Paper 28, http://www.casa.ucl.ac.uk/working_papers.htm.

Tu, Y., and J. Goldfinch. 1996. A two-stage housing choice forecasting model. *Urban Studies* 33(3): 517–537.

van de Vyvere, Y. 1994. Stated preference decompositional modeling and residential choice. *Geoforum* 25(2): 189–202.

van de Vyvere, Y., H. Oppewal, and H. Timmermans. 1998. The validity of hierarchical information integration choice experiments to model residential preference and choice. *Geographical Analysis* 30(3): 254–272.

van Dyke, G.G., H. Parunak, R. Savit, and R.L. Riolo. 1998. Agent-Based modeling vs equation-based modeling: A case study and user's guide. In J.S. Sichman, R. Conte, and N. Gilbert (eds.), *Multi-Agent systems and Agent-Based Simulation.* Springer Verlag, Lecture Notes in Artificial Intelligence 1534, 10–26.

van Ommeren, J., P. Rietveld, and P. Nijkamp. 1996. Residence and workplace relocation: A bivariate duration model approach. *Geographical Analysis* 28(4): 315–329.

van Wissen, L., and A. Rima. 1988. *Modeling Urban Housing Market Dynamics. Evolutionary Pattern of Households and Housing in Amsterdam.* Amsterdam: Elsevier Science Publishers.

Veldhuisen, J., and H. Timmermans. 1984. Specification of individual residential utility function: A comparative analysis of three measurement procedures. *Environment and Planning A* 16: 1573–1582.

White, R., and G. Engelen. 2000. High-Resolution integrated modeling of the spatial dynamics of urban and regional systems. *Computers, Environment and Urban Systems* 24: 383–400.

Wilson, W.G. 1998. Resolving discrepancies between deterministic population models and individual-based simulations. *American Naturalist* 151(2): 116–134.

Wiseman, R.F., and C.R. Roseman. 1979. A typology of elderly migration based on the decision making process. *Economic Geography* 55(4): 324–337.

Wolpert, J. 1965. Behavioral aspects of the decision to migrate. *Papers and Proceedings of the Regional Science Association* 15: 159–169.

Wrigley, N., T. Holt, D. Steel, and M. Tranmer. 1996. Analyzing, modeling, and resolving the ecological fallacy. In P. Longley, and M. Batty (eds.) *Spatial Analysis: Modeling in a GIS Environment* Cambridge, U.K.: Geoinformation International, 25–40.

5

Too Much of the Wrong Kind of Data
Implications for the Practice of Micro-Scale Spatial Modeling

David O'Sullivan

Writing at the end of the northern hemisphere's summer of 2001, in the wake of market "corrections" and the consequent subsidence of millennial excitement about a "new economy," it is easier now than it would have been even a year ago to suggest that everything has not changed utterly. Distance is still alive and kicking; personal data assistants are just electronic notebooks; and a computer is just another tool. What was that? Computers are just tools? Are you kidding?! Haven't modern computers and the attendant Internet technologies changed everything forever? Well, haven't they?

At the risk, in a complex world, of being overtaken by events, I argue in this chapter that powerful desktop computers, the rise of the Internet and World Wide Web, and the accompanying blizzard of data and "information" have not altered much that is fundamental to the process of building, testing, calibrating, exploring, and understanding mathematical or computer-based models and simulations of geographical processes and systems. Ironically, the changes that have occurred may serve to emphasize the limits to our knowledge and powers of prediction, rather than to dramatically extend them.

That is a strong claim. Certainly, it is now possible to build models of dynamic spatial processes at a level of detail and with a sophistication of design and implementation that would have been impractical even a few years ago. I refer to such detailed models below as micro-scale spatial models. This possibility has arisen out of two strong trends in the computational environment of geographic research: changes in the quantity (and quality) of spatial data, and changes in the computational resources that are routinely available for the storage, analysis, and exploration of that data. While acknowledging that a great deal has changed, I argue below that a very great deal remains unaffected even by such sweeping changes. To a considerable extent, the most reliable datasets available for use in the social sciences are very similar to those that have been available for many years. Furthermore, the requirement in micro-scale spatial modeling to precisely locate individual households—along with their demographic descriptions—runs counter to important privacy considerations, so that, even were such data readily available, their use might be questionable. Finally, thinking about how hypothetical (because impractical) individual level representations of socio-spatial phenomena might be used in practice, reveals important limitations to traditional aims of predictive modeling that it is important to acknowledge.

The context for this chapter is set by a discussion of the changes in the data and computational environments of contemporary research—the changes discussed will be familiar to most readers. The less frequently considered question of how significant those changes are is raised. Rather than make an entirely abstract argument, this discussion is extended in a description of some of the data issues encountered working alone and with colleagues on two modest dynamic spatial modeling projects. The issues are presented informally, and some of them will no doubt be familiar to others working in similar fields. In the final section, I attempt to draw out some implications of these experiences, and speculate on the appropriate use of such models in research and as decision support tools.

The Changing Research Environment

I have already flagged a degree of skepticism about the suggestion that the current research environment has been fundamentally altered by developments in computing technology. Such skepticism demands explanation, given that a great deal certainly *has* changed in the research environment. In this section I examine what has happened from two perspectives in turn: changes in the size, quality, and availability of spatially referenced datasets, and changes in the computational resources available for generating and handling such data.

Data, Data, Everywhere

It is readily apparent that in the *physical* geographic domain, continued rapid developments in remote sensing have dramatically increased the availability of data describing earth surface processes, such as climate, changes in land cover and land use, deforestation, and urbanization. Each of these new sources of physical geographic data are related to aspects of human spatial activity, but none of them can be thought of as materially augmenting more traditional social scientific data that describe the social characteristics of individuals and groups (although see Donnay et al. 2001). It is also noteworthy that such data are rarely useful without extensive 'ground-truthing,' a process that remains time-consuming and expensive (see Chapter 2, by Boucek and Moran).

Thus, notwithstanding the view that "[o]ne of the least interesting ways of looking at society is by demographic analysis" (Sayer 1992, 177), data describing household composition, age and ethnic composition, income, and so on, remain *the* essential backbone of empirical studies in the social sciences. These data allow us to describe the social changes that any social scientific theory, spatial or not, seeks to explain.

A focus on census data is appropriate here, since as David Martin remarks, "in many parts of the world, the census is the primary or only source of detailed socioeconomic data" (Martin 1998, 673). Such demographic "background" datasets are relatively unaffected by technological change. This is especially true of national censes at least in terms of what is measured and how: censes are not getting any bigger, except in the trivial sense that there are more people to be "counted." In spite of technological innovations, national censes of population remain large and complex undertakings and as a result, seem likely to remain decennial in most countries, albeit with improved prospects for annual sample-based datasets that enable estimation of intervening moments in time. Current technologies also allow the more rapid *release* of census data products (see, for example Brewer et al. 2001), but the products themselves remain very similar in form and intended purpose. Indeed, it appears that the early release of data in online forms is biased toward consumer-oriented applications, emphasizing a view of the census as a collection of disorganized and disparate "facts" (see, for example, *American FactFinder* by the U.S. Census Bureau 2001). Regardless of how they are repackaged and distributed, the underlying data remain very similar in detail to previous census forms. Indeed, a large degree of continuity is desirable to facilitate longitudinal investigation of societal change.

Additionally, in many countries access to detailed government-assembled data are subject to strict controls on use, for privacy reasons. Detailed census records at the individual household level are not routinely available to researchers. Data are available only in aggregated forms at a level of detail intended to prevent the ready association of demographic information with individual households. Even where "freedom of information" legislation is in place, it often incorporates safeguards specifically intended to make the use of individual household data difficult or impossible. Often these safeguards mean that only the individual on whom data are held may legitimately have access. In relation to census data, safeguards are often even more stringent, and detailed data are made available on a case-by-case basis to specific research projects for limited periods of time and for strictly limited purposes (see, for example, Chapter 4, Benenson). The safeguards applied are often frustrating to the academic researcher, but they exist for widely agreed civil liberties reasons.

The need for privacy in this regard extends to recent proposals for flexible "output geographies." There is a concern that astute users might be able to access data at a more disaggregate scale than intended, by repeatedly requesting data using different output geographies, and analyzing similarities and differences between the resulting maps. As a result, with regard to implementing flexible output geographies for census data "[t]he key outstanding issues concern the implementation of a sufficiently secure access model" (Martin 1998, 683). Recent interest in "surface modeling" approaches to the presentation of demographic data, in part, reflects dissatisfaction with the arbitrary nature of census tracts or other sub-divisions, together with a desire for less distorting ways of visualizing patterns in the data, while preserving the individual anonymity required in many countries (see Bracken and Martin 1995, and articles by Coombes and Raybould 2000; Martin et al. 2000; and Thurstain-Goodwin and Unwin 2000 in a recent special issue of *Transactions in GIS*).

Perhaps then, the idea that we are awash with detailed and reliable socioeconomic data at the household level is not as self-evident as it seems. What about private corporate data holdings on the individual? As Curry (1998, 111) points out, the commercial sector is often resolutely opposed to the restrictions on use of individual data that apply to the national census. In fact, privacy concerns about detailed governmental datasets seem misplaced in a world where Sun Microsystems' Chief Executive Officer Scott McNealy can say, "You have zero privacy anyway. Get over it" (Sprenger 1999). Such views are consistent with the almost mystical notion, commonplace on the Web that "Information Wants to Be Free" (Brand 1987, 202). However, implicit corporate support for the free use of data on individuals rarely extends to those who have not paid for its collection! As Brand paradoxically (and *immediately*) continues, "Information also wants to be expensive."

Corporate data holdings on individual households are certainly growing. Such data are valuable commercial assets and collection is increasingly routine—almost to the point of invisibility: we have become used to not asking why exactly our favored supermarket needs to know how many children of what age live in the house. Further, as McNealy's remark implies, even if we choose not to say, retailers can often work out for themselves the household composition, based on purchasing records. Devices commonly used to collect personal data are mail-in rebate offers, retailer loyalty cards, telecommunication company recording of numbers called, credit card company billing details, financial and insurance information, and latterly the data that is voluntarily supplied when we register for online access to information or retail services. Combining these data in order to target local niche markets effectively is precisely the purpose of the burgeoning field of geodemographics, which has generated much interest (Feng and Flowerdew 1999), along with plenty of skepticism (Voas and Williamson 2001). Such data collection methods are ubiquitous in many parts of the developed world, and as a result each of us is increasingly shadowed by a "digital individual" to use Curry's evocative term (Curry 1998, 126ff.).

However, there are several points to make about such datasets, in the context of dynamic geographic model building:

- *They are not freely available.* These data are legally the property of the corporation that collects them. For academic purposes, this means that most such data are unavailable except on terms and for purposes approved and agreed by the owner. Data that are affordable to the academic researcher are rarely of the quality required for serious research.
- *From a statistical perspective, most of these data are irretrievably flawed.* No amount of wishful thinking can avoid the fact that datasets gathered by a specific company, from stratified segments of their customers, are not random samples. It is also difficult to know what effects the flawed nature of these datasets are likely to have on their usefulness or viability for academic research (see Longley and Harris 1999; and Openshaw and Turton 1998 for conflicting views).
- *Such datasets are often poorly maintained.* This is difficult to quantify. Anyone who has recently changed address can attest to the infrequency with which datasets are updated, based on the quantity of "junk" mail received intended for the previous (or even earlier) occupants. The most serious problem here may be that the currency of data held is better for certain socioeconomic groups, particularly owner-occupiers as opposed to tenants,

who tend to move more frequently. This is another non-random mechanism affecting the quality and coverage of many corporate datasets.

It is important to be clear about the point being made. Corporate or commercial data may often be useful. For example, recently I was able to assemble quickly a point pattern analysis laboratory assignment for investigation by an undergraduate class, by downloading a certain coffee company's store locations from the corporate Web site. Although this is a neat example of the increased accessibility of much real world spatial data, it is neither a very serious case, nor one where data reliability is very important. Such convenient access to real world spatial data is undoubtedly a new phenomenon. However, it is doubtful that similar open access would be granted to the detailed demographic data held by retailers—the data are simply too commercially valuable to be released in this way.

The argument of this section rests on the idea that it is important to distinguish among changes in data quantity, changes in data quality, and changes in data accessibility. That more data on individual households are routinely gathered and stored is unquestionable. How well data are subsequently maintained, and how representative of underlying social complexities they can ever be, given that they are collected neither in the form of census nor by any satisfactory unbiased sampling technique, is much more debatable and suggests that changes in data quality are harder to characterize. It also calls into question claims as to the high quality of such data. Finally, most officially collected, often more complete datasets, remain subject to (perfectly reasonable) restrictions on access and use, while corporate data holdings are simply not generally accessible. It is important to note that increases in the convenience of access provided by the Internet and other electronic forms, while welcome, have rarely led to the "declassification" of previously unavailable data. Census data have always been available to legitimate academic researchers: that they have now become a little less arduous to make use of is not a fundamental change.

The Price of Chips

If claims about the changing data environment are overstated, it would be much harder to exaggerate the scale of the changes that have occurred in the computational resources available to contemporary spatial social scientists. Only a fool would deny that the contrast—in size, speed, memory capacity, graphic capabilities, sheer computational *oomph*—between a turn-of-the-twenty-first-century desktop computer and a 1980s minicomputer is anything other than flattering to this year's model.

A great deal of the increased computational power of computers is under-utilized most of the time, whether it is used to word process book chapters or to shop online for books, but there is undeniably considerably more computational processing power available. In the context of dynamic spatial models, whether or not there is enough processing power is dependent on the scope and scale of the models we build. Los Alamos National Laboratories (LANL) in the United States has built the ambitious TRANSIMS model, which simulates medium to large urban traffic patterns at the individual-vehicle level (see Casti 1997). More modestly, the Centre for Advanced Spatial Analysis in University College London can manage STREETS (Haklay et al. 2001). LANL's computing resources are extraordinary even by the standards that have become routine in geoinformation science laboratories at campuses worldwide. Even so, while it is unlikely that the social sciences—even the style of social science described in this volume—will ever have access to the very latest technology, raw processing power is rarely the limiting factor in contemporary research projects.

In summary, although we may reasonably argue that the computational research environment of geographic and geographical information science has dramatically changed in the last two or three decades, it is less clear that the data available for analysis in that environment—particularly the data available for pursuing social scientific research—are very much altered. This argument is made without reference to the much more thorny question of how useful data gathered for one purpose (say the national census, or tracking individual health records) is likely to be for purposes such as modeling social change in housing markets. When we consider the availability of data gathered for the specific modeling application for which it is to be used, then a social science procedure much like the "ground-truthing" of remote sensing is required: data must be collected the hard way, in the field. Such data remain in short supply and are expensive, difficult to collect, and often available (and known) only to the researchers who collected them.

Experiences with Micro-Scale Socio-Spatial Models

"Water, water everywhere,
   Nor yet a drop to drink"

We now come to the question of how changes in the computational environment of human geographical research play out in practice relative to the type of data required for the detailed micro-simulation of socio-spatial systems. The remarks in this section are reflections on my own involvement in two micro-scale modeling projects (Haklay et al. 2001; O'Sullivan 2002). Note that these are not offered as typical projects. Both were small scale, with no resources available for the collection of tailor-made data. This forced the researchers to work with whatever data could be found, so that these projects are good "test cases" for the idea that something fundamental has changed in the ready availability of *free* data. However, it may also mean that these projects are *not* good examples of what is possible when resources are available to purchase detailed corporate data sets, or when it is practical to collect precisely the data required by a model. The experiences described are therefore offered as food for thought and not as the last word on this matter.

An Agent-Based Pedestrian Model: STREETS

First we consider a simple agent-based model of pedestrian movement in a town center. For interested readers, details of the model are provided by Haklay et al. (2001). More general introductions to the agent-based modeling approach are available in a variety of places (Conte et al. 1997; Epstein and Axtell 1996; Gilbert and Conte 1995; Gilbert and Doran 1994; Resnick 1994) and in at least one recent textbook (Gilbert and Troitzsch 1999). Other examples of agent-based *pedestrian* models include work by Kerridge et al. (2001) and Helbing et al. (2001). The agent-based modeling paradigm is exemplified over several years by the *Free Agents in a Cellular Space* models of Juval Portugali (2000) and his colleagues at the University of Tel Aviv (see Chapter 2, Benenson, this volume).

The idea behind the STREETS model is to place a population of minimally intelligent, autonomous software agents in a simulated urban environment and to allow them to pursue their goals as they see fit. The goals set for the agents in this model are not open-ended. Instead, they consist of a planned or "intended" route in the urban street network, with allowance made for deviations from the route to take a closer look at interesting shops or other attractions. The envisaged purpose of a STREETS model is to allow study of the patterns of pedestrian flow in the street network under investigation. This model architecture may also be applied to investigate flows in complex buildings such as airports, railway stations, or shopping malls. A similar project (Dijkstra et al. 2001) has made considerable progress in operationalizing the approach suggested by STREETS.

Detailed land use data at the plot-level are required in STREETS or any similar model, and are usually freely available. More interesting however, than the spatial environment are the agents themselves. How are they to be represented and at what level of detail? Haklay et al. (2001, 358) suggest that a "more complete and sophisticated approach to socioeconomic variables" is required in the STREETS model. This anticipates the use of such models by planning agencies and implies that individuals with different demographic characteristics are likely to circulate in different parts of the town center represented in the model. These seem to be reasonable assumptions. However, it is also clear that the data required to represent such variation satisfactorily are hard to obtain. There are two factors at work here. First, there is no simple mapping from readily available socioeconomic data in the census to the likely shopping preferences of individuals. This mapping could only be obtained from the retailers themselves, using privately held commercial data. Second, agents in this model are not at their overnight residential addresses. These are the locations where the relevant census data are recorded. It might be possible to extrapolate from spatial census data for the wider metropolitan area to the likely socioeconomic composition of a population of individuals in the town center, but any such determination would be subject to considerable uncertainty.

In practice, therefore, it is more tenable to populate the model with a representative population of pedestrian agents. Individual agents in the model then represent nobody in particular, but collectively the agents represent a possible downtown population. Based on successive runs of the model with different representative populations, it might be possible to determine whether there are likely to be any differences in the street-level pedestrian dynamics as the demographic profile of the town center alters. More important, from the current perspective, is the suggested shift from real data to representative data. This neatly sidesteps many of the data issues raised above but does beg questions about what exactly the STREETS model is a model of! The spatial characteristics of the place are faithfully represented, but its demographic characteristics are not. This is an odd hybrid style of model, but probably one that anybody who has worked with micro-scale spatial models will recognize.

A Graph Cellular Automaton-Based Gentrification Model

Another micro-scale geographical model is the graph-based cellular automaton *Gentrification* model presented by O'Sullivan (2002). A graph-based cellular automaton (graph-CA) is a simple extension of the standard cellular automaton (CA) model architecture. In a CA, space is represented as a regular lattice of cells, typically a grid. Each cell may be in one a set of allowed discrete states. Cell states change at each model time step according to the CA rules, which operate on each cell and its immediate neighbors in the lattice. The rules define what cell state results at the next time step, given the state of a cell and of its neighbors. CA-based models of urban change have become relatively common in recent years (Batty et al. 1999; Clarke et al. 1997; Li and Yeh 2000; Ward et al. 2000; White and Engelen 2000). The graph-CA generalization of CA allows cells to be irregularly located at the vertices of a graph rather than on a regular lattice. Everything else remains the same. In particular, the rules governing model dynamics are still defined with respect to a *neighborhood* of "cells"—in this case, buildings. That is, the process rules are applied to each cell and its neighbors in the graph to determine changes in cell states. This generalization of the CA formalism may be described in terms of an algebra (Takeyama and Couclelis 1997) or using graph theoretic concepts (O'Sullivan 2001), and also appears in less general guises (Semboloni 2000; Shi and Pang 2000). The way that this type of model represents the geographical dynamics, both as a spatial structure and as a dynamic process, is summarized schematically in Figure 5.1.

In the graph-CA *Gentrification* model we must represent the physical character of buildings in the urban fabric. The U.K. Ordnance Survey's *Landline* digital datasets are a good source of the detailed, large scale, spatial data required. Even so, it is not

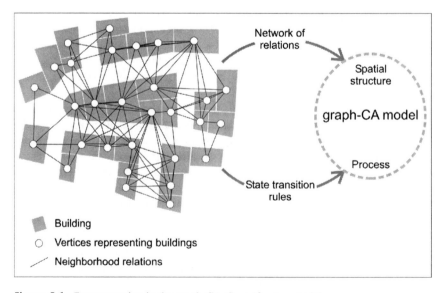

Figure 5.1. Representation in the graph-CA *Gentrification* model.

possible to set about constructing an "accurate" representation of the built fabric before facing difficult issues such as multi-occupancy buildings, and the complexity of representing built forms in all their three-dimensional reality. Therefore, even the apparently detailed representation of the urban space in this model is really an abstract two-dimensional and representative view. The apparently unambiguous hard edges of urban environments are considerably fuzzier than they at first appear (Campari 1996).

The next step in building the model is to describe the gentrification process in terms of a set of rules that can be applied to each building and its neighborhood. Implicit in this stage of the modeling process is the selection of a set of variables that describe the state of each building. Choice of these variables dictates the model data requirements. In the present case, the key variables are household income and the physical condition of each building, since these are important determinants of the building life cycle central to the rent gap model of gentrification proposed by Neil Smith (1979).

Working with these two state variables, we require details of household income for every building in the model, and again we are faced with a problem. Ignoring the particular difficulties in the United Kingdom associated with household income data (see Dorling 1999), it should be apparent that there are at least two obstacles to obtaining the required detailed data. First, for reasons of anonymity, census data are unavailable at the individual household level. Other data sources are likely to be unreliable. Second, even if census or other data were available, they only remain valid for a short time period. For these reasons, as reported elsewhere (O'Sullivan 2002), the decision was again made in this model to use *representative data* based on a surface model of a variety of demographic variables for this neighborhood (see Thurstain-Goodwin and Unwin 2000 for details).

It should be readily apparent that obtaining detailed and accurate data on the physical condition of each building in the model is also problematic. This is a problem also faced by attempts to empirically test the rent gap hypothesis (Badcock 1989; Clark 1988; Ley 1986; Yung and King 1998). Again the solution adopted in this case was to assign representative conditions to each building. It is a relatively simple matter to randomly assign values of this state variable based on the income variable, and then to experiment with different degrees of correlation between the two, as the basis for an exploration of the socio-spatial dynamics of the gentrification process.

Implications and Conclusions

In this section I draw some tentative conclusions from the modeling experiences recounted in the previous section, concentrating particularly on how the limitations of the available data affected the model building process and how we should think about and use micro-scale spatial models.

In both the examples discussed, the style of modeling ultimately adopted was strongly conditioned by the available data. Difficulties in obtaining or synthesizing demographic data at the level of individual households are thus a considerable hurdle to overcome in micro-scale model building.

As a result, determining what data are available must be one of the first questions addressed in model building. This is at odds with conventional ideas about best scientific practice, where research should be led by the questions or hypotheses we wish to explore, or by theory, rather than by the data available. The dangers of data-led enquiry are evident, since it could rapidly result in only those places for which rich data are readily available being studied. This point is well made by Taylor and Overton (1991) in their response to Openshaw's (1991, 1992) advocacy of a "GISable" geography. Using representative datasets in modeling is one way of addressing this problem. Where adequate real data are available, they can be used either directly, or to generate proxy data that represent the phenomena of interest. Failing that, modeling using entirely synthetic data is a possible approach. This allows us to build models of anywhere we please, but does profoundly affect the nature of the models we build.

Models that are representative of reality in the rather loose sense implied by the foregoing discussion demand to be used in specific ways. In the applied policy domain, it is evident that such models do not lend themselves to use as predictive tools. We should not expect to set such models up with year 2000 data and run them forward in time to 2005 or 2010, hoping to gain much insight into the likely unfolding of real events. This might be regarded as a major problem, but it is naïve to think that such predictive modeling is really feasible. On the contrary, it is important to acknowledge from the outset, that it is in the nature of the complex open systems in question that they are unpredictable in detail, by their very nature. The option of prediction is closed off by the nature of the systems we model, so that the apparent limitations of working with merely representative data need not frustrate us unduly.

A short thought experiment emphasizes the point. Imagine for a moment that accurate household-level income data were available in the gentrification model described above, and that the model were initialized at time $t = 0$ with that data. Now imagine that the model "predicts" that household A will move out in two weeks time, to be replaced by a richer household B. It is surely not even remotely plausible that such prediction is possible! If we are concerned about prediction, then this is a serious problem. In the representative style of model however, the problem disappears. A particular household's decision to leave the neighborhood in a representative model implies no prediction of a particular household's decisions. Instead, the model allows us to examine possible futures of the urban space represented. None of these possible futures are "real," but exploration of a large number of them may allow us to develop a deeper understanding of which sorts of future are likely, which are possible, and which are very unlikely in this urban space. This mode of investigation may be thought of as an exploration of the socio-spatial dynamics of the model, and by extension, of the urban space itself.

The implications of this perspective for practical policy tools are not entirely clear. Would-be predictive tools, however absurd the claims made for them, are easily justified, because the potential benefits of predicting the future are evident. A more realistic *modus operandi* however, is the creative exploration of models by policy-makers, planners, and other interested parties, with a view to improving our understanding of the ways that possible policies might affect events through the operation of system dynamics. Intriguingly, *play* may be a useful metaphor for thinking about how such models are best used. By this I mean to suggest that open-ended exploration of the behavior of dynamic models, with the aim of developing intuitive understanding or feel for the ways that real world systems behave, may be the most promising application of microscale spatial models.

In the models considered in this article, it is important to note the substantial difference between the potential for representing the spatial and socioeconomic contexts. In general, spatial context can be represented fairly well. Although I noted some complexities in the gentrification model concerning the detailed representation of the urban fabric, such problems do not seem completely insurmountable in principle. Representation of the socioeconomic context is much more likely to be partial, limited, and ultimately impoverished. This is a result of the data problems discussed earlier and is also due to the obvious limitations we face in attempting to represent human beings inside computers (see Chapter 3, Kwan and Lee, this volume). Note that how *processes* are represented is not even considered here, nor has it been considered in detail in the extensive geographic information science literature.

Nevertheless, and in spite of the impoverished representation of individuals and their motivations, it is important to emphasize the real potential for insight opened up by embedding socio-spatial models in detailed, realistic representations of real places. Abstract economic models operating either aspatially, or in simple one- or two-dimensional spaces (frequently grids), are often used to explore the dynamics of economic systems. The approach advocated here of building hybrid models—realistic spaces inhabited by merely representative populations—enables a program of research exploring "the difference that space makes" (Sayer 1985). Such research is unlikely to be easy, but it must surely be an indispensable component of any spatially integrated social science.

References

Badcock, B. 1989. An Australian view of the rent gap hypothesis. *Annals of the Association of American Geographers* 79(1): 125–145.

Batty, M., Y. Xie, and Z. Sun. 1999. Modelling urban dynamics through GIS-based cellular automata. *Computers Environment and Urban Systems* 23: 205–233.

Bracken, I., and D. Martin. 1995. Linkage of the 1981 and 1991 Censuses using surface modeling concepts. *Environment and Planning, A* 27: 379–390.

Brand, S. 1987. *The Media Lab: Inventing the Future at MIT*. New York: Viking.

Brewer, C.A., T.A. Suchan, and U.S. Census Bureau. 2001. *Mapping Census 2000: The Geography of U.S. Diversity, CENSR/01–1*. Washington, D.C.: U.S. Government Printing Office.

Campari, I. 1996. Uncertain boundaries in urban space. In P. Burrough, and A.U. Frank. (eds.), *Geographic Objects with Indeterminate Boundaries*. London: Taylor & Francis, 57–70.

Casti, J.L. 1997. *Would-be Worlds: How Simulation is Changing the Frontiers of Science*. New York: John Wiley & Sons Inc.

Clark, E. 1988. The rent gap and transformation of the built environment: Case studies in Malmö 1860–1985. *Geografiska Annaler B* 70(2): 241–254.

Clarke, K.C., S. Hoppen, and L. Gaydos. 1997. A self-modifying cellular automaton model of historical urbanization in the San Francisco Bay Area. *Environment and Planning B: Planning & Design* 24(2): 247–262.

Conte, R., R. Hegselmann, and P. Terna. (eds.) 1997. *Simulating Social Phenomena*. Vol. 456, Lecture Notes in Economics and Mathematical Systems. Berlin: Springer-Verlag.

Coombes, M., and S. Raybould. 2000. Policy-relevant surfaced data on population distribution and characteristics. *Transactions in GIS* 4(4): 319–342.

Curry, M.R. 1998. *Digital Places: Living with Geographic Information Technologies*. London: Routledge.

Dijkstra, J., H.J.P. Timmermans, and A.J. Jessurun. 2001. A multi-agent cellular automaton system for visualising simulated pedestrian activity. In S. Bandini, and T. Worsch (eds.), *Theoretical and Practical Issues on Cellular Automata: Proceedings of the 4th International Conference on Cellular Automata for Research and Industry, Karlsruhe, 4–6 October 2000*, London: Springer, 29–36.

Donnay, J.-P., M.J. Barnsley, and P.A. Longley (eds). 2001. *Remote Sensing and Urban Analysis*. London: Taylor & Francis.

Dorling, D. 1999. Who's afraid of income equality? *Environment and Planning A* 31(4): 571–574.

Epstein, J.M., and R. Axtell. 1996. *Growing Artificial Societies: Social Science from the Bottom Up*. Cambridge, Mass.: Brookings Press & MIT Press.

Feng, Z., and R. Flowerdew. 1999. The use of fuzzy classification to improve geodemographic targeting. In B.M. Gittings (ed.), *Integrating Information Infrastructures with Geographic Information Technology*. London: Taylor & Francis, 133–144.

Gilbert, N., and R. Conte. (eds.) 1995. *Artificial Societies: The Computer Simulation of Social Life*. London: UCL Press.

Gilbert, N., and J. Doran. (eds.). 1994. *Simulating Societies: The Computer Simulation of Social Phenomena*. London: UCL Press.

Gilbert, N., and K.G. Troitzsch. 1999. *Simulation for the Social Scientist*. Buckingham: Open University Press.

Haklay, M., T. Schelhorn, D. O'Sullivan, and M. Thurstain-Goodwin. 2001. So go down town: Simulating pedestrian movement in town centres. *Environment and Planning B: Planning & Design* 28(3): 343–359.

Helbing, D., P. Molnár, I.J. Farkas, and K. Bolay. 2001. Self-organizing pedestrian movement. *Environment and Planning B: Planning & Design* 28(3): 361–383.

Kerridge, J., J. Hine, and M. Wigan. 2001. Agent-based pedestrian modelling of pedestrian movements: The questions that need to be asked and answered. *Environment and Planning B: Planning & Design* 28(3): 327–341.

Ley, D. 1986. Alternative explanations for inner-city gentrification: A Canadian assessment. *Annals of the Association of American Geographers* 76(4): 521–535.

Li, X., and A.G.-O. Yeh. 2000. Modelling sustainable urban development by the integration of constrained cellular automata and GIS. *International Journal of Geographical Information Science* 14(2): 131–152.

Longley, P.A., and R.J. Harris. 1999. Towards a new digital data infrastructure for urban analysis and modelling. *Environment and Planning B: Planning & Design* 26(6): 855–878.

Martin, D. 1998. Optimizing Census geography: The separation of collection and output geographies. *International Journal of Geographical Information Science* 12(7): 673–685.

Martin, D., N.J. Tate, and M. Langford. 2000. Redefining population surface models: Experiments with Northern Ireland Census data. *Transactions in GIS,* 4(4): 343–360.

Openshaw, S. 1992. Further thoughts on geography and GIS: A reply. *Environment and Planning A* 24(4): 463–466.

Openshaw, S. 1991. A view of the GIS crisis in geography, or, using GIS to put Humpty-Dumpty back together again. *Environment and Planning A* 23(5): 621–628.

Openshaw, S., and I. Turton. 1994. *Geographical research using lifestyles databases*. Paper presented at the RGS-IBG annual conference, Kingston, England.

O'Sullivan, D. 2002. Toward micro-scale spatial modeling of gentrification, *Journal of Geographical Systems* 4(3): 251–274.

O'Sullivan, D. 2001. Graph cellular automata: A generalised discrete urban and regional model. *Environment and Planning B: Planning & Design* 28 (5): 687–705.

Portugali, J. 2000. *Self-Organisation and the City*. Berlin: Springer-Verlag.

Resnick, M. 1994. *Turtles, Termites, and Traffic Jams*. Cambridge: MIT Press.

Sayer, A. 1985. The difference that space makes. In D. Gregory, and J.Urry (eds.), *Social Relations and Spatial Structures*. London: Macmillan, 49–66.

Sayer, A. 1992. *Method in Social Science: A Realist Approach*. 2nd ed. London: Routledge.

Semboloni, F. 2000. The growth of an urban cluster into a dynamic self-modifying spatial pattern. *Environment and Planning B: Planning & Design* 27(4): 549–564.

Shi, W., and M.Y.C. Pang. 2000. Development of Voronoi-based cellular automata—an integrated dynamic model for geographical information systems. *International Journal of Geographical Information Science* 14(5): 455–474.

Smith, N. 1979. Toward a theory of gentrification: A back to the city movement by capital not people. *Journal of the American Planning Association* 45, October: 538–548.

Sprenger, P. 1999. Sun on privacy: 'get over it' *Wired News*, January 26 [cited August 29, 2002]. Available from http://www.wired.com/news/politics/0,1283,17538,00.html.

Takeyama, M., and H. Couclelis. 1997. Map dynamics: Integrating cellular automata and GIS through Geo-Algebra. *International Journal of Geographical Information Science* 11: 73–91.

Taylor, P.J., and M. Overton. 1991. Further thoughts on geography and GIS. *Environment and Planning A* 23(8): 1087–1090.

Thurstain-Goodwin, M., and D. Unwin. 2000. Defining and delineating the central areas of towns for statistical monitoring using continuous surface representations. *Transactions in GIS* 4(4): 305–318.

U.S. Census Bureau. 2001. *American FactFinder*, U.S. Census Bureau [cited August 29, 2002]. Available from http://www.census.gov/.

Voas, D., and P. Williamson. 2001. The diversity of diversity: A critique of geodemographic classification. *Area* 33(1): 63–76.

Ward, D.P., A.T. Murray, and S.R. Phinn. 2000. A stochastically constrained cellular model of urban growth. *Computers, Environment and Urban Systems* 24(6): 539–558.

White, R., and G. Engelen. 2000. High-resolution integrated modelling of the spatial dynamics of urban and regional systems. *Computers Environment and Urban Systems* 24: 383–400.

Yung, C.-F., and R.J. King. 1998. Some tests for the rent gap theory. *Environment and Planning A* 30: 523–542.

Part II

Neighborhood-Level Analysis

Neighborhood analysis constitutes a distinctive body of literature in the social sciences as well as a methodological consideration in the analysis of spatial data. The chapters in this section address issues regarding the concept of neighborhood, its meaning and delineation, especially in urban areas. It addition, this section explores analytical measures related to neighborhood effects—how a sub-area is influenced by and influences surrounding areas (its neighbors). Unlike individuals and households, a neighborhood does not necessarily constitute a decision-making unit. While it may suggest a level of compatibility, identity, and even basic homogeneity among its occupants, research about neighborhoods and about neighborhood effects is likely to be based on arbitrary data units—e.g., census blocks or census tracts, possibly supplemented with supportive survey analysis or alternate sources of data. While the problems under investigation differ, the first four chapters in this section make use of a common methodology—exploratory spatial data analysis (ESDA)—in the investigation of spatial associations across neighboring data units.

Logan and Zhang deal directly with the methodology for determining neighborhoods and their boundaries, focusing on the Filipino and Chinese populations in Los Angeles. They review traditional concepts about ethnic neighborhoods and their identity, including notions of transitional communities that move from immigrant enclaves through spatial assimilation to the majority culture. However, they see the emergence of voluntary ethnic communities that follow a different dynamic. They employ local indicators of spatial association (LISA) as a means of identifying significant spatial clusters of tract-level concentrations of these communities. The results of this method are compared with more arbitrary groupings of tracts based on an odds-ratio method of classification. Their work also demonstrates a procedure for linking information across different levels of spatial aggregation while respecting confidentiality rules. Thus, by matching individual population traits in Public Use Microdata samples with census-tract data, they are able to gain greater confidence that their models of ethnic neighborhood identification reflect reasonable residential outcomes.

Messner and Anselin research homicide patterns with concepts and measures of spatial autocorrelation. Using county-level data, their research question does not relate to the concept of neighborhood so much as it does to the general methodology of how to account for spatial dependencies across neighboring data units. The first of three chapters that analyze homicide data assembled by areal units, this chapter describes and illustrates application of methods for treating spatial dependency in measures of spatial association and in regression models. Messner and Anselin develop two case studies to illustrate the need for researchers to understand three important problems regarding the use of aggregate spatial data in social research. These include (1) ecological inference, (2) the heterogeneity of rates based on unstable variance measures that arise from differences in the populations of observation units, and (3) the interpretation of spatial autocorrelation in models. Their first study considers the diffusion of homicide over space across two time periods for county-level data in the St. Louis region. ESDA is used to dynamically link statistics, graphs, and maps of LISA values to reflect local patterns of spatial autocorrelation. The second study models homicide rates by U.S. Southern and non-southern counties across four time points from 1960 to 1990. The results of Ordinary Least Squares regression are compared with those from a spatial econometric approach. The later includes spatial-lag and spatial-error variants of a spatial regression model to permit explicit treatment of spatial effects on crime patterns and processes. These methods are shown to tease out useful insights from the data that are lost in non-spatial approaches.

Sampson and Morenoff deal with an issue that confronts many researchers at the neighborhood scale—linking data from different sources (census data, police crime data, and personal survey interviews) described for different units of spatial aggregation that cover the same area. Faced with diverse data sources and imperfect tools, they display the kind of caution that should be seen as best practice in spatial social science. Their research question deals with the spatial and functional interdependence of homicide rates in a neighborhood in relationship to the homicide rates and social characteristics of surrounding neighborhoods. Concentrated disadvantage (deprivation and inequality) and collective efficacy (institutional presence, and social ties that build trust and a sense of neighborhood control) are two social processes that the authors hypothesize as altering the risk and exposure to homicide. The authors move systematically through a set of analyses: regression with spatial dependencies accounted for, exploratory spatial data analysis, and regression-based multivariate analysis. Under a variety of controls and alternative modeling frameworks, spatial interdependence of neighborhoods persisted as a significant factor in the explanation of urban violence.

Cohen and Tita illustrate the use of LISA measures and mappings to decompose complex patterns in the spatio-temporal incidents of reported gun shots in urban neighborhoods of Pittsburgh. The authors establish a framework for identifying both contagious and hierarchical forms of diffusion in relationship to processes and patterns of neighborhood violence, youth gang activity, and crack drug markets. Data, derived from 911 calls to report shots fired, are aggregated temporally for 3-month periods over six years and spatially for 174 census tracts. The LISA measures provide a basis for assessing local-neighbor pairs of tracts for successive time periods to identify clusters of tracts with similar temporal patterns in the rates of shots fired. The authors' interpretations provide a thorough review of spatial diffusion concepts in relationship to neighborhood processes.

Eagles, Bélanger, and Calkins observe how the widely accepted and very insightful technique of social network analysis may have inadvertently and prematurely dismissed the value of a spatial perspective for research on political influence through interpersonal discussion networks. Questioning this practice, they use a GIS to analyze a geo-coded data set on discussion networks for about 500 residents distributed among designated neighborhoods in South Bend, Indiana. They seek to determine if distance between network discussants, and other spatial dimensions of the networks (e.g., concentration), influence interactions, attitudes, and political behavior. In general, interpersonal networks based on neighborhood ties were more concentrated and less dispersed than those based on family or work relationships. The analyses demonstrate that distance and neighborhood affiliations are clearly associated with network structures and political attitudes, while the impact of the spatial attributes of these networks on the transfer of political influence remains ambiguous and subject to further investigation.

The authors of this section suggest areas where significant additional work is needed. For example, neighborhood studies, though aided significantly by refined methods for measuring local effects across data units, still require support of detailed ethnographic field research. This is critical to understanding human motivations for choosing to live in an ethnic community or to assimilate. Another issue that shows up in this section is the need for researchers to operate in different software environments. While this situation is expected to change with the embedding of spatial statistics routines within GIS software packages, researchers currently face awkward transfers of results from one analytic platform to another. Another area for attention is the growing interest in the dynamics of space-time processes. In this case, researchers face problems in accounting for both spatial and temporal dependencies simultaneously, often within multiple and non-congruent software environments. Software developers seeking to design solutions to these problems must allow for inclusion of a broad range of time frames and spatial scales. As a final general observation, the chapters in this section delve deeply into the theories of neighborhood composition and meaning, crime occurrence and diffusion, and transmission of political influence. In all cases the authors see the theoretical foundation and empirical grounding of these research areas enhanced through rigorous assessment and measurement of spatial effects across units of observation over time.

6

Identifying Ethnic Neighborhoods with Census Data
Group Concentration and Spatial Clustering

John R. Logan
Wenquan Zhang

T his chapter describes and offers an example of the application of methods of spatial analysis that can be used to study ethnic neighborhoods, and by extension, to study neighborhoods defined by any other social characteristic. We use the cases of Chinese and Filipinos in Los Angeles in 1990 for illustration. Many members of these groups live in ethnic neighborhoods, and people living near these neighborhoods are very aware of their ethnic character. Surprisingly, however, there exists no consensus among social scientists about how to define an ethnic neighborhood, and there are no agreed criteria by which to distinguish a "Chinese neighborhood" from any other neighborhood that has Chinese among its residents.

We are interested in this question because American cities have always grown mainly by attracting newcomers, whose customs or language often set them apart from the majority population—never more so than in the current period of intensive immigration. Concentrated immigrant settlement areas seem to be a permanent feature of cities, yet the predominant view among social scientists is that they are also transitional places. People live in them as long as they need the affordable housing, family ties, familiar culture, and help in finding work that they provide. Then they search for areas with more amenities as soon as their economic situation improves and they become better able to function without assistance from co-ethnics, i.e., they assimilate.

In the contemporary United States, there are reasons to believe that the model of spatial assimilation (Massey 1985) does not capture important recent trends. The current immigration stream is extraordinarily diverse, ranging from refugees with peasant backgrounds to physicians and computer engineers. And notions of bilingualism and biculturalism have challenged the cultural values and ideology underlying assimilation. Under these conditions, we argue that some groups are establishing another form of neighborhood, the "ethnic community." The alternative model recognizes that some

113

groups are now able to establish enclaves in desirable locations, and that group members may choose these locations even when spatial assimilation is feasible. For some groups, therefore, the ethnic neighborhood is a starting point; for others, it may now be a destination.

The theoretical underpinnings of these alternative models are developed more fully elsewhere (Logan et al. 2002). According to the well-known theory of "spatial assimilation," segregation is natural as a group enters the United States. In the beginning, people's limited market resources and ethnically bound cultural and social capital are mutually reinforcing; they work in tandem to sustain ethnic neighborhoods. But these are transitional neighborhoods—they represent a practical and temporary phase in the incorporation of new groups into American society. Their residents search for areas with more amenities as soon as their economic situations improve, their outlooks broaden, and they learn to navigate daily life in a more mainstream setting. People with more financial resources and mainstream jobs avoid ethnic zones, and these areas are left behind by immigrants with more experience and by the second generation in search of the "Promised Land."

We use the term *immigrant enclave* to refer to such neighborhoods. Earlier in this century, Chicago School ecologists recognized immigrant enclaves and gave them names like Little Sicily, Greektown, and Chinatown. Such places are highly visible today in metropolises such as New York, Los Angeles, and Miami. Immigrant enclaves can be identified by their physical characteristics (by the usual standards of mainstream society, they are less desirable as places to live) and by the characteristics of the people who live in them (they concentrate immigrants who are recently arrived and have few socioeconomic resources). By implication, the neighborhoods to which upwardly mobile group members diffuse are less ethnically distinct and have greater economic resources.

We believe that changes in the natures of urban space and of immigration have begun to alter the function of ethnic neighborhoods for some groups or individual group members. Most important, there is now potential for acculturation and market position to be decoupled. The assimilation model was built from the experience of immigrants from the late nineteenth century. These immigrants entered American cities, in which working class people had to live near their places of employment and had little contact with people outside their neighborhood. Today, the automobile and other systems of transportation and communication have weakened the connection of home to work and enlarged the geographic scale of people's active social networks. Growing shares of immigrants live and work in suburbs (Alba et al. 1999). In addition, most immigrants of a century ago were manual laborers without the financial resources to have much control over where they lived. The contemporary immigration stream includes many immigrants with high levels of human capital who find professional or other high-status positions in the United States (Nee and Sanders 2001; Portes and Rumbaut 1990).

As a result, some groups are now able to establish enclaves in desirable locations, often in suburbia, and group members may choose these locations even when spatial assimilation is feasible. Living in an ethnic neighborhood may still be an "ethnic" behavior as posited by the assimilation model, more typical of newer immigrants with narrower horizons. But if living in these zones is not associated with low economic standing or a need to find work in the ethnic economy—that is, if it is not at the same time an adaptation to circumstance—we must reconsider whether the ethnic choice stems from constraint or from preference. We use the term *ethnic community* to refer to ethnic neighborhoods that are selected as living environments by those who have wider options based on their market resources.

The ethnic community, as we define it here, is formed through a different social process than is the immigrant enclave. It is grounded in motives associated more with taste and preference than with economic necessity, or even with the ambition, to create neighborhoods that will symbolize and sustain ethnic identity. Zhou (1992) interprets the satellite Chinatowns that have emerged in Flushing and other outlying parts of the New York region in this way. Horton (1995) describes a similar pattern for suburban Monterey Park, located not far from downtown Los Angeles, that was aggressively marketed by Chinese American developers to well-heeled immigrants and investors from Taiwan and Hong Kong.

The Chicago School ecologists noticed an element of preference as well as necessity in the creation of immigrant colonies. But because both preference and necessity operated in the same direction—because the immigrants they studied appeared to have little choice in where to live—preference was of secondary importance in their theory of spatial assimilation. What makes it potentially more significant today is the presence of immigrant groups with high levels of human and financial capital, such as Asian Indians, who have the means to translate their preferences for residing in a culturally familiar environment into residential niches in affluent areas. These are the groups for which we expect to find ethnic communities. By contrast, the areas of concentration established by low-wage labor migrant groups, such as Mexicans, are less likely to hold their more successful and more acculturated members; these areas, then, may look more like immigrant enclaves. We hypothesize that the market resources that immigrant groups bring with them are the primary determinant of the kinds of neighborhoods they establish.

Identifying Ethnic Neighborhoods

Ethnic neighborhoods are most often identified and studied through fieldwork, where the researcher typically begins with the knowledge that the ethnic character of a given locale is socially recognized—certainly by group members and perhaps also by others. This ethnic character may be visible through observation of people in public places, the names of shops or the languages found on signs or spoken by clerks or patrons, or by community institutions such as churches, social clubs, and associations.

Demographic researchers are much more limited in the information at their disposal and rely mainly on census data. There is a long tradition of directly mapping such data to show the outlines of ethnic neighborhoods, of which some of the best known are the studies of the Chicago School in the 1920s and 1930s. This is easy to accomplish in the age of computerized mapping, and the Bureau of the Census allows users to create maps interactively on its American FactFinder website http://www.census.gov.

The settlement pattern of racial and ethnic minorities is typically highly skewed in the American metropolis. The Chinese and Filipinos in the greater Los Angeles metropolitan region in 1990 (defined as the Consolidated Metropolitan Statistical Area,

Table 6.1. Distribution of group members by level of concentration, Los Angeles CMSA, 1990.

Tract – %Concentration	Chinese	% of LA Chinese	Filipinos	% of LA Filipinos
<1	25,457	8.3	25,767	8.7
1–1.99	36,876	12.0	43,549	14.8
2–4.99	66,757	21.7	94,519	32.0
5–9.99	50,942	16.6	64,275	21.8
10–19.99	47,834	15.5	42,266	14.3
20+	79,915	26.0	24,738	8.4
Group total	307,781	100.0	295,114	100.0

with a population of 14.5 million) were no exception. Each of these groups numbered around 300,000, or 2 percent of the total. The average Chinese lived in a tract that was 13.5 percent Chinese, while the average Filipino lived in a 7.3 percent Filipino tract. Consistent with these averages, Table 6.1 shows that more than a quarter of the Chinese lived in tracts where the Chinese were more than 20 percent of the total. These included only 45 of the more than 2000 census tracts in the region. Filipinos were somewhat less concentrated, but nearly a quarter of them lived in tracts that were more than 10 percent Filipino (there were only 75 such tracts). By contrast, only about 20 percent of members of either group lived in tracts where they were under-represented (that is, less than 2 percent of residents were Chinese or Filipino), though such areas covered most of the region's territory.

It is easy to distinguish a relatively small share of tracts that are candidates to be considered part of ethnic neighborhoods. But just where should we draw the line? How Chinese or Filipino must a Chinese or Filipino neighborhood be? There is no established criterion. It is widely understood that the group does not necessarily have to be a majority (a corollary is that some zones may contain "ethnic neighborhoods" of more than one group). Philpott (1978) has pointed out that the principal Swedish ghetto identified by Park and Burgess in Chicago in 1930 was only 24 percent Swedish; the German ghetto was only 32 percent German. Some places today have international reputations as ethnic neighborhoods despite having modest proportions of group members. For example, parts of Los Angeles "are so heavily identified with Armenians that when prospective emigrants in Armenia or Iran are asked about their destination, they may answer 'Hollywood' or 'Glendale,' respectively, instead of American" (Bozorgmehr et al. 1996, 368). Yet in 1990, Armenians made up only about 25 percent of residents of Hollywood and Glendale, reaching a maximum of 33 percent in their most "Armenian" tract, and only 10–15 percent in their peripheries.

Among well-known contemporary Chinese neighborhoods, the core immigrant area of Flushing (in Queens, New York) studied by Zhou (1992) was only 14 percent Chinese in 1990. Monterey Park, California, was less than 25 percent Chinese in the mid-1980s when Horton (1995) began to study it. A recent study of minority groups in Los Angeles defined Asian residential enclaves as areas that were as little as 10 percent Asian (Bobo et al. 2000).

Some recent studies have used higher minimum values. In their study of Italians,

Irish, and Germans in the New York region, Alba et al. (1997, 892) operationalized an ethnic neighborhood as "a set of contiguous tracts, which must contain at least one tract where a group is represented as 40 percent or more of the residents and whose other tracts each have a level of ethnic concentration among residents of at least 35 percent." However, only a handful of census tracts in Los Angeles meet this criterion for Chinese or Filipinos, because these groups are much smaller than the white ethnic groups in New York. This consideration suggests that concentration should be measured relative to the overall size of the group.

The Odds-Ratio Approach

We illustrate one way of achieving this, using an odds-ratio (the odds of a group member's living in a particular tract divided by the odds of a non-group member's living in the tract). The use of an odds-ratio is already well established in the ethnic economy literature as a measure of group concentration in industry sectors (Logan et al. 2000). The maps in the left-hand panels of Figure 6.1 (for Chinese) and Figure 6.2 (for Filipinos) show areas where the odds-ratio is 5.0 or above. The major "neighborhoods" defined this way correspond well with local experts' descriptions of ethnic residential patterns (e.g., Allen and Turner 1997, 146).

An early settlement area for Filipinos, dating to the 1950s, is the Temple-Alvarado area west of downtown Los Angeles, which has now extended as far north as Glendale and Eagle Rock. West Long Beach has the region's largest single concentration of Filipinos, while most recent growth is in suburban areas of the San Fernando Valley and in San Gabriel Valley.

The Chinese retain a small concentration in the traditional Chinatown adjacent to downtown. Their main settlement now is Monterey Park, which is often described as a suburban Chinatown (Horton 1995). Chinese also overlap somewhat with the suburban Filipino areas further to the east (places like Hacienda Heights, La Habra Heights, and Diamond Bar).

Spatial Clustering

Besides the level of concentration in any single tract, a striking feature of the residential pattern of many new immigrant groups is the extent to which their concentrations are spatially clustered and often spread over large areas. Clustering in adjacent tracts accentuates the ethnic character and reputation of neighborhoods by aggregating more group members in a delimited space (compared to a situation where singular tracts with high concentrations are spatially isolated). Researchers have always intuitively made use of contiguity in mapping ethnic neighborhoods.

Thanks to recent advances in spatial analysis, it is now possible to measure such clustering systematically. Responding in part to concerns about spatial autocorrelation, geographers have developed several indicators of the extent to which the spatial distribution of place characteristics departs from a random pattern. Anselin (1995) has extended this work to a class of "local indicators of spatial association" (LISA), which offer a measure for each place of the extent of *significant spatial clustering* of similar values around it. In brief, LISA indicators identify "hot spots" that take into account

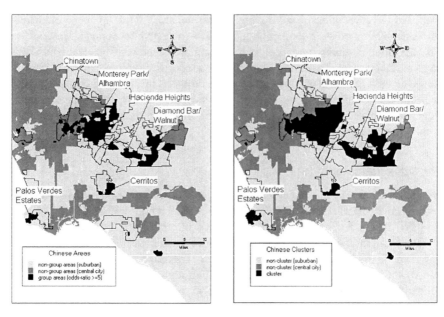

Figure 6.1. Chinese neighborhoods identified by odds-ratio (left), and spatial clusters (right).

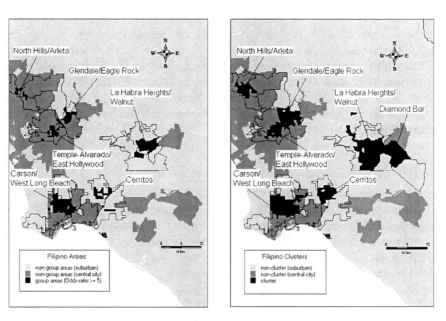

Figure 6.2. Filipino neighborhoods identified by odds-ratio (left), and spatial clusters (right).

not only unusually high or low values in a single place (such as a census tract) but also the values in nearby places. Such spatial clustering provides an alternative method of identifying ethnic neighborhoods. Compared to setting an odds-ratio or percentage criterion at an arbitrary level, it has the advantage of an underlying statistical theory through which only sets of tracts that depart significantly from a random distribution are assigned to clusters.

This is the approach advocated here. Concretely, SpaceStat exploratory spatial analysis software in conjunction with ArcView mapping software can be used to locate clusters of census tracts with statistically significant values of local Moran's I (I_i), indicating unusually high values of group presence. Following Anselin (1995, 98) the "local Moran statistic for an observation i may be defined as

$$I_i = z_i \sum_j w_{ij} z_j, \tag{1}$$

where, analogous to the global Moran's I, the observations z_i, z_j are in deviations from the mean, and the summation over j is such that only neighboring values $j \in J_i$ are included. For ease of interpretation, the [spatial] weights w_{ij} may be in row-standardized form . . . and by convention, $w_{ii} = 0$."

As measured this way, a "cluster" is made up of a single focal census tract along with all tracts that surround and share a boundary with it. We are interested in the following kinds of clusters:

1. High-high clusters: the local Moran statistic indicates a significant combination of a focal tract with a high group presence, surrounded by other tracts that on average have a high group presence.
2. High-low clusters: a significant combination of a focal tract with a high group presence, surrounded by tracts with a lower than average group presence.

High-low clusters represent locations where an ethnic neighborhood has a very well defined boundary. These are uncommon for ethnic groups in Los Angeles. In fact, most clusters are of the high-high variety, and they extend continuously over areas containing many tracts. It is usually only at the edges of these larger areas that the ethnic concentration thins out. In such clusters at the edge, where the neighborhood boundary is not sharply demarcated, we count as part of the neighborhood only those surrounding tracts in each cluster whose group concentration is equal to that of the average of the rest of the neighborhood.

The maps in the right-hand panels of Figures 6.1 and 6.2 show these spatial clusters for Chinese and Filipinos in Los Angeles.

Comparing the Results of These Two Approaches

Table 6.2 presents a comparison of the results of these two approaches to neighborhood identification. The table places census tracts into four categories: those that are part of ethnic neighborhoods for each group in the central cities and in suburbs and those that are outside ethnic neighborhoods in cities or suburbs. For each category, it provides the number of census tracts and the number of Chinese or Filipinos in them. It also

Table 6.2. Chinese and Filipino settlement areas in Los Angeles, 1990, by city or suburban location.

	Odds Ratio Method				Cluster Method			
	Group Central City	Group Suburb	Nongroup Central City	Nongroup Suburb	Group Central City	Group Suburb	Nongroup Central City	Nongroup Suburb
Chinese								
N of tracts	24	88	1048	1392	39	111	1035	1379
N of group members	23,325	108,550	65,718	110,188	28,109	117,786	60,934	100,952
% of region's group members	7.6	35.3	21.4	35.8	9.1	38.3	19.8	32.8
Mean % of group members	34.2	24.8	3.3	3.7	29.3	23.4	3.1	3.3
Filipinos								
N of tracts	51	31	1021	1449	112	75	960	1415
N of group members	41,264	28,883	93,072	131,895	65,575	50,718	68,761	110,060
% of region's group members	14.0	9.8	31.5	44.7	22.2	17.2	23.3	37.3
Mean % of group members	18.2	18.4	3.9	3.3	14.0	13.5	2.9	2.6

provides an exposure index: the average percentage of group members in each type of tract, weighted by the number of group members. The result reveals the level of ethnic concentration in the tract where the average group member lives.

Out of more than 2500 tracts in the region, the odds-ratio method classifies 24 city tracts and 88 suburban tracts as Chinese. Just under half of Chinese are in ethnic neighborhoods by this criterion, and such areas average well above 20 percent Chinese. The spatial cluster method is more expansive, including 39 city tracts and 111 in the suburbs. However, the additional tracts account for only a few extra Chinese.

There are greater differences between the two methods for classifying Filipinos. The odds-ratio approach finds 51 Filipino tracts in the city and 31 in the suburbs; exposure of Filipinos to Filipinos is close to 20 percent in both types. The cluster method more than doubles the number of Filipino tracts and increases the number of Filipinos in ethnic neighborhoods by about 50 percent. Its much broader definition includes tracts that average less than 15 percent Filipinos.

From the perspective of an urban sociologist, however, either method results in the same conclusions. First, many (but less than half) of Chinese and Filipinos in the Los Angeles region live in ethnic neighborhoods, and typically in these neighborhoods the Chinese or Filipinos are a minority of residents. Second, although both groups have about the same total size, a larger share of Chinese live in ethnic neighborhoods, and these are more intensely ethnic than is true for Filipino neighborhoods. Third, Chinese areas are considerably more weighted toward the suburbs, while Filipino zones are more likely to be located in the central cities.

The Determinants of Living in an Ethnic Neighborhood

Following either method, the next step is to build models of what kinds of group members live in them and who lives elsewhere in the metropolis. With confidential data held by the Bureau of the Census, such analyses can be completed directly. In another study (Logan et al. 2002), files maintained at the Bureau's Confidential Data Research Centers are used this way. Most social scientists, though, will be limited to publicly available data, and the problem here is that the Public Use Microdata Samples (PUMS) use relatively large areas known as PUMA's (Public Use Microdata Areas) as the smallest geographical identifier. A PUMA typically contains about 100,000 persons, some twenty times larger than a census tract. Further, in most cases it is larger than any ethnic neighborhood. Nonetheless, it is possible to use a person's PUMA location as a strong indicator of the probability of living in an ethnic neighborhood. For the models presented here, the results from public use files are very similar to those directly estimated from confidential data.

We use the following procedure. We link census tracts to their corresponding PUMAs. Then we identify which, if any, tracts within the PUMA are part of an ethnic neighborhood. In this study, we use the spatial cluster approach for this purpose. Finally, we calculate the proportion of group members in the PUMA who live in such tracts. This proportion is the probability that, if a group member lives in the PUMA, he or she lives in an ethnic neighborhood.

This procedure allows researchers to work within the limits of publicly available data to address a new range of questions about who lives where. To illustrate the procedure, consider the main Chinese concentration in and around Monterey Park, with nearly 79,000 Chinese. These account for 95 percent of the total 83,000 Chinese in the three PUMAs that include the neighborhood. Chinese residents in these PUMAs have unusually high odds (nearly 20 to 1) of living in an ethnic neighborhood; locating Chinese in these PUMAs is almost equivalent to locating them in a Chinese neighborhood.

For both Chinese and Filipinos, the probability of living in an ethnic neighborhood has a bimodal distribution among PUMAs: some PUMAs with very high values (in the range of .80 and .90), many with low values (most of which are near 0), and a smaller number in between. In light of this distribution, we treat the probability of living in an ethnic neighborhood as a three-category variable: high (.75 and above), medium (between .25 and .75), and low (.25 and below). Multinomial logistic regression is an appropriate method for modeling such a variable. We treat the low category as the reference category and ask what personal characteristics of group members predict a medium or high probability of living in an ethnic neighborhood. For the sake of parsimony, we present and discuss the logit models that predict living in the "most ethnic" category of PUMA compared to the "least ethnic." We also estimated models for living in the middle category vs. the least ethnic category; the direction of results is consistent with those presented here.

For each group, we analyze a 5 percent sample of households, selecting one group member in the household for study (choosing randomly between the householder and the householder's spouse where both belong to the group in question). We evaluate the following variables whose effects are anticipated by the spatial assimilation model:

1. Nativity. Group members born in the United States are expected to be less likely to live in ethnic neighborhoods than are immigrants; among immigrants, the most recent arrivals are expected to be most likely to live in residential enclaves. Nativity is represented by three dummy variables, with U.S.-born treated as the reference category: immigrated after 1985, between 1965 and 1985, and before 1965.

2. Language. In tandem with nativity, language is considered to be an indicator of cultural assimilation. Bilingual persons who speak English poorly are most likely to live in residential enclaves (while, at the same time, residential segregation could itself impede learning or using English). Language is represented by two dummy variables, with "speaking only English at home" treated as the reference category for language. Two dummy variables refer to those who speak another language at home: speaking English well and speaking English poorly.

3. Education. Education (years of schooling completed) is understood as an indicator of socioeconomic status. For those educated in the United States, it may also be an indicator of cultural adaptability or cultural experience.

4. Household income and homeownership. Household income (expressed in thousands of dollars) and homeownership (a dummy variable) are both considered to be indicators of socioeconomic achievement, presumed to be negatively associated with living in an ethnic neighborhood.

5. Ethnic employment. Responsive to the literature on ethnic economies, we include two indicators of position in the labor force. The first is whether any household member is self-employed. Business owners among immigrant groups (net of the effect of

their possibly higher income) may depend on connections with co-ethnics as consumers or as sources of supplies or labor; this consideration advances the hypothesis that owners are more likely to live in ethnic neighborhoods. But workers may be equally dependent on such ties in finding employment. Hence self-employment is not in itself a convincing indicator of ethnic dependency. Better are measures of the industry sectors in which people work, because ethnic economies are so often concentrated in certain sectors. Following procedures established in prior work (Logan et al. 2000), three types of ethnic sectors are identified: those in which the group is over-represented as both owners and workers (an enclave sector), those in which the group is over-represented only as owners (an entrepreneurial niche), and those in which the group is over-represented only as workers (a labor niche). Following the assimilation model, one would hypothesize that group members in any of these types of ethnic sectors would be more likely to live in ethnic neighborhoods.

Two life cycle indicators are included as control variables: the person's age and whether the person lives in a married-couple household. The theoretical models offer no clear expectations about the effects of these variables. It could be presumed that young adults will be more likely than older people of the same immigrant generation to wish to leave the enclave. But it could also be argued that older people have had more time in which to exercise this option. Married-couple households may have more residential options than single persons, although in some instances it might be expected that they would prefer—in raising their children—to live in the enclave.

We also include a variable representing city vs. suburban location. Because a few PUMAs cross city boundaries and therefore include both city and suburban portions, we define this variable as the proportion of PUMA residents in its suburban portion (ranging from 0 to 1). (Where this proportion was less than .01 or greater than .99, it was rounded to 0 or 1.) Inclusion of this variable is subject to criticism because suburbanization itself is an important residential outcome, likely to be related to other variables in the model. However, the inclusion of suburban location does not substantially change the interpretation of effects of other variables. The purpose of this variable is to test whether, having controlled for other factors, group members who live in the suburbs are less likely than those in the central city to live in residential enclaves, as traditionally supposed.

The results are presented in Table 6.3. The model for the Chinese conforms quite well to the immigrant enclave model. Recent immigrants and those who speak English as a second language are more likely to live in Chinese neighborhoods. Those with lower education and income and those who rent their homes are also more likely to be located in ethnic zones. Finally, those employed in the Chinese labor niche (where Chinese are disproportionately concentrated as workers) are also more likely to be found in a Chinese area.

The Filipinos seem to follow a different pattern. Of the variables mentioned above, the only significant predictor of living in a Filipino neighborhood is language. There is no evidence that the Filipino second generation, or those with greater choices (due to their socioeconomic success), have tended to leave ethnic zones. On the contrary, it appears likely that successful Filipinos—if they do experience residential mobility—are equally disposed to find a higher status ethnic neighborhood as to forsake ethnic ties.

Table 6.3. Predicting residence in an ethnic neighborhood (logistic regression with unstandardized coefficients and standard errors).

	Chinese		Filipinos	
Nativity				
U.S. born	—		—	
Post-1985 immigrant	0.240	(0.158)	0.430	(0.257)
1965–1985 immigrant	0.395**	(0.137)	0.186	(0.229)
Pre-1965 immigrant	−0.189	(0.179)	−0.125	(0.278)
Language				
Speaks English only	—		—	
Speaks English well	0.661***	(0.134)	0.919***	(0.190)
Speaks English poorly	1.164***	(0.163)	1.263***	(0.357)
Education	−0.079***	(0.010)	−0.002	(0.018)
Household income	−0.001	(0.001)	−0.001	(0.002)
Renter	0.388***	(0.086)	−0.086	(0.115)
Employment				
Mainstream economy	—		—	
Enclave sector	0.153	(0.127)	0.066	(0.120)
Worker Sector	0.371**	(0.140)	0.134	(0.308)
Owner Sector	0.053	(0.085)	0.029	(0.144)
Self-employment	0.003	(0.106)	−0.338	(0.222)
Age	0.003	(0.003)	0.023***	(0.004)
Married	0.021	(0.086)	−0.149	(0.118)
Suburban location	1.673***	(0.092)	−1.155***	(0.101)
Constant	−1.710***	(0.257)	−2.358***	(0.385)
Model Chi-Square	786.4		275.5	

$^*p < .05$, $^{**}p < .01$, $^{***}p < .001$

Geographic Scale in Identifying Neighborhoods

These analyses have been carried out using the census tract, an area that typically has 3000 to 4000 residents, as the unit of geography. In the study of relatively large ethnic groups in urbanized areas, we find that this is a convenient unit, because neighborhoods typically extend across many census tracts, and little error is introduced by spatial variation within tracts. In areas of very low population density, however, a census tract can include a large and socially heterogeneous territory. Also tract-level data identify only vaguely the much smaller settlement areas—indeed, micro-neighborhoods—of some groups (e.g., Syrian Jews in Brooklyn, New York). Sometimes it may be preferable to map spatial clusters at the level of block group or census blocks. However, there are also obstacles to such fine-grained analyses. The Bureau of the Census does not report some population characteristics at the block level. Also, for statistical reasons and due to data swapping procedures through which the Bureau seeks to protect confidentiality, estimates based on sample data (for items on the census long form, such as ancestry and income) are less reliable for blocks or block groups than for tracts.

Discussion and Conclusion

These analyses are intended primarily to illustrate new approaches to analyzing the phenomenon of ethnic neighborhoods. They apply a much-used tool of spatial analysis to a new domain. This tool yields results similar to those from the kinds of mapping procedures that urban sociologists have traditionally relied upon. The principal advantage is that spatial clustering is an essential characteristic of ethnic neighborhoods that should be incorporated into its definition. Additionally, the availability of statistical tests may help to allay concerns that traditional methods rely on arbitrary cutting points to define areas of high concentration.

The study also shows that it is feasible to use publicly available data to model the locational process by which some people live in one kind of place and others live in another. The very clustering that supports the use of spatial techniques as a means of identifying ethnic neighborhoods also results in a fairly clear distinction between large areas of the metropolis—PUMA's—where residents are either very likely, or very unlikely, to live in such neighborhoods.

The same methods illustrated here could be applied to other dimensions of neighborhood differentiation. An obvious extension is to other dimensions of social differentiation, such as economic class (income, homeownership). We are experimenting with small-area data on where members of different ethnic groups work, which will make it possible to identify ethnic economic enclaves in spatial terms (i.e., as an area in which a large share of the labor force is comprised of a particular group).

Substantively, the main conclusion of the present study is that urbanists need to extend their theoretical repertoire beyond the model of spatial assimilation. Not every group uses the ethnic neighborhood as an immigrant enclave, to be left behind when the individual is able to adapt successfully to living in the mainstream. For some, the ethnic neighborhood is a free choice, consistent with a preference for ethnic community. Of course, this study has not provided information on people's motives, only the residential outcomes. This is a field where quantitative and spatial studies need continuously to interact with field investigation. Hopefully the ability to identify ethnic neighborhoods and the characteristics of their residents will be a useful input for ethnographic studies, especially directing researchers toward potential sites.

Acknowledgments   This paper draws on results of a long-term collaborative project with Richard Alba. It was supported by a grant from National Science Foundation, SBR95–07920 and by the Lewis Mumford Center for Comparative Urban and Regional Research. The Center for Social and Demographic Analysis, University at Albany, provided technical and administrative support through grants from NICHD (P30 HD32041) and NSF (SBR-9512290).

References

Alba, R.D., J.R. Logan, and K. Crowder. 1997. White neighborhoods and assimilation: The greater New York region, 1980–1990. *Social Forces* 75: 883–909.
Alba, R.D., J.R. Logan, B. Stults, G. Marzan, and W. Zhang. 1999. Immigrant groups and suburbs: A reexamination of suburbanization and spatial assimilation. *American Sociological Review* 64: 6–60.

Allen, J. P., and E. Turner. 1997. *The Ethnic Quilt: Population Diversity in Southern California.* Northridge: The Center for Geographic Studies, California State University.

Anselin, L. 1995. Local indicators of spatial association—LISA. *Geographical Analysis* 27: 93–115.

Bobo, L.D., M.L. Oliver, J.H. Johnson, Jr., and A. Valenzuela. 2000. *Prismatic Metropolis: Inequality in Los Angeles.* New York: Russell Sage Foundation.

Bozorgmehr, M., C. Der-Martirosian, and G. Sabagh. 1996. Middle Easterners: A new kind of immigrant. In R. Waldinger, and M. Bozorgmehr (eds.), *Ethnic Los Angeles.* New York: Russell Sage Foundation, 345–378.

Horton, J. 1995. *The Politics of Diversity: Immigration, Resistance, and Change in Monterey Park, California.* Philadelphia: Temple University Press.

Logan, J.R., R.D. Alba, M. Dill, and M. Zhou. 2000. Ethnic segmentation in the American metropolis: Increasing divergence in economic incorporation, 1980–1990. *International Migration Review* 34: 98–132.

Logan, J.R., R.D. Alba, and W. Zhang. 2002. Immigrant enclaves and ethnic communities in New York and Los Angeles. *American Sociological Review*, 67, 299–322.

Massey, D. 1985. Ethnic residential segregation: A theoretical synthesis and empirical review. *Sociology and Social Research* 69: 315–50.

Nee, V., and J. Sanders. 2001. Understanding the diversity of immigrant incorporation: A forms of capital model. *Ethnic and Racial Studies* 24(3, May): 386–411.

Philpott, T.L. 1978. *The Slum and the Ghetto: Neighborhood Deterioration and Middle-Class Reform Chicago, 1880–1930.* New York: Oxford University Press.

Portes, A., and R. Rumbaut. 1990. *Immigrant America: A Portrait.* Berkeley: University of California Press.

Zhou, M. 1992. *Chinatown: The Socioeconomic Potential of an Urban Enclave.* Philadelphia: Temple University Press.

7

Spatial Analyses of Homicide with Areal Data

Steven F. Messner

Luc Anselin

I n a widely cited article, Land et al. (1990) noted an important development in sociological studies of crime over the previous two decades. There had been a remarkable upsurge in the volume of empirical studies seeking to explain why different areal units—e.g., cities, metropolitan areas, and states—have high or low homicide rates (Land et al. 1990, 922). Much of this research was inspired by theoretical debates surrounding a distinctively geographic issue: the historically high homicide rates in the South (Hawley and Messner 1989). However, with the exception of this focus on regional differences in overall levels of homicide, the early work on the social structural covariates of homicide rates was largely insensitive to spatial context. The field has changed dramatically in recent years, and criminologists are increasingly applying formal tools of spatial analysis to describe and explain variations in levels of homicide (and other crimes).

The purpose of the present chapter is to highlight the ways in which the application of newly developed techniques for spatial analysis contributes to our understanding of homicide. We begin with a brief historical review of the role of geographic space in the sociological study of crime. This is followed by a discussion of generic methodological issues involved in the study of areal units. We then explain the logic of important techniques for spatial analysis and illustrate their use in two empirical case studies dealing with the analysis of variation in homicide rates across U.S. counties. The chapter concludes with a brief discussion of pressing issues for future research.

Background

An interest in the geographic dimension of crime can be traced to the very beginnings of criminology as a scientific discipline. In the mid-nineteenth century, the so-called moral statisticians, Quetelet and Guerry, used the newly published criminal statistics in France to search for social forces that might underlie criminal behavior (Radzinowicz 1966, 29–38). They constructed maps of crime totals for different regions in France and observed considerable stability over time. These stable patterns suggested to them that levels of crime are, to some extent, a reflection of the larger environment (social and physical). They proceeded to examine other features of the respective regions of France, searching for covariates that could account for the geographic patterning of crime.

In the early years of the twentieth century, members of the Chicago School of sociology embraced and extended the geographic approach pioneered by Quetelet and Guerry. The human ecology perspective of Burgess et al. (1925) focused attention squarely on the spatial context for social activities, and the empirical research of Shaw and McKay (1931, 1942) documented striking similarities in the distribution of officially recorded rates of juvenile delinquency across neighborhoods and the distribution of various indicators of housing structure, economic status, and population composition (Vold et al. 1998, 144–145). The common thread underlying this early work in the sociological study of crime was the premise that social phenomena, including criminal behavior, are not randomly distributed across the physical terrain, and as a result, inquiry into the spatial patterning of these phenomena can yield unique insight into their causal dynamics.

Interest in the geographic dimension of crime waned in the middle years of the twentieth century. As Coleman (1986) explains, major innovations in survey methodology fostered an "empirical behaviorism" in the field of sociology at large. This had two important implications for sociological studies of crime. One, the analytic focus in empirical research tended to shift away from social groups and territorially based social aggregates (e.g., neighborhoods, cities) to individuals (Bursik and Grasmick 1993, ix). Rather than studying variation in crime rates across areal units, researchers increasingly concentrated on explaining differences in individual involvement in criminal or delinquent activities.

The survey paradigm also encouraged researchers to conceptualize their units of analysis as *independent* observations, consistent with the survey model of random sampling from a population (Coleman 1986, 1316). This conceptualization extended beyond studies based on actual surveys of individuals to social structural analyses employing macro-level units. Thus, the upsurge in areal studies of homicide rates that appeared in the latter decades of the twentieth century (referred to above and reviewed by Land et al. 1990; see also Parker et al. 1999) reflected an accumulation of studies based almost exclusively on analytic and statistical methods that assume independence of observations, such as regression models estimated by Ordinary Least Squares (OLS). Independent observations are just that—they are unconnected in meaningful ways, including that of location in geographic space.

In recent years, criminologists have rediscovered the importance of geographic information in the study of crime. This is driven primarily by substantive motivations, as reflected in influential place-based theories of crime such as routine activities theory (Cohen and Felson 1979; Felson 1998) and crime pattern theory (Brantingham and Brantingham 1993; see also Anselin et al. 2000). Similarly, geographic space plays a central role in the burgeoning research on crime "hot spots" (Roncek and Maier 1991; Sherman et al. 1989; Sherman and Weisburd 1995), the diffusion of violence (Cohen and Tita 1999; Messner et al. 1999; Morenoff and Sampson 1997; Rosenfeld et al. 1999; Smith et al. 2000), and neighborhood collective efficacy (Sampson et al. 1997). The non-spatial modeling characteristic of earlier macro-level studies of crime has also been increasingly replaced by approaches that are keenly sensitive to spatial dynamics (e.g., Baller et al. 2001; Morenoff et al. 2001). This resurgence of interest in space has clearly been facilitated by the increased availability of georeferenced information on crime events and the dissemination of methods of spatial analysis to the practice of empirical research in criminology. Thus, at the turn of the twenty-first century, geographic space is returning to the forefront of criminological inquiry (Abbot 1997).

Generic Methodological Issues in the Analysis of Areal Data

Areal analyses in criminology are typically based on data aggregated for administrative spatial units of observation. The use of such units raises a number of fundamental methodological concerns. We will limit our focus here to three that are particularly important for spatial analysis: the relevance of scale and the associated problem of *ecological inference*; the intrinsic *heterogeneity* of rates; and the substantive *interpretation* of spatial autocorrelation in models estimated for aggregate areal units of observation.

Ecological inference and the associated issue of the ecological fallacy pertain to problems that may occur when phenomena observed at an aggregate level are explained in terms of an individual causal mechanism (King 1997). Unless rather extreme conditions of homogeneity are satisfied, such inference is misleading or spurious. Aggregate analyses, such as the study of homicide rates at the county or census tract level, are sometimes dismissed as naturally suffering from the ecological fallacy problem. Indeed, in a naïve interpretation of aggregate results, this may well be the case. However, there are many research questions (especially those with a public policy implication) that are legitimately carried out at the scale of the administrative units to which the policies will pertain. Specifically, when dealing with homicide rates, the main interest often lies in explaining patterns and correlates for underlying risk. This risk pertains to a population at risk, which can legitimately be taken as the population of an areal unit of observation. Accordingly, it is instructive to relate the levels of risk to other characteristics of populations. However, extending such a model to the interpretation of the causal dynamics underlying individual behavior would be spurious. We argue that in sociological studies of criminal violence, where the interest lies in macro conditions or context, an areal (or ecological) perspective using administrative units is legitimate. Moreover, it allows for a much richer empirical context in terms of the range of information available on covariates.

Scale is also important due to the potential mismatch between the scale and spatial extent of units of observation for the data and the scale and spatial extent of the process at hand. This mismatch will tend to result in a statistical problem wherein error structures are spatially correlated and/or heteroskedastic. Fortunately, this statistical problem can be addressed by applying proper spatial econometric methods.

A second methodological issue encountered in the use of areal data is the intrinsic heterogeneity of rates computed for varying populations at risk. Unless the areal units all have the same population, the variance of the rate (as an estimate for the parameter in an underlying binomial random variable) will not be constant, but instead is inversely related to the size of the population (larger populations yield more precise estimates). This is mostly a problem for "small area" estimation and is especially pronounced when the risk pertains to relatively rare events, such as homicides in rural counties. There are three important implications of this variance instability for the spatial analysis of homicide rates. First, the visualization of rates for areal units such as counties or census tracts, unless properly corrected (or smoothed), may yield spurious outliers. More precisely, since the estimates of underlying risk in areas with sparse populations will have a much greater variance, "spikes" are likely to be observed, even though the areas are subject to the same risk as other, more densely populated ones. This will affect the interpretation of results in an exploratory spatial data analysis (ESDA), as outlined in the next section. Secondly, the variance instability may yield spurious indications of significant spatial autocorrelation when using traditional statistics. All familiar test statistics (such as Moran's I and Geary's c) are based on an assumption of spatial stationarity, which includes a requirement for the variance of the process to be constant. The potential of extreme variance instability for rates of small areas violates this assumption, again possibly yielding misleading inference. Finally, the non-constant variance will be intrinsic to the error term in any regression model (aside from other sources of heteroskedasticity), and inference must be properly adjusted to take this into account.

A third issue pertains to the substantive interpretation of empirical results that suggest the presence of spatial autocorrelation in areal data, especially when the data are limited to a single cross-section. In this situation, it is impossible to distinguish true contagion from apparent contagion without additional information (such as space-time data). Any spatial cluster of similar values may be the result of a process of spillover, contagion, or spatial externalities, or instead, follow from structural differences due to an intervening (unobserved) variable specific to the locations in question. It is important to keep this limitation in mind when interpreting evidence of spatial autocorrelation. Similarly, spatial autocorrelation can be embedded in regression models in a variety of ways, each of which imply different types of spatial externalities. A common characteristic of these externalities is that, even though they are modeled as spatial relations between the dependent variable of the model (e.g., homicide rates), they ultimately result from spatial relations among the explanatory variables and/or the error terms in the model (Anselin 2003). Caution must be used in cross-sectional settings not to view the models as conditional upon *observed* neighbors. This easily leads to the trap of ecological fallacy. It also suggests an interpretation that implies the availability of observations over time as well as across space. However, in a pure cross-sectional setting, this is not the case. Instead, equilibrium must be assumed, and the nature of the dynamic processes (such as contagion or diffusion) that yielded the equilibrium cannot be inferred without further information.

Spatial Analyses of U.S. County Homicide Rates

Spatial analyses are potentially useful for addressing a variety of substantive issues in criminology. For present purposes, we focus on two questions that have been of keen interest in the homicide literature. The first deals with the potential impact of homicide in one place on the likelihood of homicide in nearby locations; i.e., is the spatial patterning of homicide consistent with some kind of diffusion process? Any phenomenon that is generated by diffusion should exhibit a distinctive geographic pattern that is non-random: higher incidences of the phenomenon should be observed near the location where the initial incidents occurred (the point of origin). The theoretical possibility that *criminal violence* might spread in such a manner from one place to another has been raised prominently in the public health literature (Hollinger et al. 1987; Kellerman 1996). Loftin, for example, proposes that criminal assaults can be usefully regarded as "analogous to disease," capable of "contagious transmission" (1986, 550). With the aide of formal techniques of spatial analysis, it is possible to search for spatial imprints of homicide that are suggestive of diffusion or contagion.

A second important question in the literature concerns the possible interaction of structural factors with features of the geographic context. Are the structural determinants of homicide rates invariant across space (cf. Land et al. 1990), or do structural conditions exert differing effects on homicide levels in various sub-regions of the geography? The tools of spatial analysis facilitate the identification of spatial regimes that are likely to exhibit distinct causal processes. These tools also provide formal tests of differences in the effects of predictor variables across regimes.

We illustrate the application of spatial analysis to address these substantive questions by referring to the results from two recent studies of county-level variation in homicide rates.[1] The first entails an exploratory spatial data analysis (ESDA) applied to a case study of homicides in the St. Louis region. The second study applies the techniques of spatial econometrics to a model with structural covariates for homicides, based on data for all counties in the continental United States.

The Diffusion of Homicide in the St. Louis Region: An Application of ESDA

Despite widespread speculation about possible diffusion processes in homicide, our understanding of the nature of such processes is primitive at best. Given such limited knowledge, an exploratory data analysis (EDA) approach is an extremely valuable starting point for systematic inquiry.

EDA consists of descriptive and graphical statistical tools intended to discover patterns in data and suggest hypotheses by imposing as little prior structure as possible (Tukey 1977). Contemporary EDA methods emphasize the interaction between human cognition and computation in the form of dynamically linked statistical graphics that allow the user to manipulate directly various views of the data (e.g., Buja et al. 1996: Cleveland 1993). ESDA extends standard EDA by focusing on techniques to describe and visualize spatial distributions, identify atypical locations or spatial outliers, discover patterns of spatial association, clusters, or hot spots, and suggest spatial regimes or other forms of spatial heterogeneity (Anselin 1994, 1998, 1999a; Bailey and Gatrell 1995; Haining 1990).

ESDA is especially useful in the study of possible diffusion processes, because it has at its core a formal treatment of the notion of *spatial autocorrelation*, i.e., the phenomenon where locational similarity (observations in spatial proximity) is matched by value similarity (attribute correlation) (see Cliff and Ord 1981, and Upton and Fingleton 1985, for extensive treatments). The particular ESDA techniques used for our illustrations focus on the detection of *local* patterns of spatial autocorrelation through the implementation of so-called LISA statistics (Anselin 1995) in dynamically linked graphic windows that visualize the location, magnitude, and pattern in the data, such as box maps, Moran scatterplots, and LISA maps (Anselin 1996; Anselin and Smirnov 1999; Anselin et al. 2002).

The areal units for our case-study investigation of diffusion processes are counties in the St. Louis Metropolitan Statistical Area (MSA) and additional counties within three layers of adjacency to the MSA.[2] For each of the counties in the region, rates were based on homicide counts aggregated by the decedents' county of residence (per 100,000). To compensate for the rate instability in areas with small populations, we smoothed the data by computing averages for two periods, 1984–1988 and 1988–1993. The earlier period is one of relative stability in homicide, while the latter is a period of generally increasing homicides.

We illustrate two distinctive aspects of ESDA. First, we consider selected maps and graphical statistics for the two time periods under investigation to bring out overall trends and to identify possible outliers (see Figure 7.1).[3] The specific graphics are: (1) Box Maps, which show the location (quartile) of every county within the overall distribution of homicide rates for the period, and (2) Box Plots, which show graphically the variation of homicide rates (see Anselin 1999a). In both the maps and plots outlier counties are identified.

Visual inspection of the Box Map for the period of stable homicide rates reveals that the counties tend to fall into two general regimes, defined by a diagonal line running from the upper left of the region to the lower right. Those counties falling below the diagonal show generally higher homicide rates (third and fourth quartiles). Between 1984 and 1988, only two areas had homicide rates so extremely high that they can be considered outliers—St. Louis City and St. Clair County, IL. These basic patterns in the geographic distribution of homicide might be viewed as evidence of a spatial clustering of homicide rates; however, as will be demonstrated below, that conclusion would be premature.

The geographic distribution of homicide appears to have shifted between the periods of stable and increasing homicide. The "southwest vs. northeast" division deteriorates somewhat over time, with more high-homicide counties becoming evident in the northeast quadrant. Indeed, an especially salient characteristic of the Box Map for the latter (increasing) period is the emergence of four additional outliers—Reynolds County, MO; Bond County, IL; Macon County, IL; and Cumberland County, IL. However, the substantive importance of these four new outliers should be interpreted cautiously. Their homicide rates are far more modest than those for the two outliers that appear in both Box Maps, and closer examination reveals that three of the new outliers (all except Macon County, IL) may have achieved that status because of variance instability.

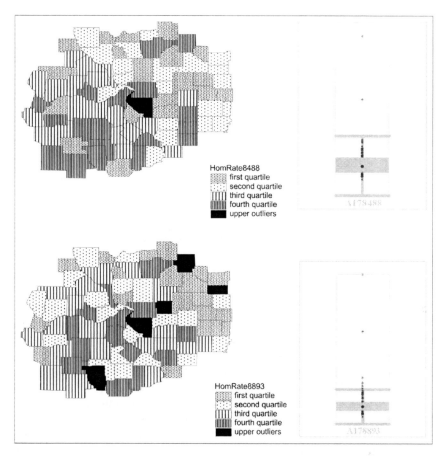

HomRate8488
- first quartile
- second quartile
- third quartile
- fourth quartile
- upper outliers

HomRate8893
- first quartile
- second quartile
- third quartile
- fourth quartile
- upper outliers

Figure 7.1. Box map (outlier map) and box plot (outlier plot) for homicide rates 1978–84 and 1988–93 in the St. Louis Region. The outliers in the Box Plot match the outlier locations in the Box Map. In a dynamically linked windows environment, these outliers are linked.

The Box Maps and Box Plots are useful for describing the general characteristics of the distribution of homicide throughout the seventy-eight-county area under study, and for revealing specific areas with exceptionally high levels of homicide. However, they are limited in their ability to identify any significant *spatial* clustering of homicide rates. To take into account the spatial arrangement of the homicide values, we make use of measures of spatial autocorrelation and specifically, local spatial autocorrelation.

Local indicators of spatial association (or LISA, an acronym coined in Anselin 1995) assess a null hypothesis of spatial randomness by comparing the values in each specific location with values in neighboring locations. Several LISA statistics can be considered, but a local version of Moran's *I* is particularly useful, in that it allows for the decomposition of the pattern of spatial association into four categories, corresponding with four quadrants in the Moran scatterplot (Anselin 1996). Two of these categories imply positive spatial association, namely, when an above-average value in

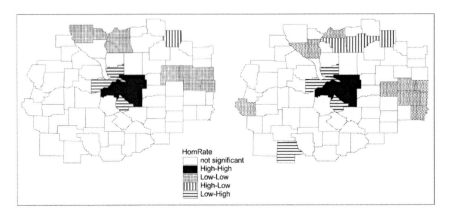

Figure 7.2. LISA maps for St. Louis region homicide rates, 1984–88 (left) and 1988–93 (right). Counties with significant Local Moran statistics are highlighted by the type of spatial association.

a location is surrounded by neighbors whose values are above average (high-high), or when a below-average value is surrounded by neighbors with below average values (low-low). By contrast, negative spatial association is implied when a high (above average) value is surrounded by low neighbors and vice versa. Both of these instances are labeled spatial outliers when the matching LISA statistics are significant. Each of the quadrants matches a different color in the so-called LISA Map, a map that shows the locations with significant LISA statistics (i.e., a rejection of the null hypothesis of spatial randomness) as well as the category of spatial association.

The classification into four categories of spatial association is illustrated by the maps in Figure 7.2. They match a Moran scatterplot (Figure 7.3), where the horizontal axis is expressed in standard deviational units for the homicide rate. The vertical axis represents the standardized spatial weighted average (average of the neighbors) for the homicide rates.[4] The slope of the linear regression through the scatterplot is the Moran's I coefficient, as shown in Anselin (1996). This allows for an easy interpretation of changes in global spatial association (the slope) as well as a focus on local spatial association (the quadrant). The scatterplot presented in Figure 7.3 also reports the Global Moran's I statistic described above as a measure of spatial autocorrelation among all counties in the analysis.

Beginning with the LISA Map for the period of stable homicide, we find evidence of spatial grouping. A cluster of counties with high homicide rates, as well as neighbors with high homicide rates, is apparent in the area around St. Louis City. This urban core of high homicide is also implicated in the three surrounding counties with low homicide rates, but high-homicide neighbors. These are suburban residential counties near the city of St. Louis. In addition, two clusters of low-homicide counties, surrounded by other counties with low homicide rates, can be seen in the northern and eastern fringes of the region. Consistent with a possible diffusion process, a distinct "hot spot" appears in the data centered on the St. Louis urban core, while "cool spots" are also detected in areas geographically removed from St. Louis.

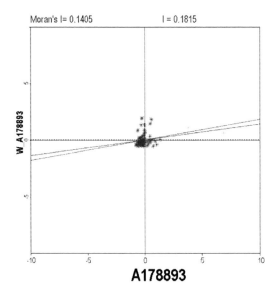

Moran's I= 0.1405   I = 0.1815

W_A178893

A178893

Figure 7.3. Moran scatterplot for
homicide rate in St. Louis region,
1988–93. Steepest slope is with two
central counties excluded. The slope
of each line is Moran's *I*.

Turning to the subsequent period during which homicide rates increased throughout
the region, the same general profile of spatial clustering appears. However, one notable
difference emerges during the later period, when both Sangamon and Morgan Counties
made the transition to high-homicide counties, surrounded by low-homicide counties.
In conjunction with Macon County, they now formed a string of counties (see the northern section of the map), suggesting the possible east-to-west diffusion of homicide out
of Macon County, as homicide in general increased throughout the region.

A final piece of evidence about the spatial clustering of homicide can be gleaned
from the Moran scatterplots. The overall clustering suggested by significant (global)
Moran's *I* statistics is not due simply to the disproportionate influence of the two neighboring counties with the highest homicide rates in the region—St. Louis City and St.
Clair County. In fact, the degree of spatial clustering *increases* for both time periods
when those two counties are omitted from the analysis, as shown in Figure 7.3 for the
later period (for further details, see Messner et al. 1999).

The application of ESDA to the St. Louis region provides suggestive evidence of a
diffusion process for homicide. The static comparisons of clustering in the two time
periods reveal a spatial imprint to be expected in the presence of past diffusion, and a
dynamic comparison across time periods indicates changes consistent with a westward
spread of homicides in a selected portion of the geography. We emphasize, however,
that ESDA is a starting point for analysis—it is explicitly *exploratory*. It permits rejection of the null hypothesis of spatial randomness, but processes other than diffusion
can produce spatial non-randomness. To illustrate the application of tools of spatial
analysis to detect some of these processes, we turn to our study based on county-level
data for the United States as a whole.

Modeling Homicide Rates across The United States: An Application of Spatial Econometrics

As noted at the beginning of this chapter, much of the initial interest in areal studies of homicide in the United States focused on the issue of regional differences and more specifically, the high homicide rate in the South. A large number of quantitative studies were conducted to determine whether the Southern effect on homicide rates persists after various social structural variables are taken into account in multivariate models. Although the results of this research are inconsistent (for a review, see Parker et al. 1999), it is hard to imagine that any serious quantitative study of homicide based on areal units for the nation at large would not take into account potential regional differences.

This interest in the geography of homicide has been largely limited to the level effect of region, i.e., whether homicide rates are higher in the South, even net of relevant control variables. Much less attention has been devoted to the possibility that geographic context might *condition* or *moderate* the effect of predictor variables (for an exception, see Messner 1983). The tools of spatial econometric modeling are especially well suited to address such an issue.

To explore the possibility of differential effects of homicide predictors across regions, we examined homicide rates calculated for each of the U.S. counties, smoothed over the three-year period centered on the Census years of 1960 to 1990 (i.e., observations for four time points). Our selection of independent variables was guided by the seminal work of Land et al. (1990). These variables include measures of resource deprivation/affluence, population structure, median age, unemployment, the percent divorced, and a dummy variable indicating Southern location (based on Census definitions). The measures of resource deprivation/affluence and population structure were constructed as composite indexes derived from principal components analysis.[5]

Before turning to spatial econometric models, consider a conventional, non-spatial model of homicide for the sample of U.S. counties. Table 7.1 presents the results of an OLS regression of homicide rates on the baseline model of predictors. Similar to the findings in Land et al. (1990), resource deprivation/affluence, population structure, and divorce are positively related to homicide rates. The negative effect of median age is also unsurprising, indicating that counties with younger populations have higher homicide rates. The negative coefficient for the percent unemployed is perhaps counterintuitive but consistent with the results of Land et al. (1990). They suggest that unemployment indicates reduced opportunity for violence (less social activity) once resource deprivation is controlled for (see also Cantor and Land 1985; Land et al. 1995). The significantly positive coefficient for the dummy variable for South reveals the often observed level effect of region—comparatively high homicide rates in the South. In general, these non-spatial results for counties mirror those found in empirical studies for other common areal units in the United States (cities, MSAs, and states).

To assess the extent of spatial effects, we carried out the usual spatial econometric battery of diagnostics for heteroskedasticity, spatial regimes, as well as *spatial lag* and *spatial error* dependence (Anselin 1988).[6] Both heteroskedasticity as well as spatial dependence were significantly present in the residuals of the OLS model.

Table 7.1. Ordinary least squares regression of county homicide rates 1960–1990.

Independent Variables	1960	1970	1980	1990
Resource dep/aff component	1.798*	2.913*	3.412*	3.872*
	[.318]	[0.396]	[0.500]	[0.583]
	(14.571)	(19.511)	(28.268)	(27.133)
Pop. structure component	.359*	0.812*	0.747*	1.353*
	[.064]	[0.111]	[0.109]	[0.204]
	(3.892)	(6.959)	(7.315)	(13.491)
Median age	−0.231*	−0.191*	−0.242*	−0.101*
	[−0.192]	[−0.130]	[−0.137]	[−0.055]
	(−11.931)	(−8.394)	(−9.671)	(−3.691)
Divorce	1.160*	1.264*	1.250*	0.583*
	[0.205]	[0.184]	[0.266]	[0.152]
	(12.233)	(12.109)	(18.586)	(10.690)
Unemployment	−0.062	−0.278*	−0.122*	−0.306*
	[−0.028]	[−0.087]	[−0.059]	[−0.141]
	(−1.762)	(−5.562)	(−3.965)	(−7.472)
South	2.639*	3.589*	2.113*	2.194*
	[0.233]	[0.243]	[0.154]	[0.165]
	(11.312)	(12.557)	(9.129)	(9.952)
Intercept	8.126*	8.653*	8.541*	6.517*
	(12.804)	(11.275)	(9.720)	(6.364)
Adj. R-squared	0.295	0.360	0.431	0.435
N	3085	3085	3085	3085

Unstandardized regression coefficients are reported (standardized regression coefficients in brackets, *t*-ratios in parentheses).

*$p < .01$ (two-tailed tests)

First, consider whether there is evidence to go beyond the simple level effect for the South. A test for structural stability of the regression coefficients across regions (a spatial Chow test; see Anselin 1990) permits a formal assessment of this (see Table 7.2). The null hypothesis of coefficient stability is clearly rejected, suggesting that the assumption of an identical (or stable) pattern of effects across regions is implausible. Moreover, an examination of the tests of individual coefficients reveals that several of the predictor variables exhibit significantly different effects in the South in comparison with the non-South. These results clearly run counter to the assumption that the same causal processes operate throughout the geography under investigation, an assumption that is implicit in non-spatial OLS analysis. Our analyses thus reveal not only that the South exhibits comparatively high homicide rates, even adjusting for social structural variables, but that the social structural variables commonly used in research *affect* homicide rates differently in the South than in other regions.

Furthermore, the estimates also indicate a larger residual variance for the model in the Southern counties, suggesting a poorer fit in this region. All of this suggests that the invariance of the Land et al. (1990) baseline model of homicide may have been

Table 7.2. Stability of regression coefficient by spatial regime—county homicide rates 1960–1990.

	1960	1970	1980	1990
Spatial Chow Test Overall stability[†]	150.527[*]	227.468[*]	162.712[*]	168.438[*]
Stability of individual coefficients (non-South versus South)[††]				
Res. dep. component	0.135	0.868	7.303[*]	36.065[*]
Pop. struc. component	0.118	0.286	32.490[*]	18.758[*]
Median Age	3.480	0.036	7.352[*]	0.982
Divorce	0.057	11.088[*]	15.822[*]	0.641
Unemployment	24.849[*]	45.870[*]	12.922[*]	28.150[*]
Heteroskedastic coefficients				
Non-South	9.776	16.016	21.750	16.209
South	36.930	54.544	30.451	34.204
Test on heteroskedasticity[††]	360.392[*]	328.375[*]	40.296[*]	164.284[*]
N (N of South)	3085 (1412)	3085 (1412)	3085 (1412)	3085 (1412)

[*] $p < .01$ (two-tailed tests)

[†] distributed as χ^2 with 6 degrees of freedom

[††] distributed as χ^2 with 1 degree of freedom

overstated. In addition, these results highlight the inadequacy of reducing spatial heterogeneity to a dummy variable for the South and the need to model regional variation in the effects of covariates explicitly.

Given the strong evidence of distinct spatial regimes in the South and non-South, we pursued a disaggregated modeling strategy by estimating separate models for each of the regions, examining the residuals for possible spatial effects and implementing a *spatial* regression model where appropriate. The spatial regression model takes the form of either a spatial lag model or a spatial error model. A spatial lag model implies that the geographic clustering of homicide is due to the influence of homicide in one place on homicide in another. This model is consistent with some kind of diffusion process. A spatial error model indicates that clustering reflects the influence of unmeasured variables. For the South, there was strong evidence of the need for a spatial lag specification in each of the years considered. In contrast, the results for the non-South suggested a lag model in 1960, but a spatial error model in the subsequent years.[7] Tables 7.3 and 7.4 summarize results for these spatial models in the Southern and non-Southern counties respectively.

Beginning with the results for the South (Table 7.3), the signs of the coefficients for structural covariates are generally consistent with those observed in non-spatial analyses for the full sample of counties. However, there are interesting changes in magnitudes (and significance) over time. The resource deprivation component is positively related to homicide rates throughout the period, but the strength of the effect steadily increases over time. The population structure variable exhibits non-significant effects in 1960 and 1970. It is only in the latter years (1980 and 1990) that the expected positive effects emerge. Divorce rates are significantly related to Southern homicide rates throughout the period, but the effect is noticeably weaker in 1990. Unemployment is

Table 7.3. Spatial lag models of Southern homicide rates 1960–1990.

Independent Variables	1960	1970	1980	1990
Resource dep/aff component	0.832**	1.792**	3.026**	4.028**
	[0.121]	[0.218]	[0.478]	[0.602]
	(3.386)	(5.820)	(13.994)	(14.814)
Pop. structure component	−0.057	0.401	1.551**	1.747**
	[−0.007]	[0.041]	[0.198]	[0.209]
	(−0.265)	(1.497)	(7.637)	(8.247)
Median age	−0.129**	−0.060	−0.150**	−0.018
	[−0.099]	[−0.039]	[−0.093]	[−0.009]
	(−2.942)	(−1.378)	(−3.736)	(−0.368)
Divorce	0.786**	0.642**	0.775**	0.482**
	[0.092]	[0.075]	[0.149]	[0.097]
	(3.241)	(3.060)	(6.302)	(4.251)
Unemployment	−0.070	−0.353**	−0.244**	−0.438**
	[−0.026]	[−0.092]	[−0.108]	[−0.191]
	(−0.897)	(−3.023)	(−4.145)	(−5.928)
Spatial lag (ρ)	0.713**	0.651**	0.182**	0.230**
	[0.379]	[0.359]	[0.100]	[0.125]
	(6.005)	(6.905)	(2.431)	(3.261)
Intercept	4.108*	4.153*	9.101**	5.249*
	(2.207)	(2.042)	(5.364)	(2.513)
Sq. corr.	0.178	0.239	0.311	0.333
N	1412	1412	1412	1412

IV estimation. Unstandardized regression coefficients are reported (standardized regression coefficients in brackets, t-ratios in parentheses)

** $p < .01$ (two-tailed tests)

negatively related to homicide rates in all years except 1960, while median age exhibits significantly negative effects sporadically.

Table 7.3 also indicates that the effects of the Southern spatial lags of homicide are positive and statistically significant in all time periods. These findings support the claim that homicides in Southern counties influence homicides in other counties, consistent with a diffusion interpretation. Note also, however, that the effects of the spatial lags generally weaken over time. An examination of the betas indicates that the spatial lags are the strongest predictors of Southern homicide in 1960 and 1970 but are eclipsed by the structural predictors in 1980 and 1990.

Turning to the non-South (Table 7.4), the results for the structural covariates are quite similar to those for all counties in the non-spatial analyses, with the exception of the unemployment variable. Resource deprivation, population structure, and divorce exhibit significantly positive effects on homicide rates, while median age yields significantly negative effects. The only significant effect for unemployment is in 1970, and it is positive, contrary to the general pattern.

With respect to spatial dependence, in every year except for 1960 the spatial error model provides a better fit in the non-South than does the spatial lag model. Substan-

Table 7.4. Spatial regression models of non-Southern homicide rates.

Independent Variables	1960	1970	1980	1990
Resource dep/aff component	1.571**	3.007**	4.143**	2.875**
	[0.275]	[0.389]	[0.467]	[0.405]
	(9.395)	(14.626)	(19.837)	(13.435)
Pop. structure component	0.386**	0.859**	0.290*	0.962**
	[0.126]	[0.211]	[0.056]	[0.229]
	(5.011)	(7.795)	(2.132)	(8.299)
Median age	−0.156**	−0.157**	−0.304**	−0.066*
	[−0.191]	[−0.163]	[−0.197]	[−0.050]
	(−7.336)	(−6.452)	(−8.607)	(−2.034)
Divorce	0.833**	1.403**	1.318**	0.572**
	[0.276]	[0.359]	[0.366]	[0.239]
	(8.552)	(13.980)	(14.560)	(9.156)
Unemployment	0.079**	−0.024	0.008	−0.045
	[0.061]	[−0.013]	[0.005]	[−0.029]
	(2.622)	(−0.502)	(0.196)	(−0.888)
Spatial lag (ρ)	0.415**	NI	NI	NI
	[.197]			
	(4.645)			
Spatial error (λ)	NI	0.243**	0.329**	0.268**
Intercept	4.832**	6.164**	9.622**	3.261**
	(6.544)	(7.309)	(7.588)	(2.621)
Sq. corr.	0.199	0.234	0.348	0.258
N	1673	1673	1673	1673

Instrumental Variables estimation in 1960, Generalized Moments in 1970–1990. Unstandardized regression coefficients are reported (standardized regression coefficients in brackets, t-ratios in parentheses). No significance is reported for the λ parameter estimated by means of the Generalized Moments technique. Significance is based on rejection of the null hypothesis in the OLS regression.

**$p < .01$ *$p < .01$ (two-tailed tests)

tively, this implies that, for the most part, the residual spatial autocorrelation in the non-South can be adequately accounted for in terms of unmeasured predictor variables. A diffusion process thus seems unlikely in non-Southern counties over recent decades.

In sum, our application of techniques of spatial modeling in the case study of U.S. counties demonstrated striking spatial patterns of homicide. Homicide researchers should attend to these patterns for at least two very important reasons: spatial dependence needs to be modeled properly to estimate the effects of non-spatial variables, and spatial dependence directs attention to potentially interesting substantive processes, such as diffusion.

Conclusion

The two case studies reviewed above illustrate the utility of exploiting an explicit spatial perspective in the analysis of homicide. Apart from purely methodological reasons to pursue such an approach, such as the inefficiency and biases in coefficient estimates that may result when spatial effects are ignored, substantive insights were gained as well.

Importantly, the explicit spatial approach allowed us to identify the incompleteness of well-accepted baseline models. It provided a way to move beyond simple dummy variable proxies for geography and permitted the assessment of the degree of regional heterogeneity in much greater detail. This points to the need for extending the baseline model of homicide with variables that can capture the suggested regional effects.

A spatial approach also allows one to shed some light on the presence of potential diffusion processes. Most importantly, the distinction between different spatial econometric specifications provides grounds to dismiss diffusion, or alternatively, to identify the types of spatial externalities or spillovers that may be instrumental in generating the observed spatial patterns.

Our approach is only the beginning, however. Powerful models of the dynamics of the space-time evolution of homicide and other violent crime still largely remain to be formulated. Recently developed methods for the spatial econometrics of panel data are very promising in this respect. The procedures for identifying clusters, outliers, and spatial regimes discussed in this chapter are only initial steps in the understanding of these patterns. Richer models and additional specifications need to be considered, and the underlying vectors of transmission yielding the spatial patterns or outliers need to be identified. Successful efforts along these lines are likely to require more sophisticated *theorizing* about the determinants of levels of homicide risk across varying populations.

Much remains to be done, but the current methods of exploratory spatial data analysis and spatial econometrics provide a solid base for further inquiry. It is our hope that the examples provided here will stimulate future work of both an inductive and deductive nature to enhance our understanding of homicide and to promote a spatially informed criminology more generally.

Acknowledgments Support for this research was provided by a grant from the National Consortium on Violence Research (NCOVR). NCOVR is supported under grant # SBR 9513040 from the National Science Foundation. Support was also provided by a grant from NSF to the Center for Spatially Integrated Social Science (BCS-9978058) and by grants to the Center for Social and Demographic Analysis (SUNY-Albany) from NICHD (P30 HD32041) and NSF (SBR-9512290). Any opinions, findings, conclusions or recommendations expressed herein are those of the authors and do not necessarily reflect the views of the funding agencies.

Notes

1. These studies are reported in Messner et al. (1999) and Baller et al. (2001). The discussion below draws upon these sources.
2. See Messner et al. (1999) for a detailed description of data sources and variable definitions.
3. Note that in a software implementation of ESDA, these graphs would be linked in real-time, to allow for interaction with the various views of the data, see Anselin et al. (2002).
4. The spatial correlation statistics were based on a spatial weights matrix that labeled counties as neighbors when their centroids (centers of gravity) were within 31.7 miles from each other; for details, see Messner et al. (1999).

5. See Baller et al. (2001), for a detailed description of data definitions and data sources.
6. All computations were carried out by means of the SpaceStat software package (Anselin 1999b).
7. For detailed results, see Baller et al. (2001).

References

Abbot, A. 1997. Of time and space: The contemporary relevance of the Chicago School. *Social Forces* 75: 1149–1182.

Anselin, L. 1988. *Spatial Econometrics: Methods and Models*. Boston: Kluwer Academic.

Anselin, L. 1990. Spatial dependence and spatial structural instability in applied regression analysis. *Journal of Regional Science* 30: 185–207.

Anselin L. 1994. Exploratory spatial data analysis and geographic information systems. In M. Painho (ed.), *New Tools for Spatial Analysis*, Luxembourg: EuroStat, 45–54.

Anselin, L. 1995. Local indicators of spatial association LISA. *Geographical Analysis* 27: 93–115.

Anselin, L. 1996. The Moran scatterplot as an ESDA tool to assess local instability in spatial association. In *Spatial Analytical Perspectives on GIS in Environmental and Socio-Economic Sciences*. London: Taylor and Francis, 111–125.

Anselin, L. 1998. Exploratory spatial data analysis in a geocomputational environment. In P.A. Longley, S. Brooks, B. Macmillan, and R. McDonnell (eds.), *Geocomputation, A Primer*, New York: John Wiley, 77–94.

Anselin, L. 1999a. Interactive techniques and exploratory spatial data analysis. In P.A. Longley, M.F. Goodchild, D.J. Maguire, and D.W. Rhind (eds.), *Geographic Information Systems: Principles, Techniques, Management and Applications*, New York: John Wiley, 251–264.

Anselin, L. 1999b. *SpaceStat Software Program for Spatial Data Analysis*, Version 1.90. Ann Arbor, Mich.: BioMedware Inc.

Anselin, L. 2003. Spatial externalities, spatial multipliers and spatial econometrics. *International Regional Science Review* 26(2): 153–166..

Anselin, L., J. Cohen, D. Cook, W. Gorr, and G. Tita. 2000. Spatial analyses of crime. In D. Duffee (ed.), *Criminal Justice 2000, Volume 4, Measurement and Analysis of Crime and Justice*. Washington, D.C.: National Institute of Justice, 213–262.

Anselin, L., and O. Smirnov. 1999. *The DynESDA Extension for ArcView 3.0*. University of Texas at Dallas. Richardson, Tex., Bruton Center.

Anselin, L., I. Syabri, O. Smirnov, and Y. Ren. 2002. Visualizing spatial autocorrelation with dynamically linked windows. *Computing Science and Statistics* 33, in press.

Bailey, T.C., and A.C. Gatrell. 1995. *Interactive Spatial Data Analysis*. New York: John Wiley.

Baller, R.D., L. Anselin, S.F. Messner, G. Deane, and D.F. Hawkins. 2001. Structural covariates of U.S. county homicide rates: Incorporating spatial effects. *Criminology* 39: 201–232.

Brantingham, P.L., and P.J. Brantingham. 1993. Environment, routine and situation: Toward a pattern theory of crime. In R.V. Clarke, and M. Felson (eds.), *Routine Activity and Rational Choice: Advances in Criminological Theory, Vol. 5*, New Brunswick, N.J.: Transaction Books, 259–294.

Buja, A., D. Cook, and D. Swayne. 1996. Interactive High Dimensional Data Visualization. *Journal of Computational and Graphical Statistics* 5: 78–99.

Burgess, E., R.E. Park, and R.D. McKenzie. 1925. *The City*. Chicago: University of Chicago Press.

Bursik, R.J. Jr., and H.G. Grasmick. 1993. *Neighborhoods and Crime: The Dimensions of Effective Community Control*. New York: Lexington Books.

Cantor, D., and K.C. Land. 1985. Unemployment and crime rates in the post-World War II United States: A theoretical and empirical analysis. *American Sociological Review* 50: 317–332.

Cleveland, W.S. 1993. *Visualizing Data.* Summit, N.J.: Hobart Press.

Cliff, A., and J.K. Ord. 1981. *Spatial Processes: Models and Applications.* London: Pion.

Cohen, J., and G. Tita. 1999. Diffusion in homicide: Exploring a general model for detecting spatial diffusion processes. *Journal of Quantitative Criminology* 15: 451–493.

Cohen, L.E., and M. Felson. 1979. Social change and crime rate trends: A routine activities approach. *American Sociological Review* 44: 588–608.

Coleman, J.S. 1986. Social theory, social research, and a theory of action. *American Journal of Sociology* 91: 1309–1335.

Felson, M. 1998. *Crime and Everyday Life, 2nd Ed.* Thousand Oaks, Calif.: Pine Forge Press.

Haining, R.F. 1990. *Spatial Data Analysis in the Social and Environmental Sciences.* Cambridge: Cambridge University Press.

Hawley, F.F., and S.F. Messner. 1989. The Southern violence construct: A review of arguments, evidence, and the normative context. *Justice Quarterly* 6: 481–511.

Hollinger, P.C., D. Offer, and E. Ostrov. 1987. An epidemiologic study of violent death, population changes, and the potential for prediction. *American Journal of Psychiatry* 144: 215–219.

Kellerman, A. 1996. *Understanding and Preventing Violence: A Public Health Perspective.* National Institute of Justice Review. Washington, D.C.: U.S. Government Printing Office.

King, G. 1997. *A Solution to the Ecological Inference Problem.* Princeton: Princeton University Press.

Land, K.C., D. Cantor, and S.T. Russell. 1995. Unemployment and crime rate fluctuations in the post-World War II United States: Statistical time-series properties and alternative models. In J. Hagan, and R.D. Peterson (eds.), *Crime and Inequality.* Stanford, Calif.: Stanford University Press, 55–79.

Land, K.C., P.L. McCall, and L.E. Cohen. 1990. Structural covariates of homicides rates: Are there any invariances across time and space. *American Journal of Sociology* 96: 1441–1463.

Loftin, C. 1986. Assaultive violence as a contagious process. *Bulletin of New York Academy of Medicine* 62: 550–555.

Messner, S.F. 1983. Regional differences in the economic correlates of the urban homicide rate: Some evidence on the importance of the cultural context. *Criminology* 21: 477–488.

Messner, S.F., L. Anselin, R.D. Baller, D.F. Hawkins, G. Deane, and S.E. Tolnay. 1999. The spatial patterning of county homicide rates: An application of exploratory spatial data analysis. *Journal of Quantitative Criminology* 15: 423–450.

Morenoff, J.D., and R.J. Sampson. 1997. Violent crime and the spatial dynamics of neighborhood transition: Chicago, 1970–1990. *Social Forces* 76: 31–64.

Morenoff, J.D., R.J. Sampson, and S.W. Raudenbush. 2001. Neighborhood inequality, collective efficacy, and the spatial dynamics of urban violence. *Criminology* 39: 517–560.

Parker, K.F., P.L. McCall, and K.C. Land. 1999. Determining social-structural predictors of homicide: Units of analysis and related methodological concerns. In M.D. Smith, and M.A. Zahn (eds.), *Homicide Studies: A Sourcebook of Social Research,* Thousand Oaks, Calif.: Sage, 107–124.

Radzinowicz, L. 1966. *Ideology and Crime.* New York: Columbia University Press.

Roncek, D.W., and P.A. Maier. 1991. Bars, blocks, and crimes revisited: Linking the theory of routine activities to the empiricism of hot spots. *Criminology* 29: 725–755.

Rosenfeld, R., T.M. Bray, and A. Egley. 1999. Facilitating violence: A comparison of gang-motivated, gang-affiliated, and nongang youth homicide. *Journal of Quantitative Criminology* 15: 495–516.

Sampson, R.J., S.W. Raudenbush, and F. Earls. 1997. Neighborhoods and violent crime: A multilevel study of collective efficacy. *Science* 277: 918–924.

Shaw, C.R., and H.D. McKay. 1931. *Social Factors in Delinquency*. Chicago: University of Chicago Press.

Shaw, C.R., and H.D. McKay. 1942. *Juvenile Delinquency and Urban Areas*. Chicago: University of Chicago Press.

Sherman, L.W., and D. Weisburd. 1995. General deterrent effects of police patrol in crime 'hot spots': A randomized, controlled trial. *Justice Quarterly* 12: 625–648.

Sherman, L.W., P.R. Gartin, and M.E. Buerger. 1989. Hot spots of predatory crime: routine activities and the criminology of place. *Criminology* 27: 27–55.

Smith, W.R., S.G. Frazee, and E.L. Davison. 2000. Furthering the integration of routine activity and social disorganization theories: small units of analysis and the study of street robbery as a diffusion process. *Criminology* 38: 489–523.

Tukey, J. 1977. *Exploratory Data Analysis*. Reading, Pa.: Addison Wesley.

Upton, G., and B. Fingleton. 1985. *Spatial Data Analysis by Example*. New York: John Wiley.

Vold, G.B., T.J. Bernard, and J.B. Snipes. 1998. *Theoretical Criminology, Fourth Edition*. New York: Oxford University Press.

8

Spatial (Dis)Advantage and Homicide in Chicago Neighborhoods

Robert J. Sampson

Jeffrey D. Morenoff

For some time now, research in the ecological tradition has demonstrated the concentration of interpersonal violence in certain neighborhoods, especially those areas characterized by poverty, the racial segregation of minority groups, and single-parent families. Still, fundamental questions remain about what it is about these communities that might explain the link between structural features of neighborhood environments and rates of violent crime. The traditional or perhaps idyllic notion of local communities as "urban villages" characterized by dense networks of personal social ties continues to pervade many theoretical perspectives on neighborhood crime. Yet such ideal typical neighborhoods bear little resemblance to contemporary cities, where weak ties prevail over strong ties and social interaction among residents is characterized by increasing instrumentality. The urban village model is also premised on the notion that networks of personal ties and associations map neatly onto the geographic boundaries of spatially defined neighborhoods, such that neighborhoods can be analyzed as independent social entities. Modern neighborhoods are often less distinctly defined, with permeable borders. Social networks in this setting are likely to traverse traditional ecological boundaries, implying a spatial interdependence among social processes.

This chapter builds on recent criminological research to integrate key dimensions of neighborhood-level structure, social processes, and spatial embeddedness to address the question of crime's ecological concentration. In particular, we examine the extra-local processes related to the spatial dynamics of violent crime, along with more local institutional processes related to voluntary associations and neighborhood organizations. We interpret these dimensions of the urban landscape with a theoretical framework highlighting the role of social control and cohesion—or what we have termed collective efficacy—and neighborhood structural inequality. Our focus on inequality

145

centers on the extreme concentration of socioeconomic resources at both the upper and lower tails of the distribution and on spatial inequality in social processes.

Spatial Dynamics

Contrary to the common assumption in ecological criminology of analytic independence, we argue that neighborhoods are *inter*dependent and characterized by a functional relationship between what happens at one point in space and what happens elsewhere. Spatial interdependence is theoretically motivated on three grounds. First, we expect it to arise as a result of the inexact correspondence between the neighborhood boundaries imposed by census geography and the ecological properties that shape social interaction. One of the biggest criticisms of neighborhood-level research to date concerns the artificiality of boundaries; for example, two families living across the street from one another may be arbitrarily assigned to live in different "neighborhoods" even though they share social ties. From the standpoint of systemic theory, it is important to account for the social and institutional ties that link residents of urban communities to other neighborhoods, particularly those that are more spatially proximate to their own neighborhood. Spatial models address this problem by recognizing the interwoven dependence among (artificial) neighborhood units. The idea of spatial dependence thus challenges the urban village model, which implicitly assumes that geographically defined neighborhoods represent intact social systems that function as islands unto themselves, isolated from the wider sociodeomographic dynamics of the city.

Second, spatial dependence is implicated by the fact that homicide offenders are disproportionately involved in acts of violence near their homes (Block 1977; Reiss and Roth 1993). From a routine activities perspective, it follows that a neighborhood's "exposure" to homicide risk is heightened by geographical proximity to places where known offenders live (see also Cohen et al. 1981). Moreover, to the extent that the risk of becoming a homicide offender is influenced by contextual factors such as concentrated poverty, concentrated affluence, and collective efficacy, spatial proximity to such conditions is also likely to influence the risk of homicide victimization in a focal neighborhood.

A third motivation for studying spatial dependence relates to the notion that interpersonal crimes such as homicide are based on social interaction and thus, subject to diffusion processes (Cohen and Tita 1999; Messner et al. 1999; Morenoff and Sampson 1997; Rosenfeld et al. 1999; Smith et al. 2000). Acts of violence may themselves instigate a sequence of events that leads to further violence in a spatially channeled way. For example, many homicides, not just gang-related, are retaliatory in nature (Black 1983; Block 1977). Thus, a homicide in one neighborhood may provide the spark that eventually leads to a retaliatory killing in a nearby neighborhood. In addition, most homicides occur among persons known to one another (Reiss and Roth 1993), usually involving networks of association that follow geographical vectors.

There is, then, reason to believe that spatial dependence arises from processes related to both diffusion and exposure, such that the characteristics of surrounding neighborhoods are, at least in theory, crucial to understanding violence in any given neighborhood. The diffusion perspective focuses on the consequences of crime itself as they are played out over time and space—crime in one neighborhood may be the cause of future crime in another neighborhood. The concept of exposure focuses on the antecedent conditions that foster crime, which are also spatially and temporally ordered. Although both concepts provide strong justification for analyzing spatial dependence, criminological research has been surprisingly slow to adapt tools of spatial analysis, especially in a regression framework that accounts for a competing explanation of clustering—selection effects based on population composition (see also Rosenfeld et al. 1999; Smith et al. 2000). In this chapter, we therefore focus on the independent effect of spatial proximity on the likelihood of homicide, accounting for key structural and social characteristics of life within the boundaries of focal neighborhoods.

Informal and Institutional Processes

Our second major goal is to integrate the study of neighborhood mechanisms with regard to informal and institutional social processes. Neighborhood-level social processes are not easy to study, of course, because the socio-demographic characteristics drawn from census data and other government statistics typically do not provide information on the collective properties of administrative units. Of those studies that have focused on social processes, most have focused on social ties and interaction to the exclusion of organizations (see Peterson et al. 2000). For example, Sampson et al.'s (1997) test of collective efficacy highlighted cohesion and mutual expectations among residents for control. But as alluded to earlier, communities can exhibit intense private ties (e.g., among friends, kin), and perhaps even shared expectations for control, yet still lack the institutional capacity to achieve social control. The institutional component of social capital is the resource stock of neighborhood organizations and their linkages with other organizations. Bursik and Grasmick (1993a) also highlight the importance of public control, defined as the capacity of community organizations to obtain extra-local resources (e.g., police protection, block grants, health services) that help sustain neighborhood stability and control. It may be that high levels of collective efficacy come about because of such controls, such as a strong institutional presence and intensity of voluntary associations. Or it may be that the presence of institutions directly accounts for lower rates of crime. Relatively few studies have examined voluntary associations, and almost none a community's organizational base (for a review see Sampson et al. 2002). In addition to incorporating the systemic dimensions of collective efficacy and social ties, we therefore address this gap by simultaneously examining institutional density and the intensity of local voluntary associations.

In short, this chapter presents a substantive and methodological framework for studying the spatial dynamics of violence in neighborhood contexts. Criminal events require the intersection in time and space of three elements—motivated offenders, suitable targets, and the absence of capable guardians (Cohen and Felson 1979). As such, crime can be ecologically concentrated because of the presence of targets and/or the absence of guardianship (e.g., collective efficacy), even if the pool of motivated offenders is more evenly distributed across the city. We are thus interested in how neighborhoods fare as units of guardianship and collective efficacy; the outcome is the rate of homicide and robbery victimization. Applying this framework, we highlight two neglected dimensions of neighborhood context: (1) spatial dynamics arising from neighborhood interdependence, and (2) social-institutional processes.

Data Sources

The data on neighborhood social processes stem from the Community Survey of the Project on Human Development in Chicago Neighborhoods (PHDCN). The extensive social-class, racial, and ethnic diversity of the population was a major reason Chicago was selected for the study. Chicago's 865 census tracts were combined to create 343 "Neighborhood Clusters" (NCs) composed of geographically contiguous and socially similar census tracts. NCs are smaller than Chicago's 77 community areas (average size = 40,000) but large enough to approximate local neighborhoods, averaging around 8,000 people. Major geographic boundaries (e.g., railroad tracks, parks, freeways), knowledge of Chicago's local neighborhoods, and cluster analyses of census data were used to guide the construction of relatively homogeneous NCs with respect to distributions of racial-ethnic mix, socio-economic status (SES), housing density, and family structure. The Community Survey (CS) of the PHDCN was conducted in 1995, when 8,782 Chicago residents representing all 343 NCs were personally interviewed in their homes.[1] The basic design for the CS had three stages: at stage 1, city blocks were sampled within each NC; at stage 2, dwelling units were sampled within blocks, and at stage 3, one adult resident (18 or older) was sampled within each selected dwelling unit. Abt Associates carried out the screening and data collection in cooperation with PHDCN, achieving an overall response rate of 75 percent.

To assess collective efficacy we replicated Sampson et al. (1997) and combined two related scales. The first is a five-item Likert-type scale of *shared expectations for social control*. Residents were asked about the likelihood that their neighbors could be counted on to take action if: children were skipping school and hanging out on a street corner, children were spray-painting graffiti on a local building, children were showing disrespect to an adult, a fight broke out in front of their house, and the fire station closest to home was threatened with budget cuts. *Social cohesion/trust* was measured by asking respondents how strongly they agreed that "People around here are willing to help their neighbors"; "This is a close-knit neighborhood"; "People in this neighborhood can be trusted"; "People in this neighborhood generally don't get along with each other" (reverse coded); and "People in this neighborhood do not share the same values" (reverse coded). Social cohesion and informal social control were strongly related across neighborhood clusters (r = .80), and following Sampson et al. (1997), were combined into a summary measure of the higher-order construct, "collective efficacy." The aggregate-level or "ecometric" reliability (see Raudenbush and Sampson 1999) of collective efficacy was .85.[2]

In addition to the cohesion and control scales that define collective efficacy, our analysis takes into account institutional neighborhood processes and social networks. *Organizations* is an index of the number of survey-reported organizations and programs in the neighborhood—the presence of community newspaper, block group or tenant association, crime prevention program, alcohol/drug treatment program, mental health center, or family health service. *Voluntary associations* taps the "social capital" involvement by residents in (1) local religious organizations, (2) neighborhood watch programs, (3) block group, tenant associations, or community council, (4) business or civic groups, (5) ethnic or nationality clubs, and (6) local political organizations. The measure of *social ties/networks* is based on the combined average of two measures capturing the number of friends and relatives living in the neighborhood.

Unlike the full-count census measures described below, our community survey measures of social process are based on only about 25 respondents per neighborhood cluster. Moreover, there are differential missing data by items in the scales. To account for measurement error and missing data we employ the empirical Bayes (EB) residuals of the key survey-based predictors—collective efficacy, social ties, organizations, and voluntary associations. EB residuals are defined as the least squares residuals regressed toward zero by a factor proportional to their unreliability (Bryk and Raudenbush 1992, 42). Using EB residuals as explanatory variables corrects for bias in regression coefficients resulting from measurement error (Whittemore 1989).

Structural Characteristics

Based on the 1990 census and our theoretical framework, we examine five neighborhood structural characteristics. All scales are based on the summation of equally weighted z-scores divided by the number of items; factor-weighted scales yielded the same results. *Concentrated disadvantage* represents economic disadvantage in racially segregated urban neighborhoods. It is defined by the percentage of families below the poverty line, percentage of families receiving public assistance, percentage of unemployed individuals in the civilian labor force, percentage of families with children that are female-headed, and percentage of residents who are black. These variables are highly interrelated and load on a single factor using either principal components or alpha-scoring factor analysis with an oblique rotation (see also Sampson et al. 1997, 920). This result makes sense ecologically, reflecting neighborhood segregation mechanisms that concentrate the poor, African-Americans, and single-parent families with children (Bursik and Grasmick 1993b; Land et al. 1990; Massey and Denton 1993; Wilson 1987).

In such a segregated context, it is problematic at best to try and separate empirically the influence of percent black from the other components of the disadvantage scale, for there are in fact no white neighborhoods that map onto the distribution of extreme disadvantage that black neighborhoods experience (Krivo and Peterson 2000; Sampson and Wilson 1995). For example, if one divides Chicago into thirds on concentrated poverty, there are no white neighborhoods in Chicago that fall into the high category (Sampson et al. 1997). Even though traditional in criminology, regression models that enter both percent black and disadvantage thus assume a reality counter to fact. We address this race issue in two ways. First, we assess whether the structural, social, and spatial processes specified in our models vary across regimes defined by racial composition. In other words, although we cannot reliably disentangle the direct effects of race and disadvantage, we address the possibility that racial composition interacts with other variables. Second, we test the robustness of main results, other than disadvantage, to traditional controls for percent black.

Focusing on the pernicious effects of concentrated disadvantage, while obviously important, may obscure the potential *protective* effects of affluent neighborhoods. After all, concentrated affluence may be more than just the absence of disadvantage. Recent years have seen the increasing separation of affluent residents from middle class areas (Massey 1996), a phenomenon not captured by traditional measures of poverty. Moreover, Brooks-Gunn et al. (1993) argue that concentrated affluence generates a separate set of protective mechanisms based on access to social and institutional resources. The resources that affluent neighborhoods can mobilize are theoretically relevant to understanding the activation of social control, regardless of dense social ties and other elements of social capital that might be present. In support of this notion, recent work has demonstrated the importance of measuring the upper tail of the SES distribution when analyzing structural characteristics and youth outcomes (Brooks-Gunn et al. 1993; Sampson et al. 1999). We thus extend our focus by introducing a measure that captures the concentration of both poverty and affluence. The index of concentration at the extremes (ICE) (Massey 2001) is defined for a given neighborhood by the following formula: [(number of affluent families − number of poor families) / total number of families], where "affluent" is defined as families with income above \$50,000, and "poor" is defined as families below the poverty line. The ICE index ranges from a theoretical value of −1 (which represents extreme poverty, namely that all families are poor) to +1 (which signals extreme affluence, namely that all families are affluent). A value of zero indicates that there is an equal share of poor and affluent families living in the neighborhood. ICE is therefore an inequality measure that taps both ends of the income distribution, or as Massey (2001, 44) argues, the *proportional* imbalance between affluence and poverty within a neighborhood.

Other structural covariates include the relative presence of *adults per child* (ratio of adults 18+ to children under 18) and *population density* (number of persons per square kilometer). We also build on Sampson et al. (1997) by examining two additional structural characteristics long noted in the ecological literature. *Residential stability* is defined as the percentage of residents five years old and older who lived in the same house five years earlier, and the percentage of homes that are owner-occupied. The second scale captures areas of *concentrated Latino immigration*, defined by the percentage of Latino residents (in Chicago approximately 70 percent of Latinos are Mexican-American) and percentage of persons foreign born.

Violence Measures

To eliminate method-induced associations between outcomes and predictors, we examine two independent measures of homicide relative to our survey-based approach to measuring social process and census-based approach to measuring structural covariates. We analyze homicide as an indicator of neighborhood violence, both because of its indisputable centrality to debates about crime, and because it is widely considered to be the most accurately recorded of all crimes. Our principal data source comes from reports of homicide incidents to the Chicago Police Department. These data consist of aggregate homicide counts that have been geo-coded to match the neighborhood cluster in which the events occurred. We use the homicide count data from two time periods, the years 1991 to 1993 and the years 1996 to 1998.[3] Because homicide is a rare event, we construct rates based on three-year counts for both periods to reduce measurement error and stabilize rates. We replicate the main analysis on a person-based measure of homicide victimization in 1996 derived from vital statistics rather than police records.[4] The original source here was death-record information found in the coroner's report and recorded in vital statistics data for Chicago, which were geocoded based on the home address of the victim.[5] To the extent that basic patterns are similar across recording systems with obviously different error structures, we can place increased confidence in the results of independently measured predictors. Nevertheless, we privilege the incident-based homicide measure from police statistics as our primary outcome, because our theoretical perspective, grounded in the social control of routine activities, places its analytic focus on the neighborhood factors that might suppress the occurrence of homicide events within its boundaries.

Sampson et al. (1997) analyzed violence measured at the same time (1995) as the survey of collective efficacy, meaning that the outcome could have influenced the alleged explanatory factors. By contrast, we assess the ability of our model to predict future variations in violence. Specifically, the census-based factors (1990) and survey-based processes (1995) were measured temporally prior to the event counts of homicide in 1996–1998. Moreover, we address the potential endogeneity of collective efficacy with respect to past violence by explicitly controlling for the rate of violent events in 1992–1993. It may be that neighborhood social trust and residents' sense of control are undermined by experiences with crime, most notably interpersonal crimes of violence and those committed in public by strangers (Bellair 2000; Liska and Bellair 1995; Skogan 1990). Ours is a strict test, because the strong temporal dependence in violence (e.g., the correlation between 1991–1993 and 1996–1998 is .79 for incidence rates) may yield unduly conservative estimates of any of the predictors. This procedure also gives us some purchase on controlling for prior sources of crime not captured in our measured variables.[6]

Statistical Models and Spatial Framework

There are three major features of our approach and data that must be represented in our statistical model: the conception of the outcome as a count of rare events (homicides); the likely unexplained variation between neighborhoods in the underlying latent event rates; and the spatial embeddedness of neighborhood processes. Our model views the homicide count Y_i for a given neighborhood as sampled from an over-dispersed Poisson distribution with mean $n_i \lambda_i$, where n_i is the population size in 100,000s of neighborhood i, and λ_i is the latent or "true" homicide rate for neighborhood i per 100,000 people. We view the log-event rates as normally distributed across neighborhoods. However, we conceive of these log-event rates as spatially auto-correlated. More specifically, using a hierarchical generalized linear model approach (McCullagh and Nelder 1989), we set the natural log link $\eta_i = \log(\lambda_i)$ equal to a mixed linear model that includes relevant neighborhood covariates, a random effect for each neighborhood, plus a spatial autocorrelation term. Thus, our model for the neighborhood log homicide rate conforms to an over-dispersed Poisson distribution (see Raudenbush and Bryk 2002).

The advantage of this approach is three-fold. First, it sensibly incorporates the skewed nature of the homicide outcome, which has many values of zero, while at the same time creating a metric that defines meaningful effect size. Namely, exponentiating the regression coefficient in such a model and multiplying the result times 100 produces the useful interpretation of "the percent increase in the homicide rate associated with a one unit increase in the predictor." Second, the approach represents unique unobserved differences between neighborhoods via random effects. To the extent that neighborhoods have unique features that affect homicide rates, these random effects are important in accounting for variation not explainable by the structural model. Third, the approach incorporates the spatial dependence of neighborhood homicide rates.

Unfortunately, software that can simultaneously handle over dispersed Poisson variates, random effects of neighborhoods, and spatial dependence is not currently available. We therefore employed a two-step approximation. First, we used a hierarchical generalized linear model without spatial dependence to compute posterior modes η_j^* of neighborhood-specific log-homicide rates given the data, the grand mean estimate for Chicago, and the estimated between-neighborhood variance in the true log-rates.[7] Next, we imported these posterior modes into software dedicated to estimating regression models with spatial dependence (SpaceStat). Using this integrated approach, regression coefficients and coefficients of spatial dependence have the desirable interpretation of the ideal model described above.

We estimate spatial dependence by constructing "spatially lagged" versions of our measures of violence. We define y_i as the homicide rate of NC_i, and w_{ij} as element i, j of a spatial weights matrix that expresses the geographical proximity of NC_i to NC_j (Anselin 1988, 11). For a given observation i, a spatial lag $\sum_i w_{ij} y_j$ is the weighted average of homicide in neighboring locations.[8] The weights matrix is expressed as first-order contiguity, which defines neighbors as those NCs that share a common border (referred to as the rook criterion).[9] Thus, $w_{ij} = 1$ if i and j are contiguous, 0 if not. We then test formally for the independent role of spatial dependence in a multivariate model by introducing the spatial lag as an explanatory variable. The spatial lag regression model is defined as

$$y = \rho W y + X\beta + \varepsilon, \tag{1}$$

where y is an N by 1 vector of observations on the dependent variable; Wy is an N by 1 vector composed of elements $\sum_j w_{ij} y_j$, the spatial lags for the dependent variable; ρ is the spatial autoregressive coefficient; X is an N by K matrix of exogenous explanatory variables with an associated K by 1 vector of regression coefficients β; and ε is an N by 1 vector of normally distributed random error terms, with means 0 and constant (homoskedastic) variances.[10]

The most straightforward interpretation of ρ is that, for a given neighborhood, i, it represents the effect of a one-unit change in the average homicide rate of i's first-order neighbors on the homicide rate of i. This interpretation would seem to suggest a diffusion process, whereby a high homicide rate in one neighborhood diffuses outward and affects homicide rates in surrounding neighborhoods. However, the notion of diffusion implies a process that occurs over time, while the spatial autocorrelation process modeled in Equation (1) is entirely cross-sectional—homicide rates are spatially interrelated across neighborhoods but simultaneously determined. Moreover, the interpretation of ρ as a pure diffusion (or feedback) mechanism—the effect of a one-unit change in Wy on y—does not capture the complexity of the spatial process specified in Equation (1). By extending the logic of Equation (1), we can demonstrate that the spatial lag model also incorporates the idea of "exposure" to the values of the measured X variables and the ε term (i.e., unmeasured characteristics) in spatially proximate neighborhoods. According to Equation (1), the value of y at location i depends on the values of X and ε at location i and on values of y in i's first-order neighbors. In turn, the first-order neighbors' values of y are functions of X and ε in i's first-order neighbors and y in i's second-order neighbors, and so on. This process continues in a step-like fashion, incorporating the neighborhood characteristics of successively higher-order neighbors of i (see also Tolnay et al. 1996). This process can be expressed mathematically by rewriting Equation (1) as follows:

$$y = X\beta + \rho W X\beta + \rho^2 W^2 X\beta + \dots$$
$$+ \rho^m W^m X\beta + \varepsilon + \rho W\varepsilon + \rho^2 W^2\varepsilon + \dots + \rho^m W^m\varepsilon, \qquad (2)$$

where $m \to \infty$. Equation (2) is also known as the "spatial multiplier" process, because it shows that the spatial regression model treats spatial dependence as a ripple effect, through which a change in X or ε at location i influences not only the value of y at location i but also (indirectly) at all other locations in Chicago.

Equation (2) also shows that the spatial effect can be decomposed into two parts: the effect of proximity to the measured X variables, and the effect of proximity to unmeasured characteristics, ε. The first component (the spatial process in the X variables) directly addresses the "proximity hypothesis" discussed above—it estimates the extent to which homicide rates are related to values of the measured X variables in spatially proximate neighborhoods.[11] The second component of Equation (2) (the spatial process in ε) is more ambiguous and depends on the model specification. In part, this component taps the effect of spatial proximity to unmeasured features in nearby neighborhoods that are associated with homicide. For example, the homicide rate of the focal neighborhood might be related to rates in surrounding areas because of overlapping social networks across arbitrary neighborhood boundaries. Another possibility is a spillover effect such that the homicide rate in the focal neighborhood is affected by the homicide rate in nearby neighborhoods directly. Therefore, the ρ coefficient from the spatial lag model captures spatial exposure to the observed X variables, spatial exposure to unobserved predictors, and endogenous feedback effects in y.

Exploratory Spatial Data Analysis

We begin our analysis by examining the geographic distributions of homicide and collective efficacy across Chicago neighborhoods in an exploratory spatial data analysis

(Anselin 1988). Consistent with much past research, homicide events are not randomly distributed with respect to geography. In fact, supplementary tabulations reveal that 70 percent of all the homicides in Chicago between 1996 and 1998 occurred in only 32 percent of the neighborhood clusters, according to the Police data. We thus examined the geographic correspondence between the distribution of neighborhood homicide rates and that of collective efficacy, a key social processes from our theoretical perspective. To facilitate such a comparison, we employ a typology of spatial association, referred to as a Moran scatterplot, which classifies each neighborhood based on its value for a given variable, y, and the weighted average of y in contiguous neighborhoods, as captured by the spatial lag term, Wy. For simplicity, neighborhoods that are above the mean on y are considered to have "high" values of y, while neighborhoods below the mean are classified as "low." The same distinction is made with respect to values of Wy for each neighborhood, resulting in a four-fold classification with the following categories: (1) low-low, for neighborhoods that have low levels of efficacy and are also proximate to neighborhoods with low levels of efficacy; (2) low-high, for neighborhoods that have low levels of efficacy but are proximate to high levels; (3) high-low, for neighborhoods that have high levels of efficacy but are proximate to low levels; and (4) high-high, for areas with high levels of efficacy that are also proximate to high levels of efficacy.

Figure 8.1 displays the results of the spatial typology for two variables: collective efficacy and the 1996–1998 EB homicide rates, constructed from the incident-based Police data.[12] This map conveys two pieces of information for each neighborhood. First, each neighborhood's value for the spatial typology of collective efficacy is denoted by a different fill pattern: light gray for low-low; dots for low-high; diagonal stripes for high-low; and dark gray for high-high.[13] Second, the symbols on the map represent values of the spatial typology of EB homicide rates, constructed from the 1996–1998 police data: black stars indicate significant high-high values (i.e., homicide "hot spots"), and gray crosses indicate significant low-low values (i.e., homicide "cold spots").

We draw two general conclusions from Figure 8.1. First, the map shows that there is a high degree of overlap between the spatial distributions of collective efficacy and homicide. For example, 67 of the 93 neighborhoods that have spatial clustering of high levels of collective efficacy (72 percent) also experience statistically significant clustering of low homicide. Most of the clustering of low homicide coupled with high collective efficacy occurs in neighborhoods located on the western boundaries of Chicago, particularly on the far northwest and southwest sides. Similarly, there is a strong correspondence between the spatial clustering of high homicide rates and low levels of collective efficacy. Of the 103 homicide hot spots, 77 (or 75 percent) also have spatial clustering of low levels of collective efficacy. Second, despite the strong association between the geographic distribution of collective efficacy and homicide, there are many observations where the two typologies are at variance with one another. For example, 14 of the 93 homicide cold spots (15 percent) appear in neighborhoods with low levels of collective efficacy that are surrounded by high levels. Moreover, 15 of 103 homicide hot spots (15 percent) are in neighborhoods that have high levels of collective efficacy but are surrounded by neighborhoods with low levels. Neighborhoods where the level

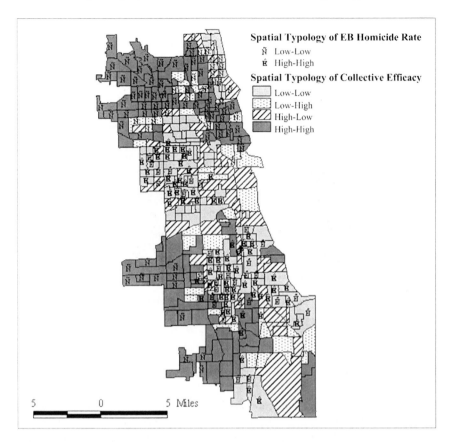

Figure 8.1. Spatial typology of collective efficacy with homicide "Hot" Spots and "Cold" Spots.

of collective efficacy is at variance with surrounding neighborhoods are important the-oretically, because they reveal concrete but often neglected forms of spatial advantage and disadvantage (Sampson et al. 1999).

The role of spatial proximity to collective efficacy is further explored in Figure 8.2, which graphs the mean homicide rate for the four categories of the collective efficacy spatial typology.[14] Figure 8.2 reveals that regardless of the level of collective efficacy in the focal neighborhood, mean homicide rates are lower among neighborhoods that are spatially proximate to high levels of collective efficacy (as indicated by the dark gray bars) than they are among neighborhoods that are spatially proximate to low levels of collective efficacy (as indicated by the dotted bars). It is therefore clear that a neighbor-hood's spatial proximity to collective efficacy conditions its homicide rate, independent of its own level of collective efficacy. In other words, knowing the local level of social organization is not enough, a proposition we now test further in a multivariate spatial analysis of homicide rates with additional covariates.

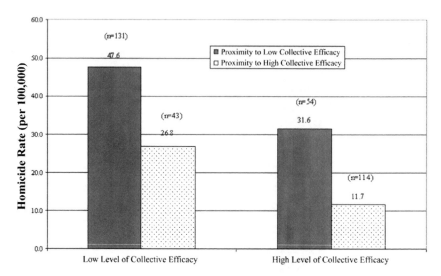

Figure 8.2. Mean homicide rate by level and spatial proximity to collective efficacy.

Multivariate Analysis

We turn to a regression framework to investigate three substantive issues in the analysis of neighborhood homicide rates: the role of multiple social processes as neighborhood mechanisms, the spatial dynamics of homicide, and the endogeneity of collective efficacy. Table 8.1 presents the results of regression models for EB homicide rates using the Chicago Police Data. The first model includes only the structural covariates. The natural log of the concentrated disadvantage index is used, because scatterplots revealed a nonlinear relationship between disadvantage and homicide. The log-transformation effectively linearizes this association.[15] The results show that all of the coefficients in this model are significant, with the exception of the ratio of adults to children. When social and institutional processes are added to the regression, in Model 2, only the effects of disadvantage (positive), residential stability (positive), and density (negative) remain significant.[16] More importantly, Model 2 also reveals that collective efficacy is negatively related to homicide rates, as anticipated by the theoretical discussion. Somewhat unexpectedly, none of the other social or institutional process variables in Model 2 are significantly related to homicide.

Models 3 and 4 represent spatial lag regressions estimated via maximum likelihood. Model 3 introduces the spatial lag term, which is positively related to homicide rates and strongly significant. The introduction of the spatial lag term in Model 3 eliminates the significance of residential stability and diminishes the effects of concentrated disadvantage (by 30 percent), population density (by 20 percent), and collective efficacy (by 16.5 percent). Model 4 adds a control for the prior neighborhood homicide rate (1991–1993) in order to address the possibility that the association between collective efficacy

Table 8.1. Coefficients from the regression of incident-based 1996–1998 empirical Bayes Poisson homicide rate on neighborhood predictors.

Variables	OLS		Maximum Likelihood			
	(1)	(2)	(3)	(4)	(5)	(6)
LN concentrated disadvantage	1.30**	1.14**	0.80**	0.54**		
	(0.07)	(0.09)	(0.10)	(0.13)		
ICE index					−1.12**	−0.68**
					(0.18)	(0.19)
Concentrated immigration	0.10**	0.06	0.03	0.04	−0.14**	−0.04
	(0.04)	(0.05)	(0.04)	(0.04)	(0.04)	(0.04)
Residential stability	0.05*	0.05*	0.03	0.03	0.03	0.03
	(0.02)	(0.02)	(0.02)	(0.02)	(0.02)	(0.02)
Adults per child†	0.01	−0.06	0.02	−0.12	−0.07	−0.16
	(0.33)	(0.33)	(0.30)	(0.30)	(0.32)	(0.32)
Population density†	−0.27**	−0.33**	−0.27**	−0.24**	−0.20**	−0.20**
	(0.09)	(0.09)	(0.08)	(0.08)	(0.09)	(0.08)
Collective efficacy		−0.65**	−0.54**	−0.47**	−0.67**	−0.47**
		(0.20)	(0.18)	(0.18)	(0.18)	(0.18)
Voluntary associations		0.18	0.15	0.13	0.15	0.14
		(0.10)	(0.09)	(0.09)	(0.09)	(0.09)
Organizations		−0.05	−0.05	−0.03	−0.02	−0.01
		(0.07)	(0.06)	(0.06)	(0.07)	(0.06)
Kin/friendship ties		0.02	−0.02	−0.05	−0.10	−0.13
		(0.16)	(0.15)	(0.15)	(0.16)	(0.16)
Spatial proximity			0.34**	0.31**	0.48**	0.30**
			(0.05)	(0.05)	(0.05)	(0.05)
Prior homicide rate (1991–1993)				0.21**		0.37**
				(0.06)		(0.05)
Constant	2.91**	6.01**	4.62**	3.87**	5.14**	3.81**
	(0.08)	(0.92)	(0.87)	(0.89)	(0.87)	(0.89)
R^2	0.68	0.70	0.72	0.73	0.69	0.73

(Standard Errors in Parentheses)

†Adults per child multiplied by 100

††Population density multiplied by 10,000

**$p < .01$; *$p < .05$

Sources: 1990–1998 Chicago Police Data; 1995 PHDCN Survey; and 1990 Census.

in 1995 and 1996–1998 homicide rates is really a reflection of the downward spiral of neighborhoods caused by prior violence.[17] The control for prior homicide reduces the magnitude of the collective efficacy coefficient (by 13 percent), but it still maintains significance. The control for prior homicide reduces the disadvantage coefficient more substantially (by 33 percent), but because 1991–1993 homicide rates and the logged disadvantage index are so highly correlated (r = .90), it is difficult to disentangle their independent effects on 1996–1998 homicide rates. More important from the standpoint of our theoretical discussion above is that collective efficacy and the spatial term maintain significant and strong associations with variations in future homicide unaccounted for by the stable patterns of violence as reflected in prior homicide.

The remaining models in Table 8.1, Models 5 and 6, offer an alternative specification of the spatial autocorrelation model with and without the control for prior homicide. What is unique about Models 5 and 6 is the substitution of the ICE index for the disadvantage index. The ICE index captures the degree of concentrated affluence relative to the concentration of poverty in a neighborhood (Massey 2001). The coefficients for collective efficacy remain statistically significant in Models 5 and 6 after controlling for prior homicide. Significant spatial dependence also remains in each of the models. Thus, even though they are conceptually distinct, substituting ICE for the disadvantage index does not alter the main findings. The larger message appears to be that concentrated inequality in socioeconomic resources is directly related to homicide.

To assess robustness, Table 8.2 replicates the same set of models using victim-based homicide rates for 1996 from the Chicago Vital Statistics data. The results are similar to those from Table 8.1 for the variables of main theoretical interest: concentrated disadvantage, collective efficacy, spatial proximity, and the ICE index. In Model 1, concentrated disadvantage is the only structural variable that has a statistical association with homicide. Unlike the results for the incident-based homicide measure, density does not have a direct relationship with victim-based homicide. This makes sense from a routine activities perspective, because it is a factor that is theoretically related to the point of the event's occurrence, not the residence of the victim.

When the social process variables are added in Model 2, we again find a significant association between homicide rates and collective efficacy, but not for social ties or any of the institutional measures. The spatial lag term, introduced in Model 3, is significant and positively related to homicide rates. The control for prior homicide is not significant in Model 4,[18] but the coefficients for disadvantage, collective efficacy, and spatial dependence maintain their significance. The effects associated with collective efficacy and spatial dependence also remain significant after the substitution of the ICE index for the disadvantage index in Models 5 and 6.

In sum, we find a fairly robust set of results across independently collected sources of homicide data: the Chicago Police Statistics and Chicago Vital Statistics. Concentrated disadvantage, collective efficacy, and the ICE index are consistently related to homicide. In particular, strong spatial effects are also evident in both data sets; these spatial effects remain after controlling for the strong stability in homicide risk over time. We believe this finding is important, for one of the biggest problems in spatially-based social research is ensuring that ρ is not spurious due to a failure to fully specify the causal processes in a focal community. The strength of our model is that the temporally lagged homicide rate essentially serves as a proxy for all such unmeasured variables. Thus, to the extent that prior homicide adjusts for the unobserved heterogeneity of causal processes, the continued strength of the ρ coefficient increases our confidence in the robustness of the effect of spatial proximity on homicide.

Although we consider homicide to be our best measure of violence, to test the robustness of our main patterns we also replicated the spatial models on a different predatory crime—robbery. Table 8.3 presents the basic models and empirical results. Overall, the same pattern obtains. The spatial proximity coefficient is significant in all models, including those that control for prior robbery. In this case, prior robbery and concurrent robbery are correlated at more than $r = .90$, meaning that there is very little residual variance left to explain. It is not clear whether a reduction in magnitude for the

Table 8.2. Coefficients from the regression of victim-based 1996 empirical Bayes Poisson homicide rate on neighborhood predictors.

Variables	OLS		Maximum Likelihood			
	(1)	(2)	(3)	(4)	(5)	(6)
LN concentrated disadvantage	0.66**	0.56**	0.44**	0.35**		
	(0.05)	(0.07)	(0.08)	(0.10)		
ICE index					−0.56**	−0.35**
					(0.15)	(0.16)
Concentrated immigration	−0.04	−0.05	−0.05	−0.04	−0.14**	−0.09**
	(0.03)	(0.04)	(0.04)	(0.04)	(0.03)	(0.04)
Residential stability	0.03	0.03	0.03	0.03	0.03	0.03
	(0.02)	(0.02)	(0.02)	(0.02)	(0.02)	(0.02)
Adults per child†	0.01	−0.03	0.01	0.02	−0.14	−0.02
	(0.27)	(0.27)	(0.26)	(0.26)	(0.27)	(0.27)
Population density†	−0.04	−0.08	−0.07	−0.07	−0.04	−0.04
	(0.07)	(0.07)	(0.07)	(0.07)	(0.07)	(0.07)
Collective efficacy		−0.48**	−0.50**	−0.47**	−0.66**	−0.52**
		(0.16)	(0.15)	(0.15)	(0.15)	(0.16)
Voluntary associations		0.13	0.14	0.13	0.13	0.12
		(0.08)	(0.07)	(0.07)	(0.08)	(0.08)
Organizations		0.05	0.04	0.04	0.05	0.05
		(0.06)	(0.05)	(0.05)	(0.06)	(0.06)
Kin/friendship ties		0.04	-0.07	0.08	0.08	0.09
		(0.13)	(0.13)	(0.13)	(0.14)	(0.14)
Spatial proximity			0.22**	0.20**	0.33**	0.18**
			(0.06)	(0.07)	(0.06)	(0.05)
Prior homicide rate (1991–1993)				0.09**		0.24**
				(0.06)		(0.06)
Constant	2.00**	4.24**	3.78**	3.38**	4.23**	3.20**
	(0.06)	(0.75)	(0.74)	(0.79)	(0.74)	(0.79)
R^2	0.50	0.52	0.53	0.53	0.50	0.52

(Standard Errors in Parentheses)

†Adults per child multiplied by 100

††Population density multiplied by 10,000

**$p < .01$; *$p < .05$

Sources: 1990–1998 Chicago Police Data; 1995 PHDCN Survey; and 1990 Census.

effects of our set of social-process predictors means that the association is mediated or is spurious. What we can see, however, is that in this conservative test, the spatial lag effect remains robust for robbery.

Further Understanding the Spatial Dynamics of Violence

To interpret more fully the results of the spatial lag models, it is important to recall that in Equation (2), homicide is related to the value of each X variable in successively higher-order neighbors by a function of ρ, the coefficient for the spatial lag term. In Figure 8.3, we use the results from Model 4 in Tables 8.1 and 8.2 to demonstrate how

Table 8.3. Coefficients from the regression of 1995 logged robbery rate on neighborhood predictors.

Variables	Maximum Likelihood	
	(1)	(2)
LN Concentrated disadvantage	0.20**	0.03
	(0.05)	(0.04)
Concentrated immigration	0.00	0.03
	(0.04)	(0.03)
Residential stability	−0.06**	0.02
	(0.02)	(0.01)
Adults per child[†]	0.11	−0.01
	(0.24)	(0.17)
Population Density[††]	−0.30**	−0.13**
	(0.07)	(0.05)
Collective efficacy	−0.29	−0.14
	(0.15)	(0.11)
Voluntary assocations	0.03	−0.02
	(0.07)	(0.05)
Organizations	−0.02	−0.01
	(0.05)	(0.04)
Kin/friendship ties	−0.26**	−0.03
	(0.13)	(0.09)
Spatial proximity	0.76**	0.27**
	(0.03)	(0.04)
Prior logged robbery rate (1993)		0.68**
		(0.04)
Constant	2.74**	0.73
	(0.70)	(0.51)
R^2	0.75	0.91

(Standard Errors in Parentheses)

[†]Adults per child multiplied by 100

[††]Population density multiplied by 10,000

**$p < .01$; *$p < .05$

this "spatial multiplier" process works with respect to two key covariates: concentrated disadvantage (which is logged) and collective efficacy.[19] The bars on the left side of the graph illustrate how the spatial multiplier process operates for concentrated disadvantage. The first set of bars in this series shows that, controlling for all other covariates in Model 4, a one-standard-deviation increase in the log of the disadvantage index *in the focal neighborhood* is associated with a 40 percent increase in the homicide rate in the focal neighborhood, according to the Police data, and a 24 percent increase according to the Vital Statistics.[20] The next set of bars reveals that all else being equal, a one-standard-deviation increase in the average level of concentrated disadvantage *in the first-order neighbors* of the focal neighborhood is associated with a 9 percent increase in the homicide rate in the focal neighborhood, according to the Police data, and a 4 percent increase according to Vital Statistics. The remaining bars show that the effects of disadvantage decrease exponentially with each succeeding level of contiguity. To gauge the cumulative effect, it is possible to add up all the bars in this series for each data set. This shows that a simultaneous one-standard-deviation increase in the log of the disadvantage index in the focal neighborhood, and in the first-, second-, and third-order neighbors, is associated with a 52 percent increase in homicide, according to Police data, and a 28 percent increase according to the Vital Statistics.

The right side of Figure 8.3 displays results for the same exercise conducted on collective efficacy. The coefficients for collective efficacy are more stable across the two data sets. A one-standard-deviation increase in the level of collective efficacy in the focal neighborhood is associated with a 12 percent reduction in the homicide rate, according to both the Police data and the Vital Statistics data. Cumulatively, a one-standard-deviation increase in collective efficacy in the focal neighborhood, and the first-, second-, and third-order neighbors is associated with a 15 percent reduction in the homicide rate of the focal neighborhood, according to the Police data, and a 14 percent drop according to the Vital Statistics.

Note that Figure 8.3 only displays the spatial effects associated with two independent variables, concentrated disadvantage and collective efficacy. A full decomposition of the spatial effect would include other variables in the model, in addition to the error term. Thus, the effects displayed in Figure 8.3 are only a fraction of the full spatial effect. What these results do show, however, is that the cumulative effects associated with both disadvantage and collective efficacy are substantively quite large, particularly when their spatial dynamics are taken into account.

Regimes of Racial Segregation

To this point our analysis has relied on an index of concentrated disadvantage that includes racial composition as one of its components. As we argued above, the high degree of racial segregation overlaid with poverty hinders our ability to disentangle the direct effects of neighborhood racial composition and neighborhood socioeconomic disadvantage in Chicago.[21] However, it is possible, and we would argue more meaningful, to examine whether the social and structural processes under study operate similarly across neighborhoods of differing racial composition. We address this issue by estimating spatial regime models (Anselin 1995a), which allow coefficients to vary across regimes defined by neighborhood racial composition while also controlling for spatial dependence.[22] To define these regimes, we divide Chicago's neighborhoods into two categories based on their 1990 racial composition: (1) less than 75 percent non-Hispanic black (henceforth referred to as "non-black" neighborhoods) and (2) 75 percent or more non-Hispanic black (henceforth referred to as "black" neighborhoods). There are 125 black neighborhoods, as defined by this typology, and they are on average 96.4 percent black, 2.5 percent white, and 2.8 percent Hispanic. There are 217 non-black neighborhoods, which on average are 54.3 percent white, 30.5 percent Hispanic, and 9.4 percent black.[23]

The results of the regime model are reported in Table 8.4. We use ICE as our inequality measure in these models, because the disadvantage index contains the percent black measure, which cannot be used both on the right-hand side of the regressions and in the definition of the regimes. Theoretically, we are interested in the propor-

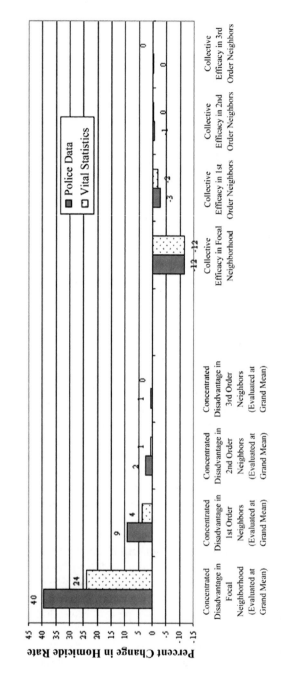

Figure 8.3. Percent change in homicide rate per standard deviation change in concentrated disadvantage and collective efficacy by spatial proximity to focal neighborhood.

Table 8.4. Coefficients from the regression of empirical Bayes Poisson homicide rates on neighborhood predictors by racial regimes.

	Incident-Based		Victim-Based	
	< 75% Black	≥ 75% Black	< 75% Black	≥ 75% Black
Variables	(1)	(2)	(3)	(4)
ICE index	-1.20^{**}	-0.87^{**}	-0.67^{**}	-0.02
	(0.28)	(0.35)	(0.23)	(0.29)
Concentrated immigration	-0.05	-0.34	-0.02	-0.69
	(0.07)	(0.48)	(0.06)	(0.39)
Residential stability	0.00	0.03	0.00	0.00
	(0.03)	(0.05)	(0.02)	(0.04)
Adults per child[†]	0.03	0.73	0.10	-1.52
	(0.34)	(2.54)	(0.28)	(2.09)
Population density[††]	-0.26	-0.24	-0.05	-0.13
	(0.10)	(0.18)	(0.08)	(0.15)
Collective efficacy	-0.56^{*}	-0.61^{*}	-0.18	-0.98^{**}
	(0.25)	(0.29)	(0.21)	(0.24)
Voluntary associations	0.19	0.08	0.14	0.27^{*}
	(0.12)	(0.15)	(0.10)	(0.13)
Organizations	0.00	-0.08	-0.03	0.17^{*}
	(0.09)	(0.11)	(0.07)	(0.09)
Kin/friendship ties	-0.13	0.20	-0.05	0.36
	(0.20)	(0.29)	(0.17)	(0.24)
Constant	5.12^{**}	3.88^{**}	2.82^{**}	5.12^{**}
	(1.08)	(1.53)	(0.89)	(1.26)
Spatial proximity		0.41^{**}		0.24^{**}
		(0.05)		(0.06)
R^2		0.71		0.54

[†]Adults per child multiplied by 100

[††]Population density multiplied by 10,000

$^{**}p < .01;\ ^{*}p < .05$

Sources: 1990–1998 Chicago Police Data; 1995 PHDCN Survey; and 1990 Census.

tional distribution of affluence and poverty within racial regimes. The first two columns display results using the incident-based homicide outcome—column 1 contains the coefficients for the non-black neighborhoods, and column 2 contains coefficients for the black neighborhoods. In general, the results do not differ very much across regimes in the incident-based homicide model.[24] The ICE index and collective efficacy have significant negative associations with the homicide incident rate in both non-black and black neighborhoods. The spatial effect, which is estimated jointly across non-black and black neighborhoods, is also significant and large. The main difference is that population density has a significant negative effect only in non-black neighborhoods.

Turning to the victim-based homicide measure (columns 3 and 4), the results yield more differences across the two regimes.[25] In the victim-based homicide model, the ICE index is significantly associated with homicide only in non-black neighborhoods, whereas the association between collective efficacy and homicide is significant only in black neighborhoods. Moreover, in black neighborhoods, the measures of voluntary associations and organizations are positively associated with homicide, whereas in non-black neighborhoods these associations are non-significant. Again, the spatial effect is significant. Although there is evidence of differing magnitudes of effect across black and non-black neighborhoods, the overall results for collective efficacy and spatial proximity are fairly robust taking both homicide outcomes into account.

Conclusion and Implications

Our results suggest that spatial embeddedness, internal structural characteristics, and social organizational processes are each important for understanding neighborhood-level variations in rates of violence. Spatial proximity to violence, collective efficacy, and alternative measures of neighborhood inequality—indices of concentrated disadvantage and concentrated extremes—emerged as the most consistent predictors of variations in homicide across a wide range of tests and empirical specifications. Moreover, our analysis of racial "spatial regimes" suggested that structural characteristics and social processes have many similar effects on homicide rates in predominantly black, compared with non-black, neighborhoods. Although we did find some evidence of differences in coefficients across regimes—and it is noteworthy that the effect of collective efficacy is strongest in black neighborhoods—overall, the results suggest that a fairly stable causal process is operating in all parts of the city. Put differently, the evidence is more favorable than not to the idea that the fundamental causes of neighborhood violence are similar across race (see also Krivo and Peterson 2000; Sampson and Wilson 1995).

A major theme of our analysis is that homicide is a spatially dependent process, and that our estimates of spatial effects are relatively large in magnitude. Indeed the spatial effects were larger than standard structural covariates and an array of neighborhood social processes. The tendency of past research has been to focus on internal neighborhood factors, but they are clearly not enough to understand homicide. Local actions and population composition make a difference, to be sure, but they are severely constrained by the spatial context of adjacent neighborhoods. Our results suggest that political economy theorists are right in insisting on models that incorporate citywide dynamics (Logan and Molotch 1987). Hope (1995, 24) makes a similar point from the criminological perspective, suggesting that many intervention efforts have failed because they did not adequately address the pressures towards crime in the community that derive from forces external to the community in the wider social structure. Although very different in research style and method, the recent ethnographic work of Pattillo-McCoy (1999) also parallels our findings and discovery of the salience of spatial vulnerability, especially for black middle-class neighborhoods (Figure 8.1).

The puzzle that remains is to further disentangle spatial processes into constituent parts. At this juncture we are unable to pinpoint the relative contributions of exposure and diffusion, an agenda we are hopeful that criminological researchers and methodologists will have an interest in tackling. We believe that better longitudinal data on crime and social processes will provide a particular boon to disentangling temporal and cross-sectional diffusion. In the meantime, it seems clear that spatial proximity cannot be ignored in theories of violence.

Acknowledgment   This paper selectively condenses previously published work; see especially Morenoff et al. 2001. We acknowledge the American Society of Criminology, publishers of the journal *Criminology*.

Notes

1. By neighborhood, the survey protocol stated: " . . . we mean the area around where you live and around your house. It may include places you shop, religious or public institutions, or a local business district. It is the general area around your house where you might perform routine tasks, such as shopping, going to the park, or visiting with neighbors."

2. Distinct from individual-level reliability (e.g., Cronbach's alpha), neighborhood reliability is defined as: $\sum \left[\tau_{00}/(\tau_{00} + \sigma^2/n_j) \right]/J$, which measures the precision of the estimate, averaged across the set of J neighborhoods, as a function of (1) the sample size (n) in each of the j neighborhoods and (2) the proportion of the total variance that is between-groups (τ_{00}) relative to the amount that is within-groups (σ^2). A magnitude of greater than .80 suggests that we are able to reliably tap parameter variance in collective efficacy at the neighborhood level. For further discussion of tools for assessing ecological context see Raudenbush and Sampson (1999).

3. We thank Richard Block for providing the police count data for 1996–1998. Homicide data from 1991–1993 were downloaded from the Chicago Homicide Data Set at the ICPSR data archive (www.icpsr.umich.edu). Homicide data from both time periods come from police counts, also compiled by Richard Block, that were geocoded based on the address where the incident occurred. The homicide counts for each neighborhood cluster include cases of non-negligent manslaughter but exclude deaths from injuries inflicted by law-enforcing agents.

4. We did not have access to vital statistics data for 1997 or 1998, so our two measures of homicide do not cover exactly the same period. Homicides in the vital statistics are coded as causes of death due to injuries inflicted by another person with intent to injure or kill, by any means. As with the police statistics, these homicide data include non-negligent manslaughter but exclude injuries inflicted by the police or other law-enforcing agents (NCHS 2000).

5. A long history of research on homicide has shown that victims tend to be killed in or very near to their neighborhoods of residence. For homicide, then, the victimization rate also serves as a proxy for homicide incidence, an assumption validated by the high correlation between vital statistics and the police-recorded incidence of homicide events. The correlation between the homicide rate calculated from vital statistics from 1996 data and that calculated from the police statistics for 1996–1998 is .71. The correlation between homicide rates calculated on the two data sets for 1991–1993 is .86.

6. An alternative approach to addressing the endogeneity of collective efficacy would be to examine simultaneous equation models, but in this procedure the choice of instrumental variables is often very difficult to justify (see discussion in Bellair 2000), and the existing literature has been harshly criticized as untenable (Fisher and Nagin 1978). The problem is that the exclusionary restrictions cannot be validated with the data at hand. We prefer to address endogeneity through a control for prior homicide on two grounds—no identifying restrictions are necessary, and it is a conservative test. The latter is true because the very high stability in homicide rates over time results in little residual variation left in the homicide rate to explain with other covariates. Also, prior levels of social process, for which we have no measures, may have influenced prior levels of crime and thus, may be mediated in their effect. However, *if* a significant association between social process and homicide maintains

after partialling the effect of prior homicide, endogeneity is an implausible inference in our panel model, since the homicide outcome is measured at a later time than the predictors; crime cannot influence the past.

7. The approximate posterior mode η_i^* for neighborhood i is a weighted average of that neighborhood's log homicide rate, estimated using only the data from that neighborhood, and the overall mode of the homicide rates estimated from the data generated by all of the neighborhoods. The weights accorded each component are proportional to their precisions. The more data collected in neighborhood i, the more precise will be the estimate based on the data from that neighborhood, and the more weight it will be accorded in composing η_i^*. The more concentrated the neighborhood rates around the overall mode, the more that overall mode will be weighted. Such approximate posterior modes are routinely produced as output from widely used statistical software for multilevel analysis (c.f., Raudenbush and Bryk 2002). The shrinkage of neighborhood-specific estimates toward an overall mode is not ideal, because it ignores prior information about how neighborhoods differ in their homicide rates. In principle, this leads to somewhat conservative estimates of the effects of neighborhood-level covariates. To assess the extent of bias, we replicated our results using standard regression analyses with the neighborhood-based rates as outcomes. Results were very similar. We chose the approach using posterior modes, because it extends better to spatial modeling. The standard approach using the neighborhood-based rates as outcomes does not extend well to the incorporation of spatial effects, because the extreme skewness of the neighborhood-specific rates contradicts the assumptions of the spatial regression procedures. Using the posterior modes solves this problem and produces stable and interpretable spatial results.

8. Spatial dependence may also be treated as a "nuisance," in the form of a spatial error model (Anselin 1988). The spatial lag model was chosen because it conforms to our theoretical approach that specifies spatial dependence as a substantive phenomenon rather than as a nuisance (see also Tolnay, Deane, and Beck 1996). Moreover, the spatial lag models generally outperformed the corresponding spatial error models in a variety of diagnostic tests.

9. Before computing the spatial lag term, we standardized the weights matrix by dividing each element in a given row by the corresponding row sum (see Anselin 1995a). Defined formally as $w_{ij}/\sum_j w_{ij}$, row standardization constrains the range of the parameter space in such a way that the resulting coefficient is no longer dependent on the scale of the distance employed in the weights matrix. The spatial lag parameter can be interpreted as the estimated effect of a one-unit change in the scale of the original variable from which it was created.

10. This model is often referred to as the simultaneous spatial autoregressive model, because the presence of the spatial lag is similar to the inclusion of endogenous explanatory variables in systems of simultaneous equations. All estimates of the spatial proximity models were derived using the program "SpaceStat" (Anselin 1995a).

11. Because ρ is multiplied by the β coefficient for each X variable in Equation (2), and $0 \leq \rho \leq 1$, it is possible to think of ρ as the rate at which the effects of each X variable are "discounted" in contiguous neighbors. Thus, if $\rho = .50$, then the effects of the average level of X in the first-order neighbors (Wx) will be half as strong as they are in the focal neighborhood. In the second-order neighbors, the effect will be reduced by one-quarter the size of $\beta(.50^2 = .25)$, and so on for each successive order of contiguity.

12. A color version of the map is displayed at the website http://www.csiss.org/best-practices.

13. It is possible to apply a test of statistical significance for the values of this typology, developed by Anselin (1995b). This test of local spatial association at each location i is referred to as the local Moran statistic, defined as $I_i = (z_i/m_2)\sum_j w_{ij}z_j$ with $m_2 = \sum_i z_i^2$, where the observations z_i and z_j are standardized values of y_i and y_j expressed as deviations from the mean (Anselin 1995a and 1995b). Under a conditional randomization approach, the

value of z_i at location i is held fixed, and the remaining values of z_j over all other neighborhoods in the city are randomly permuted in an iterative fashion. With each permutation, a new value of the quantity $\sum_j w_{ij} z_j$ is computed, and the statistic is recalculated. This permutation operationalizes the null hypothesis of complete spatial randomness. A test for pseudo significance is then constructed by comparing the original value of I_i to the empirical distribution that results from the permutation process (Anselin 1995b). We could not convey the information about statistical significance of the Moran typology for collective efficacy with the limited shading scheme of a black and white map—such a map entails an eight-fold categorization, which is better displayed in color. However, the symbols on the map representing homicide hot spots (stars) and cold spots (crosses) are based on only the statistically significant "high-high" and "low-low" values of the local Moran statistic for homicide. We have posted a more detailed color map at http://www.csiss.org/best-practices that also displays the significant spatial clustering of collective efficacy.

14. This graph does not take into account statistical significance of Moran's I, because there are very few neighborhoods that are in either the low-high or high-low categories and have statistically significant values of Moran's I (only 6 in low-high and 11 in high-low). These cell sizes are too small to generate reliable estimates of mean homicide rates.

15. Before taking its natural log, we added a constant (1.5) to the disadvantage scale to eliminate negative values.

16. The negative association between population density and homicide might go against conventional wisdom that it should be positive. The expectation of a positive association is probably more applicable to the city level (i.e., more densely populated cities may indeed have higher homicide rates), but it is less applicable to the neighborhood level, because many of the most devastated and poor areas *within* cities of the North and Midwest are those that became "depopulated" during the social dislocations of the 1970s and 1980s (Wilson 1987).

17. These prior homicide rates are also based on the over-dispersed Poisson distribution, using the same methodology described above.

18. Again, prior homicide is strongly correlated with the logged disadvantage index (.90). Consequently, as was the case in Table 8.1, we cannot reliably disentangle the independent effects of prior homicide and disadvantage on homicide in 1996.

19. In order to obtain the percentage change in the homicide rate per standard deviation change in the corresponding independent variable, we exponentiate the product of each regression coefficient and the standard deviation of the respective covariate.

20. Because the relationship between concentrated disadvantage and the homicide rate is nonlinear, the effect of a one-standard deviation increase in disadvantage depends on where in the distribution of disadvantage that change is evaluated. Figure 8.3 displays the difference in the homicide rate associated with moving from one-half of a standard deviation below the mean of disadvantage to one-half of a standard deviation above the mean on disadvantage.

21. We did attempt to re-estimate the models in Tables 8.1 and 8.2 by recalculating the disadvantage index without percent black, and instead, entering percent black as a separate covariate. Our major substantive results remained intact with this alternative specification. However, the Variance Inflation Figures increased dramatically—to over 5 in some cases for the percent black variable—indicating severe problems with multicolinearity. Nevertheless, the pattern of results for the other factors in the model was similar, especially for spatial proximity.

22. The spatial regime model is a switching regression model, in which the coefficients and constant term take on different values depending on the regime, and the coefficients of each regime are jointly estimated. The model also includes a spatial lag term that does not vary across regimes, meaning that the spatial process is assumed to be uniform across the entire city.

23. Although we specify only two regimes, we recognize that the "non-black" category encompasses a heterogeneous grouping of neighborhoods that may be predominantly white, predominantly Hispanic, or mixed. It is possible to expand the regime specification to more than two regimes, but further disaggregation of the non-black regime would result in very small sample sizes—there are only 69 neighborhood clusters that were over 75 percent white in 1990 and only 21 that were over 75 percent Hispanic. We thus present the more parsimonious two-regime specification and leave for future research the question of what explains differences across these two regimes. Our main interest here is the replicability of results in all black areas.

24. Both the overall Chow test for the structural stability of the regression model across the two regimes and the coefficient-specific Chow tests for stability across regimes reveal that there are no significant differences across regimes. This suggests that for incident-based homicide, the regression models for black and non-black neighborhoods are not significantly different.

25. In this model, the Chow test for the structural stability of the regression model across regimes indicates significant differences in the patterns of association across black and non-black neighborhoods. Coefficient-specific Chow tests indicate that the collective efficacy coefficient varies across regimes ($p = .01$), although the Chow tests for ICE ($p = .08$), concentrated immigration ($p = .09$), and organizations ($p = .08$) are all marginally significant.

References

Anselin, L. 1988. *Spatial Econometrics: Methods and Models*. Dordrecht: Kluwer Academic.

Anselin, L. 1995a. *SpaceStat Version 1.80: User's Guide*. Morgantown, W.Va.: West Virginia University.

Anselin, L. 1995b. Local indicators of spatial association—LISA. *Geographical Analysis* 27: 93–115.

Bellair, P. 2000. Informal surveillance and street crime: A complex process. *Criminology* 38: 137–170.

Black, D. 1983. Crime as social control. *American Sociological Review* 48: 34–45.

Block, R. 1977. *Violent Crime: Environment, Interaction, and Death*. Lexington, Mass.: Lexington Books.

Brooks-Gunn, J., G. Duncan, P. Kato, and N. Sealand. 1993. Do neighborhoods influence child and adolescent behavior? *American Journal of Sociology* 99: 353–395.

Bryk, A., and S.W. Raudenbush. 1992. *Hierarchical Linear Models*. Newbury Park, Calif.: Sage Publications.

Bursik, R.J., and H. Grasmick. 1993a. *Neighborhoods and Crime: The Dimensions of Effective Community Control*. New York: Lexington.

Bursik, R.J., and H. Grasmick. 1993b. Economic deprivation and neighborhood crime rates, 1960–1980. *Law and Society Review* 27: 263–284.

Cohen, L., and M. Felson. 1979. Social change and crime rate trends: A routine activity approach. *American Sociological Review* 44: 588–608.

Cohen, L., J. Kluegel, and K. Land. 1981. Social inequality and predatory criminal victimization: An exposition and test of a formal theory. *American Sociological Review* 46: 505–524.

Cohen, J., and G. Tita. 1999. Diffusion in homicide: Exploring a general method for detecting spatial diffusion processes. *Journal of Quantitative Criminology* 15: 451–493.

Fisher, F., and D. Nagin. 1978. On the feasibility of identifying the crime function in a simultaneous model of crime rates and sanction levels. In A. Blumstein, J. Cohen, and D. Nagin (eds.), *Deterrence and Incapacitation: Estimating the Effects of Criminal Sanctions on Crime Rates*. Washington, D.C.: National Academy Press, 361–399.

Hope, T. 1995. Community crime prevention. In M. Tonry, and D. Farrington (eds.), *Building a Safer Society*. Chicago: University of Chicago Press, 21–89.

Krivo, L., and R.D. Peterson. 2000. The structural context of homicide: Accounting for racial differences in process. *American Sociological Review* 65: 547–559.

Land, K., P. McCall, and L. Cohen. 1990. Structural covariates of homicide rates: Are there any invariances across time and space? *American Journal of Sociology* 95: 922–963.

Liska, A., and P. Bellair. 1995. Racial composition and crime: Convergence over time. *American Journal of Sociology* 101: 578–610.

Logan, J., and H. Molotch. 1987. *Urban Fortunes: The Political Economy of Place*. Berkeley, Calif.: University of California Press.

Massey, D.S. 1996. The age of extremes: Concentrated affluence and poverty in the twenty-first century. *Demography* 33: 395–412.

Massey, D.S. 2001. The prodigal paradigm returns: Ecology comes back to sociology. In A. Booth, and A. Crouter (eds.), *Does It Take a Village? Community Effects on Children, Adolescents, and Families*. Mahwah, N. J.: Lawrence Erlbaum Associates Publishers, 41–48.

Massey, D.S., and N. Denton. 1993. *American Apartheid: Segregation and the Making of the Underclass*. Cambridge, Mass.: Harvard University Press.

McCullagh, D.W., and J.A. Nelder. 1989. *Generalized Linear Models (2nd edition)*. London: Chapman and Hall.

Messner, S.F., L. Anselin, R.D. Baller, D.F. Hawkins, G. Deane, and S. Tolnay. 1999. The spatial patterning of county homicide rates: An application of exploratory spatial data analysis. *Journal of Quantitative Criminology* 15: 423–450.

Morenoff, J., and R.J. Sampson. 1997. Violent crime and the spatial dynamics of neighborhood transition: Chicago, 1970–1990. *Social Forces* 76: 31–64.

Morenoff, J., R.J. Sampson, and S. Raudenbush. 2001. Neighborhood inequality, collective efficacy, and the spatial dynamics of violence. *Criminology* 39: 517–560.

National Center for Health Statistics. 2000. *International Classification of Diseases, Ninth Revision* (ICD-9). http://www.cdc.gov/nchs/about/major/dvs/icd9des.htm.

Pattillo-McCoy, M.E. 1999. *Black Picket Fences: Privilege and Peril Among the Black Middle Class*. Chicago: University of Chicago Press.

Peterson, R.D., L.J. Krivo, and M.A. Harris. 2000. Disadvantage and neighborhood violent crime: Do local institutions matter? *Journal of Research in Crime and Delinquency* 37: 31–63.

Raudenbush, S., and R.J. Sampson. 1999. 'Ecometrics': toward a science of assessing ecological settings, with application to the systematic social observation of neighborhoods. *Sociological Methodology* 29: 1–41.

Raudenbush, S., and A.S. Bryk. 2002. *Hierarchical Linear Models: Applications and Data Analysis Methods*, Second Edition. Newbury Park, Calif.: Sage.

Reiss, A.J. Jr., and J. Roth (eds.). 1993. *Understanding and Preventing Violence (Volume 1)*. Washington, D.C.: National Academy Press.

Rosenfeld, R., T.M. Bray, and A. Egley. 1999. Facilitating violence: A comparison of gang-motivated, gang-affiliated, and nongang youth homicides. *Journal of Quantitative Criminology* 15(4): 495–516.

Sampson, R.J., J. Morenoff, and F. Earls. 1999. Beyond social capital: Spatial dynamics of collective efficacy for children. *American Sociological Review* 64: 633–660.

Sampson, R.J., J.D. Morenoff, and T. Gannon-Rowley. 2002. Assessing neighborhood effects: Social processes and new directions in research. *Annual Review of Sociology*, Volume 28, In Press.

Sampson, R.J., S. Raudenbush, and F. Earls. 1997. Neighborhoods and violent crime: A multilevel study of collective efficacy. *Science* 277: 918–924.

Sampson, R.J., and W.J. Wilson. 1995. Toward a theory of race, crime, and urban inequality. In J. Hagan, and R. Peterson (eds.), *Crime and Inequality*. Stanford, Calif.: Stanford University Press, 37–56.

Shaw, C., and H. McKay. 1942 (1969, 2nd edition). *Juvenile Delinquency and Urban Areas*. Chicago: University of Chicago Press.

Skogan, W. 1990. *Disorder and Decline: Crime and the Spiral of Decay in American Neighborhoods*. Berkeley, Calif.: University of California Press.

Smith, W.R., S.G. Frazee, and E.L. Davison. 2000. Furthering the integration of routine robbery as a diffusion process. *Criminology* 38: 489–523.

Tolnay, S., G. Deane, and E.M. Beck. 1996. Vicarious violence: Spatial effects on Southern lynchings, 1890–1919. *American Journal of Sociology* 102: 788–815.

Whittemore, A.S. 1989. Errors-in-variables regression using Stein estimates. *The American Statistician* 43: 226–228.

Wilson, W.J. 1987. *The Truly Disadvantaged: The Inner City, the Underclass, and Public Policy*. Chicago: University of Chicago Press.

9

Measuring Spatial Diffusion of Shots Fired Activity across City Neighborhoods

George Tita
Jacqueline Cohen

S ocial scientists interested in crime often ask one of two questions: "Why does the distribution of crime differ over place?" or "Why does the level of crime within a place change over time?" However, the social processes often posited to explain changing crime rates do not limit themselves to such an either/or proposition. That is, the mechanisms of crime (e.g., economic opportunities, social mobility, opportunity structures) are interdependent both over time and across geographic space. This is especially true for acts of interpersonal violence.

Though often only implicitly so, the interdependence of spatial and temporal factors is central to such theoretical and practical perspectives on violence as routine activities theory (Felson and Cohen 1980; Messner and Tardiff 1985), situational transactions perspective (Luckenbill 1977), drug market organization (Blumstein 1995; Blumstein and Cork 1996; Cork 1999; Wilkinson and Fagan 1996), and urban youth gangs (Bjerregaard and Lizotte 1995; Block and Block 1993; Braga et al. 2001; Cohen and Tita 1999; Maxson 1999; Rosenfeld et al. 1999). For instance, Blumstein posits a model where the adoption of guns as a tool of the trade in mid-1980s crack cocaine markets sparked the diffusion of guns from market participants, first to socially and spatially proximate inner-city youth, and then to less proximate youth and adults. This model is empirically supported by Cork's (1999) national-level examination of the arrival of crack in a city and the timing of the onset of a city's rise in homicide. Research also finds that gang conflicts often display patterns of spatial and temporal interdependence consistent with a retaliatory process (Cohen and Tita 1999; Cohen et al. 1998; Rosenfeld et al. 1999).

Cross sectional studies of spatial dynamics are only suggestive of social processes, and successfully isolating the underlying mechanisms that drive the distribution or diffusion of crime can only be accomplished by incorporating a times-series dimension into a spatial model (cf., Baller et al. 2001; Morenoff et al. 2001). The lack of explicit attention to the interdependent nature of spatial and temporal processes in empirical research arises chiefly from limitations in the ability of most multivariate statistical methods to identify the source of dependency within data on social processes. Model identification often becomes impossible when both types of dependency are present. It is possible, however, to begin to identify patterns of spatial and temporal change within an exploratory spatial data analysis framework (Cohen and Tita 1999).

Recent advances in exploratory spatial data analysis techniques (ESDA) provide social scientists with a new set of tools for distinguishing between random and non-random spatial patterns of events (Anselin 1999). One ESDA method—the Moran scatterplot—has special heuristic value because it visually displays local spatial relationships between each spatial unit and its neighbors. These early ESDA measures, however, are static and do no permit comparisons of distributions of events in the same space but across different time periods.

Our previous work extends the static cross-sectional view of the spatial distribution of events by developing a method that considers dynamic features of changes over time in spatial dependencies. The method distinguishes between *contagious diffusion* among adjoining spatial units and *hierarchical diffusion* that spreads broadly among spatial units through commonly shared influences. The identification of specific patterns of diffusion is useful for determining whether the observed patterns are consistent with specific social processes. For instance, by applying this method to homicide data, we found evidence of a contagion process in which high rates of youth-gang homicides in some census tracts are followed by increases in youth-nongang homicides in neighboring census tracts (Cohen and Tita 1999). This pattern is consistent with a social process by which guns, the predominate weapon in youth homicides, diffuse from gang members to the more general population of inner-city youth.

This chapter addresses both theoretical and methodological issues relating to the diffusion of gun violence. Distinctive features of the recent homicide epidemic (i.e., it disproportionately involved young, minority, urban males, and virtually all of the increase in homicides involved use of firearms) suggest that certain social processes—notably, illegal drug markets and gang rivalries—may be important for explaining the pattern and mechanisms of a more general spread of inter-personal gun violence among youth. To pursue this wider scope, we explore patterns of spatial diffusion in non-lethal precursors to gun violence reflected in emergency calls to police reporting "shots fired" incidents.

The remainder of the chapter is organized as follows. We first explore the distinguishing features among various types of diffusion, focusing especially on the mechanisms of diffusion and their application to incidents involving gun violence. The discussion then turns to the special features of gun incidents that make them candidates for diffusion. The focus is on identifying organizational features that tie violent incidents to specific locations. Street-level drug markets and youth gangs are especially implicated. Finally, empirical analyses explore the evidence of spatial diffusion in "shots fired." The results are suggestive about the processes of diffusion of guns and associated gun violence among youthful offenders and are of methodological value in exploring a means for detecting spatial diffusion processes that can be applied broadly to a wide array of social phenomena.

Background

It is well established that the decade following the mid-1980s was a period of sharp changes in some types of homicide in the United States. While total rates nationally were relatively stable, cycling between 8 and 10 homicides per 100,000 population, selected population groups—notably young black males in cities—experienced staggering increases in their homicide rates (Figure 9.1). Nationally, rates for black males ages 15 to 24 more than tripled between 1984 and the most recent peak year in 1993, with similar growth evident among victims (Fingerhut 1993; Fingerhut et al. 1998) and offenders (Blumstein 1995; Cook and Laub 1998, 2001; Fox 1996). Increased reliance on firearms was a distinguishing feature of the rise of homicides among young black males (Blumstein and Cork 1996; Cook and Laub 1998, 2001; Cork 1996; Wilkinson and Fagan 1996). Non-lethal forms of youthful gun violence displayed similarly escalating patterns as well (Cook and Laub 1998, 2001; Fox 1996).

The term "epidemic" is often invoked colloquially to describe this dramatic growth in homicides. In a strict mathematical or biological sense, certain structural features distinguish observed increases in social phenomena as epidemics. Simplifying somewhat, an epidemic involves non-monotonic changes, characterized first by a sudden shift to rapidly accelerating growth that is followed by slower declines. This distinctive temporal pattern depends fundamentally on the presence of some mechanism for transmitting the "infective" agent among susceptible individuals in the population. There is convincing evidence of non-linear growth and increasing concentration of gun homicides and other violent offending within a subpopulation at both the national and local levels (see Cohen and Tita 1999 for a review of these findings.) The challenge for

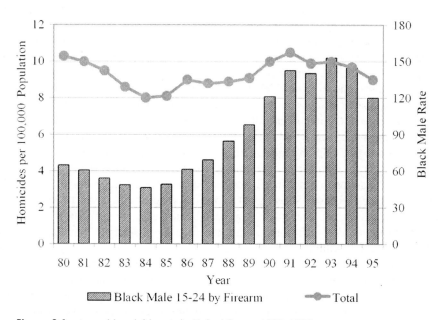

Figure 9.1. Annual homicide rate in United States, 1980–1995.

research lies in identifying the mechanisms of gun diffusion and understanding the social processes that drive the spread of related gun violence.

The concentration of growth in lethal and non-lethal violence among urban youth and firearms suggests that certain organizational and structural features—namely, growing youth participation in urban gangs and crack drug markets—may be crucial in the initial spread and subsequent decline of youthful gun violence. These youthful enterprises are likely to be especially relevant to diffusion, because they involve organizations that are sustained over time through continuing social interactions, both among participants and between participants and outsiders. The particular nature of these social interactions, with their heavy reliance on violence to maintain order, is also important, as is the explicit role that spatial locations play in each. For instance, the prevailing wisdom is that participants in crack markets quickly succumbed to the need to carry and use guns as tools of the trade. As hypothesized by Blumstein (1995) and empirically supported by Blumstein and Cork (1996), arming participants in crack markets increases the risks of violence for non-participants as well. Faced with increased risks to personal safety, youth outside crack markets increasingly carry guns and use them to settle interpersonal disputes, thereby spreading gun violence more broadly among the youth population. While spreading guns and associated gun violence to new segments of the population, early crack markets were less likely to serve as vehicles for the geographical spread of violence to new locations. As an illicit market, continued transactions often depend on maintaining stable market locations so that customers can easily locate sellers. Such markets entail strong incentives for locational persistence.

Gang locales tend to be centers of persistently high crime rates, especially violence (Block 1998; Spergel and Curry 1990; Tita 1999a). Violence is presumed to be another integral part of gang life. Used internally, it might serve as a means for maintaining control over and assuring loyalty by gang members. Used against outsiders, it may serve as a means of inflicting harm on rivals and garnering cooperation, or even submission, from the surrounding host population. Identity with a place is a strong motivating factor for gangs. Research has repeatedly demonstrated the importance that gang members attach to the specific areas in which they hang out (e.g., Klein 1995; Moore 1991; Tita et al. 1998). Spatial diffusion of gun violence involving gangs might follow two distinct paths. Because of the importance of gang turf, both symbolically and practically for gang members and their activities, we might expect the greatest spatial dependencies to occur among neighboring tracts. This pattern would be consistent with *contagious* diffusion through *expansion* from original-source innovator gangs out to imitator gangs that form in reaction to gangs in neighboring tracts and to the threat posed by gang violence in nearby locations. Alternatively, contemporaneous emergence of youth gangs in many widely spread areas might have been influenced by broad cultural influences leading to *hierarchical* diffusion with distinct youth gangs emerging simultaneously in different locations within a city.

In addition to features that facilitate the growth and spread of gun violence and its precursors, crack markets and youth gangs also involve self-limiting features that may stem the tide of an epidemic. Drug dealers realize that too much violence is bad for business, because it attracts increased police attention and encourages customers to find other less violent outlets. Technological changes also affected the operation of crack markets. Notably, new communications technology in the form of beepers, pagers, and cellular phones, and new ways of marketing these communications services through large one-time cash purchases, substantially reduced the importance of stable market locations. Rather than hawking their wares in known—and possibly increasingly dangerous—street locations, dealers could be anywhere waiting for a customer's call. The actual location of the transaction became more flexible and could be chosen to maximize dealer and customer safety.

The types of places where crack markets and youth gangs locate may also help to limit the spread of these types of violence. Continuing patterns of racial residential segregation, compounded by further segregation within minority communities along social and economic status dimensions, effectively isolate disadvantaged urban minority communities spatially and socially from contact with others. This physical and social isolation also may serve to limit the diffusion of homicides across space and more importantly, across population subgroups. To the extent that virtually all aspects of the daily social life of a population subgroup are limited to other members of the same group, there are few occasions for spreading violent encounters to other groups. This may help to explain why minority youth, especially young black males, were so susceptible during the most recent homicide epidemic. Crack and violent youth gangs first emerged and flourished in poor minority communities. Sharp differences in social and economic structure—notably in the capacity for exercising informal social control—between afflicted communities and their neighbors likely served to effectively repel the encroachment of these violent enterprises into neighboring areas.[1]

Diffusion Processes and the Role of Drug Markets and Gangs

Though often used interchangeably, the terms diffusion and contagion refer to different aspects of the processes of spread and recession of a phenomenon. Diffusion refers to the general process of movement, while contagion is one mechanism for achieving that movement. Below, we briefly define the various categories of diffusion and contagion and offer examples of how the organizational features of drug markets and urban street gangs might serve as catalysts to the spread of violence as well as those features of each that might inhibit growth.

Contagious diffusion depends on direct contact and is the classic way of spreading disease. While a single person may be responsible for infecting a large number of people with a particular infectious disease over a large geographic area, it is highly unlikely that contagious spread of violence will involve single perpetrators, or single incidents, that precipitate gun use by many others. However, when a gun attack is instigated by, or furthers the objectives of a continuing organization, organizational interests may well fuel a series of related reprisals. For example, rivalries between gangs or drug markets in the same city may lead to a series of retaliatory acts among competing enterprises. The threat of victimization these incidents pose for individuals not associated with gangs or drug markets may prompt the further spread of threats of gun violence by potentially triggering an increase in defensive gun carrying and use among populations outside the competing organizations. Furthermore, when the interests of violence-linked organizations are tied to specific locations, geographic proximity may be important in determining the extent of spread that occurs in violence and its precursors.

Two main types of contagious diffusion are possible: *relocation diffusion* and *expansion diffusion*. In *relocation diffusion* the object being diffused leaves the point of origin and spreads outward from that point. A forest fire exemplifies this type of diffusion as the fire moves along the landscape toward new fuel sources, and abandons previously affected areas as the fuel there is exhausted. Evidence of relocation diffusion in the case of gun violence might emerge following effective policing practices that displace gun violence from one location to another. Responding to a series of retaliatory strikes between rivals (gangs or drug dealers), law enforcement might focus its resources in the areas of the most recent assaults or homicides. In response, the targeted gangs or drug markets might move their activities to nearby locations just beyond the concentration of police resources. If repeated over several successive incidents, gun violence may spread out from an origin. Since spread by *relocation diffusion* involves newly active areas replacing previously active ones, currently active prevalence need not be substantially increasing in this type of diffusion.

Like relocation diffusion, *expansion diffusion* also spreads from the center, but the diffusing phenomenon continues at high rates at the place of origin. A strong attachment to a specific place is inherent to both youth gangs and drug markets. This increases the likelihood that the center of activity (gang turf or market location) will continue to exhibit high levels of associated violence. Temporary retreats from an area occur during periods of intensified attention from law enforcement or from rivals. Once attention from adversaries declines, gang members and drug dealers will likely return to reclaim a location. Expansion diffusion may also be a factor in a receding epidemic as the benefits of effective treatments are spread to populations in adjoining geographic areas. In the case of crime prevention interventions, recent evaluations have noted a previously unexpected "*diffusion of* [crime prevention] *benefits*" from treated areas to immediately adjacent untreated areas (Clarke and Weisburd 1994).

The second mechanism for the spread of gun violence is through *hierarchical diffusion*. "This [process] describes transmission through an ordered sequence of classes or places. The process is typified by the diffusion of innovations (such as new styles in women's fashions or new consumer goods, for example, television) from large metropolitan centers to remote villages" (Cliff et al. 1981, 9). In this instance, the spread of a phenomenon does not require direct contact, but rather occurs through *spontaneous innovation* or *imitation*. Transmission is through broad cultural influences that affect the general population or a particular subgroup that may be widely dispersed geographically. We are particularly interested in instances of hierarchical diffusion that occur relatively quickly in time as in the spread of fads or fashions. Within a city, the effects of hierarchical diffusion might be manifested close in time in many physically disjoint—but socially similar—neighborhoods.

Spontaneous innovation might accompany the introduction of a new product like crack cocaine that is widely accessible to potential new dealers. Because it is cheap and easy to produce, this product might spawn the simultaneous development of several new and unrelated marketing organizations in different parts of a city. Imitation may also figure prominently through mass media popularization of a distinctive lifestyle that is common in one area of the country, e.g., gang-related violence, which is then copied in other cities. There is little evidence that well-established gangs in some parts of the country (e.g., Los Angeles and Chicago) cultivated newly emerging gangs in many smaller U.S. cities (Maxson 1998). Instead, it appears that violent urban street gangs emerged independently in many cities as local youth adopted a lifestyle they saw portrayed in the media. Similarly, it is possible that the formation of gangs within cities followed a similar ordered-adoption.

Hierarchical diffusion, like contagious diffusion, may also be a factor during the receding phase of an epidemic. This is most evident in the case of passing fads that may be widely dispersed initially, but with only weak commitment by adopters, so that they quickly recede again. If highly visible lifestyle changes among new youth gang members are not accompanied by the development of an institutional infrastructure for sustaining the organization, new gangs will not be able to sustain themselves as early members leave. Popularization of newly emerging attitudes that discourage youth involvement in crack markets or gangs likewise may spread broadly throughout a population without requiring direct contact.

Patterns of Diffusion in Homicide

We previously found the following regarding the impact of drug markets and gangs on the changing levels and spatial distribution of homicide in Pittsburgh. Despite the arrival of crack markets in Pittsburgh late in 1989, the number of drug-related homicides changed hardly at all over the entire period 1987 to 1995. However, the formation of gangs, beginning in late 1991 and continuing through 1992, is associated with substantial increases in youth homicides in Pittsburgh. Consistent with hierarchical diffusion in response to widely felt cultural influences, the proliferation of youth gangs was accompanied by sharp increases in youth-gang and youth-nongang homicides in widely dispersed areas of the city. With respect to diffusion, the homicidal violence that started in gang-involved incidents apparently spread quickly from gang to non-gang youth, with non-gang homicides accounting for 38 percent of the growth during the peak year of homicides in 1993. In that year, there is evidence of contagious diffusion from tracts with high-rates of youth-gang homicides in 1992 to increased rates of youth-nongang homicides in neighboring tracts during 1993.

There is little overlap between drug- and gang-related homicides. Homicides that were both gang- and drug-involved were only 6 percent of total homicides in the period 1991 to 1995. This subset of dual drug-gang homicides represents 21 percent of total gang-related homicides and 27 percent of all drug-related homicides.

Gang-involved homicides changed in character over time. A homicide was classified as gang-related if the homicide involved some gang motivation (e.g., inter-gang disputes, initiation activities, or spontaneous drive-by killings) or any participant was a gang member. The special subclass of "member-only" homicides involved at least one gang member, but no gang motivation. From the start of youth-gang homicides in late 1991, gang-motivated homicides were about two-thirds and member-only homicides one-third of all gang-involved homicides in the city. This changed at the end of the study period in 1995 when member-only homicides—usually involving domestic disputes or robberies—increased to become 68 percent of all gang-involved homicides. This transformation in the nature of gang-involved homicides may signal a decline in active gangs in the city.

Analyzing Shots Fired

Homicides, which are the most serious form of interpersonal violence, are also relatively rare. They represent only a portion of violence generally. Because fatalities are rare, changes in violence and in the processes that underlie these changes are often difficult to detect from homicides alone. This is especially so for processes of diffusion in which acts of violence propagate further violence throughout a population, but the chain of violence is observed only intermittently in cases with fatal outcomes. Tracking a more complete series of violent incidents will provide a better basis for isolating any diffusion processes that may exist.

Police incident report data on the full array of youthful assaults, robberies, and homicides with guns would provide a more complete picture of the waxing and waning over time and space of gun violence during the period of epidemic increases in youth homicides. While police reports for a wider array of incidents involving actual or threatened gun violence would expand the numbers and types of violent incidents, police reports are themselves filtered, first by incidents not reported to police by citizens, and second by police practices governing the recording of citizen-reported offenses.

Citizen calls for emergency services—"911" calls—are an alternative to police incident reports. Call data on assaults and robberies do not improve substantially on police reports for these incidents. While call data will include incidents that police designate as "unfounded" and exclude from reported offenses, call data are equally vulnerable to victim non-reporting. Also, aside from date, time, and address, 911 call data do not include any further information on attributes of the participants or incidents. Despite these limitations, another class of calls reporting "shots fired" incidents represents an attractive opportunity.

"Shots fired" data include incidents where a gun is fired but did not result in injuries, for example, shots fired into the air or ground, or at property. While some shots fired incidents are not themselves violent, they represent a type of behavior closely related to gun violence. Other commonly used measures of gun prevalence—subscriptions to gun and sporting magazines, hunting licenses, memberships in sporting and gun advocacy groups—are quite remote from actual availability and illegal usage of guns, and such data are generally not available at levels of spatial resolution smaller than counties or states.

Shots fired incidents, by contrast, not only capture varying levels of access to *crime guns*, but also variations in willingness to use guns in a criminal manner. At its most trivial level, discharging a gun within city limits is usually a criminal violation. Criminal use escalates in seriousness when the gun is fired to damage property and reaches its highest levels of seriousness when the gun is fired to threaten or injure another person. Incident-level data on shots fired not only provide a more direct indicator of the prevalence and use of crime guns, they often do so at the level of local neighborhoods within a city.

Aside from providing direct measures of access to crime guns, variations in levels of shots fired calls also provide reasonable proxy measures of variations in more serious gun violence among youth within a city. In some instances, shots fired are directly linked to violence. The shots fired incidents may themselves be failed attempts at violence, where the shooter misses the targeted victim. In other cases, shots fired may be intended as warnings or threats of violence. And in still other instances, perpetrators are practicing to use firearms in attacks on others. The link between shots fired and violence is evident in the similar temporal and spatial patterns of shots fired and youth homicides. Figure 9.2, for example, shows how closely shots fired and youth homicides track one another, with similarly escalating rates to a citywide peak in 1993, followed by a slower downturn. The two measures also share similar spatial distributions across tracts, with youth homicides significantly more likely to occur inside tracts characterized by the highest levels of shots fired (Table 9.1).

Given the predominate role of firearms in youthful homicides and the links with violence evident in the similar spatial and temporal patterns among shots fired and youth homicides, it is reasonable to expect that many of the same social processes that underlie diffusion of youth homicides will also influence the spatial and temporal dynamics of shots fired. To the extent that such relationships do obtain, the more frequent shots fired incidents provide a more robust measure of gun violence than previously analyzed homicide data. Furthermore, because homicide is such a rare event, our previous research was limited to examining yearly changes in homicide rates. The frequency of shots fired—at about 2,500 annually—is sufficient to permit analysis of quarterly changes. This finer temporal resolution increases the potential of identifying processes of diffusion that might otherwise be masked in more aggregate annual data. Exploiting both the shots fired and homicide data, we will also explore the extent to

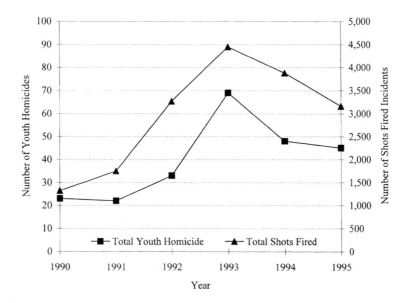

Figure 9.2. Annual citywide trends in shots fired and youth homicides.

Table 9.1. Association between annual youth homicides and levels of shots fired in census tracts in Pittsburgh, 1990–1995.

| Year | Youth Homicides | Number of Tracts by Annual Level of Shots Fired[†] | | | χ^{2}[††] |
		Low	Medium	High	
1990	None	135	17	1	17.15
	At least one	12	7	2	
1991	None	128	24	1	25.78
	At least one	11	6	4	
1992	None	108	29	9	20.97
	At least one	8	13	6	
1993	None	85	43	4	59.75
	At least one	7	16	20	
1994	None	94	44	3	71.95
	At least one	6	9	18	
1995	None	99	47	2	43.46
	At least one	8	9	9	

[†] Low tracts have no more than one shot fired call monthly (<12 annually), medium tracts about one weekly (< 55 annually), and high tracts more than one weekly ($\geq$ 59 annually).

[††] χ^{2} (2 degrees of freedom) are all statistically significant at better than .0001 level.

which changes in the level and location of shots fired may serve as a leading indicator that youth homicides are likely to follow.

Data

The analysis that follows uses calls for emergency services—"911" data—reporting shots fired (as described above) in the city of Pittsburgh for the six years from 1 January 1990 to 31 December 1995. Using the available information on date, time, and address, individual incidents can be located spatially and temporally. Shots fired incidents are aggregated to counts in 1990 census tracts. Tracts are small enough to meaningfully distinguish between areas with and without gangs and crack markets (Tita 1999b) and to observe diffusion across space. As the units of analysis increase in size and include more diverse areas within the same areal unit, it becomes more difficult to actually observe the spread of shots fired *between units,* as opposed to an undetectable redistribution among locations within the same spatial unit. With 174 tracts citywide and 24 quarters in the six years of data, the data include observations for a total of 4,176 tract-quarters.

Both the local level and rate of diffusion of shots fired will depend on the size of the population at risk in census tracts. The larger the population at risk in an area, the greater the likelihood of shots fired incidents. To better isolate the effects of spatial proximity from those of population at risk, the analysis of diffusion relies on population-based rates of gun violence, specifically rates adjusted by total population minus children under age 12. In three tracts with total populations under 100, we assigned population adjusted rates of zero shots fired to remove the unusually high rates that result when very few shots fired incidents are adjusted relative to these unusually small population bases.

We hypothesize that the two features of potentially greatest relevance for the spatial diffusion of guns and gun violence are crack drug markets and youth gangs. Because these two features arrived in the city at different times, it should be possible to isolate their separate influences on gun violence. Crack cocaine arrived in Pittsburgh during the latter half of 1989. It was accompanied by substantial increases in drug arrests (up more than 100 percent from 1988 to 1989, and an additional 61 percent from 1989 to 1990), especially arrests of younger offenders through age 20 (up 4.7-fold from 1988 to 1989, and then almost 2-fold from 1989 to 1990).

While we found little evidence that drug markets impacted levels of homicides, we continue to include the geographic location of drug markets to explore whether these markets might have served as the source of diffusion for other forms of gun violence, reflected here in shots fired, to other spatially proximate areas. Furthermore, the temporal lag between the establishment of crack markets and the emergence of gangs provides an opportunity to determine if shots fired activity diffused prior to the establishment of gangs, or whether shots fired diffused only after gangs emerged.

Local gang members reported in interviews that recent gang "sets" began emerging in Pittsburgh during the latter half of 1991 and continued forming through 1992 (Tita 1999b; Tita et al. 1998). This start-up period was confirmed in parallel interviews with youth service workers and police officers working in the affected neighborhoods, as well as by sharp increases in the volume of citizen-initiated 911 calls reporting shots fired (a common gang activity that rose by 78 percent between 1991 and 1992). The method for identifying gang locations is detailed in our earlier work (Tita 1999b; Tita et al. 1998.) This measure is static, once a gang emerges in a census tract, it does not desist prior to the end of the current study period (1995).

Since the specific locations of drug markets can be fluid, especially following the arrival of technological innovations that enabled highly mobile telephone communications, we identify drug markets separately for each year. The annual number of 911 drug calls reported to the police was aggregated to the census tract level for each year. We designated the fifteen tracts with the most drug complaints annually as the most active drug markets each year. The total tracts with youth gangs is 33 (19 percent of all tracts), and 15 tracts (9 percent of the total) have highly active drug markets each year. Because of overlap, a total of 37 tracts (21 percent of the total) include either drug markets or youth gangs sometime over the six years of data.

Table 9.2 reports the association between the locations of youth gangs and highly active drug markets in 1993 (the distribution is virtually the same in every year). As might be expected, youth gangs are 3 times more likely (39.4 percent versus 12.6 percent) to be located in tracts with highly active drug markets than in tracts without these markets. The same relationship prevails at the same level in every year. It is interesting to note that, while the extent of overlap between youth gang locales and highly active drug market remains stable over time, the specific tracts with highly active drug markets change substantially over time. For example, six of the highly active drug market tracts in 1990 are not highly active in 1995, and seven active market tracts in 1995 were not similarly active in 1990.

Table 9.2. Distribution of youth gangs and most active drug markets over Pittsburgh census tracts in 1993.[†]

		Highly Active Drug Markets		
		No	Yes	Total
Youth Gangs	No	139	2	141
	Yes	20	13	33
	Total	159	15	174
		χ^2	(df, *p*-value)	48.96 (1, <.0001)

[†]Annual totals are 33 tracts with youth gangs and 15 tracts with highly active drug markets. A total of 37 tracts have either in any of the six years.

The tracts with waxing and waning drug market activity, however, share at least one thing in common—they are home to youth gangs (in all six of the 1990 market tracts, and six of the seven 1995 market tracts). While we found very little overlap between drug-related and gang-related homicides, drug markets and youth gangs evidently do share social space, and there may be more overlap in non-lethal forms of violence associated with these two forms of criminal enterprises. We return to this theme when considering diffusion of shots fired.

Spatial Features of Shots Fired

We know from citywide data that the levels of reported shots fired changed dramatically during the study period (Figure 9.2). There are also indications that these changes in citywide totals involved both increasing concentration of shots fired in already affected locations and the dispersion of gun activity to new locations. Concentration and dispersion measures capture the breadth and depth of high-rate activity in the city. But how were the affected tracts distributed spatially in the city? Was the growth restricted primarily within clusters of neighboring tracts or distributed more broadly across the city? To answer these questions, we look first to available measures of spatial association.

Global measures of spatial dependence look for spatial associations in the distribution of some phenomenon. Positive associations exist when neighboring locations share similar levels of a variable, for example, clusters of high (or low) values in geographically proximate locations. The association is negative when neighboring locations are dissimilar, with high-level locations adjacent to low-level neighbors. One of the most commonly used measures of global spatial association is Moran's I, a statistic that measures the extent of similarity or dissimilarity in a variable across neighboring spatial units. For the combined years from 1992 to 1995, the global Moran's $I = .48$ ($p < .001$ in two-tailed test) for annual shots fired rates in each tract. A positive Moran's I indicates that tracts with similar values are reasonably spatially clustered across the city over the six years of data.

The global Moran's I statistic is most useful for detecting a single common *citywide* pattern of spatial dependency. As a global indicator, it measures the presence of a homogeneous pattern of spatial association across the entire study area. Global measures are poorly suited when there is heterogeneity in spatial dependencies, for example, a case with varying levels of association across different regions of the study area. Such nonstationarity in the association across space might be manifested in the extreme by localized "hot spots," or even positive associations in some regions and negative associations in others. Local indicators of spatial association (LISA) statistics are more appropriate for detecting such spatial instabilities (Anselin 1993, 1995a).

Local Indicators of Spatial Association

LISA statistics are especially valuable in exploratory spatial data analyses looking for patterns across space in spatial dependencies. The values of a variable for local and neighbor pairs provide the most basic representation of local spatial associations. Each pair (L, N) consists of the standardized level of a variable in the local (L) spatial unit and the standardized value of the same variable in neighboring (N) spatial units—both standardized relative to their respective mean and standard deviation across the spatial units. In this analysis, neighbor values are the simple average value of a variable in all physically adjacent units (obtained using the row-standardized version of a simple 0/1 contiguity matrix). Each element of the pair is either low (L) or high (H) relative to the distributions of the respective local and neighbor values across all observations. The standardized values locate each local-neighbor pair within a two-dimensional Euclidian space (Figure 9.3). Pairs in which both the local and neighbor values are above their respective means fall in the upper right HH quadrant. When both elements of the pair are below their means, the pair falls in the lower left LL quadrant. When the relative values of local and neighbor units differ, the pair falls in either the HL or LH quadrant.

By standardizing the local and neighbor shots fired rates relative to their respective means and standard deviations, a simple scatterplot of local-neighbor pairs like that in Figure 9.3 provides a basis for judging the relative strength of spatial relationships. While the appropriate distributional assumption for the spatial units is unknown, we invoke a simple "two-sigma" rule to approximate the tails of the distribution. In a variation from the approach suggested by Anselin (1995b), "significant" tracts fall outside the circle defined by an origin at the local and neighbor means and radius that is two standard units in length. Extreme outliers in the HH quadrant may be symptomatic of "hot spots," while those in the LL quadrant may be relatively "immune" to the phenomenon under study.

Figure 9.3 plots local-neighbor pairs for shots fired rates in the fourth quarter of 1992, one of the most active periods of reported gun activity. A total of 22 tracts in the HH and HL quadrants experienced high shots fired rates locally during this quarter relative to the overall distribution of rates across all tracts and quarters. Local rates in another 15 tracts in the LH quadrant are below the overall mean locally, but relatively high-rate neighbors surround these tracts. None of the local-neighbor pairs in the LL quadrant ever exceeds the two-sigma distance filter. Figure 9.4 displays the outlier tracts for the above period on a map. The significant local-neighbor pairs form several disjoint clusters of high-rate shots fired activity throughout the city.

The above illustrates the use of exploratory spatial data analysis to identify localized clusters of adjoining high-rate tracts. Such analyses, however, provide static views of the spatial distribution of shots fired at just one point in time. They do not address the

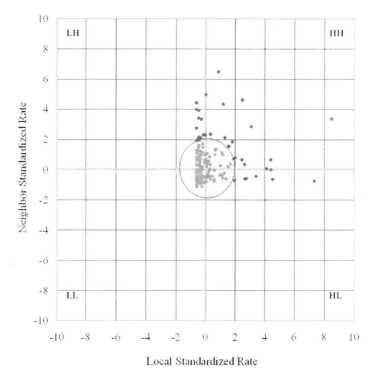

Figure 9.3. Scatterplot of local and neighbor standardized rates for shots fired, 4th quarter 1992.

dynamics of changes in that distribution over time. To partially address this limitation, we have created a Web-based exhibit to visually display animated sequences of outlier clusters in successive quarters.[2] While there are indications of some potential diffusion among neighboring census tracts, the visual displays alone do not help in discerning what types of processes might underlie the evident movement among locations. Is it just random relocations, or is some more systematic process of diffusion at work? These questions arise naturally from viewing the animations, but they are difficult to answer by relying solely on visual displays.

Dynamics of Change in Spatial Relationships

The *local-neighbor* pairs provide a simple but powerful tool for identifying spatial clusters. We introduce here a simple method for extending the analysis of these pairs to address dynamic features of changes over time in the spatial patterns. The method focuses on changes in the levels of local-neighbor pairs and looks for evidence of diffusion that involves the spread of high (or low) rates to increasing numbers of spatial units. This spread may be spatially dependent among adjoining spatial units or more general throughout non-adjoining units. We apply the method to look for evidence of

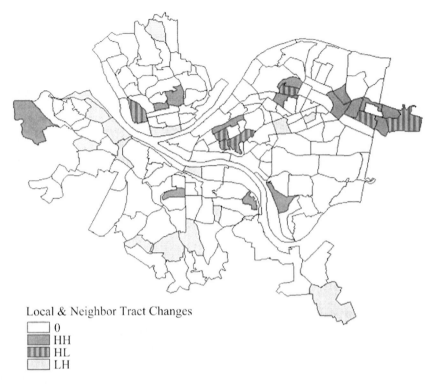

Local & Neighbor Tract Changes

☐ 0
▨ HH
▥ HL
☐ LH

Figure 9.4. Significant local and neighbor shots fired rates: Pittsburgh tracts, 4th quarter 1992.

the spatial diffusion of shots fired among census tracts within one city. The method has the potential for much wider application as a means of characterizing changes over time in spatial units.

Method for Calibrating the Extent of Diffusion

Table 9.3 identifies the full array of possible combinations of local-neighbor pairs over successive time periods. The various combinations of pairs in successive time periods are each compatible with a different type of diffusion. The types of change are distinguished in terms of the direction and mechanism of change, and whether the local spatial unit is the outcome or source of diffusion in local-neighbor pairs.

The direction of diffusion may be monotonic or non-monotonic over time. An epidemic is a particular form of non-monotonic diffusion, with an "infectious" period of rapid spread of high levels, followed by a period of slower proliferation of low levels as the epidemic recedes. We would expect to see changes in both directions in annual tract-level shots fired rates.

Four mechanisms lead to changes from low to high levels in spatial units. *Expansion* and *relocation* are forms of *contagious diffusion* in which the status among neighboring spatial units affects the future status of adjoining units, either by increasing the

Table 9.3. Dynamics of change in spatial distribution of shots fired rates over successive observations.

Direction of Change	Type of Diffusion	Mechanism of Change	Year-to-Year Change in Local-Neighbor *Pairs*	
			Local is Diffusion Outcome	Local is Diffusion Source
Changes from low to high levels	Contagious	Expansion among neighbors	LH to HH	HL to HH
		Relocation among neighbors	LH to HL	HL to LH
	Hierarchical	Isolated increase	LL to HL	LL to LH
		Global increase	LL to HH	LL to HH
Changes from high to low levels	Contagious	Expansion among neighbors	HL to LL	LH to LL
		Relocation among neighbors	HL to LH	LH to HL
	Hierarchical	Isolated decrease	HH to LH	HH to HL
		Global decrease	HH to LL	HH to LL
No change	None	Stationary		

level locally or in the neighbors located in the same local-neighbor pair. Spatial units can also change from low to high levels through *hierarchical diffusion* in the form of spontaneous increases that occur in *isolated* tracts or *globally* in many tracts simultaneously. Both types of hierarchical diffusion reflect increases that do not depend on contact with nearby high-level spatial units. Instead, individual or adjoining spatial units "heave" upward without any neighbor effects, possibly in response to broad cultural influences. Four parallel mechanisms lead to changes in the opposite direction, from high to low levels in spatial units. Finally, the spatial pattern of local-neighbor pairs may remain stationary over successive observations, with no evident changes in levels in response to high or low levels in other spatial units.

Large changes can be distinguished from small changes using the Euclidian distance, D, between successive local-neighbor pairs, (L_t, N_t) and (L_{t+1}, N_{t+1}):

$$D = \sqrt{(L_{t+1} - L_t)^2 + (N_{t+1} - N_t)^2} \tag{1}$$

where L_t = standardized value at time t of a local spatial unit, and N_t = standardized value at time t of the spatially lagged weighted average value in neighboring spatial units. Without making any strong assumptions about the appropriate distributional form for this distance measure, we invoke a simple two-sigma rule as an approximation to identify unusually large changes in either an increasing or decreasing direction. Changes over time between quadrants that involve a move of at least two standard units in the value of a local-neighbor LISA pair will be designated as "significant."

Method for Analyzing Dynamic Changes over Time in Spatial Distributions

The basic strategy is to compare the relative prevalence of transitions among the different local-neighbor LISA pairs in successive time periods. The question is whether transitions that are compatible with diffusion are more likely than expected based on the prevalence of other transitions to the same local-neighbor outcome. The spread of high shots fired rates among neighboring tracts is of special interest in the present analysis. An excess of significant transitions from LH shots fired rates at time t to HL or HH rates at time $t + 1$ is compatible with contagious diffusion of high rates of shots fired activity from neighboring tracts. In this case, the comparison transition rate is based on the prevalence of other non-stationary, significant transitions to HL and HH outcomes at time $t + 1$. A simple t-test of the difference between proportions evaluates whether the diffusion transition occurs more often than might be expected based on the prevalence of other transitions to the same outcome. A more formal treatment of this methodology follows.

The basic units of analysis used in this research are LISA (Local Indicators of Spatial Association) statistics that characterize the levels in local-neighbor pairs relative to their respective standardized distributions. Each local area and its neighbors can be L = low (i.e., below the mean) or H = high (i.e., above the mean). The LISA pair $L_t H_t$, for example, designates a spatial area that has a low level (below mean) locally and high level (above mean) in neighboring spatial areas. Spatial diffusion involves changes over time in the levels of these local-neighbor LISA pairs. Tables 9.4 and 9.5 identify the various possible transitions among local-neighbor pairs. The shaded transitions in these tables involve some form of "significant" diffusion, either in the *local* level of local-neighbor pairs (Table 9.4), or in the *neighbor* level of local-neighbor pairs (Table 9.5). The actual calculation of diffusion and comparison transition rates is in Table 9.6.

Contagious diffusion that results in increased local levels is reflected in transitions from LH rates at time t in Table 9.4. Exposure to high levels in neighboring spatial units is associated with increases in local levels, either through expansion $\left[L_t H_t \text{ to } H_{t+1} H_{t+1} \right]$ or relocation $\left[L_t H_t \text{ to } H_{t+1} L_{t+1} \right]$. Hierarchical diffusion to high local levels is reflected in transitions from LL levels at time t, through either isolated increases locally $\left[L_t L_t \text{ to } H_{t+1} L_{t+1} \right]$ or global increases in both local and neighboring spatial units $\left[L_t L_t \text{ to } H_{t+1} H_{t+1} \right]$. The cells in Table 9.4 that highlight these instances of upward diffusion from low to high levels are marked with a single dagger (†). The transitions marked by daggers († and ††) in these tables reflect analogous downward diffusion from HL or HH local-neighbor pairs at time t to low levels in the local unit at time $t + 1$.

The diagonal elements in Tables 9.4 and 9.5 are *stationary* transitions that involve no change in local-neighbor levels in successive time periods. The sixth column of these tables includes all those changes in local-neighbor LISA pairs that do not satisfy the criterion of "significant" changes. These "non-significant" cases involve non-stationary changes in LISA statistics (e.g., from LH to HH), but the Euclidian distance between the local-neighbor pairs at times t and $t + 1$ does not exceed two standard units.

One strategy for empirically gauging the relative prevalence of diffusion is simply to compare the raw counts of transitions in local-neighbor pairs from time t to $t + 1$ reflected in Tables 9.4 and 9.5. Large variations in the row totals, however, will seriously distort comparisons of counts across different rows. For example, a large count for global increases reflected in N_{14} of Table 9.4 compared to a much smaller count for expansion diffusion reflected in N_{34} of the table might be interpreted as indicating that hierarchical diffusion dominates contagious diffusion. The difference in counts, how-

Table 9.4. Possible transitions over time in local neighbor pairs: local area is outcome of diffusion.

Local-Neighbor Pairs at Time t	"Significant" Change in Local-Neighbor Pairs at $t+1$				Changes Not "Significant" at $t+1$	Total	Total Excluding Stationary Diagonals
	LL	HL	LH	HH			
LL	N_{11} Stationary	N_{12} Hierarchical Isolated Increase†	N_{13}	N_{14} Hierarchical Global Increase†	N_{15} Small changes from LL to HL, LH, or HH	$N_{1.}$ $\sum_{j=1}^5 N_{1j}$	$N_{1.} - N_{11}$
HL	N_{21} Contagious expansion in local††	N_{22} Stationary	N_{23} Contagious relocation in local††	N_{24}	N_{25} Small changes from HL to LL, LH, or HH	$N_{2.}$ $\sum_{j=1}^5 N_{2j}$	$N_{2.} - N_{22}$
LH	N_{31}	N_{32} Contagious relocation in local†	N_{33} Stationary	N_{34} Contagious expansion in local†	N_{15} Small changes from LH to LL, HL, or HH	$N_{3.}$ $\sum_{j=1}^5 N_{3j}$	$N_{3.} - N_{33}$
HH	N_{41} Hierarchical global decrease††	N_{42}	N_{43} Hierarchical isolated decrease††	N_{44} Stationary	N_{45} Small changes from HH to LL, HL, or LH	$N_{4.}$ $\sum_{j=1}^5 N_{4j}$	$N_{4.} - N_{44}$
Total	$N_{.1}$ $\sum_{i=1}^4 N_{i1}$	$N_{.2}$ $\sum_{i=1}^4 N_{i2}$	$N_{.3}$ $\sum_{i=1}^4 N_{i3}$	$N_{.4}$ $\sum_{i=1}^4 N_{i4}$	$N_{.5}$ $\sum_{i=1}^4 N_{i5}$	$N_{..}$ $\sum_{i=1}^4 \sum_{j=1}^5 N_{ij}$	
Total excluding stationary diagonals	$N_{.1} - N_{11}$	$N_{.2} - N_{22}$	$N_{.3} - N_{33}$	$N_{.4} - N_{44}$	$N_{.5}$	$N_{..} - N_{11} - N_{22} - N_{33} - N_{44}$	$N_{..} - N_{11} - N_{22} - N_{33} - N_{44}$

†Diffusion transitions to increased local rates.

††Diffusion transitions to decreased local rates.

Table 9.5. Possible transitions over time in local neighbor pairs: local area is source of diffusion.

Local-Neighbor Pairs at Time t	"Significant" Change in Local-Neighbor Pairs at $t+1$				Changes Not "Significant" at $t+1$	Total	Total Excluding Stationary Diagonals
	LL	HL	LH	HH			
LL	N_{11} Stationary	N_{12}	N_{13} Hierarchical Isolated Increase†	N_{14} Hierarchical Global Increase†	N_{15} Small changes from LL to HL, LH, or HH	$N_{1.}$ $\sum_{j=1}^{5} N_{1j}$	$N_{1.} - N_{11}$
HL	N_{21}	N_{22} Stationary	N_{23} Contagious relocation in local†	N_{24} Contagious expansion in neighbors†	N_{25} Small changes from HL to LL, LH, or HH	$N_{2.}$ $\sum_{j=1}^{5} N_{2j}$	$N_{2.} - N_{22}$
LH	N_{31} Contagious expansion in neighbors††	N_{32} Contagious relocation in neighbor††	N_{33} Stationary	N_{34}	N_{15} Small changes from LH to LL, HL, or HH	$N_{3.}$ $\sum_{j=1}^{5} N_{3j}$	$N_{3.} - N_{33}$
HH	N_{41} Hierarchical global decrease††	N_{42} Hierarchical isolated decrease††	N_{43}	N_{44} Stationary	N_{45} Small changes from HH to LL, HL, or LH	$N_{4.}$ $\sum_{j=1}^{5} N_{4j}$	$N_{4.} - N_{44}$
Total	$N_{.1}$ $\sum_{i=1}^{4} N_{i1}$	$N_{.2}$ $\sum_{i=1}^{4} N_{i2}$	$N_{.3}$ $\sum_{i=1}^{4} N_{i3}$	$N_{.4}$ $\sum_{i=1}^{4} N_{i4}$	$N_{.5}$ $\sum_{i=1}^{4} N_{i5}$	$N_{..}$ $\sum_{i=1}^{4} \sum_{j=1}^{5} N_{ij}$	$N_{..} - N_{11} - N_{22} - N_{33} - N_{44}$
Total excluding stationary diagonals	$N_{.1} - N_{11}$	$N_{.2} - N_{22}$	$N_{.3} - N_{33}$	$N_{.4} - N_{44}$	$N_{.5}$	$N_{..} - N_{11} - N_{22} - N_{33} - N_{44}$	

†Diffusion transitions to increased neighbor rates.

††Diffusion transitions to decreased rates.

Table 9.6. Calculation of diffusion and comparison transition rates in local neighbor pairs[†].

Diffusion Type [††]	Change in Local-Neighbor Pair	Diffusion Rate	Comparison Rate [†††]
A. Local Area is Outcome of Diffusion: Effect of Neighbor Level at t on Local Level at t + 1			
Hierarchical: isolated or global increases	L_tL_t to $H_{t+1}L_{t+1}$ or $H_{t+1}H_{t+1}$	$\dfrac{N_{12} + N_{14}}{N_{1.} - N_{11}}$	$\dfrac{N_{32} + N_{42} + N_{24} + N_{34}}{N^* - (N_{1.} - N_{11})}$
Contagious: expansion or relocation increases	L_tH_t to $H_{t+1}L_{t+1}$ or $H_{t+1}H_{t+1}$	$\dfrac{N_{32} + N_{34}}{N_{3.} - N_{33}}$	$\dfrac{N_{12} + N_{42} + N_{14} + N_{24}}{N^* - (N_{3.} - N_{33})}$
Contagious: expansion or relocation decreases	H_tL_t to $L_{t+1}L_{t+1}$ or $L_{t+1}H_{t+1}$	$\dfrac{N_{21} + N_{23}}{N_{2.} - N_{22}}$	$\dfrac{N_{13} + N_{43} + N_{31} + N_{41}}{N^* - (N_{2.} - N_{22})}$
Hierarchical: isolated or global decreases	H_tH_t to $L_{t+1}L_{t+1}$ or $L_{t+1}H_{t+1}$	$\dfrac{N_{41} + N_{43}}{N_{4.} - N_{44}}$	$\dfrac{N_{13} + N_{23} + N_{21} + N_{31}}{N^* - (N_{4.} - N_{44})}$
B. Local Area is Source of Diffusion: Effect of Local Level at t on Neighbor Level at t + 1			
Hierarchical: isolated or global increases	L_tL_t to $L_{t+1}H_{t+1}$ or $H_{t+1}H_{t+1}$	$\dfrac{N_{13} + N_{14}}{N_{1.} - N_{11}}$	$\dfrac{N_{23} + N_{43} + N_{24} + N_{34}}{N^* - (N_{1.} - N_{11})}$
Contagious: expansion or relocation increases	H_tL_t to $L_{t+1}H_{t+1}$ or $H_{t+1}H_{t+1}$	$\dfrac{N_{23} + N_{24}}{N_{2.} - N_{22}}$	$\dfrac{N_{13} + N_{43} + N_{14} + N_{34}}{N^* - (N_{2.} - N_{22})}$
Contagious: expansion or relocation decreases	L_tH_t to $L_{t+1}L_{t+1}$ or $H_{t+1}L_{t+1}$	$\dfrac{N_{31} + N_{32}}{N_{3.} - N_{33}}$	$\dfrac{N_{12} + N_{42} + N_{21} + N_{41}}{N^* - (N_{3.} - N_{33})}$
Hierarchical: isolated or global decreases	H_tH_t to $L_{t+1}L_{t+1}$ or $H_{t+1}L_{t+1}$	$\dfrac{N_{41} + N_{42}}{N_{4.} - N_{44}}$	$\dfrac{N_{12} + N_{32} + N_{21} + N_{31}}{N^* - (N_{4.} - N_{44})}$

[†]N_{ij} is the number of transitions from state i at time t to state j at time $t + 1$. See Tables 4 or 5 for N_{ij} designations in each transition.

[††]To avoid instability problems that can arise from small Ns, we continue to distinguish the direction of diffusion (i.e., increasing or decreasing rates), but otherwise combine the alternative types of contagious diffusion together, and the alternative types of hierarchical diffusion together.

[†††]$N^* = \sum_i \sum_j N_{ij} - N_{11} - N_{22} - N_{33} - N_{44}$

ever, might simply be due to a much larger starting prevalence of LL units at time t. One way to control for large differences in the prevalence of cases eligible for each type of transition is to rely on transition rates that scale raw counts relative to their respective row totals. Comparing the resulting transition rates across rows indicates whether a specific type of diffusion is disproportionately large or small after differences in prevalence at time t are removed.

Counts of Transitions in Shots Fired Rates

The fundamental units of observation in this study are *local-neighbor pairs* of shots fired rates—LL, LH, HL, and HH—reflecting the shots fired rate in a local tract in the

Table 9.7. Counts of quarterly transitions in local-neighbor pairs of shots fired incidents for census tracts in Pittsburgh from 1990 to 1995: cross quarter effects.

Local-Neighbor Pairs at Time t	"Significant" Change in Local-Neighbor Pairs at $t + 1$				Changes Not "Significant" at $t + 1$	Total	Percent Stationary from t to $t + 1$	Total Excluding Diagonals
	LL	HL	LH	HH				
LL	1457	9	12	6	412	1896	76.8	439
HL	4	309	5	12	223	553	55.9	244
LH	7	4	630	18	321	980	64.3	350
HH	4	8	16	338	207	573	59.0	235
Total	1472	330	663	374	1163	4002	—	1268
Total excluding stationary diagonals	15	21	33	36	1163	1268	—	—

first position and the average rate in all adjoining neighbor tracts in the second position. The rates in each tract and its neighbors are designated as low (L) or high (H) relative to the respective standardized distributions of local and neighbor rates for all tracts and all time units in the data. The analysis of diffusion focuses on the dynamics of change in these local-neighbor pairs over successive quarters. For example, a change from LH to HH in successive quarters is consistent with contagious diffusion through the expansion of neighboring high rates into the local tract in the next time period. The full array of possible transitions is described in Table 9.6.

Table 9.7 reports the total counts of census tracts experiencing transitions from local-neighbor pairs of shots fired rates at time t to local-neighbor pairs of rates at time $t+1$. Data are available for twenty-three quarterly transitions from first-quarter 1990–second-quarter 1990 through third-quarter 1994–fourth-quarter 1994. The analysis combines all quarters together to estimate overall transition rates among local-neighbor pairs. With 174 tracts and twenty-three quarterly transitions, the data include a total of 4002 possible transitions. Only those transitions that involve "significant" changes in homicide rates are treated as diffusion. To be considered significant, the Euclidian distance between a local-neighbor pair of rates at $t + 1$ must be more than 2 standard units away from the local-neighbor pair of rates in the same tract at time t. When calculating the transition rates in Table 9.8, the diagonal counts of tracts shown in Table 9.7 are excluded. The diagonal counts are stationary transitions with no change in local-neighbor pairs.

Table 9.7 reports the row totals and percentage of stationary transitions for shots fired rates examined in this paper. LL, and to a lesser extent LH local-neighbor pairs dominate. The number of observations eligible for hierarchical diffusion to higher rates through isolated or global increases from LL levels constitute nearly 50 percent of all observations. Stationary transitions at just over 75 percent also dominate among these transitions from LL levels. More than one-third of *all* transitions for shots fired rates are stationary LL transitions. The very large numbers of stationary cases can easily swamp the estimates of shots fired transition rates among local-neighbor LISA pairs. Furthermore, the very large differences in the share of stationary transitions in each row will distort row comparisons of transition rates. The large presence of stationary LL tracts will lower the range of possible hierarchical diffusion rates much more than stationary LH tracts affect possible contagious diffusion rates.

To remove the undue influence of stationary LL transitions (and to a lesser extent, of stationary LH transitions) in the row comparisons, we exclude the counts of stationary transitions from all calculations of transition rates. The analysis thus focuses on the relative magnitude of diffusion rates observed among those transitions that involve changes in LISA statistics for local-neighbor pairs. This restriction does not bias the results in favor of diffusion, since the transitions involving change are free to move to any of the three remaining nonstationary local-neighbor pairs, and the share that follows a specific diffusion path may be small or large in magnitude.

Tables 9.4 and 9.5 identify the diffusion transitions relative to the *local* spatial unit in local-neighbor pairs. The local unit is the outcome of diffusion in Table 9.4 and the source of diffusion in Table 9.5. The question is whether these diffusion transitions occur more frequently than might be expected if quarter-to-quarter changes in the levels of local-neighbor pairs are independent of the starting values of the pairs at time t. We test this by comparing the observed diffusion rate to the likelihood of nonstationary transitions into the same destination from all other starting locations. So, for example, in a test of the prevalence of upward contagious diffusion in local levels, the observed diffusion rate is obtained from the ratio $(N_{32} + N_{34})/(N_{3.} - N_{33})$ in Table 9.4. The comparison transition rate for other changes to HL or HH rates at $t + 1$ is based on the nonstationary moves from LL, HL, and HH at time t. In this case, the comparison transition rate is:

$$(N_{12} + N_{42} + N_{14} + N_{24})/(N_{1.} - N_{11} + N_{2.} - N_{22} + N_{4.} - N_{44}) \qquad (2)$$

The comparison transition rates for all other types of diffusion are calculated similarly (see Table 9.6).[3]

Use of a comparison transition rate is intended to distinguish the prevalence of changes that are compatible with diffusion from other stochastic changes in the levels of local-neighbor pairs. For example, regression to the mean effects would increase the prevalence of shifts away from unusual outlier values and back toward the mean. These stochastic shifts will be reflected in the comparison transition rate. The test for diffusion assesses the degree to which shifts compatible with diffusion are statistically more likely than other shifts to the same outcome.

Dynamics of Change in Shots Fired Data

We first examine the dynamics of spatial changes looking for evidence consistent with the various types of diffusion processes. For example, how do shots fired spread among census tracts, and is the spread among neighboring tracts more likely than expected? This diffusion of events involves the influence of local-neighbor rates at time t on subsequent shots fired rates at time $t+1$.

Table 9.8 reports the resulting tests of diffusion transitions. In each case, we test whether the diffusion transition rate is significantly larger than the rate of other non-

Table 9.8. Patterns of quarterly changes in local and neighbor tract shots fired rates in Pittsburgh from 1990 to 1995.

Diffusion Type	Proportion of Tracts with "Significant" Change in Shots Fired Rate in Successive Quarters[†]	
	Diffusion[††]	Other[†††]
Local Tract Is Outcome of Diffusion: Effect Neighbor Rate at t on Local Rate at t + 1		
General increases, spontaneous or global	.034	.051
(LL to HL, LL to HH)	(439)	(829)
Neighbor effect increases, expansion or displacement	.063[*††††]	.038
(LH to HH, LH to HL)	(350)	(918)
Neighbor effect decreases, suppression or displacement	.037	.038
(HL to LL, HL to LH)	(244)	(1024)
General decreases, spontaneous or global	.085[**††††]	.027
(HH to LH, HH to LL)	(235)	(1033)
Local Tract Is Source of Diffusion: Effect Local Rate at t on Neighbor Rate at t + 1		
General increases, spontaneous or global	.041	.062
(LL to LH, LL to HH)	(439)	(829)
Neighbor effect increases, expansion or displacement	.070	.051
(HL to LH, HL to HH)	(244)	(1024)
Neighbor effect decreases, suppression or displacement	.031	.027
(LH to HL, LH to LL)	(350)	(918)
General decreases, spontaneous or global	.051[*††††]	.023
(HH to HL, HH to LL)	(235)	(1033)

[†]The transition rates reported in this table exclude completely all stationary transitions that result in *no change* in local-neighbor pairs. The proportion stationary in each type of local-neighbor pair exceeds one-half (see Table 9.7). The number of tracts eligible for each type of transition is noted in parentheses. A change in rates for a tract is "significant" if the Euclidian distance between the local-neighbor pair of rates at time $t + 1$ is more than 2 standard units away from the local-neighbor pair of rates at time t.

[††]Transitions involving diffusion are described in the first column of the table. For example, in the analysis of outcome effects, contagious diffusion that increases local rates for shots fired calls involves transitions from LH local-neighbor pairs in year t to either HL or HH pairs in year $t + 1$. Alternatively, in the analysis of source effects, contagious diffusion that increases neighbor rates for shots fired calls involves transitions from HL local-neighbor pairs in year t to either LH or HH pairs in year $t + 1$.

[†††]The comparison group of "other" transitions includes all other "significant" non-stationary transitions to the same destination local-neighbor pair. For example, in the case of outcome effects associated with contagious increases in local shots fired rates, "other" transitions include all "significant" non-stationary changes from LL, HL, and HH at time t to HL or HH at time $t + 1$. The individual counts that are the basis for the reported transition rates are in Table 9.7.

[††††]Table reports results of one-tail test that diffusion transition rates are larger than other transition rates. Significance levels in one-tail test are: [*]$p < .05$, [**]$p < .01$, and [***]$p < .001$.

stationary transitions to the same local-neighbor pair of shots fired rates. In other words, are transitions that involve diffusion to higher or lower shots fired rates more likely than other types of transitions to the same local-neighbor pairs of shots fired rates? The results in Table 9.8 are for all tracts in all quarters combined. Combining all tracts ($n = 174$) and all pairs of adjacent quarters ($n = 23$ transitions from first quarter

1990 to second quarter 1990; second quarter 1990 to third quarter 1990; through third quarter 1995 to fourth quarter 1995), there are a total of 4002 transitions.[4]

Panel A in Table 9.8 looks for evidence of diffusion from neighbor rates to local tracts serving as the *outcomes* of diffusion. We find evidence of upward contagious diffusion where increasing shots fired in local tracts follow high neighboring rates (Row 2 in Panel A). In results compatible with hierarchical diffusion, there are significant spontaneous declines in local rates as well (Row 4 of Panel A). There is no statistically significant evidence of either hierarchical diffusion of increases or contagious diffusion of declines in rates of shots fired (Rows 1 and 3 of Panel A, respectively).

Panel B in Table 9.8 examines diffusion in the other direction to assess whether shots fired rates in local tracts serve as *sources* of diffusion to other tracts. There is no evidence of contagious diffusion in either direction. Neither upward diffusion from high local rates nor downward diffusion from low local rates is evident (Rows 2 and 3 of Panel B, respectively). There is, however, evidence that low rates emerge spontaneously in neighboring tracts (Row 4 of Panel B).

Rates of shots fired display evidence of significant diffusion in both increasing and decreasing directions, serving as both outcomes (Panel A) and sources (Panel B) of diffusion over spatial units. Contagious diffusion is only evident from high rates in neighboring tracts ($L_t H_t$) to subsequently high rates in a local tract ($H_{t+1} H_{t+1}$ or $H_{t+1} L_{t+1}$), but is not significant following locally high rates ($H_t L_t$). This suggests that contagion is more likely to occur when high rates are more pervasive among several neighboring tracts. A single isolated high rate tract is less effective in fostering spread to its neighbors. For the remainder of the discussion, we focus on increasing diffusion only.

There are some important differences between the distribution of tracts experiencing hierarchical diffusion and those experiencing contagion diffusion. The first is a period effect. Figure 9.5 displays maps of the tracts experiencing significant quarterly diffusion in direction of increasing shots fired rates during the observation period 1990 to 1995.[5] Effects consistent with upward hierarchical diffusion are displayed for the eight quarters from start of 1990 through end of 1991. Of 21 cases of significant spontaneous increases (hierarchical diffusion) over the full six-year period, 17 occurred in the first two years of the observation period, before youth gangs began to emerge in earnest at the end of 1991. Effects consistent with contagious diffusion are displayed for the twelve quarters from 1992 to 1994. Of 29 cases of significantly increasing contagious diffusion over the full six years of data, 19 occurred during the 1992–1994 period of rapidly escalating shots fired rates citywide.

Also note that tracts experiencing substantial changes in shots fired rates are widely dispersed throughout the city and not compactly clustered in just a few areas. In the early period, this spatial dispersion results from hierarchical diffusion, in which increases in shots fired rates emerge simultaneously in disjoint tracts throughout the city. Tracts exhibiting contagious diffusion are also widely dispersed in disjoint clusters throughout the city. For the most part, the contagious diffusion in the later years occurs independently of locations with prior hierarchical diffusion—only three contagious diffusion tracts (15 percent) have both types of diffusion and twelve contagious diffusion tracts (60 percent) have no contact at all with locations of prior hierarchical

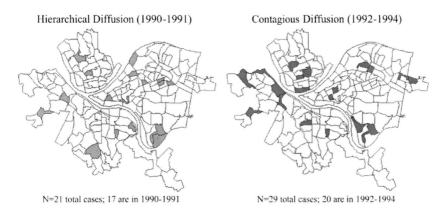

Hierarchical Diffusion (1990-1991)   Contagious Diffusion (1992-1994)

N=21 total cases; 17 are in 1990-1991   N=29 total cases; 20 are in 1992-1994

Figure 9.5. Locations of "significant" upward diffusion in shots fired: Quarterly across Pittsburgh census tracts.

diffusion. This suggests that the processes underlying the initial increases in shots fired are distinct from those contributing to contagious diffusion.

Factors Associated with Diffusion of Shots Fired—Illicit Drug Markets, Gangs, and Youth Homicides

In motivating our analysis of the spatial diffusion of shots fired, we argued that specific features of illicit drug markets and violent youth gangs—for example, their functioning as criminal enterprises without recourse to legal remedies for dispute resolution and organizational control, their ties to specific locations, and persistence of grievances over time—implicate them as potentially central factors in the recent spread of gun violence among youth. It is clear from the analysis so far that shots fired display distinctive spatial and temporal patterns, as did youth homicides (Cohen and Tita 1999). The challenge now is to relate those patterns to distinctive features of the expansion and contraction—both temporally and spatially—of drug markets and youth gangs.

A formal citywide examination of these processes is beyond the scope of this chapter. However, some compelling patterns are evident. For example, the timing of the different types of diffusion in Figure 9.5 tells a compelling story of a classic epidemic in shots fired. During the pre-gang quarters in 1990–1991, shots fired rates spontaneously increased in tracts distributed widely throughout the city. Youth gangs then form independently of the locations of prior spontaneous increases.[6] The emergence of youth gangs, however, is followed by contagious spread of shots fired activity in gang tracts or tracts adjoining them.[7] Not only is there a period of sharp rises in shots fired citywide, this increase is spatially patterned around the location of emerging youth gangs. The spatial and temporal pattern of diffusion in shots fired strongly suggests that youth gangs contribute directly to and facilitate escalating levels of shots fired activity and any forms of gun violence that accompany street gunfire. In this manner, youth gangs function in much the same way as an "infective" agent fueling an epidemic

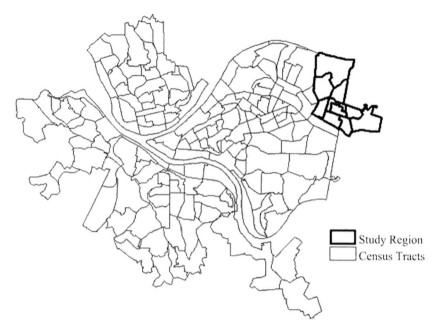

Figure 9.6. East End case-study area.

spread within a larger host population. The following case study explores further the dynamics of a contagious spread of youth gun violence.

Shots Fired—Youth Homicide Nexus: A Case Study of the East End

Above, we demonstrate that the rate of increase in both citywide reported incidents of shots fired and levels of youth homicide supports our use of shots as a precursor to inter-personal violence (see Figure 9.2 and Table 9.1). We do not know, however, whether this temporal ordering is also spatially oriented. That is, did statistically significant changes in rates of shots fired in an area precede an increase in youth homicide in the same area? We set out to examine this question by focusing only on a small, but violent, area of Pittsburgh. The study region is made up of four predominately African-American neighborhoods that experience high levels of poverty, unemployment, and most other measures of poor social and economic health. Of the ten census tracts that make up the region, three tracts only contain gang "set space" (the colloquial description by gang members of the highly localized areas where they hang out on a daily basis), and another three include both drug markets and gangs. Figure 9.6 identifies the study region, which is commonly referred to as the East End.

We focus our case study on the eight quarters in 1992 and 1993. We choose this period because it captures the first instance of statistically significant diffusion (first quarter of 1992) and because it provides sufficient time for examining changes in shots fired and youth homicide. We pay particular attention to whether source or outcome tracts involved in diffusion of shots fired are systematically related to the location of

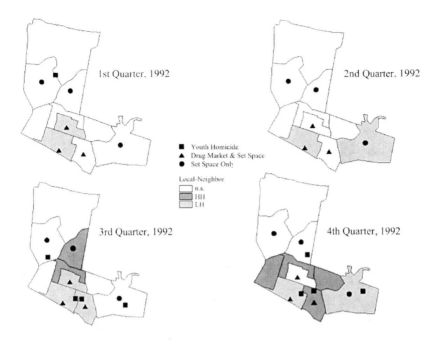

Figure 9.7. Tracts with significant local indicators of spatial association (LISA) for shots fired, East End neighborhoods, 1992 quarters.

youth homicides. Specifically, we are interested in the following set of questions. First, within the same spatial unit, do changes in shots fired precede increases in youth homicide, or do they occur contemporaneously? If these increases are not occurring at the same time and in the same place, what association is there between sources (outcomes) of diffusion and outcomes (sources) of youth homicide? Finally, what does a particular pattern suggest regarding the role of guns, drug markets, and gangs in the diffusion of lethal violence?

Figures 9.7 and 9.8 demonstrate a general pattern of increased clustering of similarly high rate areas over time as more tracts fall into the HH quadrant of the LISA statistic. This mirrors the citywide process described above, suggesting that there was both an increase in dispersion of high rate tracts and an increase in concentration of calls within high rate tracts (i.e., the mean number of calls per high-rate tract increased as well).

Increased rates of shots fired activity appear to have emerged initially through a process of hierarchical diffusion. The first significant change in local-neighbor rates occurs in the first quarter of 1992, as shots fired activity increases in the neighbors of the tract highlighted in Figure 9.9 (LISA switches from LL to significant LH for highlighted tract). The first evidence of contagious diffusion occurs in the third quarter of 1992, when shots fired increase significantly among neighbors to the north, and their LISAs switch from not significant HL to significant HH as they share local high rates with their neighbors. There is no further evidence of diffusion through the next five quarters ending in 1994.[8] This local pattern is consistent with the previously identified

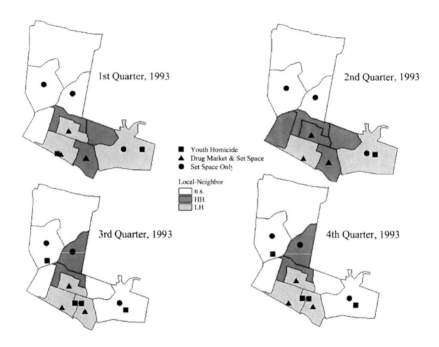

Figure 9.8. Tracts with significant local indicators of spatial association (LISA) for shots fired, East End neighborhoods, 1993 quarters.

evidence of a citywide "period effect" between hierarchical and contagious diffusion. In this case, however, the two are linked with contagious diffusion following the initial seeding of an area through hierarchical diffusion.

Next we turn our attention to the distribution of youth homicides over this period. In 1992, there were a total of ten youth homicides in the study region. What is immediately striking is that prior to the contagious diffusion of shots fired rates in the third quarter of 1992, there was only a single homicide involving a youthful participant (ages 14–24). The contagious diffusion to high rates of shots fired in Quarter Three is accompanied by four youth homicides in the same quarter and then five more homicides in the next quarter. This is compatible with the temporal lag between shots fired and youth homicides suggested in Figure 9.2, in a narrower time frame (quarterly rather than yearly). Furthermore, none of the youth homicides occur in the two HH tracts that are the sources of contagious diffusion of shots fired to their neighbors (third quarter in Figure 9.7). This suggests a process where increased shots fired activity in the source tract leads to higher levels of gun activity in surrounding tracts, some of which manifests itself in lethal violence.

In 1993 (Figure 9.8) there is no further evidence of diffusion in shots fired, but youth homicides continue at a high level in a concentrated area. Of the eleven youth homicides in 1993, ten occur in only three tracts. As in 1992, none of these homicides occurs in either of the two original HH source tracts.

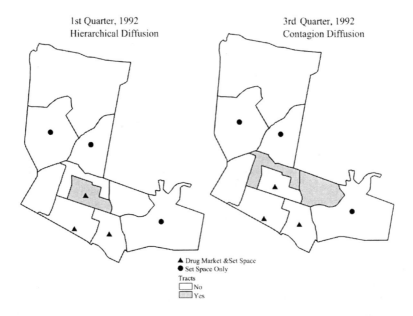

Figure 9.9. Significant diffusion changes in local neighbor rates of shots fired, East End 1992.

The census tract that initially signals hierarchical diffusion of high shots fired rates among its neighbors (see Quarter One of 1992 in Figure 9.9) contains both gang set space and an active drug market. The two census tracts that later serve as sources of contagious diffusion (Third Quarter of 1992 in Figure 9.9) have neither gangs nor drug markets, but they are neighbors to tracts with set space alone or both set space and drug markets. Absence of set space and drug markets, and of youth homicides, suggests that this area may serve as what Anderson (1999) calls a "staging ground" for local youth. With no particular group claiming dominance or control over the area, this buffer area serves as neutral turf between rival neighborhoods.

It is certainly difficult to draw strong conclusions about the role of youth gangs in the diffusion of violence from experiences in a such a small geographic area (ten census tracts) and relatively few homicides. It is notable, however, that every single youth homicide occurred in an area with either gang set space or both set space and drug markets. At this time, we are not prepared to disentangle the individual contributions of drug markets and gangs to the diffusion of guns and gun violence. That may be possible in similar analyses of experiences throughout the entire city, which we leave to future extensions from the current research.

Conclusions

This work extends and builds upon our earlier work on the youth homicide epidemic of the late 1980s and early 1990s. Previously (Cohen and Tita 1999), we found evidence of two processes of diffusion that accounted for the spread of homicide. In the case of hierarchical diffusion, we found evidence that homicide rates grew initially across spatially independent but socially similar areas (specifically, fractured, high poverty, African-American communities). In later periods, we found that youth-gang homicides seem to be the sources of contagious diffusion to neighboring areas. But rather than precipitating other gang homicides, they seem to spawn a more general class of non-gang homicides involving youth.

In that work, we implicated youth gangs, and generally exonerated crack drug markets, as the primary mechanism behind the spread of youthful homicidal violence. However, in that work, we were careful to note that the rarity of homicide undermined the robustness of our findings. It became obvious that an increase of one or two events over a one-year period in a geographic unit might be large enough in magnitude to induce statistical significance in the changes of our local-neighbor rates.

By adopting a very generous proxy for gun violence (shots fired calls) and demonstrating the validity of this measure as an indicator of a broader class of fatal and nonfatal youth violence, we are able to improve the credibility of findings generated by our method of measuring spatial-temporal changes. In validating our proxy measure, we find strong spatial association between areas with high rates of shots fired and youth homicide. More importantly, we find that the spatial and temporal changes in shots fired not only validate it as a proxy measure but hint at a temporal lag in which shots fired serve as an important leading indicator or precursor of lethal youth violence.

There are also similar trends in the patterning of hierarchical and contagious diffusion of homicide and of shots fired. In both cases, hierarchical diffusion in the form of spontaneous increases are the dominant means for spreading events during the early, low-rate periods in 1990 and 1991, while contagious diffusion dominates during the period of sharply increasing violence from 1992 to 1994. As expected, contagious spread, with its mutually reinforcing capacities, seems to be essential for rapidly escalating rates and geographic dispersion in youth violence. Initial spontaneous increases in widely dispersed geographic areas may extinguish quickly without the presence of some mechanism for sustaining spread to similarly susceptible areas.

At least in the one city examined here, much of the rise and contagious diffusion in shots fired activity accompanied a rise in urban street gangs. While the lack of increases in gun violence prior to the onset of gangs once again suggests that drug markets did not impact gun violence, we find considerable overlap of drug and gang areas. While beyond the scope of the current paper, we aim to revisit this issue in hopes of better understanding the gun-drug-gang nexus of interpersonal violence.

Recent publications in the area of spatial analysis of crime make it clear that the analysis of cross sectional data cannot identify patterns of "diffusion." The identification of true diffusion requires models that simultaneously account for spatial and temporal effects. Unfortunately, modeling space and time in a multivariate regression framework is not easily accomplished. Until such methods are commonplace, we offer this extension of existing exploratory spatial data analysis techniques as a way to identify meaningful changes in spatial distribution.

Acknowledgments   This research was partially supported by the Alfred P. Sloan Foundation and builds on earlier work funded by grants from the National Consortium on Violence Research at

Carnegie Mellon University (NCOVR is supported under Grant SBR 9513040 from the National Science Foundation) and the National Institute of Justice (#95-IJ-CX-0005). The authors thank the City of Pittsburgh Bureaus of Police and City Information Systems for their cooperation in providing data for this research. Wilpen Gorr and Piyusha Singh of Carnegie Mellon University provided vital assistance in preparing the raw data for analysis. Susan Bennett and Danielle Wallace at UC-Irvine provided research assistance. All viewpoints expressed are those of the authors alone and do not represent the official position and policies of any of the individuals or organizations mentioned above.

Notes

1. Tita et al. (1998) empirically examine differences in the economic and social structure of neighborhoods with and without violent youth gangs and find significant effects for factors often associated with social control. Also see Curry and Spergel (1988).
2. The animations are available on the web at http://www.csiss.org/best-practices/siss/09/.
3. To avoid instability problems in transition rates that can arise from small Ns, we continue to distinguish the direction of diffusion (i.e., increasing or decreasing rates), but otherwise combine the alternative types of contagious diffusion together, and the alternative types of hierarchical diffusion together.
4. The local and neighbor rates of shots fired calls in Pittsburgh are standardized relative to the distribution of rates in all tracts and all quarters combined (i.e., 174 tracts by 24 quarters = 4176 total observations). We include all quarters together when standardizing the rates so that changes in overall levels from quarter to quarter are detectable as unusually large values in standardized rates. If each quarter (or quarters in the same year) were standardized separately, then extreme values in low-rate quarters would be treated as similar to extreme values in high-rate quarters.
5. Animations of the changes over successive quarters are in the web-based exhibit accompanying this paper available at http://www.csiss.org/best-practices/siss/09/.
6. Gangs are no more likely to form in tracts with or adjoining prior spontaneous increases in shots fired than any other tract.

		Spontaneous Increase Tract	Adjoins Spontaneous Increase Tract	Other	Totals
Gang in Tract	No	16	46	79	141
	Yes	1	13	19	33
Totals		17	59	98	174

$\chi^2 = 2.27$ (2 d.f., $p = 0.332$)

7. Contagious increases in shots fired are more likely to occur in tracts with gangs or those adjoining gang tracts.

		Gang Tract	Adjoins Gang Tract	Other	Totals
Contagious Shots	No	26	44	84	154
Fired in Tract	Yes	7	9	3	19
Totals		33	53	87	173

$\chi^2 = 10.53$ (2 d.f., $p = 0.005$)

8. During the second quarter of 1995, one tract does experience diffusion, this time as an outcome as its own rate increases in relationship to its neighbors' rates.

References

Anderson, E. 1999. *Code of the Street: Decency, Violence and the Moral Life of the Inner City.* New York: W.W. Norton & Company.

Anselin, L. 1993. *The Moran Scatterplot as an ESDA Tool to Assess Local Instability in Spatial Association.* Paper presented as GISDATA Specialist Meeting on GIS and Spatial Analysis, Amsterdam, The Netherlands, December 1–5 (West Virginia University, Regional Research Institute, Research Paper 9330).

Anselin, L. 1995a. Local indicators of spatial association—LISA. *Geographical Analysis* 27: 93–115.

Anselin, L. 1995b. *SpaceStat Version 1.80 Users Guide*, Regional Research Institute. Morgantown, W. Va.: West Virginia University.

Anselin, L. 1999. Interactive techniques and exploratory spatial data analysis. In P.A. Longley, M.F. Goodchild, D.J. Maguire, and D.W. Rhind (eds.), *Georgraphic Information Systems: Principles, Techniques, Management and Applications*, New York: John Wiley and Sons, 251–264.

Baller, R.D., L. Anselin, S.F. Messner, G. Deane, and D.F. Hawkins. 2001. Structural Covariates of U.S. County Homicide Rates: Incorporating Spatial Effects. *Criminology* 39(3): 561–590.

Bjerregaard, B., and A. Lizotte. 1995. Gun Ownership and Gang Membership. *Journal of Criminal Law and Criminology* 86: 37–58.

Block, R. 1998. *Gang Activity and Overall Levels of Crime: A New Method for Defining Areas of Gang Activity Using Police Records.* Paper presented at the Annual Meetings of American Society of Criminology.

Block, C., and R. Block. 1993. *Street Gang Crime in Chicago. Research in Brief*, U.S. Department of Justice, National Institute of Justice, Washington, D.C.

Blumstein, A. 1995. Youth violence, guns, and the illicit drug industry. *The Journal of Criminal Law and Criminology* 86: 10–36.

Blumstein, A., and D. Cork 1996. Linking gun availability to youth gun violence. *Law and Contemporary Problems* 59(1): 5–24.

Braga, A., D. Kennedy and G. Tita. 2001. New Approaches to the Strategic Prevention of Gang and Group-Involved Violence. In C.R. Huff (ed.), *Gangs in America 3rd edition.* Newbury Park, Calif.: Sage Publications, 271–285.

Clarke, R.V., and D. Weisburd. 1994. Diffusion of crime control benefits: Observations on the reverse of displacement. In R.V. Clarke (ed.), *Crime and Prevention Studies Vol 2.* Monsey, N.Y.: Criminal Justice Press, 165–184.

Cliff, A.D., P. Haggett, J.K. Ord, and G.R Versey. 1981. *Spatial Diffusion: An Historical Geography of Epidemics in an Island Community*, Cambridge, U.K.: Cambridge University Press.

Cohen, J., and G. Tita. 1999. Diffusion in homicide: Exploring a general method for detecting spatial diffusion processes. *Journal of Quantitative Criminology* 15(4): 451–494.

Cohen, J., D. Cork, J. Engberg, and G. Tita. 1998. The role of drug markets and gangs in local homicide rates. *Homicide Studies* 2(3): 241–262.

Cook, P.J., and J.H. Laub. 1998. The Unprecedented Epidemic in Youth Violence. In M. Tonry, and M.H. Moore (eds.), *Youth Violence, Crime and Justice Vol 24.* Chicago: University of Chicago Press, 26–64.

Cook, P.J., and J.H. Laub. 2001. *After the Epidemic: Recent Trends in Youth Violence in the United States*. NBER Working paper 8571 (http://www.nber.org/papers/w8571).

Cork, D. 1996. *Juvenile Homicide and the Availability of Firearms*. Working paper, H. John Heinz III School of Public Policy and Management, Carnegie Mellon University, Pittsburgh, Pa.

Cork, D. 1999. Examining space-time interaction in city-level homicide data: Crack markets and the diffusion of guns among youth. *Journal of Quantitative Criminology* Vol. 5, 4: 379–406.

Curry, G.D., and I.A. Spergel. 1988. Gang homicide, delinquency, and community. *Criminology* 26(3): 381–405.

Felson, M., and L.E. Cohen. 1980. Human ecology and crime: A routine activity approach. *Human Ecology* 8 (December): 398–405.

Fingerhut, L.A. 1993. *Firearm Mortality Among Children, Youth, and Young Adults 1–34 Years of Age, Trends And Current Status: United States, 1985–90*. Advance Data 231, U.S. Department of Health and Human Services, National Center for Health Statistics, Hyattsville, Md.

Fingerhut, L.A., D. Ingram, and J. Feldman. 1998. Homicide rates among U.S. teenagers and young adults: Differences by mechanism, level of urbanization, race and sex, 1987 through 1995. *JAMA* 280(5): 423–427.

Fox, J.A. 1996. *Trends in Juvenile Violence*. A report to the United States Attorney General on Current and Future Rates of Juvenile Offending. Prepared for the U.S. Department of Justice, Bureau of Justice Statistics, March 1996. Report available at: www.ojp.usdoj.gov/bjs/pub/pdf/tjvfox2.pdf. See also Homicide Trends in the United States at: http://www.ojp.usdoj.gov/bjs/homicide/homtrnd.htm .

Klein, M. 1995. *The American Street Gang: Its Nature, Prevalence and Control*. New York: Oxford University Press.

Luckenbill, D. 1977. Criminal homicide as a situated transaction. *Social Problems* 25(2): 176–186.

Maxson, C. 1998. *Gang Members on the Move*. OJJDP Juvenile Justice Bulletin. Washington, D.C.: Office of Juvenile Justice and Delinquency Prevention, Department of Justice.

Maxson, C. 1999. Gang homicide. In M. Dwayne Smith, and M. Zahnn (eds.), *Studying and Preventing Homicide*. Thousand Oaks, Calif.: Sage Publications, 197–220.

Messner, S.F., and K. Tardiff. 1985. The social ecology of urban homicide: An application of the 'routine activities' approach. *Criminology* 23 (May): 241–267.

Morenoff, J., R.J. Sampson, and S. Raudenbush. 2001. Neighborhood inequality, collective efficacy, and the spatial dynamics of urban violence. *Criminology* 39(3): 517–560.

Moore, J. 1991. *Going Down to the Barrio: Homeboys and Homegirls in Chang*. Philadelphia: Temple University Press.

Rosenfeld, R., T. Bray, and A. Egly. 1999. Facilitating violence: A comparison of gang-motivated, gang-affiliated, and nongang youth homicide. *Journal of Quantitative Criminology* 15(4): 495–516.

Spergel, I., and D. Curry. 1990. Strategies and perceived agency effectiveness in dealing with the youth gang problem. In C.R. Huff (ed.), *Gangs in America: Diffusion, Diversity and Public Policy*. Newbury Park, Calif.: Sage Publications, 288–309.

Tita, G. 1999a. *An Ecological Study of Violent Urban Gangs and their Impact on Crime*. Unpublished Doctoral Dissertation, Carnegie Mellon University, Pittsburgh, Pa.

Tita, G.E. 1999b. Mapping the set space of urban street gangs. In E.H. Hendrix, B. Dent, and L.S. Turnbull (eds.), *The Atlas of Crime*. Phoenix, Ariz.: Oryx Press, 125–131.

Tita, G., J. Engberg, and J. Cohen. 1998. *An Ecological Study of Gangs: The Social Organization of "Set Space."* Working Paper, H. John Heinz III School of Public Policy and Management, Pittsburgh, Pa.: Carnegie Mellon University.

Wilkinson, D., and J. Fagan. 1996. Understanding the role of firearms in violence "scripts": The dynamics of gun events among adolescent males. *Law and Contemporary Problems* 59(1): 55–90.

10

The Spatial Structure of Urban Political Discussion Networks

Munroe Eagles
Paul Bélanger
Hugh W. Calkins

Interpersonal Relations and Political Behavior

Since the 1950s, most research in the field of political behavior has relied upon survey data for randomly sampled individuals (the Michigan school; see Campbell et al. 1960). As a result, theory building and explanation have traditionally been preoccupied with understanding the effects of personal and psychological factors, while community and geographic factors have been devalued. Over time, the atomistic assumptions of methodological individualism that contributed to the popularity of sample survey research came under attack (Barton 1968; Sheingold 1973). Contextual analyses, in which survey respondents were assumed to interact with those in their immediate geographic environments (the characteristics of which were usually derived from census data), became increasingly popular (Books and Prysby 1991). The local community, then, is regarded as the most suitable container to serve as a proxy for the social relations of individual survey respondents. However, this assumption has been questioned by many critics of contextual analyses, who point to such factors as the number of extra-local social ties individuals develop and maintain, the high levels of geographic mobility among Americans, and the decline of sentiments of community.[1]

More recently, social network analyses, in which primary respondents and their social interaction partners are interviewed, have enabled scholars to assess the nature and content of social influence processes directly (see Knoke 1990; Pattie and Johnston 2001). A strength of such studies is that they focus attention on the relationships between individuals regardless of their location. A common finding emerging from these analyses is that dense, spatially bounded networks typically account for a minority of an individual's important social ties (Wellman and Leighton 1979, 384). With the rise of "networked individualism," we learn that networks are increasingly being defined personally and not spatially (Wellman 2001). Network analysis allows for variability among individuals in terms of the definition of their personal environments.

While refreshingly sociological in their approach, such innovations in the survey research tradition have ironically contributed to a long-standing intellectual devaluation of space and place in quantitative analyses of political behavior (Agnew 1987). Proponents of network analysis argue that the focus on interpersonal networks better proxies the relevant social influences to which an individual is exposed than does the residential community. As Richard Merelman (1981, 252–253) has put it, "Social networks have a functional rather than a territorial locus. High rates of residential mobility, expanded educational opportunities, and access to cheap transportation make it possible for people to choose their friends on the basis of mutual interests, most of which fall into the occupational area. As a result, territorial neighborhoods no longer form the locus of social networks." Of course, the growth of the Internet and cyber communities in the last several decades has only exacerbated the tendency to see interpersonal communities as "liberated" from geography. Social network scholars argue that community itself is not in decline. Rather, what is in decline is the association of community with territory.

So widely accepted has this argument become that relatively few attempts have been made to explore the spatial dimension of interpersonal networks as something of interest in its own right. This theoretical closure is premature, however, and there are strong grounds for inquiring into the spatial dimension of social networks in political analysis. For example, even with the diminished costs of long-distance communication, only some—probably the more intimate and emotionally intense—relationships may be strong enough to be sustainable across long distances. The intimate personal communities frequently serving as the focus of network analyses are but a small subset of the much larger set of informal relationships in which individuals participate. It is entirely possible that less intimate relationships may demonstrate a stronger spatial clustering. In his recent survey of 29 Torontonians, for example, Wellman found that 23 percent of their active social ties were formed among people living within a mile of the respondent (1996, 348). Importantly, Wellman found that the frequency of interaction within local informal networks was greater than that for non-local, more intimate networks. For this reason, he concluded " . . . the preponderance of frequent contact with neighbors and workmates should lead network [analysts] to bring proximity back into their investigations of community, along with the existing criteria of intimacy and supportiveness" (Wellman 1996, 353).

Such findings are particularly important for understanding the *political* impact of social interaction. Several scholars have argued that it is the frequency of interaction and not its intimacy that accounts for the political impact of social relationships. Stephen Weatherford's (1982, 130) analysis of the political impact of social networks concluded that, after controlling for the intimacy, duration, and frequency of contact, " . . . the absence of affective factors as causal agents in political networking suggests that local political networks may be founded on weak ties and may expose individuals in them to correspondingly wide-ranging sets of alters [i.e., network partners]." Analyses of the political discussion networks of a sample of residents of South Bend, Indiana, revealed that the intimacy of the relationship is not related to the frequency of political discussion within the network (Huckfeldt and Sprague 1995, 116). Similarly, Robert Huckfeldt (1986, 130; emphasis in original) has argued that " . . . social interaction may not be persuasive because it is intensive or intimate, but rather because it is frequent and recurring: *the most important social learnings are those that are reinforced continually.*" In light of Granovetter's argument that "weak ties" are more efficacious in modifying an individual's attitudes and behavior because they are more likely to convey dissonant or new information, informal contacts may be of particular importance for political behavior. The grounds for bringing geography back in to the study of political discussion networks are therefore compelling. We do not know with precision, however, how geography figures in political discussion networks.

Our objective in this chapter is to examine the geography of political discussion networks, thereby "bringing geography back in" to the analysis of sociometric or network data. Specifically, we take up four related questions that explore for patterns in the geography of political discussion networks. What are the determinants of network dispersion or concentration? Second, to what extent are geographic areas such as neighborhoods distinctive in terms of the spatial pattern of residents' interpersonal ties? Third, do particular types of discussion networks exhibit distinctive spatial characteristics? Finally, are networks spanning shorter geographical distances more effective in transmitting political influence than those stretching over longer distances?

Measuring the Spatial Dimension of Interpersonal Networks

Addressing these questions requires an exceptionally rich and diverse body of data on individuals and their political discussion partners, and their respective geographic locations. Previous work examining the spatial-boundedness of networks has relied on impressionistic or crude measures of geographic distance covered by the network (from self-reported distance estimates, from references to ill-defined "neighborhoods," or from simple dichotomous local vs. non-local categorizations, for example). We are fortunate in having been given access to a data source that enables us to measure the spatial properties of political networks more directly and precisely than have earlier studies. In this chapter, most of our data come from a widely used three-wave survey of 1,500 South Bend, Indiana, residents in the context of the 1984 election. These data were collected by Robert Huckfeldt and John Sprague (see Huckfeldt and Sprague 1995, 33–42, for a description of the research design and data). The surveys covered a wide range of issues concerning the attitudes, associational and group ties, and political behavior of respondents. Respondents were drawn from sixteen South Bend neighborhoods (approximately 94 respondents per neighborhood), chosen to reflect a diversity of geographical and social environments within the city and to minimize diversity within the neighborhood unit. Aggregating the data from these individuals provides contextual information on the neighborhood environment. In addition to this rich body of individual-level data, census data for South Bend were obtained from the 1990 census and appended to the survey data files to provide contextual information on respondents' local environments.

A significant strength of the Huckfeldt and Sprague design is that, during the third wave of the survey, respondents were asked to provide the first names of up to three individuals with whom they "talked with most about the events of the past election year."[2] Subsequently, more than nine hundred interviews were taken with these discussants in a truncated snowball sample. These secondary respondents were asked a shorter battery of questions regarding their political orientations and behavior, and about their relationship to the primary respondent. In addition to Huckfeldt and Sprague's extensive analyses of these data, other scholars have used this extraordinary data set to investigate a variety of individual and contextual aspects of interpersonal influence on political behavior (e.g., Kenny 2001; La Due Lac 1999). To date, however, no one has attempted to explore, on a systematic basis, the geographic dimension of these discussion networks.

Using a geographic information system and the address data supplied by the study's principal investigators, we have geocoded primary respondents and their political discussion partners (see Figure 10.1). As a result, we are in a position to measure the spatial attributes of a large number of political discussion networks (most significantly, distance separating discussant pairs), and to relate these to a variety of individual and contextual factors. Missing address information for either primary respondents or their discussants reduced the number of dyads from 924 to 629, of which 502 had a distance measure of greater than zero (where the discussants mentioned did not live in the same household as the primary respondent).[3]

In the analysis that follows, we will confine our attention to these non-household discussion dyads. Figure 10.1 depicts the geographic distribution of main respondents in our sample, and also delineates the geographic footprint of the sample neighborhoods in South Bend. Since we know relatively little about the spatial dimension of political discussion networks, we begin with a consideration of some of the individual and contextual determinants of network distance.

Individual (Main Respondent) Determinants of Discussion Dyad Distance

Distance in a social (or political) network is conventionally conceptualized as a 'cost' to be borne by participants—the more distant the contact, the more costly it is to initiate and sustain (Jackson et al. 1977, 48). The ability to overcome these costs is likely to be distributed differentially across individuals in accordance with a number of characteristics. Table 10.1 presents some descriptive information on the distance separating political discussion partners in the sample of South Bend residents. These enable us to explore several hypotheses related to the ability to overcome distance in the construction of these relationships. For example, demographic characteristics are likely to influence networks. It seems likely that women—who are still more likely to be heavily involved in child-rearing and less likely to be employed outside the home than men—will have more spatially restricted political discussion networks than men. The data in the top panel of Table 10.1 confirms that this is indeed the case for our survey respondents. On average, the political discussion partners of men span distances that are a third of a mile longer than those of women in the sample (2.94 miles for men; 2.73 miles for women).

Similarly, an individual's age is likely to affect their ability and willingness to sustain far-flung political discussion networks. Other things being equal, young people are likely to be more mobile than older people, and we therefore expect to see the distance separating political discussion partners diminish with age. The second panel in Table

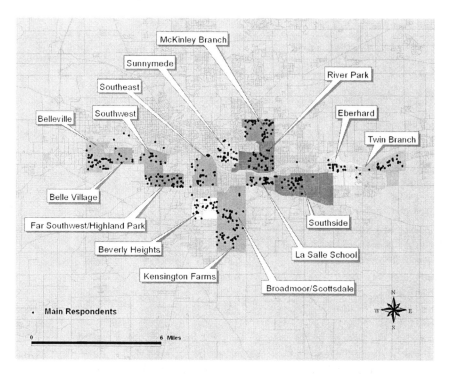

Figure 10.1. Main respondents (and neighborhoods), South Bend, Indiana.

10.1 confirms this hypothesis also. The political discussion networks of respondents below the age of 39 years spanned the greatest average distance (2.94 miles), while those of the 65-and-over age group were the most spatially concentrated (2.44 miles on average). The middle-age (40–64 years) group had discussion networks that spanned an average of 2.81 miles.

Previous research on the dispersion of contacts within social networks has suggested that individuals of lower socio-economic status construct more spatially constrained social networks than do more affluent or higher status individuals. Table 10.1 contains information on the network dyads of individuals according to two conventional measures of socio-economic status (SES), education and income. Other things being equal, we expect more highly educated individuals to be able to incur distance costs more easily than those of lower education. The data in Table 10.1 confirm this expectation rather strikingly. The relationship between education and dyad distance is monotonic across the four categories of educational attainment. Those with elementary education had political discussion networks that spanned an average of 2.55 miles, whereas those of college graduates and post-graduates spanned an average of 2.92 miles. Similarly, the hypothesis expecting an inverse relationship between family incomes and network distance is even more strongly confirmed by the data in Table 10.1. Across the three income categories, the relationship to network distance is linear and monotonic, and the differences in mean distance are quite large (more than a mile from low to high income).

Table 10.1. Individual-level patterns in dyad distance (miles).

Main Respondent Characteristic	Mean	Standard deviation	N
All dyads	2.76	2.65	502
Males	2.94	2.70	220
Females	2.73	2.60	282
Age 0–39 yrs.	2.94	2.63	170
Age 40–64 yrs.	2.81	2.55	217
Age 65+ yrs.	2.44	2.86	113
Elementary education	2.55	3.70	27
Secondary education	2.69	2.63	279
Some College	2.86	2.56	88
College graduate & postgraduate	2.92	2.46	108
Family income < $10,000	2.11	3.11	28
Family income > $10,000 and < $40,000	2.72	2.63	406
Family Income > $40,000	3.32	2.50	51
Race—White	2.75	2.59	477
Race—Black	2.31	2.35	16

Finally, the persistence of racism and racial differences in standard of living in America suggest that African-Americans might be expected to construct more spatially concentrated political discussion networks than do white Americans. The final panel of Table 10.1 confirms this hypothesis as well. Black Americans, on average, participate in political discussion networks that cover 2.31 miles, while those of white Americans span an average of 2.75 miles.

Clearly, the spatial dimensions of political discussion networks are structured by a number of individual-level characteristics. Distance appears from these data to be a cost for networks, and the ability to overcome these costs is distributed unevenly across individuals of different socio-economic and demographic characteristics. The strong and consistent patterning of these relationships suggests that the geographic dimension is theoretically tractable and interpretable using some relatively simple hypotheses. We know from other studies that residential segregation processes produce neighborhoods that are differentiated along many of these same characteristics. Because of the incorporation of neighborhoods into the primary sampling frame of the South Bend study, we can look for evidence of contextual differences in the mean distances separating political discussion partners. We turn to an exploration of this in our next section.

Neighborhood Patterns in the Geography
of Political Discussion Networks

In designing the sampling frame for primary respondents in the South Bend survey, the principal investigators incorporated a rich variety of information about the city's

Table 10.2. Neighborhood Patterns in Dyad Distance (miles).

Neighborhood	Average Family Income($)	Average House Value($)	(%) Home Owners	(%) African-American	Area in square miles	Mean Dyad Distance (# of Dyads)
River Park	25,673	39,288	59.9	3.1	1.44	1.83 ($N = 64$)
Kensington Farms	50,964	87,900	98.5	4.2	1	2.84 ($N = 44$)
Broadmoor/Scottsdale	37,264	55,800	89.4	5.3	1.88	2.62 ($N = 46$)
La Salle School	23,748	37,475	81.2	0.0	0.53	2.12 ($N = 44$)
Southside	23,208	45,750	75.0	0.5	2.21	2.20 ($N = 50$)
Eberhard	29,321	49,575	86.7	0.0	1.21	1.98 ($N = 37$)
Twin Branch	32,596	51,125	91.4	0.4	1.19	2.33 ($N = 31$)
McKinley Branch	31,685	49,400	71.2	6.9	1.04	2.37 ($N = 52$)
Far Southwest/ Highland Park	20,774	27,417	84.7	17.3	0.72	3.10 ($N = 37$)
Sunnymede	35,468	58,733	83.6	22.4	0.75	2.45 ($N = 42$)
Southeast	18,864	27,636	57.4	38.9	1.01	1.33 ($N = 53$)
Belleville	28,763	39,500	87.1	18.5	1.05	1.86 ($N = 39$)
Belle Village	19,022	27,600	72.9	47.7	0.59	2.30 ($N = 49$)
Southwest	20,050	23,875	69.1	13.2	0.86	2.06 ($N = 17$)
						1.94 ($N = 28$)

neighborhoods. Using this information, they constructed their sample so as to ensure that respondents would be concentrated in sixteen differentiated neighborhoods, representing the full range of the city's diversity on socio-economic status and ethnic lines (for a discussion of the neighborhood selection process, see Huckfeldt and Sprague 1995, 37–38). Using 1990 census tract GIS boundary files, we have delineated the spatial extent of these neighborhoods, based on the smallest aggregation of census tracts capturing the majority of main respondents for each neighborhood (see Figure 10.1).[4] As a result, we are in a position to examine neighborhood patterns in the mean distance spanned by political discussion networks to see if the relationships observed in the individual-level analysis of the preceding section are reproduced.

As Table 10.2 reveals, the principal investigators were successful in incorporating a socio-economically diverse range of neighborhoods. Across a number of measures of the socio-economic and ethnic character of each of the sixteen study neighborhoods, we see that political discussion networks are sustained at varying distances depending, in part, on neighborhood composition.

The contrast between the neighborhoods of Kensington Farms and Southeast is particularly telling. Kensington Farms, with the highest average family income, the highest average home value, and the highest proportion of homeowners, is home to main respondents that sustain, on average, the longest discussion networks at 2.84 miles. Conversely, the Southeast neighborhood has the lowest average family income, the second highest proportion of African-Americans, the fourth lowest average home value, and the smallest proportion of homeowners. Main respondents from Southeast have, as might be expected, the most compact political discussion networks with an average distance less than one-half (or 1.33 miles) of respondents from Kensington Farms. As

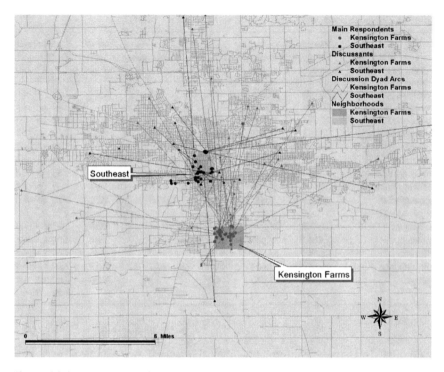

Figure 10.2. Discussion dyad arcs of two neighborhoods.

Figure 10.2 depicts, the difference in the average dyad distance of main respondents from these two neighborhoods is readily apparent. Note finally, the complete absence of discussion networks between these two neighborhoods.

Dyad Properties and Dyad Distance

To this point we have explored for patterns in dyad distance that are related to the individual and neighborhood properties of the main respondent. In this section we explore for evidence of relationships between a variety of dyad characteristics and the distance separating the discussion partners. Do relationships formed from initial contacts in different kinds of venues differ in their physical distance spanned? Does distance vary with the intimacy of the tie? Is the frequency of talk in general, and political talk in particular, related to the distance a network encompasses? Finally, is dyad distance related to the level of agreement or disagreement in a network?

Table 10.3 presents evidence bearing on these questions. The top-most panel provides the mean dyad distance for networks formed at work, church, the neighborhood, through the family, in casual social situations, and in the schools. Of these, we might hypothesize that neighborhood-based networks would have the lowest distance measures, and this turns out to be the case. Neighborhood-initiated dyads, on average, span

Table 10.3. Dyad characteristics and dyad distance (miles).

		Dyad Distance	N
How met?	Work	3.55	146
	Church	3.13	37
	Neighborhood	.46	77
	Family	3.84	10
	Casual social situation	2.54	27
	School	3.07	17
Intimacy	Close friend	2.67	204
	Friend	2.56	98
	Just regular contact	2.46	32
Talk frequency	Daily	1.76	301
	Once or twice a week	2.63	270
	Once or twice a month	2.87	50
	Less than once a month	1.14	5
Frequency of political talk	Most times	1.88	41
	Fairly often	1.82	145
	Only once in awhile	2.40	416
Frequency of disagreement	Often	2.46	71
	Sometimes	2.29	269
	Rarely	2.11	182
	Never	2.03	80

distances of less than half a mile, by far the shortest distance of all the different origins. By contrast, networks formed around the family (3.84 miles) and workplace (3.55 miles) have the average longest distance measures. Perhaps not surprisingly, the two types of networks that formed as a result of routine or casual interaction (among neighbors or casual social acquaintances), as opposed to those that arose from purposeful or familial activities, spanned the shortest distances.

In light of the hypothesis introduced earlier, in which dyad distance was conceptualized as a cost to be incurred, we might expect the distance spanned by a dyad to be a partial function of the intimacy of the tie. In particular, we might anticipate that respondents might be more willing to bear the costs associated with longer distances for close friends than mere acquaintances. The second panel in Table 10.3 confirms these expectations as well, revealing a modest but consistent relationship between dyad distance and the intimacy of the network. The mean distance spanned by discussion networks involving close friends was 2.67 miles, as opposed to 2.46 miles for "just regular contacts."

We might expect the frequency of interaction and political discussion across networks to vary as a function of the distance they span, such that closer discussion partners interact more frequently than more distant ones. These expectations are borne out in the third and fourth panels of Table 10.3. Those in daily contact live, on average, 1.76 miles apart, whereas those interacting only once or twice a month live an average of just below three miles apart (2.87). Surprisingly, the data suggest that those interacting less than once a month live only 1.14 miles apart, but this is likely to be an unreliable result produced by the extremely small number of cases ($N = 5$) falling into this category. Political discussion is more frequent among those living near one another, but the relationship is not linear. Those discussing politics "fairly often" live slightly closer together (1.82 miles) than those discussing politics frequently (1.88 miles), but these two categories are both lower than the mean distance for those discussing politics only "once in a while" (2.40 miles).

Finally, is there any evidence that the level of agreement or disagreement in a discussion network is related to the distances these relationships span? The bottom-most panel of Table 10.3 suggests that there is a linear relationship between the amount of conflict in a dyad and its spatial dimension. It is clear that more conflictual ties span longer distances than more consensual ones. This interesting finding is open to several interpretations. On the one hand, these results could reflect the operation of residential segregation processes that produce local neighborhoods that are more homogeneous than the functional (church, job, etc.) or family ties that individuals form with others outside the residential neighborhood. In this respect, the distance spanned by a discussion network may be analogous to Granovetter's (1973) "weak ties" argument, with longer distances serving to increase the heterogeneity of information flow along the network. On the other hand, individuals may be more selective in their choice of political discussion partners when interacting with their neighbors in order to avoid potentially conflictual relationships with those with whom they are in most frequent casual contact.

Does Dyad Distance Matter for the Transmission of Political Influence?

The foregoing has demonstrated that, while network analysis can overcome the limitations of geographically based research designs and focus attention on the politically salient ties formed by individuals regardless of their location, there remains a distinctive spatial patterning of the political discussion networks people construct. Geography does not determine anything about political discussion networks, yet our analyses demonstrate that space is a constraint that interacts in a series of predictable and theoretically tractable ways with a variety of individual, contextual, and dyad characteristics. Perhaps most interestingly, the analysis above suggests that discussion dyads characterized by higher levels of conflict tend to span the longest average distances. This finding invites us to question whether, *ceteris paribus*, the distances covered by political discussion networks makes any difference to their effectiveness in transmitting political influence. Answering this question definitively is beyond the scope of the present analysis. However, even a provisional response requires a more complicated estimation strategy than the simple tests we've presented to this point.

To estimate whether the distance separating dyad partners has any independent impact on the likelihood that the partners will adopt similar political behaviors, we constructed two dummy variables to measure different dimensions of the political homogeneity of the dyad. The first, a "mobilization" measure, is scored one if both members of the network either voted or did not vote, with all other cases scored as a zero. The second dummy variable measures partisan homogeneity and was scored one if both partners voted the same way in the Presidential election, and zero if they did not. With respect to our key independent variable of interest, the measure of dyad distance, we hypothesize that, net of other factors, the closer the proximity of the discussants, the more likely they will adopt the same political behavior.

To determine if physical proximity matters for political homogeneity, it is important to control for a range of other possible sources of political similarity. For this purpose we constructed a number of variables based on a series of comparisons of main respondents and their discussion partners. We created a series of dummy variables that were scored one if both respondent and discussant shared levels of education, religious affiliation, income, and partisanship and had union members in their respective households. We calculated a "difference in age" variable by subtracting the discussant's age in years from that of the main respondent. Since we are solely interested in the size of the age gap, we took the absolute value of this difference in ages. To control for the intimacy of the relationship, we included a three-category "closeness" variable, in which scores of one signify that the discussant is simply a "regular contact," three indicates that they are "friends," and five indicates that they are "close friends." Along with these control variables, we have included our measure of dyad distance, in miles.

The dichotomous nature of the dependent variable suggests the use of binary logistic regression to estimate these relationships. The results of the two parallel analyses of our two measures of dyad political homogeneity are presented in Table 10.4. The model performs much better in measuring the partisan homogeneity of the network than it does for the question of equal mobilization (compare the Cox and Snell R^2 figures of .053 for the mobilization model and .226 for the partisanship model).[5] This undoubtedly reflects the fact that most discussants and respondents both consistently reported voting or not voting in the survey instrument (only 14.1 percent of dyads reported differences in voting/not voting), thus providing relatively little variance for the model to explain. Only the difference in age variable has any significant impact on the likelihood that a dyad is homogeneously mobilized in the 1984 campaign, and as might be expected, the greater the age difference, the less likely both partners behaved the same. The distance separating discussion partners registered no significant impact on the propensity of dyad members to turn out at the polls.

With respect to consistent dyad partisanship, however, the model performs more strongly. Sharing religious preferences, intimacy, partisanship, and union households all contribute to explaining variations in dyad partisan homogeneity. However, here again the distance measure failed to contribute to the explanation of the partisan homogeneity of a dyad. Clearly, net of other explanatory factors, the distance separating discussion partners does not exert any systematic or statistically significant impact on the likelihood of partisan homogeneity within a political discussion network. While this suggests that the spatial dimension of political discussion networks is not associated with a direct impact on the political character of the network (at least in terms of its homogeneity), this does not imply that there are not important ways in which the geography of these networks might condition the transmission of partisan influence. A full exploration of these possibilities is beyond the scope of the present analysis.

Table 10.4. Determinants of dyad political homogeneity logistic regression coefficient / S.E.).

	Turnout (1 = same; 0=different)	Same Presidential Vote (1=same; 0=different)
Same level of education dummy	−.28	−.13
	(.41)	(.34)
Same income level dummy	.44	−.05
	(.53)	(.39)
Absolute value of age difference	−.05**	.03
	(.02)	(.02)
Same religious preference dummy	.59	.65*
	(.42)	(.36)
Intimacy (1–5; high scores = closer friends)	−.01	.28*
	(.15)	(.14)
Same partisanship dummy	.43	1.53***
	(.54)	(.37)
Union members in both households dummy	.53	−1.87**
	(.59)	(.65)
Distance (miles)	−.05	.04
	(.07)	(.14)
Constant	2.15**	−2.56***
	(.78)	(.73)
Correctly classified	87.6	72.6
−2 log likelihood	166.47	213.09
Cox & Snell R-squared	.053	.226

*** $p < .000$; ** $p < .05$; * $p < .10$.

Conclusion

Network analysis of political behavior has become popular as a means of analyzing the sociological dimension of political life without making assumptions about the geographic containers that encompass these sociological processes. In this chapter we have deliberately tried to "bring geography back in" to the analysis of political networks, to explore the geography of political discussion networks. Using a powerful data set that combines information on main respondents, their political discussion partners, and their respective locations, we have demonstrated that the spatial dimension of these networks is regular and ordered.

Specifically, we have shown that dyad distance varies by a range of individual, neighborhood, and dyad properties. In terms of the former, it appears as though the distance between discussion partners exists as a "cost" for maintaining the relationship, and we have shown that these costs are more easily met by males, by the young, by whites, and by the more educated and affluent. Similarly, we demonstrated that residential segregation processes that result in neighborhoods differentiated by socioeconomic status and race are also associated with distinctive patterns of political discussion networks. Poorer and less white neighborhoods appear, on average, to have discussion networks that span less distance than their more affluent and white counterparts do. Finally, we demonstrate that the character of the discussion network also varies according to where the discussion partners met, by the level of intimacy in the network, and by the frequency of interaction and political talk. We also saw that disagreement was more common in networks that spanned longer distances.

While the latter finding suggests that the spatial dimension of political discussion networks might be a centrally important property governing the political effectiveness of the discussion along it, our exploratory analysis of the determinants of two dimensions (mobilization and partisanship) of dyad political homogeneity failed to turn up any systematic distance effects. This is a relatively crude and demanding test of the direct effects of distance on networks, however. On the strength of the various analyses presented in this chapter, however, we are convinced that, despite their explicitly a-spatial definition, people respond to spatial constraints and opportunities in the construction of their personal political networks. This spatial dimension is subsumed in conventional network analysis, and as a result, we know relatively little about the interaction of geography and networks as they combine to influence political orientations and behavior. By drawing attention to an important underlying spatial dimension to political discussion networks, we hope to have established the need to explore the interactions of individuals across space in order to fully understand the nature of this interaction.

Acknowledgments   We would like to thank Robert Huckfeldt and John Sprague for generously giving us access to their primary data, and for working with us to prepare their survey data for spatial analysis. Of course, neither of these principal investigators bears any responsibility for the use we make of their data.

Notes

1. As Kevin Cox (1969: 159–160) has argued, " . . . implicit in much of the work using the contextual model is the assumption that the individual who is being affected by the context of an influence process confines his friends and associational contacts to the ecological unit chosen for analysis. Yet intuitively one knows that is not necessarily so; not only will the number of external contacts increase with decreasing the areal size of ecological units but those having contacts outside the ecological unit are less likely to be influenced by the context within the ecological unit."

2. The name generator read: "Can you give me the FIRST names of the three people you talked with most about the events of the past election year? These people might be from your family, from work, from the neighborhood, from church, from some other organization you belong to, or they might be from somewhere else."

3. Since the geocoding of respondents in one neighborhood resulted in a very small sample, our analyses are confined to the remaining fifteen neighborhoods.

4. All 1990 census tract data were sourced from the U.S. Census Bureau's web site, http://www.census.gov and the census tract GIS boundary file was sourced from *ESRI Data & Maps* CD-ROM data collection by Environmental Systems Research Institute, Inc.

5. Cox-Snell R^2 is one of a family of measures of goodness of fit for logistic regression models. Like other "pseudo-R^2" measures that are analogous to conventional regression's R^2 statistics, poor model fits generate scores near zero, with excellent fits associated with scores near 1. It is calculated as Cox-Snell $R^2 = 1 - \exp(-\text{Model } L^2/N)$.

References

Agnew, J.A. 1987. *Place and Politics: The Geographical Mediation of State and Society*. London: Allen and Unwin.

Barton, A.H. 1968. Bringing society back in: Survey research and macro-methodology. *American Behavioral Scientist*, XII, 2 November–December: 1–9.

Books, J.W., and C.L. Prysby. 1991. *Political Behavior and the Local Context*. New York: Praeger.

Campbell, A., P.E. Converse, W.E. Miller, and D. Stokes. 1960. *The American Voter*. New York: John Wiley and Sons.

Cox, K.R. 1969. The spatial structuring of information flow and partisan attitudes. In M. Dogan, and S. Rokkan (eds.), *Quantitative Ecological Analysis in the Social Sciences*. Cambridge, MA: MIT Press, 157–185.

Granovetter, M. 1973. The strength of weak ties. *American Journal of Sociology* 78: 1360–1380.

Huckfeldt, R.R. 1986. *Politics in Context: Assimilation and Conflict in Urban Neighborhoods*. New York: Agathon.

Huckfeldt, R.R., and J. Sprague. 1995. *Citizens, Contexts, and Social Communication: Information and Influence in an Election Campaign*. New York: Cambridge University Press.

Jackson, R.M., C.S. Fischer, and L. McCallister Jones. 1977. The dimensions of social networks. In C.S. Fischer, R.M. Jackson, C.A. Stueve, K. Gerson, L.M. Jones, with M. Baldassare (eds.), *Networks and Places: Social Relations in the Urban Setting*. New York: The Free Press, 39–58.

Kenny, C. 2001. *Social Influence in the Beginning: Disagreement and the Construction of Political Information Networks*. Paper presented to the American Political Science Association annual conference, San Francisco, Calif., August 30–September 1.

Knoke, D. 1990. *Political Networks: The Structural Perspective*, New York: Cambridge University Press.

La Due Lac, R. 1999. *Social Capital in Context: Implications of Social Network Structure and Neighborhood Context on Civic and Political Participation*. Paper presented to the American Political Science Association annual meeting, Atlanta, Ga., September 2–5.

Merelman, R.M. 1981. Politics and social structure, In S. Long (ed.) *The Handbook of Political Behavior*, Volume 3. New York: Plenum Press.

Pattie, C., and R. Johnston. 2001. Talk as a political context: Conversation and electoral change in British elections, 1992–1997. *Electoral Studies* 20 (1), March: 17–40.

Sheingold, C.A. 1973. Social networks and voting: The resurrection of a research agenda. *American Sociological Review* 38, 6 December: 712–720.

Weatherford, M.S. 1982. Interpersonal networks and political behavior. *American Journal of Political Science* 26, 1 February: 117–143.

Wellman, B. 1996. Are personal communities local? A dumptarian reconsideration. *Social Networks* 18: 347–354.

Wellman, B. 2001. Physical place and cyberplace: The rise of personalized networking. *International Journal of Urban and Regional Research* 25, 2 March: 227–252.

Wellman, B., and B. Leighton. 1979. Networks, neighborhoods, and communities: Approaches to the study of the community question. *Urban Affairs Quarterly* 14, 3 March: 363–390.

Part III

Region-Level Analysis

In popular parlance and in much of the social science literature, the term "region" describes an area at a level that is above that of a functional neighborhood. Hence, cities and counties may be seen as regions, based on political frameworks for decision-making and jurisdiction over a diverse set of interdependent processes. Metropolitan areas are regions defined in relationship to a collection of jurisdictions that interact with one another and share common interest as a consequence of such interactions. Similarly, the interactions of people across space may define a region based on culture, shared beliefs, or functional interdependence. It is possible to think in terms of cultural regions, linguistic regions, and political regions, to name a few. The analytical issues for regional analysis, however, parallel closely those discussed in Part II on neighborhoods, e.g., in the chapter by Messner and Anselin. Some of the same methods apply and derive their analytic value from preservation of local variation across a region. In this section, Sweeney and Feser review the special problems of analyzing point data and areal data in a regional context. In addition, Serge Rey introduces the modifiable areal unit problem (MAUP) and the prospect that analytic results can vary as one shifts from one set of data units to another within the same study area. Regional analysis is also fundamental to many planning and policy issues where the intent is to define boundaries that capture the process that one is trying to control or direct, or to fashion a holistic perspective on the character of the region and on possible solutions to its problems.

The chapter by Câmara et al. investigates patterns and processes of social exclusion in the teeming metropolis of São Paulo. Concepts and measurements of social exclusion are discussed with reference to practices used in the United Kingdom and with regard to defining a methodology appropriate to the special conditions of Brazil. Global and local spatial autocorrelation measures are used to assess levels of spatial dependency in the data and to map clusters of social exclusion and social inclusion. To explain the patterns, the authors compare different spatial regression approaches, including a spatial-regimes model based on three distinct areas of the city. This method, which recognizes the non-stationarity of process relationships across space, yielded a better fit to the data and a stronger accounting for local circumstances. Câmara et al. also illustrate a geostatistical technique to model trend surfaces in the city's homicide rates for 1996 and 1999. This approach to regional analysis dissolves the boundaries of the district crime data into a continuous distribution for which a trend surface is interpolated and mapped. The results show crime increasing and spreading into wealthier parts of the city. The research in this chapter has had significant press exposure in Brazil, has influenced social policy measures in São Paulo, and has raised general awareness about the value of spatial analysis in social science.

Sweeney and Feser provide an exhaustive account of index measures of industry concentration and of different global and local indicators of spatial autocorrelation as applied to areal data (e.g., Moran's *I*, Geary's *c*, and the Getis-Ord *G* statistic) and to point-location data (*K*-function, Getis-Ord *G*, and the *D*-function). Their analysis evaluates these alternative measures for exploring the proximity of firms and their tendencies to seek business externalities by locating near one another in spatial clusters. The data consists of the street addresses and employment levels of firms in six different industry groups for the Los Angeles and Atlanta regions in 1997. Construct and content validity are at the core of their analysis. In seeking to determine if the measures are congruent with the concepts, they face challenges of whether or not measures of spatial clustering can account for alternative origins of clusters and whether or not the measures are sensitive to co-location processes that operate at different geographic scales. The point location data are aggregated to three different levels of areal resolution for the area measures of co-location and to 2-, 5-, and 10-kilometer resolutions for the point-based measures. These procedures permit an assessment of how the measures vary at different scales and how they relate to the distance sensitivity of spatial externalities for firms in different industry groups in different urban regions. The authors explore options for visualizing the results on maps, and illustrate how the measures perform at different distance resolutions and under different boundary conditions. This chapter provides an excellent overview of alternative measures, identifying the strong points and weaknesses of each.

Shen considers the regional context of accessibility to jobs for low-income labor markets and the role of telecommunications in urban travel behavior and residential location choice. He reviews the importance of treating distance in a functional sense to represent the effort required to overcome spatial separation, and he sees transportation and communication technologies as transforming the spatial relationships among places in complex ways. He uses a least-squares regression model to analyze the commuting behavior of more than 3,000 workers in the Boston Metropolitan Area. This provides a basis for assessing the controversial spatial-mismatch hypothesis regarding the central-city residence of most low-income workers far from suburban jobs. Using accessibility measures that account for functional distance, he finds that low-income workers are disadvantaged more by reliance on public transportation than by geographical position of residence, especially in a dispersing metropolitan economy that favors automobile users. He concludes with a research plan for exploring the impact of telecommuting options and of virtual transactions on metropolitan form and related changes in accessibility patterns for residents.

Rey documents an analysis of regional income inequality for the United States over a 72-year period, providing explicit treatment of spatial dependence and exposing the problems of interpretation that arise from using data at different spatial scales. In addition, he develops an analytic approach for inferential examination of research hypotheses regarding regional inequality. A thorough review of the literature reveals insufficient attention to these methodological issues. Rey also addresses the modifiable areal unit problem (MAUP), whereby changes in spatial scale for the basic data unit may influence the measures of regional inequality. His comparison of inequality measures and spatial dependency for state-level and for county-level data for the 48 states reveals notable differences. Partitions of the data by regional divisions (e.g., the four U.S. Census Regions, nine U.S. Census Divisions, or the eight regions used by the Bureau of Economic Analysis) yield contrasting results in the share of global inequality accounted for by the interregional versus the intraregional component of inequality. This scale issue warrants careful consideration in spatial approaches to social science research.

Bradshaw and Muller review the application of spatial analysis in policy formulation for land use planning at state and county levels in California. Their chapter features two interesting research projects that have influenced policy directions. The first concerned the expansion of a state program to guarantee bank loans for small businesses. This entailed use of the service-area concept and a location-allocation method to determine where to locate new community financial development corporations. The second research project used the Alternative Growth Futures (AGF) modeling framework to assess the influence of land use conversions on the costs, profitability, and other impacts to local agricultural economies and environments from different possible urban forms for Monterey and Santa Cruz counties. GIS is an important component for application of this modeling framework and for communicating alternative development scenarios to policy makers and the general public. The scenarios provided a basis for discussion aimed at identifying conflict potentials and achieving compromise in a highly politicized environment. The experiences of Bradshaw and Muller raise interesting questions about the boundaries between science and the public uses of science. Community sentiment, ambiguity of purpose, political power, multiple effects of decisions, and variable levels of understanding of spatial analysis co-mingle in the world of state and regional politics. Land use models and GIS tools, though of considerable help, are limited in their capacities to capture the complexities of many public policy issues. Nonetheless, they play an important role in policy formulation and are increasingly in demand, providing interesting areas for research and participation by social scientists trained in the methods of spatial thinking.

So far, the chapters in Part III have explored contemporary issues, mostly related to urban-based regions and socio-economic concerns. The final chapter explores a very different problem but, nonetheless, one that presents formal attention to spatial organization at a regional level. Archaeologist John Kantner examines evidence of prehistoric roadways of the Chaco Anasazi as clues to cultural values of past civilizations. The evidence of these roadways, dating from about 1000 years ago, includes linear features that show up in remote sensing imagery and in shallow swales in field surveys.

At issue is whether they formed an extensive network that connected Chaco Canyon to other locations in the American Southwest, consisted of only short road segments to serve local functional needs, or served symbolic and cosmological purposes. Kantner reviews hypotheses and research about the genesis of these past geographic patterns. He uses GIS to compare the locations of known road segments with simulated patterns based on alternate hypotheses about the underlying motivations for the roadways. The simulations involve spatial optimization methods applied to digital elevation models to estimate walking time from a hiking algorithm developed by Waldo Tobler. Kantner's evaluation of the results points to the primary cosmological basis for the roadway networks—drawing attention to locations and features of known religious significance. Kantner also provides an insightful overview of the spatial methodologies that have aided archaeologists in reconstructing and interpreting ancient landscapes. These include graph theory, central place theory, location-allocation algorithms, and network simulation models.

This section reinforces some of the methodologies discussed in Part II regarding areal data. However, it also introduces other issues that are critical to the proper use and assessment of spatially oriented research in the social sciences. These include questions about aggregation and analysis of point-data, choice of measures, analytic impact of the modifiable areal unit problem, and interpolation of data values in instances where the basic data units are not spatially correspondent. The chapters in Part III provide some excellent examples of operational solutions to these problems.

11

Mapping Social Exclusion and Inclusion in Developing Countries
Spatial Patterns of São Paulo in the 1990s

Gilberto Câmara

Aldaiza Sposati

Dirce Koga

Antonio Miguel Monteiro

Frederico Roman Ramos

Eduardo Camargo

Suzana Druck Fuks

The concept of social exclusion was born in Europe, motivated by the sharp increase in the number of poor, whose numbers in the twelve countries of the EEC went from 38 million in 1975 to 53 million in 1992. First conceived in the 1960s in France (Klanfer 1965), in the last two decades social exclusion has become a major category of social thinking (Duffy 1995; Paugam 1991). Poverty implies exclusion from goods and services; social exclusion goes beyond income inequalities, to encompass denial or non-realization of civil, political, and social rights of citizenship (Room 1995). Social exclusion is therefore linked to the approach proposed by Nobel laureate Amartya Sen (1992), which considers that removal of inequalities in modern societies is determined by the access to basic capabilities such as the ability to be healthy, well-fed, housed, and integrated into the community, to participate in community and public life, and to enjoy social bases of self-respect.

Social exclusion has become a major policy issue in both developing and developed nations. In Europe, the U.K. government has established a "Social Exclusion Unit," set up by the Prime Minister in 1997, and has produced the "indices of deprivation" for the United Kingdom (DETR 2000). The Council of Europe carried out a project on "Human Dignity and Social Exclusion." In the United States, initiatives include the "National Neighborhood Indicators Partnership," which aims to use geographical information as a means of improving the awareness of citizens and urban planners about the different dimensions of deprived urban areas (Kingsley et al. 1997).

Since most of the socioeconomic data used in social exclusion studies are associated with geographical locations and aggregated into areas such as census tracts or boroughs, maps are a natural way of portraying local social and economical conditions. In this way, the perception of social exclusion is enhanced with the visualization of "problem-areas," which, more often that not, tend to exhibit some type of cluster patterns. Notwithstanding the impact of maps in promoting awareness about deprivation, the role of space in the patterns of social exclusion indicators has received considerably less attention. In most cities and countries, the social and economical phenomena that cause social exclusion will tend to be space-related, since the very nature of wealth concentration in most modern societies tends to produce large inequalities in land allocation and in land and house prices. Therefore, it is very relevant to inquire (following Bailey 2001): *Are the patterns of social exclusion conditioned by factors that are spatially dependent?* Or to put it directly, *why are these spatial patterns there, and how will they change if we intervene in a particular way?* Answering these questions requires using statistical methods that are spatially explicit; it also requires handling data sources at different levels of spatial aggregation and using different ways of depicting spatial information.

Given this motivation, this work examines the use of spatial analytical techniques to explore patterns of social exclusion. The basis for the work is a set of indices of social exclusion/inclusion for the Brazilian city of São Paulo, which have had a major impact on policy makers and the public (Sposati 1996, 2000). Taking the maps of social exclusion/inclusion as a basis, we have set out to address the question: *Can the explicit use of space in our analytical techniques enhance our comprehension of social exclusion in São Paulo?* This general concern was broken down in the following issues:

1. *Are the patterns of social exclusion spatially dependent? Or are there "pockets" of local variation where social exclusion/inclusion differs significantly from the overall trends in the city?* To address these questions, we have used global and local spatial autocorrelation indices to explore the properties of the social exclusion patterns in São Paulo and to identify clusters of social exclusion and social inclusion in São Paulo.

2. *Given the many dimensions and components of the social exclusion/inclusion indices, what is the relative influence of the individual components to the overall social exclusion? Is there a single factor that is highly correlated to the overall pattern of social exclusion? Is this correlation spatially dependent?* This is a very relevant question for public policy, since its helps to ascertain and direct the use of public funds. To address this question, we have used spatial regression techniques, which show that the conditioning factors of social exclusion vary considerably within the city.

3. *How can spatio-temporal trends in the components of social exclusion best be portrayed? Can we gain insight into the spatio-temporal trends of social exclusion by freeing ourselves from "the tyranny of zones" (Spiekermann and Wegener 2000)?* To address this question, we have mapped spatio-temporal trends in the evolution of crime in São Paulo using geostatistics.

Each of these questions has been addressed with the use of spatial analysis techniques, as described in the next sections. These examples show how spatial analytical techniques can enhance substantially the understanding of social exclusion and inclusion patterns in large cities of the developing world.

Measuring Social Exclusion/Inclusion in São Paulo

The development of indicators for the measurement of deprivation and social exclusion has been subject to intense debate recently (for reviews of the problem, see, e.g.,

Gordon and Townsend 2000, and Senior 2002). Most approaches to the calculation of social exclusion indices are based on the premise that social exclusion is made up of separate dimensions, or "domains" of deprivation, where each domain is made up of a number of components that cover aspects of social exclusion as comprehensively as possible. For example, the United Kingdom's deprivation index (DETR 2000) is made of six dimensions, calculated for each ward: (a) income deprivation, (b) employment deprivation, (c) health deprivation and disability, (d) education, skills, and training deprivation, (e) housing deprivation, and (f) geographical access to services. Each index is computed, and the different areas are ranked. Then, a normalization procedure is applied for expressing each dimension in the same scale, and all indexes are transformed to ensure that each domain is transformed to a common distribution. Finally, the indexes are added up according to a weighting rule that reflects the relative importance of each factor (DETR 2000).

The United Kingdom's and similar deprivation indicators are based on the implicit assumption that "social exclusion" tends to be associated with processes of *social disqualification* and on economical and social problems that impact urban areas, many of which have had previously better living conditions. In the definition of United Kingdom's Social Exclusion Unit, "*social exclusion is a shorthand term for what can happen when people or areas suffer from a combination of linked problems such as unemployment, poor skills, low incomes, poor housing, high crime environments, bad health and family breakdown*" (Blair 1998). This assumption of social disqualification is implicit in the methodological procedures applied: for each "dimension" of the deprivation index, wards are *ranked* and then *normalized*. The implicit assumption is that the average values for the country represent an "acceptable" level of social inclusion and that social policies should be geared toward "regeneration" of areas that have the lowest deprivation indices.

In lower income countries (LIC), social exclusion has a completely different setting. Their deprived populations have never had acceptable living conditions, and there is no social protection typical of the Welfare State societies of the twentieth century. In these countries, social exclusion is the result of *social apartheid* and of strong inequalities in income distribution. Therefore, measurement of social exclusion in the developing world requires a different strategy than indicators such as United Kingdom's Indices of Deprivation, which are based on *ranking* and do not provide an objective measure of whether the citizens of an area have achieved an acceptable standard of living. In LICs, social exclusion indices have to consider that the average values of dimensions such as income, health deprivation, and housing quality may represent unsatisfactory living conditions. Therefore, social exclusion indices in LICs have to convey not only the *relative* position of an area (e.g., an electoral ward) in relation to a study area (e.g., a country), but also the *absolute* situation of this area in relation to the attainment of acceptable living conditions. The social exclusion/inclusion index developed by the authors starts by defining *a basic living standard*, which includes needs that are considered basic and universal according to a collective ethic of life and that incorporates attainable goals for public policy (Sposati 1996).

Our proposed *social exclusion/inclusion index* is aggregated by areal units, with four components: income, quality of life, human development, and gender equality. Each component is captured by a set of variables obtained from census and field data collection, described in Table 11.1. For each variable, we propose a *reference value* that marks the attainment of *a basic standard of inclusion*. Areas that achieve such levels are assigned a value of 0 (zero), whereas areas with values above such reference are mapped linearly to a positive [0 to 1] scale, and areas below such reference are assigned negative values on a [−1 to 0] scale. Therefore, each of the components has a range between −1 (total exclusion) and 1 (total inclusion). The social exclusion index is obtained by averaging its four components.

This methodology was used to assess the evolution of the city of São Paulo during the 1990s. São Paulo presents an important challenge to social and urban planners, a city that is simultaneously one of the world's largest (9 million people), Brazil's richest (as measured by the industrial and service goods output), and the one that includes the largest number of socially excluded citizens in Brazil. To allow for a common geographical basis for the different data sets, the study used the official division of São Paulo in 96 districts. The data sets used included: (a) the 1991 census and the 1996 population assessment, from IBGE (Brazil's Bureau of Census); (b) the 1987 and 1997 living conditions surveys by the Companhia do Metropolitano de São Paulo (Subway Authority); (c) the 1996 and 1999 homicide rates produced by Fundação SEADE (São Paulo State Statistics Bureau); (d) information on infant mortality rates by PROAIM (Public Safety Secretariat of the São Paulo city).

We have produced the "Map of Social Exclusion/Inclusion of São Paulo—1995," which used data available from 1987 to 1995 to produce indicators for the earlier part of the 1990s (Sposati 1996), and the "Map of Social Exclusion/Inclusion of São Paulo—2000," which concentrated on trends on population, employment, and quality of life indicators during the 1990s (Sposati 2000). The 1995 map showed a significant gap between the social exclusion and the social inclusion regions of São Paulo, where 2/3 of its districts are below acceptable levels of living standards, as depicted in Figure 11.1.

The main findings of the 2000 Map were a significant change in population dynamics and a strong relation between education and unemployment trends. Although there has been only a small increase of the overall population from 1991 to 1996 (from 9,646,185 inhabitants to 9,839,066 inhabitants or a 2 percent growth), the poorest regions of the city have registered population increases up to 130 percent. This trend is also markedly skewed in the range of 15- to 24-year-olds, which has grown by 75,000 people, mostly in deprived neighborhoods. One consequence has been a large increase in violence and homicide rates, since youngsters have access to information, but do not have the means to obtain consumer goods. Therefore, teenage violence has grown markedly in São Paulo during the 1990s.

Exploring the Patterns of Social Exclusion/Inclusion for Spatial Dependence

Taking the "Map of Social Exclusion/Inclusion of São Paulo" as our basic data set, we have set out to explore a number of questions regarding the role of space in the social exclusion patterns. Our first concern was to address the nature of spatial dependence in these patterns. As a starting point, it was necessary to determine the possible existence

Table 11.1. Composition of the social exclusion/inclusion index.

Index	Subcategory	Census Variables	Reference Values
Income index	Poor family survival conditions	Family heads below the poverty limit (without income)	0 percent
	Income autonomy	Income per family head	3–5 minimum wage
		Job offer	0.55
	Street population	Adult poverty rate	0 percent
		Children-at-risk rate	0 percent
Quality of life index	Environmental quality	Houses with poor water service	0.5 percent
		Houses with poor sewer service	0.5 percent
		Houses with poor garbage collection	0.3 percent
	Sanitation comfort	Habitation density	4 person/house
		Bathroom/house offer	1 bathroom/house
		Bathroom/person density	3 persons/bathroom
	Privacy comfort	Bedroom/house	2 bedrooms/house
		Bedroom/person density	2 persons/room
	Poor housing	Percentage of population who lives in poor housing	0.5 percent
	Time to work	Average time spent to work	56 minutes
	Social services deficit	Basic health services access potential	40 percent access
		Day care access potential	in day care
		Kindergarten education access potential	100 percent access
		First level access potential	100 percent access
Human develop. index	Poor literacy	Illiterate family heads	0 percent illiteracy rate
	Educational development	Years of education of family head	8 years of education
	Death risk	Percentage of population over 70	3 percent
		Children mortality	25 per 1,000 births
		Youth mortality	3.76 per 100,000
		Potential of lost life years	43
	Violence	Larceny cases	0 cases
		Robbery cases	0 cases
		Vehicle robbery cases	0 cases
		Homicide cases	0 cases
Gender equality index		Concentration of women as family heads	2 percent
		Concentration of illiterate women as family heads	0.4 percent

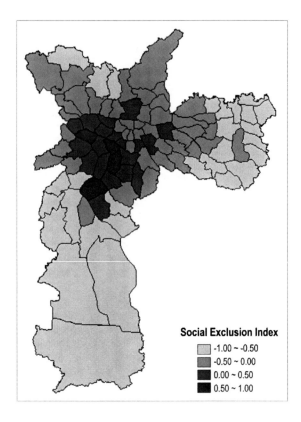

Figure 11.1. Social Exclusion Index in São Paulo obtained by the 1995 Social Exclusion/ Inclusion Map (96 districts). Values vary from −1 (extreme exclusion) to +1 (extreme inclusion).

Social Exclusion Index
- -1.00 ~ -0.50
- -0.50 ~ 0.00
- 0.00 ~ 0.50
- 0.50 ~ 1.00

of regional trends in the data; estimation is necessary, since, if the data exhibit a trend, it would cause the indices to be naturally spatially autocorrelated. The regression fit for the trend surface was very poor ($R^2 = 0.12$), and it can be inferred that there are no strong spatial trends in the data. The next step was to estimate the global spatial autocorrelation in the social exclusion index, by using Moran's I index:

$$I = \frac{\sum_{i=1}^{n}\sum_{j=1}^{n} w_{ij}(x_i - \bar{x})(x_j - \bar{x})}{\sum_{i=1}^{n}(x_i - \bar{x})^2} \tag{1}$$

In this equation, n is the number of areas, x_i is the value of the attribute in area i, $\bar{x}$ is the mean value of the attribute for the whole region, and the weights w_{ij} are such that they are $1/neigh_i$ if area i and area j are contiguous and 0 (zero) otherwise, where $neigh_i$ is the number of neighbors of area i. The Moran index is a global correlation coefficient, where a value of 0 would indicate no spatial correlation and a value of 1 a complete spatial dependency. For the composite social exclusion/inclusion index, we have obtained a Moran's I index of 0.642. In order to test the significance of this index, we have used a permutation test, where the values of the attributes associated with the regions are shuffled in random fashion, generating 999 new spatial arrangements (Anselin 1992). The Moran index associated with each new spatial arrangement is computed, producing an empirical distribution of 1000 values, from which we can determine if the value obtained is significant within a 99 percent confidence interval. Based on the pseudo-distribution, it was estimated that the spatial autocorrelation index was significant at the 99 percent level.

Given the existence of a strong global pattern of spatial association for the social exclusion/inclusion index in São Paulo, the next question to be asked concerns the regional distribution of this index: *Are there "pockets" of local variation where social exclusion/inclusion differs significantly from the overall trends in the city?* The idea is to find clusters of local variation where the social exclusion/inclusion index has a stronger association than the overall trends in the city. To address these questions, we have used two exploratory data analysis tools: the Moran scatterplot and the Local Moran spatial autocorrelation index.

The *Moran scatterplot* (Anselin 1996) is a tool for visualizing patterns of spatial autocorrelation. The idea is to compare the spatial distributions of an *attribute* and its *local mean*. As a first step, both variables are *normalized*, subtracting values from the global mean and dividing by the standard deviation. The resulting normalized variables will have a mean of 0 and a standard deviation of 1. Following Anselin (1996), we refer to the normalized variable as Z and to its local mean as WZ, where W is the normalized weights matrix, as described in Equation (1). By constructing a graph of Z versus WZ (Figure 11.2), we can express four different types of spatial association:

- Quadrant Q1 ("High-High"), showing areas where both normalized values and local mean values are positive;
- Quadrant Q2 ("Low-Low"), showing areas where both normalized values and local mean values are negative;
- Quadrant Q3 ("High-Low"), with positive values and negative local means; and
- Quadrant Q4 ("Low-High"), with negative values and positive local means.

The interpretation of the Moran scatterplot map in this context is that most of the districts of the city are located in quadrants Q1 and Q2, which are areas of positive spatial association. However, a significant number of districts are located in quadrants Q3 and Q4 and can be considered as areas that do not follow the same pattern of spatial association. These districts can therefore be considered as transition regions between regions of social inclusion (the "high-high" districts) and regions of social exclusion (the "low-low" areas). To investigate this hypothesis, we have created a map, Figure 11.3, in which each district is labeled according to the quadrant occupied by its social exclusion/inclusion index in its Moran scatterplot. Such a map is called a "Moran scatterplot map" (Anselin 1996), and shows that Q1 ("high-high") districts are all located in the center of São Paulo, and Q2 ("low-low") districts are mostly located in the eastern and southern parts of the city, which are the regions of greater social exclusion. Districts in quadrants Q3 ("high-low") and Q4 ("low-high") are mostly associated with intermediary regions between the city's center and its two great regions of social exclusion.

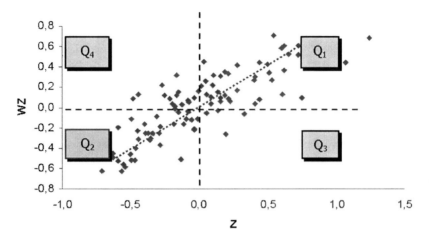

Figure 11.2. Moran scatterplot for the social exclusion/inclusion index of São Paulo, 1995.

The Moran scatterplot map indicates strong patterns of spatial association and, therefore, suggests the presence of clusters on the distribution of the social exclusion/inclusion index. To find such clusters, we used the *local Moran index* (Anselin 1995):

$$I_i = \frac{(x_i - \bar{x}) \sum\limits_{j=1}^{n} w_{ij}(x_j - \bar{x})}{\sum\limits_{j=1}^{n}(x_j - \bar{x})^2} \tag{2}$$

where the terms are defined as in Equation (1). To establish the significance of the local Moran index, we simulated a pseudo-distribution by permutation of the attribute values among the areas; statistical tests were then used to establish confidence intervals. Local index values with significance of 95 percent, 99 percent, and 99.9 percent were then mapped and posited as "hot-spots" of local non-stationarity (Anselin 1995). We found two "hot spots" of social exclusion, located in the south and east of the city, and one "hot spot" of social inclusion located in the center of the city, as shown in Figure 11.4.

The clusters in Figure 11.4 correspond to areas that concentrate a significant amount of the city's disparities: (a) the so-called "Deep South" and the "Far East" regions of São Paulo, areas of high social exclusion; and (b) the center of the city, an area of high social inclusion. The two most excluded regions of the city differ in the causes for such exclusion. The city's "Deep South" region has had an explosive growth in recent times. Migrant workers have come to São Paulo from other parts of the country and have occupied the region, resulting in population growth rates of over 100 percent in most areas. This process has not been matched by public investment, and as a result, its inhabitants have the worst conditions of the city in terms of public services (health, education, and social care). In the "Far East" of São Paulo, concentration of low-income population is a direct consequence of public policies of the 1970s and 1980s, which removed poor people from slums located in the central (and wealthiest) part of the city

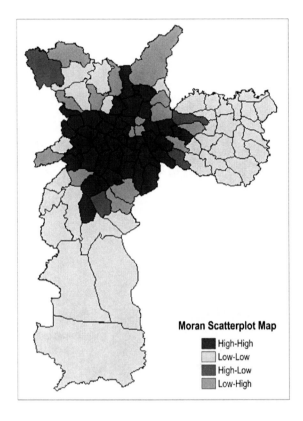

Moran Scatterplot Map
- High-High
- Low-Low
- High-Low
- Low-High

Figure 11.3. Moran scatterplot map for social exclusion/ inclusion index of the "Map of Social Exclusion/ Inclusion of São Paulo—1995."

to publicly-built housing estates in the eastern periphery. These housing estates were inadequately built and rapidly degraded into crime-infested areas. By contrast, in the center of São Paulo, the map shows a significant cluster of high-income areas, where the wealthiest part of the population lives. Consequently, the exploratory data analysis tools have proven effective in distinguishing the extreme concentrations of wealth and poverty in São Paulo.

Analysis of Social Exclusion Factors by Spatial Econometrics

The investigation of social exclusion process in São Paulo also requires an assessment of the relative influence of the factors that produce the overall index. The 1995 Map used 45 variables, but such a large data set may not be always available for researchers in developing nations. This raises an important question: *what is the minimum set of variables that can still produce a credible result for the social exclusion/inclusion index? Is there a variable that is a determinant factor for social exclusion?* To establish a relation between the relevant factors and the composite indices, we investigated three different types of spatial regression models: the *spatial autoregressive lag* model, *the spatial autoregressive error* model, and the *spatial regimes* regression. Each of these

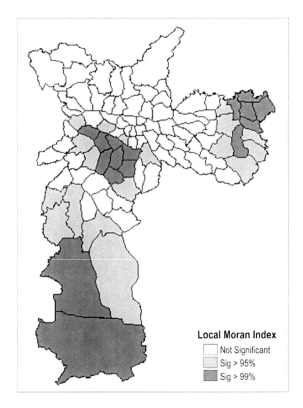

Local Moran Index
☐ Not Significant
▨ Sig > 95%
▧ Sig > 99%

Figure 11.4. Significant values
of local Moran index for social
exclusion/inclusion index for
São Paulo, 1995.

models is briefly described, following Anselin (1988). The linear regression model
formulation can be described as

$$Y = X\beta + \varepsilon, \varepsilon \sim \tilde{N}(0, \sigma^2) \tag{3}$$

or

$$
\begin{bmatrix} y_1 \\ y_2 \\ .. \\ .. \\ y_n \end{bmatrix} = \begin{bmatrix} 1 & x_{11} & .. & x_{1k-1} \\ 1 & x_{21} & .. & x_{2k-1} \\ .. & .. & .. & .. \\ .. & .. & .. & .. \\ 1 & x_{n1} & .. & x_{nk-1} \end{bmatrix} \begin{bmatrix} \beta_0 \\ \beta_1 \\ .. \\ .. \\ \beta_{k-1} \end{bmatrix} + \begin{bmatrix} \varepsilon_1 \\ \varepsilon_2 \\ .. \\ .. \\ \varepsilon_n \end{bmatrix} \tag{4}
$$

where Y is an $(n \times 1)$ vector of observations on a dependent variable taken at each of
n locations, X is an $(n \times k)$ matrix of exogenous variables, β is an $(k \times 1)$ vector of
parameters, and ϵ is an $(n \times 1)$ vector of disturbances. The *spatial lag model* includes a
spatial dependence term, through a new term that incorporates spatial autocorrelation
as part of the explanatory component of the model:

$$Y = \rho WY + X\beta + \varepsilon \tag{5}$$

where W is the spatial weights matrix, as described in Equation (1), and the product WY expresses the spatial dependence on Y, where ρ is the *spatial autoregressive*

coefficient. The *spatial autoregressive error model* considers that the spatial effects are a perturbation that should be removed. In this case, the spatial effects are associated with the error term, and the model is expressed as

$$Y = X\beta + \varepsilon, \varepsilon = \lambda W + \xi \tag{6}$$

where λ is a scalar spatial error parameter, and ϵ is a spatially autocorrelated disturbance vector. The spatial autoregressive lag model and the spatial autoregressive error model both aim at exploring the global patterns of spatial autocorrelation in the data set. These global spatial regression models are based on the hypothesis that the spatial process whose observations are being analyzed is stationary. This implies that the spatial autocorrelation patterns can be captured in a single regression term. In practice, medium-to-large sized data sets, such as the São Paulo ones, exhibit different patterns of spatial dependence, as seen in the previous section, and suggest the use of regression techniques suitable for non-stationary spatial processes, whose regression coefficients must reflect the spatial heterogeneity. One possibility is to model the spatial trends in a discrete fashion, subdividing the study region into in sub-regions, called *spatial regimes* (Anselin 1988). Each spatial regime is posited to have its own spatial pattern and its own coefficients. For example, consider the case where the study region is divided in two subregions:

$$Y = X_1\beta_1 + X_2\beta_2 + \varepsilon \tag{7}$$

In this model, the non-zero values of vector X_1 are only those values of X for areas that are within the first spatial regime, as expressed in:

$$
\begin{bmatrix} y_1 \\ y_2 \\ .. \\ .. \\ y_n \end{bmatrix} =
\begin{bmatrix} 1 & x_{11} & .. & x_{2k-1} \\ 1 & x_{21} & .. & x_{2k-1} \\ .. & .. & .. & .. \\ .. & .. & .. & .. \\ 0 & 0 & .. & 0 \end{bmatrix}
\begin{bmatrix} \beta_0^1 \\ \beta_1^1 \\ .. \\ .. \\ \beta_{k-1}^1 \end{bmatrix}
$$
$$
+ \begin{bmatrix} 0 & 0 & 0 & 0 \\ 0 & 0 & 0 & 0 \\ .. & .. & .. & .. \\ .. & .. & .. & x_{n-1,k-1} \\ 1 & x_{n1} & .. & x_{n,k-1} \end{bmatrix}
\begin{bmatrix} \beta_0^2 \\ \beta_1^2 \\ .. \\ .. \\ \beta_{k-1}^2 \end{bmatrix}
+ \begin{bmatrix} \varepsilon_1 \\ \varepsilon_2 \\ .. \\ .. \\ \varepsilon_n \end{bmatrix} \tag{8}
$$

As an initial approximation to the spatial regimes for the São Paulo data set, we used the exploratory techniques described in the previous section and divided the city into three distinct regions, as shown in Figure 11.5: the city's center, which is a locus of social inclusion, the southern and eastern parts of the city (extremes of social inclusion), and a transition region, which contains most areas that do not follow the main spatial dependence trend, and which fall into quadrants Q3 and Q4 of the Moran map (see Figure 11.3).

We performed a regression analysis on the correlation between the percentage of family heads[1] with more than 15 years of schooling (as the independent variable) with the social exclusion index (as the dependent variable). Four regression techniques were used: standard OLS regression, spatial lag model, spatial error model, and the spatial

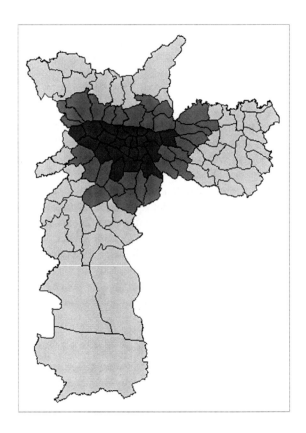

Figure 11.5. Spatial regimes
for the city of São Paulo.

regimes, as shown in Figure 11.5. The results are summarized in Table 11.2, based on
four comparison criteria: (a) R^2—the standard "goodness-of-fit" measure, which is inadequate for spatially dependent data, as discussed in Anselin (1988); (b) *Likelihood*—
maximized log-likelihood assessment of model fit, a preferred measure according to
Anselin (1992); (c) *MI-error*—global spatial autocorrelation indicator of residuals; (d)
LM-error—Lagrange Multiplier indicator (assesses the extent to which there remains
spatial autocorrelation in the residuals), a test proposed by Anselin (1992).

The spatial regimes regression was significantly superior to the other regression
models; it had a better fit to the observed data, and the model residuals exhibited significantly less spatial autocorrelation. This performance is explained by the existence
of different regimes of spatial association for the social exclusion/inclusion index in
São Paulo. Since the spatial error and the spatial lag regression techniques only model
the global autocorrelation patterns, they fail to account for local instabilities.

The practical implication of this regression study is that a significant proportion
of the social exclusion/inclusion index can be related to the education of the family
head, when the spatial dependence is taken into account. In fact, similar regressions
indicated that, out of all 45 basic variables, education has the strongest relation to the
social exclusion/inclusion index. In São Paulo's poor regions, our results indicate that

Table 11.2. Education X social exclusion in São Pulo (results from regression models).

	OLS	Spatial Lag	Spatial Error	Spatial Regimes
R^2	0.75	0.77	0.79	0.86
Likelihood	14.9	20.53	26.68	47.86
MI-error	0.384	—	—	−0.007
LM-error	29.43	12.19	16.58	0.006

a small increase in years of schooling will most often be translated into a substantial improvement in social inclusion.

Trend Surfaces of Homicide Rates in São Paulo

Spatial data models for socioeconomic phenomena usually involve aggregation of census-type data over area units. The boundaries of such areas are defined by operational or political criteria and are, therefore, essentially unrelated to the phenomena being modeled (Martin 1996). This fact leads to the idea of dissolving zonal data into continuous surfaces; these surfaces provide a useful framework for the spatial analysis of socioeconomic data. For the social scientist, the removal of the boundaries is not as important as the information gained by having a distribution that depicts the major trends of a variable (or a set of variables) over the entire study area (Goodchild et al. 1993; Spiekermann and Wegener 2000).

We used geostatistical techniques to produce trend surfaces for the homicide rates in São Paulo in 1996 and 1999, as shown in Figure 11.6. The original data consisted of estimates of homicide rate per 100,000 inhabitants, aggregated by the 96 districts. To produce these maps, we obtained a sample set by assigning a sample at the center of each district. These samples were then used as a basis for computing a variogram that models the spatial correlation structure, and a surface was interpolated by ordinary kriging (Bailey and Gatrell 1995). The trend surfaces depict a significant decrease in the areas with lowest homicide rates (below 30 deaths per 100,000 inhabitants) in 1999 in relation to 1996. Since the lower homicide rates correlate very strongly with the wealthiest regions of the city (compare with Figures 11.1 and 11.2), these results indicate a spatial spreading of crime. Violence is, thus, not confined to the poorest areas of the city, and the inhabitants of richer areas are increasingly prone to be victims of violent assaults. These results have had a major impact on public awareness of the spatial trends of crime in the city; *Folha de São Paulo*, Brazil's largest newspaper, ran a major story with Figure 11.6 on its front page.

Despite its usefulness for estimating trend surfaces, there is a potential problem of using ordinary kriging techniques in connection with this type of socioeconomic data. Ordinary kriging relies on the normal distribution hypothesis, which is not the most appropriate assumption for data sets such as homicide rates. Given the characteristics of homicides as rare events, a more appropriate assumption would be a Poisson or a binomial probability distribution (Bailey and Gatrell 1995). An alternative to kriging

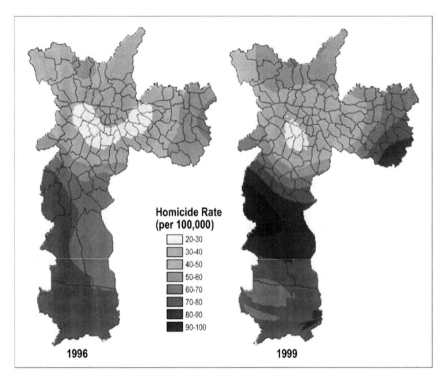

Figure 11.6. Trend surfaces for homicide rates in São Paulo, with values shown as homicides per 100,000 population. Left: 1996 data. Right: 1999.

this kind of phenomenon would be to use corrections proposed by McNeil (1991) and Oliver et al. (1998). These corrections estimate the "risk" of homicide, expressed as the probability that an individual in an area will be killed by homicide. Another alternative would be to use "model-based geostatistics," a set of kriging estimators for distributions other than the normal (Diggle et al. 1998). Unfortunately, such techniques are not widely available in connection with GIS packages, a situation we hope will be solved in the near future.

Conclusions and Future Work

What can be gained in social exclusion studies by using spatial analytical techniques? A lot, as it turns out. Exploratory techniques, such as global and local Moran indexes and Moran scatterplot maps, are very useful to indicate the existence of global trends of spatial autocorrelation for social exclusion patterns and to point out regions where this trend was significantly weaker or stronger. Spatial regression analysis (especially the spatial regimes technique) enables measuring the relation between the various phenomena that comprise social exclusion and can help establish how the relationships between the components of social exclusion and the combined indices vary in space.

Finally, by freeing ourselves from the "tyranny of zones," surfaces provide a powerful means for apprehension of spatial variation.

Further work being carried out by the authors concerns one specific limitation of our data set: the use of 96 districts, which represent an aggregated perspective of most areas. In countries with great social contrasts, such as Brazil, it is frequent that different social groups are aggregated in the same administrative areas, resulting in indices that can misrepresent the diversity of these populations. The reason for the use of the district-level data was its availability at this spatial level of aggregation, for the 1991 and 1995 data sets. Detailed data from the 2000 Census are currently being made available to the authors, who will refine and review the indices for São Paulo, using data at the census-tract level.

The work related to the "Map of Social Exclusion/Inclusion of São Paulo" has had a large impact on increasing political and academic awareness of the issue of social exclusion in São Paulo. Many researchers and public policy administrators have been using its results; the "Social Exclusion/Inclusion" maps have appeared in more than 50 news articles since 1995. The current mayor of São Paulo is using its results to subsidize public policy and government investment in the city, and one of the authors (Sposati) has been appointed as Social Services Secretary of São Paulo, during the 2000–2004 period. The practical impact of the work only enhances the benefits than can be gained by spatially aware social science research.

Acknowledgments   Gilberto Câmara, Antonio Miguel Monteiro, Frederico Roman Ramos, and Eduardo Camargo, are affiliated with the Image Processing Division, National Institute for Space Research (INPE); Aldaiza Sposati and Dirce Koga are affiliated with the Center for Research on Social Security and Social Assistance, Catholic University of São Paulo (PUC/SP), Rua Monte Alegre, 984, São Paulo, Brazil. Suzana Druck Fuks is affiliated with the Brazilian Agricultural Research Agency (EMBRAPA), Rodovia Brasília-Fortaleza, BR 020, Km 18, Planaltina, Brazil.

The results presented in this paper have mostly been financed by FAPESP (Fundação de Amparo à Pesquisa em São Paulo), by grant 00/01965-0. The research of Gilberto Câmara and Antonio Miguel Monteiro is also supported by CNPq (National Research Council of Brazil—award number CNPq 480322/99) and by Brazil's MCT/PCTGE (Ministry of Science and Technology—Program for Science and Technology on Ecosystems Management). The data sets used in this work are available on the Internet, on the Web page http://www.dpi.inpe.br/geopro/exclusao. The software used in this work was *SPRING*, a free GIS available on the Internet (www.dpi.inpe.br/spring) developed by INPE (Câmara et al. 1996) and *SpaceStat*, a spatial analytical software developed by Luc Anselin (Anselin 1992).

Note

1. In the Brazilian census, a "family head" is the person of the family who is responsible for bringing the most income into the family (usually, but not always, the father).

References

Anselin, L. 1988. Spatial Econometrics: Methods and Models. Dordrecht: Kluwer.
Anselin, L. 1992. *SpaceStat tutorial: A Workbook for Using Spacestat in the Analysis of Spatial Data*. Santa Barbara: NCGIA (National Center for Geographic Information and Analysis).

Anselin, L. 1995. Local indicators of spatial association—LISA. *Geographical Analysis* 27: 91–115.

Anselin, L. 1996. The Moran scatterplot as ESDA tool to assess local instability in spatial association. In M. Fisher, H.J. Scholten, and D. Unwin (eds.), *Spatial Analytical Perspectives on GIS*. London: Taylor & Francis, 25–32.

Bailey, T. 2001. Debate on paper by G. Câmara and and A.M.V. Monteiro, Geocomputation techniques for spatial analysis: Are they relevant to health data? *Cadernos de Saúde Pública* 17(5): 1059–1081, set/out. 2001.

Bailey, T., and A. Gatrell. 1995. *Spatial Data Analysis by Example*. London: Longman.

Blair, A. 1998. Bringing Britain together: A national strategy for neighbourhood renewal. London: U.K. Cabinet Office Social Exclusion Unit, *CM Report 4045*.

Câmara, G., R. Souza, U. Freitas, and J. Garrido. 1996. SPRING: Integrating remote sensing and gis with object-oriented data modelling. *Computers and Graphics* 15(6): 13–22.

DETR. 2000. Indices of Deprivation 2000. U.K. Department of Environment, Transport, and Regions Research Summary 31. London: DETR.

Diggle, P., R. Moyeed, and J. Tawn. 1998. Model-based geostatistics. *Applied Statistics* 47: 299–350.

Duffy, K. 1995. *Social Exclusion and Human Dignity in Europe*. Strasbourg: Council of Europe.

Goodchild, M., L. Anselin, and U. Deichmann. 1993. A framework for the areal interpolation of socioeconomic data. *Environment and Planning A* 25: 383–397.

Gordon, D., and Townsend, P. (eds). 2000. *Breadline Europe: The Measurement of Poverty*. Bristol: The Policy Press.

Kingsley, T., C.J. Coulton, M. Barndt, D.S. Sawicki, and P. Tatian. 1997. *Mapping Your Community: Using Geographic Information to Strengthen Community Initiatives*. Washington, D.C.: U.S. Department of Housing and Urban Development.

Klanfer, J. 1965. *L'Exclusion sociale. Étude de la marginalité dans les sociétés occidentales* (The social exclusion. Study on the marginality on the western societies). Paris: Bureau de Recherches Sociales.

Martin, D. 1996. An assessment of surface and zonal models of population. *International Journal of Geographical Information Systems* 10: 973–989.

McNeill, L. 1991. Interpolation and smoothing of binomial data for the Southern African Bird Atlas project. *South African Statistical Journal* 25: 129–146.

Oliver, M., R. Webster, C. Lajaunie, and K. Muir. 1998. Binomial cokriging for estimating and mapping the risk of childhood cancer. *IMA Journal of Mathematics Applied in Medicine and Biology* 15: 279–297.

Paugam, S. 1991. *La Disqualification sociale. Essai sur la nouvelle pauvreté* (Social disqualification. Essay on the new poverty). Paris: Presses Universitaries de France.

Room, G. 1995. *Beyond the Threshold. The Measurement and Analysis of Social Exclusion*. Bristol: Polity Press.

Sen, A. 1992. *Inequality Reexamined*. Cambridge: Harvard University Press.

Senior, M. 2002. Deprivation indicators. In P. Rees, D. Martin, and P. Williamson (eds.), *The Census Data System*. Chichester: John Wiley, 123–138.

Spiekermann, K., and M. Wegener. 2000. Freedom from the tyranny of zones: Towards new GIS-based models. In A.S. Fotheringham, and M. Wegener (eds.), *Spatial Models and GIS. New Potential and New Models*. London: Taylor & Francis, 45–60.

Sposati, A. 1996. *Mapa de Exclusão/Inclusão Social de São Paulo*. São Paulo: EDUC.

Sposati, A. 2000. *Map of Social Exclusion/Inclusion for São Paulo—2000. Social Dynamics of the 1990s*. São Paulo: Catholic University.

12

Business Location and Spatial Externalities
Tying Concepts to Measures

Stuart H. Sweeney
Edward J. Feser

The notion that firms enjoy inherent and significant benefits from co-location is both intuitively persuasive and empirically challenging. Positive spatial business externalities (or localized business spillovers) are cost savings or productivity benefits that accrue to firms as a direct result of their geographic proximity to other businesses. Such externalities are a source of increasing returns, which help explain sustained economic growth in endogenous growth models, the geographical concentration of industrial activity, the ability of some regions to buck convergence and maintain dominant economic positions vis-à-vis other regions, and patterns of intraregional and international trade. Business externalities and spillovers are the subject of considerable research of late and are at the core of an emerging field that spans geography and economics (the so-called new economic geography; see Clark et al. 2000).

Business externalities, which may not be reflected in prevailing prices (i.e., they can be either pecuniary or non-pecuniary in nature), generally derive from *access* to a productive factor, technology, or innovation. For example, companies in a given region benefit from pools of skilled and unskilled labor that are jointly attracted and sustained by neighboring businesses. They may also benefit from ready access to plentiful input supplies or producer services and faster rates of innovation diffusion and information sharing (so-called knowledge spillovers). Closely related is the concept of an agglomeration economy, a notion that encompasses benefits from interfirm proximity (termed localization economies), as well as general advantages associated with the size of urban areas (termed urbanization economies). The dimension of accessibility behind spatial business externalities was largely viewed in terms of distance and scale (a large number of tightly co-located businesses were presumed to enjoy more externalities than a smaller number of more dispersed firms) early in the urban and regional economics literatures. More recently, researchers have emphasized the nature of the conduits via which localized business and labor interactions flow, including prevailing social and cultural norms, regulatory frameworks, contracting practices within commodity chains, and important intermediary institutions such as universities and colleges, government laboratories, and employment agencies. There is strong evidence that such factors heavily mediate the influence of geographic proximity on business cost, productivity, and innovation.

Externalities are notoriously difficult to measure, and existing research is only partially successful in isolating their practical significance and character. The most common empirical approaches include the use of regional cost and production functions, hedonic pricing models, simplified growth models, models of technology adoption and diffusion, and models of regional wage and amenity differentials (Feser 1998, Hanson 2000). More recently, researchers have turned to the analysis of the spatial distribution of employment and businesses as a means of quantifying externalities and increasing returns. Such work is propelled by the increasing availability of economic data at higher levels of geographic resolution, as well as rapid developments in spatial statistics, geo-computation, and related software. Research in the strategic management literature that links industry co-location to national and international economic competitiveness under the rubric of industry clusters has also been influential (e.g., Porter 1990, 2000). Indeed, a massive applied and academic literature on industry clusters has developed as cities, regions, and states around the world have sought to exploit cluster concepts in their own development strategies and policies (Bergman et al. 2001; Roelandt and den Hertog 1999; Steiner 1998).

If positive business externalities truly reduce costs or improve productivity, they should be detectable either directly with applied production models and methods or indirectly via observed regional differences in wages, growth rates, and innovation rates. Positive externalities should also encourage firms to concentrate or cluster geographically, *ceteris paribus*, as firms take the benefits of co-location into account in their location decisions. It is this last sort of evidence that we are chiefly concerned with here. Spatial proximity among businesses may also generate negative externalities, which will offset positive effects to some degree. In the end, spatial business externalities may be positive or negative in the net, leading to spatial concentration or dispersion. In the agglomeration economies literature, the notion of net economies drives empirical models of optimal city size.

The chapter is concerned chiefly with revealed industry location as a source of evidence of externalities. We begin by developing a map of the conceptual domain of spatial externalities, in a sense establishing "bounds" on the notion of a spatial economic cluster as a theoretical construct. Establishing those bounds permits an assessment of the construct validity of competing measures of business co-location. We then undertake a kind of controlled comparison of a set of such measures, using micro data for selected industries in Los Angeles and Atlanta. From the baseline data, which are point referenced, we construct three spatial resolutions of areal data to look for differences among the measures as the scale of the analysis changes. The objective of the comparison is not to analyze the Los Angeles and Atlanta economies per se, but rather to assess the variation in results generated by the indicators. A small (large) variation in the findings suggests that differences in the conceptual validity of the measures are small (large). The paper closes with a general assessment of the measures, a summary of unresolved methodological issues, and recommendations for future research.

More generally, the problems that surround the current state of empirical measurement of externalities are illustrative of a set of common challenges that face attempts to draw inferences about socio-economic spatial behavior from cross-sectional areal data. In principle, spatial externalities, like many other behavioral phenomena of interest to geographers and regional scientists, are best studied with dynamic models and time-series methods and data. However, appropriate models and methodologies are in their infancy, and time-series data with sufficient geographic resolution, while improving, remain severely limited. Researchers are heavily dependent on areal data in particular, which are ordinarily only indirectly representative of the phenomena under study, usually in cross-sections. As a result, strong assumptions are generally required to draw inferences. Over time, as those assumptions are invoked repeatedly in numerous studies, they are often subject to less and less scrutiny. By revisiting the assumptions and approaches common to the study of one particular area of study, business externalities, we hope to contribute to a better understanding of the strengths and limitations of cross-sectional areal analysis more broadly.

Relating Concepts to Measures

Long-standing academic and policy interest in spatial business externalities has yielded a large literature on the topic. Although the conceptual terrain has clearly advanced from decades of work, the literature is also characterized by significant redundancy among core concepts. Much of the current literature has its origins in Marshall (1920). We will not attempt to review those conceptual roots here, both because it would take us too far afield and because there are extensive reviews already available (Feser 1998; Gordon and McCann 2000). The goal of this paper is to consider the value of co-location measures that have been or might be employed to empirically evaluate the concept of spatial business externalities.

For social scientific research to be of value, theory and measurement must proceed in balance. Elaborate theorizing is vacuous if it fails to produce empirically testable hypotheses. Similarly, blind empiricism in the absence of theory yields only meaningless arrays of disjointed facts. The domain of research design concerned with maintaining that balance is measurement theory and, more specifically, the concept of construct validity. The criterion of construct validity is highly pragmatic: it is the evaluation of operationalized measures based on whether they measure the concepts they purport to measure. According to Trochim (2001, 64), construct validity allows one to assess the "degree to which inferences can legitimately be made from the operationalizations in [the] study to the theoretical constructs on which those operationalizations are based."

The notion of construct validity provides a useful framework for evaluating the relative utility of geographic measures of business location—including simple concentration measures and indicators of spatial association—for understanding business externalities. A particularly relevant type of construct validity is content validity, or the degree to which an operational measure matches the full conceptual domain of the pertinent construct (i.e., "the extent to which a measure adequately measures all facets of a concept," Singleton et al. 1988, 118). Content validity is described by Trochim (2001) as a kind of translation validity, where the latter is concerned with how the construct is translated into an operationalization. Put differently, a good measure is one that reflects all critical dimensions of the concept in question.

Assessment of content validity requires a clear definition of the construct as a basis for an evaluation. Based on the literature, spatial business exernalities are changes in the productivity or costs of individual enterprises that result from co-location of multiple businesses at a meaningful regional scale:

1. They may be compensated (pecuniary) or uncompensated (technological);
2. They may be positive or negative;
3. They may accrue during a single time period, or over multiple time periods with increasing or decreasing effect;
4. They may accrue to all industries in a location, to a single industry, or to a subset of linked or related industries;
5. They derive not from scale or size per se (the number of establishments or volume of production in a place) but from changes in the organization of work and division of labor that business co-location (and implied increasing scale) permits;
6. *They originate from different sources (e.g., shared infrastructure, labor pools, knowledge spillovers), and resulting business concentration or dispersion may be realized for different spatial scales, types of industries, and forms of business organization (small firms, large firms, singly-owned versus multi-establishment businesses, vertically versus horizontally integrated companies, and so on);*
7. *Their spatial and temporal extensiveness may depend on several factors including:*

   - *The nature of the local institutional and regulatory environment;*
   - *Prevailing social and cultural norms;*
   - *The character of industrial organization in a place;*
   - *Regional and urban spatial structure.*

Measures of business co-location have the potential to shed light on the dimensions of the externalities concept that are identified in italics. But there are two significant challenges for researchers working along these lines. The first is that the identification of spatial clustering (or dispersion) alone says nothing about whether businesses derive cost or productivity advantages (or disadvantages) from co-location. Clustering or dispersion itself is not evidence of spatial externalities; natural resource or transportation advantages (harbors, canals, rail, roads), accessibility to sources of demand (population concentration), and simple dumb luck followed by historical lock-in effects can easily explain observed patterns of industrial concentration (Ellison and Glaeser 1997). Dispersion might be explained by explicit market and pricing strategies or the distribution of natural resources. The relative utility of geographic measures of business location for understanding externalities turns on whether they can accommodate those alternative explanations.

The second major challenge is that the range, or spatial scale, over which such externalities are likely to operate is not uniform. In general, one would expect that some types of cross-business interactions generate externalities at the scale of neighborhoods or small districts, while others are binding at the level of the regional labor market or metropolitan area. Since the issue of scale is an open empirical question, the best co-location measures will admit inspection over a range of scales. To complicate matters, the scale of externality effects will likely vary among industries and metropolitan areas according to differences in industrial organization, urban form, and institutional structure. The ideal measure would admit controls for characteristics of establishments and the overall spatial structure of the built environment.

These two challenges can be summarized as follows: observed business concentrations or spatial clusters (or patterns of dispersion) are both time- and place-dependent. Relative location is an important determinant of development. Some areas are climatically or geologically blessed, and the values attached to those blessings change over time. In short, historical processes leave a footprint on the spatial structure of cities and regions. Any cross-sectional snapshot of a city will reveal the aggregate impact of past industrial location decisions. In assessing business spatial externalities, we must separate such historical processes from the interactions among industries that drive business locations in the current period. In terms of measurement, that means that the optimal data and measures would emerge from longitudinal data that record observed location decisions over several periods. In the absence of such data, measures should isolate the second-order characteristics (or covariance) of the location process from the first-order (or mean).[1]

Alternative Measures

Table 12.1 partitions several potential business co-location measures according to the nature of their input data and treatment of space. The indicators use either point data, which reveal the exact locations of establishments, or areal data, which effectively aggregate points into spatial zones and, thereby, impose the assumption that externalities operate at a scale at least as large as the spatial unit of analysis (e.g., zip codes, counties, metro areas, or states). Area-based measures have been used most extensively to study business co-location, since establishment-level data are rare. Some of the indicators use space explicitly in the form of distances or a contiguity matrix, while others simply treat it as a nominal regional identifier. Each has already been used in research on business externalities and industry clustering (indicated in bold face type in Table 12.1) or falls into a general class of indicators potentially useful for such research. In the discussion that follows, we focus on the former, each of which is defined formally in Table 12.2. Our concern is with the content validity of the measures; details of their statistical properties are available elsewhere (Cliff and Ord 1973; Diggle and Chetwynd 1991; Ellison and Glaeser 1997; Getis 1984; Getis and Ord 1992; Ord and Getis 1995; Ripley 1977).

Area Data, Implicit Treatment of Space

The measures with the weakest content validity are those in the lower right quadrant of Table 12.1. They use areal data but do not explicitly account for spatial proximity. Instead, they effectively assign area labels as a categorical variable, characterizing differences in distributions over the areal labels between an industry of interest and a referent group.[2] The three measures used to examine industry co-location are the coefficient of localization (dating back to Hoover's work on the shoe industry; Hoover

Table 12.1. Types of measures.

		Use of space	
		Explicit	Implicit
Type of input data	Point	**Second moment distance statistics ($G(s)$, $K(s)$, $D(s)$)** and nearest neighbor statistics	Morris, Bernhardt, and Handcock's (1994) inequality measure
	Area	**LISAs ($G(s)$ & I), global measures of autocorrelation ($G(s)$, Moran's I, and Geary's c),** quadrat methods, White's (1983) inequality measure.	**Ellison's and Glaeser's (1997), location quotient, coefficient of localization,** inequality measures (entropy, Simpson's index, dissimilarity, kappa, etc.)

1948), location quotients, and Ellison and Glaeser's γ (1997). The coefficient of localization is simply the halved sum of absolute differences between a subregional industry share and a subregional total employment share, where the shares are with respect to some referent region. The γ is effectively a coefficient of localization that incorporates information about the size distribution of the industry via a Herfindahl index. Both the coefficient of localization and γ take low values when the industry distribution and referent distributions are similar and high values when the distributions are dissimilar. Dissimilarity is interpreted as concentration, though as we will see below, the interpretation is opaque, since either positive or negative distributional deviations yield high values.[3]

Area Data, Explicit Treatment of Space

Among area-based co-location measures, the most theoretically appealing are those that incorporate space explicitly, either as intercentroid distances or as a contiguity matrix (lower left quadrant in Table 12.1). Such measures have traditionally been the workhorses of social science research on spatial processes, again mainly because the bulk of available data is area-based. Ord and Getis (1995) and Anselin (1995) both make a distinction between global and local measures. Global measures of spatial autocorrelation attempt to measure second-order properties of a spatial pattern. The second-order interactions are measured slightly differently in these measures. Both the Moran's I and Geary's c rely on deviations from means whereas Getis and Ord's G uses cross-products.

The local statistics of spatial autocorrelation, termed LISAs by Anselin, have been proposed as a means to identify "hot spots" or pockets of spatial autocorrelation. Computationally, this is accomplished by parsing out the contribution of each areal unit to the overall global statistic. Maps of the values can then be used to locate important pockets of spatial interaction. An example of an industrial location application is Feser et al. (2003). The advantage of the LISAs is that it is often relevant both to determine whether business clustering exists over some threshold and to identify the number and

Table 12.2. Selected formulae for assessing business externalities.

Measure	Estimator	Reference(s)	Comments
K function	$K(s) = \dfrac{A}{n(n-1)} \sum_i \sum_j w_{ij} I(d_{ij} < s)$	Ripley (1977), Besag (1977), Diggle (1983	Measures clustering or dispersion with respect to complete spatial randomness.
D function	$D(s) = K_{case}(s) - K_{control}(s)$	Diggle and Chetwynd (1991)	Indicates clustering or dispersion as a deviation from the overall spatial inhomogeneity of the population.
G function	$G(s) = \dfrac{\sum_i \sum_j w_{ij}(d_{ij} < s)x_i x_j}{\sum_i \sum_j x_i x_j}$	Getis and Ord (1992), Ord and Getis (1995)	Measures clustering or dispersion with respect to complete spatial randomness.
Coefficient of localization	$COL_j = 0.5 \sum_i |p_{ij} - p_{i+}|$ p_{ij} = proportion of industry j in region i p_{i+} = proportion of all industry in region i	Hoover (1948), Duncan and Duncan (1955), Duncan (1957), Isard (1965)	High values indicate a deviation from the reference distribution.
γ	$\gamma_j = \dfrac{\sum_i (p_{ij} - p_{i+})^2 - (1 - \sum_i p_{i+}^2)(\sum_k p_k^{-2})}{(1 - \sum_i p_{i+}^2)(1 - \sum_k p_k^{-2})}$ p_{ij}, p_{i+} as defined above. p_k = proportion of national industry employment in establishments of size quantile k	Ellison and Glaeser (1997)	High values indicate a deviation from the reference distribution. Control for national industry size distribution.

precise location of such clusters. Conceptually, the local statistics are an important adjunct to other indicators of spatial clustering and dispersion.

Getis and Ord's G can also be used for areal data where distances are constructed from the centroids of the areal units. The measure reports positive values for clustering and negative values for dispersion. This contrasts with the Moran's I or Geary's c, where either high or low values both imply positive spatial autocorrelation. The G also produces values over a range of scales down to a minimum scale equal to the size of the basic areal unit of analysis.[4] As a content valid indicator of externalities, $G(s)$ therefore fares better than other spatially explicit areal measures and is far superior to the spatially inexplicit metrics.

A major shortcoming of all areal measures is that they obscure the underlying location pattern through spatial aggregation and the imposition of arbitrary administrative boundary definitions. Spatial aggregation is problematic, since the rank order of results may shift or reverse at different levels of aggregation.[5] Moreover, the results may also change under different boundary definitions. This is the modifiable areal unit problem (MAUP). Although the influence of aggregation and boundary definitions on results is certainly an undesirable property, social scientists are often forced to work with areal data.

Another problem is that areal data necessarily impose a minimum spatial scale over which clustering can be observed. Although region-scale industry clustering, say at the metropolitan level, may be of academic or policy interest in some cases, its relevance to spatial externalities as a theoretical construct is questionable. One can make a strong case that some types of inter-business interaction that drive externalities would likely take place at a sub-metropolitan, or even sub-county, scale. An example is the exchange of informal or tacit knowledge between firms that yields productivity increases or other improvements in business performance. There is even less relevance to the state scale, which has actually been studied most extensively (particularly in the agglomeration economies literature), since data are readily available. Redressing or solving such problems requires either pure point data (business locations coded to street address) or synthetic point data (business locations at very small geographic scales, such as zip codes or census tracts).

Point Data, Explicit Treatment of Space

The measures contained in the upper left quadrant of Table 12.1 use the most detailed spatial data and distance formulations. Ripley (1977) is credited with developing the K function, the first distance-based second-moment measure in spatial statistics. As with all of the measures in the upper left quadrant, the K function indicates the degree of spatial clustering or dispersion over a range of distances, s. As noted above, this is one of the desired properties of a measure, since the range of clustering (or dispersion) is something that can only be assessed empirically, though we may have hypotheses about relevant scales from theory. The various measures in the quadrant differ mainly in the referent used to assess whether a pattern is clustered or dispersed. Both the K function and Getis and Ord's G (used with point data) employ complete spatial randomness as the referent.[6] Strictly speaking, that means that the measures only yield valid results when they are used to assess spatial patterns where there is no large-scale (first-order) variation in the mean of the process. Otherwise, the first- and second-order properties of the spatial pattern are confounded in the measurement. That is clearly not desirable in the business location context, since all human settlements are characterized by first-order variation; that is, we observe cities and towns in any region and employment districts in any metropolitan area. Since Getis and Ord's G allows for the use of positive rational numbers as weights, it is possible to partially account for such first-order variation (Feser et al. 2003).

The D function, in contrast, was explicitly designed to measure clustering in the presence of first-order variation (Diggle and Chetwynd 1991). The D function is constructed as the difference between two K functions, one of which measures the second-order properties of a subpopulation of interest ("cases") and the other of which measures the second-order properties of a random sample of objects from the general population ("controls"). The D function indicates whether a subpopulation is more or less clustered (i.e., dispersed) than the overall clustering (or dispersion) in the population as a whole.

Of all the measures in Table 12.1, the D function—which is really more of a methodological framework than an individual measure—exhibits the most content validity with respect to the measurement of business externalities. First, the control group provides a means of capturing the general spatial structure of a given city or region. Second, stratified random sampling can assure that the control group matches the case group along certain confounding dimensions (Feser and Sweeney 2000, 2002b, 2002c; Sweeney and Feser 1998). Third, the D function takes advantage of the rich spatial detail inherent in point data and therefore can search over various spatial scales. Fourth, the framework has an intuitively appealing economic interpretation. If one views industry locations as choices on an unobserved spatially-continuous profit surface, the control group may be viewed as characterizing the general properties of the profit surface faced by all firms, while the case group reveals the attributes unique to that reduced set of industries. In an agglomeration-economies context, the control group might be thought of as measuring urbanization economies, in which case the D function itself identifies the increment in clustering associated with localization economies (Feser and Sweeney 2000). It is important to note that there is no reason why the control framework of the D function could not also be applied to $G(s)$. Employed in the same way, the D function and $G(s)$ should yield similar results.

An Empirical Assessment

If we had outside information about the precise pattern of clustering (or dispersion) of businesses in a given location, as well as the degree to which externalities played a role in generating the observed spatial pattern, we could formally evaluate the performance and accuracy of the co-location measures. Absent such information, we conduct a kind of controlled comparison to assess the variation in substantive findings yielded by the measures and to illustrate their interpretation. By "controlled" comparison, we mean the use of point data that can be aggregated to standardized areal units of our choosing (e.g., grids) so that we can generate findings at different scales for both the area and point-based measures.

Our data are the street address and total employment of business establishments in six manufacturing industries in Atlanta and Los Angeles, as reported in the U.S. Bureau of Labor Statistics' confidential ES-202 files. The industries—electronics, textiles and apparel, motor vehicles, petrochemicals, aerospace, and publishing—were selected to include both high tech and traditional manufacturing activity. Details of the procedures and success rates of matching ES-202 addresses to approximate latitude and longitude coordinates are reported elsewhere (Feser and Sweeney 2002a). Briefly, the ES-202 file contains employment and payroll data for all businesses subject to employment security law, an estimated 90 percent of U.S. firms. It excludes sole proprietorships. For 1997, the year used in this analysis, some 65 percent of ES-202 records contain physical addresses. We were able to establish longitude and latitude coordinates for over 70 percent of those records in Atlanta and Los Angeles, yielding a net match rate of 46 percent. In other words, we were able to locate nearly half of business units in the six industries in the two study regions, a substantial sample size in industry location analysis by conventional standards. Sample bias is modest. It is mainly associated with location; address match rates are lower in the fastest growing or more rural parts of the metro areas. To minimize the problem, we focus on a reduced core area of the two cities by drawing a box that captures the major clusters of industries when we plot the locations of all manufacturers. In general, however, bias is a minimal concern in the current application, since our purpose is primarily to assess the variation in findings across measures rather than to study the Los Angeles and Atlanta economies per se.

An important question is the appropriate indicator of economic activity. Cases have been made in the literature for both establishments and employment.[7] Some of the measures, e.g., $D(s)$ and $G(s)$, will work for establishments or employment, while others, such as γ, are restricted to examining employment. The case for employment rests primarily on the notion that size is an important barometer of concentration or clustering, i.e., that a couple of firms with 10,000 employees apiece constitutes a more significant concentration of activity than 10 firms with 15 employees apiece. Establishments, on the other hand, are the principal units between which externality-inducing interactions are likely to occur (implying that the more enterprises in a given place, the more likely they are to enjoy positive externalities based on co-location). In the absence of a compelling argument excluding either approach, we calculate the results using both employment and establishments where possible.

We aggregated the point data set to three levels: a 2-kilometer resolution, a 5-kilometer resolution, and a 10-kilometer resolution. We then used the point data set and three sets of areal data to calculate the point- and area-based co-location measures. Before comparing results, several visualizations of the data help set the stage by identifying the location and frequency of manufacturing clusters.

Visualizing Industry Location.   Figure 12.1 displays three visualizations of manufacturing locations in Los Angeles: a point map, a choropleth map, and a kernel smoothed map. The point and basic choropleth maps are the simplest means of characterizing the general spatial pattern of manufacturing establishments in Los Angeles.[8] However, they suffer from too much and too little detail, respectively. The lower panel of Figure 12.1 is generated by applying kernel smoothing techniques, developed for bivariate statistical distributions, and then mapping the results. The kernel smoothed images identify three, or perhaps four, centers of manufacturing activity in the study region. The images can be altered based on the properties of the kernel smoothing algorithm and the number of bins used to map colors onto the map. Appendix 1 contains several versions of kernel smoothed images for the six study industries in the two cities.

Figure 12.2 displays choropleth maps of the local G for manufacturing establishments in the two study cities. The maps are more granular than the kernel images but also easily identify the same centers. There are two advantages of the G over the kernel smoothers. First, the local G can be calculated over different spatial scales, resulting in different images, a process roughly akin to altering the bandwidth in the kernel smoothing algorithm. Thus, the results can be used to investigate a series of prior

Point map

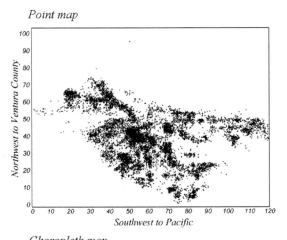

Choropleth map

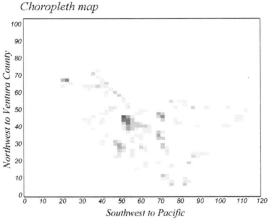

Kernel smoothed surface

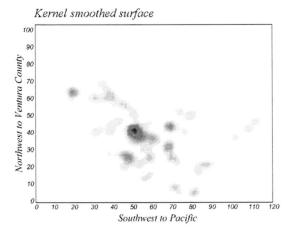

Figure 12.1. Visualization techniques for Los Angeles establishments.

249

beliefs about the nature and scale of business clustering. Second, the local G is scaled in standard scores (Z-scores) so statistical significance of the mapped clusters can also be assessed. In this application, using the underlying 2-kilometer resolution data, we chose a 5-kilometer scale of influence. Los Angeles, somewhat unexpectedly given its reputation for sprawl, displays a very prominent central cluster with perhaps two subordinate centers, whereas Atlanta displays three dominant manufacturing centers.

Figures 12.3a and 12.3b display choropleth maps of the local G for establishments for the six study industries in the two cities. The maps are suggestive of general tendencies toward concentration or deconcentration and provide some insight to the location and frequency of clusters. In Los Angeles, for example (Figure 12.3a), both textiles/apparel and publishing are highly concentrated. In contrast, the motor vehicles industry is at the other end of the spectrum with a fairly diffuse pattern. Both aerospace and electronics are clustered in locations away from the central core of the city, with the electronics located in a dominant node in the San Fernando Valley. The contrast between Los Angeles and Atlanta is also striking. In Atlanta (Figure 12.3b), the electronics industry is more centralized, with both a single node and a location near the city center. Textiles and apparel manufacturing, in contrast, are more dispersed in Atlanta than Los Angeles.

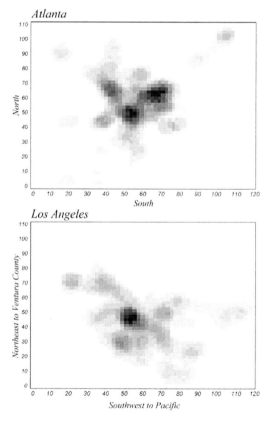

Figure 12.2. Local $G(5)$ using establishments and 2-km grid resolution.

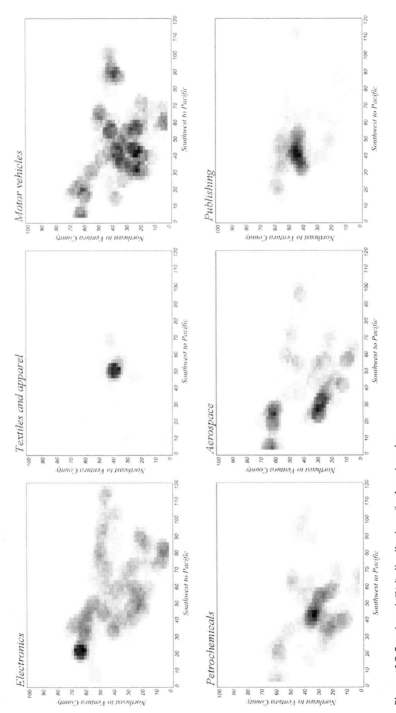

Figure 12.3a. Local $G(d)$ distributions for Los Angeles.

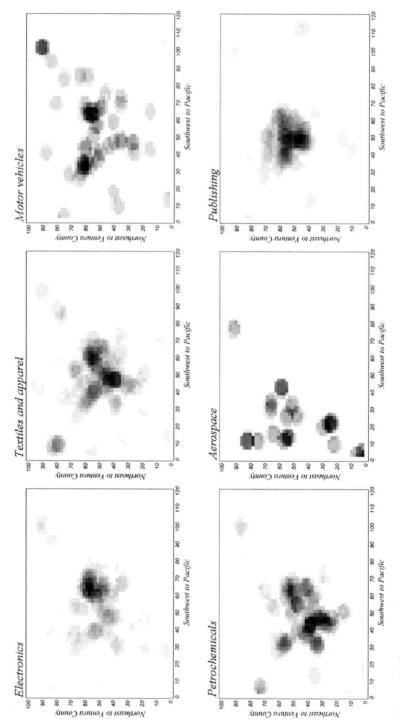

Figure 12.3b. Local $G(d)$ distributions for Atlanta.

Aggregate Tendencies toward Clustering/Dispersion

Though the visual depiction of business locations is useful as a starting point, aggregate measures that characterize the spatial pattern of economic activity for statistically significant clustering or dispersion, as well as provide a means of assessing the influences behind the observed pattern (such as externalities), have considerable advantages. In this section we interpret and compare findings generated with four co-location measures—$D(s)$, $G(s)$, the coefficient of localization (COL), and γ—for both establishment counts and employment.

Table 12.3 reports COL results based on three spatial grids (2, 5, and 10 kilometer). Results for the γ statistic are provided over the same range of spatial scales (2, 5, and 10 kilometer grids) in Table 12.4.[9] Recall from the discussion above that γ is defined only for employment counts, while COL can be calculated for both establishments and employment.

For establishments, the COL takes the highest values in both cities for the aerospace and motor vehicles industries. The rankings for employment are similar, though aerospace slips to third in Los Angeles at the two and five kilometer resolutions. The lowest values are posted for publishing and electronics in Atlanta and textiles and electronics in Los Angeles. Strictly speaking, high values of the COL indicate only a deviation from the baseline distribution (all manufacturing employment or establishments). If the baseline is relatively clustered, then any distribution either more clustered or more dispersed will yield high values for the index. Motor vehicles likely generates a high value because it is more dispersed than the baseline (contrast the patterns for motor vehicles in Figures 12.3a and 12.3b with the overall manufacturing patterns in Figure 12.2). In general, the ambiguity of the results means that collateral information is needed to determine whether the measure is indicative of dispersion or clustering.

The high COL for aerospace (and highest γ for all spatial scales in both cities) reflects a more serious problem with the two measures. The explanation is that aerospace is a comparatively small industry in both places (relative to the other five study sectors), and the employment, or establishment, surface contains a large number of zero cells. In the abstract, this means that, even if an industry locates in a region according to the exact same probability surface shared by other industries, an industry with a small number of establishments will register a higher index value (either COL or γ) because of the zero cells. More generally, this relates to the problem noted by Besag and Newell (1991) that small populations in cells have higher variances that lead to spurious results. This problem is alleviated by using higher levels of spatial aggregation; higher cell counts essentially stabilize the cell proportions. But increased spatial aggregation mitigates against detecting spatial clustering or dispersion at the smaller geographical scales appropriate for testing hypotheses about externalities.

There are two other noteworthy aspects of the findings in Tables 12.3 and 12.4. First, the rank orderings shift over the three spatial scales. For example, using γ, the Los Angeles textiles and apparel sector is tied for third at the 2-kilometer resolution, and shifts to second at both the 5- and 10-kilometer resolutions. That the textiles and apparel sector could be ranked either second or third is surprising, given the visual dominance of that sector in Figure 12.3a (as we will see below, both $G(s)$ and $D(s)$ functions detect that dominance). While most of the rank shifts are slight, they illustrate

Table 12.3. Coefficients of localization[†]

Spatial Resolution	Industry	Establishments				Employment			
		Atlanta		Los Angeles		Atlanta		Los Angeles	
		COL	Rank[††]	COL	Rank	COL	Rank	COL	Rank
2 km.	1. Electronics	0.0083	4	0.0287	5	0.2572	5	0.5191	5
	2. Textiles	0.0083	5	0.0279	6	0.2584	3	0.5181	6
	3. Motor Vehicles	0.0085	2	0.0300	2	0.2598	2	0.5589	2
	4. Petrochemicals	0.0084	3	0.0298	3	0.2583	4	0.5592	1
	5. Aerospace	0.0085	1	0.0301	1	0.2608	1	0.5583	3
	6. Publishing	0.0081	6	0.0293	4	0.2560	6	0.5460	4
5 km.	1. Electronics	0.0413	4	0.1288	5	0.5980	6	0.6051	6
	2. Textiles	0.0406	5	0.1210	6	0.6221	3	0.6344	5
	3. Motor Vehicles	0.0425	2	0.1357	2	0.6283	2	0.7940	2
	4. Petrochemicals	0.0414	3	0.1347	3	0.6114	4	0.8123	1
	5. Aerospace	0.0430	1	0.1361	1	0.6448	1	0.7931	3
	6. Publishing	0.0396	6	0.1326	4	0.6109	5	0.7641	4
10 km.	1. Electronics	0.1266	3	0.3101	5	0.7045	6	0.4546	6
	2. Textiles	0.1231	5	0.2860	6	0.7187	4	0.5330	5
	3. Motor Vehicles	0.1309	2	0.3309	2	0.7966	2	0.7386	2
	4. Petrochemicals	0.1264	4	0.3259	3	0.7257	3	0.7250	3
	5. Aerospace	0.1326	1	0.3317	1	0.8477	1	0.8060	1
	6. Publishing	0.1188	6	0.3215	4	0.7093	5	0.6973	4

[†]The Coefficient of localization (COL) ranges between 0 and 1 with high values indicating concentration.

[††]Values indicate an ordinal ranking from the highest relative concentration (difference in distribution) for low ordinal values, 1, to lowest relative concentration (similarity in distribution) for high ordinal values, 6.

the effects of the modifiable areal unit problem nonetheless: the ordering of results depends on both the size and configuration of the areal units. It follows that the results from applied business cluster studies that use administrative boundaries to define the spatial polygons are suspect, since the scale of observations will often vary at both intra- and inter-metropolitan scales.

Second, the γ is extremely sensitive to the choice of quantile used to construct the Herfindahl index. As noted above, Ellison and Glaeser's γ metric is a function of the Herfindahl index, which evaluates an industry's size distribution as the sum of squared inverse proportions of industry employment in a given employment size quantile. The columns of Table 12.4 contain the results of evaluating γ using 5, 20, 100, and then observation-wise quantiles to construct the Herfindahl. For many choices, the γ, which is only defined for positive values, takes negative values, thereby rendering the metric uninterpretable.

Illustrative results for the global $G(s)$ and $D(s)$ are shown in Figure 12.4. A complete set of figures showing the results for all industries, in both metropolitan areas, and for both establishments and employment are available on the Web site associated with this book. Note that for $G(s)$, the value for total employment is included as a reference. Also, recall that the referent for $G(s)$ is complete spatial randomness, whereas

Table 12.4. Ellison-Glaeser γ, sensitivity to industry and spatial aggregation.[†]

Spatial Resolution	Industry	γ_{raw}	$\gamma\,[H(5)]$	$\gamma\,[H(20)]$	$\gamma\,[H(100)]$	$\gamma\,[H(i)]$	ordinal $\gamma\,[H(i)]$[††]
			Atlanta, GA				
2 km.	1. Electronics	0.111	−2.296	−0.358	0.005	0.112	3
	2. Textiles	0.100	−1.790	−0.265	0.029	0.101	4
	3. Motor Vehicles	0.325	−2.509	−0.173	0.218	0.329	2
	4. Petrochemicals	0.057	−2.270	−0.438	−0.055	0.057	5
	5. Aerospace	0.859	0.216	0.732	0.836	0.871	1
	6. Publishing	0.047	−2.911	−0.624	−0.109	0.047	6
5 km.	1. Electronics	0.127	−2.231	−0.331	0.025	0.130	3
	2. Textiles	0.117	−1.728	−0.237	0.050	0.121	4
	3. Motor Vehicles	0.337	−2.417	−0.142	0.238	0.347	2
	4. Petrochemicals	0.068	−2.229	−0.421	−0.042	0.068	6
	5. Aerospace	0.903	0.578	0.856	0.912	0.931	1
	6. Publishing	0.075	−2.792	−0.574	−0.075	0.076	5
10 km.	1. Electronics	0.135	−2.188	−0.313	0.038	0.141	3
	2. Textiles	0.122	−1.704	−0.226	0.059	0.128	4
	3. Motor Vehicles	0.340	−2.367	−0.125	0.250	0.356	2
	4. Petrochemicals	0.090	−2.140	−0.382	−0.013	0.094	5
	5. Aerospace	0.919	0.799	0.931	0.958	0.967	1
	6. Publishing	0.079	−2.767	−0.564	−0.068	0.082	6
			Los Angeles, CA				
2 km.	1. Electronics	0.017	−2.654	−0.505	−0.103	0.016	5
	2. Textiles	0.033	−2.000	−0.360	−0.045	0.033	3
	3. Motor Vehicles	0.034	−4.059	−0.691	−0.128	0.033	3
	4. Petrochemicals	0.023	−2.391	−0.492	−0.094	0.022	4
	5. Aerospace	0.073	−4.694	−0.949	−0.188	0.066	1
	6. Publishing	0.049	−2.907	−0.622	−0.108	0.048	2
5 km.	1. Electronics	0.017	−2.653	−0.505	−0.103	0.016	6
	2. Textiles	0.102	−1.781	−0.261	0.032	0.103	2
	3. Motor Vehicles	0.049	−3.979	−0.664	−0.110	0.048	5
	4. Petrochemicals	0.049	−2.297	−0.451	−0.064	0.049	4
	5. Aerospace	0.134	−4.310	−0.817	−0.108	0.129	1
	6. Publishing	0.060	−2.856	−0.601	−0.093	0.061	3
10 km.	1. Electronics	0.018	−2.646	−0.502	−0.101	0.018	6
	2. Textiles	0.128	−1.691	−0.220	0.063	0.133	2
	3. Motor Vehicles	0.065	−3.887	−0.633	−0.089	0.065	4
	4. Petrochemicals	0.055	−2.272	−0.439	−0.056	0.056	5
	5. Aerospace	0.224	−3.716	−0.614	0.016	0.226	1
	6. Publishing	0.073	−2.797	−0.576	−0.077	0.075	3

[†]The γ metric is composed of two components: a raw concentration measure and a industry employment size distribution measure (the Herfindahl). The notation above displays γ as a function of the Herfindahl index evaluated using a given number of quantiles of the employment size distribution. For examples, $\gamma\,[H(5)]$ is evaluated using quintiles of the employment size distribution whereas $\gamma\,[H(i)]$ is evaluated at the observation level.

[††]Values indicate an ordinal ranking from the highest relative concentration (difference in distribution) for low ordinal values, 1, to lowest relative concentration (similarity in distribution) for high ordinal values, 6.

$D(s)$ employs a case-control framework. In Figure 12.4, the dashed horizontal lines at approximately 2 and -2 indicate confidence bands. Reading from left to right, the path traced by $G(s)$ or $D(s)$ indicates the degree of spatial clustering at the scale indicated by the kilometers on the horizontal axis. The $G(s)$ has a minimum scale imposed by the 2-km grid resolution. The results are similar but do lead to qualitatively different interpretations. Though textiles shows clear indications of strong spatial clustering, the results for electronics and aerospace are at odds with each other.

Overall, the findings for the complete set of $G(s)$ and $D(s)$ statistics are roughly in accord with the visualizations. In Los Angeles, textiles is most clustered, followed by publishing and then petrochemicals. The electronics industry shows some significant clustering at a small spatial scale (< 5 kilometers). Motor vehicles, as anticipated, is most dispersed (even statistically significantly dispersed at a small spatial scale). For Atlanta, both publishing and electronics are identified as the most clustered, though aerospace is identified as more dispersed than vehicle manufacturing. In comparison to the total employment $G(s)$ values, only the textiles and apparel sectors in Los Angeles indicate some clustering in excess of the general spatial pattern of establishments in the study region.

In short, $G(s)$ provides subjectively appealing rankings but cannot answer the question that $D(s)$ is constructed to answer: is the observed clustering beyond the general level of establishments in the region? Moreover, the $G(s)$ does not control for any of the confounding factors associated with business location decisions. As discussed above, the case-control framework of $D(s)$ employs stratified proportionate sampling to construct a control group of industries that match the "case" industry sectors' attributes associated with location decisions. In theory, the framework produces two sets of sample industry locations, such that the industries in the two samples only differ along a single dimension of interest. The hypothesis test simply evaluates whether the observed differences in spatial patterns are significantly different. For example, one facet of the localization economies notion could be tested by identifying "case" industries that share intermediate input suppliers and a set of controls that match the case industry attributes *except* for their connectivity in input suppliers space. In practice, the stratified sampling is limited by the scope of variables in a data set.

The $D(s)$ results are constructed using establishments in an industry group (e.g., electronics) as the cases and (proportionately to employment-size distribution) a matched sample of controls from the rest of the population of manufacturing establishments. We also use a supplemental set of analyses to identify and remove industry sectors with extreme leverage on the results of $D(s)$, parallel to the concept of outlier observation detection in regression.[10] It is clear that the $D(s)$ generates richer information about clustering and dispersion than the other measures. For example, in both Atlanta and Los Angeles, the estimated $D(s)$ for establishment counts reveals high levels of clustering in the aerospace industry at very small spatial scales (< 2 km). Petrochemicals displays a similar pattern in Atlanta. For employment in Atlanta, the variation in $D(s)$ over the range of spatial scales is even more pronounced. Moreover, by construction, $D(s)$ indicates clustering or dispersion in excess of the background population. The dispersion evident in the visualizations for the motor vehicles industry in both Los Angeles and Atlanta is shown to be broadly characteristic of the overall

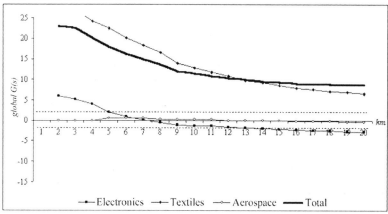

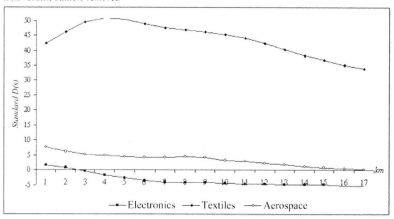

Figure 12.4. $G(s)$ and $D(s)$ results for Los Angeles establishments.

spatial pattern of establishments in each study region; that is, the spatial pattern of establishments of motor vehicles is statistically insignificant (neither clustered nor dispersed).

It is difficult to assess the general pattern of results across all of the measures from the separate graphs and tables. Tables 12.5 and 12.6 summarize the findings by assigning ranks for each of the four measures.[11] The results for Los Angeles (Table 12.5) clarify some of the points made above. The first three orderings for the establishment $G(s)$ and $D(s)$ are identical, but the measures disagree on the pattern for electronics. The establishment-based industry rankings for the COL make little sense, as noted above. The employment-based industry rankings show less agreement between $G(s)$ and $D(s)$, especially with regard to aerospace. For the Atlanta employment-based results (Table 12.6), aerospace and vehicles are ranked first and second by $G(s)$,

Table 12.5. Rank orderings for Los Angeles.

Establishments:

		Industry					
Statistic	Spatial Res.[†]	*clustered (dissimilar)* ———————————————————— *dispersed (similar)*					
Localization	2	aerospace	vehicles	petrochem	publishing	electronics	Textiles
	5	aerospace	vehicles	petrochem	publishing	electronics	Textiles
	10	aerospace	vehicles	petrochem	publishing	electronics	Textiles
γ	2	—	—	—	—	—	—
	5	—	—	—	—	—	—
	10	—	—	—	—	—	—
$G(s)$	2, s	textiles	publishing	petrochem	electronics	aerospace*‖	Vehicles
$D(s)$	s	textiles	publishing	petrochem	aerospace	vehicles*‖	Electronics

Employment:

		Industry					
Statistic	Spatial Res.	*clustered (dissimilar)* ———————————————————— *dispersed (similar)*					
Localization	2	petrochem	vehicles	aerospace	publishing	electronics	Textiles
	5	petrochem	vehicles	aerospace	publishing	textiles	Electronics
	10	aerospace	vehicles	petrochem	publishing	textiles	Electronics
γ	2	aerospace	publishing	textiles	vehicles	petrochem	Electronics
	5	aerospace	textiles	publishing	petrochem	vehicles	Electronics
	10	aerospace	textiles	publishing	petrochem	petrochem	electronics
$G(s)$	2, s	textiles	aerospace	petrochem	publishing	vehicles	electronics‖
$D(s)$	s	textiles	publishing	petrochem	vehicles*	electronics*‖	aerospace

Note: ‖ indicates division between clustering and dispersion

* indicates statistical insignificance

[†]The spatial resolutions for $D(s)$ and $G(s)$ are over a range of distances, s, though $G(s)$ has a mimimum resolution of 2 km given its reliance on a grid.

COL, and γ, while $D(s)$ ranks the same two industries, respectively, as dispersed and insignificant. It is difficult to say why $G(s)$ and $D(s)$ disagree so completely on those two industries. In general, $D(s)$ assigns very little significant spatial clustering to any industries in Atlanta except at the very smallest spatial scales. It could be that the failure of $G(s)$ to account for the background variation is the reason for the divergent results.

Overall, both $G(s)$ and $D(s)$ get at the nuances of clustering or dispersion over a range of spatial scales, but only $D(s)$ provides some control for the background pattern of variation in the study region. This is fundamentally important, since externality-related clustering should be something in excess of the normal spatial patterns of co-location among establishments. The COL and γ also both use a reference distribution to gauge deviation in pattern, but the use of areal proportions proves problematic at spatial scales relevant for externality-related clustering.

Table 12.6. Rank orderings for Atlanta.

Establishments:

Statistic	Spatial Res.[†]	Industry					
		clustered (dissimilar) ———————————————— *dispersed (similar)*					
Localization	2	aerospace	vehicles	petrochem	electronics	textiles	publishing
	5	aerospace	vehicles	petrochem	electronics	textiles	publishing
	10	aerospace	vehicles	electronics	petrochem	textiles	publishing
γ	2	—	—	—	—	—	—
	5	—	—	—	—	—	—
	10	—	—	—	—	—	—
$G(s)$	2, s	publishing	electronics	textiles‖	petrochem	vehicles	aerospace
$D(s)$	s	publishing	petrochem	electronics	textiles	aerospace	vehicles*‖

Employment:

Statistic	Spatial Res.	Industry					
		clustered (dissimilar) ———————————————— *dispersed (similar)*					
Localization	2	aerospace	vehicles	textiles	petrochem	electronics	publishing
	5	aerospace	vehicles	textiles	petrochem	electronics	publishing
	10	aerospace	vehicles	petrochem	textiles	electronics	publishing
γ	2	aerospace	vehicles	electronics	textiles	petrochem	publishing
	5	aerospace	vehicles	electronics	textiles	publishing	petrochem
	10	aerospace	vehicles	electronics	textiles	petrochem	publishing
$G(s)$	2, s	aerospace	vehicles	publishing	electronics	textiles	petrochem
$D(s)$	s	petrochem	electronics	publishing	textiles*‖	vehicles*	aerospace

Note: ‖ indicates division between clustering and dispersion

* indicates statistical insignificance

[†]The spatial resolutions for $D(s)$ and $G(s)$ are over a range of distances, s, though $G(s)$ has a mimimum resolution of 2 km given its reliance on a grid.

Conclusion

In this chapter, we consider the issues and pitfalls associated with the use of various indicators of co-location and industry association to study business clustering and, more specifically, spatial business externalities. We should restate at this point that the role of such measures does not get at the totality of research questions about business clustering. The primary economic elements, cost reductions or productivity enhancements, are not and cannot be measured using these purely spatial methods. In general, a multi-method approach is probably warranted. The two most promising indicators discussed here are the local $G(s)$ and the $D(s)$: the first because of its ability to identify the locations of clusters, and the second because of its ability to control for the general locational tendencies of industries in a given study region. It may also be useful to adapt the global $G(s)$ into the case-control framework, since its multiplicative, or cross-product, approach provides a slightly different way to measure spatial interaction.

Spatially inexplicit areal co-location indicators are considerably less promising for studying spatial business externalities. Though such measures have been the work-horses of segregation and income inequality research, they have little construct validity in the present context. The attempt to use patterns of business clustering and dispersion to reveal information about positive and negative externalities is extraordinarily diffi-cult against a background of concentrated human settlement. These areal measures are simply not up to the task.

Notes

1. *First-* and *second*-order properties of a spatial process are akin to the first- and second-moment terminology common to basic statistics. With spatial processes it is desirable to remove the dependence of the mean and covariance on the size of spatial units by rescaling to per-unit-area measures. The first-order properties describe the mean number of events per unit area and the second-order properties describe the dependence between events in two different areas.
2. The industry co-location measures in the lower right quadrant of Table 12.1 are members of a large family of measures designed to assess distributional differences. Common applications are to income inequality (the Gini and Theil indices) and residential segregation. The coefficient of localization of regional science is identical to the dissimilarity index of the sociology literature. A small sociology literature assesses the construct validity of such measures. Excellent reviews include Allison (1978), Massey and Denton (1988), and White (1983). The comparison of distributions dates back to work by Gini (1914), Lorenz (1905), Pearson (1895), and Yntema (1933), among others.
3. An additional problem with measures that use subregional shares is that the variance over the set of regions is heteroskedastic, as noted by Besag and Newell (1991). This means that small population areas may register high values, thus making large contributions toward concentration, even when the underlying probability of locating in the given area is equal to larger population areas.
4. The validity of areal co-location measures increases as the spatial scale of the data decreases, although there is an exception to the rule for measures using shares, since the point estimates of those shares are less stable at smaller spatial scales.
5. Simpson's paradox is the name commonly applied to such aggregation-induced reversals.
6. Complete spatial randomness (CSR) describes a process that distributes events in space such that the mean number of events per unit area is constant. CSR is usually characterized by a homogeneous Poisson process with a constant parameter, γ.
7. Of course, other measures are also possible (e.g., output, value-added, wages, etc.). How-ever, employment and establishments dominate applications to date.
8. The point map is only an approximate simulation based on the areal data. Our data use agreement with the Bureau of Labor Statistics forbids us from publishing the real point map.
9. Employment size quantiles are used to construct the Herfindahl component of the γ index ($\sum_k p_k^{-2}$ in Table 12.2).
10. The method of identifying outliers is discussed elsewhere (Feser and Sweeney 2001a; Sweeney and Feser 2001). The results with the outliers included can be viewed at the Web site associated with this book.
11. It is somewhat problematic assigning a single rank to the results of $D(s)$ and $G(s)$, since

the rankings change over the range of scales. In the tables, the rankings for $D(s)$ and $G(s)$ are based on small-scale orderings (< 5 kilometers).

Acknowledgments   The research reported in this paper was supported by grants from the National Science Foundation (BCS-9986541 and BCS-9986561) and the Center for Spatially Integrated Social Sciences at UC Santa Barbara. Data are used with special permission from the U.S. Bureau of Labor Statistics (BLS). Research results and conclusions expressed are the authors' and do not necessarily indicate concurrence by the BLS. We would like to thank Rick Clayton, Mike Searson, Tim Pivetz, and Holly Olson for providing access to the BLS data and supporting our research. We also thank Henry Renski for assistance with data preparation and to Art Getis for access to his point pattern analysis program for generating the local $G(s)$ statistics.

References

Allison, P. 1978. Measures of inequality. *American Sociological Review* 43: 865–881.

Anselin, L. 1995. Local indicators of spatial autocorrelation—LISA. *Geographical Analysis* 27: 93–115.

Bergman, E.M., D. Charles, and P. den Hertog (eds.). 2001. *Innovative Clusters: Drivers of National Innovation Systems*. Paris: Organisation for Economic Cooperation and Development.

Besag, J. 1977. Comment on Ripley's modelling spatial patterns. *Journal of the Royal Statistical Society B* 39: 172–212.

Besag, J., and J. Newell. 1991. The detection of clusters in rare diseases. *Journal of the Royal Statistical Society, Series A* 154: 143–155.

Clark, G.L., M.P. Feldman, and M.S. Gertler (eds.). 2000. *The Oxford Handbook of Economic Geography*. Oxford, U.K.: Oxford University Press.

Cliff, A., and K. Ord. 1973. *Spatial Autocorrelation*. London: Pion.

Diggle, P. 1983. *Statistical Analysis of Spatial Point Patterns*. London and New York: Academic Press.

Diggle, P., and A. Chetwynd. 1991. Second-order analysis of spatial clustering for inhomogenous populations. *Biometrics* 47: 1155–1163.

Duncan, O.D. 1957. The measurement of population distribution. *Population Studies* 11: 27–45.

Duncan, O.D., and B. Duncan. 1955. A methodological analysis of segregation indices. *American Sociological Review* 20: 210–217.

Ellison, G., and E.L. Glaeser. 1997. Geographic concentration in U.S. manufacturing industries: A dartboard approach. *Journal of Political Economy* 1055: 889–927.

Feser, E.J. 1998. Enterprises, externalities and economic development. *Journal of Planning Literature* 123: 283–302.

Feser, E.J., and S.H. Sweeney. 2000. A test for the coincident economic and spatial clustering of business enterprises. *Journal of Geographical Systems* 2: 349–373.

Feser, E.J., and S.H. Sweeney. 2002a. *The Geography of the U.S. ES-202 file: Prospects for Small area Data Analysis*. Unpublished manuscript, Department of City and Regional Planning, University of North Carolina at Chapel Hill.

Feser, E.J., and S.H. Sweeney. 2002b. Spatially binding linkages in manufacturing product chains. In R. McNaughton, and M. Green (eds.), *Global Competition and Local Networks*. Hampshire, U.K.: Ashgate, 111–130.

Feser, E.J., and S.H. Sweeney. 2002c. Theory, methods, and a cross-metropolitan comparison of business clustering, In P. McCann (ed.), *Industrial Location Economics*. Cheltenham: Edward Elgar, 222–262.

Feser, E.J., S.H. Sweeney, and H.C. Renski. 2003. A descriptive analysis of discrete U.S. indus-trial complexes. *Journal of Regional Science*. In Press.

Getis, A. 1984. Interaction modeling using second-order analysis. *Environment and Planning A* 16: 173–183.

Getis, A., and J.K. Ord. 1992. The analysis of spatial association by use of distance statistics. *Geographical Analysis* 243: 189–206.

Gini, Corrado. 1914. Sula misura della concentrazione e della variabilita dei caratteri, *Atti del R. Istituto Veneto di Scienze, Lettere ed Arti* 73: 1203–1248.

Gordon, I.R., and P. McCann. 2000. Industrial clusters: Complexes, agglomeration and/or social networks? *Urban Studies* 373: 513–532.

Hanson, G.H. 2000. Firms, workers, and the geographic concentration of economic activity. In G.L. Clark, M.P. Feldman, and M.S. Gertler (eds.), *The Oxford Handbook of Economic Geography*. Oxford, UK: Oxford University Press, 477–494.

Hoover, E. 1948. *The Location of Economic Activity*. New York: McGraw-Hill.

Isard, W. 1965. *Location and Space Economy*. Cambridge: MIT Press.

Lorenz, M. 1905. Methods of measuring the concentration of wealth. *Journal of the American Statistical Association* 70 June, 209–219.

Marshall, A. 1920. *Principles of Economics: An Introductory Volume*. New York: Free Press.

Massey, D., and N. Denton. 1988. The dimensions of residential segregation. *Social Forces* 672: 281–315.

Morris, M., A. Bernhardt, and M. Handcock. 1994. Economic inequality: New methods for new trends. *American Sociological Review* 59 April: 205–219.

Ord, J.K., and A. Getis. 1995. Local spatial autocorrelation statistics: Distributional issues and an application. *Geographical Analysis* 274: 286–306.

Pearson, K. 1895. Regression, heredity, and panmixia. *Philosophical Transactions of the Royal Society of London, Ser. A* 187: 253–318.

Porter, M.E. 1990. *The Competitive Advantage of Nations*. New York: Free Press.

Porter, M.E. 2000. Location, competition, and economic development: Local clusters in a global economy. *Economic Development Quarterly* 141: 15–34.

Ripley, B.D. 1977. Modelling spatial patterns. *Journal of the Royal Statistical Society B* 39: 172–212.

Roelandt, T.J.A., and P. den Hertog (eds.). 1999. *Boosting Innovation: The Cluster Approach*. Paris: Organisation for Economic Co-operation and Development.

Singleton, R., B.C. Straits, M.M. Straits, and R.J. McAllister. 1988. *Approaches to Social Research*. New York: Oxford University Press.

Steiner, M. (ed.). 1998. *Clusters and Regional Specialisation Vol. 8*. London: Pion.

Sweeney, S., and E. Feser. 1998. Plant size and clustering of manufacturing activity. *Geographical Analysis* 301: 45–64.

Sweeney, S., and E. Feser. 2001. *Detecting the influence of outliers in second moment measures of spatial point patterns*. Unpublished manuscript. University of California, Santa Barbara, Department of Geography.

Trochim, W. 2001. *The Research Methods Knowledge Base*. Cincinnati, Ohio: Atomic Dog Publishing.

White, M. 1983. The measurement of spatial segregation. *American Journal of Sociology* 885: 453–468.

Yntema, D. 1933. Measures of the inequality in the personal distribution of wealth or income. *Journal of the American Statistical Association* 28 December: 423–433.

13

Updating Spatial Perspectives and Analytical Frameworks in Urban Research

Qing Shen

A spatial perspective is essential for understanding many kinds of urban problems. Current literature on urban issues reflects the continued prevalence of what might be called "the conventional spatial perspective"—the customary view that physical distance is a primary determinant, as well as a principal measure, of spatial relationship.[1] Since the distance between any two objects on the surface of the earth is determined by their geographic locations, from this conventional perspective geographic location is the key to understanding how an object is spatially related to others. Although more sophisticated notions of distance have been introduced over the last century by many scholars (see, for example, Brown and Horton 1970; Isard 1956, 1960; Sack 1980), the conventional perspective still has a major influence on how urban researchers usually approach questions regarding potential and actual interactions among people, organizations, or communities. Consciously or unconsciously, many urban researchers often assume physical distance, and hence geographic location, to be the most important variable for describing and explaining spatial phenomena in the city.

As an indication of the prevalence of the conventional spatial perspective, in academic publications as well as in daily life, the words "spatial" and "geographic" are often used synonymously. It is particularly worth noting the pervasiveness of this conventional perspective in urban economics and urban geography, which provide the most important theoretical foundations and analytical tools for urban research. The notion that physical distance can effectively describe and fundamentally explain the spatial distribution of economic activities is central to virtually all existing location theories and models.[2] This notion also is embodied in numerous models of spatial interaction and urban growth, ranging from traditional gravity models to recent cellular automata models.[3]

In the meantime, the literature—especially the part addressing urban issues closely related to telecommunications, such as globalization and social networks—also shows an increasing presence of views that underplay, or even totally dismiss, the importance of geographic location and physical distance. These views, collectively called "the radical spatial perspective" here, for the lack of a better term, reflect the fact that transportation and communications technologies have drastically modified spatial relationships that were once largely dependent on physical distance. But they tend to exaggerate the impacts. The radical spatial perspective has found various channels to spread, including books by some well-known postindustrial theorists (see, for example, Toffler 1980) and commentaries by many journalists working for popular newspapers and magazines.

The pervasiveness of the conventional spatial perspective is at odds with the technology-enabled transformation of geographic space that the world has been witnessing, whereas the radical spatial perspective is in conflict with the shared experiences of people, organizations, and communities whose interactions with others are still at least partly influenced by geographic factors. These contradictions call for a careful reexamination of spatial perspectives and analytical frameworks.

In this chapter, I present an alternative spatial perspective that differs significantly from both the conventional one and the radical one and apply this perspective to address key issues in two important areas of urban research—urban low-income labor markets and telecommuting. The chapter starts with an introduction of several concepts that are essential for describing the alternative view. A theoretical discussion of this perspective, which encompasses technologic, socioeconomic, and geographic dimensions, is followed by an empirical analysis of commuting data for the Boston Metropolitan Area to illustrate the wide range of important factors influencing spatial interaction. Next, the alternative spatial perspective is shown to help in analyzing urban low-income labor markets. The analysis sheds new light on the debate over the "spatial mismatch" hypothesis by advancing understanding about the roles of transportation mode and residential location in determining workers' access to economic opportunities. Finally, the usefulness of this alternative perspective in exploring effects of telecommunications on households' travel behavior and location choice is illustrated. By incorporating both the physical and virtual elements of activity space into an integrated analytical framework, new capacity is created for modeling the impacts of telecommunications under different scenarios.

An Alternative Spatial Perspective

The alternative spatial perspective involves several key concepts. The first is "functional distance," which is often described as distance measured by taking into consideration the time and effort required to move certain material, information, or people from one geographic location to another. Brown and Horton (1970) defined it as "a measure of the distance separating any two nodes such that it reflects the net effect of nodal properties upon their propensity to interact." In comparison with physical distance, which is a quantification of the unique and symmetrical geometric relation between any pair of objects, functional distance is a more general and sophisticated measure. It depends on "nodal properties" (e.g., low-income and high-income groups, transit and auto commuters) as well as "associational properties" (e.g., highway and transit links) that include physical distance as a basic element. It can represent multiple and asymmetrical spatial relations resulting from different interactions between nodal properties and associational properties. Obviously, functional distance changes when any relevant nodal property or associational property is changed.

The second concept is "spatial position," which refers to the comparative advantage or disadvantage of a place (e.g., a central-city neighborhood) or a locator (e.g., a low-income worker) in reaching certain desirable destinations by overcoming the functional distances in between.[4] It should be distinguished conceptually from geographic advantage or disadvantage, which is determined on the basis of physical distances to desirable destinations. Spatial position is often measured in terms of accessibility. The spatial position of a place or a locator may change not only absolutely, but also relatively, when the functional distances to desirable destinations are changed.

The third concept is "spatial order," which describes the hierarchy of places or locators according to their spatial positions. The spatial order of places or locators changes when their spatial positions are altered relatively to one another.

The technology-enabled transformation of geographic space implies the weakening correlation between physical distance and functional distance. Indeed, one may argue that this transformation is essentially a process of reestablishing the spatial orders of places and locators through shortening some—but not all—functional distances. Innovations in transportation and communications often bring new, desirable "associational properties" to selected places and locators that possess certain "nodal properties." For example, the construction of a modern inter-European transportation system has improved substantially the transportation connections among major political and economic centers in Europe. Consequently, the spatial positions of these major cities have been elevated both absolutely and relatively, whereas many places that are unconnected with the system have fallen to lower positions in the new spatial order (Spiekermann and Wegener 1994). Generally speaking, as transportation and communications technologies become more advanced, they are capable of generating greater differential impacts.

When physical distance is no longer representative of functional distance, the conventional spatial perspective becomes rather inadequate for understanding spatial phenomena and is potentially misleading. Alternative spatial perspectives must then be sought. What distinguishes an appropriate alternative perspective from the conventional one is its focus on functional distance instead of physical distance as the basis for determining the spatial position of a place or locator. The importance of this distinction was illustrated by Brown and Horton (1970), who showed that geographic location and population size did not provide a satisfactory explanation for observed patterns of inter-metropolitan migration. Even though geographic location and population size were the factors used traditionally to predict movement of people, Brown and Horton found that these factors did not represent appropriately the functional distances for people migrating between cities.

It follows that a spatial perspective appropriate for understanding contemporary cities must encompass multiple dimensions, rather than only the geographic dimension. Urban areas are becoming increasingly diverse and complex. Various combinations of nodal properties and associational properties are at work in determining the functional distances for different population groups, organizations, and communities. Consequently, multiple spatial orders of places and locators exist in any urban area. Some of these spatial orders may show little correspondence with each other geographically.

The spatial perspective of this chapter views geographic location and physical distance as basic elements for forming spatial relationships, transportation and communications technologies as the driving forces for transforming spatial relationships, and relevant socioeconomic factors as the intervening variables in technology-driven spatial transformations. These technological, socioeconomic, and geographic dimensions determine jointly the spatial position of each place and locator by manipulating the functional distances to desirable destinations, and thus establish the spatial orders of places and locators. What technological and socioeconomic factors are important is an empirical question for which the answer is context-dependent. Unlike some post-industrial theorists' radical view, this spatial perspective does not overlook the role of geographic location and physical distance. From this perspective, functional distance and physical distance would be equivalent if technological and socioeconomic factors affected all functional distances proportionately.

Understanding contemporary urban issues requires not only an updated spatial perspective, but also updated analytical approaches. The shortage of satisfactory spatial analytical tools is especially evident in the face of the ongoing dramatic transformation of geographic space caused by an explosion in the application of digital information and communications technologies, particularly the Internet (Janelle and Hodge 2000). In general, an appropriate spatial analytical framework is built on the basis of properly estimated functional distances. This requires that all important factors influencing functional distance in a particular context be identified and their effects be quantified. Unlike geometric distance, functional distance usually cannot be straightforwardly measured; instead, it is estimated. Rigorous estimation of function distance can be obtained by analyzing observed patterns of spatial interaction (Brown and Horton 1970). However, this approach is often extremely complicated, and therefore less sophisticated approaches are frequently taken. For example, Isard (1956) proposed the use of transportation cost as a measure of "economic distance." Many researchers used travel time as a simplified representation of functional distance for the same reason. If these simplified quantifications of spatial separation are differentiated appropriately for different population groups, they can adequately approximate functional distances.

Effects of Technological, Socioeconomic, and Geographic Factors

The purpose of this section is two-fold: (1) to illustrate the importance of technological and socioeconomic factors in influencing spatial relationship and (2) to provide an example of identifying and assessing the relevant factors in a particular context. The discussion is based on an analysis of commuting behaviors of workers in the Boston Metropolitan Area. The primary data used for this analysis came from the 1995 Nationwide Personal Travel Survey (NPTS). The supplementary data, matrices of intrametropolitan origin-destination travel times for auto and public transit, were obtained from the Central Transportation Planning Staff in Boston. The combined database contains records for more than three thousand workers. Each worker's commuting distance and duration, modal choice, and socioeconomic attributes are measured at the individual level, and each worker's residential location is geo-coded at the zip code level.

Commuting distance and duration describe a worker's spatial interaction with employment opportunities in an urban economy. They are useful—although not ideal—measures of a worker's spatial position in a metropolitan labor market.[5] The research hypothesis is that commuting distance and duration are influenced not only by the geographic location factor, but also by transportation (technological) and socioeconomic factors.

A two-equation regression model is specified and estimated. Equation (1) represents commuting distance as a function of geographic location, transportation mobility, and the commuter's socioeconomic characteristics. The geographic location factor considered here is the number of employment opportunities within 30 minutes of automobile travel from each worker's residential location.[6] The transportation mobility factors included in the model are travel mode, auto ownership, and peak-hour and weekend commuting. The relevant socioeconomic characteristics of the commuter are income, education, race, age, gender, and presence of one or more young children in the household.

Equation (2) expresses commuting duration as a function of commuting distance and several factors that can affect travel speed, which include travel mode, congestion level, and the worker's age and gender. Congestion level is measured indirectly by whether the commuting trip was taken during peak hours or on a weekend, and on whether or not it originated in an area of high employment concentration (represented by number of employment opportunities within 30 minutes of automobile travel).

$$
\begin{aligned}
\text{distance} = {} & \alpha_0 + \alpha_1 \text{emp\_opp} + \alpha_2 \text{transit} + \alpha_3 \text{walk} + \alpha_4 \text{other\_mode} \\
& + \alpha_5 \text{own\_auto} + \alpha_6 \text{peak\_hour} + \alpha_7 \text{weekend} + \alpha_8 \text{income} + \alpha_9 \text{edu\_12} \\
& + \alpha_{10} \text{edu\_16} + \alpha_{11} \text{black} + \alpha_{12} \text{asian} + \alpha_{13} \text{other\_race} + \alpha_{14} \text{age\_18} \\
& + \alpha_{15} \text{age\_61} + \alpha_{16} \text{female} + \alpha_{17} \text{children}
\end{aligned}
\tag{1}
$$

$$
\begin{aligned}
\text{duration} = {} & \beta_0 + \beta_1 \text{distance} + \beta_2 \text{transit} + \beta_3 \text{walk} + \beta_4 \text{other\_mode} \\
& + \beta_5 \text{peak\_hour} + \beta_6 \text{weekend} + \beta_7 \text{emp\_opp} + \beta_8 \text{age\_18} \\
& + \beta_9 \text{age\_61} + \beta_{10} \text{female}
\end{aligned}
\tag{2}
$$

Even though both commuting distance and duration are endogenous variables, Equation (1) contains only one of them. Therefore, Equations (1) and (2) are recursive and can be estimated sequentially. Equation (1) is estimated using the ordinary least squares. The estimated distance from Equation (1) is then used as an independent variable in Equation (2). This procedure is equivalent to applying the two-stage least-squares method to estimate the regression equation for commuting duration. Many alternative model specifications were tested, and the main results were highly consistent with the findings reported in Table 13.1 and Table 13.2.

Table 13.1. Regression outcome for commuting distance.

Variable	Coefficient	Beta	*T* Statistic
Employment opportunities	−1.20E-05	−.25	−13.29
Using public transit	4.93	.09	4.95
Walking	−6.14	−.04	−2.47
Using other mode	−3.16	−.02	−1.07
Owning automobile	2.79	.03	1.75
Peak-hour trip	−2.88	−.11	−6.18
Weekend trip	−1.09	−.03	−1.57
Income	6.35E-05	.12	6.38
High school education (12 years) or less	−3.50	−.07	−3.06
College education (16 years) or more	3.28	.12	6.52
Black	−.53	−.01	−.36
Asian	.00	.00	.00
Other Race	.32	.01	.27
Age 18 or younger	−5.66	−.08	−3.96
Age 61 or older	−1.19	−.02	−1.09
Female	−3.61	−.14	−7.99
Having young children	1.50	.05	2.76
(Constant)	13.34		7.91
		R^2:	.15
		No. of cases:	3025

The output of the first regression shows that, if everything else is the same:

1. Living in geographic location with more employment opportunities nearby shortens commute;
2. In comparison with driving, using public transit increases, whereas walking decreases, commuting distance;
3. Owning automobile increases commuting distance;
4. Peak-hour commutes have shorter distances;
5. Higher income workers choose longer commutes for better housing;

Table 13.2. Regression outcome for commuting duration.

Variable	Coefficient	Beta	*T* Statistic
Estimated commuting distance	1.34	.37	11.97
Using public transit	17.24	.23	12.12
Walking	12.59	.06	3.55
Using other mode	8.43	.03	2.03
Peak-hour trip	1.75	.05	2.60
Weekend trip	−.10	−.00	−.11
Employment opportunities	5.11E-06	.08	2.86
Age 18 or younger	−1.35	−.01	−.69
Age 61 or older	1.45	.02	.94
Female	.94	.03	1.20
(Constant)	2.63		1.09
		R^2:	.16
		No. of cases:	3025

6. More educated workers have a more extensive labor market;
7. Teenagers tend to work nearby home;
8. Females tend to work nearby home; and
9. Workers with young children choose longer commutes for better housing.

The outcome of the second regression indicates that commuting time is affected not only by the estimated commuting distance, but also by travel mode and congestion level. The most striking result is that, in comparison with workers who use automobile, those using public transit spend, on average, an extra 17 minutes on each commuting trip. Because, for all workers, the average commuting distance is approximately 14 miles, and the average duration is approximately 25 minutes, the comparative spatial disadvantage of public transit riders is quite enormous.

These results indicate the significance of transportation mobility and socioeconomic characteristics, as well as residential location, in influencing workers' spatial position and travel behavior in a metropolitan economy. They show that, due to the influences of transportation technologies and intervening socioeconomic variables, physical distance translates into very different functional distances for different people. These results are generally consistent with what many researchers found previously in different contexts or with different data (Hanson and Pratt 1995; Rosenbloom and Burns 1993; Shen 1998, 2000a).

It is important to note that the regression models have rather low R^2 values (0.15 and 0.16), indicating that only slightly more than 15 percent of variance in workers' commuting behavior is explained. This means that workers in contemporary metropolitan areas have great flexibility in deciding home and work locations. Modern transportation, particularly private automobile, has made it possible to be flexible in location choice. In contrast workers who are dependent on public transit enjoy much less such flexibility. This is indicated by much higher R^2 values (above 0.30) resulting from running the regressions only for workers who do not commute by auto. Residential location is much more powerful for explaining the commuting behaviors of workers who have a relatively low level of transportation mobility.

Obtaining New Insights to Inform Ongoing Debates

The spatial perspectives adopted in this chapter can help to advance understanding about kinds of unresolved urban problems. This is illustrated for two problems in this section: (1) research on low-income labor markets, focusing on issues concerning access to employment opportunities in dispersing metropolitan economies, and (2) research on telecommuting, focusing on the effects of telecommunications on travel behavior and residential location choice.

Reexamining Urban Low-Income Labor Markets

For more than three decades, a focal point for debate in this important field of urban research has been the question of whether the high level of concentration of poverty in American central cities is caused partly by central-city residents' spatial disadvantage in access to suitable employment opportunities. The mainstream view, shared by most researchers, is articulated in the so-called "spatial mismatch theory." According to this theory, suburbanization of employment, racial discrimination in the suburban housing market, and post-industrial restructuring of the urban economy have jointly created a mismatch between where low-income people reside and where employment opportunities suitable for them are located (see, e.g., Kain 1992; Kasarda 1995; Wilson 1987). While low-income people are highly concentrated in the central city, available jobs are believed to mostly situate in the suburbs. Therefore, proponents of the spatial mismatch theory argue that a central-city residential location translates into spatial disadvantage for low-income people living there, and that the resulting spatial disadvantage is an important causal factor of unemployment and poverty. They suggest that the problem of unemployment would be alleviated if low-income and minority central-city residents were able to follow employment decentralization by relocating to suburban areas (Holzer 1991).

On the other hand, some researchers reject the notion that unemployment and poverty among central-city residents is attributable to spatial mismatch between low-income people and jobs suitable for them (Ellwood 1986; Gordon et al. 1989; Harrison 1974). They contend that central-city residents do not have spatial disadvantage in access to jobs. For example, Gordon et al. presented this argument based on observed commuting behaviors of workers who traveled by private vehicles. They categorized workers by income, race, and residential location. Their data showed that the average commuting duration of low-income and minority workers living in the central city was not significantly longer than the averages for other groups. This finding led these researchers to the conclusion that the concentration of poverty in central cities is caused by factors other than spatial barriers.

Despite a large volume of completed research on this subject, neither the advocates nor the detractors of the spatial mismatch theory have been able to explain satisfactorily basic patterns of spatial interaction in contemporary metropolitan labor markets. If it were true, as proponents of the mismatch theory have argued, that central-city low-income residents suffered from a location disadvantage because employment opportunities were mostly located in the suburbs, then their average commuting distance would be longer than the average for other residents. But empirical studies have shown that, on the contrary, suburban and high-income residents tend to commute longer distances.[7] A relevant observation is that long commuting distance does not seem to discourage a large number of people who reside at the periphery of a metropolitan area or beyond from finding and keeping jobs located in the central city. This suggests that geographic location and physical distance may not be the most critical determinant of job accessibility in urban labor markets.

Arguments made by some opponents of the mismatch theory are as unconvincing. If it were true, as these opponents have contended, that low-income central-city residents were not spatially disadvantaged in terms of access to employment opportunities, then their average commuting duration would be similar to that of other residents. However, empirical evidence shows that residents of central-city low-income neighborhoods, especially those who live in the poorest neighborhoods, tend to spend significantly longer times on journeys to and from work.[8] In other words, the data indicate that the residents of central-city low-income neighborhoods *are* spatially disadvantaged in terms of access to employment.

The inability of both groups of researchers to provide a satisfactory explanation for these seemingly contradictory phenomena reveals the limitation of the conventional spatial perspective, which has dictated these researchers' conceptualization and empirical testing of the spatial mismatch hypothesis. Both groups of researchers have equated disadvantage in spatial position with disadvantage in geographic location. They have focused narrowly on the geographic factors, i.e., residential location, employment location, and home-to-work distance, in their spatial analyses of urban labor markets. Many relevant transportation and socioeconomic factors have been overlooked.

New insights about urban low-income labor markets are required to help resolve the fundamental disagreement on spatial mismatch. Can a better understanding of spatial barriers in these labor markets be obtained using the alternative spatial perspective?

A number of researchers have shown that new insights can be obtained by changing the spatial perspective. In their study of workers' commuting patterns in American metropolitan areas, Taylor and Ong (1995) proposed and tested the hypothesis that travel mode, instead of geographic location of residence, is the primary determinant of a worker's spatial position. Using data from the American Housing Surveys in the late 1970s and the mid 1980s, they found that workers living in predominantly minority areas had shorter commuting distances, and that these workers' commuting distances increased more slowly between the two time periods. These results contradict the spatial mismatch theory. On the other hand, they found that commuting times for public transit riders averaged 75 percent longer than commuting times for auto drivers. Since low-income and minority workers are much more likely to be dependent on public transit, their access to employment is much reduced.

Taylor and Ong essentially obtained important statistics about metropolitan low-income labor markets simply by applying a more updated spatial perspective. Examining commuting patterns explicitly along technological (in this case, automobile availability) and social dimensions, they found an explanation for the seemingly contradictory co-existence of shorter commuting distances and longer commuting times for low-income workers. They showed that the spatial barrier facing low-income and minority workers living in central cities is caused not by their residential location, but by their dependence on public transportation. For people who do not have a car and hence rely on slow public transit, geometric distance translates into relatively long functional distance.

In a study of the location characteristics of inner-city areas and employment accessibility for low-income workers in Boston, Shen (1998) developed an analytical framework that is coherent with the alternative spatial perspective described in this chapter. This framework, consisting of a set of accessibility measures, takes into consideration the geographic distribution of suitable opportunities, the geographic distribution of opportunity seekers, the travel time between each pair of locations for each transportation mode, and the mode split of opportunity seekers in each location. It can be generally represented by two equations. The first, Equation (3), measures residents' employment accessibility for each location and each transportation mode:

$$Ai^m = \sum_j \frac{O_j \times f(C_{ij}^m)}{\sum_m \sum_k \left[P_k^m \times f(C_{kj}^m) \right]} \tag{3}$$

where:

A_i^m is accessibility of people living in location i and traveling by mode m;

O_j is number of relevant opportunities in location j;

P_k^m is number of people living in location k and traveling by mode m in seeking the opportunities;

$f(C_{ij}^m)$ and $f(C_{kj}^m)$ are the impedance functions for traveling by mode m between locations i and j and between locations k and j, respectively;

For an urban or regional system with N locations, $i, j, k = 1, 2, \ldots, N$;

For an urban or regional system with M modes, $m = 1, 2, \ldots, M$.

The second, Equation (4), calculates the general (i.e., weighted average) employment accessibility for all residents of each location:

$$A_i^G = \sum_m \left[(P_i^m / P_i) \times A_i^m \right] \tag{4}$$

where:

A_i^G is general accessibility for all groups of people living in location i;

P_i^m is number of people in location i traveling by mode m seeking the opportunities;

P_i is the total number of people in location i;

For an urban or regional system with M modes, $m = 1, 2, \ldots, M$.

Equation (3) seeks to describe the relative contributions of residential location and transportation option to a low-income worker's spatial position in an urban labor market. Using primarily 1990 Census demographic and journey-to-work data, Shen found that a central-city location of residence still gives low-income workers some advantage, so far as employment accessibility is concerned. For a given transportation mode, workers living in central-city locations generally have higher accessibility than those living in suburban locations. However, he found that auto ownership is a much more important determinant of workers' spatial position in a dispersing metropolitan economy. Specifically, for workers who commute by auto, the majority of residential locations in the metropolitan area would give them above-average employment accessibility. For workers who commute by public transit, on the other hand, only a few residential locations near the central business district would give them above-average employment accessibility. The limited geographic advantage of a central-city location is in most cases not sufficient to compensate the mobility disadvantage of public transportation.

Based on the Equation (4), the overall spatial position of all residents can be determined for each location. Shen showed that, because a disproportionately high percentage of low-income workers living in central-city locations do not own automobiles, the weighted average employment accessibility is relatively low for the central city, especially its low-income neighborhoods. This led to the conclusion that low-income residents of the central city are spatially disadvantaged despite having some location advantage.

The spatial perspective embodied in Shen's analytical framework contributes additional insights about the spatial structure of urban low-income labor markets. By differentiating accessibility measurement for workers commuting by different transportation modes, belonging to different income and occupation groups, and residing in different locations, it takes into account technological, socioeconomic, and geographic factors in understanding the spatial order of labor markets. The results—especially the finding that the central city is a geographically advantaged residential location but that central-city residents are spatially disadvantaged commuters—shed new light on the debate over the relationship between spatial barriers and urban unemployment.

Updated spatial perspectives are reflected in other studies of urban low-income labor markets. The recent study by Kawabata (2001) is especially worth mentioning. Kawabata extended Shen's Boston study to examine factors influencing low-income workers' spatial positions in the labor markets of the Los Angeles and San Francisco metropolitan areas. Her findings were generally consistent with those reported by Shen. In addition, she estimated logit models to explain low-income workers' labor market outcomes in terms of employment status, and found that the differentiated measures of employment accessibility for transit commuters and for auto commuters add significant explanatory power to the models.

Exploring the Spatial Effects of Telecommunications

The recent convergence of digital information and communications technologies (ICT) marked the beginning of a new phase in the transformation of geographic space. It is characterized by a dramatic increase in the importance of remote interactions—which involve processing information using computers and exchanging information through communications networks—in people's economic and social lives. This ICT-enabled transformation of geographic space is so significant that some scholars (see, e.g., Castells 2000) consider it as what fundamentally defines our historic time.

The ICT change raises new questions about cities—their people, organizations, and communities. However, the conventional spatial perspective and analytical methods appear rather powerless in addressing these new questions, because physical distance creates practically no impedance to interactions taking place over telecommunications networks. Many authors, especially some commentators in the popular press, see this as the arrival of a "spaceless economy." But this radical spatial perspective is not an adequate replacement for the traditional frameworks that have become obsolete. There is a shortage of appropriate spatial perspectives and related analytical tools for understanding the effects of telecommunications.

The question to be addressed in this section is whether the spatial perspective described in this chapter is useful for understanding urban problems in the age of advanced information and communications technologies.

Over the past five decades, a considerable number of scholars have made serious efforts to develop and/or apply refreshing spatial perspectives for examining the effects of telecommunications on travel behavior, location choice, and urban form and function (Gottmann 1983; Janelle 1995; Meier 1962; Nilles 1991; Pool 1979; Salomon 1986; Webber 1964). Many of them either explicitly or implicitly explored the idea of including technological, socioeconomic, and geographical dimensions in the analysis of new patterns of spatial interaction. For example, Webber (1964) viewed the desire for interaction among people with shared interest as the essence of the city and believed that telecommunications would lead to the formation of "urban realms" based on socioeconomic considerations rather than geographic proximity. Similarly, Gottmann (1983) predicted a telecommunications-facilitated redistribution of firms in the city based primarily on each firm's level of dependence on face-to-face interaction in business operations. Focusing on the effects of telecommunications on travel, Pool (1979) conjectured that remote interaction may either increase or decrease travel, depending on whether or not the communication leads to future travel (i.e., the secondary effect) that exceeds the travel it initially reduced (i.e., the direct effect).

The past decade has witnessed the development of new analytical capacity for understanding the impact of ICT, especially the partial substitution of telecommunications for travel. For example, Mokhtarian and Salomon (1996) analyzed the extent to which telecommuting can potentially replace commuting trips. They found that there are many institutional and personal constraints on the adoption of telecommuting. Because of these constraints, for the majority of employees telecommuting is a preferred but impossible alternative. Based on a survey of California state employees, it was shown that telecommuting is possible, preferred, and chosen for only 11 percent of the entire sample. In a study published two years later, Mokhtarian (1998) developed an innovative approach to estimate the overall level of adoption of telecommuting and the aggregate impact on travel. Using a multiplicative model, she took into consideration factors such as workers' occupational suitability for telecommuting, their willingness to work at home, and their telecommuting frequency. Her estimation indicated that the percentage of workers telecommuting on any given day would be fairly small, and that the resulting impact of telecommuting on travel demand would be quite limited for the foreseeable future.

The research by Mokhtarian and Salomon once again reveals the importance of socioeconomic factors, which are basic components of nodal properties, in determining functional distances. ICT only shortens the functional distances for those who can actually choose to use the technologies. Their findings are generally consistent with observations made by many other researchers, including Gillespie and Richardson (2000) and Wheeler et al. (2000), that the impacts of telecommuting have long been overestimated. Some of the constraints may be removed in the future because of technological advances and because of changes in individuals' lifestyle and workplace culture. These changes could render estimates of impacts obsolete in the future. However, the process of technology substituting for traditional forms of spatial interaction will continue to be influenced by socioeconomic forces.

To explore changing spatial positions of geographically and socio-economically defined urban residents, Shen (1999) extended his analytical framework to include telecommunications as an option for spatial interaction. He defined three categories of spatially distributed opportunities: (1) those existing in the cyberspace and accessed through telecommunications, at least in part, (2) those existing in the hybrid space and accessed through either transportation or telecommunications, and (3) those belonging exclusively to the physical space, and therefore accessed through transportation only. Seekers of these opportunities were categorized by their travel mode and telecommunications capabilities, which reflect their income, occupation, and education status.

Effects of telecommunications technologies on workers' spatial position in the information economy were reflected in the redistribution of opportunities among the three categories and in the reduced functional distance between home and workplace for workers who partially substitute telecommuting for commuting trips. The spatial position for seekers who do not have telecommunications capabilities is measured as follows:

$$A_i^m = A_i^{m(1)} + A_i^{m(2)} \tag{5}$$

The spatial position for seekers who have telecommunications capabilities, on the other hand, is measured as follows:

$$A_i^m = A_i^{m(1)} + A_i^{cm(2)} + A_i^{cm(3)} \tag{6}$$

where:

$A_i^{m(1)}$ is accessibility to opportunities that are accessed through transportation only;

$A_i^{m(2)}$ is accessibility to opportunities that can be accessed through either transportation or telecommunications, as measured for people who can use transportation only;

$A_i^{cm(2)}$ is accessibility to opportunities that can be accessed through either transportation or telecommunications, as measured for people who can use telecommunications;

$A_i^{cm(3)}$ is accessibility to opportunities that are accessed through telecommunications.

Impedance for telecommunications is defined by assuming that people who use telecommunications to access opportunities still make at least some supplementary trips. If these people typically travel once every τ days, instead of everyday, a *perceived average daily travel time* can be calculated for them:

$$t_{ij}^{cm} = \sigma(1/\tau)t_{ij}^m \tag{7}$$

Note that there are two variables that determine the impedance for an opportunity seeker who has telecommunications capabilities. One is the frequency of using transportation for opportunity-seeking trips, and the other is the location-to-location travel times (t_{ij}^m) for the transportation mode used. Note also that σ is a parameter that converts an *actual* average daily travel time into a *perceived* average daily travel time.

Again, technological forces, socioeconomic factors, and geographic location are included in the analytical framework as essential elements. They are connected to each other by considering the ways in which communications technology changes the distribution of opportunities between physical space and cyberspace and reduces certain functional distances. The basic premise is that, while contemporary urban activities can assume many forms, they all either take place in some physical location or are logistically and functionally related to location-based activities. This relationship allows joint measurement of impedance for a group of related activities.

This work is a preliminary effort to develop formal representation and analytical tools for human activity spaces in an information society. It has shown that it is possible to develop operational measures of spatial relationship, spatial position, and spatial order that take into consideration the influence of telecommunications. In addition, it has facilitated the exploration of the spatial consequence of the digital divide.[9] With the resulting modeling capacity, the differential effects of ICT on the spatial positions and residential location flexibility of individuals with different combinations of transportation and telecommunications options and socioeconomic characteristics can be analyzed systematically. Simulation exercises using this analytical tool indicate that households with both automobile and telecommunications capabilities are gaining residential location flexibility, and that their gain may result in loss for households who depend on public transit (Shen 2000b). The differential spatial effects are significant and the long-term implications should not be overlooked.

Conclusion

An updated spatial perspective is required for understanding many problems in contemporary cities. Physical distance and geographic location are still essential elements for defining human activity spaces. But it is functional distance and spatial position that ultimately determine patterns of spatial interaction. Transportation and communications technologies can drastically modify functional distances and change the relative spatial positions of places and of people, organizations, and communities located in these places. Furthermore, many socioeconomic factors, such as income, education, and health, intervene in the technology-driven spatial transformation. It is no longer sufficient to focus narrowly on physical distance and geographic location as the variables for describing and explaining spatial phenomena. As shown in the debate over low-income workers' spatial position in metropolitan labor markets, by overlooking the technological dimensions, a conventional spatial perspective can lead to serious misunderstanding of urban problems, which in turn may lead to ineffective urban policies. On the other hand, it is also inadequate to overstate the significance of advanced technologies while neglecting the continued importance of the traditional geographic dimension in the spatial organization of economic and social activities. A radical spatial perspective without a geographic foundation is undoubtedly partial, and likely misleading.

If urban researchers are to appropriately inform urban planning and policymaking, they must update not only their spatial perspectives, but also their analytical approaches. The improved approaches must enable relevant technological and socioeconomic variables to be incorporated—along with traditional geographic variables—into analysis of spatial phenomena. Several recent studies on spatial barriers in urban low-income labor markets and on the spatial impacts of telecommuting provided illustrative examples. Using the resulting analytical tools, the researchers were able to obtain new insights about these issues to inform ongoing debates.

Notes

1. In this chapter, "the conventional spatial perspective" collectively refers to all spatial perspectives that mirror this customary view.
2. Heilbrun (1987) and O'Sullivan (2000) provide good overviews of location theories and models.

3. See, for example, Cechini (1996).
4. In this chapter, a "place" is conceptually distinguished from a "geographic location." A place is a physical setting in an environment either created by or influenced by human activities, whereas a geographic location is a position in a geometric space.
5. Commuting distance and duration are not ideal measures of a worker's spatial position because they can be interpreted quite differently depending on the circumstances. A longer commuting distance, for instance, can be either a result of a high-income worker's conscious decision to trade higher accessibility for better housing or a result of a low-income worker living in a place that does not have suitable employment opportunities nearby. But commuting distance and duration are still useful measures because, as shown in the next paragraphs, they allow statistical analyses on the factors that affect workers' patterns of spatial interaction.
6. A better measure, more consistent with the notion of geographic location used in the chapter, would be the number of employment opportunities within a certain geometric distance—such as 5 miles—from a worker's residence. Due to time and resource constraints, a threshold travel time of 30 minutes, which could be readily applied through the available origin-destination time matrices, was used to identify employment opportunities within reach from a worker's residential location.
7. Many researchers, including Taylor and Ong (1995) and Shen (2000a), have shown that the average commuting distances of suburban and high-income residents are significantly longer than that of central-city low-income residents.
8. Using the 1990 U.S. Census data, Shen (2000a) shows that commuting duration tends to be longer for low-income neighborhoods of central cities than it is for most other parts of metropolitan areas. Shen's finding contradicts the finding of Gordon et al. (1989), whose data include only commuting distances and times of people who travel by private vehicles.
9. Digital divide refers to uneven social distribution of access to ICT caused by financial, educational, and other barriers. There is a large volume of literature on this problem (see, for example, Dertouzos 1999 and Hoffman and Novak 1998).

References

Brown, L.A., and F.E. Horton. 1970. Functional distance: An operational approach. *Geographical Analysis* 2: 76–83.
Castells, M. 2000. Grassrooting the space of flow. In J.O. Wheeler, Y. Aoyama, and B. Warf (eds.), *Cities in the Telecommunications Age: The Fracturing of Geographies.* New York: Routledge, 18–27.
Cechini, A. 1996. Urban modelling by means of cellular automata: Generalised urban automata with the help on-line (AUGH) model. *Environment and Planning B* 23: 721–732.
Dertouzos, M. 1999. The rich people's computers? *Technology Review* No. 1, 22.
Ellwood, D.T. 1986. The spatial mismatch hypothesis: Are there teenage jobs missing in the ghetto? In R.B. Freeman and H.J. Holzer (eds.), *The Black Youth Employment Crisis.* Chicago: University of Chicago Press.
Gillespie, A., and R. Richardson. 2000. Teleworking and the city: Myths of workplace transcendence and travel reduction. In J.O. Wheeler, Y. Aoyama, and B. Warf (eds.), *Cities in The Telecommunications Age: The Fracturing Of Geographies.* New York: Routledge, 228–245.
Gordon, P., A. Kumar, and H. Richardson. 1989. The spatial mismatch hypothesis: Some new evidence. *Urban Studies* 26: 315–326.

Gottmann, J. 1983. *The Coming of the Transactional City*. College Park, Md.: Institute of Urban Studies, University of Maryland.

Hanson, S., and G. Pratt. 1995. *Gender, Work and Space*. New York: Routledge.

Harrison, B. 1974. *Urban Economic Development: Suburbanization, Minority Opportunity, and the Condition of the Central City*. Washington, D.C.: The Urban Institute.

Heilbrun, J. 1987. *Urban Economics and Public Policy*. 3rd edition. New York: St. Martin's Press.

Hoffman, D.L., and T.P. Novak. 1998. Bridging the racial divide on the Internet. *Science* 280: 390–391.

Holzer, H. 1991. The spatial mismatch hypothesis: What has the evidence shown? *Urban Studies* 28: 105–122.

Isard, W. 1960. *Methods of Regional Analysis: An Introduction to Regional Science*. New York: John Wiley.

Isard, W. 1956. *Location and Space-Economy*. New York: John Wiley.

Janelle, D.G. 1995. Metropolitan expansion, commuting and transportation. In S. Hanson (ed.) *The Geography of Urban Transportation*. 2nd edition. New York: The Guilford Press, 407–434.

Janelle, D.G., and D.C. Hodge. 2000. Information, place, cyberspace, and accessibility. In D.G. Janelle and D.C. Hodge (eds.), *Information, Place, and Cyberspace: Issues In Accessibility*. New York: Springer, 3–11.

Kain, J.F. 1992. The spatial mismatch hypothesis: Three decades later. *Housing Policy Debate* 3: 371–460.

Kasarda, J. 1995. Industrial restructuring and changing location of jobs. In R. Farley (ed.) *State of the Union: America in the 1990s, Volume I: Economic Trends*. New York: Russell Sage Foundation, 215–266.

Kawabata, M. 2001. *Job Accessibility and Employment Outcomes for Low-Skilled Autoless Workers in U.S. Metropolitan Areas*. Paper presented at the 43rd Annual Conference of the Association of Collegiate Schools of Planning. November 8–11, Cleveland, Ohio.

Meier, R.L. 1962. *A Communications Theory of Urban Growth*. Cambridge, Mass.: MIT Press.

Mokhtarian, P.L. 1998. A synthetic approach to estimating the impacts of telecommuting on travel. *Urban Studies* 35: 215–241.

Mokhtarian, P.L., and I. Salomon. 1996. Modeling the choice of telecommuting 2: A case of the preferred impossible alternative. *Environment and Planning A* 28: 1859–1876.

Nilles, J.M. 1991. Telecommuting and urban sprawl: Mitigator or inciter? *Transportation* 18: 411–432.

O'Sullivan, A. 2000. *Urban Economics*. 4th edition. New York: Urwin McGraw-Hill.

Pool, I. 1979. The communications/transportation tradeoff. In A. Altshuler (ed.), *Current Issues in Transportation Policy*. Lexington, Mass.: Lexington Books.

Rosenbloom, S., and E. Burns. 1993. Gender differences in commuter travel in Tucson: Implications for travel demand management programs. *Transportation Research Record* 1404: 82–90.

Sack, R.D. 1980. *Conceptions of Space in Social Thought*. Minneapolis, Minn.: University of Minnesota Press.

Salomon, I. 1986. Telecommunication and travel relationships: A review. *Transportation Research A* 20: 223–238.

Shen, Q. 1998. Location characteristics of inner-city neighborhoods and employment accessibility of low-wage workers. *Environment and Planning B* 25: 345–365.

Shen, Q. 1999. Transportation, telecommunications, and the changing geography of opportunity. *Urban Geography* 20: 334–355.

Shen, Q. 2000a. Spatial and social dimensions of commuting. *Journal of the American Planning Association* 66: 68–82.

Shen, Q. 2000b. New telecommunications and residential location flexibility. *Environment and Planning A* 32: 1445–1463.

Spiekermann, K., and M. Wegener. 1994. The shrinking continent: New time-space maps of Europe. *Environment and Planning B* 21: 653–673.

Taylor, B., and Ong, P. 1995. Spatial mismatch or automobile mismatch? An examination of race, residence and commuting in U.S. metropolitan areas. *Urban Studies* 32: 1453–1473.

Toffler, A. 1980. *The Third Wave*. New York: William Morrow.

Webber, M.M. 1964. The urban place and the nonplace urban realm. In M.M. Webber (ed.), *Explorations Into Urban Structure*. Philadelphia, Pa.: University of Pennsylvania Press.

Wheeler, J.O., Y. Aoyama, and B. Warf. 2000. City space, industrial space, and cyberspace. In J.O. Wheeler, Y. Aoyama, and B. Warf (eds.), *Cities in the Telecommunications Age: The Fracturing of Geographies*. New York: Routledge, 3–17.

Wilson, W. 1987. *The Truly Disadvantaged*. Chicago: University of Chicago Press.

14

Spatial Analysis of Regional Income Inequality

Sergio J. Rey

Just over a decade ago, Barro and Sala-i-Martin (1991) reintroduced main-stream macroeconomics to the concept of a region. That introduction set off an explosion of research on the question of regional economic convergence.[1] Much of this research represented a shift in focus from studying the dynamics of international income disparities to the analysis of intranational dynamics. That is, whether incomes between regions within a given nation state become more, or less, similar over time.

Despite the rich geographical dimensions underlying the data used in regional income convergence analysis, the role of spatial effects has only recently begun to attract attention (Armstrong and Vickerman 1995; Chatterji and Dewhurst 1996; Cuadrado-Roura et al. 1999; Fingleton 1999). These studies demonstrate how the analysis of spatial dependence and spatial heterogeneity can add to a richer understanding of regional economic growth processes (Goodchild et al. 2000).

The study of regional inequality offers interesting contrasts to, as well as similarities with, the literature on regional convergence. Regional income inequality analysis has its origins in the study of personal income inequality. The latter is "a scalar numerical representation of the interpersonal differences in income within a given population" (Cowell 1995, 12). Kuznets (1955) hypothesized an inverted-U relationship between the level of development and personal income inequality. In early stages of development, the concentration of income-generating wealth in the hands of a subset of individuals in the population was seen as a required condition for the accumulation of capital that fueled the expansion of industrial activity. In subsequent stages of development, benefits of growth were passed on to other members of society as higher wages and increased income. Personal income inequality would then begin to slow and eventually decline.

Williamson (1965) applied the inverted-U pattern to the question of unequal regional development. Here the focus is on the distribution of regional incomes, and not the incomes of individuals. Initial concentrations of income in certain geographic regions were attributed to unequal natural resource endowments. Williamson argued that these concentrations attracted selective skilled labor migration from the peripheral regions and generated rapid income growth in the core regions. This led to widening differentials in per capita incomes between the core and peripheral regions. Over time, however, a diffusion of income-generating factors leads to the subsequent slowing and eventual decline in regional income inequality.

There has been a great deal of work investigating the inverted-U pattern of regional income inequality in national systems.[2] Most of this work relies on descriptive analysis using measures of dispersion in regional income distributions and relates these to a measure of development. This stands in marked contrast to work on regional economic convergence, where there has been a tight linkage between model specification and one or more growth theories. As a result, the empirical analysis of regional inequality relies more heavily on exploratory and descriptive methods, in contrast to the more confirmatory and inferential approaches in regional convergence studies.

An important similarity that the inequality literature shares with the convergence literature is a general neglect of the spatial dimensions of the data underlying the empirical analysis. More specifically, a number of issues associated with spatial effects in regional income inequality analysis remain overlooked by previous studies. These surround the relationship between regional inequality and spatial dependence, and the sensitivity of inferences on regional inequality to the choice of spatial scale. Moreover, applications of inequality analysis at the regional scale are currently lacking an inferential basis.

These neglected issues are important for both analytical and substantive reasons. Analytically, the extension of regional convergence analysis to fully consider spatial effects has provided important insights to regional growth processes. It remains to be seen if a similar result will hold for regional inequality analysis.

From a substantive perspective, spatial inequalities in income have been identified as a destabilizing force in societies throughout human history.[3] Space can also matter a great deal to policies targeted at reducing regional income disparities. As the work of Baker and Grosh (1994) has shown, not only is the question of the delineation of regional boundaries important, but the level of geographic unit chosen can have an influence on targeting outcomes. At the same time, the spatial distribution of regional incomes, as well as the degree of inequality, need to be considered jointly. This is because social tensions arising from income inequalities may be heightened by geographical concentration of poorer social groups.

As Zhang and Kanbur (2001) have argued, it is important to move beyond single scalar measures of inequality to consider more disaggregate movements within the income distribution. For example, it is possible that incomes become polarized across groups in a society. If incomes within each of these groups become similar, yet the differences among the mean incomes from each group increase, then an overall index of inequality can in fact decline while polarization increases. Although Zhang and Kanbur (2001) focus on personal income distributions, their concerns can be extended to the case of regional income distributions. A focus on the evolution of the overall measure of regional inequality could mask very important developments within the distribution. Some of these developments could have spatially explicit manifestations reflecting poverty traps (Esteban and Ray 1994), convergence clubs (Chatterji and Dewhurst 1996), and other forms of geographical clustering that are not captured by an overall regional inequality measure.

This chapter aims to contribute to the regional inequality literature by investigating several spatial dimensions that have been largely ignored. It focuses on three extensions of regional inequality analysis:

- an exploration of the relationship between regional inequality and spatial dependence,
- the analysis of the role of spatial scale and its impact on inequality measurement,
- alternative inferential strategies for regional inequality analysis.

The plan of this chapter is as follows. The next section provides an overview of recent work on regional inequality measurement. This is followed by a discussion of several issues related to the spatial characteristics of the data that have been largely overlooked in existing studies. The chapter presents an empirical investigation of some of these issues using data for the United States over the 1929–2000 period and concludes with a summary of the key findings.

Regional Inequality Analysis

Measurement

A wide number of inequality measures are available in the literature.[4] In regional inequality analysis, a popular choice has been Theil's inequality measure (Theil 1967), given as:

$$T = \sum_{i=1}^{n} s_i \log(ns_i) \tag{1}$$

where n is the number of regions, y_i is per capita income in region i, and:

$$s_i = y_i / \sum_{i=1}^{n} y_i. \tag{2}$$

T is bounded on the interval $[0, \log(n)]$, with 0 reflecting perfect equality (i.e., $y_i = y_j \forall i, j$), and a value of $\log(n)$ occurring when all the income is concentrated in one region. T measures systematic or, as what we shall refer to now as, global inequality incomes across the regional observations at one point in time.[5]

As T is a member of a generalized entropy class of inequality measures, it has the quality of being additively decomposable (Shorrocks 1984). This is desirable for both analytic and arithmetic reasons. Substantively, the ability to measure the contribution to global inequality (1) that is attributable to inequality between and within different partitions of the observational units can provide a deeper understanding of global inequality. For example, in studies of wage inequality, the partitions are sometimes defined according to industry groupings, such as manufacturing versus agriculture.

Mathematically, the decomposition is exhaustive, meaning that the global inequality is completely separated into the two components.

In studies of regional income inequality, the decompositional property has been exploited to investigate the extent to which global inequality is attributable to inequality "between" or "within" regional groupings.[6] By partitioning the n spatial observations into ω mutually exclusive and exhaustive groups, T can be decomposed as follows:

$$T = \sum_{g=1}^{\omega} s_g \log(n/n_g s_g) + \sum_{g=1}^{\omega} s_g \sum_{i \in g} s_{i,g} \log(n_g s_{i,g}) \tag{3}$$

where n_g is the number of observations in group g (and $\sum_g n_g = n$), $s_g = \sum_{i \in g} y_{i,g} / \sum_i^n y_i$ is the share of total income accounted for by group g, and $s_{i,g} = y_{i,g} / \sum_{i=1}^{n_g} y_{i,g}$ is region i's share of group g's income.

The first term on the right hand side of (3) is the "between-group" component of inequality, while the second term is the "within-group" component of inequality. In other words:

$$T = T_B + T_W. \tag{4}$$

In a spatial context, the within-group term measures intraregional inequality, while the between-group component captures interregional inequality. Put another way, the interregional term measures the distance between the mean incomes of the aggregate groups. The intraregional term measures distances between the incomes of regions belonging to the same group.

Existing Studies

Fan and Casetti (1994) analyzed United States income inequality using four Census Divisions to define the partitions of the states. The within-region component was found to account for the largest share of state income inequality over the 1950–1989 period. Using the same partitioning, but county rather than state data, Conceição and Ferreira (2000) also conclude that the within component of inequality was the most important share over the 1969–1996 period. Nissan and Carter (1999) analyzed state income inequality over the 1969–1995 period. A regional inequality decomposition was employed for the states as a whole, as well as for the subset of metropolitan and the subset of rural states. Inequality between regions was found to decline in the early 1970s, but increased through the 1980s, followed again by convergence in the 1990s. At the same time, they found strong evidence that within-region inequality showed a much stronger decline over the study period. This was true for all states, as well as metropolitan and rural states.

Inequality decomposition has been applied in several regional analyses outside of the United States as well. Fujita and Hu (2001) analyzed regional income disparities in China over the 1984–1994 period, using a coastal-interior partitioning of 30 provinces. They find that overall regional inequality was fairly stable, exhibiting a slight decline in the 1980s. The overall decline was driven by the decline in intraregional inequality, the latter being larger than interregional inequality until the last three years of their sample, accounting for between 77 percent and 43 percent of overall inequality.

Azzoni (2001) explored inequality in 20 Brazilian states over the 1939–1995 period. Overall regional inequality was substantial up until 1965, at which point a steady decrease began. Partitioning the states into 5 groups revealed that interregional inequality was the most important contributor to overall regional disparities. Moreover, the interregional component accounted for an increasing share of total inequality, starting from 60 percent and ending at 87 percent.

Geographical decomposition of inequality has been applied at the international as well as intranational scale. Theil (1996) applied a decompositional analysis to 100 countries over 1950–1990 and found that the majority (roughly 88%) of global inequality was due to differences between, rather than within, regional groupings of countries. In a similar study Levy and Chowdhury (1995) report that the relative importance of the two components has varied over the 1960–1990 period, with the between-region component dominating from 1960–1967, the within region component being larger from 1967–1983, and a second reversal from 1983–1990.

These studies have illuminated the spatial structure underlying the dynamics of regional inequality in different contexts. However, there is much variation across the studies with respect to the relative importance of the interregional versus intraregional inequality components. What is currently unknown, however, is to what extent that variation is due to differences in the structure of the economies in the different studies or to the articulation of methodological issues across the studies. These issues include the choice of regional partitioning and the spatial scale of the observational units.

At the same time there are several limitations in these studies having to do with a lack of an inferential basis that require additional attention. Moreover, it is possible that much more can be said about the geographical dimensions of regional inequality. In the remainder of the chapter these issues are more fully discussed, and an initial attempt at addressing these concerns is presented.

Spatial Effects in Regional Inequality Analysis

Spatial Dependence

Spatial dependence occurs when the values for some phenomenon measured at one location are associated with the values measured at other locations (Anselin 1988). The issues that spatial dependence raise for econometric analysis of regional income convergence have received recent attention (Fingleton 2003; Rey and Montouri 1999), yet the role of spatial dependence in studies of regional inequality has been largely ignored.

The issues associated with spatial dependence may be conveniently split into two groups. From a substantive perspective, spatial dependence can play an important role in shaping the geographical distribution of incomes. From a nuisance perspective, spatial dependence can complicate the application of traditional statistical methods designed to analyze regional inequality.

Lucas (1993) suggests a model that allows for cross-economy interactions in the form of human capital spillovers. The presence of these spillovers (i.e., learning by doing) can radically alter the patterns of cross-economy growth from those suggested by a traditional neoclassical growth model. The basic idea is that if economies interact via human capital spillovers, and if the interacting economies form groups, it is likely that within-group spillovers will be stronger than between-group spillovers. This would result in within-group convergence but, potentially, divergence between groups.

From a nuisance perspective, the presence of spatial dependence presents a challenge to the use of statistical inference in inequality analysis. This is because the existing approaches to inference are based on an assumption of random sampling which is violated by the presence of spatial dependence. This issue is taken up further below. Spatial dependence of a nuisance form can also arise from a mismatch between the regional boundaries used to organize the data and the boundaries of the actual socioeconomic process under study. In regional inequality analysis, this could be reflected in a misspecified partitioning, whereby the partitioning imposed by the researcher fails to match the natural groupings of the regional observations.

Interestingly, global inequality measures are insensitive to the underlying spatial distribution of the income values. This reflects a focus on the dispersion of the distribution only. This also brings up an intriguing question regarding the relationship between the level of spatial dependence in regional incomes and spatial income inequality. At first glance it would appear that strong positive spatial autocorrelation would lead to increasing global inequality, given that we would be able to see clusters of similar incomes on a map. However, the analysis of spatial autocorrelation rests on the assumption of spatial stationarity. Loosely speaking, this requires the mean and variance of the distribution to be constant over space. At the same time, it is well known that the presence of spatial dependence can induce a form of heteroskedasticity in the error terms of spatial econometric models (Anselin 1988). The question then becomes one of being able to disentangle any apparent spatial heterogeneity induced by the dependence, from true heterogeneity reflecting a lack of spatial stationarity. This would allow one to distinguish between increasing inequality owing to increasing variance in a distribution versus inequality attributable to the mixing of different distributions.

Spatial Scale in Regional Convergence Analysis

As is well known in other areas of spatial analysis, the modifiable areal unit problem (MAUP) arises when the inferences drawn about the process under study are sensitive to the spatial scale and partitioning of the data at hand (Openshaw and Alvanides 1999). Given the wide scope for selecting a spatial partitioning as well as the unit of observation in regional inequality analysis, it would appear that the MAUP would attract much attention. This, however, has not been the case.

That inequality measures will be subject to the MAUP can be seen by an examination of the bounds for the the global T. The theoretical upper bound of T is $\log(n)$. Any change in spatial scale, say from the state level to the county level, will change the number of observational units and affect the upper bound of the statistic. The question of how this affects the comparison of inferences drawn about inequality at the two different scales has gone unexamined in the literature.

In addition to affecting the upper bound of the global T, a change in spatial scale may also impact the decomposition of the global measure into its intra and interregional components. Here again, this issue has been neglected in previous regional studies. These issues are taken up in the empirical analysis.

Inferential Issues

In regional applications of inequality measures the focus is typically on a descriptive analysis, either reporting the value of the measure at one point in time, tracking the statistic over time, or decomposing global regional inequality into its intra and interregional shares. An important omission in the regional literature is the use of inferential methods that allow for formal hypothesis testing regarding inequality measures. There are several interesting hypotheses regarding regional inequality that could be examined from an inferential perspective:

- Is the coefficient different from what would be expected under perfect regional equality?
- Is any empirical change in an inequality measure over time significantly different from zero?
- Is the share of intraregional inequality significantly different from some hypothesized value?
- In comparing two (or more) economic systems over time (i.e., the United States versus the European Union) is the difference in regional inequality significant?
- Are the within- and between-regional inequality components significantly different between the two systems?

In the wider inequality literature two general approaches towards inference have been used. The first rests on theoretical results regarding the asymptotic distributions of different inequality statistics (Maasoumi 1997). Application of these results to the small samples used in most regional settings is problematic for two main reasons. First, the inequality statistics are typically truncated at 0. Use of asymptotic standard errors to construct confidence intervals around the empirical value for the statistic may produce inadmissible interval bounds. The second problem is that the small sample properties of these statistics are unknown, and as such, the usefulness of asymptotic results is uncertain.

The second approach to inference in inequality analysis rests on computational procedures. Mills and Zandvakili (1997) suggest the use of a bootstrap to construct empirical sampling distributions for inequality measures. At first glance this may appear to offer a way to introduce an inferential component into regional inequality analysis. Unfortunately, regional income data often display a high degree of spatial autocorrelation (Rey and Montouri 1999). The presence of such dependence violates the random sampling assumption at the heart of the bootstrap methodology. A similar difficulty applies to the asymptotic results.[7]

Because the presence of spatial dependence rules out the use of asymptotics or bootstrapping, an alternative approach to inference is required. The approach suggested here is based on random spatial permutations of the actual incomes for a given map pattern. This can be used to test hypotheses regarding the decomposition of global inequality into its interregional and intraregional components. This is accomplished with the following steps:

1. Calculate decomposition:

$$T^* = T_W^* + T_B^* \tag{5}$$

2. Randomly reassign incomes to new locations.

3. Calculate decomposition for permutated map:

$$T^P = T_W^P + T_B^P \tag{6}$$

4. Repeat steps 2 and 3, K times.

The values for the global inequality measure T^P will be the same for any permutation in a given time period. Because the observations are being randomly reassigned to different regional groupings in each permutation, however, the values for the intraregional (T_W^P) and interregional (T_B^P) are likely to vary across the permutations. The actual inequality measure T_W^* can then be compared against the value it would have been expected to take on if regional incomes were randomly distributed in space. The latter would be obtained as the average of the empirically generated measures from Step 3:

$$\bar{T}_W = \frac{1}{K} \sum_{P=1}^{K} T_W^P \tag{7}$$

Differences between the actual statistic and its expected value could be compared against the empirical sampling distribution in one of two ways. The first would be based on the assumption that the empirical sampling distribution is approximately normal, in which case the standard deviation for that distribution, given as:

$$s_{T_W} = \frac{1}{K} \sum_{P=1}^{K} \left(T_W^P - \bar{T}_W \right)^2 \tag{8}$$

could be used to define a confidence interval.

The second approach to inference using the random spatial permutations is to use a percentile approach. This simply sorts the empirically generated T_W^P values and then develops a pseudo significance level by calculating the share of the empirical values that are more extreme than the actual value:

$$p(T_W) = \frac{1}{K} \sum_{P=1}^{K} \psi_P \tag{9}$$

where $\psi_P = 1$ if T_W^P is more extreme than T_W, $\psi_P = 0$ otherwise. The advantage of this approach over the first is that the problem of inadmissible interval bounds is avoided.

The permutation approach provides a framework from which inferences about the relative importance of the interregional and intraregional components of global inequality can be drawn. Because the global inequality measure is invariant to the spatial arrangement of regional incomes, the random permutation approach cannot be used to test inferences regarding the global measure. Future work will focus on developing methods of inference for the global measure in the presence of spatial dependence. Such methods will also be required for the comparison of the inequality components across regional systems with different levels of global inequality.

Empirical Illustration

To explore some of these issues we focus on United States per capita income over the 1929–2000 period for the 48 lower states.[8] Attention is first directed towards the relationship between regional income inequality and spatial dependence. This is followed by an analysis of how changes in spatial scale may affect the measures of regional inequality. Finally, approaches to statistical inference in regional inequality analysis are examined.[9,10]

Inequality and Spatial Dependence

Figure 14.1 portrays the relationship between regional inequality and spatial autocorrelation. Inequality is measured using the global T from (1). Clearly, the long-term trend has been one of declining regional income inequality in the United States, with the majority of the decline coming during the war years in the early 1940s. A slight turnaround toward increasing regional inequality is seen through the 1980s, for which numerous explanations have been put forth (Amos 1988; Fan and Casetti 1994). However, these explanations focus on United States specific causes and ignore the presence of a similar turnaround in other national systems occurring during the same period (Paci and Pigliaru 1997).

Spatial autocorrelation is measured using Moran's I, defined as:

$$I = \frac{n}{\sum_i \sum_j w_{ij}} \frac{\sum_i \sum_j w_{ij} (y_i - \bar{y}) (y_j - \bar{y})}{\sum_i (y_i - \bar{y})^2} \tag{10}$$

where $w_{i,j}$ is an element of a binary spatial contiguity matrix with elements taking on the value of 1 if states i and j are first-order neighbors (i.e., share a border), 0 otherwise. y_i is per capita income in state i and $\bar{y}$ is the average per capita income for the 48 states. Moran's I has an expected value and variance that are function of the structure of the spatial weights matrix only, and are not influenced by the value of the variate in question. As such the moments of I are constant each year: $E[I] = -0.213$, $V[I] = 0.009$.[11] Basing inference regarding I on a normality assumption results in the statistic being significant in each year in this sample. Thus, personal incomes are highly autocorrelated across the states.

Figure 14.1 also reveals a strong positive relationship between the inequality measure and the autocorrelation index. The simple correlation between these two statistics over the 72 years is 0.798. It should be noted, however, that a simple re-shuffling of the actual income values about the map for a given year would leave the measure of inequality unchanged, while Moran's I would vary. This highlights the difference in emphasis between the two statistics and suggests that their joint application to the analysis of regional income growth might produce important complementarities offering insights not obtainable when either is used in isolation.

Figure 14.2 displays the global T and its decomposition into the interregional and intraregional components. The partitioning of the 48 states is based on the United States Census Regions which are defined in Table 14.1. This is the same partitioning as used in Fan and Casetti (1994), although our sample includes a larger number of years. In

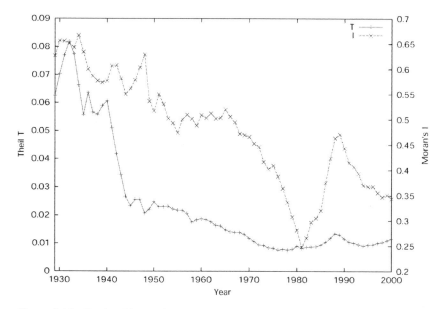

Figure 14.1. Regional inequality and spatial dependence: U.S. states.

each of the 72 years, the intraregional component exceeds that of the interregional share. These results are in agreement with those reported by Fan and Casetti (1994).

Figure 14.3 shows the effect of changing the partitioning scheme from the four Census regions to the nine Census Divisions, as defined in Table 14.2. The relative importance of the two components of inequality is reversed, with the interregional component now dominating. This reflects an increase in the internal homogeneity of the regions, largely due to the decrease in the number of states found in each region.

Figure 14.4 shows the effect of changing the partitioning scheme to the eight regions defined by the Bureau of Economic Analysis (BEA) and listed in Table 14.3.

Table 14.1. Census Regions.

Region	States
Northeast	Connecticut, Maine, Massachusetts, New Hampshire, New Jersey, New York, Pennsylvania, Rhode Island, Vermont
Midwest	Illinois, Indiana, Iowa, Kansas, Michigan, Minnesota, Missouri, Nebraska, North Dakota, Ohio, South Dakota, Wisconsin
South	Alabama, Arkansas, Delaware, Florida, Georgia, Kentucky, Louisiana, Maryland, Mississippi, North Carolina, Oklahoma, South Carolina, Tennessee, Texas, Virginia, West Virginia
West	Arizona, California, Colorado, Idaho, Wyoming, Nevada, New Mexico, Oregon, Utah, Washington, Wyoming

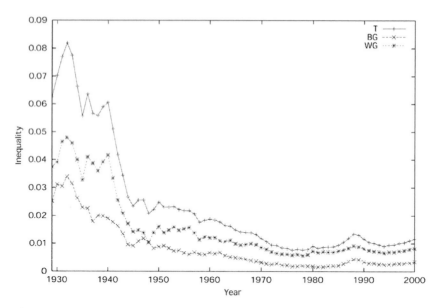

Figure 14.2. Regional inequality decomposition: Census Regions.

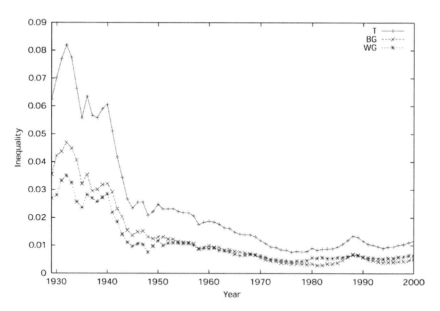

Figure 14.3. Regional inequality decomposition: Census Divisions.

Table 14.2. Census Divisions.

Division	States
Northeast	Connecticut, Maine, Massachusetts, New Hampshire, Rhode Island, Vermont
Middle Atlantic	New Jersey, New York, Pennsylvania
East North Central	Illinois, Indiana, Michigan, Ohio, Wisconsin
West North Central	Iowa, Kansas, Minnesota, Missouri, Nebraska, North Dakota, South Dakota
South Atlantic	Delaware, Florida, Georgia, Maryland, North Carolina, South Carolina, Virginia, West Virginia
East South Central	Alabama, Kentucky, Mississippi, Tennessee
West South Central	Arkansas, Louisiana, Oklahoma, Texas
Mountain	Arizona, Colorado, Idaho, Montana, Nevada, New Mexico, Utah, Wyoming
Pacific	California, Oregon, Washington

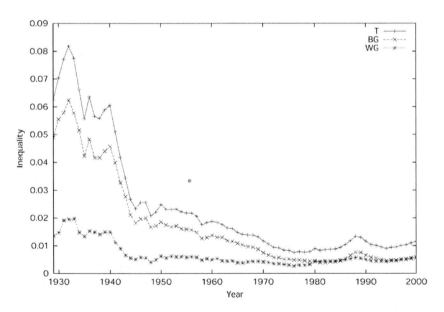

Figure 14.4. Regional inequality decomposition: BEA Regions.

Table 14.3. BEA Regions.

Region	States
Northeast	Connecticut, Maine, Massachusetts, New Hampshire, Rhode Island, Vermont
Mideast	Delaware, Maryland, New Jersey, New York, Pennsylvania
Great Lakes	Illinois, Indiana, Michigan, Ohio, Wisconsin
Plains	Iowa, Kansas, Minnesota, Missouri, Nebraska, North Dakota, South Dakota
Southeast	Alabama, Arkansas, Florida, Georgia, Kentucky, Louisiana, Mississippi, North Carolina, South Carolina, Tennessee, Virginia, West Virginia
Southwest	Arizona, New Mexico, Oklahoma, Texas
Rocky Mountains	Colorado, Idaho, Montana, Utah, Wyoming
Far West	California, Nevada, Oregon, Washington

The reversal in the relative importance of the two components of inequality is even more pronounced. Although there is a high degree of similarity between the Census Divisions and the BEA Regions, the interregional inequality component is substantially higher in the latter partitioning. Moreover, the share claimed by the interregional component using the BEA Regions in the first half of the study period is higher than that claimed by the intraregional component during the same period when the Census Divisions are used.

These interregional components are isolated in Figure 14.5, revealing the much higher interregional share each year in the sample when the partitioning is based on the BEA regions. The larger number of groups in the BEA Regions and Census Divisions relative to the Census Regions explains why the former have larger interregional components than the latter. However, the BEA Regions have higher interregional inequality than the Census Divisions, despite having a smaller number of groups of states. Consequently, the interregional share is not a simple function of the number of regional groupings used.

The rankings of the three partitions with respect to the share of total inequality claimed by the interregional component is consistent across the entire 72-year period, with the BEA scheme at the top and the Census Region partition at the bottom. Because an increase in the interregional inequality is due to differences in the mean values becoming more important than intraregional differences, the patterns in Figure 14.5 suggest that the homogeneity of the BEA regions is stronger than that found in the other two sets of regions.

In comparing the results across these three partitions of the states, it is important to keep in mind that the number and definitions of the groupings of states varies, while the number of states is held constant. Variation in the number of areal units being grouped would complicate the comparison of global inequality measures across the three different partitions. With the number of states fixed across the three regionalization schemes, insights as to the relative importance of the interregional and intraregional inequality components are made possible.

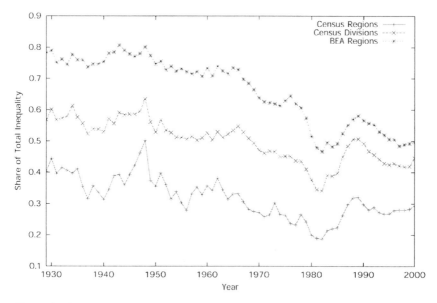

Figure 14.5. Interregional inequality components.

Despite the differences in magnitudes, all three partitions yield interregional inequality shares that are generally declining over time. This general decline was also seen in both the global inequality measure and the level of spatial dependence in Figure 14.1. The three interregional inequality series also display an increase during the 1980s, which is much more pronounced than was the case for the global inequality measure. This coincides with the sharp increase displayed by Moran's I in Figure 14.1. In fact, each of the interregional inequality shares has a strong positive correlation with the measure of spatial dependence. [12]

Spatial Scale and Regional Inequality

The results from the previous section indicate that the choice of the partition can fundamentally change the inequality decomposition, both quantitatively and qualitatively. In this section, attention shifts to the effect that a change in the spatial scale of the observational unit may have on the inferences regarding inequality. This is accomplished by using county rather than state data for the 48 lower states.

Moving to the county level of analysis required a truncation of the time series that could be considered. Annual data on per capita income was only available from 1969 through 1999. Despite this shorter time period, the use of counties as the observational units has two important benefits. First, it vastly increases the number of spatial units, from 48 states to 3079 counties. The second benefit is that a fourth level of partitioning can now be used, as the counties can be assigned to their states, while the states are nested in the three partitions examined in the previous section.

Figure 14.6 plots the interregional inequality shares for the counties using these

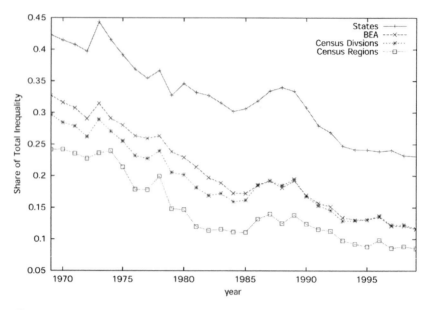

Figure 14.6. Interregional inequality: County unit of observation.

four partitions. The most striking pattern is the substantially higher share found for the state partition compared to those for the other three. Intuitively, this reflects the stronger homogeneity of the states.[13] The relative ranking of the three other partitions is in general agreement with that found when the states were the unit of analysis, although the pattern is less clear from 1995 onward.

An important difference between the state and county level analysis is that the intraregional inequality component dominates the global decomposition at the county scale. This is true for all of the four partitions. When using the states as the unit of observation, the only partition for which the intraregional component was the largest each year was the Census Regions (see Figure 14.5). For the BEA regions and Census Divisions, the interregional share was the largest for the majority of the years, again using states. If the focus is on the post-1969 period, the interregional component remains dominant for the states only for the BEA regions partition.

Inference

The final issue examined is the role of inference in regional inequality analysis. This is an important issue, as often interest centers on how much inequality the particular decomposition accounts for. Cowell and Jenkins (1995) suggest a simple measure to get at this question:

$$R(B) = T_B/T \tag{11}$$

where T_B and T are as defined above, and $R(B)$ is the share of inequality accounted for by the between group component. This is similar to the polarization index recently suggested by Zhang and Kanbur (2001):

$$P = T_B / T_W \qquad (12)$$

Unfortunately, neither of these studies developed an inferential basis against which the measures could be evaluated, and instead used their measure in a descriptive fashion. At this point it could be asked why inference is needed, since the dominance of one component over the other is sometimes readily apparent; for example, the interregional component for the states using the Census Region partition is dominated by the intraregional share (See Figure 14.2). The response is that this question misses an important point. Finding that the interregional component accounts for a smaller share of global inequality should not be taken to mean that the interregional component is irrelevant, or that the partition that it is based upon is somehow erroneous. The question should instead be rephrased as follows: "For a given partition and spatial scale of observation, is the interregional share observed different from what could be expected by random chance?"

Figure 14.7 provides an answer to this question. It depicts the actual value of the interregional inequality component for the states using the Census Regions as the partition. Also shown are the error bars associated with ± 2 standard deviations around the average values for the shares from 1,000 random spatial permutations of the incomes for each year. In each year of the sample, the interregional share is significantly greater than what would be expected if incomes were randomly distributed in space. This re-

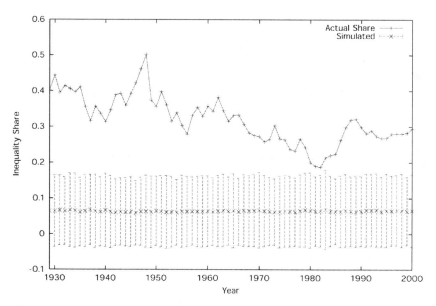

Figure 14.7. Simulated versus actual interregional inequality, Census Regions: State unit of observation.

sult is of particular interest, as it was the Census Regions partition that had a smaller interregional share relative to its intraregional share. By extending the traditional decompositional analysis to include an inferential component we find that, although this interregional inequality component is relatively small, the Census Regions do capture some aspect of spatial structure. Without the inferential test, this partition might have been viewed as irrelevant or misspecified, given that the interregional share was found to be stronger in the other partitions.

Conclusion

In their overview of recent empirical work on economic growth, Durlauf and Quah (1999) conclude that the field remains in its infancy. One sign of increasing maturity is the recent attention given to the geographical dimensions of economic growth (Barro and Sala-i-Martin 1991; Krugman 1991; Nijkamp and Poot 1998). Application of recently developed methods of spatial econometrics to the question of regional convergence has yielded a more comprehensive and multidimensional view of regional economic growth (Goodchild et al. 2000).

The literature on regional income inequality, although somewhat older than the convergence literature, has been slower to adopt new spatially explicit methods of data analysis. This chapter has attempted to contribute to such an adoption by investigating the role of spatial dependence and spatial scale in the analysis of regional income inequality in the United States over the 1929–2000 period. The key findings with regard to spatial dependence include:

- A strong positive relationship between measures of inequality in state incomes and the degree of spatial autocorrelation.
- A strong positive relationship between the interregional inequality share (as opposed to intraregional inequality) and spatial clustering.

The analysis of the role of the spatial scale of the observational unit and the choice of regional partitioning of the units revealed the following:

- The qualitative and quantitative results of inequality decomposition are highly sensitive to the scale of the observational unit. Interregional inequality is dominant when state data are used, yet intraregional inequality is most important when county level data are used.
- The relative importance of the interregional inequality component is *not* a simple function of the number of groups used in a partitioning of the regional observations.

Finally, the study also suggested an approach to inference in the decomposition analysis of regional income inequality, offering an important complement to the existing literature that has relied exclusively on descriptive methods.

Notes

1. For a recent survey of empirical work on convergence see Durlauf and Quah (1999).
2. Alonso (19-80); Amos (1983); Maxwell and Peter (1988); Tsui (1993); Fan and Casetti

(1994); Kanbur and Zhang (1999); Nissan and Carter (1999); Azzoni (2001); Zhang and Kanbur (2001).

3. "Large income and wealth differences between countries and regions generated acts of aggression which inflicted considerable human suffering, loss of resources and knowledge, destruction of civilizations and environmental damage" (Levy and Chowdgury 1995, 17).

4. See Cowell (1995) for a recent overview.

5. In what follows, time subscripts are omitted unless explicitly noted.

6. The decomposition has also been used to study the contribution of different components of income, such as transfer payments versus wages, and how regional inequalities in these components contribute to overall regional inequality. See for example Eff (1999).

7. In testing for changes in personal income inequality indices over time, the two temporal samples may be dependent, since the same individuals may be included in both periods. The focus here is on testing a single regional distribution at one point in time, so this issue is not addressed. For further details see Zheng and Cushing (2001).

8. The state and county income data used in this study were obtained from the 3 May 2001 release of the BEA state and local personal income series.

9. The empirical analysis was carried out using the package STARS (Rey 2001).

10. Excellent surveys of the historical events and policies influencing United States regional income dynamics are provided by Easterlin (1960), Williamson (1965), and Coughlin and Mandelbaum (1988).

11. For the detailed expressions for the moments of I under the normality assumption, see Cliff and Ord (1973).

12. The correlations with Moran's I are: 0.63 (Census Regions), 0.66 (Census Divisions), and 0.64 (BEA Regions).

13. In the limiting case when the number of groups is equal to n, intraregional inequality vanishes as global inequality becomes equivalent to interregional inequality. This is because each group would contain only a single state.

References

Alonso, W. 1980. Five bell shapes in regional development. *Papers of the Regional Science Association* 45: 5–16.

Amos, Jr., O. 1983. The relationship betwen personal income inequality, regional income inequality, and development. *Regional Science Perspectives* 13: 3–14.

Amos, Jr., O. 1988. Unbalanced regional growth and regional income inequality in the latter stages of development. *Regional Science and Urban Economics* 18: 549–566.

Anselin, L. 1988. *Spatial Econometrics: Methods and Models*. Boston: Kluwer.

Armstrong, H., and R. Vickerman. 1995. *Convergence and Divergence Among European Regions*. London: Pion.

Azzoni, C.R. 2001. Economic growth and income inequality in Brazil. *Annals of Regional Science* 311: 133–152.

Baker, J.L., and M.E. Grosh. 1994. Measuring the effects of geographic targeting on poverty reduction. *World Bank Living Standards Measurement Study*. Washington, D.C.: The World Bank.

Barro, R., and X. Sala-i-Martin. 1991. Convergence across states and regions. *Brookings Papers on Economic Activity* 1: 107–182.

Chatterji, M., and J. Dewhurst. 1996. Convergence clubs and relative economic performance in Great Britan. *Regional Studies* 30: 31–40.

Cliff, A., and J. Ord. 1973. *Spatial Autocorrelation*. London: Pion.

Conceição, P. and Ferreira, P. 2000. The young person's guide to the Theil index: Suggesting intuitive interpretations and exploring analytical applications. University of Texas Inequality Project Working Paper 14.

Coughlin, C.C., and T.B. Mandelbaum. 1988. Why have state per-capita incomes diverged recently? *Review of the Federal Reserve Bank of St. Louis* 70: 24–36.

Cowell, F.A. 1995. *Measuring Inequality*. London: Prentice Hall.

Cowell, F.A., and S.P. Jenkins. 1995. How much inequality can we explain? Methodology and an application to the United States. *The Economic Journal* 105429: 421–430.

Cuadrado-Roura, J., B. Garcia-Greciano, and J. Raymond. 1999. Regional convergence in productivity and productivity structure: The Spanish case. *International Regional Science Review* 22: 35–53.

Durlauf, S.N., and D.T. Quah. 1999. The new empirics of economic growth. In J.B. Taylor and M. Woodford, (ed.), *Handbook of Macroeconomics: Volume 1A*. Amsterdam: Elsevier. 235–308.

Easterlin, R. 1960. Regional growth of income. In S. Kuznets, A. Miller, and R. Easterlin, (eds.), *Population redistribution and economic growth in the United States, 1870–1950*. Philadelphia: American Philosophical Society.

Eff, E.A. 1999. Myrdal contra Ohlin: Accounting for sources of U.S. county per capita income convergence using a flexible decomposition approach. *Review of Regional Studies* 291: 13–36.

Esteban, J.-M. and D. Ray. 1994. On the measurement of polarization. *Econometrica* 624: 819–851.

Fan, C.C., and E. Casetti. 1994. The spatial and temporal dynamics of US regional income inequality, 1950-1989. *Annals of Regional Science* 28: 177–196.

Fingleton, B. 1999. Estimates of time to economic convergence: An analysis of regions of the Eurpean Union. *International Regional Science Review* 22: 5–35.

Fingleton, B. 2003. Regional economic growth and convergence: insights from a spatial econometric perspective. In L. Anselin, R. Florax, and S.J. Rey. (eds.), *Advances in Spatial Econometrics*. Berlin: Springer-Verlag. Forthcoming.

Fujita, M., and D. Hu. 2001. Regional disparity in China 1985–1994: The effects of globalization and economic liberalization. *Annals of Regional Science* 35: 3–37.

Goodchild, M., L. Anselin, R. Applebaum, and B.H. Harthorn. 2000. Towards a spatially integrated social science. *International Regional Science Review* 23: 139–159.

Kanbur, R., and X. Zhang. 1999. Which regional inequality? The evolution of rural-urban and inland-coastal inequality in China, 1983-1995. *Journal of Comparative Economics* 27: 686–701.

Krugman, P. 1991. *Geography and Trade*. Cambridge: MIT Press.

Kuznets, S. 1955. Economic growth and income equality. *American Economic Review* 45: 1–28.

Levy, A., and K. Chowdhury. 1995. A geographical decomposition of intercountry income inequality. *Comparative Economic Studies* 37: 1–17.

Lucas, R.E. 1993. Making a miracle. *Econometrica* 612: 251–271.

Maasoumi, E. 1997. Empirical analysis of inequality and welfare. In M. Pesaran and P. Schmnidt, (eds.), *Handbook of Applied Econometrics, Volume II, Microeconomics*. London: Blackwell Publishers Ltd. 202–245.

Maxwell, P., and M. Peter. 1988. Income inequality in small regions: A study of Australian statistical divisions. *The Review of Regional Studies* 18: 19–27.

Mills, J.A., and S. Zandvakili. 1997. Statistical inference via bootstrapping for measures of inequality. *Journal of Applied Econometrics* 122: 133–150.

Nijkamp, P., and J. Poot. 1998. Spatial perspectives on new theories of economic growth. *Annals of Regional Science* 32: 407–437.

Nissan, E., and G. Carter. 1999. Spatial and temporal metropolitan and nonmetropolitan trends in income inequality. *Growth and Change* 303: 407–415.

Opensaw, S. and S. Alvanides. 1999. Applying geocomputation to the anaylsis of spatial distributions. In P. Longley, M. Goodchild, D. Maguire, and D. Rhind, (eds.) *Geographic Information Systems Volume I: Principles and Technical Issues*. New York: John Wiley. 267–282.

Paci, F., and F. Pigliaru. 1997. Structural change and convergence: An Italian perspective. *Structural Change and Economic Dynamics* 8: 297–318.

Rey, S.J. 2001. Space-time analysis of regional systems: STARS. Technical report, Department of Geography, San Diego State University.

Rey, S.J., and B.D. Montouri. 1999. U.S. regional income convergence: A spatial econometric perspective. *Regional Studies* 33: 143–156.

Shorrocks, A.F. 1984. Inequality decomposition by population subgroups. *Econometrica* 526: 1369–1385.

Theil, H. 1967. *Economics and Information Theory*. Amsterdam: North Holland.

Theil, H. 1996. *Studies in Global Econometrics*. Dordrecht: Kluwer Academic Publishers.

Tsui, K.Y. 1993. Decomposition of China's regional inequalities. *Journal of Comparative Economics* 17: 600–627.

Williamson, J. 1965. Regional inequality and the process of national development. *Economic Development and Cultural Change* 4: 3–47.

Zhang, X., and R. Kanbur. 2001. What difference do polarisation measures make? An application to China. *Journal of Development Studies* 37: 85–98.

Zheng, B., and B.J. Cushing. 2001. Statistical inference for testing inequality indices with dependent samples. *Journal of Econometrics* 101: 315–335.

15

Shaping Policy Decisions
with Spatial Analysis

Ted K. Bradshaw
Brian Muller

S patial analysis has been a part of urban and land use planning at least
since the 1960s. In certain arenas, such as transportation planning and
preparation of comprehensive plans, local governments and land use agencies have
come to rely heavily on spatial data (Harris and Batty 1993). Until recently, analytical
applications were concentrated in a few areas such as demand modeling under federal
transportation statutes. During the 1990s, however, adoption of GIS technologies in
public agencies, and creation of GIS-based resource and asset inventories, expanded
the scope of analytical opportunities. A new generation of applications has emerged
with branches in many fields. These applications have the potential to capture more
effectively the complexity and interconnectedness of policy problems facing officials
and planners. Researchers, planners, and software vendors are making significant new
claims for the feasibility and value of applying spatial research to policy problems
(Brail and Klosterman 2001; Kammeier 1998; Roper and Muller 2002).

There are several perspectives on the rate and manner in which spatial analytical
methods are adopted in policy and planning. One perspective focuses on the potential uses of expanded technological capacity, such as processing speeds, memory and
storage; the emergence of the web; and development of software such as relational
databases. A key factor in this technological evolution is the growing versatility of
spatial software. Spatial technology has proven to be a "big tent" that can support a
range of analytical practices and theoretical frameworks. As the technology evolves,
new analytical opportunities and relationships to policy processes are uncovered, such
as multiplying types of resource suitability analysis. The strength of spatial technologies, ultimately, may lie precisely in their capacity to encompass and integrate varied
policy applications (Krygier 1998). With respect to the Web, researchers are interested
in its capacities for on-line analytical processing and collaborative planning methods

supported by multimedia applications (Carlson and Turban 2002; Shiffer 1995; Shim et al. 2002). From a more critical stance, researchers are concerned about the usability of spatial tools and social psychological issues regarding the interaction between humans and computers (Beynon et al. 2002). User-oriented problems include cognitive limitations, emotional responses such as frustration, and suitability of technical support (Carlson and Turban 2002).

A second perspective concerns the evolving structure of problems in urban, environmental, and land use arenas. These problems are often highly complex in terms of the number of factors that need to be considered, and they are ambiguous with respect to selection, ranking, and interaction of these factors. Some of this complexity is inherently spatial; for example, environmental impact assessment practitioners have a growing interest in analysis of cumulative, spillover, and equity effects. Moreover, complex decision environments pose an opportunity for use of computational tools that integrate multi-attribute assessment of diverse effects. Other types of problems may be less suited to analysis based in GIS (Hopkins 1999). In addition, a major effort has evolved to overcome the limitations in simplistic use of techniques such as descriptive images or linear impact assessment (Beynon et al. 2002; Montazemi et al. 1996). A significant accomplishment in this area (and one which is demonstrated below) is the integration of locally developed, policy-relevant information into models that have typically been based on standardized and published data. Because of the complexity of spatial problems as they appear in real policy environments, modelers interested in creating useable policy applications are often confronted by the need to collect messy, qualitative data, such as descriptions of jurisdictional objectives and administrative practices, spatially-related cost factors, producer or resident evaluations of environmental processes, and community values or interests.

A third approach in this literature focuses on the relationship between spatial analysis and changing organizational structures and institutional systems. Research in this framework tends to emphasize the parallel evolution of analytical sciences and social practices (Innes and Simpson 1993). In part, statutes and administrative practices that create new demands for spatial analysis guide this parallel evolution. For example, the 1991 Intermodal Surface Transportation Efficiency Act (ISTEA) requires that Metropolitan Planning Organizations develop integrated land use–transportation models (Johnston and Shabazian 2002). Guidelines for the National Environmental Policy Act (NEPA) indicate that agencies should evaluate secondary and cumulative effects of major federal projects, such as spatially proximate spillover impacts from highway development. Organizational factors, such as leadership and management structure, may also influence the rate and manner in which spatial analysis is adopted by local planning agencies (Budic 1994; Nedovic-Budic 1998).

A fourth research perspective concerns public participation and the contribution of spatial technologies to collaborative and advocacy planning (Shim et al. 2002; Simonovic and Bender 1996). There are several ways in which spatial analysis can become a vehicle for enhanced participation (Harris et al. 1995). First, residents can participate in agenda-setting, including involvement in research design. Second, residents can participate in data collection based on local knowledge of conditions and social or natural processes (Talen 1998). Finally, planning support systems provide a mechanism to help citizens comment on plans and assess alternatives (Roper and Muller

2002). Some researchers argue that planning support systems can usher in a new and invigorated mode of democracy (Redburn and Buss 2002).

Human ecology and urban microeconomic theories underpin much of the work in spatial analysis undertaken by policy researchers over the past few decades. Urban ecological spaces are organized through the interaction of social communities and microsystems across a defined geography, such as a metropolitan region or a neighborhood. In ecological analysis, policy problems are described according to spatial distributions within and between these communities. Social events are interdependent across space: changes in one component have cascading impacts on other components. Microeconomic spatial analysis assumes a similar form of spatial competition, although rooted in evaluation of location and transportation costs, economic equilibration, and decision-making by individual homeowners, developers, commuters, public managers, and others actors. For each of these approaches, the spatial distributions of such factors as infrastructure and service costs, environmental impact, or livability provide the basis for important policy tools.

Beginning in the 1970s, the growing use of spatial analysis has been accompanied by criticisms from multiple directions. One body of criticism follows from Lee's skepticism about the efficacy of modeling and its appropriateness to planning problems (Harris 1998; Lee 1994). Another type of criticism flows from the commentary among planners and geographers about potential social and political impacts from the adoption of geographic information systems (Harris and Weiner 1998; Obermeyer 1998; Sheppard 1995). A third criticism concerns social theory underlying spatial analysis, expressed sharply in the argument that microeconomic and social ecological description fails to capture the significant dimensions of social space (Castells 1977; Scott 1980). Other issues include data availability, difficulty in obtaining consensus, limits to organizational capacity, and rate of change in planning institutions (Batty 1994; Kammeier 1998). The enthusiasm for the recent wave of spatial methods is tempered by a general sense of uncertainty among planners about the effectiveness of scientific approaches, "reflecting a more conservative and less ambitious quest for a science of planning than those of a generation earlier" (Batty 1994).

In this chapter we explore issues in the use of spatial analysis to address urban and land use policy problems at the state and local level. We present two case studies based on our own work. First, we report on recent research regarding the spatial distribution of services supporting small business loan guarantees. In this case, we use a location-allocation method to evaluate site alternatives for a public facility (a community financial development corporation). California state policy makers were interested in finding new locations in currently underserved areas for the offices that arrange loan guarantees. Using data on the spatial distribution of small businesses and on the locations of banks, we identify potential service areas for the expanded program. In the second case, we build a developer location-choice model to examine urban growth alternatives under defined policy constraints. This model enables us to evaluate indicators of urban form including servicing costs and effects on the local resource economy.

In both cases, we emphasize theory drawn from urban sociology as well as microeconomic and ecological approaches. Each of these applications had an influence on a narrowly defined policy process, although we make no specific claims about the extent of this influence. The purpose of this chapter is to explore concepts and methods that mediate between spatial analysis and land use or urban policy. We show these cases as examples of how policy analysis needs to link specific political or administrative processes, such as legal mandates or political requisites, to predictive models. We find that we need to include data (including mental maps or other perceptions of spatial processes) gathered directly from constituents of the policy process and mediate the quantitative framework to accommodate these local perspectives. We also note that the spatial analytical method must be tailored substantially to the policy context, and that the process of learning about the policy context must be incorporated into the model.

Understanding How Propinquity Affects Program Delivery: Expanding the State Small Business Guaranteed Loans

The first issue for policy makers is to assure that services are allocated spatially in accordance with need, so that program delivery can be as effective and efficient as possible. Many distribution decisions are made every day on the basis of presumed density of users or need, whether it is the location of fire stations or the distribution of citizenship classes targeting specific ethnic groups. Models used by consultants to help builders select the location of shopping centers use the service area concept to assist in pinpointing areas from which customers will come. However, outside of helping to decide where to build something, policy makers have not very often looked at the way services can be distributed to meet public needs.

Research in this field has been rooted in several principles. First, location decisions in a public arena are qualitatively different from private location decisions (Teitz 1968). The normative objective of public facility location under a neoclassical welfare framework is to balance tradeoffs between efficient and equitable locations (DeVerteuil 2000; Teitz 1968). More recent work in a welfare framework emphasizes differential travel costs to alternative public facility locations (Thisse and Wildasin 1992). Recent research has also been conducted in political-economic and behavioral frameworks (Lober 1995). The availability of GIS software creates technical opportunities for the use of a variety of methods, such as contour mapping and formal optimization; these are applied to problems, such as the location of hospitals or park-and-ride facilities (Church 2002; Horner and Grubesic 2001).

A starting point in thinking about the role of spatial analysis in public policy is to distinguish policy arenas where service must be provided locally and is therefore dependent on the density of demand, from those where service can be provided from a distance. Many policies can be implemented from a distance with little loss of policy effectiveness and efficiency, such as environmental research laboratories or state tax collection bureaucracies. Others are closely tied to the distribution of demand, such as trash collection, mosquito abatement, or calibration of scales and gasoline pumps. The ability to serve local areas changes with technology and often follows contentious policy decisions about the importance of local service, such as school bussing, which allows closure of rural schools, or improved medical transport, which consolidates patients in centralized hospital facilities for specialized treatments. The key to effective policy making is to distinguish between those policies that are best distributed, according to the density of users and need, and those which can be located according to other criteria, such as the availability of key personnel. Making this distinction is not obvious, however, as the following case will show.

With the centralization of banking in the United States, one might assume that delivering loans is amenable to concentration of services in a few central locations. Fewer people go into banks for financial transactions, and loans are based on credit scores, which are processed centrally from information provided by national credit checking corporations. Business loans are especially shaped by central processing because the amounts are greater, and large central banks have greater access to needed capital. Against this presumed pressure for cost savings associated with concentration, local communities argue strongly for their local branch bank, and many local banks are created to fill voids when the large banks pull out (Conger 1998; Grzywinski 1991; Lacker 1995; Sower 1992). Local economic development agencies and organizations still argue (with limited and disputed evidence) that local banks are necessary for growth.

Small business lending is particularly risky. While failure rates are not as high as some myths suggest, the smallest businesses have survival rates in the range of 65 percent over five years, compared to nearly 98 percent for the largest businesses (Bradshaw 2002). Even so, many small businesses with growth and profitability over three to five years are excellent credit risks. At the other extreme, a highly problematic group of newly started businesses, or those without a history of profit and growth, collateral, and solid business plans are poor credit risks under any circumstance. From an economic development policy perspective, most firms that cannot qualify for bank loans cannot be helped, because the public cannot take that much risk on businesses that may fail. However, a small number of small businesses each year make the transition from risky to stable businesses, and many of them need credit to do so. Justifiably, banks may not be willing to assume the risk for these businesses that nearly qualify, but it may be good policy for public programs to help them establish a credit record and grow so that they can qualify in the future. This is where state policy becomes involved.

The California Loan Guarantee Program

In California, the state established a loan guarantee program that has a large trust fund by which qualified small businesses can obtain guaranteed loans after being turned down by their bank (Bradshaw 1998). The program guaranteed bank loans up to $350,000 to qualified small businesses that could not obtain bank loans without a guarantee. Generally, the firm must nearly qualify for the bank loan, meaning that the firm has most of the qualifications for a loan, such as collateral, being in business for 3–5 years, being profitable, and having a strong business plan. The guarantee can be up to 90 percent of the loan amount, and firms must pay a two percent fee. The costs and shared risk keep guarantees from being used by banks unless they are really needed. Typically the interest rate is the bank's normal rate. Founded in 1968, the California State Loan Guarantee Program (SLGP) guarantees the bank loans with a $33 million fund. The fund can be leveraged on a four-to-one basis, giving the state the capacity to guarantee about $120 million in loans. As the loans are paid off, the funds are available to guarantee other loans. Over the last ten years, the SLGP has had a default rate of only about two percent, which is above what banks consider acceptable (usually only a half percent), but below other programs such as the U.S. Small Business Administration small business loans (see Bradshaw 2002).

Eight regional development corporations administer the SLGP. These corporations are chartered to work with small businesses and their banks and to help them obtain guarantees, if needed. The corporations often offer other small business services, but they try to help firms capable of repaying their loan that, nonetheless, have been turned down by their bank. From 1990 to 1998, the corporations made some 2,000 loan guarantees in California, guaranteeing over $176 million in bank loans to small businesses. The corporations are located in Sacramento, Oakland, Fresno, Salinas, Santa Rosa, Los Angeles (2), and San Diego, and they have branches in six more cities. During the 1990s the loans have helped firms expand, generating an average of 40 percent increase in employment and increasing sales and tax revenues to largely pay state costs for the program (Bradshaw 2002). The spatial issue arose when a number of other cities wanted to get some benefit as well, and legislation was introduced to expand the number of corporations and increase the loan fund. Instead of putting corporations in the districts of the most vocal legislators, a study was called for to determine where the expansion would be most favorable.

Loan Locations as a Spatial Question

The question, then, of where to expand this program called for a number of new spatial analysis strategies that linked data on the distribution of demand with policy-relevant considerations. The first step was to understand the loan guarantee process and the conditions under which guarantees were made. A series of interviews and focus group meetings were held to try to discover the process by which demand for loans was linked with availability of guarantees. Based on the data collection, we learned that most small businesses, if asked, would say that they need additional capital, but that, realistically, most small businesses are appropriately cautious about acquiring debt. Similarly, most banks are perhaps "overly" cautious about making small business loans with any risk according to their criteria, and they turn down many small business applications that are not quite qualified but would probably be good loans anyway.[1] This intermediate risk category includes about 15 percent of loan applications, or about 30,000 applications[2] that might qualify for guarantees according to focus group estimates (Bradshaw 1998, 36). In addition, we learned that small business loans are costly for banks to process—the staff time to process a loan application is almost the same for a $50,000 small business loan and a $1 million loan to a larger business. It is hard to recover processing and administration costs from small loans, and the banks told us they need to simplify evaluation of smaller loans by using credit scoring and objective decision making. From the bank point of view, they have a lot of money to invest in business loans, but they cannot afford to go out of their way for small loans.

In sum, the people we interviewed who make loans and loan guarantees agreed that a very large number of small businesses could use additional capital, and they would be very likely able to repay a loan. The opportunity for investing public funds in small business loan guarantees is thus widespread and far in excess of program capacity. However, this is not a market the banks want. Most bankers acknowledged that they do small business loan guarantees as community service and to meet Community Reinvestment Act criteria. Thus, the key limitation to the expansion of the guaranteed loan program was neither the lack of small businesses that needed capital nor the banks' financial reserves, but the network created by the guarantee programs that linked highly motivated small businesses with banks willing to participate in a public program to reduce their risk on some small business loans.

Moreover, in interviews we learned that the majority of the loan guarantees originate with a banker who has prior knowledge about the guarantee program through personal ties to the loan officers at the corporations. Typically, bankers who know about the loan guarantees inform small business applicants whose loan application has been denied. Given the pressures on bank loan officers to meet high loan quotas (up to several million dollars a month), their willingness to seek a guarantee for a small loan must be seen as special service, and it is usually based on close working relations between bank officers and corporation staff, and these ties diminish with distance.[3]

Thus, banks may centralize evaluation of small business loans for established firms, but it is a decentralized spatial network that links loan guarantees to specially motivated businesses unable to get credit and banks willing to participate in the guarantee program. Our quantitative analysis aimed to represent this network spatially, to assess the extent of the spatial network that linked businesses and loan guarantees and to identify areas that are underserved.

Data were entered into a GIS analysis based on zip codes. The data were selected to address five interrelated factors that constitute demand.

1. The number of small businesses. For this research we used state employment data identifying firms with 50 or fewer employees. Demand for small business loans crosses all industrial categories; interest in guaranteed loans is assumed to vary with the number of businesses.
2. The rate of growth in small businesses, measured by the change from 1990 to 1996. Areas with growth in small businesses would be more likely to need loans, since new businesses are more likely to need guarantees at some stage.
3. Need for and availability of small business bank loans. A proxy for this is the number of federal SBA loan guarantees. The federal program is much better known than the state program, and the use of the SBA program is an indicator of the interest small businesses have in guarantees. However, because of important differences between the SBA and SLGP, there is minor overlap in coverage and limited competition between the two programs.
4. The availability of partner banks. The majority of loan guarantees came through state chartered banks, rather than federal chartered banks that have many branches in several states. Larger numbers of banks located in the area indicates partnership possibilities for the program.
5. The unmet need for state guaranteed loans, based on the ratio of SLGP borrowers to the total number of small businesses, where a low ratio indicates a high demand for more loan services.

These five factors helped to identify areas that had large numbers of small businesses needing loans, available partner banks, and low levels of existing service by the program.

Identifying Areas of Unmet Needs

The first step was to determine the extent to which the current program served businesses and banks that could be nurtured by close contact to a corporation loan officer. Using calculations of the distance between center points of zip codes, we discovered that the median distance from a corporation office to firm was only 12 miles, and the median distance between the corporation and the banks making the loans was only nine miles. In urban areas of California, which spread for 50 to 75 miles, this leaves large areas underserved.

To be consistent, all corporation service areas were set at a radius of twice the median distance from their corporation office to firms with a loan guarantee. This included nearly 80 percent of the loans. We assumed that the existing corporations would continue to serve firms within this circle.

Next, twelve candidate alternative locations were identified for expansion of the network of corporation offices based on examination of maps and consideration of where capacity would be found to operate a new corporation. These alternative locations constituted different independent scenarios for expansion, expecting that the state would add four new corporation locations initially in the areas with the greatest unmet need.

Using ArcView, circles with a 25-mile radius were drawn around candidate new locations, and the five factors were calculated for the area not already in the circle of an existing corporation. Rankings were then taken of the factors, and the ranks summed to give the priority for each new location. The data and the rankings are presented in Table 15.1, and the areas are shown in Figure 15.1. From these data it is easy to see that the priority for new locations would be sites where the region not already served by an existing corporation included

- a large number of small businesses,
- rapid growth in small businesses,
- previous history of businesses needing and getting SBA loans,
- a large number of state chartered banks, and
- a low rate of existing SLGP loans per 10,000 small business establishments.

Based on this analysis, new corporations were proposed for San Jose, Santa Anna, San Fernando, and Thousand Oaks. After some debate, the state proceeded to establish corporations in these locations.

This brief example demonstrates that spatial analysis can be used in a systematic and quick way to assist policy makers in allocating scarce resources. However, for this to be successful, there must be an underlying theory that space makes a difference. In this case, we had to rely on interview and subjective data that showed that loan guarantees were most frequently made by corporation officials and bankers knowing each other and the program before a client needed a guarantee, and that these relations were easiest to make when the distance was smaller. Moreover, the loan activity was greatest where there were more state chartered banks in the area serving more small businesses, especially in areas where there was growth in small business. Density and proximity to a loan office were crucial variables in making the decisions about where to expand the program.

Table 15.1. Rankings Of Alternative Service Regions.

Corporation Location	Zip Code	Area (mi²)	Small Business Establishments, 1996	Rank	Percentage Change in No. of Small Business Establishments, 1991 to 1996	Rank	SBA Borrowers	Rank	State-Chartered Banks	Rank	No. of SLGP Borrowers/ 10,000 Small Business Establishments	Rank	Total of Rankings
San Jose	95110	1,390	48,755	2	15.1	4	7,626	3	152	2	11.1	4	15
Santa Ana	92701	819	69,151	1	13.4	5	5,659	4	211	1	13.3	7	18
San Fernando	91340	1,088	9,426	6	24.9	2	15,481	1	20	7	15.9	9	25
Thousand Oaks	91362	890	16,290	4	17.5	3	13,781	2	42	5	31.3	12	26
Ontario	91764	700	22,068	3	9.5	9	2,068	6	73	3	15.0	8	29
Modesto	95354	1,727	11,564	5	6.2	10	785	8	59	4	9.5	3	30
Lancaster	93534	2,525	4,410	9	10.8	7	2,535	5	12	10	11.3	5	36
Riverside	92501	111	794	12	38.6	1	58	12	1	12	0.0	1	38
Escondido	92025	661	7,130	7	10.5	8	834	7	20	7	22.4	11	40
Fairfield	94533	89	2,225	11	11.0	6	199	11	5	11	9.0	2	41
Redding	96002	2,398	4,934	8	4.4	11	494	9	26	6	18.2	10	44
El Centro	92243	1,028	2,562	10	4.4	12	201	10	13	9	11.7	6	47

Note: The San Jose region includes some zip codes that were previously part of the Santa Cruz region.

Sources: Banks—California Department of Financial Institutions; Small businesses—EDD; SBA borrowers—SBA; SLGP borrowers—TCA; calculations by author.

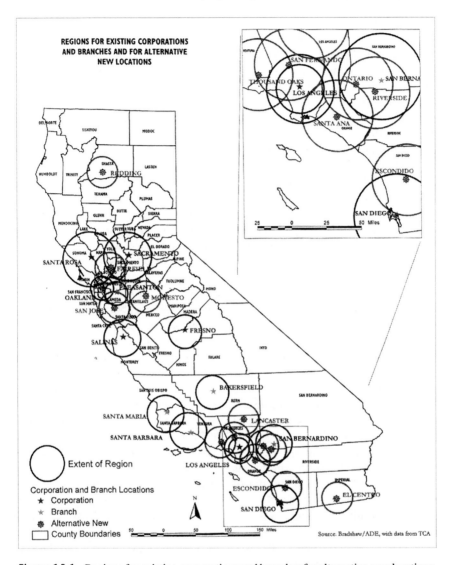

Figure 15.1. Regions for existing corporations and branches for alternative new locations.

Projecting Development for Planning: Land Use Modeling

The second example suggests a slightly different policy question. Whereas, in the bank guarantee case we asked "where" something should be located, in urban land use change modeling we generally ask "how much impact" a policy will have on socially valued spatial assets. The "how much" question is a cornerstone of land use and environmental planning, particularly for local comprehensive planning and environmental impact analysis. It is typically used to steer an evaluation of prospective alternatives and thus, helps in the formation of policy to control these alternatives

A variety of models have been developed to help evaluate the effects of alternative urban growth patterns on consumption of resources and the health of cities. These generally include two parts: a core model of development processes and linked models of impact on natural or social systems. Several types of development process models have emerged over the past decade. These are broadly similar, in the sense that they rely on a GIS and disaggregated spatial data, but otherwise diverse, built on varied theoretical foundations and with divergent capabilities. One model type emphasizes decision rules to allocate development across major land use categories (Johnston and Shabazian 2002; Klosterman 1997). Another relies on cellular automata to disseminate settlement through various propagation, dispersion, and proximity-based mechanisms, as well as suitability rules (White and Engelen 1993, 1997). More comprehensive models include interlocking components addressing multiple dimensions of urban change, such as economic transition, demographic transition, household location choice, and mobility (Waddell 2002). An even greater variety of linked impact models have been developed or modified over the past decade to process the outputs of urban growth models. These are used to evaluate effects, such as wildfire risk, cost of services, transportation demand, environmental footprint, habitat loss, neighborhood livability, quality of life, and urban performance, measured by indicators such as pattern density.

The model described in this chapter is built on discrete choice theory (McFadden 1973). It assumes that developers are boundedly rational and operate in an environment of limited information. The model, in effect, mimics the calculations of a developer who is surveying and comparing raw land sites within a market area. A logit regression is used to evaluate influences on land conversion between two historical points. These influences can be interpreted as variables that define the development profitability of alternative sites (Bradshaw and Muller 1998; Landis 1994, 1995; Landis and Zhang 1998). Variables include network accessibility, land regulation, jurisdiction type, urban proximity, neighborhood, and site attributes.

In an earlier study we employed a similar model to examine the land use consequences of projected urban fringe development within the fertile agricultural breadbasket of the California Central Valley (Bradshaw and Muller 1998). We used a GIS vector overlay process to configure an eleven-county area of the San Joaquin and lower Sacramento valleys into about 750,000 developable land units. We analyzed historical development experience through a regression and generated development probabilities for each land unit. These probabilities were used to rank developable land units and allocate forecasted population increases at set densities across the study area. This model was then applied to a specific policy problem, the evaluation of agricultural land loss under alternative growth scenarios. We found that the forecasted population increase (tripling of population from 1990 to 2040) would consume about one million acres of farmland if growth were to continue at current average densities. This growth would consume about 600,000 acres of prime farmland, 12.5 percent of all prime agricultural land in the study counties. However, we also showed that, if policies were established leading to increased densities for new development, which we pegged at six units per acre based on an assessment of new subdivisions in the area, the same population could be accommodated on 470,000 acres. Only 265,000 of prime land would be lost under this more compact scenario.

Our policy purpose in this study was very general education about the implications of growth and alternative land use regulations. Its findings received considerable attention in the Central Valley, as well as in California and national media. While we have not systematically evaluated the outcomes of the project, we feel it played a useful role in focusing public discussion on consequences of current development rates and patterns over a long planning horizon. The American Farmland Trust estimates that they presented the study in more than 100 public meetings; they trace several institutional outcomes to discussions generated by the study, including the formation of the Fresno Growth Alliance.

Continuing Innovations: The Salinas-Pajaro AGF Model

A group at the University of Colorado has continued to refine the Alternative Growth Futures (AGF) method through case studies in selected California and Colorado communities. (Muller and Yin 2001; Muller et al. 2002a,b). Over the past three years, we have constructed AGF models for 16 counties in the central coast of California, recreation-based Colorado mountain communities, and rapidly urbanizing areas of Colorado's Front Range. These projects were designed around various types of local planning processes. In this section of the chapter, we focus on the design and policy context for an AGF model developed by this team in a comprehensive planning context in Monterey and Santa Cruz Counties of California.

This Monterey-Santa Cruz study was designed for a rather different policy purpose than the Central Valley research described above. Its intention was to aid farm organizations, local land trusts, environmental groups, and county planners in preparation for a county general plan update.[4] Development politics in this region encapsulate an important dimension of the postwar development story in coastal California: land use competition between heavily-capitalized agricultural industries, development pressures from rapid population growth, and demands for recreation based in natural amenities. On the one hand, the Salinas Valley in Monterey County and southern Santa Cruz County are the home of a specialized agricultural complex producing commodities, such as fresh-pack lettuce, strawberries, flowers, organic vegetables, and wine. The major cities, including Watsonville and Salinas, have high housing densities and large immigrant populations attracted by agricultural jobs. On the other hand, even with the recent downturn, residential spillover from Silicon Valley is placing new development pressures on the eastern parts of the two counties. The area also contains well-known recreational destinations, such as the Monterey Peninsula, associated with demands for retirement housing and high-end second homes. Finally, the region has significant habitat resources, notably Monterey Bay. The purpose of the Monterey-Santa Cruz study was to design a model to span the interests of these varied land users, and to begin to identify areas of potential conflict and compromise based on modeling outputs and discussions.

This model relies on the statistical method described above, but introduces several innovations to meet the particular demands of the Monterey-Santa Cruz policy environment. The statistical method used to generate a surface of development probabilities has been discussed elsewhere (see above). We focus here on the adaptation of this method to a complex planning application sensitive to local policy considerations and landscape values. In part, the framework we designed in this project parallels research on public participation GIS and use of planning support systems as a public participation tool. In this discussion, however, we focus not on problems of general public participation but on the knowledge and interests of specific public and private groups, who we determined were likely to be influential in the process leading up to the general plan. The model was designed, in large measure, to support the internal debate among primary actors, in many cases people who were knowledgeable about technical issues and political dynamics behind land use decision-making in the area. The policy environment in the two counties and our project objectives led us to design a modeling framework with the following five elements.

First, because of the "high resolution" of planning debate in Monterey and Santa Cruz counties with respect to specific locations and parcels, we found it necessary to use fine-grained data. This approach is possible in the region because counties and cities, the Coastal Commission, and other organizations develop significant data locally. With fine-grained data, impact analysis can yield results that illuminate problems at a neighborhood level and of interest to geographically focused policy constituencies. For example, using disaggregated crop production data, we were able to closely analyze the consequences of different patterns of urbanization on specific agricultural industries.[5] If growth in Monterey County is pushed to the northern part of the county, significant strawberry acreage will be lost, whereas other crops would suffer if growth is pushed elsewhere.

Second, we found that published data were inadequate to capture significant definitions of land value and use in the eyes of local planners and environmental and agricultural communities. In this model we focused on three local data collection problems: local definition of resource values; delineation of areas that are unlikely to receive development because of negative externalities;and description of current policy ideas and arrangements. The definition of "prime" agricultural land (derived from the relative valuation of different combinations of productive conditions) was debated intensively in Monterey and Santa Cruz Counties at the time this project was underway. Still, many people in the agricultural community argued that USDA definitions of prime land are inadequate. To address these concerns, we developed a map mark-up for identifying the "super-prime" areas. Local project participants also argued that we should include locally unwanted land uses (LULUs) in the model as development inhibitors, and we used a similar approach to delineate areas that might be affected by LULUs. Finally, published data did not shed much light on the spatial definition of current development objectives in city and county governments. For example, many of the city comprehensive plans in the region were out of date. In each of these areas, we addressed data gaps by organizing and recording spatially explicit discussions with selected groups and individuals in the two counties and transposing these discussions into digital maps. We used two qualitative methods in our research: key informant interviews regarding current local government policy and growth objectives, and focus groups with local agricultural and environmental organizations leading to map mark-ups describing land values.

A third feature of model design for this project relates to disaggregated demographic forecasts. We configured our model according to the tract-level forecasting geography used by local planners. This feature of the model permits us to compare our findings with local forecasts and most important, incorporate local forecasts into the development of scenarios. Disaggregated demographic projections have become a focal point for debate within and among jurisdictions in many parts of the United States. Population projections at a state and even a regional level are controversial because of their policy implications. By using official forecasts, prepared at a state level by the California Department of Finance and at the multi-county level by the Council of Government, we locate our model in the framework of the state's formal growth assessment system. In addition, this method creates a bridge between our research and debates among local governments about how growth should be allocated among jurisdictions through instruments such as annexation rules.

In this project, we also found it necessary to consider a relatively broad range of factors in the construction of policy scenarios. Scenario construction is a policy art that is strictly limited by the tools available in spatial analytical software; nonetheless, modelers have dramatically extended the scope of scenario tests to new types and scales of problems. Scenario design is time-consuming because it reaches for the heart of the trade-offs and compromises that are available in a specific political and technical environment. In this project, we attempted to create scenarios that represent generic elements of the local policy debate but at the same time span key interests and values identified through the research. We incorporated a variety of dimensions in our scenarios, including potential water infrastructure investments, growth objectives in local governments, and agricultural land value.

Finally, we included a fiscal and agricultural industry analysis in our calculation of the impacts of land use change. The fiscal analysis focused on the costs of servicing alternative urban forms defined in terms of relative compactness and fragmentation. In the agricultural industry analysis, we evaluated the loss or gain of agricultural revenues associated with the amount of land likely to be available for production of specific crops. Our work on the fiscal analysis paralleled much of the method employed in the general growth impact model, in the sense that we relied heavily on interviews to define servicing costs for individual jurisdictions.

The Monterey-Santa Cruz Case

The case study being reported on here is along the coast in the Salinas and Pajaro valleys of Monterey and Santa Cruz Counties, 75–100 miles south of San Francisco. The farmland in these coastal plains and valleys is limited to several hundred thousand acres, rather than 14 million acres in the central valley, and the fertile soils and unique climate caused by regular dense summer fog make it a unique resource for specialty crops such as summer lettuce and cool weather vegetables, artichokes, broccoli, and strawberries. The area is the major producer of some of these crops and is thus of national interest.

At the same time, tourism is a major industry in nearby Santa Cruz, Monterey, Carmel, and the Big Sur coastal area. Moreover, both counties are just south of the rapidly growing Silicon Valley around San Jose, where booming economic and population growth made for some of the nation's highest priced housing. Commuters and retirement or recreation settlement are conspicuous, with growth in all the major cities as well as along the roads leading in and out of the valleys. A huge military base closure (Fort Ord) seemed to open development options rather than cause economic catastrophe (Bradshaw 1999). In spite of growth pressures, it is also an area with strong environmental values, and concern is strong about finding options to rampant growth. These conditions made growth modeling highly challenging because it was extremely politicized, visible, and contentious. It also made it essential because so much valuable land was at stake.

We constructed four scenarios to represent the variety of interests in these areas.

1. The *Low-Density Scenario* assumes that growth occurs at current, average development densities and according to current market patterns. It permits relaxation of zoning ordinances under the assumption that these will not necessarily be sustained over a long planning horizon.

2. The *Local-Government Scenario* assumes that individual jurisdictions are each able to achieve current, long-term growth and planning objectives without interference from other local jurisdictions or entities such as the Coastal Commission or the state of California. This scenario is based on interviews and map mark-ups with planners and local officials in city and county government. It permits varying development densities according to local market conditions and policies. This scenario suggests a modeling framework that could be used in a more formal system to mediate boundary and annexation disputes among local jurisdictions.[6]

3. The *Compact-Growth Scenario* assumes that new policies are enacted in multiple jurisdictions with the combined effect of encouraging development at significantly higher densities across the entire region. We peg compact densities at a level that permits separate houses on small lots, generally at the denser end of what local planners consider to be desirable and marketable subdivision types within the region. This scenario could be implemented through policy changes such as revised zoning ordinances, establishment of growth boundaries, restrictions on water supply and infrastructure development, and the use of density bonuses.

4. The *Farmland-Protection Scenario* prioritizes protection of the best agricultural lands. These lands were delineated through interviews and focus groups within the agricultural community to identify both attributes and locations of valuable lands. This scenario assumes policy changes such as highly restrictive zoning alongside non-governmental efforts such as expanded easement purchase programs.

Population growth is held constant throughout the four scenarios, and it is based on revised projections from the California Department of Finance in 1998. The population is projected to more than double in 40 years, somewhat slower growth than expected in the Central Valley. In total, the two counties are expected to gain nearly 700,000 persons, though much of that growth will go into the cities of Monterey and Santa Cruz, as well as reuse of the Fort Ord military base. The urban and base reuse is held constant across all scenarios according to local plan. For the most part, these areas are away from the important agricultural land, and planning issues there will have limited impact on the rest of the county. A constant estimate for household size (2.5 persons) was used except for the Local-Government Scenario, where local planner estimates for individual jurisdictions were used. The household size reflects a balance between retirement and recreational development (smaller household size) and farmworker or immigrant populations (larger household size). Density of housing units per acre varied according to scenario. Current development densities are about four housing units per acre, the figure used for the low-density scenario. Compact growth is set at eight units per acre. This figure is deemed attainable under current market practices (and there are examples at this density), while presenting a challenge to local governments. The Low-Density Scenario reflects variable densities as set by local planners, generally ranging between the low density and compact density scenarios. Infill of urban areas of 15 percent is projected for compact growth and farmland protection scenarios, but no infill is projected for the other scenarios.

In addition to the four scenarios the model had to accommodate many local planning realities, such as plans for the reuse of the Fort Ord military base and strong agricultural protections around Watsonville. No growth is permitted in areas of the Coastal Zone that are under special growth controls. Water is a major constraint. While water from the Central Valley eventually may be brought into the area, it is now reliant on wells and limited runoff. The compact and farmland-protection scenarios recognize that development will not displace enough agricultural water to handle urban uses, especially in areas well away from existing infrastructure. Thus, these scenarios assume additional water development. Finally, many environmentally sensitive areas are prohibited from development, and the model additionally assumes that some sensitive areas not under current protections will eventually be excluded from development.

The reason for discussing these details is mainly to illustrate the specificity at which models must operate if they are to be used directly in city and county planning processes. Statewide or Central Valley-scale models assume that local variations in such factors average out, shifting development from one place to another with minimal consequence. But when used in practice by planners, city officials, and landowners whose farmland or speculative housing tracts are being affected, the model must be sensitive to relevant details at a high level of resolution.

Project findings illustrate the effect of density-related policies and market trends on raw land consumption. Development in the low-density and local-government scenarios consumes 60,000–70,000 acres; the compact and farmland-protection scenarios only convert about 29,000 acres of raw land. In addition, the model results suggest that current local government policies are keyed already to protection of valuable agricultural land. The low-density scenario converts 37,000 acres of prime farmland to development, compared to 26,000 acres in the local-government scenario. The model also shows that simply opting for the compact-growth scenario reduces farmland loss to 15,000 acres. These effects are in large part the result of spatial patterns produced by the different iterations of the model. Most important, low-density growth is shown by the model to create a new metropolitan region dominating the best agricultural area, which runs north-to-south through the Salinas Valley (see Figure 15.2). The other scenarios tend to distribute population more evenly.

In the farmland protection scenario, growth is forced away from places where it would go if other "good planning" criteria were applied, such as cost-of-services or urban compactness measures (see Figure 15.3). For example, around the city of Salinas, which is centered in prime agricultural land, agricultural land protection effectively created a greenbelt, pushing growth into foothills some distance from town. Similarly, in King City, strong agricultural protection pushes urban development across the river

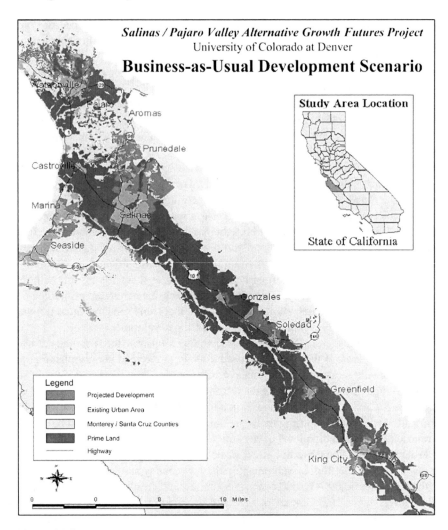

Figure 15.2. Business-as-usual development scenarios.

and away from the main part of the city. Moreover, the low density and compact alternatives favor growth in cities, with 80 and 85 percent of growth within expected city limits. The agricultural land protection scenario, however, shifts most growth outside the cities, leaving only about 30 percent within city limits, because the cities in this area are largely surrounded by prime farmland.

What are the implications of the fiscal analysis? Based on current tax rates, a compact or agriculture protection growth pattern will lead to the highest overall tax benefit to the growing municipalities, while holding down the loss to the economy, whereas low density development and the continuation of current planning efforts will lead to significant loss of land, agricultural jobs, and economic productivity.

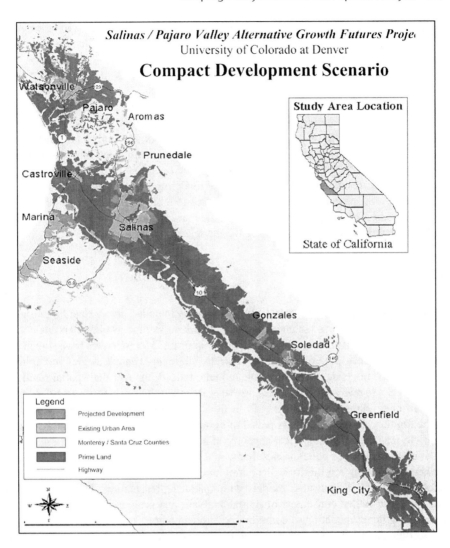

Salinas / Pajaro Valley Alternative Growth Futures Proje
University of Colorado at Denver

Compact Development Scenario

Watsonville

Pajaro
Aromas

Prunedale

Castroville

Marina

Salinas

Seaside

Gonzales

Soledad

Greenfield

King City

Study Area Location

State of California

Legend
Projected Development
Existing Urban Area
Monterey / Santa Cruz Counties
Prime Land
Highway

Figure 15.3. Compact development scenarios.

The local-government scenario most closely represents current planning policy. Interestingly, this is the least attractive option from a fiscal point of view. Across cities and counties over 40 years, it shows a surplus of $43.2 million a year. However, the farmland-protection scenario shows a balance of $86.5 million a year in revenues over expenses. These findings parallel previous findings that compact growth costs less than sprawl. On the other hand, these municipal costs are dwarfed by the losses to the agricultural industry. In the low-density scenario, which uses the most agricultural land, over 7,200 jobs would be lost and industry output would fall $502 million. In contrast, with farmland protection only 745 jobs would be lost and output would fall $46 million. This impact is based on losses to agriculture plus multipliers based on actual crops grown on developed land. It makes no assumption about additional jobs in other parts of the economy, because these will largely develop independently of land use, though variations could be explored outside the scope of this study.

In sum, land use modeling can include significant amounts of input from policy makers in the process of generating quantitative outputs as is shown by this case. Moreover, this process is ongoing, as the policy process continues to use and improve public involvement in the planning process. In Monterey County, the cost-of-service calculations in particular were of strong interest to policymakers; the analysis of impacts on the agricultural industry received less attention. Discussions around interim findings and map mark-ups appear to have greater influence than final results, because debate in the two counties moved faster than the final modeling process and production of an approved report. Monterey County has continued to build on the approach defined by the project through funding a web-based public participation and monitoring program linked to a similar type of land use change model.

Conclusion

This chapter has argued that spatial analysis is being included in an expanding number of public policy areas as technical capacity and data become available and as policy makers want to benefit from new analytical capabilities. Moreover, we have shown examples of practices that effectively incorporate public input and strategies and options that are shaped outside the quantitative models. Indeed, the fact that spatial relations are important to many public policies provides an impetus to apply the basic knowledge demonstrated in the other chapters of this book to public decision-making. Returning to the four key perspectives that opened this chapter, several conclusions can be made.

First, increasing technological capacity of hardware and software allows more sophisticated analysis of policy issues than could have been done previously, and policy makers are gaining familiarity with spatial models and the representation of complex relations using GIS and other models with spatial representation. The public is becoming more skilled consumers of spatial analysis, and progressive officials are even demanding better modeling of complex social phenomena.

Second, the models are getting better, as illustrated by the greater sophistication of land use models, but they still need input of qualitative data to reflect public interests, political power, or community inertia. The number of factors included in the analysis increases as the models get more specific at the local level, and criticisms of oversimplification are less common from policy makers. However, the complexity of policy issues still exceeds the ability of models to model properly the greater understanding we have of how the many determinants of social policy work out in real social space.

Third, the examples demonstrate the potential for using land use change and public facility location models as a formal element of policy processes. For example, land use change and impact modeling could be incorporated formally into the decision-making process of Local Area Formation Commissions, by running the models on alternative annexation proposals and evaluating outcomes.

Finally, both examples show how spatial analysis contributes to more effective means of increasing public participation in policy decision-making. In one case the constituencies of programs helped identify what was important to model, and in the other they gave modelers important information on local priorities and constraints, factors that would not be easily included in purely quantitative models. Then, in both cases, the results were utilized by policy makers as advisory, with results that left room for political judgment and interpretation. The land use model became part of the on-going process of regional planning, whereas the banking example involved discussion over several alternatives of selecting locations that ranked just below the top four. The analysis thus was input to policy rather than a determinant of outcome. However, the analysis enabled greater and more informed public participation, which is the ultimate goal of good policy making.

Overall, then, in spite of the limitations of the models and the data, spatial models are demonstrated as increasingly relevant to the policy process because they better represent the complex policy reality that leaders know, compared to models that do not take into consideration issues such as density, intensity, diversity, and interdependence. The ecology of policy issues does not lend itself to overt "scientific" policy analyses that systematically disregard how the complex social phenomena work out in real community and regional settings.

Notes

1. Otherwise qualified businesses may be denied loans because they are new businesses with special expertise, businesses with minor and explainable deficits in their credit report, successful businesses that have never had to establish a credit record, or unusual businesses such as nonprofit corporations.
2. This is compared to current capability to fund at most 1000 loan guarantees per year.
3. The fact that loans are offered through person-to-person ties does not imply that this is the most effective way for the program to run. Changes in the operation of the program that would establish more centralized administration and broader marketing to banks are an alternative to the current program design.
4. Muller and colleagues developed the urban growth model and growth policy analysis; Bradshaw and colleagues developed the cost-of-services model and financial analysis. The urban growth model and its findings are detailed in Muller and Yin (2001), and in a forthcoming article.
5. These data are available from the California Department of Natural Resources.
6. In California, boundary disputes among local governments are managed by the Local Area Formation Commissions (LAFCOs) made up of representatives of city and county governments within each county. Use of a growth model might enable these jurisdictions to better understand the consequences of alternative annexation strategies.

References

Batty, M. 1994. A chronicle of scientific planning: The Anglo American modeling experience. *Journal of the American Planning Association* 60(1): 7–16.

Beynon, M., S. Rasmequan, and S. Russ. 2002. A new paradigm for computer-based decision support. *Decision Support Systems* 33: 127–142.

Bradshaw, T.K. 1998. *Assessment of Regions Underserved by the California State Guaranteed Loan Program*. Sacramento, Calif.: State Trade and Commerce Agency and Berkeley: Applied Development Economics. Mimeo.

Bradshaw, T.K. 1999. Communities not fazed. *Journal of the American Planning Association* 65(2): 193–206.

Bradshaw, T.K. 2002. The contribution of small business loan guarantees to economic development. *Economic Development Quarterly* 16: 360–369.

Bradshaw, T.K., and B. Muller. 1998. Impacts of rapid urban growth on farmland conservation: Application of new regional land use policy models and geographic information systems. *Rural Sociology* 63(1): 1–25.

Brail, R.K., and R.E. Klosterman (eds.). 2001. *Planning Support Systems: Integrating Geographic Information Systems, Models, and Visualization Tools.* Redlands, Calif.: ESRI Press.

Budic, Z.D. 1994. Effectiveness of geographic information systems in local planning. *Journal of the American Planning Association* 60(2): 244–263.

Carlson, C., and E. Turban. 2002. DSS: Directions for a new decade. *Decision Support Systems* 33: 105–110.

Castells, M. 1977. *The Urban Question: A Marxist Approach.* Cambridge, Mass.: MIT Press.

Church, R.L. 2002. Geographical information systems and location science. *Computers & Operations Research* 29(6): 541–562.

Conger, L. 1998. Think Big, Lend Small. *Ford Foundation Report* 29(2): 15–17.

DeVerteuil, G. 2000. Reconsidering the legacy of urban public facility location theory in human geography. *Progress in Human Geography* 24(1): 47–69.

Grzywinski, R. 1991. The new old-fashioned banking. *Harvard Business Review*, May 1: 87–98.

Harris, B. 1998. The real issues concerning Lee's requiem. *Journal of the American Planning Association* 60(1): 31–34.

Harris, B., and M. Batty. 1993. Locational models, geographic information and planning support systems. *Journal of Planning and Education Research* 12:184–198.

Harris, T., and D. Weiner. 1998. Empowerment, marginalization, and "Community-Integrated" GIS. *Cartography and Geographic Information Systems* 25(2): 67–76.

Harris, T.M., D. Weiner, T. Warner, and R. Levin. 1995. Pursuing social goals through participatory GIS: Redressing South Africa's historical political ecology. In J. Pickles (ed.), *Ground Truth*. New York: Guilford.

Hopkins, L. 1999. Structure of a planning support system for urban development. *Environment and Planning B: Planning and Design* 26: 333–343.

Horner, M.W., and T.H. Grubesic. 2001. A GIS-Based planning approach to locating urban rail terminals. *Transportation* 28(1): 55–77.

Innes, J.E., and D.M. Simpson. 1993. Implementing GIS for planning: Lessons from the history of technological innovation. *Journal of the American Planning Association* 59: 230–236.

Johnston, R.A., and D.R. Shabazian. 2002. *UPlan: A Versatile Urban Growth Model for Transportation Planning.* Submitted to the Transportation Research Board for presentation at the Annual Meeting, January 2003.

Kammeier, H.D. 1998. A computer-aided strategic approach to decision making in urban planning: An exploratory case study in Thailand. *Cities* 15(2): 105–119.

Klosterman, R. 1997. Planning support systems: A new perspective on computer-aided planning. *Journal of Planning Education and Research* 17(1): 45–54.

Krygier, J.B. 1998. *The Praxis of Public Participation GIS and Visualization.* Paper presented at Project Varenius Specialist Meeting: *Empowerment, Marginalization, and Public Participation GIS.* http://www.ncgia.ucsb.edu/varenius/ppgis/papers/. Access Date: April 3, 2002.

Lacker, J.M. 1995. Neighborhoods and banking. *Economic Development Quarterly* 8(2): 13–39.

Landis, J. 1994. The California urban futures model: A new generation of metropolitan simulation models. *Environment and Planning B: Planning and Design* 21(3): 399–420.

Landis J. 1995. Imagining land use futures: Applying the California urban futures model. *Journal of the American Planning Association* 61(4): 438–457.

Landis, J., and M. Zhang. 1998. The second generation of the California urban futures model. Part 2: Specification and calibration results of the land-use change submodel. *Environment and Planning B* (25): 795–824.

Lee, D.B. 1994. Retrospective on large-scale urban models. *Journal of the American Planning Association* 60: 35–40.

Lober, D.J. 1995. Resolving the siting impasse: Modeling social and environmental locational critieria with a geographic information system. *Journal of the American Planning Association* 61(4): 482–495.

McFadden, D. 1973. Modelling the choice of residential location. In A. Karlqvist, L. Lundqvist, F. Snickars, and J. Weibull (eds.), *Spatial Interaction and Planning Models*, Amsterdam: North Holland.

Montazemi, A., F. Wang, S.M.K. Nainar, and C.K. Bart. 1996. On the effectiveness of decisional guidance. *Decision Support Systems* 18: 181–198.

Muller, B., and L. Yin. 2001. *Salinas-Pajaro Alternative Growth Futures Project: Analysis of Growth Patterns and Alternatives*. Washington, D.C.: American Farmland Trust, Working Paper. University of Colorado at Denver: Mimeo.

Muller, B., C. Bertron, and L. Yin. 2002a. *Alternatives for Future Growth in the Tri-River Region*. Washington, D.C.: American Farmland Trust.

Muller, B., K. Puccio, H. Baker, and L. Yin. 2002b. *Custer County, Colorado: Alternative Growth Futures*. Tucson, Arizona: Sonoran Institute, in press.

Nedovic-Budic. Z. 1998. The impact of GIS technology. *Environment and Planning B: Planning and Design* 25: 681–692.

Obermeyer, N. 1998. The evolution of public participation GIS. *Cartography and Geographic Information Systems* 25(2): 65–66.

Redburn, S.R., and T.F. Buss. 2002. *Modernizing Democracy*. April (report).

Roper, W., and B.H.F. Muller. 2002. Envisioning rural futures: Using innovative software for community planning. In J. Levitt (ed.), *Conservation in the Internet Age: Threats and Opportunities*. Washington, D.C.: Island Press, in press.

Scott, A.J. 1980. *The Urban Land Nexus and the State*. London: Pion.

Sheppard, E. 1995. GIS and society: Toward a research agenda. *Cartography and Geographic Information Systems*. Vol. 22(1): 5–16.

Shiffer, M. 1995. Interactive multimedia planning support: Moving from stand-alone systems to the World Wide Web. *Environment and Planning B: Planning and Design* 22: 649–664.

Shim, J.P., M. Warkentin, J.F. Courtney, D.J. Power, R. Sharda, and C. Carlsson 2002. Past, present and future of decision support technology. *Decision Support Systems* 33: 111–126.

Simonovic, S.P., and M.J. Bender. 1996. Collaborative planning support system: An approach for determining evaluation criteria. *Journal of Hydrology* 177: 237–251.

Sower, J. 1992. Bank CDC's: A new source of affordable housing finance. *Journal of Housing*: 49(May—June): 149–52.

Talen, E. 1998. Visualizing fairness: Equity maps for planners *Journal of the American Planning Association* 64: 22–38.

Teitz, M.B. 1968. Toward a theory of public facility location. *Papers of the Regional Science Association* 21: 35–52.

Thisse, J.F., and D.E. Wildasin. 1992. Public facility location and urban spatial structure: Equilibrium and welfare analysis. *Journal of Public Economics* 48(1): 83–118.

Waddell, P. 2002. Urbanism: Modeling urban development for land use, transportation, and environmental planning. *Journal of the American Planning Association* 68(3) summer: 297–314.

White, R., and G. Engelen. 1993. Cellular automata and fractal urban form: A cellular modeling approach to the evolution of urban land use patterns. *Environment and Planning A* (25): 1175–1199.

White, R., and G. Engelen. 1997. The use of constrained cellular automata for high-resolution modelling of urban land use dynamics. *Environment and Planning B* (24): 323–343.

16

Geographical Approaches for Reconstructing Past Human Behavior from Prehistoric Roadways

John Kantner

A rchaeologists have always employed geographical techniques in efforts to reconstruct human behavior (Kantner 2003). In our investigations of the static and badly eroded cultural deposits from the past, a source of information that we rely upon to interpret the past is the spatial relationships between the material remains. Sometimes we look at spatial associations within an archaeological site; other times we examine the patterns of past human settlement across vast landscapes. Accordingly, archaeology has always looked to geography to provide us with new formal techniques for building sound spatial relationships and effectively interpreting them.

The advent of geographical information systems (GIS) has proven very useful for archaeologists, both for addressing research problems and for managing data. Archaeologists were relatively quick to add GIS to the suite of technologies used for investigating the past, although we may not have been quite so quick at effectively using GIS to do more than serve as a database management system. In 1990, for example, a popular edited volume on GIS in archaeology (Allen et al. 1990) mostly focused on database development and management issues. In recent years, however, archaeological applications employing GIS-based techniques such as viewshed or cost-surface analyses have become increasingly sophisticated (see Aldenderfer and Maschner 1996; Maschner 1996; Westcott and Brandon 2000; Wheatley and Gillings 2002). Archaeologists are using GIS to facilitate complex predictive modeling, model landscape relationships, and generate three-dimensional landscapes. One of the areas of spatial inquiry employed by an increasing number of archaeologists is cost-surface analysis, which has been used to enhance catchment analyses and to model prehistoric road networks. This chapter focuses on the latter, discussing how model spatial relationships help archaeologists in the investigations of ancient roadways and how sophisticated and powerful GIS technology is now promoting a greater understanding of past human interaction.

Research on Ancient Roadways

In many contemporary applications, network analysis is used to evaluate existing or planned modern roadways. The goal is either to construct idealized transportation networks or to identify the shortest routes along existing road networks. These analyses are guided by knowledge of the organization and goals of the social, political, and economic entities that construct and manage the networks. Archaeologists, however, usually work in reverse, using transportation networks identified in the archaeological record to reconstruct the sociopolitical and economic organization and goals of past societies. While some examples of road network analysis in archaeology focus on the reconstruction of past economic behavior (e.g., Santley 1991), most applications are primarily interested in identifying past sociopolitical organization and political economy (e.g., Bell and Church 1985; Bell et al. 1988; Ebert and Hitchcock 1977; Kantner 1997). Gibson's (2000) discussion of central places in Late Medieval Irish chiefdoms, for example, notes that roadways connected tower-houses, confirming their importance in structuring sociopolitical relationships.

Assessing Prehistoric Roadway Networks

When networks of ancient roadways are identifiable, graph theory provides a more structured framework for reconstructing their role in regional organization. Graph theory features formal mathematical techniques for characterizing a network through the analysis of schematic diagrams or matrices that indicate whether or not any two nodes in a network are directly connected and how accessible each node is. These abstractions of the actual network can be mathematically distilled into various indices that measure the network's characteristics, such as the primacy of particular nodes in the network (Gorenflo and Bell 1991, 81–83). This information can assist archaeologists trying to reconstruct regional organization. Drawing on an understanding of graph theory as well as central-place theory, Carol Smith (1976) proposed several models of regional economic networks that archaeologists have employed for understanding regional hierarchies. For example, Smith's "bounded" network reflects a completely decentralized sociopolitical system, while her "dendritic" network model represents centralized administrative systems (for a critique, see Hodges 1987, 122–127). Graph theory and Smith's idealized models have been employed in a number of examples, such as Ebert and Hitchcock's study (1977) of Chaco Anasazi road networks, which identified a dendritic network suggestive of a highly centralized sociopolitical system (see also Santley 1991).

Archaeologically identifiable networks can also be examined using location-allocation analysis, a specific kind of locational analysis that relies on operations modeling. Geographers employ location-allocation analyses to identify where nodes should be located on a network in order to optimize specific objectives. Archaeologists can reverse this analysis, reconstructing the goals and objectives of a past network's creators according to where nodes were located (Gorenflo and Bell 1991, 83–84). In one such study, Bell and colleagues (1988) applied a "multiobjective maximal covering" location-allocation model to understand the motivations behind Aztec regional organization. The network was first identified by combining knowledge of site locations with Colonial period maps, and then several maximal covering models were generated, each emphasizing a different objective that could have shaped the Aztec network. The results showed that Aztec administrative organization was suboptimal, directing the researchers to possible explanations for this inefficiency (Bell et al. 1988, 191–195).

Simulating Prehistoric Road Networks

Another approach to investigating past networks is to focus on the paths or roads themselves rather than on the nodes they are connecting. The goal of this research is most often to identify the criteria that guided where paths were established. This form of network analysis is what Gorenflo and Bell (1991, 89) call the "simulation of network configurations," as the goal is to recreate an entire hypothetical network of paths according to a defined goal and known regional characteristics; the simulated network can then be compared with the real, known one. Early network simulations relied on simple distance measurements between all known nodes, often weighted by node size and perhaps constrained by obvious topographical features (Gorenflo and Bell 1991, 85–87). These simulations then attempted to optimize one or more variables, such as minimizing total distance or maximizing connectivity.

More recent approaches for analyzing prehistoric roadways are facilitated by newer computer technologies, such as GIS, which allow the simulation of entire ancient landscapes. Various computer algorithms can be employed to produce "cost-surfaces" that represent the relative or absolute cost of travel over each unit of space, with cost measured either by units of time or energy (van Leusen 1999; Wheatley and Gillings 2002, 151–159). Optimal "cost-paths" through this simulated landscape can then be generated according to one or more criteria, and entire networks can be modeled. Archaeological applications have employed a few different algorithms for generating both cost-surfaces and the cost-paths through them. Almost all of these applications depend on slope to calculate the cost of movement through a digital landscape covered with a grid of equal-sized cells. Some approaches are quite simple, simulating a cost-path between two points by moving from one cell to another according to which neighboring cell represents the least amount of slope (e.g., Anderson and Gillam 2000, 47). This kind of approach, often equated with "drainage algorithms" used in hydrology, is similar to that employed by the cost-path module in GRASS, which is used in Madry and Rakos's (1996, 113) analysis of Celtic hillfort interaction in France (see also Madry and Crumley 1990). Madry and Rakos note that this type of algorithm necessarily selects an iterative least-cost path rather than the path with the least cumulative cost, similar to how water will find the path of least resistance. The iterative or drainage approach no doubt inadequately mirrors how humans select paths; cost-path algorithms in which the cumulative values are considered are likely to be more realistic.

The cost of human travel is also unlikely to have a simple linear relationship with slope. A variety of algorithms for generating more complex cost-surfaces are available, but many have no clear articulation with realistic human movement. For example, Limp (1990; see also Hartley and Vawser 1994) generated cost-surfaces for his study in Arkansas based on an arbitrary algorithm in which cost increases as the square of the slope. In his study of movement from Archaic base camps, Savage (1990, 344) relies on the first derivative of slope to develop a cost surface. Wheatley (1996, 100) employs a function in the software package IDRISI that calculates the difference between the minimum and maximum slopes in a digital landscape and then divides this difference by ten to create ten distinct bands for the cost-surface; van Leusen (1999, 217) describes a similar algorithm. In Wheatley's study, the slope never exceeded 70 percent, so the IDRISI function determined that seven times more effort was needed to cross such a grade than was needed to cross flat terrain; for the next band in the cost-surface, six times the effort was estimated for a 60 percent slope; and so forth. These bands were then used to generate cost-paths with the least cumulative cost. Wheatley (1996, 100) recognizes that this approach for generating cost-surfaces, while heuristically useful and perfectly appropriate to answer some research questions, is unsubstantiated with empirical studies of actual human movement.

Cost-surface and cost-path algorithms also differ according to whether they assume that the costs to travel across a given space should be isotropic—the same no matter in which direction the space is crossed—or anisotropic (Wheatley and Gillings 2002, 152–153). The majority of analyses have implicitly or explicitly assumed that travel cost is isotropic, usually because most software packages do not readily accommodate anisotropic modeling. However, intuition suggests that the cost of traveling down a slope is less than trudging uphill, and a few attempts to develop anisotropic algorithms have been attempted. Ericson and Goldstein (1980) employ the following calculation to accommodate anisotropic movement:

$$W = F \sum dr + k_u F \sum dz_u + k_d F \sum dz_d \qquad (1)$$

where W is work, F is force, dr is horizontal distance, dz_u is vertical distance up, dz_d is vertical distance down, and k_u and k_d are "equivalence factors," constants that make the algorithm anisotropic. For their study, Ericson and Goldstein (1980) used standards established in backpacking for their equivalence factors, assigning values of 3 for k_u and 1.2 for k_d.

Wheatley and Gillings (2002, 152–153) describe another anisotropic cost-surface algorithm available in the IDRISI software package:

$$\text{Cost} = \text{Cost}_{\text{base}} F_{\text{max}}^{\cos^k(\alpha)} \qquad (2)$$

where $\text{Cost}_{\text{base}}$ is the base cost of movement across flat terrain, F_{max} is the greatest amount of friction possible, α is the angle between the direction of travel and the direction of friction, and k is a constant used to adjust how rapidly increasing α impacts the friction values. Using the cosine value allows this algorithm to recognize that moving across the slope (as opposed to down or up it) will have no more cost than moving across flat terrain, while moving down the slope will decrease this base cost. Like many cost-surface algorithms, how effectively this one mirrors actual human movement is not explicitly described.

Anisotropic algorithms do appear to more realistically represent the energetic costs of traversing a landscape, but simply assigning different costs to uphill and downhill movement does not make the algorithm an accurate representation of human movement. Empirical observations have in fact suggested that the time it takes to move up and down slopes are perhaps more symmetrical than intuition would suggest. This is especially true in topographically complex terrain, where a traveler could spend nearly as much energy braking against a downhill slope as he or she would spend ascending that same slope (e.g., Marble 1996, Figure 1; Wheatley and Gillings 2002, Figure 7.4). To better represent human anisotropic movement, Tobler (1993) derived an empirically derived "hiking function" based on marching data from the Swiss military as reported by Imhof (1950):

$$V = 6e^{-3.5|s+.05|} \tag{3}$$

where V is walking velocity in km/hr, e is the base of natural logarithms, and s is the slope measured in vertical change over horizontal distance. The function predicts a maximum velocity of six km/hr when going down a slope of approximately five to seven degrees, but steeper slopes compel the walker to slow down. The function is therefore roughly symmetrical, albeit offset from the zero slope to acknowledge the faster speeds one can walk on a slightly negative slope.

Tobler's hiking function is consistent with independent assessments of human movement costs, although the majority are laboratory-based experiments that tend to identify lower costs for traveling downhill than are indicated in Imhof's real-world data (Marble 1996, 4–5). Aldenderfer (1998, 12–15) tested Tobler's hiking function in Andean South America and found that it is a reasonably good estimator of travel times in rough terrain, although factors such as weight carried and path condition impact its accuracy (see also Brannan 1992). An algorithm that acknowledges weight and terrain type was generated by Duggan and Haisman (1992) based on laboratory evaluations of human movement:

$$M = 1.5W + 2.0(W + L)(L/W)^2 + n(W + L)(1.5V^2 + 0.35VG) \tag{4}$$

where M is metabolic rate in watts, W is the weight of the unclothed person in kilograms, L is the load carried by the person in kilograms, n is a value reflecting the terrain across which the person is moving, V is the speed of walking in km/hr, and G is the percentage grade. Unfortunately, many archaeological applications cannot take advantage of this more elaborate algorithm due to the number of variables that would be unknowable; holding them constant would undermine the utility of this particular algorithm.

Evaluating Cost-Surface and Cost-Path Approaches

As this discussion has highlighted, choosing an algorithm for generating a cost-surface through which cost-paths will be selected requires a number of decisions. First, does the researcher wish to calculate realistic travel costs, or will relative estimates adequately meet the goals of the research? Relative algorithms are plentiful, but functions that estimate actual travel times are few, and their use requires substantial control over factors that could impact their accuracy. A thorough assessment of how different relative algorithms impact cost-surfaces and cost-path generation is needed. Similarly, the researcher should be aware of the limitations of selecting optimal cost-paths through a simulated landscape in which the surface is divided into a grid of cells. Not only does cell size impact the results, with larger cells obscuring topographic details, but the cost-path algorithms that determine optimal travel from cell to cell are necessarily also artificial. The so-called "Queen's case" is most frequently used to determine the possible moves from any given cell: a traveler can move horizontally or diagonally, providing eight possible directions. Humans, of course, do not make such jerky movements across a landscape, and Goodchild (1977) demonstrates that these cost-path algorithms on raster surfaces identify routes that are suboptimal compared with real-world, vector-oriented movement. A possible solution is the implementation of a "Knight's case" algorithm (Wheatley and Gillings 2002, 157–159).

Another question to consider when evaluating potential approaches for simulating paths is which actual measure of cost should be employed, for the measure used for estimating travel costs is likely to impact the results, even when the researcher is only interested in relative rather than absolute costs. If the researcher wants to determine a path that someone might choose to walk from one point to another, the important question is whether humans choose the path that takes the least energy or the path that takes the least time. For shorter distances, energetic cost may well be the criterion used, while for longer distances, travel time is likely to be important. People traveling to collect and transport food may be more cognizant of how much energy they are expending relative to the amount of food they are gathering (e.g., Brannan 1992; Jones and Madsen 1989). The distinction between time and energy is critical, since measures of energetic costs, such as calories, are slightly anisotropic, but different functions that are perhaps even more anisotropic are likely to better represent temporal costs. The selection of an appropriate algorithm, therefore, requires an assessment of the context of movement.

The researcher should also consider other factors that might affect human movement across a landscape. Numerous cultural and practical considerations will often cause people to alter their path, making it unlikely that anyone in any landscape will follow an optimal route. Prohibited areas such as graveyards, cultivated farmlands, or political boundaries are impediments just as real to the traveler as a steep slope. The locations of springs or other sources of water are also important considerations for someone traveling long distances, especially in an arid environment. Although archaeologists can never completely account for all possible factors that impact human movement, characteristics of the cultural and physical landscape should be assessed, especially when an optimal cost-path does not seem to match the actual archaeological signatures of past human movement.

Despite the unresolved issues in cost-surface and cost-path research, these analytical techniques are still very useful for addressing archaeological problems. Simulated routes can be generated and then compared with the remains of actual roads, paths, or even specific types of sites. By altering the various variables used to generate cost-surfaces and cost-paths, potential criteria that actually guided the placement of the prehistoric remains can be evaluated. To demonstrate the utility of this approach, a case study is presented that demonstrates both how cost-surfaces and cost-paths can be very useful, as well as the questions that need to be considered before engaging in this kind of research.

Case Study: Chaco Anasazi Roadways

Background

In the final few decades of the ninth century AD, small villages in the northern American Southwest began to experience similar social, political, and economic changes. The emerging cultural system, often referred to as the "Chaco Anasazi" tradition, was centered in the middle of the vast and arid San Juan Basin in a shallow wash known as Chaco Canyon. Over the ensuing 250 years, this canyon would be the focus of increasing complexity as monumental architecture was built, astronomical observatories designed, extensive trade networks established, and a small class of elites emerged. Due to the aridity of the region, preservation of the prehistoric remains of this tradition is excellent, feeding an extensive amount of archaeological research on the Chaco Anasazi (e.g., Doyel and Lekson 1992; Kantner and Mahoney 2000; Lekson 1984, 1999; Marshall et al. 1979; Powers et al. 1983; Sebastian 1992; Stuart 2000; Vivian 1990).

One of the major discoveries that have profoundly impacted the study of the Chaco Anasazi is the extensive prehistoric roadways that have been found throughout the northern Southwest (Figure 16.1). While early explorers and archaeologists had described some of the roads at least as long ago as the nineteenth century, the extensive use of remote sensing techniques in the 1970s and 1980s initiated a surge of interest in the topic (Obenauf 1980, 1991; Sever and Wagner 1991). Although most of the roads are shallow swales where dirt and rubble simply was cleared away (Figure 16.2), researchers were astounded at the linearity of the roadways, many of which continue their trajectories over or through any obstacle. Soon, archaeologists were using linear features identified in aerial photographs to define a large-scale road network that presumably connected Chaco Canyon to communities elsewhere in the Southwest.

The enthusiasm in roads research led to proposals that the roadways formed a dendritic exchange system managed by bureaucrats in Chaco Canyon (Ebert and Hitchcock 1977; Mathien 1991). The economic function of the roadways was promoted by research such as the unpublished study in 1977 by E. Pierre Morenon showing that movement on the roads was much easier than moving through the brush alongside them (Stuart 2000, 81–82). These economic interpretations persevere today in many contemporary models of Chaco Anasazi development (e.g., Fish 1999, 49–50; Stuart 2000). Snygg and Windes (1998), for example, argue that the longer roadways facilitated the movement of large timbers needed for constructing the monumental architecture in Chaco Canyon. These interpretations have made their way into the popular understanding of Chaco (e.g., Dent and Coleman 1997; Schreiber 1997).

Unfortunately, the enthusiasm with which researchers accepted the systemic nature of the roadways has been challenged by ground-truthing, in which the road swales identified through remote sensing techniques are checked on the ground (Figure 16.1). This research is finding that many of the suspected roadways are either historic or unverifiable (e.g., Nials et al. 1987). Windes (1991) further suggests that roads in Chaco Canyon itself were primarily short segments that only served local functions, including providing access to springs and terraced fields and facilitating local rather than regional interaction. Roney (1992) similarly finds that roadways throughout the northern Southwest tend to be short segments located only in the immediate vicinity of prehistoric

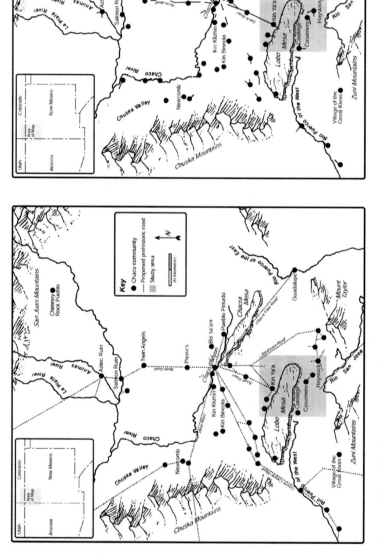

Figure 16.1. The Chaco Anasazi tradition extended over a large area centered on Chaco Canyon in northern New Mexico from A.D. 900–1150. This figure illustrates a few of the over 200 communities and many of the longer prehistoric roads. The map on the left shows the proposed extent of the road network, much of it extrapolated from aerial reconnaissance. In contrast, the map on the right reveals where road segments have actually been confirmed. (Maps based on Gabriel 1991; Nials, et al. 1987; Powers 1984, 54; Roney 1992.)

Figure 16.2. The ancient roadways emanating from the Haystack great house can be seen in this aerial photograph. The eroded roadway extending southwest of the ruins is the most visible, but two more short segments can be found northwest and east of the great house. This photo was taken in the early morning, when the long shadows enhance the visibility of the roadways. (Photograph courtesy of John Roney, Bureau of Land Management.)

communities, perhaps simply connecting different neighborhoods or isolated hamlets with the monumental masonry "great houses" or massive subterranean "great kivas" found in each major community. These results are suggesting that the scale and connectedness of the currently visible roadway system is not nearly as extensive as was once thought (see also Vivian 1997a,b).

These challenges have been countered with suggestions that many of the routes between destinations were never formalized visible roadways—or perhaps they were planned but never constructed. Lekson (1999, 115), for example, contends that road segments were built to connect communities together and with Chaco Canyon, even if spaces between them were not completed. Other suggestions are that modern development or geological processes such as alluviation have destroyed the extensively linked roadways that once existed. An alternative view developed in the past decade is that the short road segments were mostly symbolic links, although researchers disagree as to what they may have been linking together. Perhaps the roadways extended towards other communities or nearby clusters of habitations, only establishing visual ties between them to demonstrate sociopolitical connections (e.g., Roney 1992). Some archaeologists have suggested that the roadways were symbolic "roads through time" that legitimized active great houses and great kivas by connecting them with older, abandoned monumental architecture that had served the same function during earlier times (Fowler and Stein 1992).

A popular proposal is that the roadways served a cosmographic function, symbolically representing the worldview of the Chaco Anasazi through connections with the ideologically charged landscape (Doxtater 1991; Marshall 1997; Sofaer et al. 1989). Proponents of this perspective focus on the alignment of a few roads with cardinal directions, the axial oppositions that some roads form with one another, and the role of Chaco Canyon as a "middle place" from which many roads emanate. Physical connection to prominent geological features with assumed cosmographic roles is also seen as important in these explanations. Cosmographic roads are argued to be completely straight, with no consideration for minimizing either the effort to construct the road or the costs of traveling on them. The most commonly cited example is the North Road, which not only exhibits a northern alignment (Figure 16.1) but also articulates with prominent geological features on the otherwise flat San Juan Basin (Sofaer et al. 1989).

The unresolved issues related to the prehistoric Chaco Anasazi roadways can be distilled into three basic questions. First, are the roadways we see now the remains of a once extensive network that connected Chacoan communities with one another as well as with the center at Chaco Canyon? If so, was the network created to facilitate movement between the communities, or did it just symbolize their integration? If not, did the disconnected road segments serve local social or economic functions, or did they serve a symbolic or cosmographic function at a larger cultural or regional level? To contribute to the evaluation of these issues, a GIS-based cost-surface analysis of roadways in a portion of the Chaco Anasazi region was conducted (see also Kantner 1997).

Methodology

The region exhibiting Chaco Anasazi roadways is enormous, arguably measuring 120,000 km^2 and containing over 135 road segments (estimated from Kantner et al.

2002; Roney 1992; Till 2001). For this reason, this study focused on a 2,500-km^2 study area situated approximately 50 km south of Chaco Canyon and centered on Hosta Butte, a prominent geological feature located between the modern cities of Grants and Gallup, New Mexico (Figure 16.1). Previous investigations in this area have discovered over 2,000 habitations occupied during the Chaco era (approximately AD 900–1100), with most located in about a dozen communities on the northern and southern sides of a large plateau known as Lobo Mesa. As in other parts of the Chacoan world, monumental great houses and great kivas similar to those seen in Chaco Canyon are found in each of the communities within the study area (Kantner 1996, 1999). Numerous roads have also been identified, although most are only short sections that may or may not have once been longer, and several that were originally identified through remote sensing were determined to be historic roads after ground-truthing (Nials et al. 1987).

For this study, the possible functions of the road segments were evaluated by simulating the routes that they should have taken if the hypotheses commonly used to explain their existence are correct. The cost-surface used for this simulation was developed from 7.5-minute USGS Digital Elevation Models (DEMs) using ESRI's Arc/Info software. Each DEM consists of a grid of points that record elevation at 30-m horizontal intervals. Using these data, a new grid of points was generated using a revised version of Waldo Tobler's "hiking function" that is solved for time rather than velocity:

$$T = dr/6e^{-3.5|s+.05|} \tag{5}$$

where T equals the time in hours, dr is the distance in kilometers (converted from meters, the DEM's spatial unit), e is the base of natural logarithms, and s is the slope measured as vertical change over horizontal distance.

Tobler's formula was selected for three important reasons. First, the algorithm is derived from empirical data from a real-world context, and it has received additional empirical support in laboratory and real-world settings. Second, the hiking function is anisotropic and thus more likely to reflect real human movement costs; even though the function is only slightly anisotropic, Marble (1996, 9) found that it generated cost-surfaces that differed substantially from those created with isotropic algorithms. Finally, the hiking function uses time as its measure for travel, and this was thought useful for a region in which travel between many of the communities would have been around a long day's travel; minimizing time might make the difference between arriving at the destination in a day's time or having to make camp for the night. Such a consideration would be especially important, considering the scarcity of water sources in the region. In this context, caloric expenditure would likely be less important.

Application of the hiking function to the basic DEM produced a cost-surface grid indicating the amount of time it would take to cross each 30-m cell. This was then used to evaluate different models of road function. Based on expectations for each model of where roads in the study area should begin and end, idealized "cost-paths" were generated and compared with the actual road segments. For example, to evaluate whether the roadways were designed to ease foot travel and economic exchange between Chaco communities, the GIS software could select the cumulative routes that minimized travel time between every pair of communities in the study area. The resulting cost-path network (Figure 16.3) could then be compared with the prehistoric cultural features to see how closely the modeled paths fit the actual routes of the Chaco Anasazi roads. This

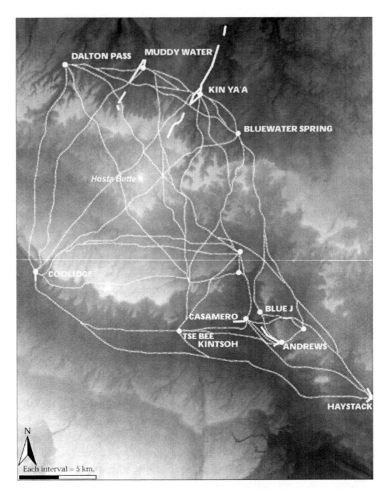

Figure 16.3. The area chosen for the cost-surface analysis includes 13 Chaco-era communities situated on two sides of a prominent mesa. The dotted lines represent the computer-generated network of cost-paths that minimize travel time between the communities, while the solid lines indicate a few of the longer prehistoric road segments. The variable gray background is derived from the Digital Elevation Model; the darker the gray, the lower the elevations, while the lighter grays represent higher elevations.

approach was employed to evaluate each of the proposed road functions described above.

Results

The first issue to investigate is whether the roadways were constructed to economically facilitate travel between Chaco Anasazi communities. For this study, the economic model of road function was evaluated by determining how closely the visible road segments corresponded with optimal cost-paths that the GIS predicted should exist between Chaco communities. The results are fairly unequivocal, for virtually none of the road segments in the study area come even close to aligning with the idealized cost-paths. Figure 16.4 provides one example: dashed lines represent optimal cost-paths between the community of Muddy Water and every other community in the study area, and the prehistoric road segments do not align with any of these projected routes. In fact, out of the 17 roadway segments examined, only three could reasonably fit the economic model of road function. The first is the famous South Road that originates in Chaco Canyon and enters the community of Kin Ya'a (Figures 16.1 and 16.3). This road no doubt served a larger regional role, but because it extends out of the study area, cost-paths for evaluating its function could not be generated. The two other cases that may fit the economic model are very short segments that do align fairly well with cost-paths connecting communities. Whether these alignments are coincidental is difficult to determine, but the poor fit between all other road segments and intercommunity cost-paths suggests that they may be.

The next issue to consider is whether or not the roadways were non-economical, symbolic links between the region's Chacoan communities. Road segments fulfilling this function would be expected to not follow economical cost-paths but would instead simply follow straight-paths between each participating village. An examination of the roadway trajectories in the study area reveal only two possible examples (Figure 16.3): a segment extending west from Casamero could symbolize a connection with Tse Bee Kintsoh, while a segment to the southeast of Casamero could link with Andrews. However, even these examples are not compelling, and both roads fit other modeled functions as well. This suggests that the vast majority of roadways in the study area were not constructed to symbolize linkages with related Chaco Anasazi communities.

While road segments may not have facilitated intercommunity travel or symbolized regional interaction, many appear to have served local economic or sociopolitical roles. For example, a road segment originating in Muddy Water leads to the cliffs at the base of Lobo Mesa where a spring is believed to have once existed (Figure 16.4). Archaeologists investigating this road identified numerous pot fragments along the road and suggested that these vessels were used to obtain water (Nials et al. 1987, 140–141; Windes 1991). The majority of other segments appear to fit with optimal cost-paths generated between the monumental great houses and different neighborhoods found in the Chaco communities. For example, a road segment extending west from Andrews corresponds with the cost-path between the community's great house and a nearby cluster of homes. Similarly, in the community of Tse Bee Kintsoh, a road segment may go around a small mesa to connect a great house with a large concentration of dwellings on the east side of the community. In a few cases, such as at Casamero, short roads extend beyond community boundaries and connect with isolated clusters of habitations known as "hamlets."

If the majority of the road segments match the predicted cost-paths for serving local functions, do any fit either the symbolic or the cosmographic models? A few segments in the study area do support the hypothesis that they symbolically connected important architectural features on the local landscape. In these cases, idealized cost-paths generated between great houses and great kivas correspond with prehistoric roads, such as

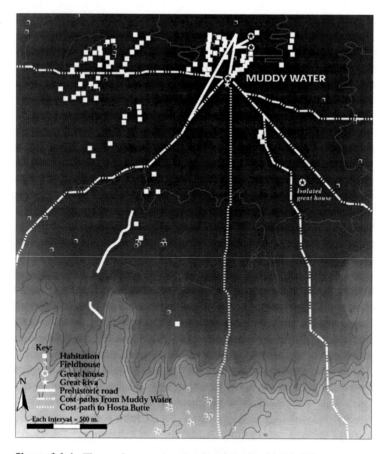

Figure 16.4. The road segments extending from the Muddy Water community do not align with any of the computer-generated cost-paths that minimize travel time between communities. The evidence instead suggests that the longer roadway facilitated travel to a nearby spring, while the other short segments articulate with the monumental great houses. The variable gray background in this figure represents increasing travel cost as one moves away from Muddy Water; as the gray becomes lighter, the travel time increases.

in the community of Andrews, where a segment extending west from the great house appears to connect with a nearby great kiva. Another short segment in Tse Bee Kintsoh exhibits the same pattern, as do roadways in Coolidge (Figure 16.3). However, at least in the case of Tse Bee Kintsoh, the architectural features at either end of the roadway were occupied at the same time, suggesting that not all thoroughfares of this type served as "roads through time."

    In the cosmographic model, roads are seen as symbolic representations of Chaco cosmology writ large on the landscape. This model of road function is difficult to evaluate without a clear idea of the range of possible cosmographical expressions that the Chaco Anasazi might have symbolized. None of the roads in the study area are axial opposites of one another, and none align with any of the cardinal directions. Even the so-called South Road, which originates in Chaco Canyon, strays significantly from a perfect southerly projection as it enters the prehistoric community of Kin Ya'a (Figure 16.3). However, the South Road and at least three other segments do appear to be directed towards Hosta Butte, a prominent geological feature visible as far away as Chaco Canyon. The South Road aligns both with a GIS-generated cost-path between Kin Ya'a and Hosta Butte and with a straight alignment connecting these two points. An identical pattern is found for a road segment emanating northwest from the Andrews community towards Hosta Butte (Figure 16.3). Hosta Butte is an important feature in the cosmography of indigenous groups living in the area, and small shrines with offerings have been found on top. The road segments suggest that the mesa was also a significant point on the prehistoric religious landscape.

Discussion

Archaeologist John Roney (1992) proposes that Chaco Anasazi roads functioned to integrate local Anasazi populations over small areas. His model is based on the scarcity of road segments longer than a kilometer or two as well as on the fact that a great house or great kiva is found at one end of most Chaco road segments. According to Roney (1992, 129), this pattern suggests that the function of roads must have been closely tied to the function of the related architectural features. By assuming that great houses served to locally unify members of each community, Roney hypothesizes that the roads directed attention, both symbolically and physically, towards this integrative architecture (Roney 1992, 130). In essence, his view sees roads as drawing people from surrounding areas and guiding them towards a particular monumental great house or great kiva.

These ideas receive considerable support from the cost-surface analysis of prehistoric roads in the study area (Figure 16.5). Although the specific function may be economic, integrative, or symbolic/cosmographic, virtually all of the roads in the study area appear to have served each community independently from the others. Only the South Road indisputably serves a larger regional role involving several different Chacoan communities, but whether this road minimized travel time or functioned in some other way is unknown, although it does articulate fairly clearly with Hosta Butte. While Roney emphasizes how roadways focused attention on monumental architecture, the segments in the study area were just as likely to emphasize connections with other prominent features in the landscape, from older abandoned great kivas to important geographic locations. Very few of the road segments suggest an important role in the daily economic lives of the Chacoan people.

Adding support to these conclusions are some unexpected patterns that the cost-surface analyses revealed. While the cost-path network optimizing travel between all of the communities in the study area did not match with the actual prehistoric road segments, the routes do correspond with other features. For example, the computer-generated routes run within 100 m of 11 of the 13 stone-circle shrines found in the study area, and the routes often cross at the exact point where isolated hamlets—small clusters of houses not near the larger communities—emerged late in Chacoan prehistory

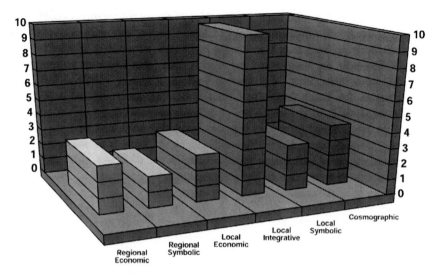

Figure 16.5. Most Chaco-era road segments in the study area appear to have served local functions. Most common are roadways that physically connect monumental architecture with different parts of the community, while symbolic and cosmographic functions also seem likely for some roads. More rare are road segments that served larger regional functions. Note that some of the 17 road segments fit the expectations of more than one model.

(Figure 16.6). In contrast, the formal road segments are clearly not associated with either the stone-circle shrines or the small, isolated hamlets. These patterns suggest that the prehistoric inhabitants of the study area were aware of and regularly used optimal routes for traveling between communities, establishing shrines and small hamlets along these well-traveled paths. The fact that the formal roadways were not built along these routes further supports the contention that they did not provide an economic function, but rather served local religious and sociopolitical purposes.

Concluding Comments

The determination that ancient roadways in the U.S. Southwest were primarily symbolic rather than functional in an economic sense has been anticipated by other scholars (e.g., Earle 1991, 13; Roney 1992). Roads and paths are not the same thing, and people created and used both in prehistory. In the Chaco Anasazi region, roads were most often associated with monumental architecture, and they appear to have been prominent features in the ideological landscape, functioning much like the Neolithic cursuses of England (Harding 1991), the sacbes of the Maya (Folan 1991), or the National Mall in Washington, D.C. The Chacoan roadways were built not to make travel along them easy, but to locally direct community attention to the most important ideological features across space and time, whether geological features associated with important historic events, great kivas used and abandoned generations ago, or monumental great

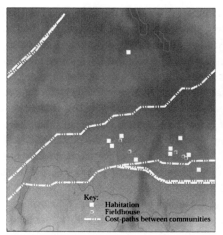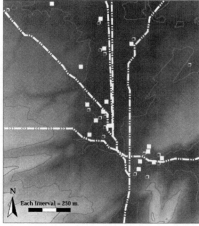

Figure 16.6. The appearance of small isolated hamlets on Lobo Mesa late in the prehistory of the area was once difficult to explain. The cost-surface analyses, however, reveal that these hamlets correspond with points where numerous cost-paths optimizing travel between communities cross one another. Perhaps these hamlets emerged to take advantage of increasing interaction between Chaco communities. Note that formal roadways are not associated with these optimal cost-paths. The hamlet on the left is northeast of Coolidge, while the one on the right is north of Tse Bee Kintsoh.

houses in current use. This does not mean that the road segments were not used for other purposes, and no doubt people traveled along them for other reasons when appropriate. But less formal yet more efficiently placed paths facilitated travel between communities.

Despite the apparent success of the Chaco Anasazi case study described in this chapter, a number of methodological problems remain to be resolved for the use of simulated cost-path networks to be most effective in archaeological research. As in any modeling technique that relies on assumptions of optimization, the researcher must consider the possibility that people were indeed trying to situate roadways to minimize the cost of travel between communities, but their efforts were simply suboptimal for any number of reasons, from technological constraints to limitations on human sensitivity to cost differences. Whether the establishment of paths and roads was shaped by considerations of time or by concerns with caloric expenditure might also have a significant impact on the modeling. Human decision-making does not consider time and energy in the same way, and different cultures may emphasize the value of one over another. Consider, for example, the difference between a traveling salesperson in the United States compared with an Inuit hunter and the routes each might choose to negotiate through a landscape.

A perhaps more substantial problem with the use of simulated cost-paths to evaluate road function is developing a technique to evaluate how closely the simulated route needs to match the actual pathway before the two can be considered as equivalent. Generating a means of evaluation comparable to a confidence interval is a complex issue.

In this study, a subjective assessment of "closeness" between the simulated cost-paths and actual roads was used to evaluate the fit between the two. However, a road that is only slightly suboptimal may actually follow a completely different route, perhaps turning up a different canyon or going over a minor obstacle that the optimal simulated cost-path avoids. Conversely, a simulated optimal cost-path and actual road segment might be spatially quite close to one another but in fact yield completely different travel times or energetic costs. "Closeness" is therefore not the most effective evaluation of the fit between a simulated network and actual road system. Future research might consider additional techniques to better evaluate the fit between the modeled and real landscape, such as Monte Carlo sensitivity analysis or another formal method to compare the objective function values of the optimal and suboptimal cost-paths (Michael Goodchild, personal communication, 2002).

Despite the unresolved issues, the Chaco Anasazi case study still illustrates how GIS-assisted spatial analyses can be useful for evaluating the possible functions of prehistoric roadways. Not only can the GIS help to determine which points on the landscape the roads connected, but it can also suggest whether the routes were designed to ease transportation or whether they may have served another less obvious function. Other investigations of prehistoric roadways may find a GIS-based approach useful for identifying the point in time when simple pathways expediting movement began to be turned into more formal roads such as those built in the prehistoric Andes (e.g., Schreiber 1991). Certainly, there are caveats to be acknowledged in this kind of research, but as long as the researcher is cognizant of available approaches and the abilities and problems of each, the use of spatial analytical techniques for investigating ancient roadways can address many unsolved archaeological problems.

Acknowledgments Numerous people have provided comments and suggestions that have significantly improved this paper and the research on Chacoan roads. Special thanks go to Mark Aldenderfer, Mike Goodchild, Cynthia Herhahn, Ron Hobgood, Don Janelle, Steve Lekson, John Roney, Waldo Tobler, Gwinn Vivian, and Tom Windes. While conducting this research, the author was supported by the University of California, Santa Barbara, the Jacob K. Javits Fellowship Program, and the Crow Canyon Archaeological Center's Lister Fellowship Program.

References

Aldenderfer, M.S. 1998. Montane Foragers: Asana and the South-Central Andean Archaic. Iowa City: University of Iowa Press.

Aldenderfer, M.S., and H.D.G. Maschner (eds.). 1996. *Anthropology, Space, and Geographic Information Systems*. Oxford: Oxford University Press.

Allen, K.M.S., Stanton W. Green, and E.B.W. Zubrow. 1990. *Interpreting Space: GIS and Archaeology*. London: Taylor & Francis.

Anderson, D. G., and J.C. Gillam. 2000. Paleoindian colonization of the Americas: Implications from an examination of physiography, demography, and artifact distribution. *American Antiquity* 65(1): 43–66.

Bell, T.L., and R.L. Church. 1985. Location-allocation modeling in archaeological settlement pattern research: Some preliminary applications. *World Archaeology* 16(3): 354–371.

Bell, T.L., R.L. Church, and L. Gorenflo. 1988. Late Horizon regional efficiency in the northeastern basin of Mexico: A location-allocation perspective. *Journal of Anthropological Archaeology* 7: 163–202.

Brannan, J.A. 1992. On modeling resource transport costs: Suggested refinements. *Current Anthropology* 33(1): 56–60.

Dent, S.D., and B. Coleman. 1997. A planner's primer: Lessons from Chaco. In B.H. Morrow and V.B. Price (eds.), *Anasazi Architecture and American Design*. Albuquerque: University of New Mexico Press, 53–61.

Doxtater, D. 1991. Reflections of the Anasazi cosmos. In O. Gron, E. Engelstad, and I. Lindblom (eds.), *Social Space: Human Spatial Behavior in Dwellings and Settlements*. Odense, Denmark: Odense University Press, 155–184.

Doyel, D.E., and S.H. Lekson. 1992. Regional organization in the American Southwest. In D.E. Doyel (ed.), *Anasazi Regional Organization and the Chaco System*. Albuquerque, N. Mex.: Maxwell Museum of Anthropology, 15–22.

Duggan, A., and M.F. Haisman. 1992. Prediction of the metabolic cost of walking with and without loads. *Ergonomics* 35(4): 417–426.

Earle, T.K. 1991. Paths and roads in evolutionary perspective. In C.D. Trombold (ed.), *Ancient Road Networks and Settlement Hierarchies in the New World*. Cambridge: Cambridge University Press, 10–16.

Ebert, J.I., and R.K. Hitchcock. 1977. Locational modelling in the analysis of the prehistoric roadway system at and around Chaco Canyon, New Mexico. In T.R. Lyons and R.K. Hitchcock (eds.), *Aerial Remote Sensing Techniques in Archeology*. Albuquerque, N. Mex.: National Park Service and University of New Mexico, 169–207.

Ericson, J.E., and R. Goldstein. 1980. Work space: A new approach to the analysis of energy expenditure within site catchments. In F.J. Findlow and J.E. Ericson (eds.), *Catchment Analysis: Essays on Prehistoric Resource Space*. Los Angeles: University of California, 21–30.

Fish, S.K. 1999. How complex were the Southwestern great towns' polities? In J.E. Neitzel (ed.), *Great Towns and Regional Polities in the Prehistoric American Southwest and Southeast*. Albuquerque: University of New Mexico Press, 45–58.

Folan, W.J. 1991. Sacbes of the northern Maya. In C.D. Trombold (ed.), *Ancient Road Networks and Settlement Hierarchies in the New World*. Cambridge: Cambridge University Press, 222–229.

Fowler, A.P., and J.R. Stein. 1992. The Anasazi great house in space, time, and paradigm. In D.E. Doyel (ed.), *Anasazi Regional Organization and the Chaco System*. Albuquerque, N. Mex.: Maxwell Museum of Anthropology, 101–122.

Gabriel, K. 1991. Roads to Center Place: A Cultural Atlas of Chaco Canyon and the Anasazi. Boulder, Colo.: Johnson Publishing.

Gibson, D.B. 2000. Nearer, my chieftain, to thee: Central place theory and chiefdoms, revisited. In M.W. Diehl (ed.), *Hierarchies in Action: Cui Bono*. Carbondale: Center for Archaeological Investigations, Southern Illinois University, 241–263.

Goodchild, M.F. 1977. An evaluation of lattice solutions to the corridor location problem. *Environment and Planning A* 9: 727–738.

Gorenflo, L.J., and T.L. Bell. 1991. Network analysis and the study of past regional organization. In C.D. Trombold (ed.), *Ancient Road Networks and Settlement Hierarchies in the New World*. Cambridge: Cambridge University Press, 80–98.

Harding, J. 1991. Using the unique as the typical: Monuments and the ritual landscape. In P. Garwood, D. Jennings, R. Skeates, and J. Toms (eds.), *Sacred and Profane: Proceedings of the Conference on Archaeology, Ritual and Religion*. Oxford: Oxford University, 141–151.

Hartley, R.J., and A.W. Vawser. 1994. Wayfinding in The Desert: Evaluating the Role of Rock Art Through GIS. Paper read at 1994 International Rock Art Congress, at Flagstaff, Ariz.

Hodges, R. 1987. Spatial models, anthropology and archaeology. In J.M. Wagstaff (ed.), *Landscape and Culture: Geographical and Archaeological Perspectives.* Oxford: Basil Blackwell, 118–133.

Imhof, E. 1950. *Gelaende und Karte.* Zurich, Germany: Rentsch.

Jones, K.T., and D.B. Madsen. 1989. Calculating the cost of resource transportation: A Great Basin example. *Current Anthropology* 30(4): 529–534.

Kantner, J. 1996. Political competition among the Chaco Anasazi of the American Southwest. *Journal of Anthropological Archaeology* 15: 41–105.

Kantner, J. 1997. Ancient roads, modern mapping: Evaluating prehistoric Chaco Anasazi roadways using GIS technology. *Expedition Magazine* 39(3): 49–62.

Kantner, J. 1999. The Influence of Self-Interested Behavior on Sociopolitical Change: The Evolution of the Chaco Anasazi in the Prehistoric American Southwest. Ph.D. dissertation, Department of Anthropology, University of California at Santa Barbara, Santa Barbara.

Kantner, J. 2003. Regional analysis in archaeology. In H.D.G. Maschner and C. Chippendale (eds.), *Handbook of Archaeological Methods.* Lanham, Md.: Altamira Press. In Press.

Kantner, J., and N.M. Mahoney. (eds.). 2000. *Great House Communities Across the Chacoan Landscape.* Vol. 64, Anthropological Papers. Tucson: University of Arizona Press.

Kantner, J., D. Gilpin, N. Mahoney, K.R. Durand, and R. Van Dyke. 2002. The Chaco World Great House Database. Access Date 5/12/2002. Available from http://sipapu.gsu.edu/chacoworld.html.

Lekson, S.H. 1984. *Great Pueblo Architecture of Chaco Canyon.* Vol. 18b, Publications in Archaeology. Albuquerque, New Mexico: National Park Service.

Lekson, S.H. 1999. *The Chaco Meridian: Centers of Political Power in the Ancient Southwest.* Walnut Creek, Calif.: AltaMira Press.

Limp, W.F. 1990. Intersite analysis: Aboriginal use of the Rush Locality. In G.I. Sabo (ed.), *Archaeological Investigations at 3MR80-Area D in the Rush Development Area, Buffalo National River, Arkansas.* Santa Fe, N. Mex.: Southwest Cultural Resources Center, U.S. National Park Service, 295–345.

Madry, S.L.H., and C.L. Crumley. 1990. An application of remote sensing and GIS in a regional archaeological settlement pattern analysis: The Arroux River valley, Burgundy, France. In K.M. S. Allen, S.W. Green, and E.B.W. Zubrow (eds.), *Interpreting Space: GIS and Archaeology.* London: Taylor & Francis, 364–380.

Madry, S.L.H., and L. Rakos. 1996. Line-of-sight and cost-surface techniques for regional research in the Arroux River Valley. In H.D. G. Maschner (ed.), *New Methods, Old Problems: Geographic Information Systems in Modern Archaeological Research.* Carbondale: Southern Illinois University, 104–126.

Marble, D.F. 1996. *The Human Effort Involved in Movement over Natural Terrain: A Working Bibliography.* Part I of the Final Report submitted under National Park Service Contract 6115-4-8031, Columbus, Ohio: Ohio State University.

Marshall, M.P. 1997. The Chacoan roads: A cosmological interpretation. In B.H. Morrow and V.B. Price (eds.), *Anasazi Architecture and American Design.* Albuquerque: University of New Mexico Press, 62–74.

Marshall, M.P., J.R. Stein, R.W. Loose, and J.E. Novotny. 1979. *Anasazi Communities of the San Juan Basin.* Santa Fe: Public Service Company of New Mexico and New Mexico Historic Preservation Division.

Maschner, H.D. G. (ed.). 1996. *New Methods, Old Problems: Geographic Information Systems in Modern Archaeological Research.* Vol. 23, Occasional Paper. Carbondale: Southern Illinois University.

Mathien, F.J. 1991. Political, Economic, and Demographic Implications of the Chaco road network. In C.D. Trombold (ed.), *Ancient Road Networks and Settlement Hierarchies in the New World*. Cambridge: Cambridge University Press, 99–110.

Nials, F., J. Stein, and J. Roney. 1987. *Chacoan Roads in the Southern Periphery: Results of Phase II of the BLM Chaco Roads Project*. Vol. 1, Cultural Resources Series. Santa Fe: Bureau of Land Management, New Mexico State Office.

Obenauf, M.S. 1980. A history of research on the Chacoan roadway system. In T.R. Lyons and F.J. Mathien (eds.), *Cultural Resources Remote Sensing*. Washington, D.C.: National Park Service, Cultural Resources Management Division, 123–167.

Obenauf, M.S. 1991. Photointerpretation of Chacoan roads. In C.D. Trombold (ed.), *Ancient Road Networks and Settlement Hierarchies in the New World*. Cambridge: Cambridge University Press, 34–41.

Powers, R.P. 1984. Regional interaction in the San Juan Basin: The Chacoan outlier system. In W.J. Judge and J.D. Schelberg (eds.), *Recent Research on Chaco Prehistory*. Albuquerque, New Mexico: National Park Service, Division of Cultural Research, 23–36.

Powers, R.P., W.B. Gillespie, and S.H. Lekson. 1983. *The Outlier Survey: A Regional View of Settlement in the San Juan Basin*. Vol. 3, Reports of the Chaco Center. Albuquerque, New Mexico: Division of Cultural Research, National Park Service, U.S. Department of the Interior.

Roney, J.R. 1992. Prehistoric roads and regional integration in the Chacoan system. In D.E. Doyel (ed.), *Anasazi Regional Organization and the Chaco System*. Albuquerque, N. Mex.: Maxwell Museum of Anthropology, 123–131.

Santley, R.S. 1991. The structure of the Aztec transport network. In C.D. Trombold (ed.), *Ancient Road Networks and Settlement Hierarchies in the New World*. Cambridge: Cambridge University Press, 198–210.

Savage, S.H. 1990. Modelling the Late Archaic social landscape. In Kathleen M.S. Allen, Stanton W. Green, and Ezra B.W. Zubrow (eds.), *Interpreting Space: GIS and Archaeology*. New York: Taylor & Francis, 330–355.

Schreiber, K.J. 1991. The association between roads and polities: Evidence for Wari roads in Peru. In C.D. Trombold (ed.). *Ancient Road Networks and Settlement Hierarchies in the New World*. Cambridge: Cambridge University Press, 243–252.

Schreiber, S.D. 1997. Engineering feats of the Anasazi: Buildings, roads, and dams. In B.H. Morrow and V.B. Price (eds.). *Anasazi Architecture and American Design*. Albuquerque: University of New Mexico Press, 77–87.

Sebastian, L. 1992. The Chaco Anasazi: Sociopolitical Evolution in the Prehistoric Southwest. Cambridge: Cambridge University Press.

Sever, T.L., and D.W. Wagner. 1991. Analysis of prehistoric roadways in Chaco Canyon using remotely sensed digital data. In C.D. Trombold (ed.), *Ancient Road Networks and Settlement Hierarchies in the New World*. Cambridge: Cambridge University Press, 42–52.

Smith, C.A. 1976. Regional economic systems: Linking geographic models and socioeconomic models. In C.A. Smith (ed.), *Regional Analysis*. New York: Academic Press, 3–63.

Snygg, J., and T. Windes. 1998. Long, wide roads and great kiva roofs. *Kiva* 64 (1): 7–25.

Sofaer, A P., M.P. Marshall, and R.M. Sinclair. 1989. The Great North Road: A cosmographic expression of the Chaco culture of New Mexico. In A.F. Aveni (ed.), *World Archaeoastronomy*. Cambridge: Cambridge University Press, 88–132.

Stuart, D.E. 2000. *Anasazi America*. Albuquerque: University of New Mexico.

Till, J.D. 2001. *Chacoan Roads and Road-Associated Sites in The Lower San Juan Region: Assessing the Role of Chacoan Influences in the Northwestern Periphery*. Unpublished M.A. thesis, Department of Anthropology, Anthropology: University of Colorado, Boulder.

Tobler, W. 1993. Three presentations on geographical analysis and modeling. Vol. 93–1, Technical Report. Santa Barbara: University of California at Santa Barbara.

Van Leusen, M. 1999. Viewshed and cost surface analysis using GIS. In J.A. Barcelo, I. Briz and A. Vila (eds.), *New Techniques for Old Times. CAA98. Computer Applications and Quantitative Methods in Archaeology*. Oxford: BAR, 215–223.

Vivian, R.G. 1990. *The Chacoan Prehistory of the San Juan Basin*. San Diego: Academic Press.

Vivian, R.G. 1997a. Chacoan roads: Function. *Kiva* 63 (1): 35–68.

Vivian, R.G. 1997b. Chacoan roads: Morphology. *Kiva* 63 (1): 7–34.

Westcott, K.L., and R. Joe Brandon. (eds.). 2000. *Practical Applications of GIS for Archaeologists: A Predictive Modeling Kit*. London: Taylor & Francis.

Wheatley, D. 1996. The use of GIS to understand regional variation in earlier Neolithic Wessex. In H.D.G. Maschner (ed.). *New Methods, Old Problems: Geographic Information Systems in Modern Archaeological Research*. Carbondale: Southern Illinois University, 75–103.

Wheatley, D., and M. Gillings. 2002. Spatial Technology and Archaeology: The Archaeological Applications of GIS. New York: Taylor & Francis.

Windes, T.C. 1991. The prehistoric road network at Pueblo Alto, Chaco Canyon, New Mexico. In C.D. Trombold (ed.), *Ancient Road Networks and Settlement Hierarchies in the New World*. Cambridge: Cambridge University Press, 111–131.

Part IV

Multi-Scale Spatial Perspectives

The fourth and final section of the book builds on the theme of scale, but departs from the single-scale themes of previous chapters by including studies that make use of multiple scales. Scale is such a pervasive theme in any spatial approach to social science that it is perhaps not obvious that considering several scales at once can have substantial value. Yet the chapters in this section clearly demonstrate the added value that can be obtained by comparing analyses at different scales and by examining systems and processes that operate at multiple scales. For example, an analyst who chooses to look at a social system at several distinct spatial scales may often find that patterns at one scale show little relationship to patterns at other scales and may even be in direct conflict. An analysis of census data at the census-tract scale may reveal patterns that are not evident at all at the block-group scale and vice versa. One of the recurring themes of this section is the difficulty of reasoning and inference across scales. Social scientists have long been aware of the ecological fallacy—the impossibility, or at least extreme difficulty, of making inferences about individual behavior from data about aggregates.

In the first chapter in this section, Daly and Lock survey the recent history of GIS applications in archaeology and contrast contemporary thinking about GIS and spatial perspectives with earlier work almost 15 years ago. While early applications of GIS used the technology to automate conventional modes of analysis, more recent thinking has focused on new perspectives that are possible only with GIS—in essence, GIS has changed the questions that archaeologists ask, just as the telescope changed the questions that seventeenth-century scientists were able to ask about the cosmos. So, while early work using GIS tended to be quantitative, automating the quantitative analyses in vogue at that time, more recent work has emphasized qualitative description and has opened the possibility of analysis at multiple scales. Today, archaeologists are able to use GIS and spatial methods to examine deposits at many scales and to use them to reveal multi-scale interactions in ancient social systems. Unlike many of the chapters in this book, which emphasize the value of spatial perspectives in providing context to observations, this chapter stresses the importance of time in addition to space, and the role of context in both space and time.

In Chapter 18, Gatrell and Rigby undertake an ambitious survey of the role of spatial perspectives in health studies and the importance of location and place in shaping health. Space is the key to estimating the exposures to environmental and social factors that influence human health, and GIS has played a major role in correlating health outcomes to exposure. Space is also the key to accurate assessment of human access to goods and services, and hence, to an important aspect of the quality of health services. The authors elaborate on these two themes at multiple spatial scales, examining, for example, the influence of various scales of human movement—commuting, migration, and vacation travel—on the spread of diseases such as AIDS. Analysis of patterns of health at multiple scales can help us to understand the importance of different factors impacting human health, and they illustrate these issues by reference to breast cancer and skin disease, in addition to HIV/AIDS.

Weeks argues in Chapter 19 that one of the most important drivers of increasing interest in spatial approaches in demography is the availability of data—that more and more data are available in georeferenced form, inviting spatial analysis. He provides a thorough overview of how different data resources at different levels of spatial resolution can aid in the analysis of demographic processes. He also reviews the importance of context, particularly the built and natural environments in demographic processes, and argues that aggregate population patterns are often no more than the expression of vast numbers of local decisions, conditioned by local factors. Weeks illustrates these points through a space-time analysis of fertility patterns based on village-level data for a densely populated rural governorate of Egypt. The research shows how it is possible to investigate the fertility transition at multiple scales and is an excellent demonstration of the integration of spatial methodologies, including GIS, remote sensing, and spatial statistics.

The final two chapters of this last section move away from analysis, into spatially explicit modeling. The first, by Guldmann, introduces the reader to the spatial interaction model, a class of models dating back to the nineteenth century and widely used to analyze and theorize about interactions in space. Spatial interaction models have been applied to flows of goods, migrants, commuters, shoppers, and many other phenomena, but Guldmann focuses on their use in understanding patterns of international telecommunications traffic.

Although the spatial interaction model was originally derived by analogy to Newton's inverse-square Law of Gravity, predicting that interactions between two places would decline with the square of distance, ceteris paribus, modern thinking has defined several justifications for the model, and placed it on a sound theoretical basis. The model can be derived from a simple argument about utilities and choices, or from an entropy-maximizing argument that the model is no more than the most likely arrangement given the known constraints. The author shows the value of applying the model to international telecommunications traffic, predicting that the interaction between any pair of countries (and by extension any other origin and destination) is the product of a factor unique to the origin, a factor unique to the destination, and an inverse function of the distance between them. Deviations from this model can be used to identify anomalies and patterns and to link them to particular behaviors and effects.

Chapter 21 forms a fitting last chapter, because it illustrates a new generation of research that brings together many of the themes of the book. Cellular automata (CA) were devised, in part, as a means of modeling complex systems and of discovering *emergent properties*, properties of the aggregate behavior of such systems that could not be readily deduced from knowledge of the processes occurring in the system. Cellular automata are now widely applied in spatial settings. A series of simple rules is devised to represent the most important aspects of the complex processes impacting the space. Boundary conditions are defined to represent the space and provide it with characteristics typical of real geographic spaces—for example, varying topography or the presence of transportation arteries. The rules are then executed in a series of iterations, and the states of the system are tracked through time. Such CA models are being applied to areas as different as the prediction of urban growth, land use transition, and the development of urban heat islands. They provide very general environments for the modeling of processes and for the imposition of constraints, through the boundary conditions or through the rules themselves.

The authors describe two major models of the Dutch social landscape. As with many such projects, there is no realistic possibility that the true future landscape will exactly match predictions; instead, interest focuses on the aggregate properties of the predictions and, often, on their spatial patterns. It is important, for example, to know the conditions under which the future landscape will be more fragmented, because of the implications of habitat fragmentation for the survival of species. Similarly, it is important to know average travel distances and levels of transport congestion.

All such models raise interesting questions of validation and of epistemology. How do we know that a model's predictions are accurate or that one model's predictions are more accurate than another's? What, exactly, does the construction and execution of a model tell us about social processes, and does it lead to explanation and understanding in the traditional scientific senses of those words? These are important questions, and it is fitting that they are asked in the last chapter and in one that focuses on such an important and emerging area of social science.

17

Time, Space, and Archaeological Landscapes
Establishing Connections in the First Millennium BC

Patrick Daly

Gary Lock

O ver the past ten years or so, an increasing number of archaeologists have recognized the importance of the work of social theorists such as Bourdieu (1977) and Giddens (1984) in providing a framework for addressing the construction of cultural landscapes (Ashmore and Knapp 1999; Hirsch and O'Hanlon 1995). The general lines of inquiry stemming from this approach question how the human condition is reproduced across space and time, from individual acts of practice to complex webs of social behavior. The manifestations of cultural information, which form the basis for archaeology and anthropology, are clearly multifaceted. While these include direct forms of explicit communication such as speech and written text, when dealing with non-literate societies and extended temporal spans the shortcomings of both of these for passing on knowledge to subsequent generations is obvious[1].

For most of human history, cultures have persevered because large amounts of cultural information are conveyed through a range of socially directed, necessitated, and recognized practices. Both the physical and cognitive "knowledge" necessary to make tools, farm the land, navigate from place to place, build dwellings and monuments, relate both within and with other groups, etc., are learned through association with, and, most importantly, involvement in, some form of practice. In addition, the social institutions that give cultures definition, stability, trajectory, and endurance all are equally dependant upon networks of both ritual and pragmatic social practices for their substance and "flow." This involvement may be any combination of discursive and non-discursive, conscious and sub-conscious, meditated and spontaneous practices. It is within the enactment of this range of practice, regardless of how tightly prescribed, that opportunities for development and change occur.

Fundamental to all of this is the material world and hence the potential of archaeology. It is now generally accepted that the landscape and mobile elements of material culture are not just the setting and props within which people live and interact (Barrett 1994), thus acknowledging both the agency of people and the agency of materiality. A range of factors, from the naturally endowed characteristics of material objects, to social values placed upon them, gives objects unique roles within people's lives, the enactment of social practice, and therefore, the definition and construction of cultural landscapes.

An inextricable combination of materiality and cultural significance leads to complex and unique variations of structuration at a range of different scales, from the filling of individual postholes, through the layout of settlements, to the spatial organization of the landscape itself. Structuration theory is based upon the premise that all cultural and social activity occurs within structural paradigms that direct the possibilities for action and development of newer structures. Social agents do not operate within totally confined ranges of possibilities, but rather, all human decisions have some grounding within a nexus of practices and materiality inherited from the past and intentions for the future (Gosden 1994). All aspects of human activity, while in some way having to consider and contend with the natural characteristics of the physical environment, are shaped by engagements with elements of materiality endowed with social meaning, producing social response. The landscape at any point in time exerts pressures, sometime much more dominate than those based upon pure environmental restrictions, reflecting the cultural aspects of material residue, built up through social practices.

While there has been a great deal of theoretic musing about such issues within archaeology generally and landscape archaeology in particular, it is clear that there is a lack of formalized structures and methodologies for developing these new approaches. In fact, much of the debate seems to center upon words and intuition rather than on data and analysis, a dichotomy that is reflected more generally within the arena of GIS-based archaeological landscape studies (Lock 2002). Because GIS has become fundamental to much of landscape archaeology, it is of relevance here to briefly explore this tension through the historical development of GIS applications within archaeology. We then move on to offer a way forward, through the construction of a formalized approach to the structuration of cultural landscapes and social practice using the Hillforts of the Ridgeway Project as a case study.

It is now just over ten years since the landmark volume on GIS and archaeology introduced the technology and its applications to the discipline (Allen et al. 1990). A considerable literature since then has described an increasing variety of applications and demonstrated the strengths and weaknesses of the technology, together with methodological and theoretical concerns. Periodic reviews of these developments can be found in the main texts and need not be rehearsed here in detail (Aldenderfer and Maschner 1996; Johnson and North 1997; Lock 2000; Lock and Stančič 1995; Maschner 1996; Peterson 1998; Slapšak 2001; Wescott and Brandon 2000).

The early adopters of a new technology often use that technology to reproduce tasks that are already being performed in other ways. This was certainly true of GIS in archaeology, where the first applications were focused on predictive modeling of site locations within North American Cultural Resource Management (CRM), a major area of interest pre-dating GIS, as shown by a survey citing over seventy papers on the topic (Kohler and Parker 1986). One underlying assumption is that past peoples did not locate their sites at random but employed logical decision-making processes. It follows, therefore, that if the variables involved in that decision-making can be identified and measured, then predictions of site location can be made based on the characteristics of known sites (Kvamme 1990). The main criticism of predictive modeling has been the charge of environmental determinism, and related functionalist interpretations, generally seen as a retrogressive step in terms of embracing humanist theory (Gaffney and van Leusen 1995). Cultural and social considerations of site location are not incorporated into these models, producing an unacceptably reductionist version of complex social decision-making. Here we can see a soft technological determinism, as it is much easier to digitize environmental variables such as elevation, soil type, and distance from water than it is "social variables." Indeed, it is somewhat difficult even identifying what constitutes aspects of social awareness that could be included within a GIS study.

These criticisms of GIS as a predictive modeling tool, and the so-called return to environmental determinism, fed into wider debates about the epistemology of the technology. Another stimulus for these discussions was the publication of the first integrated landscape analysis using GIS (Gaffney and Stančič 1991), which established GIS more centrally within the interests of landscape analysis through the case study of Hvar, a small island off the coast of Dalmatia. During the early- to mid-1990s, however, these initial applications of GIS to landscape archaeology suffered from a variety of criticisms, with Hvar-type analyses seen as being rooted in the overly mechanistic spatial modeling of the 1970s, supporting an agenda of quantitative reductionism with an emphasis on functionalism and economic explanations. This was at odds with the humanistic approaches to landscape, for example, as presented to a wide audience in Tilley's influential *A Phenomenology of Landscape* (1994). The essence of this tension is often presented as the "space versus place" argument, where space is characterized as a void in which human activities took place, the same everywhere and at any point through time, a neutral backdrop for spatial modeling. Places, on the other hand, are culturally meaningful locales that act as a medium for practice by being part of human experience and activity. Places, therefore, are fluid and capable of taking on different meaning at different times but are always formative within personal and social practice.

Whereas geographical models are relatively methodologically concise and reproducible within a GIS context (through buffering, overlaying, and statistical tests of association, for example), the text-rich description that forms the basis of humanistic landscape work is focused on descriptive theory rather than methodology. This dichotomy has been established since at least 1993 (Wheatley 1993) and has produced a growing literature concerned with the theorizing of archaeological GIS (e.g., Wheatley 2000; Wise 2000; Witcher 1999), although, it must be said, very few innovative applications that have moved far beyond the theorizing. Developments have concentrated on notions of landscape perception mainly through visibility studies (Wheatley and Gillings 2000) or through the modeling of movement based on various forms of cost-surface formulae (Llobera 1996, 2000).

While these have been innovative in moving away from earlier functionalist methodologies, we feel that they still fall short of addressing the central concerns of landscape archaeology. Perhaps most serious is the failure to confront the multi-scalar nature of archaeological data and the complexity of the data itself. To do this, we propose to shift the emphasis away from the phenomenological "perception" of the landscape toward the structuration of the archaeological landscape as displayed through data. This entails interpretation through notions of social practice, with particular attention being paid to the different levels of structuration represented by artifacts, the contextuality of their deposition and discovery, connections that create sites, and wider connections that create landscapes. Weaving together this complex web of relationships is not only spatiality but also temporality, an axis of analysis that has been poorly served by archaeological GIS despite being a fundamental underpinning of any archaeological endeavor. Since the early days of archaeological GIS, it has been recognized that incorporating temporal analysis is problematic (Castleford 1992), and again, we propose that a way forward is through the structuring of data to create multi-scalar temporal connections.

Of course these concerns are not limited to archaeological applications of GIS and, to a large extent, equate with Curry's classification of GIS into PaleoGIS and GIS_2 (Curry 1998) and reflect a wider GIS discourse (Lock and Harris 2000). There are many strands to the GIS and Society debate that are of relevance here, including the social construction of data and its bias toward scientific data-driven, as opposed to theory-driven, representation (Mark 1993).

Scales of Materiality

The material world consists of an almost infinite range of material elements, implicating all scales of possible human activity. Any investigation of past social practices drawing upon material evidence has to understand both the role of material culture within the lives of people in the past and how traces of this are manifested in the deposits of cultural material that we uncover through excavation. To this end, an integrated approach is needed, bringing together data from different physical scales, while recognizing the complex relationships that exist within and between them. Here we focus on five scales of materiality: the object, feature, deposit, site, and landscape.

Objects are the most conceptually straightforward, defined as individual elements of material culture, pottery sherds being one of the most common categories. Features are the structural components of various forms of human activity. For the present case study they largely consist of sub-surface elements such as storage pits, postholes, and ditches, but can also include aboveground entities, for example earthworks and walls. Many of these features either are the result of various forms of deposition or get filled by deposits. Deposits are the most potentially complicated scale, as these are both the venue within which objects are discarded and ultimately recovered, and also the physical point of contact where all scales were brought together through the practice of constructing the deposit. A site is defined as a complex of features, objects, and deposits that form a coherent physical and social entity. Similarly, landscape is constructed from a web of connections that have meaning through their physicality but also through their potential for analysis and interpretation. While this division of scale is sensible against the backdrop of most archaeological evidence, it must be kept in mind that the boundaries are often very fluid, based as much upon context as physical criteria. A posthole may be viewed as a feature, containing distinct deposits and objects, while also being one of many components of a single dwelling structure, with its own unique characteristics binding it, and all of its parts, together into a single entity.

All of these scales are interwoven, and mutually define each other. Therefore, any investigation has to focus upon sets of relationships between scales to understand any of the elements, as well as the wider practices of social activity that they represent. Furthermore, the biographical aspects of materiality need to be appreciated, as material culture is not static (Appadurai 1986). All elements of materiality have durations of creation, use-life and discard, and it is very common for them to play different roles during different parts of their lives, reflecting the constantly shifting flow of social context. All aspects of materiality, and the practices associated with these, can mean a variety of things to different people, in different places, social contexts, and times. After a brief description of the Ridgeway database below, we move on to explore some examples of practice, with regards to data management and structure at different scales.

Toward a Digital Ridgeway

The Hillforts of the Ridgeway Project began a campaign of fieldwork, together with background research, in 1994, resulting in one of the most intensively studied areas of archaeological landscape in England. The study area comprises 150 km^2 in southern Oxfordshire, united by the ancient Ridgeway track running approximately east–west through it (Figure 17.1). This follows the northern scarp of the chalk massif and has a series of Later Prehistoric hillforts positioned along it, overlooking the Vale of the White Horse to the north (Bell and Lock 2000). Hillforts are large banked and ditched enclosures that have been variously interpreted as settlements, fortified sites, and ritual enclosures, their social role having been re-interpreted several times over the last few decades (Hill 1996). In the study area, the hillforts are Liddington Castle, Hardwell Camp, Uffington Castle, Rams Hill, and Segsbury Camp. The temporal focus of the project is the Later Prehistoric and Romano-British periods (approximately 1000 BC to AD 450), resulting in one and a half millennia of landscape development and use. Both north and south of the Ridgeway are complex archaeological landscapes of farmsteads, larger settlements, field systems, and extensive linear ditches spanning the period and known from a rich source of aerial photographic evidence, fieldwalking surveys, and previous excavation.

Excavation carried out by the Project[2] has centered on Uffington (1994–1995), Segsbury (1996–1997), Alfred's Castle, a small hillfort just to the south of the Ridgeway (1998–2000), and Marcham/Frilford (2001 and ongoing), a later prehistoric and Romano-British settlement situated in the lower environment of the Vale. A remarkably complex picture of diversity and similarities is emerging from this work, drawing attention to how the physicality of landscape can be used through social memory to sustain long periods of discontinuous use and re-use of particular places (Gosden and Lock 1998). Central to this work has been the creation of a digital archive, which is powerful and flexible enough to create an environment for data management, analysis, and presentation. The challenge is to incorporate data obtained through excavation (vertical data) and data spread across the landscape (horizontal data), both producing a wide range of data types, sources, and resolutions. The solution is outlined below

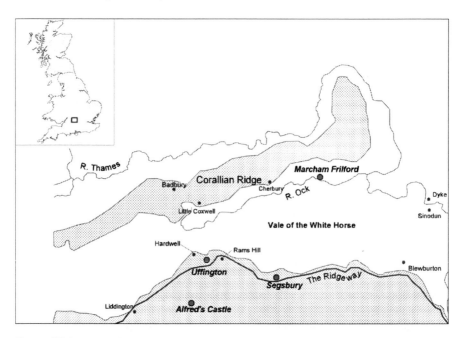

Figure 17.1. The Hillforts of the Ridgeway study area, showing the sites excavated, large circles, and other hillforts, including those mentioned in the text. High ground is shown shaded. (© Crown Copyright Ordnance Survey. An EDINA Digimap/JISC supplied service.)

before we move on to demonstrate how some of the theoretical ideas above can be approached using notions of structuration and social practice.

The Spatial Dataset

The framework for the spatial dataset was obtained from the Ordnance Survey Digimap program[3] in the form of six 1:10,000 OS quarter sheets, with both raster information and vector contour and elevation data covering an area of 150 square km. Within this setting, all of the known archaeological sites in the case-study area were georeferenced. For all excavated sites, their outlines and features visible on the surface were digitized, as well as the plans of the excavated areas, showing all of the features within. Furthermore, all of the vertical section drawings from the excavation of these features were digitized.[4] The coordinates of roughly 500 areas of archaeological interest, ranging from isolated artifact finds to field systems and settlement sites, were obtained from the Oxfordshire Sites and Monuments Record (SMR), a county-wide depository for local heritage information. Finally, the English Heritage National Mapping Programme provided a highly detailed digital coverage, mapped from aerial photographs and rectified by computer, of the case-study area showing all traces of earthworks and crop marks that might indicate features of archaeological interest in the landscape. The end result is 150 square km of archaeology in digital form, with all visible and known indications of archaeological evidence included to some level.

The Ridgeway Database

A large amount of archaeological information, derived from excavations, archives, the SMR, and other sources, has been collated and included within the Ridgeway database. The general structure of the database reflects the scales of practice and materiality outlined above, so that all tables have a unique identifier for all possible scales of representation; object, deposit, feature, trench, site numbers, and so on. Starting from the object level, which is the most atomic level of material culture found during excavation, and building up through deposit and feature levels, the data tables all have fields for the levels "above" them in scale. This also enables varying degrees of spatial connectivity as some degree of map element occurs for each level. The object level table has fields for context, feature, trench, and site ID, while the feature data table has fields for the trench and site, so that a query made at any scale will resonate through the chain of scale. For example, for an object-level query, the map elements representing all selected objects and their contexts, features, trenches, and sites respond visually.

The majority of the information contained in the database is based upon material recovered from excavations and subsequent specialist analysis (such as artifacts, faunal and human remains, samples for scientific dating), in addition to data about the composition of depositions (e.g., soil consistency, grain size, inclusions), and the physical characteristics of features (e.g., depth, diameter, width, length, volume).

The Ridgeway GIS

Both the spatial and attribute dataset come together within the Ridgeway GIS. While a range of computing tasks is farmed out to ArcInfo (such as building topologies), ArcView provides the basis for most of the work. The digitized sections and plans were converted into coverage files in ArcInfo, exported as SHAPEFILES, and imported into ArcView. Using SQL CONNECT, all of the relevant data tables were imported into ArcView, and the attribute tables of all relevant SHAPEFILES were JOINED to the imported data tables. The final step to fully integrating the data into one comprehensive tool for both intra- and inter-site analysis was to LINK the various tables in a way that enabled queries at one level to resonate at all scales. As discussed above, data tables for the object, deposit, and feature levels,[5] contain fields for all other levels. Tables for these three scales were imported into ArcView and LINKed together by their respective id numbers and then were further linked to the same fields in the SHAPEFILE attribute files for both the plan map view (with all features evident in plan) and the section view. Hotlinks were established based upon the "line" of where the section originated on the plan. This allows, with the simple click of a mouse, jumping from the plan view to the individual section views, both of which respond graphically to data queries. The end product allows for queries to be addressed to the object, context, and feature databases, and the results be shown graphically and simultaneously, at multiple levels.

Examples of Practice

As mentioned above, these individual scales are interwoven and mutually define each other, and it is through understanding the relationship between scales that interpretation can move fluidly from objects, through deposits, features, and sites to landscapes. These scales link together the individual in the past with the social. The breaking of a pot and its deposition within the fill of a pit, for example, may be an individual action, but if the material patterning it produces is repeated within deposits and features across a site, and then within several sites across a landscape, it becomes a structured activity representative of social practice that warrants interpretation. The examples presented below explore the interplay between scales further.

Structured Objects

There are little obvious differences between the majority of deposits that make up the archaeological record from later prehistoric Britain, and traditionally all layers in pits and ditches, the most common prehistoric features, have been viewed as dumps of rubbish or natural infill. Consequently, the material culture associated with these features was only useful as dating evidence. However, through very careful study of the positioning of objects and the relationships between different types of material culture, it has recently been suggested that deposition within such features is guided by forms of highly structured social practices (Hill 1995). Unfortunately, the recording systems used on most archaeological sites have not kept pace with this change of focus and are not sensitive to the subtle patterning of material within contexts, therefore, potentially excluding any social practices that may be reflected.

Our approach to exploring these relationships is demonstrated in Figure 17.2, which shows cut Feature 12003, a small Roman furnace at the site of Marcham-Frilford. On-site recording employed digital surveying, with database capture of attribute information, and digital photography, resulting in the shape of the cut and its physical characteristics being displayed in 3D, together with the boundary between the two deposits that fill it and the objects found within it. Digital photography was used extensively to record the positioning and arrangement of material *in situ*, as well as contextual information such as soil composition, color, and inclusions. The physical characteristics of the feature and deposits, including large amounts of ash, burnt material, and metal finds in various stages of completion make its function as a furnace clear. However, the arrangement of the artifacts within the fills of the feature, in particular the differences between the ceramic material (not directly associated with the primary purpose of the furnace), and metal finds (very much related with the primary purpose), show different patterns of deposition in the secondary phase of the furnace's life history. After its active life ended, at least two intentional processes of infilling occurred, each of which contained different sediments and objects. While analysis is ongoing, and a final interpretation has not yet been reached, this example serves to illustrate the possibilities of such an approach. The post excavation analysis of the artifacts, coupled with detailed information about the placement of, and relationships between, objects and objects, objects and deposits, and objects and features, will allow for new levels of interpretation to be possible within a formalized methodology.

It is clear that such techniques allow for a number of breakthroughs in archaeological recording, specialist analysis, interpretation, and publication. For example, this approach radically alters the decontextualizing of material artifacts that characterize much of specialist analysis in archaeology. The myriad of specialists typical of post-

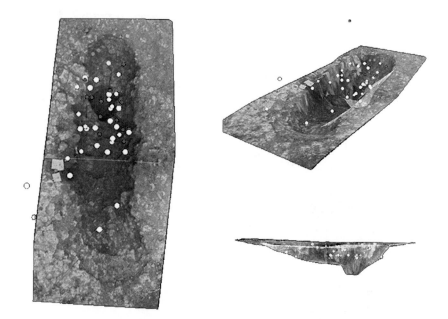

Figure 17.2. Cut Feature 12003 at Marcham-Frilford. A small Romano-British furnace modeled from digitally surveyed data and photography. The contained objects are: white, pottery; light grey, metalwork; and dark grey, bones. When viewed interactively the interfaces between deposits within the feature can be shown.

excavation work (pottery, metal work, faunal remains, sediments, etc.) can access important information about the environment that their material came from, providing the next best option to having all specialists in the field, participating in the collection of data. Furthermore, the establishment of a digital platform for recording archaeological investigations at this level allows for new and innovative opportunities for multi-media publication (Richards 2001). A combination of database-driven Web sites, navigated by "virtually" interacting with the excavation plans and sections in a GIS map server, in addition to text descriptions and interpretation, reduces the distinction between final publication and data archive and allows all interested parties to view the raw data in its full context.

Structured Features, Deposits, and Sites

As we have stressed, the enactment of activity within sites is dependent upon human decision making, grounded in social concerns, and detectable through material patterning. This is illustrated in Figures 17.3 and 17.4, which show Segsbury Camp, an Iron Age hillfort built in the Early Iron Age, sixth century BC, and occupied sporadically for several centuries. A combination of excavation and geophysical survey has shown that there are a number of areas of activity within the interior of the encircling ramparts,

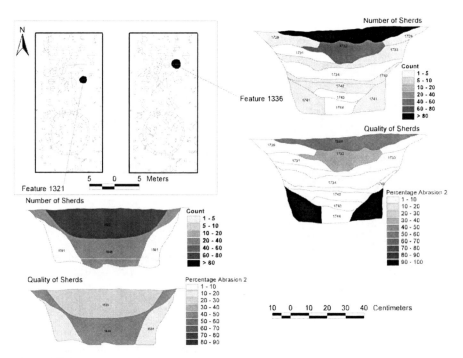

Figure 17.3. Objects, deposits and features within Trench 1 at Segsbury Camp hillfort. A comparison of the stratigraphy within two pits, the upper section shows the number of pottery sherds per deposit, and the lower the level of sherd abrasion.

consisting of circular ditched gullies (the remains of a common form of Middle Iron Age roundhouse) and associated clusters of pits (traditionally interpreted as grain storage pits that then get used for rubbish disposal). Most of this activity occurs within the central and eastern areas of the interior, perhaps significant, as the one surviving original entrance to the site is through the eastern ramparts. The complex inter-cutting of features suggests long sequences of occupation; the roundhouse gullies, for example, tend to be of two types. The more ephemeral, such as in the northern part of Trench 1, are older and located within clusters of often inter-cutting later pits and are themselves often cut by the pits. The better preserved, and later gullies, tend to be about ten meters from a pit cluster, although they are sometimes cut by still later pits.

Trench 1 shows the complexity of the relationships between objects, the deposits they are contained within, features and the deposits that fill them, and the way these elements fit together to create the structure of a site. Figures 17.3 and 17.4 show a small selection of the possible analyses exploring material culture patterning both within individual features and across features at the trench and site scale. Sections of individual selected pits are shown in Figure 17.3, displaying the number of sherds and an index developed to quantify the "quality" of the pottery for each deposit making up the pit's fill. The quality index is a dual function of both the size of the sherds and their surface condition, and reflects the exposure to post-depositional processes that the pottery

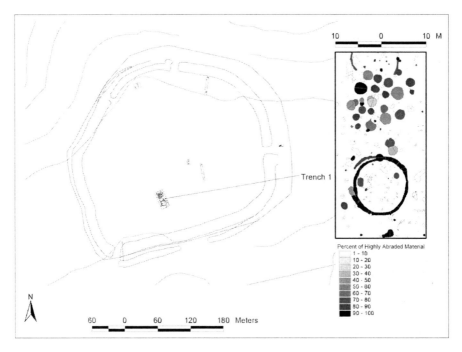

Figure 17.4. Segsbury Camp hillfort showing the location of excavation trenches. The features within Trench 1 are coded to show the percentage of highly abraded sherds per feature.

might have had prior to its final deposition within the pit. We hypothesize that more deliberate deposits of material culture, as part of overt and discursive social practices specific to this period, result in higher qualities of material being interred. The detailed results of this analysis suggest that there are differences in the fill histories of pits between different parts of the clustering, based upon both the stratigraphy and the quality of the pottery.

It is also of interest to look at the contents of features at a trench-wide and site-wide scale to establish patterns based on temporal trends or on aspects of material characteristics. Figure 17.4 shows the plan of Segsbury Camp, with the excavation trenches together with the features within Trench 1 coded to show the percentage of material in the most highly abraded category of assessment, based on the sum of all deposits within each feature. This suggests definite distinctions: for example, the gullies, while containing large amounts of material, are characterized by the highly fragmentary and poor quality of their assemblages. The pits overlying the early gully in the north end of the trench contain high percentages of low grade material, while there is a group of pits further to the south and associated with the later roundhouse that contain much lower percentages of highly abraded material.

It is always important in archaeology to appreciate temporal structuring, not just of the material excavated but also of the individual and social lives of the people who created what we excavate. Social practices incorporate the past to create the present, and this is evident within Trench 1, where deposition is shaped by the presence of previous areas of activity, for example, the circular gullies. The locations of later episodes of activity and feature construction were influenced by the remnants of earlier dwelling structures, visible mainly as partially infilled gullies, with houses positioned in some proximity to earlier ones. The pits most likely associated with the later activity also respected the previous order of the site so that large pits, containing many layers of highly abraded material, were clustered on the location of previous houses, but the smaller and richer deposits of material were located several meters away. It seems that the boundaries of structures were respected long after the features ceased to be functioning entities, and that the filling of pits within those areas involved different material, and different practices, from those located further away. The higher quality material seems to indicate repeated intentional deposition directly into the pit, perhaps as a part of votive ritual connected with the earth, crop fertility, and the agricultural cycle (Cunliffe 1992), whereas the highly abraded sherds had been exposed for considerable lengths of time, perhaps on the surface, before ending up as casual deposits within slowly filling disused pits. By combining the wider picture presented in Figure 17.4 with the stratigraphic detail of the sections in Figure 17.3, it is possible to begin to understand these spatial and temporal relationships.

Structured Landscape

Feature deposits and sites form landscapes through complex interactions based on people's activities and needs. When considering the structuration of human practices at the landscape scale, we would emphasize the importance of embedded history within it and the influence of existing landscape features on contemporary action. Today it is impossible to pass through the landscape of Oxfordshire without encountering indications of past human activity; evidence of the past is everywhere manifested in the remains of medieval settlements and field systems, Anglo Saxon and Roman land boundaries, interspersed with prehistoric monuments. This certainly would have been even more the case in the past, not only relatively recently—prior to the massive landscape alteration caused by plowing and development since the 1950s—but further back into prehistoric time, when fresher cultural connections to elements within the landscape would have existed. It has been proposed elsewhere that many of the clearly visible elements of landscape use had some presence within the local understandings of the world in the first millennium BC (Gosden and Lock 1998). Accumulation of cultural residue caused various areas and sites to be re-occupied at different times, and because of the role of physical remains and activity carried out in association with these, historical relations were fostered, communicated, and re-negotiated. This model of structuration over extended time periods across the landscape has been argued as a central mechanism for social reproduction through much of later prehistory (Barrett 1994).

To look in more detail at the case-study area, one of the most significant features within it is the Ridgeway itself, a present day track-way that has its origins in early prehistory. It runs east—west along the upper edge of the Berkshire Downs, and, as shown in Figure 17.5, has a number of different relationships with many of the important sites in the area, including hillforts. Detailed pathway analysis conducted in ArcView showing the least-cost passage through the landscape based upon a variety of topographic

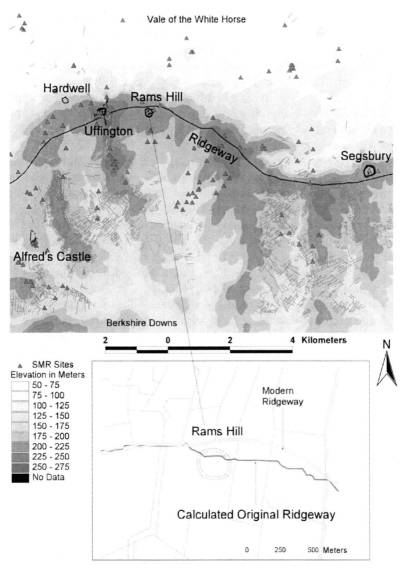

Figure 17.5. The study area showing aerial photographic evidence for prehistoric and Romano-British field systems together with data from the Oxfordshire Sites and Monuments Record. The area around Rams Hill is highlighted to demonstrate landscape detail, in this case the suggested route of the early Ridgeway track and its current route. (© Crown Copyright Ordnance Survey. An EDINA Digimap/JISC supplied service. Aerial photographic data is © English Heritage National Mapping Programme.)

considerations concluded that optimal routing across the Downs broadly reflects the known course of the Ridgeway (Bell and Lock 2000). Interestingly, the results of the computer modeling show that the optimal path passes through the original entrances of several of the hillforts, aligned east—west, something the modern-day Ridgeway does not do. It is likely that these sites were located across an already existing Ridgeway in the eighth to sixth centuries BC to take advantage of the route. Evidence from excavation shows that several centuries later some of the original entrances were blocked during a phase of remodeling, suggesting that the Ridgeway was diverted at this time, perhaps to its current route (Figure 17.5).

Long-term history is represented by this spatial and temporal structuration. Movement through the landscape was initially responsive to topographic considerations, quite possibly due to the pastoral need to move, or follow, herds of animals through the landscape. This led to the creation of corridors that were more and more heavily trafficked, resulting in an accumulation of cultural awareness of the area and its features and places, as shown by the range of archaeological features that exist in close proximity to the Ridgeway (Figure 17.5). However, while the path might have been instrumental in the creation of the sites and maintaining connections between them, it was not beyond the influence of cultural considerations. The deviation of the Ridgeway was caused by changes of social practices within the hillforts, resulting in the blocking of entrances through the restructuring of activities within those contained spaces. Although the Ridgeway gave structure to the Berkshire Downs in its earliest form, by aiding and also confining the flow of people through the landscape, each new element of materiality added to the landscape as a result of this was a response to this structure, while at the same time, serving to redefine it. Gradually, the wider landscape was banded together by the spread of cultivation, with its infrastructure of land divisions and field systems.

Conclusions

The tension within modern archaeology reflects attempts to move beyond the empirical consideration of material culture and material remains into the realms of past social practices and social reproduction. Archaeology is a pragmatic discipline based upon fieldwork and the generation of large spatially and temporally complex datasets, while at the same time being influenced by the changing theoretical winds blowing through the social sciences more widely. Post-modern considerations of what it means to be human and how, as humans, we construct and maintain social relationships and cultural values have to be related to the pot sherds and the other cultural debris that we excavate. We argue that a productive approach is to identify spatial and temporal patterning within the data that represents social practices. While time and space are two axes that structure past behavior, they are also scale critical and it is scale, and moving between scales of data and analysis, that form the lubrication enabling the two axes to work together. The examples described above have shown how the deposition of artifacts within the fill of a cut feature can be as historically contingent as the routing of a trackway that runs for many kilometers across the landscape. Both are a material representation of a prehistoric awareness of the past, and it is through the considered and subtle use of GIS technology that we can begin to approach these complex life stories.

Notes

1. There are many examples where rich traditions of orally based communication allow for a great deal of cultural information to be transmitted through rather impressive spans of time. However, it has been shown that there is a ceiling on how long such practices can exist and still be successful (Ballard 1994). Furthermore, such traditions almost always occur in tandem with other forms of activity or, as is discussed below, are anchored to materiality.
2. Interim reports appear annually in South Midlands Archaeology and are also online at http://athens.arch.ox.ac.uk/~glock/fieldwork/ridgeway/index.htm .
3. http://edina.ac.uk/digimap/ .
4. In all, six detailed site plans are fully digital, with over a thousand features, and most of their sections.
5. Most features are identified by the context number of the cut, as the majority of features are intrusive.

References

Aldenderfer, M., and H.D.G. Maschner (eds.). 1996. *Anthropology, Space, and Geographic Information Systems*. New York: Oxford University Press.

Allen, K.M.S., S.W. Green, and E.B.W. Zubrow. 1990. *Interpreting Space: GIS and Archaeology*. London: Taylor and Francis.

Appadurai, A. (ed.). 1986. *The Social Life of Things*. Cambridge: Cambridge University Press.

Ashmore, W., and A.B. Knapp. (eds.). 1999. *Archaeologies of Landscape. Contemporary Perspectives*. Oxford: Blackwell.

Ballard, C. 1994. The centre cannot hold: Trade networks and sacred geography in the Papua New Guinea Highlands. In L. Head, C. Gosden, and J.P. White (eds.), *Social Landscapes, Archaeology in Oceania* 29: 130–148.

Barrett, J.C. 1994. *Fragments from Antiquity: An Archaeology of Social Life in Britain, 2900–1200 BC*. Oxford: Blackwell.

Bell. T., and G. Lock. 2000. Topographic and cultural influences on walking the Ridgeway in later prehistoric times. In G. Lock (ed.), *Beyond the Map: Archaeology and Spatial Technologies*. Amsterdam: IOS Press.

Bourdieu, P. 1977. *Outline of a Theory of Practice*. Cambridge: Cambridge University Press.

Castleford, J. 1992. Archaeology, GIS and the time dimension: An overview. In G. Lock, and J. Moffett (eds.), *Computer Applications and Quantitative Methods in Archaeology 1991*. Oxford: Tempus Reparatum, British Archaeological Reports International Series S577: 95–106.

Cunliffe, B.W. 1992. Pits, preconceptions, and propitiation in the British Iron Age. *Oxford Journal of Archaeology* 11: 69–84.

Curry, M.R. 1998. *Digital Places: Living with Geographical Information Technologies*. London: Routledge.

Gaffney, V., and Z. Stančič. 1991. *GIS Approaches to Regional Analysis: A Case Study of the Island of Hvar, Znanstveni inštitut Filozofske fakultete*. Yugoslavia: University of Ljubljana, (reprinted 1996).

Gaffney, V., and P.M. van Leusen. 1995. GIS, environmental determinism and archaeology. In G. Lock and Z. Stančič (eds.), *Archaeology and Geographic Information Systems: A European Perspective*. London: Taylor and Francis, 367–382.

Giddens, A. 1984. *The Constitution of Society: an Outline of the Theory of Structuration*. Berkeley: University of California Press.

Gosden, C. 1994. *Social Being and Time*. Oxford: Blackwell.

Gosden, C., and G. Lock. 1998. Prehistoric histories. *World Archaeology*, 30(1): 2–12.

Hill, J.D. 1995. *Ritual and Rubbish in the Iron Age of Wessex. A Study on the Formation of a Specific Archaeological Record*. Oxford: Tempus Reparatum. British Archaeological Reports British series 242.

Hill, J.D. 1996. Hillforts and the Iron Age of Wessex. In T.C. Champion and J.R. Collis (eds.), *The Iron Age in Britain and Ireland: Recent Trends*. Sheffield: J.R. Collis Publications, 95–116.

Hirsch, E., and M. O'Hanlon (eds.). 1995. *The Anthropology of Landscape: Perspectives on Place and Space*. Oxford: Clarendon Press.

Johnson, I., and M. North (eds.) 1997. *Archaeological Applications of GIS*: Proceedings of Colloquium II, UISPP XIIIth Congress, Forli, Italy, September 1996. Sydney: University of Sydney, Archaeological Methods Series.

Kohler, T.A. and S.C. Parker. 1986. Predictive models for archaeological resource location. In M.B. Schiffer. (ed.), *Advances in Archaeological Method and Theory, Vol. 9*. New York: Academic Press, 397–452.

Kvamme, K.L. 1990. The fundamental principles and practice of predictive modelling. In A. Voorrips (ed.), Mathematics and Information Science in Archaeology: A Flexible Framework. Bonn: *Studies in Modern Archaeology* 3, Holos-Verlag, 257–295.

Llobera, M. 1996. Exploring the topography of mind: GIS, social space and archaeology, *Antiquity* 70. 269: 612–622.

Llobera, M. 2000. Understanding movement: A pilot model towards the sociology of movement. In G. Lock (ed.), *Beyond the Map: Archaeology and Spatial Technologies*. Amsterdam: IOS Press, 65–84.

Lock, G. (ed.). 2000. *Beyond the Map: Archaeology and Spatial Technologies*. Amsterdam: IOS Press.

Lock, G. 2002. Theorising the practice or practicing the theory: Archaeology and GIS. *Archaeologia Polona* 39: 152–164.

Lock, G., and T. Harris. 2000. Introduction: Return to Ravello. In G. Lock (ed.), *Beyond the Map: Archaeology and Spatial Technologies*. Amsterdam: IOS Press, xiii-xxv.

Lock, G., and Z. Stančič (eds.). 1995. *Archaeology and Geographic Information Systems: A European Perspective*. London: Taylor and Francis.

Mark, D.M. 1993. On the ethics of representation: Or whose world is it anyway? *Geographic Information and Society: A Workshop*. National Center for Geographic Information and Analysis, unpublished.

Maschner, H.D.G. (ed.). 1996. *New Methods, Old Problems. Geographic Information Systems in Modern Archaeological Research*. Carbondale: Southern Illinois University, Center for Archaeological Investigations, Occasional Paper No. 23.

Peterson, J. (ed.). 1998. *The Use of Geographic Information Systems in The Study of Ancient Landscapes and Features Related to Ancient Land Use*. Luxembourg: EC COST ACTION G2.

Richards, J. 2001. *Rethinking Publication: Going Digital. ADS Online*. York: Archaeology Data Service. Online at http://ads.ahds.ac.uk/newsletter/issue9.html#rethinking .

Slapšak, B. (ed.). 2001. *On the good use of Geographic Information Systems in Archaeological Landscape Studies*. Luxembourg: EC COST ACTION G2.

Tilley, C. 1994. *A Phenomenology of Landscape. Places, Paths and Monuments*. Oxford: Berg.

Westcott, K.L., and R.J. Brandon (eds.). 2000. *Practical applications of GIS for Archaeologists. A Predictive Modeling Kit*. London: Taylor and Francis.

Wheatley, D.W. 1993. Going over old ground: GIS, archaeological theory and the act of perception. In J. Andresen, T. Madsen, and I. Scollar (eds.), *Computing the Past: Computer Applications and Quantitative Methods in Archaeology CAA92*. Aarhus, Denmark: Aarhus University Press, 133–138.

Wheatley, D.W. 2000. Spatial technology and archaeological theory revisited. In K. Lockyear, T.J.T. Sly, and V. Mihăilescu-Bîrliba (eds.), *CAA96. Computer Applications and Quantitative Methods in Archaeology*. Oxford: BAR International Series 845: 123–32.

Wheatley, D., and M. Gillings. 2000. Vision, perception and GIS: Developing enriched approaches to the study of archaeological visibility. In G. Lock (ed.), *Beyond the Map: Archaeology and Spatial Technologies*. Amsterdam: IOS Press, 1–27.

Wise, A.L. 2000. Building theory into GIS-based landscape analysis. In K. Lockyear, T.J.T. Sly, and V. Mihăilescu-Bîrliba (eds.), *CAA96. Computer Applications and Quantitative Methods in Archaeology*. Oxford: BAR International Series 845: 141–148.

Witcher, R. 1999. GIS and Landscapes of perception. In M. Gillings, D. Mattingly, and J. van Dalen (eds.), *Geographical Information Systems and Landscape Archaeology. The Archaeology of Mediterranean Landscapes Vol 3*. Oxford: Oxbow Books, 13–22.

18

Spatial Perspectives in Public Health

Anthony C. Gatrell
Janette E. Rigby

There is now a wealth of compelling evidence to suggest that location and place shape our health, our exposure to environmental features that impact upon our health, and our access to those goods and services that either promote our health or treat episodes of disease or illness that we all encounter. Moreover, the research evidence to support these claims comes from a wide range of settings across the developed and the developing worlds and at a variety of spatial scales (Gatrell 2002). Whether we are attempting to: predict the likely impact of global environmental change on vector-borne diseases such as malaria or dengue fever (Hay et al. 2000); examine the associations between radon gas emissions and the incidence of lung cancer in countries such as Sweden and the United States (Lubin and Boice 1995; Teppo 1998); or assess how proximity influences access to pre-natal (ante-natal) and other health screening services (Bentham et al. 1995; Gatrell et al. 1998) at more local scales, we cannot escape the fact that spatial context provides a backcloth against which these issues are projected.

That there are "spatial perspectives in public health" is, therefore, well established. Our purpose in this chapter is to develop that argument and to illustrate it with a small number of selected examples. Before doing so, it is appropriate to consider what is meant by "public health." It is now accepted that this covers considerable ground. It is far broader than a concern with the incidence of disease or with patterns of mortality, or with the introduction of interventions (such as sanitation schemes) to reduce the burden of disease. While these remain a concern of public health, the contemporary view is of a focus on population groups, not individuals, and on a very broad set of factors that may shape population health. These would include a focus on the social as well as the physical environment, and the broad structural determinants of health. A focus on health inequalities or "divides" features prominently in contemporary work (Shaw et al.

1999). In this way, public health is genuinely multi-disciplinary, with epidemiology, sociology, ecology, economics, psychology, law, and geography among a variety of disciplines that are needed to understand the health of the public. While the skills of biomedical scientists are required, so too are the perspectives and skills of social and environmental scientists.

One implication of this is that it is a somewhat daunting task to convey, in a short chapter, the richness of a spatial perspective on public health! Inevitably, we must be extremely selective. Our selectivity manifests itself in the following way. First, we take three broad areas of disease and consider how a spatial—and spatial analytic—perspective helps illuminate our understanding of these diseases. Here, we consider geographic research on HIV/AIDS, at a variety of spatial scales; next, we look at some research on breast cancer, examining some of the analytic methods that geographers and epidemiologists have brought to bear; last, we review some research into skin disease, showing what progress has been made in understanding links to environment. In the second main section we turn our attention to the social patterning of health, explaining how a spatial perspective sheds light on our understanding of health inequalities. We do so in two broad sections: one that considers inequalities at a regional scale; and a second section that illustrates more local spatial variation in access to those features of the built landscape that impact on health.

Understanding Disease Distributions

HIV/AIDS

As Meade and Earickson (2000, 286) observe, among the "plethora of emergent and reemergent infections . . . the diffusion of no other agent in recent time has had nearly the profound impact on people and their societies as has human immunodeficiency virus (HIV) and the acquired immunodeficiency syndrome (AIDS) it causes." As of December 2000, there were an estimated global total of 36.1 million persons living with HIV/AIDS (WHO 2000). But this is geographically differentiated, with by far the most (25.3 million) in sub-Saharan Africa, a smaller proportion (5.8 million) in south and Southeast Asia, and relatively small (in global terms) numbers in North America (920,000) and western Europe (540,000). What contribution can a spatial perspective make to our understanding of the spread and patterning of HIV and AIDS?

As both Gould (1993) and Meade and Earickson (2000) observe, getting epidemiologists to take space seriously in HIV/AIDS modeling has taken many years. "Health professionals of all kinds, and most of the public, perceive an epidemic spreading through a population over time, but they do not envision the process as happening over space or having geographic consequences" (Meade and Earickson 2000, 289–290). In an endeavor to convince skeptics of the value of a geographic approach, Gould produced a sequence of maps of disease spread across the United States, demonstrating evidence of both hierarchical diffusion (spread from the major cities to smaller cities and city-regions) and subsequent local, "contagious" diffusion (Gould and Wallace 1994).

Before his untimely death, Gould was at the forefront of attempts to understand the spatial structure of HIV spread at different spatial scales. For the United States as a whole, he took 102 of the largest cities and constructed a matrix of air passenger flows; this was converted into a matrix of contact probabilities, a transition matrix that inevitably shows high probabilities of interaction between major centers. Taking the number of AIDS cases in 1986 as a state vector, we may multiply this by the transition matrix to yield a likely distribution of cases in 1998; successive multiplication of projected state vectors by the transition matrix yields year-on-year predictions of the distribution of cases. Results show a close correspondence between the observed number of cases and those predicted by this Markov chain model. In other work, at the city-region scale, he applied the same ideas to the distribution of HIV infection over 24 boroughs and counties of New York City (Gould and Wallace 1994). Here, the transition matrix is obtained from data on flows of commuters, a justification being that there is a close correspondence between AIDS rates and the percentage of the workforce commuting from counties to Manhattan. A property of Markov chains is the eventual convergence to an equilibrium (fixed point vector), which here shows that 61 percent of cases are likely to be concentrated in Manhattan and much lower proportions elsewhere. Gould and Wallace (1994, 110) argue that "the daily commuting pattern is a spatial scavenger, sucking the HIV into the center, where it may multiply rapidly, only to be redistributed over the entire region by the very process that concentrated it."

But Gould also argued that we need to map disease distributions, and the spread of disease, in new kinds of epidemiological spaces. One technique for doing so is multidimensional scaling (MDS). Here, conventionally we take a lower triangular matrix of "dissimilarities" between a set of objects; these might be a set of towns or cities, between which are estimated travel times. MDS seeks a new space of minimum dimensionality in which the objects are located so as to best fit the original dissimilarities; typically, so that the distances in the new space preserve, so far as is possible, the rank order of the original dissimilarities. A monotonic regression of distance on dissimilarity produces a residual sum-of-squares statistic, known as "stress." This will always be lower in a space of higher dimensionality, but usually we seek a low stress solution in two dimensions. How is this useful in HIV/AIDS research? Gould proposes that, instead of taking dissimilarities as input to the scaling procedure, we use predicted spatial interaction as a measure of the "similarity" between pairs of places. If we do so, a conventional geographical space (e.g., Ohio: Figure 18.1a) is transformed into a new "disease space" in which large cities are located close together, and the smaller population centers are dispersed (Figure 18.1b). We can use this new space in order to show that HIV infection spreads "contagiously" away from the origin.

Breast Cancer

As a disease with high (and increasing) incidence in many developed countries, breast cancer has seen considerable research investment in all aspects of disease studies. These include causation (using biomedical, environmental, and behavioral approaches), survival analysis, and access to treatment, in addition to sensitive psychosocial studies on the effects of the disease on patients and carers. Spatial perspectives impinge on many of these studies. As well as issues of spatial scale and the nature of the basic spatial units used for data collection and referencing, we have to deal with the often-complex interaction between disease latency (the time elapsing between when a

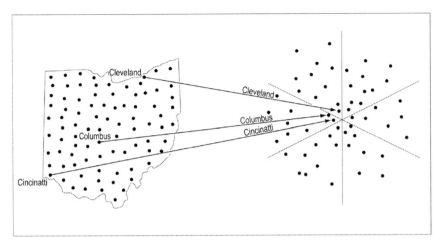

Figure 18.1. AIDS in Ohio in (a) geographic and (b) interaction space. Reprinted from Gould (1993) with permission from Blackwell Publishers Ltd.

disease is initiated and when it is diagnosed) and migration; this too is a fundamentally spatial issue.

In addition to looking at variations in disease rates represented simply in tabular form, more information can often be gained by examining *where* these rates vary, and where high and low rates occur in relation to others. Disease rates can be mapped at a variety of scales in a search for spatial patterns (Cliff and Haggett 1988). The last ten years have seen exciting developments in geographic visualization, made possible by improved computing power and functionality. For example, quite detailed data on geographic variation in breast cancer at the county scale, for both white and black females, is available in the U.S. Atlas of Cancer Mortality (Devesa et al. 1999; also online at http://cancer.gov/atlasplus/new.html). However, at more detailed spatial scales the numbers of cases may be relatively small, particularly in sparsely populated rural areas, where extremely high apparent risks can emerge from small numbers of cases. As a consequence, empirical Bayes estimates, which adjust the relative risks according to our confidence in their reliability, are increasingly used in such mapping (see Gatrell 2002 for further details and Langford 1994 for an implementation method; Clayton and Bernardinelli (1992); Rigby and Gatrell (2000) for application to breast cancer rates).

Disease mapping of breast cancer incidence at a variety of spatial scales in part of northern England was undertaken by Rigby and Gatrell (2000). An initial examination of rates over quite sizeable administrative areas (whose populations numbered a few thousands) revealed little by way of spatial patterning, and this was confirmed by a low spatial autocorrelation (Moran) coefficient. However, spatial autocorrelation generates a single measure for the entire map, and to explore whether there might be some more local processes operating, methods for detecting local association (*G* statistics) were used (Anselin 1995; Getis and Ord 1999). These can identify whether there are any areas whose rates are closely aligned to those in adjacent areas. This technique identified a small group of neighboring rural areas in one part of the study region, all with low incidence rates of breast cancer (Figure 18.2).

There are situations where individual, address-based, data can be used for spatial analyses; here we draw upon the literature on spatial point pattern analysis, rather than on methods for handling area data. There are a number of possible approaches, including that developed by Openshaw (1990), an innovative approach to exploring whether cases of a disease were clustered or not. The approach was based on investigating the probability of whether the observed number of cancer cases within a circle of radius r, centered on a point (x,y) could have occurred by chance. The study area was overlain with a lattice structure, and the intersections of the lattice points used as the (x,y) points. Hence, circles were constructed, and the number of cases in each could be determined. Where a circle was considered *significant*, it was drawn on a map. The whole process was automated, so that repeated runs could be made using circles of varying radii. A recent version, GAM/K, is available over the Web, whereby users can experiment with a sample dataset, or enter their own data and receive cluster results by return (Openshaw and Turton, www.ccg.leeds.ac.uk/smart/intro.html). In an application to the data referred to earlier, GAM/K identified several significant clusters of high rates across the study region.

This procedure has been developed in new ways by Kulldorff, who has proposed a "spatial scan statistic" that searches for clusters of disease cases. He has applied this method in a variety of contexts, including breast cancer mortality at county level in the northeastern United States. His approach was to impose circular windows on the region, centered on county geographical centroids, and then vary the radius so that different groupings of neighborhood counties were captured. His results (Kulldorff et al. 1997) indicated that the most likely cluster of breast cancer mortality was in the New York City/ Philadelphia metropolitan area, with a strong subcluster on Long Island, which was an existing concern to health professionals. Kulldorff has also facilitated availability to his spatial scan software via the web (SaTScan at www.nci.nih.gov).

Breast cancer on Long Island was also the subject of a study by Timander and McLafferty (1998). Here, point data were derived from the residential addresses of women who responded to a survey of breast cancer incidence. A clustering technique based on that developed by Besag and Newell (1991) was used to identify significant clusters of disease incidence. Whereas Openshaw's approach uses circular windows moved across the entire study area, Timander and McLafferty searched for clusters in the neighborhood of known cases by centering their circles on each case. The resultant significant circles were all in the same geographical area, possibly suggesting a link with an environmental exposure. Following the approach of Kingham et al. (1995), data from the survey relating to established risk factors for breast cancer were used to run a logistic regression, which explained 30 percent of the disease incidence. The clustering process was then repeated using the residuals from the regression. This yielded no significant findings; hence an environmental link could not be pursued.

A fundamental issue in all spatial epidemiology, of which these studies are representative, is the need to consider migration. People move house quite frequently. If we are investigating a disease that may have commenced some ten years or more earlier, then it is inappropriate to research the current place of residence. More imaginative approaches are needed (Sabel et al. 2000).

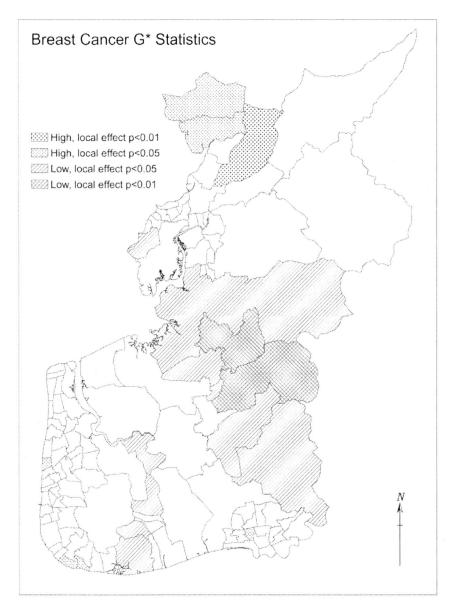

Figure 18.2. *G* statistics for breast cancer (Rigby and Gatrell, 2000).*

Skin Disease

Consider first the spatial distribution of skin cancer, of which the most serious form is malignant melanoma. This shows considerable geographic variation over a variety of scales. In Europe, for example, age-standardized incidence varies from 12.9 per

100,000 in Denmark, to only 1.9 per 100,000 in Greece. Within individual countries there is latitudinal variation (see, for example, Bulliard et al. 1994 on New Zealand). Within particular regions, such as Ontario, Canada, there is variation from district to district. Indeed, in Ontario there is evidence of regional aggregation or autocorrelation (Walter et al. 1999). For both men and women there is a significant tendency for districts with high rates to be adjacent to other high-rate districts (Moran's $I = 0.39$ for men, 0.41 for women).

Having established spatial aggregation using exploratory techniques such as autocorrelation measures merely describes a map pattern; it does not explain anything, since such a pattern can arise in a number of different ways. Indeed, a starting point in any model-based spatial analysis must surely be to examine the extent to which a range of variables "soak up" regional variation. Only if residual autocorrelation remains will it be necessary to fit a model with spatial effects, one that builds in the correlation between values in nearby zones. In the Ontario study a non-spatial regression model suggests that incidence is positively associated with employment in farming and inversely associated with income and latitude. Having established these as possible explanatory factors, a geographic analysis of residuals reveals no significant residual autocorrelation. In research within Scandinavia, similar non-spatial regression analyses have been undertaken to explain spatial variation (Aase and Bentham 1994; Bentham and Aase 1996). These reveal that estimated exposure to ultraviolet B radiation is a significant predictor of incidence, as are patterns of vacationing abroad. The authors consider what the possible impact might be of increases in UVB radiation (resulting from ozone depletion), a kind of "what if" approach that is valuable in predicting a range of possible health outcomes and in planning the demand for health services (cancer care in this context).

There is some evidence from geographical epidemiology that the hardness of water (the presence of high concentrations of calcium and magnesium salts) is a risk factor for the development of eczema in children. In a study in Nottingham, U.K. (McNally et al. 1998) researchers asked parents of children aged 4–16 years about the occurrence of "itchy skin rash" during the previous year and at any time during the child's life. Home addresses were geo-coded and assigned, using a point-in-polygon routine, to one of 33 water quality zones, for each of which mean water hardness readings were available. There is considerable spatial variation in water hardness across the city, with soft water in the north and much harder water in the south.

The proportion reporting eczema varied significantly across four categories of water hardness (Table 18.1) and logistic regression analysis confirms that the risk of eczema increases with water hardness after adjusting for other possible variables that might "confound" the relationship; these include age, sex, socio-economic status, and proximity to health centers. The interpretation of an odds ratio of 1.54 is that a child living in a hard water zone is 54 percent more likely to report eczema than one living in a soft water zone. However, this relationship holds only for younger children (under 11 years). A possible explanation is that calcium and magnesium in domestic water supplies irritate the skin.

The question then arises of what policy interventions can be introduced to mitigate the burden of disease and illness. These interventions are typically focused at the level of the individual, with exhortations to change lifestyles and behaviors: to adopt "safe

Table 18.1. Water hardness and prevalence of eczema (reported during past year) among primary schoolchildren in Nottingham, U.K.

Water Hardness Category	Number Reporting Eczema	Prevalence (%)	Odds Ratio	Confidence Interval (95%)
1	94	12.0	1.00	
2	103	14.1	1.19	0.88–1.62
3	163	14.6	1.32	1.00–1.76
4	261	17.3	1.54	1.19–1.99

Source: McNally et al. (1998, 529), with permission from Elsevier Science (*The Lancet*, 1998, vol 352, page 529).

sex" practices, to improve diet, or to avoid over-exposure to direct sunlight, for example. However, interventions will invariably be required that are more broadly based. For example, water parameters are open to modification, while global agreements have been reached to halt ozone depletion.

Understanding Health Inequalities

We are all aware of considerable variations in the health status of the world's population. At their most stark, these are portrayed by figures from the annual Human Development Report (United Nations Development Programme 2001). The most recent public health indicators include life expectancy ranging from to 37 in Sierra Leone up to 80 in Japan, the infant mortality rate (per 1000 live births) ranging from 3 in Sweden, through 4–6 in many developed countries, to 132 in Malawi, and 182 in Sierra Leone. The maternal mortality ratio (per 100,000 live births) ranges from an estimate of 1 in Greece, through 8 in the United States, to 440 in Bangladesh, to 1100 in Mozambique and the Central African Republic. The largest single cause is poverty, which can manifest itself as malnutrition, absence of sanitation, and lack of access to clean drinking water and to health care. However, even in countries within the developed world there are substantial variations, again at a variety of spatial scales.

Regional Perspectives

Poverty assumes rather different guises in more affluent societies, but inequalities in health status persist at sub-national levels, demonstrating a clear need for policies to alleviate it. For example, latest estimates of male life expectancy in the United Kingdom vary from 79 in parts of southern England, to 69 in parts of urban Scotland (Office for National Statistics 2001). Figures for the United States (National Center for Health Statistics 1997) show that, for all races combined, male life expectancy varies from 75.4 in Hawaii to 68.9 in Mississippi; the figure for black males in Washington, D.C. is only 57.5 years.

Recent work in the United Kingdom (Shaw et al. 1999) has used geographic visualization to reveal the nature and spatial extent of health inequalities. This work was based on the calculation of premature mortality (deaths under 65 years of age, standardized according to the related age and sex structures) and supported by a wide range of other social indicators. The units of analysis were electoral constituencies, and the report compared the 15 constituencies with the highest rates of premature mortality with 13 "best health" constituencies. The 15 "worst health" constituencies could clearly be seen to have poorer levels of employment, education qualifications, child health, and average household income. Displaying the data on maps (see Figure 18.3), 12 of the 13 "best health" constituencies, and only one of the "worst health" constituencies, were situated in the affluent south of Britain.

A major consideration within the health inequalities debate is that of equity of access to health care. In countries where there is no substantive public health care system, income will be the primary determinant of access. Here, the term "health care" may be the most basic provision of a hospital, or the proximity of a family doctor or other health professional, but it also incorporates access to preventive services such as immunization and screening, contraception and maternity services, and palliative care throughout a terminal illness.

The development of geographical information systems has supported increasingly sophisticated and robust modeling of access to health care. A fundamental issue is how we quantify the distance between a "demand point" (usually a person's home) and a "supply point," for example, a doctor's surgery. Early work simply used the straight-line distance between the two points. These calculations were often inaccurate reflections of the travel involved, for example, artificially shortening a journey that might involve a tortuous route around a river estuary. Conversely, a journey that allowed fast travel on a multi-lane highway might prove more efficient than a model for the Euclidean plane suggested. Road networks can be easily represented within a GIS, and estimates of travel times between points generated by applying different speeds to the different classes of roads encountered along the route. Jones and Bentham (1995) were concerned that a policy of centralizing emergency health services might not be the best approach for a large rural area. Taking a database of the locations and outcomes (fatalities or otherwise) of road traffic accidents, they used the road network within a GIS to simulate the route of an ambulance from the nearest ambulance station to each geo-coded accident, and then the route from the scene of the accident to the nearest hospital accident and emergency department. This allowed them to assess the distance traveled by the ambulance in connection with the outcome of the accident, and they found that the relationship between access time and health outcome was not significant. If the road networks are not explicitly classified (for example motorway, dual carriageway, minor road), measures of sinuosity (bendiness) can be calculated, which indicate that the speed of vehicles will be restricted (Lauder et al. 2001). Such work has an important role in the allocation of funding for health resources where the costs of healthcare provision to populations in remote areas are a concern.

Local Perspectives

We want here to consider three examples of work where a spatial perspective can inform our understanding of local variation in health outcomes. Consider first research in

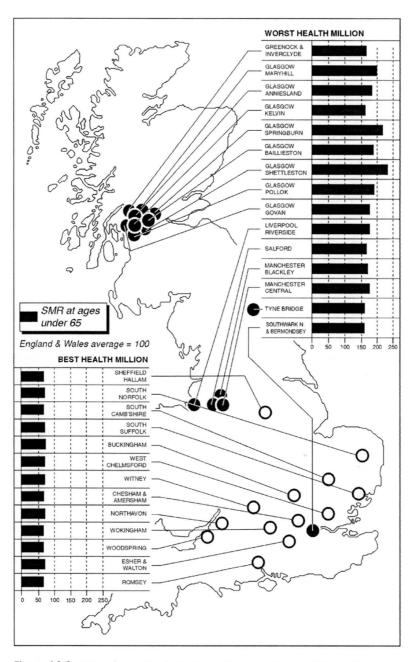

Figure 18.3. Map of mortality in U.K. constituencies. Reprinted from Shaw et al. (1999) with permission from The Policy Press, University of Bristol.

Glasgow, Scotland, that has sought to explain intra-urban variation in a variety of health outcomes, including self-reported health and mental health in particular (Macintyre et al. 1993; Sooman and Macintyre 1995). Four localities within the city are studied, two in the relatively affluent northwest and two in the more deprived southwest. Broadly speaking, health is better in the two northwest localities (Table 18.2). The explanation lies, in part, in differences in the local social environment, including both the extent to which there is poor infrastructure and a variety of reported social problems. While in the northwest there is good access to local services and facilities, such as public transport, health services, and retail outlets, in the southwest these are more sparsely provided. A genuine "mapping" of public health therefore needs to document the availability of those "goods" that may impact on population health.

At the other extreme, we need to focus on proximity to environmental "bads" as well as access to health-promoting services. Here, the research effort has been driven by those working in North America, under the heading of "environmental justice." This imperative is that people have equitable access to environmental resources and that the burden of environmental costs should be shared in a reasonably equitable way. This, quite manifestly, does not happen, with political power (held differentially by local groups and institutions) and externality effects conspiring to ensure that the spatial distribution of pollution, for example, is socially patterned. Jerrett et al. (2001) have shown how to use spatial analytic methods to assess the nature of the problem. They take monitored data on particulate air pollution from 23 monitoring stations in Hamilton, Ontario. From the measurements they construct a spatially continuous surface of pollution using the geostatistical technique of kriging (see Bailey and Gatrell 1995,

Table 18.2. Local social environment and health outcomes in Glasgow, Scotland.

Area Indicator	West End (NW)	Garscadden (NW)	Mosspark (SW)	Pollok (SW)
Access to services				
Pharmacy[†]	97.9	96.0	87.2	92.0
Post office[†]	98.4	97.7	89.4	96.4
Grocery store[†]	99.5	99.4	97.9	98.5
Reported problems				
Discarded needles[††]	4.3	8.5	10.8	18.0
Poor public transport[††]	13.4	16.7	20.5	18.8
Assaults and muggings[††]	28.2	34.5	47.9	56.1
Health outcomes				
Health for age[†††]	35.1	22.6	29.8	13.2
HADS anxiety[††††]	16.5	17.7	29.8	25.6

[†]percentages of respondents reporting amenities within half a mile

[††]percentage of respondents reporting selected problems

[†††]percentage of respondents reporting health as excellent

[††††]percentage of respondents reporting anxiety

Source: Sooman and Macintyre (1995), with permission from Elsevier Science (*Health and Place*, vol. 1, 1995, pages 15–26).

for an introduction). The pollution surface is overlain on census tracts, and regression analyses conducted to determine the relationship between pollution levels and socio-economic variables such as dwelling value, household income, and unemployment. All the latter exert a significant influence on pollution exposure, though analysis of residuals shows evidence of autocorrelation, and a spatially autoregressive model is required to remove this. The conclusion is that poorer groups are significantly more exposed to pollution than higher status populations (Figure 18.4). Research such as this has led other authors (Falit-Baiamonte and Osleeb 2000) to consider a new form of location model, one that determines a configuration of noxious facilities such that the burdens associated with hazardous plants are shared as equitably as possible among sub-regions.

As noted earlier, there is now a rich vein of work emerging that demonstrates an association between mortality or morbidity and the distribution of resources (usually income) within a study region. Unequal shares of income seem to contribute to population ill health. In a local British context, Ben-Shlomo and his colleagues (1996) demonstrated that mortality was associated with variability in socio-economic status. Those local authorities in which there was high variation in deprivation (a mix of deprived and affluent small areas) had poorer health than those that were more homogeneous, once overall levels of deprivation had been controlled for. Gatrell (1997) and Boyle and colleagues (1999) have sought to introduce an explicit spatial dimension to this research. They argue, and then demonstrate, that we may look at variability (heterogeneity) not solely within a single administrative area, but also among contiguous areas. They show that morbidity is associated with variations in deprivation within small areas and their neighbors. From the perspective of an individual, one's health is shaped to some extent by income, but it is also shaped by whether one is surrounded by generally better-off, or generally worse-off neighbors.

This overtly spatial context has yet to be fully exploited by public health researchers seeking to understand health inequalities. However, there is a substantial body of research now on the impact of "context" on health. By this is meant the effect of neighborhood or local social characteristics on health. It is argued that to understand health outcomes at the individual level one needs not solely "compositional" variables (on smoking behavior, for example) but also contextual influences that are "supra-individual." For example, if seeking to predict the incidence of childhood asthma, one could hypothesize that this is shaped in part by household-level factors (dampness in the home, prevalence of smokers in the household), but also by factors operating at another level (such as the number of vehicles traveling along the road outside, or the average level of outside air pollution in the neighborhood).

The existence of health determinants at different "levels" (individual, household, neighborhood) has led to the now quite extensive use of multi-level modeling to take account of these wider spatial contexts. For example, O'Campo and her colleagues (1997) explain geographic variation in low birth weight both in terms of individual-level determinants (such as late initiation of pre-natal care) and neighborhood-level influences (such as levels of crime). The evidence from this and many similar studies is that "area-level" variables contribute some explanatory power over and above factors operating at the individual level.

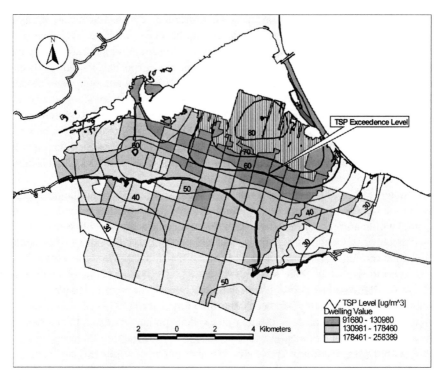

Figure 18.4. Dwelling values and total suspended particulates in Hamilton, Ontario, 1985–94. Reprinted from Jerrett et al. (2001, 966) with permission from Pion Limited, London.

Concluding Remarks

We have but scratched the surface of a growing, and rich literature on the geography of health (or "medical geography"), a literature that demonstrates quite convincingly that space and place figure prominently in epidemiology and public health. While this connection has a history stretching back into the nineteenth century and beyond, only quite recently has spatial context begun to re-emerge. In part this is due to the emergence of geo-referenced data and the technical advances offered by GIS and contemporary spatial analysis. Striking advances have been made in geographic visualization, exploratory spatial data analysis, and geographic modeling. Of course, these insights offer only a partial picture, and we must turn to other methodological perspectives—including qualitative methods—to gain a fuller understanding of ill health. We need to progress in other directions too, of which an understanding of health and disease "through the life-course" is paramount. As we have hinted here, a spatial perspective will continue to figure prominently.

References

Aase, A., and G. Bentham. 1994. The geography of malignant melanoma in the Nordic countries: The implications of stratospheric ozone depletion. *Geografiska Annaler* 76B: 129–139.

Anselin, L. 1995. Local indicators of spatial association. *Geographical Analysis* 27: 93–115.

Bailey, T.C., and A.C. Gatrell. 1995. *Interactive Spatial Data Analysis*. Harlow: Addison Wesley Longman.

Ben-Shlomo, Y., I. White, and M. Marmot. 1996. Does the variation in the socio-economic characteristics of an area affect mortality? *British Medical Journal* 312: 1013–1014.

Bentham, G., and A. Aase. 1996. Incidence of malignant melanoma of the skin in Norway, 1955–1989: Associations with solar radiation, income, and holidays abroad. *International Journal of Epidemiology* 25: 1132–1138.

Bentham, G., J. Hinton, R. Haynes, A. Lovett, and C. Bestwick. 1995. Factors affecting nonresponse to cervical cytology screening in Norfolk, England. *Social Science and Medicine* 40: 131–135.

Besag, J., and J. Newell. 1991. The detection of clusters in rare diseases. *Journal of the Royal Statistical Society Series A* 154: 143–155.

Boyle, P., A.C. Gatrell, and O. Duke-Williams. 1999. The effect on morbidity of variability in deprivation and population stability in England and Wales: An investigation at small-area level. *Social Science and Medicine* 49: 791–799.

Bulliard, J-L., B. Cox, and J.M. Elwood. 1994. Latitude gradients in melanoma incidence and mortality in the non-Maori population of New Zealand. *Cancer Causes and Control* 5: 234–240.

Clayton, D., and L. Bernardinelli. 1992. Bayesian methods for mapping disease risk. In P. Elliott, J. Cuzick, D. English, and R. Stern. (eds.), *Geographical and Environmental Epidemiology*. Oxford: Oxford University Press, 205–200.

Cliff, A.D., and P. Haggett. 1988. *Atlas of Disease Distributions*. Oxford: Oxford University Press.

Devesa, S.S., D.J. Grauman, W.J. Blot, G.A. Pennello, R.N. Hoover, and J.F. Fraumeni, Jr. 1999. *Atlas of Cancer Mortality in the United States 1950–94*. Washington, D.C: National Institutes of Health.

Falit-Baiamonte, A., and J.B. Osleeb. 2000. An equity model for locating environmentally hazardous facilities. *Geographical Analysis* 32: 351–368.

Gatrell, A.C. 1997. Structures of geographical and social space and their consequences for human health. *Geografiska Annaler* 79B: 141–154.

Gatrell, A.C. 2002. *Geographies of Health*. Oxford: Blackwell Publishers.

Gatrell, A.C., S. Garnett, J. Rigby, A. Maddocks, and M. Kirwan. 1998. Uptake of screening for breast cancer in South Lancashire. *Public Health* 112: 297–301.

Getis, A., and J.K. Ord. 1999. Spatial modelling of disease dispersion using a local statistic: The case of AIDS. In D.A. Griffith, C.G. Amrhein, and J.M. Huriot (eds.), *Econometric Advances in Spatial Modelling and Methodology: Essays in Honour of Jean Paelinck*. Dordrecht: Kluwer, 143–158.

Gould, P.R. 1993. *The Slow Plague*. Oxford: Blackwell.

Gould, P., and R. Wallace. 1994. Spatial structures and scientific paradoxes in the AIDS pandemic. *Geografiska Annaler* 76B: 105–116.

Hay, S.I., S.E. Randolph, and D.J. Rogers (eds.), 2000. *Remote Sensing and GIS in Epidemiology*. London: Academic Press.

Jerrett, M., R.T. Burnett, P. Kanaroglou, J. Eyles, N. Finkelstein, C. Giovis, and J.R. Brook. 2001. A GIS-environmental justice analysis of particulate air pollution in Hamilton, Canada. *Environment and Planning A* 33: 955–973.

Jones, A.P., and G. Bentham. 1995. Emergency medical service accessibility and outcome from road traffic accidents. *Public Health* 109: 169–177.

Kingham, S., A. Gatrell, and B. Rowlinson. 1995. Testing for clustering of health events within a geographical information system framework. *Environment and Planning A* 27: 809–821.

Kulldorff, M., E.J. Feuer, B.A. Miller, and L.S. Freedman. 1997. Breast cancer in northeastern United States: A geographical analysis. *American Journal of Epidemiology* 146: 161–170.

Langford, I.H. 1994. Using empirical Bayes estimates in the geographical analysis of disease risk. *Area* 22:142–149.

Lauder, C., C. Skelly, and L. Brabyn 2001. Developing and validating a road travel time network for cost path analysis. *Proceedings of SIRC 2001*. University of Otago, New Zealand, 2–5 December 2001: 225–231.

Lubin, J.H., and J.D. Boice. 1997. Lung cancer risk from residential radon: Meta-analysis of eight epidemiologic studies. *Journal of the National Cancer Institute* 89: 49–57.

Macintyre, S., S. Maciver, and A. Sooman. 1993. Area, class and health: Should we be focusing on places or people? *Journal of Social Policy* 22: 213–234.

McNally, N.J., H.C. Williams, D.R. Phillips, M. Smallman-Raynor, S. Lewis, A. Venn, and J. Britton. 1998. Atopic eczema and domestic water hardness. *The Lancet* 352: 527–531.

Meade, M.S., and R.J. Earickson. 2000. *Medical Geography*. 2nd edition. New York: Guilford Press.

National Center for Health Statistics. 1997. *US Decennial Life Tables for 1989–91*. Washington, D.C.: U.S. Government Printing Office.

O'Campo, P., X. Xue, M-C. Wang, and M. Caughy. 1997. Neighborhood risk factors for low birthweight in Baltimore: A multilevel analysis. *American Journal of Public Health* 87: 1113–1118.

Office for National Statistics. 2001. *Health Statistics Quarterly, Autumn 2001*. London: The Stationery Office.

Openshaw, S. 1990. Automating the search for cancer clusters: A review of problems, progress and opportunities. In R.W. Thomas (ed.), *Spatial Epidemiology*. London: Pion, 48–78.

Rigby, J.E., and A.C. Gatrell. 2000. Spatial patterns in breast cancer incidence in northwest Lancashire. *Area* 32: 71–78.

Sabel, C.E., A.C. Gatrell, M. Löytönen, P. Maasilta, and M. Jokelainen. 2000. Modelling exposure opportunities: Estimating relative risk for motor neurone disease in Finland. *Social Science and Medicine* 50: 1121–1137.

Shaw, M., D. Dorling, D. Gordon, and G.D. Smith. 1999. *The widening gap: Health inequalities and policy in Britain*. Bristol: The Policy Press.

Sooman, A., and S. Macintyre. 1995. Health and perceptions of the local environment in socially contrasting neighbourhoods in Glasgow. *Health and Place* 1: 15–26.

Teppo, L. 1998. Problems and possibilities in the use of cancer data by GIS: Experience in Finland. In A.C. Gatrell and M. Löytönen (ed.), *GIS and Health*. London: Taylor and Francis, 167–77.

Timander, L.M., and S. McLafferty. 1998. Breast cancer in West Islip, NY: A spatial clustering analysis with covariates. *Social Science and Medicine* 46: 1623–1635.

United Nations Development Programme. 2001. *Human Development Report 2001*. New York: Oxford University Press.

Walter, S.D., S.M. Taylor, and L.D. Marrett. 1999. An analysis of determinants of regional variation in cancer incidence: Ontario, Canada, In A. Lawson, A. Biggeri, D. Böhning, E. Lesafre, J.F. Viel, and R. Bertollini (ed.), *Disease Mapping and Risk Assessment for Public Health*. Chichester: John Wiley, 365–381.

WHO. 2000. *Report on the Global HIV/AIDS Epidemic*. Geneva: World Health Organisation.

19

The Role of Spatial Analysis in Demographic Research

John R. Weeks

D emography is an inherently spatial science, since it almost always deals with human populations in a defined geographic region, but spatial analysis has thus far played only a small role in the development and testing of demographic theory. There are several reasons for this, including the recency of many of the more useful spatial statistical approaches, and the fact that most people practicing demographic science are not in geography and have not been encouraged to think spatially. Yet, even in geography, few population specialists adopt specifically spatial approaches to their research beyond the measurement of the movement of people from one region to another, or the comparison of demographic trends among different regions.

In the past few decades, demographic research has focused particularly on the analysis of survey data drawn from interviews conducted at the household level, and as a consequence, theory has focused heavily on individual-level influences on demographic behavior. The development of surveys such as the National Survey of Family Growth in the United States, and the U.S.-funded Demographic and Health Surveys in less developed nations represented an important step in demographic research because the previous heavy reliance on aggregated data, especially from censuses and vital statistics, left gaps in our knowledge about how individuals think and behave. Now, however, the confluence of powerful geographic information system technologies, advances in the design of spatial statistics, and the increasing availability of georeferenced databases has improved vastly the ability of demographers to think spatially. As a result, there is a reawakening of interest in models of human behavior that place individuals in the environmental context of space and time.

Demography is not only spatial, but it is also by nature interdisciplinary. The demographic transition, which provides the organizing framework for most demographic research, is really a complex set of transitions, each of which draws upon expertise in differing social science and health-related disciplines. The demographic transition usually begins with the epidemiological transition, which is the shift over time from high death rates, with deaths clustered at the younger ages and caused largely by communicable diseases, to low death rates, with deaths clustered at the older ages and caused largely by degenerative, non-communicable diseases. This sets in motion a train of other transitions. The fertility transition represents the change from high fertility levels over which people have relatively little direct control to low fertility over which people have considerable control. The migration transition is initially the response to population growth in rural areas, which causes people to seek opportunity elsewhere, typically urban places, thus unleashing the urban transition, in which a population moves from being largely rural to being largely urban. The age structure transition is a predictable result of changes in mortality and fertility in which high mortality and high fertility produce a very young age structure that is pyramid-shaped, whereas the declines in both mortality and fertility produce bulges in the young adult ages, leading eventually to a barrel-shaped age structure. The family and household transition represents the change from complex forms of family and household structure when mortality and fertility are both high, to less variability in the middle of the transition, to new forms of complexity when both fertility and mortality are low. Finally, of course, there is the overall transition in population size that occurs when mortality declines sooner than fertility (the usual pattern in the demographic transition) from which massive changes follow with respect to resource use and allocation.

Each of these interrelated aspects of demographic change has a spatiotemporal component, which, when understood, adds to our knowledge of how and why these transitions occur. Furthermore, each of these different aspects of the demographic transition draws attention, as appropriate, from sociologists, economists, geographers, regional scientists, public health researchers and practitioners, and a host of other disciplines. In fact, very few people in the field of demography actually have advanced degrees in the named field of demography, and there are very few academic departments of demography in the world. Instead, demographic research is conducted as a sub-discipline of nearly every one of the social and health sciences fields, and researchers in these various disciplines are then frequently associated with academically based population centers.

The fact that demography is spatial by nature means that much, if not most, of the demographic research that is conducted has a spatial "awareness," even if relatively little of it engages spatial "analysis" in any formal sense. Spatially aware research understands that demographic behavior will differ by geographic region—that population characteristics and change are different in urban than in rural places; that countries in sub-Saharan Africa with a high proportion of Muslims have lower HIV/AIDS prevalence rates than predominantly non-Muslim nations; that East Asian countries have experienced a different fertility transition than South Asian countries. All migration research—which has historically been the staple of population geographers—has a built-in spatial awareness, because the analyses focus on the places from which migrants come and the places to which they go. Migration matrices and multi-regional life tables have been created as tools that increase our quantitative understanding of these changes involved in migration. But such spatial awareness is not quite the same as spatial analysis because it is not typically associated with underlying theories and hypotheses about spatial patterns that are designed to be tested for their specific spatial content.

In this chapter, I first offer a general framework for the application of spatial analysis to demographic research as a way of integrating and better understanding the different transitional components of the overall demographic transition. Then I discuss the kinds of data that are required for spatial demographic analysis, allowing researchers to use the concepts and tools of spatial analysis to test theories emerging from the general framework that I have laid out. Finally, I summarize some of the work that I and my colleagues have been doing in Egypt, searching for an improved understanding of the Arab fertility transition through the testing of explicitly spatial hypotheses about the timing and tempo of fertility change.

General Framework for Spatial Analysis in Demography

Spatial analysis can be defined as a quantitative data analysis in which the focus is on the role of space and which relies on explicitly spatial variables in the explanation or prediction of the phenomenon under investigation (Chou 1997; Cressie 1993). Spatial analysis in the social sciences tests theories that where you are makes a difference in social attitudes and behavior, and that observed differences in the social world are not distributed in a spatially random pattern. Cressie (1993) argues that the classical, non-spatial data analysis should actually be seen as a special case of spatial data analysis. Viewed in this way, the underlying logic is that each random variable (z) is associated with locational attributes (x and y). In spatial data analysis, the researcher uses geostatistics to glean information from the x and y coordinates, whereas in classical statistical analysis the researcher ignores those coordinates (often not even realizing that they might exist). More to the point, in classical statistical analysis, the locational attributes are considered to be a nuisance, rather than representing useful information. Spatial autocorrelation follows Tobler's "First Law of Geography": Everything is related to everything else, but near places are more related than far places (Tobler 1970). In classical statistical analysis, this is something to be gotten rid of, or controlled for, whereas in spatial data analysis it becomes an object of investigation. If spatial autocorrelation exists, then there may be spatial dependence, and thus, something of interest spatially that is occurring.

The comments about spatial autocorrelation also apply to temporal autocorrelation (things that are close to one another temporally are more likely to be similar than things that are more temporally distant). Econometricians have developed autoregressive models to account for the temporal autocorrelation that is typically found in time-series data that constitute the backbone of much of economic analysis. Time is a disturbance to be controlled, not an effect to be studied.

To think spatially with regard to demographic research, it is useful to keep in mind the suggestion of Star and Estes (1990) that spatial analysis can be divided into two "families": (1) analysis that is concerned with *local or neighborhood characteristics*; and (2) analysis that is concerned with *connections* among locations. This distinction provides a useful way of organizing our thinking into a general framework, as is illustrated in Figure 19.1. In demographic research we can think of the neighborhood

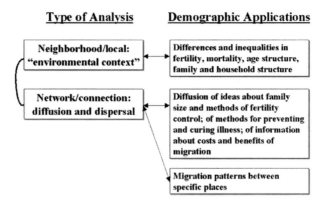

Figure 19.1. A framework for spatial analysis in demographic research.

characteristics as representing aspects of the context in which demographic decisions are made and demographic behavior is manifested. Spatial analysis then looks for place-specific factors that influence the behavior of otherwise similar people. The connections relate to the kinds of networking and interaction that lead both to *diffusion* (the spread of ideas) and *dispersal* (the geographic redistribution of people). Spatial analysis then searches for the timing and direction of the connections and seeks to understand their causes and consequences. Let me discuss these general concepts in more detail.

Spatial Analysis Based on Environmental Context

One of the theoretically more robust ways in which spatial analysis is beginning to enter demography theory is in an updated version of human ecology that is often referred to in the literature as "environmental context." From a human ecological perspective, this means that population size and characteristics interact with social organization, and with the environment and technology, to produce the behavior that constitutes human society. In turn, human behavior influences population, organization, the environment, and technology, and for this reason, the concept is that of a system, a human ecosystem (Micklin and Sly 1998; Namboodiri 1988).

Social scientists tend to focus on the population and social organizational parts of this system and spend less time thinking about the environment in which these parts are embedded. In particular, sociologists and demographers are generally vague, if not dismissive, of the built environment—of the buildings, parks, roads, bridges, and the associated infrastructure that humans create out of the natural environment and which become the places where everyday life takes place. Micklin and Sly (1998) put the built environment under technology, representing one set of "tools" available to human society. Yet, the built environment is more than that—it is the actual environment in which a large fraction of humans spend their entire lives. The natural environment is so transformed by urbanization that the majority of urban residents spend little time touching soil and interacting with flora and fauna. Even more importantly, the built environment is not just a product of human activity; it is also a very important element of what Namboodiri (1988, 622) has called the goal of human ecology, which is "to identify the linkage between the dynamics of human interdependence and the pursuit of the art of living."

There can be little doubt, of course, that national and regional events affect things like fertility levels regardless of where a person lives (see, e.g., Fargues 1997), and that events outside an area can be instrumental in producing change at the local level (Courbage 1994). But ultimately, it is at the local level that the actual decisions are made that lead to the specific behavior that determines what the regional and national fertility levels are going to be. Duncan made the classic statement of this in 1959:

> A concrete human population exists not in limbo but in an environment. Moreover, to continue to exist, it must cope with the problems posed by an environment that is indifferent to its survival but offering (in varying degree) resources potentially useful for the maintenance of life. By mere occupancy of an environment, as well as by the exploitation of its resources, a human population modifies its environment to a greater or lesser degree, introducing environmental changes additional to those produced by other organisms, geological processes, and the like. Thus, in the language of bioecology, one may say that not only does the environment "act" upon the population but also the human population "reacts" upon its environment. . . . The adjustment of a population to its environment, therefore, is not a state of being or static equilibrium but a continuing, dynamic process (Duncan 1959, 681–682).

When Duncan uses the word "environment" he is referring to the natural environment, in the way that human ecologists have tended to do. But, a substitution of "built environment" for "environment" keeps the meaning while applying it specifically to human life as organized in cities, towns, and villages throughout the world. And when we use the term local context or local environment, we mean the complex of social activities that are taking place within a given built environment, situated within a specific natural environment.

Local context has emerged as an important way of conceptualizing inequalities in the social world (Tickamyer 2000), and this approach is exemplified in this volume by the chapters by Logan and Zhang, Sampson and Morenoff, and Messner and Anselin. With respect to demographic research, this approach offers a way of exploring differences and inequalities in fertility, mortality, age structure, and family and household structure. Note that I have put a two-headed arrow in Figure 19.1 to indicate the reciprocal nature of these relationships. If you want to understand spatial inequality in fertility, for example, you must realize that part of the context of that fertility behavior will be in terms of local health and mortality levels, the local age structure (influencing cohort size distortions), and the prevailing family and household structures, all of which will be related to local issues of gender equality and empowerment.

Relatively little attention has been paid thus far to analyses of fertility at the local spatial scale. There is a vast literature on fertility differentials, to be sure, but attention is paid largely to characteristics of individuals without regard to where they live. At first glance, it might seem that this is simply evidence that population geographers believe that where you live is not related to fertility. There is the nearly universal finding that fertility differs by social class (defined sometimes by income differences, by occupational distributions, by education, and sometimes by racial/ethnic differences). Since there is a tendency for there to be a geographic sorting process by social class, the spatial dimension of fertility is implicitly incorporated into that model, but little attention is otherwise given to the demographic and social variability in fertility across space. That is to say, little attention is paid to the ecology of fertility, even among human ecologists. Rather, the emphasis is on examining fertility levels at the individual level, using data from surveys that, by and large, do not permit a neighborhood analysis. These studies, of necessity, focus attention on national comparisons or at regional differences within a country.

Scale becomes an important issue in such research, because as fertility declines over time, regional differences may disappear, even though local variations remain. Indeed, even under conditions of relatively high fertility, this confounding may occur. Wilson and Woods (1991, 414) show that in Victorian England and Wales "demographic conditions were local, rather than regional. These local patterns tend to be masked when counties, or combinations of counties, are made the framework for analysis." Weeks et al. (2001) found the same issues of scale in the spatial patterning of fertility in Egypt, based on an analysis of Demographic and Health Survey data. Using data at the governorate (state) level, only the most general pattern of a north-south fertility differential was observable. However, within Cairo, where the sample size was sufficient for a within-state analysis, clear spatial patterns did in fact emerge.

More attention has been paid to spatial differences in various causes of disease and death. Communicable diseases, by their very nature, are susceptible to local differences in infrastructure and population structure. Langford et al. (1999) have examined some general issues related to spatial patterns of mortality in Scotland, whereas Wallace and Fullilove (1991) examined the local spatial context of AIDS deaths in the Bronx in the 1980s. Reid (1997) used data from the 1911 census of England and Wales to show that infant and child mortality at the beginning of the twentieth century was influenced by a combination of the parents' characteristics (especially the father's occupation) and where the child lived. LeClere et al. (1998) show that neighborhood context is related to death from heart disease among women in the United States; Robert (1998) has shown that the socioeconomic status of a person's community affects adult health over and above an individual's own sociodemographic characteristics; and Peak and Weeks (2002) have demonstrated that living in a Mexican ethnic enclave improves reproductive outcomes of Mexican-origin women in California. Gatrell and Rigby discuss similar types of studies in this volume.

Although the local environmental context may be the focus of a particular spatial analysis, there may well be overlap with the diffusion/dispersal aspects of analysis. To be sure, one of the reasons why change may occur at the local level is because of the influence of networks and connections between different places. For this reason, Figure 19.1 shows a link between these types of analysis.

Spatial Analysis Based on Networks and Connections

Demographic transition theory rests as least partially on the concept of the diffusion of innovations—including ways of preventing death, preventing births, and organizing migration flows and chains. These are processes that spread over space and across time and are naturally prone to spatial analysis. Early references to this spatially demographic way of viewing the world include a study of fertility change in Nigeria by van de Walle (1965), the study of fertility differences in Spain by Leasure (1962) that actually ignited the Princeton European Fertility Project, and the later results from that project that emphasized the process of diffusion in the European fertility transition (Coale and Watkins 1986; Watkins 1991). However, all of these studies would fall into the category of "spatial awareness" rather than spatial analysis. Casterline and his colleagues used pooled time series data to demonstrate the diffusion of the fertility transition in Taiwan (Montgomery and Casterline 1993) and in Costa Rica (Rosero-Bixby and Casterline 1994). More recent studies have benefited from the availability of GIS, including especially the work of Bocquet-Appel and Jakobi (1998, 199), who used kriging and other techniques of spatial interpolation to show that Peebles, in lowland Scotland, quite possibly served in the mid-nineteenth century as the "detonator to what appears to be a 'Big Bang' in the introduction of contraception in Great Britain."

A potentially important subset of diffusion is the idea of networks. Diffusion is usually measured, as in the Bocquet-Appel and Jakobi study, at the aggregate level. If areas A and B are not alike on characteristic z at time 1, but are more alike at time 2, even after controlling for endogenous sociocultural changes, then we infer that diffusion has occurred from area A to area B (Tolnay 1995). Some sources of change do occur at the regional level, especially those affecting mortality (such as cleaning up the water supply or controlling mosquito populations), but some occur at the individual level, especially innovative behavior like fertility limitation or migration decisions. The influences here may be linked to networks, which have an important spatial component, even though most theorizing about human networks has been done without taking location into account (see Burt 1992, 1999), and most analyses in demographic research can be best described as spatially aware, rather than spatially analytic (see, for example, Kohler et al. 2001). A major exception to this statement is the study by Entwisle et al. (1997), which used spatial network analysis to study the accessibility of family planning services in a rural population in Thailand.

Data Requirements for Spatial Analysis in Demographic Research

Demographic research that employs spatial analysis obviously requires data that are georeferenced. If data are not assigned to a location, then spatial analysis is not possible. The most precise locational attributes are points with precise longitude (x) and latitude (y) coordinates. The coordinates may be measured from a Global Positioning System (GPS), or they may be mapped from addresses that are referenced to a map and which can be matched to the map coordinates through address matching software that is built into most GIS applications. This kind of point information affords the opportunity for the most powerful and sophisticated type of spatial data analysis, which is known as point pattern analysis (PPA). The least precise spatial attributes refer to data that are aggregated into areas (polygons) and for which relative distances from other places are known, even if the exact location of the polygon is not provided. Thus, we may know simply that area A is contiguous to area B, but not contiguous to area C. Even this much spatial information offers the opportunity for at least limited kinds of spatial data analysis, such as area pattern analysis.

Virtually all demographic data have some georeferencing associated with them: it is largely a question of scale. Data are almost always recorded at least at the country level (although some United Nations publications aggregate data only to the regional level), and so this provides a way of assessing spatial patterns among and between different regions of the world. Indeed, spatial clustering is a way of *defining* regions. Places that are relatively homogenous and share important characteristics in common are often called *formal* regions, whereas places that exhibit some kind of mutual interdependence, even if they are not otherwise similar, can be defined as *functional* regions (Noronha and Goodchild 1992). Northern Africa is a formal region in the sense that countries of northern Africa all share in common an ethnicity (Arab), a language (Arabic), and a religion (Islam) and so they are relatively homogeneous in that regard. On the other hand, metropolitan areas in North America and Europe are typically defined by combining contiguous places that share commuters (evidence of economic interdependence) no matter how different those places might otherwise be from one another.

There is a limit to the usefulness of data at the national level for spatial analysis, especially given the relatively small number of countries in the world. Demographic theories are likely to be more readily tested using geographic units at the sub-national level, especially if such data are available for more than one country, so that regional patterns can still be discerned, but at a finer scale. Such data work their way down to a level equivalent to the census tract in the United States, or in some instances, a sub-unit of the tract, such as a block or block group. Most data that are georeferenced to these types of administrative units are also aggregated statistically in order to preserve confidentiality, creating classical problems of ecological inference: Do the results summarized for many people reflect anything about the behavior of the individuals themselves?

The ecological fallacy can be thought of as a sub-set of a larger issue that arises regularly in spatial analysis—the modifiable areal unit problem (MAUP)—which has two components (Fotheringham et al. 2000, 237): (1) *the scale effect* (different results can be obtained from the same statistical analysis at different levels of spatial resolution), and (2) *the zoning effect* (different results can be obtained owing to the regrouping of zones at a given scale). The scale effect represents the core issue of the ecological fallacy, in which different correlation coefficients can result from using the same data, but at different levels of aggregation. Thus, one set of correlations may hold for individuals, another for individuals grouped in households, another for individuals aggregated at the census tract level, another for individuals aggregated at the county level, and so on. The only real solution to this problem is to conduct a sensitivity analysis by repeating the analysis at several different scales and see if similar results are obtained. If so, the findings are robust; if not, then further research will be required to determine what influences the variability in results at different resolutions.

The zoning effect is produced by the arbitrariness with which boundaries may be drawn around areas that then become the units of analysis for some set of data. Different boundaries might produce different results because of the different people who would be captured within the different zone. This effect can be studied by moving different "windows" over a set of data to see the effect of aggregating zones in different ways (Openshaw and Rao 1995), and this is the concept underlying the Geographically Weighted Regression algorithm developed by Fotheringham and his associates (Fotheringham et al. 1998).

The only real solution to both aspects of the MAUP is to begin with individual level data that are geocoded to specific locations, and thus, be able to aggregate the data to any scale that the researcher desires, and delimit any set of boundaries that the researcher believes is appropriate to the data. Demographic data are rarely available in that format, however, because of issues of confidentiality. The closest that demographers tend to come to this is through the use of samples of individual records from the Census. Files such as the public use microdata samples (PUMS) in the United States and Mexico, and the SARs (Samples of Anonymised Records) in the United Kingdom represent data for individuals, so that analysis can be run without aggregation, albeit at the cost of some geographic specificity, since privacy demands that you not be able to locate the person whose census record you are studying. Areal units for the samples are typically larger (sometimes much larger) than census tracts, and so spatial questions can be answered only in very general terms.

The PUMS and SAR data are samples from the complete set of census data, and in that sense they are little different from survey data, except that the sample size is typically large enough to provide a reasonable amount of geographic detail. A sample of a thousand people may be quite representative of the entire voting population of the United States, but it is not large enough to tell us anything at the sub-national level. Larger samples are capable of being georeferenced, however, and the Demographic and Health Surveys (DHS) have been leaders in this direction. The design of the DHS has always been based on a cluster sample, in which a fairly large number of households in each village or neighborhood in a city will be included in the sample. This has permitted these data to be linked back to administrative units such as census tracts, so that respondents could be located within their neighborhood context. Since 1999, the DHS has supplied interviewers in several of its surveys with GPS units so that the location of each geographic cluster in which households are located can be recorded. Nonetheless, privacy concerns limit the geographic specificity of those data, just as they do of the PUMS or SAR data. Administratively-derived data, such as birth and death certificates, often have addresses associated with them that permit location to be calculated by matching with street addresses, such as the TIGER file created by the U.S. Census Bureau.

The data from remotely sensed images provide new opportunities to apply spatial analysis to demographic research. There is a long history in demography of using aerial photographs to aid in the estimation of population size (see, e.g., Noin 1970). The general strategy is to count the number of households observed from the air, and then apply an average number of persons per household to estimate the total population. Although this does not automatically use spatial analysis, new variations on the old theme do incorporate spatial analysis to increase the accuracy of the estimation process (Lo 1995), including the use of night-time imagery to measure population density (Sutton 1997).

More sophisticated uses of new multi-spectral imagery offer the prospect of enhancing our understanding of spatial processes for demographic purposes (Rindfuss and Stern 1998). Some of the applications include: (1) linking changes in vegetation to changes in population distribution and characteristics; (2) measuring the spread of urban areas, and measuring the environmental impact of that spread (see, e.g., Longley and Mesev 2001; Ridd 1995; Ward et al. 2000); (3) classifying human settlements to derive proxies for social structural variables (see Moran, this volume); and (4) using night-time light images as a proxy for levels of rural development in less developed settings.

Remotely sensed imagery can also be used to help physically locate where populations may be concentrated within the boundaries of an otherwise much larger administrative unit. This can be an important in spatial analysis, because spatial statistics tend to be much more powerful when the unit of analysis is a point rather than an area. For this reason, it is common in spatial data analysis to convert polygons to points using some algorithm for determining a point that is most appropriate to the data within the area. If no information exists about the distribution of data, then one might assume a uniform distribution of data across space and calculate the centroid (the geometric center) of a polygon as the point which will then represent all of the data within that area and which will be used as the value for calculating distances between other polygons for purposes of determining the size and nature of any spatial association. If the data refer to human populations, then we can infer that people will be disproportionately found in built areas, which can be identified through the classification of satellite imagery. If only one built area is found in the larger administrative unit, then the geometric center of the built area can be used as the point that best represents the polygon. If more than one built area exists, then we can make an assumption that the size of each built area is proportional to the size of the population itself, and we can use this information to calculate a weighted mean center for the polygon. These techniques can be especially useful in the analysis of data for rural areas, as we have demonstrated with data for a rural governorate of Egypt.

Illustration: Spatial Analysis of Fertility Change in Egypt

In analyzing fertility change in Egypt, my colleagues and I (Weeks et al. 2000) have borrowed from Gadalla (1978), Namboodiri (1988), Entwisle et al. (1989), Hill (1997), and Crenshaw and his associates (2000) the idea that an account of fertility decline must "nest fertility decision-making and micro-level behavior in their environmental contexts" (Crenshaw et al. 2000, 371). The model that guides our research incorporates the assumptions that (1) the built environment represents something tangible about the social environment; (2) the social environment influences the social and human capital variables that more directly influence the demand for children; (3) the reproductive behavior of some people within a neighborhood will influence the behavior of others, even net of the human capital opportunities that objectively exist in the neighborhood; and (4) these influences operate on reproductive levels through the mechanisms of the proximate determinants of fertility, such as age at marriage and the use of contraceptives within marriage, to determine fertility at the local level; but (5) changes in reproductive behavior at the local level may be influenced by changes in, and reciprocally influence changes in, other neighboring regions, resulting in spatial patterns of fertility transition; the consequences of which (6) ultimately determine the overall societal level of reproduction, thus creating the wider phenomenon of a fertility transition.

In this research we are interested in the extent to which the variation in fertility from one rural village (the local context) to another may be explained by a process of diffusion of behavior from some villages to others, net of the human capital variables, such as education, that may exist within the village. We lack direct evidence of such spatial diffusion, but can infer it from the spatial and temporal patterning of reproductive behavior. First we must show that proximity matters, and then we must show that changes occurred over time in a sequence that is consistent with spread or diffusion.

We illustrate this procedure using data for a rural governorate of Egypt (Menoufia) for 1976 and 1986. Menoufia is one of the 26 governorates that comprise the administrative regions of Egypt, roughly equivalent to states in the United States, although perhaps more analogous to counties in the United Kingdom. For decades Menoufia has been one of the most rural and most densely populated rural areas of Egypt (Gadalla et al. 1987). It has been, and remains, predominantly agricultural, and the high rate of population growth has increased the redundancy of the rural labor force and encouraged out-migration—to Cairo or to other Arab (especially oil-producing) nations.

The demographic data used for this study come from the 1976 and 1986 censuses of Egypt. Data were coded from the Arabic-language publications using the smallest geographic unit available in the Egyptian censuses—the shiakha or village. The "shiakha" literally refers to the area controlled by a sheikh, but in more practical terms it is the area serviced by a police post. The dependent variable is the level of fertility in each shiakha, which is an estimate of the total fertility rate, derived from age data in the census. It is measured as the net reproduction rate, which takes mortality into account, for a measure that represents the actual "supply" of children. See Arriaga (1994) for a review of the methods that we employed in these calculations. The human capital variables derived from the census included adult female illiteracy and female labor force participation rates, with a control for the percent of women who were currently married.

In attempting to model the diffusion of fertility and/or its antecedents (the human capital variables) using census data, we had to deal with the problem mentioned earlier of how best to convert census areas to points so that we could apply the statistical techniques of point pattern analysis. In almost every instance demographic information is gathered at some arbitrarily defined geographic level such as a census tract or enumeration district. However, unless this area defines a small and heavily built area, its areal boundaries will include space in which people do not reside. This is especially true in agricultural areas where most space is devoted to crop, orchard, or pastureland. Thus, a rural village, even if densely populated within its own boundaries, may consume only a small portion of the administrative boundaries to which the demographic data are attached. We dealt with this problem through the use of remotely sensed images, which we employed to classify land cover by built/non-built use in order to undertake what is sometimes known as dasymetric mapping (Langford and Unwin 1994), in which information inside a zone is used to map the population density or distribution within that zone. The advantage of a classification of data from a remotely sensed image that spatially defines built areas is that it frees us from the "tyranny of an arbitrary imposed and fixed set of census geographies" (Openshaw and Rao 1995, 425). The results of the classification of the image allowed us to determine a unique location for each village in Menoufia, and this set of coordinates for each village was then used in the spatial analysis. The details of this process are discussed in Weeks et al. (2000).

The first question of interest was whether, in fact, fertility exhibited a spatially dependent pattern in Menoufia in each of the years under study. We used the global spatial statistic, Moran's I, to test the null hypothesis of spatial independence. In 1976, the normalized random z-score for Moran's I for the net reproduction rate (NRR) was 6.82, indicating a statistically significant amount of spatial autocorrelation, thus leading us to reject the null hypothesis that fertility is spatially independent in Menoufia. In 1986, the NRR produced a normalized random z-score for Moran's I of 5.50, again indicating a statistically significant level of spatial autocorrelation.

The $G_i^*(d)$ statistic (see Getis 1995; Getis and Ord 1992, 1996) provides a more precise local test for spatial dependence. For any given cell in the grid, its statistically significant difference from spatial independence is given by the ratio of the $G_i^*(d)$ statistic relative to its expected value at a calculated critical distance d. We calculated the critical distance as that distance at which a spatial filtering algorithm had removed the spatial autocorrelation (measured by Moran's I) from the variable (Scott 1999).

Any cell with a $G_i^*(d)$ value that is statistically significant at the .05 level would cause us to reject the null hypothesis of no clustering and would assign that cell to a cluster of either high or low fertility, depending upon the sign of G^*. In 1976 the critical distance was 5 km, indicating that, on average, villages that were clustered were more similar in fertility levels to those that were within a 5-km radius than they were to villages beyond that distance. In 1986 the critical distance was 4 km. In both 1976 and 1986 the villages clustered around low fertility also exhibited, as expected, lower than average proportions married, lower proportions of illiterate women, and lower adult sex ratios. In 1986, but not in 1976, the lower fertility clusters were associated with more populous villages (which we used as a proxy for level of urbanization). On each characteristic the villages clustered around high fertility exhibited the opposite patterns—higher proportions married, higher proportions of illiterate women, and higher adult sex ratios, again consistent with our theoretical expectations.

Panel A of Figure 19.2 shows the spatial clustering of high and low fertility in 1976, where villages in high clusters were those whose normalized z-scores for the $G_i^*(d)$ statistic were above 2, villages in low cluster were those whose normalized z-scores for the $G_i^*(d)$ statistic were below –2, and those villages with normalized z-scores between –2 and 2 were considered not to be clustered. A kriging function was applied to smooth the data for purposes of enhanced visualization of the results. In 1976 the clusters of low fertility were found in the north and northeast, while the clusters of high fertility were concentrated in the south and southwest of the governorate.

Although the pattern of clustering shown in Figure 19.2 could be interpreted as being influenced by edge effects, the clustering in 1986, shown in Panel B of Figure 19.2, seems to belie that explanation. In 1986 the clustering of low fertility had moved toward the middle of the governorate, although still concentrated in the north, whereas the clustering of high fertility was more concentrated in the southern portion of the governorate. Although the southern portion of Menoufia is closest to Cairo, it is also the site of the Nile Delta Barrage—the dam that controls the flow of water from the Nile River as it enters the Delta region. This is rich agricultural land with centuries, if not millennia, of rural tradition that almost certainly contributes to the maintenance of low levels of education, low levels of female labor force participation, and higher-than-average levels of fertility.

The data in Panel C of Figure 19.2 illustrate the change in the pattern of clustering between 1976 and 1986. Villages were categorized according to the combinations of

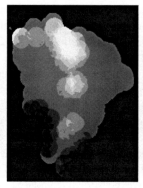

Figure 19.2. Spatial clustering of fertility in Menoufia, Egypt (left: 1976; middle: 1986; right: changes from 1976–1986). Lighter shading indicates clustering around low fertility, whereas darker shading indicates clustering around high fertility. Clustering is based on G_i^* scores. Source: Weeks et al. 2000, figures 5, 6, 7.

clustering in the two time periods. Thus, the lightest shades of clustering are assigned to villages that were in low fertility clusters in both 1976 and 1986, while the next lighter shade indicates villages that moved from not being clustered in 1976 to low fertility in 1986. The data thus show the concentration of lower fertility in the north, and the diffusion of lower fertility in that region. At the other extreme, the darkest shading is assigned to villages that were in high fertility clusters in both 1976 and 1986 and the next darker shading reflects villages that went from not being clustered in 1976 to being in a high fertility cluster in 1986. These villages are concentrated in the southern portion of the region. In general, the changes between 1976 and 1986 exhibit a spatial diffusion effect, with a spread of higher-than-average fertility to contiguous villages, and a spread of lower-than-average fertility to contiguous villages.

It is clear from Figure 19.2 that spatial variability in fertility exists in Menoufia. It does matter where you are—lower fertility is clustered in the north, and higher fertility is clustered in the south. How important is this spatial effect as a determinant of fertility levels? We used the technique of spatial filtering of variables in a regression model to try to answer this question. First we developed an Ordinary Least Squares (OLS) regression model that did not include a spatial component, echoing the typical such model in demographic analysis. This model had a statistically significant level of spatial autocorrelation in the residuals, indicating a poorly specified model, in the classical sense, but also indicating the presence of the kind of spatial dependence that was apparent visually in Figure 19.2. We filtered the statistically significant predictor variables to assess the importance of the spatial effect.

The basic non-spatial model is that the fertility level in a village is a function of female illiteracy, controlling for the sex ratio at the reproductive ages (as a control for the effect of out-migration), the percentage of adult women who are currently married (as a control for the effect of marital status on the measure of fertility that we calculated) and for total population size (as a control for urbanness). Two of the predictor variables— female illiteracy and proportion married—have statistically significant levels of spatial autocorrelation, whereas the other two predictor variables do not. The two with spatial autocorrelation were then filtered to decompose the spatial component from the non-spatial (called the "filtered") component, using the method described in Getis (1995). The regression results produce an overall adjusted R^2 of 0.393, as summarized in Table 19.1. The filtered component of the proportion married has a standardized beta coefficient that is virtually the same as the spatial component of that variable, indicating that the spatial component explains about half of that variable's relationship to fertility levels. The spatial component of female illiteracy is slightly more important than the filtered component, as can be seen in Table 19.1. The standardized beta coefficients in regression analysis represent the partial correlation coefficient of that independent variable to the dependent variable, controlling for all other independent variables in the equation. The ratio of the square of the beta coefficients for any two independent variables then gives us a quantitative measure of the relative contribution of each variable to the prediction of the dependent variable. Thus, we can note that the spatial component of the percent married was five times more important as a predictor of the net reproduction rate in 1976 than was the non-spatial component of female literacy, but almost equally important a predictor as the non-spatial component of the percent married.

In 1986 the female illiteracy variable was a more important predictor of fertility than was the percent married, and neither the adult sex ratio nor the total population size was statistically significantly related. The spatial component was also more noticeable than in 1976 because all four predictor variables exhibited spatial autocorrelation and the residuals were also spatially autocorrelated. All four predictor variables were filtered in 1986, and the resulting regression model is shown in the lower panel of Table 19.1. Filtering raised the explained variation from .482 in the original model (not shown) to .513 in the spatial model, although female illiteracy and the proportion of women married remained as the only statistically significant variables in the equation. In 1986 the most important predictor was the filtered (non-spatial) component of female illiteracy, followed by the spatial component of the proportion married, then the filtered component of the proportion married, and the spatial component of female illiteracy. If we once again square the standardized beta coefficients of the predictor variables, we find that the non-spatial component of female illiteracy was 2.3 times more important as a predictor of fertility in 1986 than was the spatial component of the percent married. This turnabout from the 1976 pattern suggests that changes were taking place in Menoufia during this period of time that would not have been observable in the absence of the spatial analysis.

The period from 1976 to 1986 was a period of overall relative stability in fertility levels in rural Egypt, yet it is obvious that at least by 1976 there were clear spatial patterns to fertility in Menoufia, and our analysis suggests that these spatial patterns were even more definitive in 1986 than they had been in 1976, with the southern portion of the governorate being more obviously the location of higher-than-average fertility in 1986 than had been true in 1976. Analysis of data from the 1996 census has revealed that this spatial pattern continued into the 1990s, and that the decline in fertility that did occur between 1986 and 1996 was found especially in those places that had been clustered around high levels of fertility in 1986 (Weeks et al. 2002). In other words, the decline of fertility had a clear spatial component to it. Because fertility declined faster in the high fertility villages than in the lower fertility villages, there was less variability, and slightly less clustering of fertility at both ends of the spectrum in 1996

Table 19.1. Spatially filtered OLS regression results.

	1976				
	Unstandardized	Standardized		Significance	
Variable	Coefficient	Beta	*t*	of *t*	$Z(I)$
Dependent variable: NRR					6.82
Filtered female illiteracy	.417	.149	2.699	.007	−0.99
Filtered proportion married	1.724	.329	5.907	.000	0.48
Spatial female illiteracy	.640	.167	2.563	.011	10.92
Spatial Proportion married	2.322	.331	5.024	.000	11.76
Sex ratio at reproductive ages	.178	.060	1.223	.222	1.30
Population size	−.00005	−.148	−3.111	.002	0.96
R	.637				
Adjusted R^2	.393				
$Z(I)$ for residuals	0.67				

	1986				
	Unstandardized	Standardized		Significance	
Variable	Coefficient	Beta	*t*	of *t*	$Z(I)$
Dependent variable: NRR					5.50
Filtered female illiteracy	1.920	.480	9.496	.000	−.64
Filtered proportion married	1.057	.170	3.587	.000	−.36
Filtered sex ratio at reproductive ages	.002	.006	0.136	.892	−.58
Filtered population size	−.00000008	−.063	−.379	.705	.03
Spatial female illiteracy	.913	.157	2.716	.007	26.80
Spatial Proportion married	3.352	.317	4.755	.000	25.72
Spatial sex ratio at reproductive ages	.640	.051	0.332	.332	28.96
Spatial population size	−.00000004	−.021	−.131	.896	.22
R	.717				
Adjusted R^2	.513				
$Z(I)$ for residuals	1.32				

Source: Weeks, J. R., M. S. Gadalla, T. Rashed, J. Stanforth, and A. G. Hill. 2000. "Spatial variability in fertility in Menoufia, Egypt, assessed through the application of remote sensing and GIS technologies," *Environment and Planning A*, (32): 695–714: Tables 5 and 7. Reproduced with permission from Pion Limited, London.

than in 1986. However, between those two dates there was very little change in marriage patterns anywhere in Menoufia, so that could not have contributed much to the fertility decline. Those places with the most rapidly declining fertility remained as the places with the highest percentage of women who were married (implying no change in the age at marriage). The major improvements in the education of females, which we had previously taken note of for the 1976–86 period, continued unabated between 1986 and 1996, but this seems to have been a governorate-wide initiative, because the absolute decline in the percentage of women who are illiterate was nearly identical across all fertility clustering categories.

These data suggest that it was not changes in the human capital variables that were the underlying causes of the differential rate of fertility decline in Menoufia between 1986 and 1996. By default, the explanation must lie in the family planning arena, in the more rapid spread of the use of modern contraceptives among women, especially younger women, in the higher fertility areas. This suggests a combination of targeted family planning effort and the diffusion of the use of contraception in those high fertility areas that essentially overrode the underlying characteristics of marriage patterns, education, and employment of women. The limited data available to us from the Demographic and Health Survey for Egypt (El-Zanaty and Way 2001) seem to be consistent with this idea.

There is not space in this chapter, obviously, to detail all of the nuances of this type of analysis, but the important point to be made here is that there is a clearly established spatial component to fertility levels and fertility change in rural Egypt. From a theoretical perspective, the spatial analysis helps us to quantify the roles that human capital and diffusion factors may be playing in the fertility transition in rural Egypt. From a research perspective, the spatial analysis helps to identify places where things are clearly different and where additional research ought to be focused. From a policy perspective, the spatial analysis helps planners and providers to know where programs of reproductive health and rural redevelopment are likely to have the greatest impact on fertility change.

Conclusion

Demographic research is moving inexorably from its long-standing pattern of spatial awareness to an increased appreciation for the value and utility of spatial analysis. In this chapter I have emphasized the role that spatial analysis can play in the testing of propositions that are central to demographic theory. I would be remiss to not also mention the importance of spatial analysis in models that link population growth and distribution to global issues such as land, water, and atmospheric degradation and change. The resources consumed locally are increasingly derived from non-local sources; and the polluting side effects of resource consumption may occur locally, but their impact can spread well beyond that. Understanding these and other kinds of global population-environment interactions requires the application of large-scale GIS models, following the lead of organizations such as the International Institute for Applied Systems Analysis (IIASA) in Austria. Thus far, demographers have been only minimally involved in this kind of research (see Findlay and Hoy 2000), and the modeling that has been done has not involved intensive use of spatial analysis *per se*. This combination seems to signal an area ripe for potential growth in the level of sophistication with which the consequences of population growth and change can be researched.

Acknowledgments   This work was supported by grants from the Andrew Mellon Foundation and the National Science Foundation (Grant No. BCS-0095641).

References

Arriaga, E.E., P.D. Johnson, and E. Jamison. 1994. *Population Analysis With Microcomputers.* Washington, D.C.: U.S. Bureau of the Census.

Bocquet-Appel, J.P., and L. Jakobi. 1998. Evidence for a spatial diffusion of contraception at the onset of the fertility transition in Victorian Britain. *Population: An English Selection* 10: 181–204.

Burt, R.S. 1992. *Structural Holes: The Social Structure of Competition*. Cambridge: Harvard University Press.

Burt, R.S. 1999. The social capital of opinion leaders. *Annals of the American Academy of Political and Social Sciences* 566: 37–54.

Chou, Y.H. 1997. *Exploring Spatial Analysis in Geographic Information Systems*. Santa Fe, N. Mex.: OnWard120 Press.

Coale, A., and S.C. Watkins. 1986. *The Decline of Fertility in Europe*. Princeton, N. J.: Princeton University Press.

Courbage, Y. 1994. Demographic change in the Arab world: The impact of migration, education, and taxes in Egypt and Morocco. *Middle East Report* 24: 19–22.

Crenshaw, E., M. Christenson, and D.R. Oakey. 2000. Demographic transition in ecological focus. *American Sociological Review* 65: 371–391.

Cressie, N.A.C. 1993. *Statistics for Spatial Data: Revised Edition*. New York: John Wiley & Sons.

Duncan, O.D. 1959. Human ecology and population studies. In P.M. Hauser and O.D. Duncan (eds.), *The Study of Population: An Inventory and Appraisal*. Chicago: University of Chicago Press, 678–716.

El-Zanaty, F., and A.A. Way. 2001. *Egypt Demographic and Health Survey 2000*. Calverton, MD: Ministry of Health and Population (Egypt), National Population Council and ORC Macro.

Entwisle, B., J. Casterline, and H.A.A. Sayed. 1989. Villages as contexts for contraceptive behavior in rural Egypt. *American Sociological Review* 54: 1019–1034.

Entwisle, B., R.R. Rindfuss, S.J. Walsh, T.P. Evans, and S.R. Curran. 1997. Geographic information systems, spatial network analysis, and contraceptive choice. *Demography* 34: 171–188.

Fargues, P. 1997. State policies and the birth rate in Egypt: From socialism to liberalism. *Population and Development Review* 23: 115–138.

Findlay, A.M., and C. Hoy. 2000. Global population issues: Towards a geographical research agenda. *Applied Geography* 20: 207–219.

Fotheringham, A.S., C. Brunsdon, and M.E. Charlton. 2000. *Quantitative Geography: Perspectives on Spatial Data Analysis*. London: Sage Publications.

Fotheringham, A.S., M.E. Charlton, and C. Brunsdon. 1998. Geographically weighted regression: A natural evolution of the expansion method for spatial data analysis. *Environment and Planning A* 30: 1905–1927.

Gadalla, S. 1978. *Is There Hope? Fertility and Family Planning in a Rural Community in Egypt*. Chapel Hill, N.C.: Carolina Population Center, University of North Carolina.

Gadalla, S., J. McCarthy, and N. Kak. 1987. The determinants of fertility in rural Egypt: A study of Menoufia and Beni-Suef. *Journal of Biosocial Science* 19: 195–207.

Getis, A. 1995. Spatial filtering in a regression framework: Examples using data on urban crime, regional inequality, and government expenditures. In L. Anselin and R. Florax (eds.), *New Directions in Spatial Econometrics*. Berlin: Spriger-Verlag, 172–185.

Getis, A., and J.K. Ord. 1992. The analysis of spatial association by use of distance statistics. *Geographical Analysis* 24:189–206.

Getis, A., and J.K. Ord. 1996. Local spatial statistics: An overview. In P. Longley and M. Batty (eds.), *Spatial Analysis: Modelling in a GIS Environment*. Cambridge, England: GeoInformation International, 261–277.

Hill, A.G. 1997. Truth lies in the eye of the beholder: The nature of evidence in demography and anthropology. In D. Kertzer and T. Fricke (eds.), *Anthropological Demography: Toward a New Synthesis*. Chicago: University of Chicago Press, 223–247.

Kohler, H.P., J.R. Behrman, and S.C. Watkins. 2001. The density of social networks and fertility decisions: Evidence from South Nyanza District, Kenya. *Demography* 38: 43–58.

Langford, I.H., A.H. Leyland, J. Rasbash, and H. Goldstein. 1999. Multilevel modelling of the geographical distributions of diseases. *Journal of the Royal Statistical Society, Series C: Applied Statistics* 48: 253–68.

Langford, M., and D.J. Unwin. 1994. Generating and mapping population density surfaces within a geographical information system. *Cartographic Journal* 31: 21–25.

Leasure, J.W. 1962. *Factors Involved in the Decline of Fertility in Spain: 1900–1950*. Doctoral thesis in Economics, Princeton University, Princeton, N.J.

LeClere, F.B., R.G. Rogers, and K. Peters. 1998. Neighborhood social context and racial differences in women's heart disease mortality. *Journal of Health and Social Behavior* 39: 91–107.

Lo, C.P. 1995. Automated population and dwelling unit estimation from high-resolution satellite images: A GIS approach. *International Journal of Remote Sensing* 16: 17–34.

Longley, P., and V. Mesev. 2001. Measuring urban morphology using remotely-sensed imagery. In J.P. Donnay, M.J. Barnsley, and P. Longley (eds.), *Remote Sensing and Urban Analysis*. London: Taylor & Francis, 163–224.

Micklin, M., and D.F. Sly. 1998. The ecological complex: A conceptual elaboration. In M. Micklin and D.L. Poston (eds.), *Continuities in Human Ecology*. New York: Plenum Press, 51–84.

Montgomery, M.R., and J.B. Casterline. 1993. The diffusion of fertility control in Taiwan: Evidence from pooled cross-section time-series models. *Population Studies* 47: 457–479.

Namboodiri, K. 1988. Ecological demography: Its place in sociology. *American Sociological Review* 53: 619–633.

Noin, D. 1970. *La Population Rurale du Maroc*. Paris: Presses Universitaires de France.

Noronha, V.T., and M.F. Goodchild. 1992. Modeling interregional interaction: Implications for defining functional regions. *Annals of the Association of American Geographers* 82: 86–102.

Openshaw, S., and L. Rao. 1995. Algorithms for reengineering 1991 Census geography. *Environment and Planning A* 27: 425–446.

Peak, C., and J.R. Weeks. 2002. Does community context influence reproductive outcomes of Mexican origin women in San Diego, California? *Journal of Immigrant Health* 4: 125–136.

Reid, A. 1997. Locality or class? Spatial and social differences in infant and child mortality in England and Wales, 1895–1911. In C.A. Corsini and P.P. Viazzo (eds.), *The Decline of Infant and Child Mortality. The European Experience: 1750–1990*. Dordrecht, Netherlands: Martinus Nijhoff, 129–154.

Ridd, M. 1995. Exploring a V-I-S (vegetation-imperious surface-soil) model or urban ecosystem analysis through remote sensing: Comparative anatomy of cities. *International Journal of Remote Sensing* 16: 2165–2185.

Rindfuss, R.R., and P.C. Stern. 1998. Linking remote sensing and social science: The need and the challenges. In D. Liverman, E.F. Moran, R.R. Rindfuss, and P.C. Stern (eds.), *People and Pixels: Linking Remote Sensing and Social Science*. Washington, D.C: National Academy Press, 1–27.

Robert, S.A. 1998. Community-level socioeconomic status effects on adult health. *Journal of Health and Social Behavior* 39: 18–37.

Rosero-Bixby, L., and J.B. Casterline. 1994. Interaction diffusion and fertility transition in Costa Rica. *Social Forces* 73: 435–62.

Scott, L. 1999. *The Accessible City: Employment Opportunities in Time and Space*. Ph.D. Dissertation, Department of Geography, San Diego State University, San Diego.

Star, J., and J. Estes. 1990. *Geographic Information Systems: An Introduction*. Englewood Cliffs, N.J.: Prentice Hall.

Sutton, P. 1997. Modeling population density with night-time satellite imagery and GIS. *Computing, Environment and Urban Systems* 21: 227–244.

Tickamyer, A.R. 2000. Space matters! Spatial inequality in future sociology. *Contemporary Sociology* 29: 805–812.

Tobler, W. 1970. A computer movie simulating urban growth in the Detroit region. *Economic Geography* 26: 234–40.

Tolnay, S.E. 1995. The spatial diffusion of fertility: A cross-sectional analysis of counties in the American South, 1940. *American Sociological Review* 60: 299–308.

van de Walle, E. 1965. An approach to the study of fertility in Nigeria. *Population Studies* 19: 5–16.

Wallace, R., and M.T. Fullilove. 1991. AIDS deaths in the Bronx 1983–1988: Spatiotemporal analysis from a sociodemographic perspective. *Environment and Planning A* 23: 701–23.

Ward, D., S.R. Phinn, and A.T. Murray. 2000. Monitoring growth in rapidly urbanizing areas using remotely sensed data. *The Professional Geographer* 52: 371–385.

Watkins, S.C. 1991. *From Provinces Into Nations: Demographic Integration in Western Europe, 1870–1960*. Princeton, N. J.: Princeton University Press.

Weeks, J., M.S. Gadalla, and A.G. Hill. 2001. The environmental context of fertility in Egypt: Evidence from demographic and health surveys. Presented at *Annual Meeting of the Association of American Geographers*, New York.

Weeks, J.R., M.S. Gadalla, T. Rashed, J. Stanforth, and A.G. Hill. 2000. Spatial variability in fertility in Menoufia, Egypt, assessed through the application of remote sensing and GIS technologies. *Environment and Planning A* 32: 695–714.

Weeks, J.R., X. Yang, A. Getis, M.S. Gadalla, and A.G. Hill. 2002. Spatial patterns as predictors of fertility change in rural Egypt. Presented at *Annual Meeting of the Population Association of America*, Atlanta, Ga.

Wilson, C., and R. Woods. 1991. Fertility in England: A long-term perspective. *Population Studies* 45: 399–415.

20

Spatial Interaction Models of International Telecommunication Flows

Jean-Michel Guldmann

International telecommunication flows have increased significantly in recent years. For instance, the total traffic over the public international network has grown from 14.8 billion minutes in 1985 to 60 billion minutes in 1995, at an annual rate of 15 percent (ITU and TGI 1996). With important technological advances leading to decreasing costs, international telephone calls have become more frequent, though shorter, and have virtually eliminated once-competing telegraph and telex services. While we are clearly moving towards an international information economy, it is, however, surprising that there is relatively little recent research on the determinants of international telecommunications and the geographical distribution of this traffic. This is consistent with the general observation of several analysts, who have noted a relative scarcity of research on telecommunication flows. As Staple and Mullins (1989) put it, telecommunications circuits are the electronic highways of the modern economy, but little is known about the volume and character of the traffic they carry.

Why is research on international telecommunication flows worth performing, and what can we learn from its results? The analogy between telecommunications and transportation provides a useful framework to answer this question. Telecommunication systems carry information over space in the same way that transportation systems carry goods and people. In both cases, these movements are necessary to complete economic and social transactions and can be viewed as derived demands, which are necessary inputs to both production and social interaction processes. Telecommunication flows analysis may therefore provide empirical insights into existing patterns of spatial interactions between individuals, businesses, cities, regions, and countries and may also help predict how new technologies are likely to modify these patterns in the future. At the international level, research might help answer the following questions: (1) What is the impact on telecommunications of the growth of international trade and global firms, with their need for rapid information transfer? Do telecommunications, in turn, spur such growth? (2) What is the relationship between telecommunications and human movements, such as tourism and migrations, both short-term and long-term? (3) Do countries with cultural, sociological, or political affinities, such as common language and religion, or membership in a political union, talk more with each other? (4) How does the level of telecommunications technology in a country impact its international interactions? In particular, what is the role of new information technologies and services, such as the Internet? (5) What is the impact on telecommunications of geographical factors, such as country-to-country distances, country isolation from or closeness to other countries, continental or sub-continental memberships, and more generally, the overall international spatial structure? The extensive scope of the previous questions underscores the need for an integrated methodological approach, with most social sciences, to various extents, involved in such research, in particular economics, political science, sociology, and geography.

Spatial interaction modeling is the methodology to be used to analyze international telecommunications flows, in conjunction with a new set of flow data, much larger than any data set used in past research, and involving 103 origin and 204 destination countries. These data are matched with several country-related technological and socio-economic data, making up a very rich set of exploratory variables, allowing for analyses of the effects of telecommunication equipment, including Internet access, trade and tourism, income per capita, geographical distance, isolation, and contiguity, language, cultural, religious, political, and geographical commonalities, and the international spatial structure.

The remainder of the chapter is organized as follows. The next section reviews the literature, and this is followed with an overview of spatial interaction modeling. Empirical analyses are presented, along with data sources, functional specification, and results. Conclusions and areas for further research are outlined in the final section.

Literature Review

This review focuses exclusively on empirically based studies of country-to-country telecommunication flows, as measured in number of messages or conversation minutes. These studies extend to the international realm the intra-country point-to-point flow studies reviewed in Guldmann (1999). The general modeling framework is the generalized unconstrained spatial interaction model (SIM), with a variety of statistical techniques used to estimate it (e.g., standard least-squares regression, simultaneous equations systems, etc.). Two streams of SIM research can be distinguished: (1) standard analyses, and (2) analyses with reverse flows.

Standard SIM specifications are of the form:

$$F_{AB} = G(W_A, W_B, R_{AB}), \tag{1}$$

where F_{AB} is the telecommunication flow from country A to country B, the vectors W_A and W_B include demographic, economic, and technological characteristics of countries A and B, respectively, that affect flows both positively and negatively (e.g., population, GDP, industrial activity, telecommunication facilities, etc.), and the vector R_{AB}

includes facilitation and resistance variables, such as distance, telephone prices, people and trade flows, and language, political, and cultural affinities, that are expected to influence flows both positively and negatively.

Early such models were developed by Lago (1970), using 73 observations on telecommunication flows between the United States and 23 countries over the period 1962–1964, Naleszkiewicz (1970), using similar data, and Yatrakis (1972), using the numbers of calls over 46 international routes in 1967. These studies include separate equations for telephone, telegraph, and telex services, as these services were then substitutable one for the other, to some extent. The variables considered in these models, while making intuitive sense, are not introduced with a strong theoretical backing. They include

- the volume of trade between the countries,
- the flows of capital, as proxied by foreign assets and liabilities,
- national incomes and gross national products (GNP),
- per capita income,
- country wealth, as measured by money supply and demand for deposits,
- country industrialization, as measured by industrial production,
- the percentages of a country GDP attributable to the extractive and manufacturing sectors,
- the number of ships of 1,000 tons capacity registered with the origin country,
- government expenditures as a percentage of the GDP,
- the average annual dividends paid and received on foreign investments,
- the value of travel expenditures,
- the average fare of a first-class airline round trip,
- the numbers of emigrants to and immigrants from destination countries,
- the population with ancestry roots in the other country,
- the percentage of the population living in urban centers,
- measures of language similarity and spatial contiguity,
- the number of telephone sets,
- dummy variables related to use of radio circuits,
- the speed of service (all connections were operator-assisted),
- the number of common hours during a working day schedule between the two countries,
- the price of a 3-minute call,
- the cost per telegram word,
- the telex cost for 3 minutes,
- the monthly rental cost of leased telegraph circuit service.

All these contributions involve ordinary least squares regressions (OLS).

More sophisticated are the later works of Rea and Lage (1978), who use the error component regression model to deal with cross-section time-series data on the number of outgoing messages from the United States to 37 major countries over the period 1964–1973, and Fiebig and Bewley (1987), who use the Box-Cox transformation in the estimation of a lagged model for telephone traffic between Australia and ten foreign countries. The lagged endogenous variable is used to capture habit formation and inertia effects and also provides a way to distinguish between short-term and long-term elasticities. Bewley and Fiebig (1988) further analyze Australia-originating international telephone calls by modeling how the numbers of calls and conversation minutes are shared among the following three services: (1) direct dialing, (2) operator-connected station-to-station, and (3) operator-connected person-to-person. Rietveld and Janssen (1990), analyzing telephone flows between the Netherlands and 27 foreign countries, focus on the barrier effect of borders. Kellerman (1990) analyzes the outgoing telephone calls from 18 countries to their 10 most frequently called destinations, relating these flows to imports, exports, and arriving tourists. In a related study, Dokmeci and Berkoz (1996) analyze international telephone calls from Turkey over the period 1963–1990, regressing them on incoming tourism, exports, and the GNP. Finally, Hackl and Westlund (1995), departing from the traditional assumption of constant price elasticity, estimate equations with time-varying coefficients, using the moving local regression technique and monthly data over the period 1976–1990 for telecommunications between Sweden and its major trading partners.

The SIM specification with reverse flow is of the form:

$$F_{AB} = H(W_A, W_B, R_{AB}, F_{BA}), \tag{2}$$

based on the framework first proposed by Larson et al. (1990) in their study of point-to-point routes within the United States, wherein the phenomenon of call stimulation or substitution (or callback effect) is accounted for (if applicable) by including the return telephone flow in the estimated equation. Except for the return flow variable F_{BA}, the other variables are generally similar to those used in the standard SIMs.

Acton and Vogelsang (1992) analyze the annual telephone traffic between the United States and 17 West European countries over the period 1979–1986. Instead of using a simultaneous equation approach, they estimate a reduced form of the equation, where the demand for calls (minutes) from the United States to a foreign country is a function of the originating and terminating prices of both telephone and telex services, the United States and foreign country gross domestic products (GDP), the number of European telephones, trade volumes, and the composition of production in the destination country. Appelbe and Dineen (1993) present the results of a similar analysis of Canada-Overseas flows, using quarterly data for the period 1988 to 1991. They report a low callback coefficient of 0.10. Sandbach (1996) estimates an origin-destination model with traffic data on 154 routes between developed countries. The non-price variables include, among others, dummy variables related to language commonality and the Germany-Turkey routes (picking up the impact of the German guest worker community). The price variables include the difference between incoming and outgoing call prices, but this effect turns out to be not statistically significant, probably because of the limited price disparity. Garin-Munoz and Perez-Amaral (1998) estimate demand functions for outgoing telephone traffic from Spain to 27 African and Oriental countries over the period 1982–1991 and use instrumental variables to control for the simultaneity between outgoing and incoming calls. Finally, Karikari and Gyimah-Brempong (1999), using traffic data between the United States and 45 African countries over the 1992–1996 period, implement a simultaneous equations approach. In addition to the standard explanatory variables, they use the product of the number of households in both countries as a measure of the community of interest.

Except for Yatrakis (1972), Kellerman (1990), and Sandbach (1996), all the previous studies involve only one origin country, and generally small samples, which makes it difficult to generalize the results with a strong degree of certainty. The number and type of explanatory variables vary from study to study, and their choice is generally not related to a clear theoretical framework, except for the role of telephone prices (Taylor

1980) and callback effects (Larson et al. 1990). Communities of interest, whether related to trade, culture, language, religion, politics, or geography, are poorly accounted for. The impacts of emerging telecommunications technologies (e.g., the Internet) are not assessed, nor is the possible impact of the international spatial structure and related competition and/or agglomeration effects.

Overview of Spatial Interaction Modeling

Spatial interaction modeling (SIM) is best viewed as the generic name of various models used to explain and predict movements over space, including airline passenger transport, commuting, migrations, interregional commodity flows, international trade, shopping travel, and telecommunications. SIM ranges from the gravity model to Wilson's entropy models to discrete choice models. The gravity model, based on an analogy with the Newtonian model of the force of attraction between two bodies, constitutes the oldest and fundamental paradigm of SIM, with:

$$T_{ij} = k W_i W_j / d_{ij}^a \tag{3}$$

where T_{ij} is the flow from origin i to destination j, W_i and W_j are measures of the sizes of the origin and destination, respectively, d_{ij} is the distance between them, a is a positive parameter characterizing the distance friction, and k a calibration parameter. The size variables are proxies for the abilities of the origin to generate flows and of the destination to attract them. Generalized versions of Equation (3) have been used widely, wherein several variables are used to characterize the origin and destination, and several variables measure friction effects that impede the flow. Generally, these variables are characterized by unknown exponents, which are estimated through regression analysis. This type of SIM has also been termed unconstrained SIM. The standard international telecommunications models described in Section 2 all fit this generalized SIM, and so do several other telecommunications models at the regional/national scale, as reviewed in Guldmann (1999).

The unconstrained approach is probably best when the modeling objective is primarily explanatory. However, if the total outflow from i, O_i, and the total inflow into j, D_j, are known, with

$$\sum_j T_{ij} = O_i, \tag{4}$$

$$\sum_i T_{ij} = D_j, \tag{5}$$

and if the modeling objective is to incorporate the knowledge of these marginal totals into the model, then we obtain the doubly-constrained or production-attraction constrained model, with

$$T_{ij} = A_i O_i B_j D_j W_i W_j / d_{ij}^a, \tag{6}$$

where A_i and B_j are balancing factors guaranteeing the proper summations of the flows, with:

$$A_i = \left(\sum_j B_j D_j W_i W_j / d_{ij}^a \right)^{-1} \tag{7}$$

$$B_j = \left(\sum_i A_i O_i W_i W_j / d_{ij}^a \right)^{-1} \tag{8}$$

Separate formulations are derived easily to deal with attraction-only or production-only constraints. Wilson (1967) has provided a theoretical framework for SIM by showing that equations similar to (6) can be derived from the maximization of an entropy measure of the pattern of flows, subject to the total inflow and outflow constraints and to a trip expenditures linear constraint. In this formulation, the exponential friction factor $\exp(-\beta d_{ij})$ replaces the power-based factor in Equation (6). Double-constraint or single-constraint SIM is particularly appropriate when the model objective is allocative rather than explanatory. Further discussions of the entropy-maximization approach can be found in Fotheringham and O'Kelly (1989).

Another theoretical interpretation of SIM is related to discrete choice models, stressing the importance of stochastic utility maximization, and using disaggregate data at the level of the decision maker. Consider a decision maker i facing choice k, and let the corresponding utility be expressed as a linear function of variables characterizing both the decision maker (S_i) and the choice itself (X_k), with, in addition, a random error term. Suppose that the other choices are noted by j. Then, the probability P_{ik} of decision maker i choosing alternative k is expressed as

$$P_{ik} = \text{Prob } (U_{ik} > U_{ij}) \text{ for any } j \neq k \tag{9}$$

Under the assumption that the error term follows a Weibull distribution, McFadden (1973) has shown that P_{ik} is expressed as a multinomial logit model, with

$$P_{ik} = \exp[V_{ik}(X_k, S_i)] / \sum_j \exp[(V_{ij}(X_j, S_i)], \tag{10}$$

where V_{ik} is the non-random component of the utility. This model can be used to analyze spatial choices. Let the choice set be a set of destinations contemplated by a decision maker located at origin i. If O_i is the total number of decision makers at i, then the total flow from i to k is simply

$$T_{ik} = P_{ik} O_i \tag{11}$$

Equation (11) is structurally similar to the production-constrained SIM discussed earlier. Anas (1981) argues that the gravity/entropy and multinomial logit approaches are two equivalent views of the same problem.

However, both approaches suffer from the problem of independence from irrelevant alternatives. The nested multinomial logit model resolves this problem by introducing hierarchy into the decision-making process and by assuming that decision makers make choices sequentially. The gravity/entropy SIM literature suggests that improved models can be obtained by accounting for the effects of the spatial structure, particularly in eliminating the estimation bias of the distance parameter. One approach, proposed by Fotheringham (1983), is to introduce into the model a competing destination (CD) factor that measures the accessibility of the destination j to all (or a subset of) the other destinations. If the interaction decreases with this factor, competition is deemed to exist among the destinations, and the closer a specific destination j is to other destinations, the smaller the interaction terminating at j. In the opposite case, agglomeration effects are deemed to take place. CD factors are used, among others, by Ishikawa (1987) in modeling migration and university enrollments in Japan, Guy (1987) in modeling shopping travel, Fik and Mulligan (1990) in modeling airline traffic, and Fik et al. (1992) in modeling interstate labor migration. Both competition and agglomeration effects are uncovered in these different studies. Another approach involves the use of an intervening opportunities (IO) factor, based on the ideas developed by Stouffer (1940, 1960), who argues that the observed attenuating effects of distance represent the absorbing effects of those opportunities located between the origin and the destination. IO factors are used, among others, by Barber and Milne (1988) in modeling internal migration in Kenya, by Fik and Mulligan (1990) and Fik et al. (1992), together with CD factors, and by Conçalves and Ulysséa-Neto (1993) in modeling public transportation flows. In the area of telecommunications interactions, Leinbach (1973) and Hirst (1975) account implicitly for the effect of the spatial structure on telephone flows within West Malaysia and Tanzania, and Guldmann (1999) does so explicitly in his analysis of telephone flows within a U.S. region.

While reviewing the above studies, one can observe a significant variability in the formulation of the CD/IO factors and in the definition of the geographical space over which they are computed. [See Guldmann (1999) for further discussion of this issue]. As the literature provides little guidance, and because the international geographical space (i.e., the whole planet) has never been, to the best of our knowledge, investigated with regard to the possible effects of the spatial structure, several alternative factors should be considered, in the spirit of exploratory analysis. Let X_k be a variable characterizing the competing or intervening country k, and D_{km} the distance between countries k and m. The spatial structure variable SS_m characterizing country m is computed as follows:

$$SS_m = \sum_k X_k/(D_{km})^\lambda \tag{12}$$

The set of countries k selected in the summation of Equation (12) is an important decision variable. It could represent all countries (except m), or countries within a given distance from m, or countries with specific cultural or other characteristics, irrespective of their locations. The distance exponent λ is either selected exogenously, or a sensitivity analysis is conducted, with the chosen value maximizing the explanatory power of the model. If the variable SS_m is linked to the origin country i, it naturally represents an IO factor. If it is attached to the destination country j, it represents a CD factor. Both types of effects may be present.

Empirical Analyses

Data

Country-to-country traffic data, in minutes of conversation, have been obtained for the year 1995 from the International Telecommunications Union (ITU) through Telegeography, Inc. (TGI), and include 4,137 origin-destination routes, with 103 origin and 204 destination countries. These countries are listed in Table 20.1, regrouped by continent and subcontinent. The actual numbers of outgoing and incoming links and flows are provided for each of these countries at http://www.csiss.org/best-practices/siss/20/. This sample covers 52.3 billion minutes, or about 87 percent of the total worldwide traffic flow in 1995. The peak and off-peak rates, in U.S. dollars, for a 3-minute direct-dialed call from 55 countries to their top 20 destinations have been drawn from ITU and TGI (1996), providing a match for 952 traffic routes (or 23 percent). A second set of telecommunications data, also obtained from the ITU, includes country-level indicators such as numbers of different types of lines and phones, aggregate local, national, and international traffic, various prices and connection charges, numbers of subscribers to advanced telecommunication features (e.g., ISDN, facsimile, radio-paging), demographic and socio-economic variables (e.g., GDP, population, households, radio and television receivers, etc.), and financial information on the country telecommunication companies. While the number of variables is very large, there are many missing data, particularly for developing countries, which reduces the overall usefulness of this data source. A third set of data has been derived from the *World Factbook*, compiled by the CIA, and includes quasi-complete data on each country's population, age, and gender structure, literacy rate, religion, languages, labor force, unemployment rate, GDP purchasing power parity, and the shares of the GDP among agriculture, industry, and services. Memberships in various international organizations and economic, trade, and cultural groups, have also been derived from the *World Factbook*. Their definitions and compositions are available at http://www.csiss.org/best-practices/siss/20/. Each country has been assigned to a continent and a subcontinent, as defined in the *World Factbook* (see Table 20.1). Exports and imports data have been drawn from a database maintained by the International Monetary Fund (IMF). International tourism data have been drawn from the U.N. *Statistical Yearbook* (43rd Edition, 1996). Finally, the latitudes and longitudes of the capitals or main cities of all countries have been drawn from the ArcWorld GIS coverage produced by the Environmental Systems Research Institute, Inc. (ESRI), and used as inputs to compute great-circle distances. The time zones of all countries have been drawn from the Web site of the Time Service Department, United States Naval Observatory (http://tycho.usno.navy.mil) and used to compute the time difference between each pair of countries.

Model Specification

In order to explain the variations in the independent variable—the country-to-country telephone traffic flow F in 1995—the following categories of independent variables have been considered:

TEL : vector of Telecommunication Equipment variables,

ECD : vector of Economic Development variables,

ITR : vector of International Trade variables,

ITO : vector of International Tourism variables,

CUL : vector of Cultural Relationships variables,

POL : vector of Political Relationships variables,

SEP : vector of Geographical Separation variables,

CON : vector of Continent/Subcontinent Membership variables, and

SPS : vector of Spatial Structure variables.

The general model specification is then:

$$F = G(TEL, ECD, ITR, ITO, CUL, POL, SEP, CON, SPS) \tag{13}$$

The specific variables included in the above vectors are defined in Table 20.2. Some characterize the origin (A) and destination (B) countries separately, and others characterize the combination of countries (A, B); some are continuous and others are dummy variables. Basic descriptive statistics on the continuous dependent (flow) and independent variables are presented in Table 20.3, and the frequency distributions of the dummy variables are available in Table 20.4

The TEL variables have been drawn from the ITU Indicators data set. While the access line (MTL) variable is fairly standard (Sandbach 1996), the two other variables (INTHS, ISDN) have never been used before. In addition to measuring the level of sophistication of a country in information technologies (IT), they may also point to substitution and complementary effects. For instance, the availability of Internet access may stimulate phone calls, or may provide a way to reduce them through alternatives such as e-mail or search of information on the World Wide Web (WWW). The ECD variables have been drawn from the ITU and CIA databases. It is worth noting that the INC variable is based on purchasing power parity GDP (CIA database), and not simply on the conversion of the GDP, measured in local currency, into U.S. dollars, using exchange rates, as has been the case in past studies. The INC variable can thus better reflect the role of income in telephone usage decisions. The variable PBML (ITU database) is important because it reflects the size of the economic sector in a country, and also because businesses generate a much larger volume of calls per line than residential users. The ADEC variable reflects the general role of economic development in international telecommunications. In addition to the actual export and import flows, the ITR vector includes several dummy variables to characterize mutual membership in a trade group. Such variables have long been used in trade gravity models (e.g., Bröcker and Rohweder 1990; Zhang and Kristensen 1995; Frankel and Wei 1998). The tourism vector ITO only includes the number of international visitors in each country, as detailed country-to-country tourist flows data are not available to match telephone flows. (The UN *Statistical Yearbook* provides only continent-to-country tourist flows). The dummy variables in the CUL and POL vectors were derived from the CIA database, and are self-explanatory. In the SEP vector, the distance (DIS) variable is a standard one in most trade gravity models, but has been used only by Rietveld and Janssen (1970) and Sandbach (1996). Moreover, Sandbach restricts the relationship to be linear in the inverse of distance. The ΔTIME variable was also used by Sandbach and, in a modified form (number of common working hours between countries A and B), by Lago (1970). The contiguity variable (ADJ) has often been used, but the ISLA variable never. The underlying assumption regarding the island status of a country is that it creates a special barrier to telecommunications, whether outgoing or incoming. There are 62 island

Table 20.1. Countries By Continent/Subcontinent.

Africa/Central Africa
Burundi, Central African Republic, Chad, Rwanda, Zaire
Africa/Eastern Africa
Djibouti, Ethiopia, Kenya, Seychelles, Somalia, Tanzania, Uganda
Africa/Northern Africa
Algeria, Egypt, Libya, Mauritania, Morocco, Sudan, Tunisia
Africa/Southern Africa
Angola, Botswana, Comoros, Lesotho, Madagascar, Malawi, Mauritius, Mayotte, Mozambique,
Namibia, Reunion, South Africa, Swaziland, Zambia, Zimbabwe
Africa/Western Africa
Benin, Burkina Faso, Cameroon, Cape Verde, Congo, Cote D'Ivoire, Equatorial Guinea, Gabon,
Gambia, Ghana, Guinea, Guinea-Bissau, Liberia, Mali, Niger, Nigeria,
Sao Tome and Principe, Senegal, Sierra Leone, Togo
America/Caribbean
Antigua And Barbuda, Aruba, Bahamas, Barbados, Cuba, Dominica,
Dominican Republic, Grenada, Guadeloupe, Haiti, Jamaica, Martinique,
Netherlands Antilles, Puerto Rico, Saint Kitts and Nevis, Saint Lucia,
St. Vincent and Grenadines, Trinidad and Tobago, Virgin Islands (U.S.)
America/Central South America
Bolivia, Paraguay
America/Eastern South America
Brazil
America/Middle America
Belize, Costa Rica, El Salvador, Guatemala, Honduras, Mexico, Nicaragua, Panama
America/North America
Bermuda, United States
America/Northern North America
Canada, Greenland
America/Northern South America
Columbia, Guiana, Guyana, Suriname, Venezuela
America/Southern South America
Argentina, Chile, Uruguay
America/Western South America
Equador, Peru
Asia/Central Asia
Kazakhstan, Kyrgyzstan, Tajikistan, Turkmenistan, Uzbekistan
Asia/Eastern Asia
China, DPR Korea, Hong Kong, Japan, Korea (Rep. of), Macau, Taiwan
Asia/Middle East
Bahrain, Cyprus, Iran (Islamic Rep. of), Iraq, Israel, Jordan, Kuwait, Lebanon, Oman, Qatar, Saudi
Arabia, Syria, United Arab Emirates, Yemen
Asia/Northern Asia
Mongolia, Russia
Asia/Southeastern Asia
Brunei Darussalam, Cambodia, Indonesia, Lao P.D.R., Malaysia, Myanmar,
Papua New Guinea, Philippines, Singapore, Thailand, Viet Nam
Asia/Southern Asia
Afghanistan, Bangladesh, Bhutan, India, Maldives, Nepal, Pakistan, Sri Lanka
Asia/Southwestern Asia
Armenia, Azerbaijan, Georgia, Turkey
Europe/Central Europe
Austria, Czech Republic, Germany, Hungary, Liechtenstein, Poland, Slovak Republic, Switzerland

Table 20.1. *Continued*

Europe/Eastern Europe
Belarus, Estonia, Latvia, Lithuania, Moldova, Ukraine
Europe/Northern Europe
Denmark, Faroe Islands, Finland, Iceland, Norway, Sweden
Europe/Southeastern Europe
Albania, Bosnia and Herzogovina, Bulgaria, Croatia, Romania, Slovenia,
T.F.Y.R. Macedonia, Yugoslavia
Europe/Southern Europe
Greece, Italy, Malta
Europe/Southwestern Europe
Andorra, Gibraltar, Portugal, Spain
Europe/Western Europe
Belgium, France, Ireland, Luxembourg, Netherlands, United Kingdom
Oceania
American Samoa, Australia, Fiji, French Polynesia, Guam, Kiribati, Marshall Islands, Micronesia
(Fed. States), New Caledonia, New Zealand, Solomon Islands, Tonga, Vanuatu, Western Samoa

---

Note: The number of originating and terminating links for each country are provided on this book's Web page, at
http://www.csiss.org/best-practices/siss/20/.

countries in the sample, which makes it feasible to test for this effect. The dummy variables in the vector CON are self-explanatory. The list of continents and subcontinents, and their country memberships, is available in Table 20.1. The variables in the SPS vector have been computed based on the formulation in Equation (12), under the following considerations: (1) the distance between countries k and m is the great-circle distance; (2) the number of main access lines is taken as the measure of a country size; (3) two definitions of the sets of countries k associated to country m in the summation have been considered: (a) all countries in the world, except country m (SSC); and (2) all countries that share the same main language as m (SSL), irrespective of their locations. (Other groupings were tested, such as continent and subcontinent memberships, and countries contiguous to country m, but the results were insignificant, and are not reported here).

The estimated model is linear in the logarithms of the dependent (F) and the continuous independent variables (MTLA, MTLB, INTHSA, INTHSB, ISDNA, ISDNB, PBMLA, PBMLB, INCA, INCB, EXP, IMP, TOURA, TOURB, DIS), linear in the dummy variables and in the time zone difference variable, and linear in the logarithms of the spatial structure variables. A few missing values were estimated for the variables TOUR, PBML, and ISDN, using regression relations between the number of business lines and the number of ISDN subscribers, on one side, and the number of main access lines, MTL, on the other side (with R^2 of 0.97 and 0.70, respectively). The number of tourists was regressed on the variables MTL and INC, with an R^2 of 0.76. Also, because the variables INTHS, ISDN, EXP, and IMP take a value of zero in several countries (mostly developing or small countries), the Box-Cox transformation, with a parameter $\alpha = 0.001$, was used for these variables to approximate their logarithms, with:

$$X(\alpha) = (X^\alpha - 1)/\alpha \qquad (14)$$

Table 20.2. Independent variable name and definition.

Name	Definition
Telecommunication Equipment	
MTLA	Number of main access lines in country A
MTLB	Number of main access lines in country B
INTHSA	Number of Internet hosts in country A
INTHSB	Number of Internet hosts in country B
ISDNA	Number of ISDN subscribers in country A
ISDNB	Number of ISDN subscribers in country B
Economic Development	
INCA	Gross Domestic Product (GDP) per capita in country A
INCB	Gross Domestic Product (GDP) per capita in country B
PBMLA	Percentage of business access lines in country A
PBMLB	Percentage of business access lines in country B
ADEC	Dummy variable = 1 if countries A and B belong to the Advanced Economies Group (IMF definition)
International Trade	
EXP	Exports from country A to country B
IMP	Imports by country A from country B
ANDEAN	=1 if A and B belong to the Andean Community of Nations
APEC	=1 if A and B belong to the Asia-Pacific Economic Cooperation
ASEAN	=1 if A and B belong to the Association of Southeast Asian Nations
CACM	=1 if A and B belong to the Central America Common Market
CAEU	=1 if A and B belong to the Council of Arab Economic Unity
ECWAS	=1 if A and B belong to the Economic Community of West African States
EFTA	=1 if A and B belong to the European Free Trade Association
EU	=1 if A and B belong to the European Union
LAIA	=1 if A and B belong to the Latin American Integration Association
MERCOS	=1 if A and B belong to the Southern Cone Common Market
NAFTA	=1 if A and B belong to the North American Free Trade Association
International Tourism	
TOURA	Number of international tourists visiting country A
TOURB	Number of international tourists visiting country B
Cultural Relationships	
LANG	=1 if A and B speak the same main language
RELIG	=1 if A and B have the same major religion
ACCT	=1 if A and B belong to the Agency for the French Speaking Community
Political and Former Colonial Relationships	
CMWTH	=1 if A and B belong to the Commonwealth of Nations
CBSS	=1 if A and B belong to the Council of Baltic Sea States
FSU	=1 if A and B belong to the Former Soviet Union
FZ	=1 if A and B belong to the Franc Zone
OPEC	=1 if A and B belong to the Organization of Petroleum Exporting Countries
Geographical Separation	
DIS	Great-circle distance between the capitals of countries A and B
ΔTIME	Time zone difference between countries A and B (hours)
ADJ	=1 if countries A and B share a common border
ISLA	=1 if neither country A nor country B is an island

Table 20.2. *Continued*

Name	Definition
Continent/Subcontinent Memberships	
CONT	=1 if countries A and B belong to continent CONT
SCONT	=1 if countries A and B belong to subcontinent SCONT
Spatial Structure	
SSCA	Spatial structure variable associated to country A and computed over all countries in the world (except A)
SSCB	Spatial structure variable associated to country B and computed over all countries in the world (except B)
SSLA	Spatial structure variable associated to country A and computed over all countries with the same language as A (except A)
SSLB	Spatial structure variable associated to country B and computed over all countries with the same language as B (except B)

Table 20.3. Basic statistics—telephone flows and related variables.

Variable	Number of Observations	Mean	Minimum	Maximum
Origin—Destination				
Telephone flow (minutes)	4137	12,642,770	1	3,046,125,000
Exports ($ million)	4137	877	0	152,896
Imports ($ million)	4137	893	0	148,304
Distance (kilometers)	4137	2,880.5	39.9	11,784.0
Time zone difference (hours)	4137	2.46	0	12
Origin Country				
Number of main lines	103	5,779,647	2,503	164,624,400
Number of internet hosts	103	88,766	0	6,054,959
Number of ISDN subscribers	103	23,112	0	961,610
Percentage of business lines	103	30.90	9.00	70.00
Income per capita ($)	103	8,730	591	27,575
International tourists	103	4,972	2	60,033
Destination Country				
Number of main lines	204	3,399,471	2025	164,624,400
Number of internet hosts	204	46,514	0	6,054,959
Number of ISDN subscribers	204	14,371	0	961,610
Percentage of business lines	204	30.87	7.05	77.00
Income per capita ($)	204	6,827	374	29,045
International tourists	204	2,777	1	60,033

Results

All regression analyses are performed with OLS. The results are reported in Table 20.5. In a first stage, a benchmark model without spatial structure variables (Model 1) was estimated, with $R^2 = 0.863$. Several dummy variables associated with various groups,

Table 20.4. Frequency distributions of dummy variables.

Dummy Variable	# Cases = 1 (out of 4137)	Percentage (%)
A. Geographic Separation		
Contiguity (ADJ)	279	6.74
No Island (ISLA)	2741	66.26
B. Language/Religion		
Main Language (LANG)	814	19.68
Agency for the French-Speaking Community (ACCT)	388	9.38
Religion (RELIG)	906	21.90
C. Trade/Cultural Groups		
Advanced Economies (IMF Definition—ADEC)	410	9.91
Asia-Pacific Economic Cooperation (APEC)	195	4.71
Economic Community of West African States	59	1.43
(ECWAS)	78	1.89
Latin American Integration Association (LAIA)	92	2.22
Franc Zone (FZ)	58	1.40
Former Soviet Union (FSU)	241	5.83
Commonwealth of Nations (CMWTH)	16	0.39
Southern Cone Common Market MERCOSUR	2	0.05
(MERCOS)	14	0.34
European Free Trade Association (EFTA)	30	0.73
Andean Community of Nations (ANDEAN)	5	0.12
Association of Southeast Asian Nations (ASEAN)	6	0.15
Central America Common Market (CACM)	38	0.92
North American Free Trade Associatin (NAFTA)	172	4.16
Organization of Petroleum Exporting Countries	64	1.55
(OPEC)	75	1.81
European Union (EU)		
Council of Arab Economic Unity (CAEU)		
Council of Baltic Sea States (CBSS)		
D. Continents		
America	493	11.92
Europe	677	16.36
Africa	693	16.75
Asia	459	11.09
Oceania	39	0.94
E. Subcontinents		
Caribbean	35	0.85
Central South America	0	0
Eastern South America	0	0
Middle America	16	0.39
North America	1	0.02
Northern North America	0	0
Northern South America	9	0.22
Southern South America	6	0.15
Western South America	1	0.02
Northern Europe	15	0.36
Central Europe	23	0.56
Eastern Europe	19	0.46
Southeastern Europe	30	0.73
Southern Europe	6	0.15
Southwestern Europe	3	0.07
Western Europe	27	0.65

Table 20.4. *Continued*

Dummy Variable	# Cases = 1 (out of 4137)	Percentage (%)
Northern Africa	24	0.58
Central Africa	12	0.29
Eastern Africa	9	0.22
Western Africa	99	2.39
Southern Africa	36	0.87
Central Asia	4	0.10
Eastern Asia	27	0.65
Middle East	93	2.25
Northern Asia	1	0.02
Southeastern Asia	33	0.80
Southern Asia	7	0.17
Southweastern Asia	2	0.05

continent, and subcontinents were deleted because they turned out to be insignificant. Among the Telecommunication Equipment variables, the effects of the access lines variables, MTLA and MTLB, are highly significant, very close, and surprisingly similar to those obtained by Sandbach (1996). The coefficients of the Internet variables, INTHSA and INTHSB, are significant (at the 5 percent level), negative for country A, and positive for country B. The negative sign suggests that electronic mail and WWW browsing (although admittedly in its infancy in 1995) substitute for telephone calls from country A, while the availability of Internet hosts (hence Web sites) in country B stimulates calls from A, possibly as a result of newly gathered WWW information, and the need for further complementary information. The coefficients of the ISDN variables are both positive, pointing to stimulation effects. Among the Economic Development variables, the shares of business lines in both countries, PBMLA and PBMLB, have significant and positive effects, with lines in country A having, nevertheless, a stronger impact, as expected. The coefficient of the income-per-capita variable INCA is highly significant and positive, as expected, but the variable INCB turned out to be completely insignificant, and was deleted. The dummy variable ADEC, which characterizes interactions between advanced economies, is significant and positive, pointing to specific telecommunications interactions among these countries. Among the International Trade variables, the coefficients of the actual export and import flows, EXP and IMP, are highly significant and positive, but in a 1:2 ratio, suggesting that trade-related calls from A to B pertain more heavily to imports by A from B. Only four trade group dummy variables turn out to be significant (APEC, ECWAS, LAIA, and MERCOS). As LAIA includes all South-American countries, its negative sign may point to overall lesser telephone interactions on this continent, irrespective of trade, whose effect is primarily taking place among the Southern Cone Common Market countries (MERCOS). Among the International Tourism variables, only TOURA has a significant and positive effect, suggesting that visitors in A call home in B, but that no one from A calls the visitors in B (assumedly sailing from A). The Geographic Separation variables have all significant effects, with the expected sign. Island status clearly creates a barrier for telecommunications, while contiguity enhances them. Distances and time zone differences appear to have distinct, negative effects. All the Cultural Relationships variables have significant and positive effects. Among languages, it appears that French may play a specific and enhanced role, as measured by ACCT. The impact of religion commonality is uncovered here for the first time. Among the Political and Former Colonial Relationships variables, only CMWTH, FSU, and FZ have strong and positive effects. Finally, the Continent Membership variables are significant for all continents, except Asia. The negative coefficients for America and Europe may reflect a compensation effect, counterbalancing the possibly excessive and positive influences of some other variables, such as income per capita or the level of telecommunication equipment and technology. The Subcontinent Membership variables point to networks with positive interactions in the cases of Northern, Western, and Southeastern Europe, Eastern Africa, the Middle East, and Southern Asia. However, there is no clear explanation for the negative coefficient for Northern Africa.

As discussed earlier, data on telephone call prices from country A to country B are available for 952 pairs of countries (about 23 percent of the sample). Model 1 specification was expanded to include the logarithm of this price as an additional independent variable, and was re-estimated with the reduced sample. The coefficient of the price variable turned out to be positive, but insignificant ($t = 0.87$), probably as a result of the correlation between distance and price, and the inability of the regression to disentangle both effects. We therefore retained Model 1 specification over the whole sample, and expanded it by considering the spatial structure variable

While considering separately each of the two spatial structure variables (SSC, SSL), we have attached each one to both the origin country A (SSCA, SSLA) and the destination country B (SSCB, SSLB). In each case, we use the same distance exponent λ for all the spatial structure variables. We have conducted a sensitivity analysis over λ and selected the specification yielding the highest R^2. The optimal λ is reported at the bottom of Table 20.5. Model 2 includes the variables SSCA and SSCB, which involve all the countries in the world, except countries A and B, respectively. The coefficients of both variables are negative and highly significant, although they only add marginally to the explanatory power of the model ($R^2 = 0.865$). Model 3 includes the variables SSLA and SSLB, which have positive, and highly significant, coefficients, pointing to the complex and synergistic effect of language commonality, which was already uncovered in benchmark Model 1. These results suggest that having clusters of countries with similar language in proximity encourages the generation of telephone conversation. Finally, we have combined the specifications of Model 2 and Model 3 into Model 4. The coefficients of all four variables are estimated precisely, and with the same original signs. Overall, we can conclude that there are spatial structure effects in international telecommunications, both competitive and agglomerative.

Conclusions

Spatial interaction models of international telephone flows have been estimated, using a much larger data set than in past studies, as well as explanatory variables hitherto unavailable. The results point to both the stimulation and substitution effects of new technologies (Internet, ISDN), suggesting that electronic mail via the Internet may

Table 20.5. Regression models of international telephone flows.

Variable	Model 1 Benchmark	Model 2 Spatial Structure Whole World	Model 3 Spatial Structure Language Commonality	Model 4 Combination of Models 2 and 3
Intercept	3.242	5.188	2.954	4.193
	(4.08)[1]	(6.25)	(3.75)	(5.25)
In MTLA	0.633	0.609	0.642	0.607
	(31.75)	(30.29)	(32.50)	(30.11)
In MTLB	0.685	0.694	0.687	0.689
	(45.94)	(46.59)	(46.48)	(47.10)
In INTHSA	−0.00028	−0.00031	−0.00020	−0.00021
	(3.71)	(4.10)	(2.67)	(2.79)
In INTHSB	0.00026	0.00028	0.00027	0.00030
	(3.80)	(4.09)	(3.92)	(4.36)
In ISDNA	0.00013	0.00010	0.00016	0.00016
	(1.89)	(1.47)	(2.41)	(2.32)
In ISDNB	0.00016	0.00018	0.00014	0.00022
	(2.63)	(3.05)	(2.38)	(3.67)
In PBMLA	0.996	0.755	0.920	0.674
	(12.35)	(8.66)	(11.45)	(7.65)
In PBMLB	0.512	0.490	0.482	0.413
	(6.39)	(6.12)	(6.06)	(5.19)
In INCA	0.591	0.627	0.564	0.600
	(14.26)	(15.11)	(13.59)	(14.52)
ADEC	0.349	0.413	0.229	0.258
	(3.66)	(4.34)	(2.40)	(2.74)
In EXP	0.000372	0.000380	0.000378	0.000392
	(4.92)	(5.05)	(5.05)	(5.28)
In IMP	0.000742	0.000717	0.000737	0.000717
	(9.65)	(9.37)	(9.68)	(9.51)
APEC	0.814	0.649	0.829	0.656
	(7.24)	(5.68)	(7.46)	(5.88)
ECWAS	0.800	0.764	0.760	0.774
	(3.97)	(3.81)	(3.81)	(3.91)
LAIA	−0.505	−0.646	−0.418	−0.612
	(2.50)	(3.20)	(2.09)	(3.07)
MERCOS	1.124	1.077	1.048	1.057
	(2.83)	(2.73)	(2.67)	(2.72)
TOURA	0.176	0.220	0.152	0.195
	(7.38)	(8.98)	(6.42)	(7.98)
In DIS	−1.059	−1.131	−1.099	−1.173
	(22.70)[1]	(23.91)	(23.70)	(25.13)
ΔTIME	−0.047	−0.046	−0.043	−0.046
	(3.44)	(3.40)	(3.21)	(3.42)
ADJ	0.376	0.279	0.377	0.288
	(3.62)	(2.68)	(3.67)	(2.81)
ISLA	0.133	0.220	0.124	0.227
	(2.45)	(3.97)	(2.31)	(4.17)
LANG	1.470	1.480	1.359	1.350
	(21.36)	(21.65)	(19.66)	(19.71)
ACCT	0.716	0.761	0.664	0.700
	(7.57)	(8.06)	(7.09)	(7.54)

Table 20.5. *Continued*

Variable	Model 1 Benchmark	Model 2 Spatial Structure Whole World	Model 3 Spatial Structure Language Commonality	Model 4 Combination of Models 2 and 3
RELIG	0.186	0.157	0.178	0.136
	(3.08)	(2.62)	(2.99)	(2.30)
CMWTH	0.765	0.656	0.762	0.658
	(7.12)	(6.10)	(7.18)	(6.22)
FSU	1.336	1.518	1.706	1.949
	(6.77)	(7.67)	(8.57)	(9.78)
FZ	1.204	1.213	1.311	1.289
	(6.77)	(6.87)	(7.44)	(7.39)
AMERICA	−0.311	−0.418	−0.527	−0.643
	(3.35)	(4.49)	(5.57)	(6.80)
CARIBBEAN	1.637	1.664	1.617	1.688
	(6.39)	(6.54)	(6.39)	(6.73)
EUROPE	−0.706	−0.550	−0.539	−0.408
	(7.47)	(5.72)	(5.66)	(4.29)
NORTHERN EUROPE	0.970	0.893	1.332	1.346
	(2.58)	(2.39)	(3.56)	(3.64)
WESTERN EUROPE	0.608	−0.044	−1.020	−0.955
	(2.10)	(1.54)	(3.53)	(3.33)
SOUTHEAST EUROPE	1.643	1.590	1.586	1.547
	(6.00)	(5.84)	(5.84)	(5.75)
AFRICA	0.494	0.402	0.389	0.291
	(5.10)[1]	(4.10)	(4.04)	(3.01)
NORTHERN AFRICA	−1.543	−1.437	−1.518	−1.487
	(5.09)	(4.77)	(5.06)	(5.01)
EASTERN AFRICA	1.221	1.118	1.281	1.103
	(2.57)	(2.37)	(2.73)	(2.37)
MIDDLE EAST	0.630	0.578	0.436	0.350
	(3.74)	(3.46)	(2.60)	(2.10)
SOUTHERN ASIA	1.728	1.494	1.927	1.729
	(3.20)	(2.78)	(3.60)	(3.26)
OCEANIA	2.015	1.594	2.006	1.487
	(8.45)	(6.52)	(8.50)	(6.16)
SSCA	—	−0.1381	—	−0.0831
		(7.18)		(7.33)
SSCB	—	−0.0506	—	−0.0605
		(3.46)		(6.50)
SSLA	—	—	0.0240	0.0303
			(7.73)	(8.70)
SSLB	—	—	0.0149	0.0247
			(5.93)	(8.03)
R^2	0.863	0.865	0.866	0.869
Optimal Distance Exponent λ	N.A.	2.6	3.2	3.8

Note: The *t* statistics are in parentheses.

substitute for international telephone flows. The results also underscore the critical role of a country's level of telecommunication equipment, size of the business sector, exports and imports, and tourists attraction, the importance of membership in trade, political, and cultural groups, the impacts of language and religion commonalities, and, of course, the role of geography, as measured by great-circle distances, contiguity, time zone differences, island status, and spatial structure variables.

Further research should involve new explanatory variables related to international migrations and ancestry stock, alternative functional specifications, as well as a multi-period sample of inter-country telephone flows. While trade and tourism have a demonstrable effect on telecommunication flows, further research could focus on analyzing the reverse effects, that is, whether telecommunications do spur trade and tourism, and thus provide an impetus for economic growth, particularly in developing countries.

Acknowledgments Support from the Ameritech Foundation through an Ameritech Faculty Fellowship is gratefully acknowledged.

References

Acton, J.P., and I. Vogelsang. 1992. Telephone demand over the Atlantic: Evidence from country-pair data. *The Journal of Industrial Economics* 40(3): 305–323.

Anas, A. 1981. Discrete choice theory, information theory, and the multinomial logit and gravity models. Paper presented at the *North American Meetings of the Regional Science Association*, November: Montreal, Canada.

Applebe, T.W., and C. Dineen. 1993. A point-to-point econometric model of Canada-overseas mts demand. Paper presented at the *National Telecommunication Forecasting Conference*, July 1993: Washington, D.C.

Barber, G.M., and W.J. Milne. 1988. Modeling internal migration in Kenya: An econometric analysis with limited data. *Environment and Planning A* 20: 1185–1196.

Bewley, R., and D.G. Fiebig. 1988. Estimation of price elasticities for an international telephone demand model. *The Journal of Industrial Economics* 36(4): 393–409.

Bröcker, J., and H.C. Rohweder. 1990. Barriers to international trade—methods of measurement and empirical evidence. *Annals of Regional Science* 24: 289–305.

Conçalves, M.B., and I. Ulysséa-Neto. 1993. The development of a new gravity-opportunity model for trip distribution. *Environment and Planning* A 25: 817–826.

Dokmeci, V., and L. Berkoz. 1996. International telecommunications in Turkey. *Telecommunications Policy* 20 (2): 125–130.

Fik, T.J., and G.F. Mulligan. 1990. Spatial flows and competing central places: Towards a general theory of hierarchical interaction. *Environment and Planning A* 22: 527–549.

Fik, T.J., R. G. Amey, and G.F. Mulligan. 1992. Labor migration among hierarchically competing and intervening origins and destinations. *Environment and Planning A* 24: 1271–1290.

Fiebig, D.G., and R. Bewley. 1987. International telecommunications forecasting: An investigation of alternative functional forms. *Applied Economics* 19: 949–960.

Fotheringham, A.S. 1983. A new set of spatial-interaction models: The theory of competing destinations. *Environment and Planning A* 15: 15–36.

Fotheringham, A.S., and M.E. O'Kelly. 1989. *Spatial Interaction Models: Formulations and Applications.* Kluwer: Dordrecht.

Frankel, J.A., and S.J. Wei. 1998. Regionalization of world trade and currencies: Economics and politics. In J.A. Frankel (ed.) *The Regionalization of the World Economy.* Chicago: The University of Chicago Press, 189–219.

Garin-Munoz, T., and T. Perez-Amaral. 1998. Econometric modeling of Spanish very long distance international calling. *Information Economics and Policy* 10: 237–252.

Guldmann, J.-M. 1999. Competing destinations and intervening opportunities interaction models of inter-city telecommunication flows. *Papers in Regional Science* 78: 179–194.

Guy, C.M. 1987. Recent advances in spatial interaction modeling: An application to the forecasting of shopping travel. *Environment and Planning A* 19: 173–186.

Hackl, P., and A.H. Westlund. 1995. On the price elasticity of international telecommunication demand. *Information Economics and Policy* 7: 27–36.

Hirst, M.A. 1975. Telephone transactions, regional inequality and urban growth in East Africa. *Tijdschrift voor Economische en Sociale Geografie* 66: 277–293.

Ishikawa, Y. 1987. An empirical study of the competing destinations model using Japanese interaction data. *Environment and Planning A* 19: 1359–1373.

ITU and TGI. 1996. Direction of traffic—trends in international telephone tariffs. Washington, D.C.: International Telecommunication Union and Telegeography, Inc.

Karikari, J.A., and K. Gyimah-Brempong. 1999. Demand for international telephone services between U.S. and Africa. *Information Economics and Policy* 11: 407–435.

Kellerman, A. 1990. International telecommunications around the world—a flow analysis. *Telecommuncations Policy* 14: 461–475.

Lago, A.M. 1970. Demand forecasting model of international telecommunications and their policy implications. *The Journal of Industrial Economics* 19: 6–21.

Larson, A.C., D.E. Lehman, and D.L. Weisman. 1990. A general theory of point-to-point long distance demand. In A. De Fontenay, M.H. Shugard, and D.S. Sibley (eds.), *Telecommunications Demand Modeling—An Integrated View*. Amsterdam: Elsevier Science Publishers, 299–318.

Leinbach, T.R. 1973. Distance, information flows and modernization: Some observation from West Malaysia. *The Professional Geographer* 25: 7–11.

McFadden, D. 1973. Conditional logit analyses of qualitative choice behavior. In P. Zarembka (ed.), *Frontiers in Econometrics*. New York: Academic Press.

Naleszkiewicz, W. 1970. International telecommunications—testing a forecasting model of demand. *Telecommunication Journal* 37(9): 635–638.

Rea, J.D., and G.M. Lage. 1978. Estimates of demand elasticities for international telecommunications services. *The Journal of Industrial Economics* 26(4): 363–381.

Rietveld, P., and L. Janssen. 1990. Telephone calls and communication barriers—the case of The Netherlands. *The Annals of Regional Science* 24: 307–318.

Sandbach, J. 1996. International telephone traffic, callback, and policy implications. *Telecommunications Policy* 20(7): 507–515.

Staple, G.C., and M. Mullins. 1989. Telecom traffic statistics—MiTT matter: Improving economic forecasting and regulatory policy. *Telecommunications Policy* 13(2): 105–128.

Stouffer, S.A. 1940. Intervening opportunities: A theory relating mobility and distance. *American Sociological Review* 5: 845–867.

Stouffer, S.A. 1960. Intervening opportunities and competing migrants. *Journal of Regional Science* 2: 1–26.

Taylor, L.D . 1980. *Telecommunications Demand: A Survey and Critique*. Cambridge, Mass.: Ballinger Publishing Company.

Wilson, A.G. 1967. A statistical theory of spatial distribution models. *Transportation Research* 1: 253–269.

Yatrakis, P.G. 1972. Determinants of the demand for international telecommunications. *Telecommunication Journal* 39 (12): 732–746.

Zhang, J., and G. Kristensen. 1995. A gravity model with variable coefficients: The EEC trade with third countries. *Geographical Analysis* 27(4): 307–320.

21

Planning Scenario Visualization and Assessment

A Cellular Automata Based Integrated Spatial Decision Support System

Roger White

Bas Straatman

Guy Engelen

P lanners and policy makers face a difficult task. The world they must deal with is complex, interconnected, and ever changing. Coastal zone management, urban planning, and the design of policies for sustainable economic development all pose the problem of dealing with systems in which natural and human factors are thoroughly intertwined. Understanding the processes driving change in these systems is essential in the formulation of effective policies.

Four aspects of such systems are of particular importance. First, and most importantly, these systems are *integrated wholes*. Thus, while a planner or policy maker may intervene directly in only a limited part of the system, linkages will transmit consequences of the policy to many other parts of the system. Conversely, the problems the planner is dealing with may have had their origins in actions that were taken in other parts of the system in an attempt to resolve other problems.

Second, human systems, and the natural systems in which they are imbedded, are *dynamic and evolving*; they are never in equilibrium. Policy makers thus intervene in a changing system, and at certain critical points, the consequences of even a small intervention may be both unanticipated and of major importance.

Third, these systems are *inherently spatial*. Both natural and human systems are structured in geographic space to optimize levels of interaction among components; clustering increases opportunities for interaction, while dispersal provides protection from the effects of interaction. The consequences of planning policies depend on the spatial context within which they are implemented, as well as on the way they alter that context.

Fourth, the world is one of *uncertainty*, and while increased knowledge and improved modeling tools may lessen that uncertainty, they cannot eliminate it. Plans and policies, therefore, need to be designed to incorporate and work with the uncertainty, rather than assume that it does not exist.

In light of these considerations, if a model is to be a useful and reliable decision support tool, it should have several characteristics. It should, first of all, incorporate an integrated treatment of as many of the primary system components as possible. The natural and human systems should both be represented—for example by including sub-models for such domains as wildlife habitat, demographics, and economics. In addition, the model should be fully dynamic and spatial. Many planning problems are, of course, explicitly spatial. But even policies that have no spatial component will typically face spatial constraints in their implementation and will have spatial consequences. Finally, the model should facilitate the exploration of the merits and problems of alternative policy or planning options. This is a useful objective, which can be attained with models that recognize a degree of inherent unpredictability in the world, and it avoids the unrealistic approach of calculating an "optimum" solution to a planning problem. It is also one that accommodates interaction among participants in a planning process, rather than pre-empting such participation as a calculated "optimum" solution does.

In this chapter we present two closely related models designed to support urban and regional planning and policy development. The first, the LeefOmgevingsVerkenner (LOV), was developed originally for the Dutch National Institute for Health and Environment (RIVM) to support the development and assessment of policies for improving the quality of the lived environment in the Netherlands. It consists of an integrated dynamic spatial simulation model augmented with decision support tools. The heart of the model is a constrained cellular automaton (CA) representing land use dynamics. The CA is linked to GIS data layers representing the various aspects of land quality that affect land use, such as physical characteristics, accessibility, and zoning. The CA is driven by a linked, regionalized model of macro-scale dynamics treating demographic and economic activities. Changes in land use generated by the CA are fed back to the linked macro-scale model, so the behavior of the economic-demographic model is altered by the land use dynamics. The entire model is imbedded in a decision support framework that facilitates the construction of scenarios representing alternative problems and policy options and enhances the interpretation and use of the output. The whole of the Netherlands is modeled.

The second model, BabyLOV, was developed for the Visions project of the European Union. The Visions project supported the development of integrated visions for a sustainable Europe for the years 2020 and 2050; scenarios were developed independently for both the whole of Europe and for three regions: the northwest of England, Venice, and the Green Heart of the Netherlands; subsequently the independent scenarios were reconciled to develop a series of integrated visions for Europe and the regions. The process of integrating the visions revealed many inconsistencies between the independently developed scenarios. BabyLOV was created from LOV by replacing the macro-scale model that drives the CA with a user-supplied scenario, and by adding tools to facilitate translation of a qualitative "story-line" scenario into a quantitative one that can drive the CA land use model. Only the Green Heart region of the Netherlands is modeled by BabyLOV.

This chapter focuses on the BabyLOV model and the scenario visualization and assessment problem it is designed to handle. For this reason the LOV model will be described only to the extent necessary to understand BabyLOV. In particular, since the model of macro-scale dynamics, which is such an important part of LOV, is replaced in BabyLOV by a scenario, it will receive only cursory treatment. But the constrained CA land use model will receive detailed treatment, since it constitutes the heart of both models.[1]

The Cellular Automaton Based Land Use Model

Cellular Automata are among the simplest representations of dynamical systems, and hence computationally efficient; they are, moreover, inherently spatial. These two characteristics make them an ideal modeling tool for land use dynamics. Tobler (1979) was the first to recognize this. Couclelis (1985, 1988, 1989) and Phipps (1989) later used CA to gain insights into general characteristics of spatial processes. Applications aimed specifically at detailed land use modeling began in the 1990s (Batty and Xie 1994; Cecchini 1996; Clarke et al. 1997; Engelen et al. 1993, 1995, 1996, 1997; Portugali 2000; Portugali and Benenson 1995, 1997; White and Engelen 1993a,b, 1994, 1997; White et al. 1997; Wu 1998a,b; Xie 1996). For an overview see White (1998).

A typical CA consists of a grid, or cell space, in which cell states represent some characteristic of interest like land use, together with a set of state transition rules. A cell changes state as a function of the states of cells within its neighborhood, as specified by the transition rules. The CA thus fully captures the idea of spatial dynamics, since the dynamic itself is defined in terms of spatial relations within a neighborhood in the grid space. A conventional CA can be described more fully as consisting of

1. A cell space—typically a homogeneous Euclidean raster;
2. A set of discrete cell states;
3. A definition of a cell neighborhood (e.g., the four adjacent cells);
4. A set of transition rules determining the state of a cell as a function of the states of the cells in its neighborhood;
5. A discrete time step, with all cells updated simultaneously at each time step.

However, in two respects a stand-alone CA is not suited to model geographical phenomena. First, in a pure CA the number of cells in any particular state at each time period is the result of the internal dynamics generated by the transition rules. Thus, in a pure CA land use model, the total number of cells of, say, housing, would be the cumulative result simply of local neighborhood dynamics. But in reality, the total area of housing depends not on local neighborhood effects but on global quantities of supply and demand, which are not represented within the CA. This points to the need to embed applied CA models within a larger contextualizing framework that will constrain the CA dynamics. The result of such an embedding is a *constrained* CA. In general the constraining framework will consist of other, linked models, as in LOV, but may, as in BabyLOV, be as simple as a file specifying the number of cells required to be in each state at each time period. The constraints act on, and in effect become part of, the transition rules.

Secondly, the assumption that the cell space is homogeneous is not a good one for geographical applications, since actual space is characterized by many properties, both physical and institutional, that may affect the cell state. Thus the cell space must be modified to reflect the varying properties of the land, and the transition rules include a number of factors other than the state of the cell neighborhood.

The CA that constitutes the heart of both the LeefOmgevingsVerkenner and Baby-LOV is thus much more specific than a classical CA. It functions in the context of both global constraints, supplied either by a macro-scale model (LOV) or by a scenario of macro-scale trends (BabyLOV), and local constraints, provided by an inhomogeneous cell space representing site specific conditions. Key features of this CA are designed specifically to facilitate this integration with exogenous micro- and macro-scale data. The model is specified as follows.

Cell Space

The cells represent units of land 500 m on a side, i.e., areas of 25 ha. Smaller cells could be used to achieve higher resolution, but model run times increase. In the interest of realism, we use an inhomogeneous space representing differences in intrinsic land quality (e.g., slope, soil type), institutionally determined differences (e.g., zoning), and other factors, such as accessibility. This provides one of the two major links between the cellular model and other components of the integrated model. In particular, the grid of cell space is structurally similar to the space representation of a raster GIS. This similarity permits an easy linkage between a GIS and the CA model, both conceptually and technically.

The inhomogeneity of cell space can be conceptualized in terms of the over-all suitability of a cell for various types of land use. However, in order to facilitate use of the model in practical applications, three types of inhomogeneities are treated separately.

1. Cell suitabilities S_j are calculated from data on some 15 factors such as soil type, slope, other physical and environmental characteristics like noise levels, and historical occupation. These calculations are made by techniques such as weighted sums or products as appropriate, using standard GIS operations; they are normalized to the range $0 \leq S_j \leq 1$. Each cell is thus characterized by a vector of suitabilities, one suitability for each possible land use, representing the intrinsic capacity of the cell to support the particular land use.
2. Each cell has a vector of zoning status values Z_j associated with it, one value for each possible land use, normalized to $0 \leq Z_j \leq 1$. Zoning status is established on the basis of zoning maps, in combination with data on other legal and institutional restrictions on the use of the land. Zoning status maps for future periods may represent planning proposals that are to be investigated or tested in the model. Zoning maps may be specified for three periods specified by the user (e.g., 1990–2005, 2005–2015, and 2015–2030); the model provides a smoothing of the transition between zoning maps to represent a phasing in of new zoning regulations.
3. Finally, each cell is characterized by a vector of local accessibility factors, A_j, again, one for each land use (Figure 21.1). These factors represent the importance of accessibility to the transport network for the various land use activities. Some activities, like commerce, require better access to the network than others, like recreation. Most natural land cover types benefit from low access, because of less likelihood of

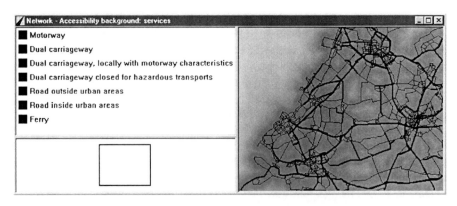

Figure 21.1. Accessibility map for services. Darker areas are more accessible; motorways have the widest impact, other classes of road have shorter-range effects.

disturbance and fragmentation of habitat. The transport networks are represented by cell-centered vectors and are superimposed on the cell grid. The highway network is based on the LMS network used by the Netherlands Ministry of Transport, Public Works, and Water Management and consists of motorways, national highways, and regional roads. For both the motorway network and the passenger rail network, access is only possible at certain points—specifically the interchanges and the rail stations. The effect of accessibility to these points is represented on the suitability maps in the form of higher suitabilities near the interchanges or stations. Nevertheless, proximity to the network itself may still be an important locational factor, for example because of increased noise. The transport networks are updated during simulation runs to reflect planned additions and modifications.

Accessibilities are calculated as a function of distance from the cell to the nearest point on the network, and normalized to $0 \leq A_j \leq 1$. For land uses benefiting from access to the network,

$$A_j = a_j/(d + a_j) \tag{1}$$

and for land uses and land covers benefiting from poor access,

$$A_j = d/(d + a_j) \tag{2}$$

where

A_j = the accessibility factor of the cell for land use j;

d = the Euclidean distance for the cell to the nearest cell through which the network passes;

a_j = a coefficient representing the importance of accessibility to the network for land use j. In some versions of the model this coefficient is a function of the kind of network or the type of link within the network.

Cell States

The cell state typically represents the dominant land use type in the cell. However, in this application, since land use data were resampled from a higher resolution (25 m) source for use in the model at a lower resolution (500 m), there are a few exceptions. Land use and land cover state definitions are the same at both scales. However, in order to preserve total areas occupied by each land use, a few 500-m cells are assigned states different from that of the dominant land use in the cell. For modeling purposes, two major classes of land use are distinguished: land use *functions*, consisting of land uses that may change state by means of the CA dynamic (e.g., industry), and land use *features*, comprising land uses that are static, and cannot be changed by the CA (e.g., the sea, or parks). In the LOV model there are 10 function states and 12 feature states. The CA transition rules need only be implemented for cell states representing functions, but features, if they appear in a cell neighborhood, may appear in the argument of a transition rule and thus affect the state transition probabilities of functions. The model can handle a maximum of 32 states—16 functions and 16 features.

Neighborhood Effect

The cell neighborhood used here is defined as the 196 cells within a radius of eight cells; in other words, the cell neighborhood has a radius of four kilometers. This is assumed to be sufficiently large to capture the effect of most local processes, including those depending on a perception of "neighborhood." The fundamental idea of a CA is that the state of a cell depends on the state of the cells within its neighborhood. Thus a neighborhood effect is calculated for each of the possible states that a cell can acquire—i.e., each function state. This effect is calculated as a weighted sum of the cells in the neighborhood, where the weights depend on the cell state and the distance from the cell for which the effect is being calculated (Figure 21.2):

$$N_j = \sum_d \sum_x w_{s(x),j,d} \tag{3}$$

where

N_j = the neighborhood effect for transitions to land use j;

$w_{s(x),j,d}$ = the weighting parameter applied to cell x, with state (land use) $s(x) = k$ in distance zone d.

The effect of a cell in the neighborhood on the potential for transition to land use j depends on the weighting parameters w_{kjd}. These sets of parameters permit various attraction and repulsion effects among land uses to be represented in the transition rules: A positive value for a weight represents an attraction between land uses, and a negative value represents a repulsion effect. Typically the strength of an attraction or repulsion effect will decrease with distance, hence the distance-specific weights. In some cases a weight may change from positive to negative or vice versa with increasing distance.

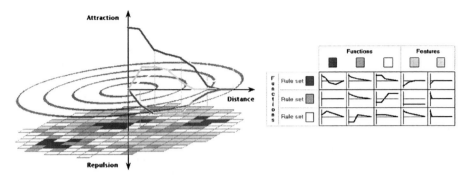

Figure 21.2. Schematic representation of the calculation of the neighborhood effect. For each function, the effect is calculated as the weighted sum of the influence of each cell in the 196-cell neighborhood. Cells are weighted according to their state and distance from the center of the neighborhood. One set of weighting parameters is shown superimposed on the neighborhood map; all sets are shown graphically in the right-hand panel.

Transition Rules

A vector of transition potentials—one potential for each possible land use—is calculated for each active cell—i.e., each cell occupied by a function state. Each transition potential is calculated by combining the neighborhood effect with the suitability, zoning, and accessibility factors, and introducing a random perturbation:

$$P_j = v S_j Z_j A_j N_j \tag{4}$$

where

    P_j = the potential of the cell for land use j;

    v = a scalable random perturbation term;

    S_j = the intrinsic suitability of the cell for land use j;

    Z_j = the zoning status of the cell for land use j;

    A_j = the local accessibility factor of the cell for land use j;

    N_j = the neighborhood effect of the cell for land use j.

The transition rule is as follows:

Change each cell to the land use for which it has the highest potential, subject to the constraint that the number of cells of each land use must be equal to the number required by the macro model at that iteration.

In applying the rule, all cells are ranked by their highest potential, which may in principle be for any land use, and cell transitions begin with the highest ranked cell and proceed downward. When the required number of cells for a particular land use has been attained, potentials for that land use are subsequently ignored. Thus, some cells will be converted to a land use other than the one for which their potential is highest. One consequence of this transition rule is that a particular land use may not appear on the cells with the highest potential for it, since those cells may have a higher potential for another land use. Also, note that most cell transitions are from a state to the same state—that is, the cell retains its previous land use.

Macro-Scale Dynamics

In LeefOmgevingsVerkenner (LOV), economic and demographic dynamics are represented at three scales: national, regional, and local. National trends are described by projections generated by various government ministries for each of several scenarios. These national totals are fed into a dynamic model representing the interactions among 40 urban-centered regions. In this model, competition among regions results in the migration of people and economic activities from one region to another, so that the model generates predictions of both population and sectoral economic activity levels for each region for each year. These population and economic activity figures are then converted (via land productivity or density functions) into demands for land for housing and for the various economic activities. It is these demands for land that constrain the CA model in the transition rule. Thus, in the LOV, the CA model is also regionalized so that, in each region, the CA is constrained by the regional cell requirements generated by the macro model. In other words, the macro model provides regionalized demands for land use that the cellular model satisfies by converting cells to the use for which the potential is highest.

In the basic LOV model, scenarios are introduced only at the national level. However, the model is constructed in such a way that scenarios for particular regions can be introduced as well—for example, by specifying a certain amount of growth in the industrial sector in the Amsterdam region during the period 2008–2025. This approach could be used to model developments in the Green Heart. But since the primary objective of the Visions project is to explore the use of flexible scenario specification and visualization as an aid to policy development and planning, in BabyLOV the regionalized macro model is replaced by a scenario for the Green Heart; it is this scenario that drives the CA, and the CA covers only the Green Heart region. This approach greatly simplifies the application of the model, since it is no longer necessary to work with data for the whole of the Netherlands, nor is it necessary to calibrate a regionalized macro model.

It is generally assumed that the result of linking several models, each one of which is characterized by a certain level of error, will be a compounding of the errors, perhaps to the point where the integrated model is useless. But when complementary models are linked, the result is more typically that one model limits the size of errors that the other can produce. Thus, the land use predictions of the constrained CA, whether driven by a full macro-scale model, as in LOV, or by a scenario, as in BabyLOV, are in general less subject to error, whether quantitative (as shown by cell-by-cell comparison) or qualitative (as shown by comparison of patterns) than those produced by an unconstrained model. Similarly, the performance of the macro-scale model in LOV, as measured by comparison with actual population and economic data, is enhanced by the constraints provided by the land use model; and in BabyLOV the output of the CA is used explicitly to improve the quality of the scenarios.

The BabyLOV Model

The BabyLOV model has two main components: a scenario specification and verification tool, and the CA land use model, which is driven and constrained by the scenario and which, in turn, provides a visualization of the detailed spatial consequences of the scenario.

The scenario specification feature is designed to facilitate the translation of a verbal scenario, a "storyline," into appropriate—i.e., numerical—model input, and to ensure that all necessary input is specified. It operates by accepting qualitative input from the user in the form of indications of no change, or low, medium, or high rates of growth or decline in various economic sectors and demographic categories during various periods specified by the user, and translating these to percentage rates of change. The numerical values then drive the CA land use model.

The dynamic land use maps or land use animations produced by the CA permit a user to visualize the spatial consequences of the scenario. At this point it may become evident that the scenario as specified contains unrealistic elements, or even inconsistencies, and so should be modified. This process of visualization, assessment, and modification of scenarios accommodates and, indeed, encourages interaction among the individuals and groups engaged in scenario development and should, thus, lead both to more reasonable scenarios and to enhanced cooperation among users of the software.

Scenario Extraction and Translation

The user must translate the story line of the verbal scenario into trends for each land use activity that is modeled. The model itself permits each activity to evolve independently, but in reality, activities are frequently related to each other, and in this case, the user must make sure that the relations are reflected in the scenario specification. Thus the user has to build an image of the verbal scenario that reflects the answers to such questions as the following: Which sectors grow? Which ones decline? When do they grow or decline, and by how much? Are the activity levels of various sectors related? Are these relations kept intact by the evolutions extracted from the scenario? By means of dialogue boxes in the user interface of the model, the user is assisted in translating the answers to these questions into numerical values that then constitute the input to the model.

The dialogue box requests information on growth, decline, or no change in activity for each sector for each time period specified; this is entered in the form of $+$, $-$, or 0, with greater rates of change being indicated by multiple plus or minus signs. The symbol inputs are then converted to percentage rates of growth, with the user being able to specify rates corresponding to each possible entry—e.g., one plus sign $= 2$ percent growth, two plus signs $= 5$ percent, three plus signs $= 10$ percent (Figure 21.3, top). When the model is run, the total area of land devoted to each activity changes as specified in the scenario, and for each activity the amount of land occupied over the simulation period is displayed as a graph (Figure 21.3, bottom). If the land use trends do not seem appropriate to the user, either because they do not seem to reflect what is understood to be in the verbal scenario, perhaps by violating assumed relationships between activities, or because they seem unrealistic, the scenario specification can be altered in any of three ways. Either the +, −, and 0 entries can be edited; the specified percentage rates associated with each symbol group can be altered; or the graphs of total area (i.e., the cell count graphs) can be adjusted directly (Figure 21.4) and used to drive future runs of the model.

While the verbal scenarios essentially deal with macro-trends, some scenario elements may require modifications to the specification of the cellular model. Some scenarios call for new land uses to appear, or for existing land uses, which are too unimportant to be treated explicitly, to become important and thus require representation in the model. For example, one scenario suggests that low income ghettos will appear in the large cities and become an important phenomenon. Since current land use data does not include such a category, it is necessary to add such a land use type to the CA model, together with the set of weighting parameters w_{kjd} that are required to calculate the neighborhood effect for this new activity. The parameter sets for the other land uses must also be augmented with values to represent the effect of this new activity on the neighborhood quality for those activities. Initially, the values for these parameters will be established on the basis of clues in the scenario—that is, the scenario should give some indication of the kinds of relations between the new land use and existing ones; e.g., low density housing may be repelled by ghettos. But the initial values will be adjusted in the light of simulation output until the resulting land use patterns are consistent with the scenario. In addition, suitability, zoning, and accessibility maps for the new land use must be provided; these too are initially tentative, and may be adjusted so that the model output is in accord with the scenario.

The Application to the Green Heart

The Green Heart of the Netherlands is a largely agricultural area situated within the ring of cities constituting the Randstad: Utrecht, Amsterdam, Leiden, the Hague, and Rotterdam. To preserve the area as open space and maintain its cultural, historical, and recreational value in the face of severe development pressures, the region is at present protected by comprehensive planning regulations that strictly limit development. But what is the future of the Green Heart? The purpose of the Visions project is to explore its possible future under three scenarios:

Scenario 1: Technology Rules. Economic growth continues; the rate of innovation in bio- nano- and information technology accelerates. The influence of the national government diminishes; market forces strengthen, with businesses and NGOs becoming increasingly important players. The income gap between social groups widens, accompanied by a growing spatial segregation of the poor.

Scenario 2: Europe Leading. Europe plays a dominant role; legislative power is transferred from the national to the European level. The European Union expands to include countries in central and eastern Europe. EU environmental policy is intensified, but

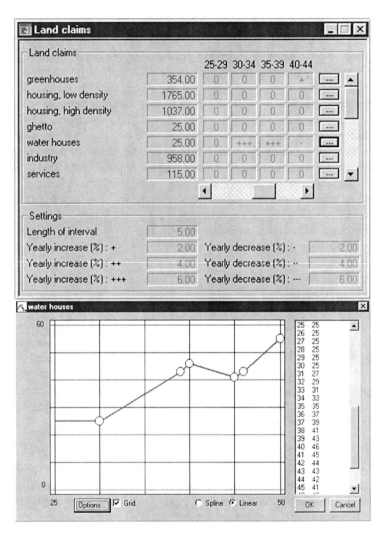

Figure 21.3. Entering a scenario in the GUI. Relative growth rates of the activities are entered using plus and minus signs; these are quantified by entering corresponding percentage rates below. The resulting trend in land area for one activity is shown graphically on the bottom.

European agricultural support decreases, and agriculture disappears from the Green Heart. The Green Heart is increasingly fragmented as the restrictive development policy is weakened. A European revitalization program has to turn the tide.

Scenario 3: Water Guiding. Global warming results in rising sea levels. Traditional measures to control water are no longer effective; safety becomes an issue; and businesses and people leave the Green Heart. A solution has to be found in a new way of

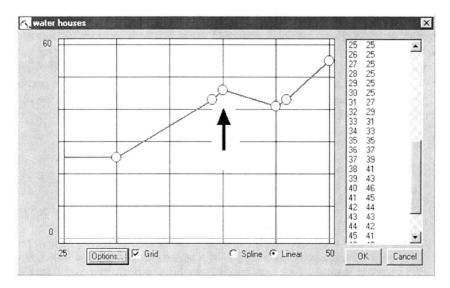

Figure 21.4. Scenario adjustment. The growth scenario can be adjusted directly by click-ing and dragging to reshape the land use graph directly.

thinking: don't fight the water, live with it. Parts of the Green Heart are flooded; new forms of housing and infrastructure emerge; farming is replaced by fish farming. But unforeseen problems appear, like vector-borne diseases.

For all three scenarios, applications of BabyLOV are based on the full LOV model for the whole of the Netherlands. LOV was calibrated to data for the period 1989–1994. Data for 1989 supplied the initial conditions for the model, and model parameters were adjusted until predictions for land use, population, and regionalized sectoral economic data were as close as possible to actual 1994 values. However, the calibration also involved runs of the model to the year 2050 to ensure that the calibrated model would not run away over the longer period. One measure of land use pattern that tends to be stable over long periods is the cluster size—frequency spectrum for various land uses; this was used to test that long run results were qualitatively similar to current conditions. The calibration procedure itself is largely heuristic, although a calibration algorithm is being developed for the cellular module (Straatman et al.2002).

Essentially all of the initial conditions for the cellular model of BabyLOV are taken from the LOV calibration. Specifically, both the accessibility parameters and the weighting parameters for the neighborhood effect are taken from this calibration, as are the initial land use, zoning, and suitability maps, although these must be augmented or modified in light of specific developments mentioned in the scenarios. One advantage of this procedure is that a full calibration of BabyLOV is not necessary. In addition, the calibrated LOV is run for the period 2000–2050 to produce a baseline or "business as usual" result against which to specify and evaluate the results of the Visions scenarios.

Here we describe an application of the *Technology Rules* scenario. The complete scenario consists of a "storyline" of some several pages. The first step is to analyze the scenario to extract elements (called *clues* in this exercise) that are relevant for the simulation model. However, some scenario themes cannot be directly translated into model input, since it is not clear how they would affect model parameters or trends in driving variables. Examples are innovations in energy resources, privatization of public services, advances in genetic engineering, and transfer of power from one level of government to another. The result of this exercise results in the following list of scenario elements or clues:

The period from 2000 to 2020

1. Economic growth continues at about the rate of the 1990s.
2. Both industry and commercial and non-commercial services flourish.
3. Agriculture remains a healthy economic sector.
4. In agriculture a noticeable shift towards organic products occurs.
5. Technological research companies flourish.
6. The service and industrial sectors experience labor shortages.
7. In 2005 a wave of economic and political refugees starts moving from Africa and eastern European countries; there are 200,000 refugees a year, mainly moving to the Randstad cities, putting pressure on the housing market.
8. Neighborhoods with cheap housing appear; some of these become overcrowded and deteriorate.
9. Around the year 2000 population growth was slowing down, but now population is growing at a higher rate.
10. People want to leave the overcrowded Randstad cities, but this is only possible for the affluent.
11. Increased demand for housing outside the cities puts great strains on the maintenance of the restrictive development policy in the Green Heart area.
12. A forest development plan and a nature development plan create the desired green living environment for the affluent.
13. New lakes are created in response to the increased demand for recreational areas.
14. Global warming affects the lower parts of the Green Heart; dikes are reinforced and flood areas are designated.
15. More scattered dwellings appear in the Green Heart.
16. Weekend recreation for inhabitants of the cities is demanded.
17. The Betuwelijn, a freight rail line connecting the port of Rotterdam with the Ruhrgebiet in Germany, is completed in 2010.
18. Air traffic increases steadily.

The period from 2020 until 2050

19. The economy is still growing but at a lesser pace.
20. The service sector is still growing strongly, with new locations next to the main infrastructural arteries.
21. Farmers remain in the Green Heart.
22. Unemployment leads to less attractive neighborhoods in the cities.
23. Wealthier people do not want to live in the proximity of existing cities.
24. "Park-like" urbanization appears, with free-standing villas scattered in a green environment; a typical density is three villas per hectare.
25. The Green Heart becomes an exclusive residential area for which the peripheral city dwellers provide the services.

26. The rich inhabitants of the Green Heart prevent the lifting of the restrictive building policy.
27. Around 2030 the influx of immigrants comes to a halt.
28. To meet the enormous demand for space, islands in the North Sea are developed; these islands are located 10 km offshore and measure 10 km^2.
29. Both residential and work islands are developed.
30. Schiphol and other airports grow steadily.
31. Shops for consumer products begin to disappear.
32. Climate change is no longer an issue; by the year 2040 the water level and temperature are no longer increasing.
33. The socio-economic status of the population living in cities has further declined.

These elements of the scenario, suitably quantified, in effect constitute the macro model that drives the land use model in BabyLOV. The first step in quantifying the scenario is to decide on a time period to be used. In this application, a five-year interval is used in scenario quantification, since that level of detail permits all the temporal information in the scenario to be captured. Next, clues are translated into land use change trends: does the scenario imply growth or decline? rapid or slow? when? Answers to these questions are entered in the form of plus or minus signs, with more signs representing more rapid change. No entry is interpreted as no change. Signs are entered for each land use, for each five-year interval over the 50-year simulation period (Table 21.1).

As described above, these qualitative growth estimates are further quantified by specifying corresponding percentage rates, and then, using cell counts from the initial land use map, graphs are generated showing the amount of land to be occupied by each land use over the 50 year period. Each graph, in effect, represents a hypothesis about total land use claims by a particular activity through the years covered by the simulation. In the current application, these graphs were discussed with the scenario developers to discover whether our interpretations reflected their intentions. Their comments were used to alter the graphs, both by altering the input table and by changing the land use graphs directly by adding, removing, or dragging points, until curves with the intended shapes were obtained. The result was the set of land use graphs shown in Figure 21.5. However, these graphs should not be treated as final. They can—and should—be changed in light of simulation results, or simply as part of an analysis of the robustness of the scenario model. In other words, they should be treated as a working hypothesis of scenario interpretation.

Since several of the scenario elements imply land uses other than those inherited from LOV, these land uses must be added to the model. Specifically, the scenario calls for *islands* in the north sea (Clue 28), and two new residential categories, *villas* (Clue 24) and *ghettos* (Clue 8), so these need to be specified in the model, though they do not appear on the initial year land use map. In addition, to make possible the appearance of the islands, a dummy land use, *potential island*, must be established on the initial land use map, since the sea is treated as a feature in the model and cannot change state by the endogenous dynamics.

The new land uses must be given neighborhood-effect weighting parameters to describe their relationships with other land use functions and features. This means both establishing complete sets of weighting parameters for the new land uses to show the

Table 21.1. Qualitative representation of technology rules scenario.

LAND USE	PERIOD									
	2000–2005	2005–2010	2010–2015	2015–2020	2020–2025	2025–2030	2030–2035	2035–2040	2040–2045	2045–2050
Greenhouses	+ (clue 2)	+ (clue 2)	+ (clue 2)				+ (clue 27)	+ (clue 27)	+ (clue 27)	+ (clue 27)
Housing-low d.	0 (clue 9)	+ (clue 7)	+ (clue 7)	+ (clue 7)	+ (clue 7)		+ (clue 27)	+ (clue 27)	+ (clue 27)	+ (clue 27)
Housing-high d.	0 (clue 9)	+ (clue 7)	+ (clue 7)						++ (clue 33)	++ (clue 33)
Ghettos	0 (clue 9)	++ (clue 7)	++ (clue 8)		++ (clue 22)					
Villas			++ (clue 15)	++ (clue 15)	++ (clue 23)	++ (clue 24)	++ (clue 25)	++ (clue 26)	++ (clue 26)	++ (clue 26)
Industry	+ (clue 2)	+ (clue 2)	+ (clue 2)	+ (clue 2)	+ (clue 19)	0 (clue 19)	+ (clue 19)	0 (clue 19)	+ (clue 19)	0 (clue 19)
Services	+ (clue 2)	+ (clue 2)	+ (clue 2)	+ (clue 2)	+ (clue 20)	+ (clue 20)	+ (clue 20)	+ (clue 20)	+ (clue 20)	+ (clue 20)
Sociocultural	+ (clue 2)	0 (clue 2)	+ (clue 2)	0 (clue 2)	+ (clue 20)	+ (clue 20)	0 (clue 20)	+ (clue 20)	0 (clue 20)	+ (clue 20)
Forest			+ (clue 12)	+ (clue 12)		+ (clue 24)	+ (clue 24)			
Wetlands			+ (clue 14)	+ (clue 14)	+ (clue 14)	0 (clue 14)	+ (clue 14)	0 (clue 32)	0 (clue 32)	0 (clue 32)
Drylands										
Recreation				+ (clue 16)						
Airports			+ (clue 18)				+ (clue 30)	+ (clue 30)		
Freshwater			+ (clue 13)			0 (clue 14)	+ (clue 14)	0 (clue 32)	0 (clue 32)	0 (clue 32)
New islands				+ (clue 13)			+ (clue 28)	+ (clue 28)	+ (clue 28)	+ (clue 28)

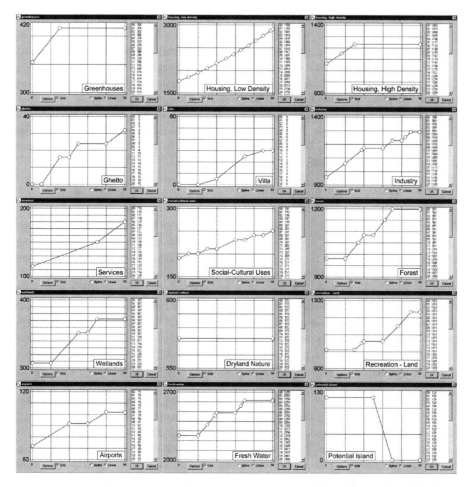

Figure 21.5. Overview of the Technology Rules scenario, showing postulated activity levels. *Top row*: greenhouses, low-density residential, high-density residential; *second row*: ghettos, villas, industry; *third row*: services, socio-cultural activities, forest; *fourth row*: wetlands, dryland nature, recreation; *bottom row*: airports, fresh water, potential islands. (*NB*: the scale on the vertical axis differs from graph to graph; the horizontal axis shows the fifty-year time scale for each graph).

effects of other land uses on them, and also, where appropriate, augmenting the parameter sets of existing land uses with parameters describing the effects of the new land uses on the existing ones. In addition, some existing influence parameters must be changed to reflect assumptions specified in the scenario. For example, recreation must be characterized as attracted to fresh water. These parameters can be entered most simply in the form of influence curves, as shown in Figure 21.1.

The new land uses also require suitability and zoning maps. In addition, updated suitability and zoning maps for both existing and new land uses can be introduced at specified points during the simulation to implement certain elements of the scenario. For example, the suitability of the area around Schiphol airport for housing is increased after the date at which the scenario suggests that quieter aircraft will be introduced. Dated zoning maps are used to implement airport expansion and construction of the North Sea islands, since these are planned projects initiated by government rather than spontaneous, incremental changes in land use.

Finally, parameters representing the importance of accessibility to the road and rail networks must be entered for the new land uses. In addition, the accessibility maps must be updated as appropriate. For example, the Betuwelijn freight railway is introduced to the network map in 2010.

Model Output

The model generates a new land use map for each year of the simulation period. Maps for 2000, 2020, and 2050 are shown in Figure 21.6; the latter two years are the dates specified in the VISIONS project as those for which images of the designated regions should be produced. In addition, using a tool integrated with the modeling software, land use maps may be compared with each other on a cell-by-cell basis to see changes from one year to another during a simulation or to see differences between two different simulations. The comparison tool displays a map of each land use showing which cells were the same in the two simulation maps being compared, which were in the first map but not the second, and which were in the second but not the first. The comparison tool also, of course, permits change over time within a given simulation to be visualized. In addition, it provides a matrix of cell differences together with Kappa statistics. These comparison maps make it very easy to see the evolving patterns of a particular land use or to see the effect of a change in scenario specification on a land use. Figure 21.7 shows a comparison of industrial land use for 2000 and 2050.

In order to provide information on the simulation results at a somewhat higher level of abstraction, the model also generates several spatial indicators. The user can define the specific calculation of the indicators by setting parameters. These are as follows:

Cluster size. A cluster is defined as a set of adjacent cells that have a specific characteristic in common. The user can specify the characteristic, such as a specific land use, or all cells defined as "built up." A minimum cluster size can be specified, and it is possible to specify that cells that are separated by a road are not adjacent. For this indicator, as well as the maps showing the clusters, graphs are available showing the time evolution of the number of clusters, the total area of the clusters, and the average cluster size, for both the Green Heart proper and for the surrounding Randstad region.

Potentials. These indicators show the accessibility or availability of several classes of activity. Specifically, three potentials can be calculated: a job potential, a recreation potential, and a socio-cultural potential. The user specifies which land uses correspond to or provide each type of activity, and also a radius within which the activity is assumed to be available. Within the specified distance, the number of cells providing the activity (e.g., jobs) is determined, as is the number of cells demanding the activity (e.g., residential cells), and the quotient of these two cell counts is the indicator of the

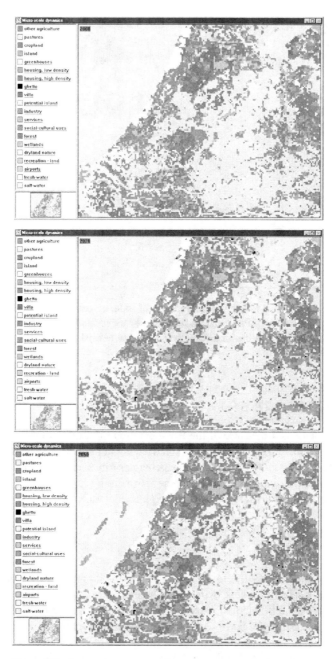

Figure 21.6. Results of the Technology Rules scenario: land use maps for the years 2000 (top), 2020 (center), and 2050 (bottom).

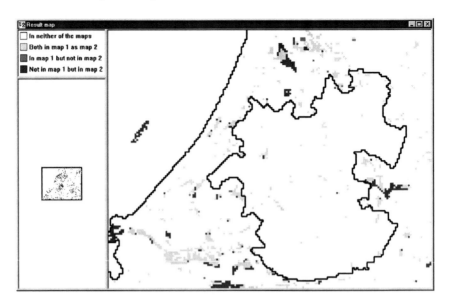

Figure 21.7. Predicted change in the location of industry between 2000 and 2050. Although the industrial area increased, most new industry located outside the Green Heart; the demand for space was met in part by the creation of new islands in the North Sea.

relative availability of an activity at a particular cell. The potentials are displayed as maps for each year of the simulation.

Contiguity.   This is a measure of the fragmentation of natural areas and is aimed at wildlife management. It is based on work carried out at the Dutch environmental institute, RIVM (Klepper 1997). The algorithm generates a measure of the size of connected natural areas, taking into account that some fragmenting land uses (e.g., agriculture) are easier for wildlife to cross than others (e.g., residential).

Discussion

The BabyLOV model was developed specifically to explore the use of simulation modeling as a tool for facilitating scenario development and evaluation by a diverse group of users. In this context, the first requirement was that BabyLOV be sufficiently flexible to capture a substantial portion of the developments described in a typical scenario storyline. This proved to be the case. However, not all elements in the scenarios were capable of being represented in the model directly. For example, the transfer of powers from national governments to regional and EU bodies is likely to have important consequences, but these cannot be expressed directly in terms of sectoral growth rates or zoning policies. This problem was resolved by having the modelers and the scenario developers work together to imagine possible spatial consequences of non-spatial elements; this amounted to generating sub-scenarios to fill in the links.

Once a scenario was implemented in BabyLOV and the model run, thorough inspection of the land use maps revealed that certain scenario elements, at least as specified, were inconsistent. In the Water Guiding scenario, for example, it is not possible to have significant agricultural growth while substantial areas are being flooded. Similarly, maintenance of land use policies specified in zoning maps is not possible in high-growth scenarios; Either growth in the modeled region must be lower than assumed in the scenario, perhaps occurring elsewhere in The Netherlands, or land use policies reflected in zoning maps must be changed, for example by allowing more growth in the Green Heart. In other words, while the story line of a scenario is usually logical at a qualitative level, it may be unable to represent the logic of secondary interactions among phenomena, nor is it able to include the effects of detailed spatial constraints. One result of this project was that the scenario developers were guided by the simulation results to revise their scenario specifications.

When, finally, realistic and consistent scenarios were obtained and implemented, they were presented in workshops to interested parties. The visualizations of the scenarios provided by the model output generated strong reactions and much discussion. Some participants criticized the scenarios themselves; others took issue with the way they were translated into model input. The discussion frequently led to suggestions for hybrid scenarios. Formulating such new scenarios and exploring their logic to ensure their basic reasonableness usually took considerably longer than entering the new versions into the model. Thus the model, used as a scenario visualization tool, proved to be a valuable stimulus to group discussion. Furthermore, it made clear to many participants the usefulness of an integrated modeling approach, because viewing the results of a scenario run showed that the future implied by a scenario was less obvious than they had imagined.

Conclusions

The full LOV model of the Netherlands was developed to show, in as much detail as possible, the spatial manifestations of national demographic and economic growth. In this role it functions first of all as a predictive tool, but its ultimate purpose is to provide a platform for performing "what-if" experiments to assist in the development and testing of spatial plans and policies. Clearly, the more accurate and reliable the predictions, the more useful the model will be in the latter role. For relatively short periods—on the order, perhaps, of ten years—the model apparently performs well, because fundamental conditions, like transport technology, do not usually change drastically. But the longer the period simulated, the more likely it is that some major, unforeseen event like war or a new technology will radically alter the basic conditions that are implicitly reflected in the structure and parameterization of the model. It would be foolish to think of the results of a simulation over such a long period as a prediction.

For longer periods, then, the model must accommodate in some way the major developments, whether anticipated or unforeseen, that are likely to alter present conditions and trends in a radical way at some point in the future. BabyLOV was developed to do this, and that is why it differs both structurally and operationally from its parent. First, the dynamics represented in the macro-scale model in LOV are the ones most likely to be altered in a fundamental way by major new developments. Thus in BabyLOV the macro model is replaced by the scenario, or rather by a set of scenarios. The scenarios can—indeed should—be far-reaching in terms of the kinds of events they anticipate, so that a wide range of possible futures can be explored.

Secondly, and most importantly, BabyLOV is used in a different way for a different purpose. Whereas LOV can be used to test alternative versions of a plan for their likely consequences, BabyLOV functions more as an aid in developing future scenarios, by stimulating thought and the discussion of possibilities, and might at a later stage provide guidance as to what kinds of policies should be explored. In short, a model of this sort could be described as a tool for giving shape to the imagination, and for this function, the possibilities for visualizing and assessing the consequences of a scenario play a key role.

Ultimately, however, the approaches embodied in the two models have much in common. They both depend to a significant degree on a predictive model, and they both involve the use of scenarios. Perhaps the most important lesson to be carried back from an application like BabyLOV to a more conventional one like LOV is that the latter kind of model should not be used simply as a tool to select the "best" solution to a planning or policy problem, for such an approach is overly optimistic, relying too heavily on model results that can never be certain. A more appropriate approach would be to treat such a model as a tool for developing and informing users' intuitions concerning the behavior of the system being modeled, for as noted in the introduction to this chapter, the behavior of complex, integrated, dynamic systems like cities and regions is difficult to understand and frequently counter-intuitive. A decision made by a planner working *with* a model is likely to be better than one made *by* a model for the planner.

Acknowledgments   This work was carried out with the financial support of DGXII of the European Commission, in collaboration with the National Institute of Public Health and the Environment (RIVM) of The Netherlands and the International Centre for Integrative Studies (ICIS) of the University of Maastricht.

Note

1. Interested readers are invited to experiment with the BabyLOV software, available at http://www.csiss.org/best-practices/siss/21/. This software was developed by the Research Institute for Knowledge Systems (RIKS), Maastricht, The Netherlands, as part of the VISIONS project of the European Union.

References

Batty, M., and Y. Xie. 1994. From cells to cities. *Environment and Planning B* 21: s31—s48.
Cecchini, A. 1996. Approaching generalized automata with help on line (AUGH). In E. Besussi and A. Cechini (eds.), *Artificial Worlds and Urban Studies*. Venice: DAEST, 231–248.
Clark, K., S. Hoppen, and I. Gaydos. 1997. A self-modifying cellular automaton model of historical urbanization in the San Francisco Bay Area. *Environment and Planning B* 24: 247–261.

Couclelis, H. 1985. Cellular worlds: A framework for modeling micro-macro dynamics. *Environment and Planning A* 17: 585–596.

Couclelis, H. 1988. Of mice and men: What rodent populations can teach us about complex spatial dynamics. *Environment and Planning A* 20: 99–109.

Couclelis, H. 1989. Macrostructure and microbehavior in a metropolitan area. *Environment and Planning B: Planning and Design* 16: 141–154.

Engelen, G., R. White, and I. Uljee. 1993. Exploratory modelling of socio-economic impacts of climate change. In G. Maul (ed.), *Climatic Change in the Intra-Americas Sea*. New York: Edward Arnold, 350–368.

Engelen, G., R. White, I. Uljee, and P. Drazan. 1995. Using cellular automata for integrated modelling of socio-environmental systems. *Environmental Monitoring and Assessment* 34: 203–214.

Engelen, G., R. White, I. Uljee, and S. Wargnies. 1996. Numerical modelling of small island socio-economics to achieve sustainable development. In G. Maul (ed.), *Small Islands: Marine Science and Sustainable Development (Coastal and Estuarine Studies Series, v. 51)*. Washington, D.C.: American Geophysical Union, 437–463.

Engelen, G., R. White, and I. Uljee. 1997. Integrating constrained cellular automata models, GIS and decision support tools for urban and regional planning and policy making. In H. Timmermans (ed.), *Decision Support Systems in Urban Planning*. London: E&FN Spon, 125–155.

Klepper, O. 1997. Stapeling van milieuthema's in termen van kans op voorkomen, *ECO-notitie*. Bilthoven, The Netherlands: RIVM, 97–101.

Phipps, M. 1989. Dynamical behaviour of cellular automata under constraints of neighbourhood coherence. *Geographical Analysis* 21: 197–215.

Portugali, J. 2000. *Self-Organization and the City*. Berlin: Springer-Verlag.

Portugali, J., and I. Benenson. 1995. Artificial planning experience by means of a heuristic cell-space model: Simulating international migration in the urban process. *Environment and Planning A* 27: 1647–1665.

Portugali, J, and I. Benenson. 1997. Human agents between local and global forces in a self-organizing city. In F. Schweitzer and H. Haken (eds.), *Self-Organization of Complex Structures: From Individual to Collective Dynamics*. London: Gordon and Breach, 537–546.

Straatman, B., R. White, and G. Engelen. 2002. Towards an automatic calibration procedure for constrained cellular automata. *Environment and Planning B*. (in press).

Tobler, W. 1979. Cellular geography. In S. Gale and G. Olsson (eds.), *Philosophy in Geography*, Dordrecht, Holland: Reidel Publishing Company, 379–386.

White, R. 1998. Cities and cellular automata. *Discrete Dynamics in Nature and Society* 2: 111–125.

White, R., and G. Engelen. 1993a. Cellular dynamics and GIS: Modelling spatial complexity *Geographical Systems* 1: 237–253.

White, R., and G. Engelen. 1993b. Fractal urban land use patterns: A cellular automata approach. *Environment and Planning A* 25: 1175–1199.

White, R., and G. Engelen. 1994. Urban systems dynamics and cellular automata: Fractal structures between order and chaos. *Chaos, Solitons, and Fractals* 4: 563–583.

White, R., and G. Engelen. 1997. Cellular automata as the basis of integrated dynamic regional modelling. *Environment and Planning B* 24: 235–246.

White, R., G. Engelen, and I. Uljee. 1997. The use of constrained cellular automata for high-resolution modelling of urban land-use dynamics. *Environment and Planning B* 24: 323–343.

Wu, F. 1998a. An experiment on the generic polycentricity of urban growth in a cellular automatic city. *Environment and Planning B* 25: 731–752.

Wu, F. 1998b. SimLand: A prototype to simulate land conversion through the integrated GIS and CA with AHP-derived transition rule. *International Journal of Geographical Information Science* 12: 63–82.

Xie, Y. 1996. A generalized model for cellular urban dynamics. *Geographical Analysis* 28: 350–373.

Epilogue
Spatial Analysis in Retrospect and Prospect

Brian J. L. Berry

During the early years of geography's "quantitative revolution" Duane Marble and I conceived of a volume that might serve as a benchmark for an ancient but rapidly transforming field. The result was *Spatial Analysis. A Reader in Statistical Geography* (Berry and Marble 1968). In this book, we explored the roots of spatial analysis and drew together papers that examined fundamental spatial concepts, the nature of spatial data and statistics, methods for analyzing spatial distribution, ways to study spatial association, and new procedures for both formal and functional regionalization. Difficult issues that were noted, in addition to those of handling large datasets on the mainframe computers of the time, included the problems of modifiable units, ecological correlation, contiguity, and spatial dependence. There were more than 30 contributors, of whom a little more than half were geographers. The rest were a mix of demographers, sociologists, econometricians, geologists, and meteorologists.

In the four decades that have passed since we conceived of *Spatial Analysis* fundamental change has occurred that now positions the field to make contributions to the social sciences that are as fundamental as those that occurred in geography itself in the 1960s. If we compare *Spatially Integrated Social Science* with *Spatial Analysis*, the dimensions of this shift become apparent. *SISS* has almost 40 contributors, a little less than half of whom are geographers, and the rest a mix of demographers, sociologists, anthropologists, archaeologists, city planners, and others. But it is not the disciplinary home or mix that matters, however; it is what is ignored, what is taken for granted, what is assumed, and what is considered to be important (recognizing that there will be a 40-author companion volume entitled *Advances in Spatial Econometric Modeling*).

First, issues of computation using massive geographic data sets have largely gone away with the morphing of computer graphics into geographic information systems and GIS into GIScience. Many things that presented fundamental obstacles forty years ago are among today's trivia, handled in passing in beginning undergraduate classes and taken to be self-evident by the research community.

Second, it now is accepted as axiomatic, not simply by geographers but also by the broader social science community, that *space matters*, that geographic units cannot be treated as independent units of observation, that spatial autocorrelation is important, that it is much more difficult to handle than time-series dependence, and that it cannot be ignored if statistical models are to be efficient and properly specified.

Third, there is also a sense that the new rich data streams made available by remote sensors are now just as much taken for granted as are modern computation and information science. This contrasts markedly with when Duane and I conceived of *Spatial Analysis*. Then, Corona was at work but its output was highly classified, and locational referencing of most datasets was in its infancy.

Fourth, with increasing freedom from computational constraints, there appears to be a welcome affirmation of the Jeffersonian belief that statistics are matters of state—that science should be use-oriented, concerned with practical applications, and attempting to resolve important policy issues.

Fifth, there is the advent of creative play and experimentation with ideas. One need only refer to the opportunities for experimentation offered by agent-based modeling and cellular automata. In 1968, Duane and I had only Hägerstrand's notions of spatial diffusion to draw on. Now, Wolfram goes so far as to argue that such methods have created "a new kind of science" (Wolfram 2002).

All of this is to the good. The rapid rise and diffusion of Geographic Information Science is one of the most remarkable features of the academic landscape in the last decade of the twentieth century. So where do we go from here? Will the convergence of new data and methods, together with an emergent cooperation that transcends traditional disciplinary boundaries in new and perhaps lasting ways, provide the necessary and sufficient conditions for both conceptual growth and more powerful practical applications?

When we prepared *Spatial Analysis* it was clear that it was spatial theory, even though limited, that had proceeded far beyond the technical capabilities of the field. After four decades of heady technical change, the situation may be reversed. Progress in developing well-grounded spatial theory—note the emphasis upon groundedness, in contrast to the verbal abstractions of self-proclaimed armchair "social theorists"— has been slow. There clearly is need for new rounds of spatial theory that will be as dramatic in their consequences over the decades to come as have been the changes in technology over the past 40 years. This theory cannot be static, a limitation of the strictly geographical approach, but must be fully spatio-temporal and positioned so as to enhance the creative tension that should exist between theory and practice. It must be multidimensional and therefore multidisciplinary, transcending the constraints of traditional disciplinary agendas and casting light on the interstices where today's important problems are located. And it must involve not simply the human sciences, but all those sciences that meet at the human-environmental interface. There is much that has been achieved. Yet in a world that is never static, there is yet more to be accomplished, and what is most exciting is that there is the momentum to get there.

References

Berry, B.J.L., and D.F. Marble.1968. *Spatial Analysis. A Reader in Statistical Geography.* Englewood Cliffs, N. J.: Prentice-Hall, Inc.
Wolfram, S. 2002. *A New Kind of Science.* Champaign, Ill.: Wolfram Media Inc.

Index